Summary of Common Linux C

COMMAND	ACTION
`egrep`	"Extended" version
`eject`	Eject the media fror
`expr`	Evaluate Boolean a
`false`	Return nonzero (*fal*
`fgrep`	"Fast" version of grep
`file`	Report type of file
`find`	Find matching files and perform specified actions
`finger`	Report user information
`format`	Format disks and cartridge tapes
`ftp`	Transfer files to and from remote systems
`grep`	Search files for regular expression matches
`groff`	Format files for printing
`head`	Display first few lines of a file
`insmod`	Load a kernel module
`join`	Display the join (lines with common field) of two files
`kill`	Send a signal to process (by default, terminate the process)
`ksh`	Invoke the Korn shell
`line`	Read a line (shell script usage)
`ln`	Create link to a file
`logname`	Get login name
`lp, lpr`	Send request to printer
`lpc`	Administer printer queues
`lprm`	Remove print jobs from the print queue
`lpq`	Report printer status
`ls`	List contents of a directory
`lsmod`	List loaded kernel modules
`mail`	Send and receive mail
`man`	Print reference pages from online manual
`mesg`	Grant or deny permission to receive write messages from other users
`mkdir`	Create a new directory
`mknod`	Build a special file
`more`	Display a file one page at a time
`mount`	Mount a special file, or report its status
`mtools`	Read and write MS-DOS or Windows disks
`mv`	Move (rename) a file

CONTINUED →

Linux Complete

Linux Complete

Linux Documentation Project
Compiled by Grant Taylor

San Francisco ▸ Paris ▸ Düsseldorf ▸ Soest ▸ London

Associate Publisher: Gary Masters

Contracts and Licensing Manager: Kristine O'Callaghan

Acquisitions & Developmental Editor: Ellen L. Dendy

Editors: Jeremy Crawford, Linda Stephenson, Lisa Duran

Project Editor: Brianne Hope Agatep

Book Designer: Maureen Forys, Happenstance Type-O-Rama

Interior Art Designer: Chris Gillespie

Graphic Illustrator: Tony Jonick

Electronic Publishing Specialist: Maureen Forys, Happenstance Type-O-Rama

Project Team Leader: Leslie Higbee

Proofreaders: Leslie Higbee, Rich Ganis

Indexer: John S. Lewis

Cover Designer: Design Site

Cover Illustrator/Photographer: The Image Bank

Library of Congress Card Number: 99-62576

ISBN: 0-7821-2567-0

Printed in Canada

10 9 8 7 6 5

ACKNOWLEDGMENTS

Thanks are due to all the Sybex editors who worked with me on this project, including Ellen Dendy, Jeremy Crawford, and Brianne Agatep. Thanks to Leslie Higbee, Maureen Forys, Rich Ganis, Tony Jonick, and Alan Smithee for their tireless work on this project. Thanks, too, are due to Sybex itself; we of the Linux Documentation Project will be getting a reasonable chunk of money from this book, not to mention an even nicer chunk of corrections to our texts.

Speaking of the LDP, author David Lawyer deserves my thanks, if not an apology; he went the extra mile to get his HOWTO updated in time for this book, only to have it dropped for lack of space. Remind me to buy you a beer someday, David...

RMS, Larry, and Linus deserve a tip of the hat; in Emacs, Perl and Linux, they've unleashed some mighty fine software without which I would probably have majored in English (but would no doubt still be writing 1000-page books).

Finally, extra special thanks are due to Kelley, who almost single-handedly planned and executed our wedding while I put together this very book. I love you, and I promise to do a short book next time!

—Grant Taylor
`gtaylor+lc@picante.com`

CONTENTS AT A GLANCE

TABLE OF CONTENTS

Part III ▸ Networking 147

Appendices 653

INTRODUCTION

Linux Complete is a one-of-a-kind computer book—valuable both for the breadth of its content and for its low price. This thousand-page collection of information compiled from the Linux Documentation Project (`http://metalab.unc.edu/LDP/index.html`) provides comprehensive coverage of the Linux operating system.

Linux Complete is designed to provide all the essential information you'll need to get the most from Linux.

WHO CAN BENEFIT FROM THIS BOOK?

Linux Complete is designed to meet the needs of a wide range of computer users. Therefore, while you could read this book from beginning to end, all of you may not need to read every chapter. The table of contents and the index will guide you to the subjects you're looking for.

Beginners Even if Linux is new to you, this book will help to get you up and running with the operating system.

Intermediate Users Chances are, you already know how to perform routine operations with Linux. You also know that there is always more to learn about working effectively, and you want to get up to speed on new features, like GNOME. Throughout this book, you'll find instructions that take you beyond the basics.

Advanced Users If you've worked extensively with Linux, you'll appreciate this book as a reference and as a guide to further work with the operating system.

HOW THIS BOOK IS ORGANIZED

Linux Complete has 16 chapters and four appendixes.

Part I: Getting Started

This first part of the book has two goals: to provide a quick introduction to Linux and to provide some information on how to obtain and install Linux.

It's fairly easy to provide an introduction to Linux, and I've done so. Unfortunately, there are so many ways to obtain and install Linux that I could fill this book with documents describing them all and still have techniques and distributions go unmentioned. Rather than pursue this impossible goal, I've included just two small documents: one lists some of the many available Linux distributions with some contact information and the other gives an overview of a typical installation process.

This section contains several chapters:

- Chapter 1, *Introduction to Linux*, is reprinted from the Linux Documentation Project's Guide *Linux Installation & Getting Started*. It provides an introduction to Linux and some other information you'll need before you begin running Linux yourself.
- Chapter 2, *Unix and Internet Fundamentals*, contains the Unix and Internet Fundamentals HOWTO by Eric Raymond. It provides an overview of PC hardware, Unix-like operating systems, and the operation of the Internet. All of these topics will be of interest if you wish to get the most out of your Linux experience.
- Chapter 3, *Distributions*, contains a discussion of available Linux distributions and information to help you decide which one suits you. Most Linux distributions are available free over the Internet, on CDs that cost as little as a few dollars, or preinstalled on new computers from companies like VA Research or Penguin Computing.
- Chapter 4, *Installing Linux*, contains the complete text of the Installation HOWTO, also by Eric Raymond. It gives a distribution-neutral overview of the procedure for installing Linux onto a PC. After reading this *and* the documentation that comes with your distribution, you should be all set for a successful install.

Part II: Hardware

Once you've completed the basic installation of Linux, you'll want to configure your new system to take full advantage of your hardware. As was the case in Part I, there isn't enough room to document all types of hardware or all ways to use that hardware. Appendix C lists sources of documentation for other peripheral devices and hardware configurations such as IrDA ports, Plug-and-Play devices, CD-ROM drives, SCSI adapters, etc.

This part of the book includes the following chapters:

- Chapter 5, *XFree86*, covers the installation and configuration of the XFree86 implementation of the X Window system on Linux. The X Window system provides access to your video hardware for graphical software; these programs may be running on your Linux machine or on any other machine (which need not be running Linux) on the network.
- Chapter 6, *Printers*, covers printing under Linux. This includes a list of supported and unsupported printers and the configuration of the lpd print spooler.

Part III: Networking

The most popular reason to run Linux seems to be for its networking capabilities, many of which Windows can't match, even with an assortment of expensive third-party programs. Unfortunately, Linux has inherited Unix's reputation of being difficult to configure, so many home users are scared away and spend money on mediocre Windows software to solve problems that are really not all that hard to solve for free with Linux.

For those of you using Linux at home, home networking is in many ways similar to networking in an office environment, but there are several important differences. The biggest one is that your Internet connection will be a much smaller affair–you'll have a PPP dial-in to an ISP, or perhaps a cable modem or DSL connection. Businesses tend to have more expensive dedicated lines.

In this part of *Linux Complete*, you'll learn about the many things Linux's networking tools can do and then delve into further detail on the things you might encounter: PPP, cable modems, or xDSL. We'll also cover the related topic of DHCP–an Internet protocol you may need to use with your Internet connection.

Again, we didn't have space to include everything here, but Chapter 7, *Networking Overview*, provides a very good introduction to most Linux networking capabilities, along with a complete list of references to other documents that will help you.

This part of the book contains these chapters:

- Chapter 7, *Networking Overview*, provides a complete overview of Linux's networking capabilities, as well as pointers to more information on everything.

- Chapter 8, *Linux Networking*, provides an in-depth description of how Linux's Internet networking software is configured. For most situations, this chapter's information will be *more* than you need, but it does make for interesting reading.
- Chapter 9, *PPP*, describes how to connect a Linux box to an Internet Service Provider using a regular phone line and modem. This connection will function as your lifeline to the Internet.
- Chapter 10, *Cable Modems*, describes how to connect to the Internet using a cable modem. Cable modems are generally the fastest way to connect a home today; they are similar in speed to xDSL connections but are somewhat more uniformly available in the areas where they are offered.
- Chapter 11, *DHCP*, describes the use of the internetworking Dynamic Host Configuration Protocol. Your Linux box will be a DHCP client of your provider's server, or you might need to run a server to allocate Internet Protocol addresses to your internal hosts. This chapter tells you how to do both.
- Chapter 12, *IP Masquerading*, describes how to connect multiple machines on your LAN to the Internet through your "residential" connection that was designed for one host at a time.

Part IV: Security

Security is very important in Linux. This part contains two chapters:

- Chapter 13, *Security*, provides a good overview of security issues, including physical security, user-level security, network security, intrusion recovery, and tips on how to keep abreast of the latest security happenings.
- Chapter 14, *IP Chains*, covers the packet filtering mechanisms of Linux 2.2, which you'll use to construct a firewall if you have this kernel. Linux 2 used a filtering system known as ipfw; Linux 2.2 replaced that with the more flexible ipchains.

Part V: Linux on the Desktop

Because of Linux's Unix heritage, you don't need to use a graphical, metaphorical interface, but you can if you want to.

The two most popular graphical desktops for Linux are the "K" Desktop Environment–KDE–and the GNU Network Object Model

Environment–GNOME. Both offer a graphical interface for basic things as well as a complete toolkit for the building of further user applications. They differ in various implementation details and in age–KDE is slightly older than GNOME and is, at the moment at least, a bit more stable (in part because it is based on a commercial toolkit). On the other hand, GNOME was initially designed with a more powerful infrastructure and the initial releases show great promise.

This section contains two chapters:

- Chapter 15, *GNOME*, describes the basics of GNOME. GNOME 1 was released March 2, 1999 and has already seen several minor updates. This is the latest User's Guide available in time for this book–version 1.0.5.
- Chapter 16, *The K Desktop Environment*, describes the basics of KDE. KDE 1.1 was released at roughly the same time as the initial release of GNOME 1. Stable versions of both systems will be available in most Linux distributions by the time you read this.

Appendixes

This book contains four appendixes:

- Appendix A is a Command Reference of common user commands, file formats, and administrative commands.
- Appendix B contains essential book-length references for Linux and Unix.
- Appendix C lists the currently available Linux HOWTOs–documents which describe in detail a certain aspect of configuring or using Linux.
- Appendix D is the GNU General Public License.

A Few Typographical Conventions

When an operation requires a series of choices from menus or dialog boxes, the ➢ symbol is used to guide you through the instructions, like this: " Select Programs ➢ Accessories ➢ System Tools ➢ System Information." The items the ➢ symbol separates may be menu names, toolbar icons, check boxes, or other elements of the Linux interface–anyplace you can make a selection.

`This typeface` is used to identify filenames and paths, Internet URLs, and program code. **Boldface type** is used whenever you need to type something into a text box.

You'll find these types of special notes throughout the book:

TIP

You'll see tips—quicker and smarter ways to accomplish a task, which the authors have based on their experience using Linux.

NOTE

You'll see these types of notes, too. They usually represent alternate ways to accomplish a task or some additional information that needs to be highlighted.

WARNING

In a few places, you'll see a warning like this one. When you see a warning, pay attention to it!

For More Information...

See the Linux Documentation Project Web site, `http://metalab.unc.edu/LDP/`, to learn more about the documentation that went into *Linux Complete*.

We hope you enjoy this book and find it useful. Happy computing!

PART I
Getting Started

ipfwadm -O
V your static
outgoing
ipfwadm
such as ip masq
define the
/bin:/usr/
CONFIG

Chapter 1

Introduction to Linux

This chapter provides an introduction to Linux, including its history, features, and hardware requirements. The chapter also looks at copyright issues associated with Linux and how it differs from other operating systems. The chapter concludes by providing some online Linux resources and how to find help.

"Introduction to Linux" is reprinted from the Linux Documentation Project's book *Linux Installation & Getting Started* by Matt Welsh and others (Specialized Systems Consultants, 1998).

What Is Linux?

Linux is quite possibly the most important free software achievement since the original Space War or, more recently, emacs. It has developed into an operating system for business, education, and personal productivity. Linux is no longer only for Unix wizards who sit for hours in front of a glowing console (although we assure you that many users fall into this category). This book will help you get the most from Linux.

Linux (pronounced with a short *i*, as in LIH-nucks) is a Unix operating system clone that runs on a variety of platforms, especially personal computers with Intel 80386 or better processors. It supports a wide range of software, from TeX, to the X Window System, to the GNU C/C++ compiler, to TCP/IP. It's a versatile, bona fide implementation of Unix, freely distributed under the terms of the GNU General Public License (see Appendix D).

Linux can turn any 80386 or better personal computer into a workstation that puts the full power of Unix at your fingertips. Businesses install Linux on entire networks of machines and use the operating system to manage financial and hospital records, distributed computing environments, and telecommunications. Universities worldwide use Linux to teach courses on operating system programming and design. Computing enthusiasts everywhere use Linux at home for programming, productivity, and all-around hacking.

What makes Linux so different is that it is a free implementation of Unix. It was and still is developed cooperatively by a group of volunteers, primarily on the Internet, who exchange code, report bugs, and fix problems in an open-ended environment. Anyone is welcome to join the Linux development effort. All it takes is interest in hacking a free Unix clone and some programming know-how. The book in your hands is your tour guide.

A Brief History of Linux

Unix is one of the most popular operating systems worldwide because of its large support base and distribution. It was originally developed at ATT as a multitasking system for minicomputers and mainframes in the 1970s but has since grown to become one of the most widely used operating systems anywhere, despite its sometimes confusing interface and lack of central standardization.

Many hackers feel that Unix is the Right Thing—the One True Operating System. Hence, the development of Linux by an expanding group of Unix hackers who want to get their hands dirty with their own system.

Versions of Unix exist for many systems, from personal computers to supercomputers like the Cray Y-MP. Most versions of Unix for personal computers are expensive and cumbersome. At the time of this writing, a one-machine version of Unix System V for the 386 runs about $1,500 US.

Linux is a free version of Unix developed primarily by Linus Torvalds at the University of Helsinki in Finland, with the help of many Unix programmers and wizards across the Internet. Anyone with enough know-how and gumption can develop and change the system. The Linux kernel uses no code from ATT or any other proprietary source, and much of the software available for Linux was developed by the GNU project of the Free Software Foundation in Cambridge, Massachusetts. However, programmers from all over the world have contributed to the growing pool of Linux software.

Linux was originally developed as a hobby project by Linus Torvalds. It was inspired by Minix, a small Unix system developed by Andy Tanenbaum. The first discussions about Linux were on the Usenet newsgroup `comp.os.minix`. These discussions were concerned mostly with the development of a small, academic Unix system for Minix users who wanted more.

The very early development of Linux mostly dealt with the task-switching features of the 80386 protected-mode interface, all written in assembly code. Linus writes,

> **After that it was plain sailing: hairy coding still, but I had some devices, and debugging was easier. I started using C at this stage, and it certainly speeds up development. This is also when I started to get serious about my megalomaniac ideas to make "a better Minix than Minix." I was hoping I'd be able to recompile GCC under Linux someday....**
>
> **Two months for basic setup, but then only slightly longer until I had a disk driver (seriously buggy, but it happened to work on my machine) and a small file system. That was about when I made 0.01 available (around late August of 1991): it wasn't pretty, it had no floppy driver, and it couldn't do much of anything. I don't think anybody ever compiled that version. But by then I was hooked, and didn't want to stop until I could chuck out Minix.**

No announcement was ever made for Linux version 0.01. The 0.01 sources weren't even executable. They contained only the bare rudiments of the kernel source and assumed that you had access to a Minix machine to compile and experiment with them.

On October 5, 1991, Linus announced the first "official" version of Linux, which was version 0.02. At that point, Linus was able to run bash (the GNU Bourne Again Shell) and GCC (the GNU C compiler) but not much else. Again, this was intended as a hacker's system. The primary focus was kernel development—user support, documentation, and distribution had not yet been addressed. Today, the Linux community still seems to treat these issues as secondary to "real programming"—kernel development.

As Linus wrote in `comp.os.minix`,

> **Do you pine for the nice days of Minix 1.1, when men were men and wrote their own device drivers? Are you without a nice project and just dying to cut your teeth on an OS you can try to modify for your needs? Are you finding it frustrating when everything works on Minix? No more all-nighters to get a nifty program working? Then this post might be just for you.**
>
> **As I mentioned a month ago, I'm working on a free version of a Minix-look-alike for AT-386 computers. It has finally reached the stage where it's even usable (though may not be, depending on what you want), and I am willing to put out the sources for wider distribution. It is just version 0.02...but I've successfully run bash, GCC, gnu-make, gnu-sed, compress, etc. under it.**

After version 0.03, Linus bumped up the version number to 0.10, as more people started to work on the system. After several further revisions, Linus increased the version number to 0.95 in March 1992 to reflect his expectation that the system was ready for an official release soon. (Generally, software is not assigned the version number 1.0 until it is theoretically complete or bug-free.) Almost a year and a half later, in late December of 1993, the Linux kernel was still at version 0.99.pl14—asymptotically approaching 1.0. At the time of this writing, the current stable kernel version is 2.0 patchlevel 33, and version 2.1 is under development.

Most of the major, free Unix software packages have been ported to Linux, and commercial software is also available. More hardware is supported than in the original kernel versions. Many people have executed benchmarks on 80486 Linux systems and found them comparable with mid-range workstations from Sun Microsystems and Digital Equipment Corporation. Who would have ever guessed that this "little" Unix clone would have grown up to take on the entire world of personal computing?

System Features

Linux supports features found in other implementations of Unix and many which aren't found elsewhere. In this section, we'll take a nickel tour of the features of the Linux kernel.

Linux is a complete multitasking, multiuser operating system, as are all other versions of Unix. This means that many users can log into and run programs on the same machine simultaneously.

The Linux system is mostly compatible with several Unix standards (inasmuch as Unix has standards) at the source level, including IEEE POSIX.1, Unix System V, and Berkeley System Distribution Unix. Linux was developed with source code portability in mind, and it's easy to find commonly used features that are shared by more than one platform. Much of the free Unix software available on the Internet and elsewhere compiles under Linux right out of the box. In addition, all of the source code for the Linux system, including the kernel, device drivers, libraries, user programs, and development tools, is freely distributable.

Other specific internal features of Linux include POSIX job control (used by shells like csh and bash), pseudoterminals (pty devices), and support for dynamically loadable national or customized keyboard drivers. Linux supports virtual consoles that let you switch between login sessions on the same system console. Users of the screen program will find the Linux virtual console implementation familiar.

The kernel can emulate 387-FPU instructions, and systems without a math coprocessor can run programs that require floating-point math capability.

Linux supports various file systems for storing data, like the ext2 file system, which was developed specifically for Linux. The Xenix and Unix System V file systems are also supported, as well as the Microsoft MS-DOS and Windows 95 VFAT file systems on a hard drive or floppy. The ISO 9660 CD-ROM file system is also supported. We'll talk more about file systems later.

Linux provides a complete implementation of TCP/IP networking software. This includes device drivers for many popular Ethernet cards, SLIP (Serial Line Internet Protocol), and PPP (Point-to-Point Protocol), which provide access to a TCP/IP network via a serial connection, PLIP (Parallel Line Internet Protocol), and NFS (Network File System). The complete range of TCP/IP clients and services is also supported, which includes FTP, Telnet, NNTP, and SMTP. We'll talk more about networking later.

The Linux kernel is developed to use protected-mode features of Intel 80386 and better processors. In particular, Linux uses the protected-mode, descriptor based, memory-management paradigm, and other advanced features. Anyone familiar with 80386 protected-mode programming knows that this chip was designed for multitasking systems like Unix. Linux exploits this functionality.

The kernel supports demand-paged, loaded executables. Only those segments of a program that are actually in use are read into memory from disk. Also, copy-on-write pages are shared among executables. If several instances of a program are running at once, they share physical memory, which reduces overall usage.

In order to increase the amount of available memory, Linux also implements disk paging. Up to one gigabyte of swap space may be allocated on disk (up to 8 partitions of 128 megabytes each). When the system requires more physical memory, it swaps inactive pages to disk, letting you run larger applications and support more users. However, swapping data to disk is no substitute for physical RAM, which is much faster.

The Linux kernel also implements a unified memory pool for user programs and disk cache. All free memory is used by the cache, which is reduced when running large programs.

Executables use dynamically linked, shared libraries–code from a single library on disk. This is not unlike the SunOS shared library mechanism. Executable files occupy less disk space, especially those that use many library functions. There are also statically linked libraries for object debugging and maintaining complete binary files when shared libraries are not installed. The libraries are dynamically linked at runtime, and the programmer can use his or her own routines in place of the standard library routines.

To facilitate debugging, the kernel generates core dumps for post-mortem analysis. A core dump and an executable linked with debugging support allows a developer to determine what caused a program to crash.

Software Features

Virtually every utility one would expect of a standard Unix implementation has been ported to Linux, including basic commands like `ls`, `awk`, `tr`, `sed`, `bc`, and more. The familiar working environment of other Unix systems is duplicated on Linux. All standard commands and utilities are included. (Novice Unix or Linux users should see Appendix B for books with an introduction to basic Unix commands.)

Many text editors are available, including vi, ex, pico, jove, and GNU emacs, and variants like Lucid emacs, which incorporates extensions of the X Window System, and joe. The text editor you're accustomed to using has more than likely been ported to Linux.

The choice of a text editor is an interesting one. Many Unix users prefer simple editors like vi. (The original author wrote this with vi.) But vi has many limitations due to its age, and modern editors like emacs have gained popularity. Emacs supports a complete Lisp-based macro language and interpreter, powerful command syntax, and other extensions. There are emacs macro packages that let you read electronic mail and news, edit directory contents, and even engage in artificially intelligent psychotherapy sessions (indispensable for stressed-out Linux hackers).

Most of the basic Linux utilities are GNU software. GNU utilities support advanced features that are not found in the standard versions of BSD and Unix System Vprograms. For example, the GNU vi clone elvis includes a structured macro language that differs from the original implementation. However, GNU utilities are intended to remain compatible with their BSD and System V counterparts. Many people consider the GNU versions to be superior to the originals.

A *shell* is a program that reads and executes commands from the user. In addition, many shells provide features like job control, managing several processes at once, input and output redirection, and a command language for writing *shell scripts*. A shell script is a program in the shell's command language and is analogous to an MS-DOS batch file.

Many types of shells are available for Linux. The most important difference between shells is the command language. For example, the C Shell (csh) uses a command language similar to the C programming language. The classic Bourne Shell sh uses another command language. The choice of a shell is often based on the command language it provides, and determines, to a large extent, the qualities of your working environment under Linux.

The GNU Bourne Again Shell (bash) is a variation of the Bourne Shell, which includes many advanced features like job control, command history, command and filename completion, an emacs-like interface for editing command lines, and other powerful extensions to the standard Bourne Shell language. Another popular shell is tcsh, a version of the C Shell with advanced functionality similar to that found in bash. Other shells include zsh, a small Bourne-like shell; the Korn Shell (ksh); BSD's ash; and rc, the Plan 9 shell.

If you're the only person using the system and prefer to use vi and bash exclusively as your editor and shell, there's no reason to install other editors or shells. This do-it-yourself attitude is prevalent among Linux hackers and users.

Text Processing and Word Processing

Almost every computer user needs a method of preparing documents. In the world of personal computers, word processing is the norm. It comprises editing and manipulating text in a What-You-See-Is-What-You-Get (WYSIWYG) environment and producing printed copies of the text, complete with graphics, tables, and ornamentation.

Commercial word processors from Corel, Applix, and Star Division are available in the Unix world, but text processing, which is quite different conceptually, is more common. In text processing systems, text is entered in a page-description language, which describes how the text should be formatted. Rather than enter text within a special word processing environment, you can modify text with any editor, like vi or emacs. Once you finish entering the source text (in the typesetting language), a separate program converts the source to a format suitable for printing. This is somewhat analogous to programming in a language like C and compiling the document into printable form.

Many text processing systems are available for Linux. One is groff, the GNU version of the classic troff text formatter originally developed by Bell Labs and still used on many Unix systems worldwide. Another modern text processing system is TeX, developed by Donald Knuth of computer science fame. Dialects of TeX, like LaTeX, are also available.

Text processors like TeX and groff differ mostly in the syntax of their formatting languages. The choice of one formatting system over another is based upon what utilities are available to satisfy your needs, as well as personal taste.

Many people consider groff's formatting language to be a bit obscure and find TeX more readable. However, groff produces ASCII output that can be viewed on a terminal more easily, while TeX is intended primarily for output to a printing device. Various add-on programs are required to produce ASCII output from TeX formatted documents or convert TeX input to groff format.

Another program is texinfo, an extension to TeX that is used for software documentation developed by the Free Software Foundation. Texinfo can produce printed output or an online-browsable hypertext Info document from a single source file. Info files are the main format of documentation used in GNU software like emacs.

Text processors are used widely in the computing community for producing papers, theses, magazine articles, and books. (This chapter was written in LaTeX.) The ability to process source language as a text file opens the door to many extensions of the text processor itself. Because a source document is not stored in an obscure format that only one word processor can read, programmers can write parsers and translators for the formatting language and thus extend the system.

What does a formatting language look like? In general, a formatted source file consists mostly of the text itself, with control codes to produce effects like font and margin changes, and list formatting.

Consider the following text:

> Mr. Torvalds:
>
> We are very upset with your current plans to implement *post-hypnotic suggestions* in the **Linux** terminal driver code. We feel this way for three reasons:
>
> 1. Planting subliminal messages in the terminal driver is not only immoral; it is a waste of time;
> 2. It has been proven that post-hypnotic suggestions are ineffective when used upon unsuspecting Unix hackers;
> 3. We have already implemented high-voltage electric shocks, as a security measure, in the code for login.
>
> We hope you will reconsider.

This text might appear in the LaTeX formatting language as the following:

```
\begin{quote}
Mr. Torvalds:

We are very upset with your current plans to implement
{\em post-hypnotic suggestions\/} in the {\bf Linux} terminal
driver code. We feel this way for three reasons:
\begin{enumerate}
\item Planting subliminal messages in the terminal driver is
   not only immoral; it is a waste of time;
\item It has been proven that post-hypnotic suggestions
   are ineffective when used upon unsuspecting Unix
   hackers;
\item We have already implemented high-voltage electric
   shocks, as a security measure, in the code for {\tt
   login}.
\end{enumerate}
We hope you will reconsider.
end{quote}
```

The author enters the text using any text editor and generates formatted output by processing the source with LaTeX. At first glance, the typesetting language may appear to be obscure, but it's actually quite easy to understand. Using a text processing system enforces typographical standards when writing. All the enumerated lists within a document will look the same, unless the author modifies the definition of an enumerated list. The goal is to allow the author to concentrate on the text, not typesetting conventions.

When writing with a text editor, one generally does not think about how the printed text will appear. The writer learns to visualize the finished text's appearance from the formatting commands in the source.

WYSIWYG word processors are attractive for many reasons. They provide an easy-to-use visual interface for editing documents. But this interface is limited to aspects of text layout that are accessible to the user. For example, many word processors still provide a special format language for producing complicated expressions like mathematical formulae. This is text processing, albeit on a much smaller scale.

A not-so-subtle benefit of text processing is that you specify exactly which format you need. In many cases, the text processing system requires a format specification. Text processing systems also allow source text to be edited with any text editor, instead of relying on format codes that are hidden beneath a word processor's opaque user interface. Further, the source text is easily converted to other formats. The tradeoff for this flexibility and power is the lack of WYSIWYG formatting.

Some programs let you preview the formatted document on a graphics display device before printing. The xdvi program displays a device-independent file generated by the TeX system under X. Applications like xfig and gimp provide WYSIWYG graphics interfaces for drawing figures and diagrams, which are subsequently converted to text processing language for inclusion in your document.

Text processors like troff were around long before WYSIWYG word processing was available. Many people still prefer their versatility and independence from a graphics environment.

Many text-processing-related utilities are available. The powerful METAFONT system, which is used to design fonts for TeX, is included in the Linux port of TeX. Other programs include ispell, an interactive spelling checker and corrector; makeindex, which generates indices in LaTeX documents; and many other groff and TeX-based macro packages that format many types of technical and mathematical texts. Conversion programs that translate between TeX or groff source and a myriad of other formats are also available.

A newcomer to text formatting is YODL, written by Karel Kubat. YODL is an easy-to-learn language with filters to produce various output formats, like LaTeX, SGML, and HTML.

Programming Languages and Utilities

Linux provides a complete Unix programming environment, which includes all of the standard libraries, programming tools, compilers, and debuggers you would expect of other Unix systems.

Standards like POSIX.1 are supported, which allows software written for Linux to be easily ported to other systems. Professional Unix programmers and system administrators use Linux to develop software at home, then transfer the software to Unix systems at work. This not only saves a great deal of time and money, but also lets you work in the comfort of your own home. (One of the authors uses his system to develop and test X Window System applications at home, which can be directly compiled on workstations elsewhere.) Computer science students learn Unix programming and explore other aspects of the system, like kernel architecture.

With Linux, you have access to the complete set of libraries and programming utilities and the complete kernel and library source code.

Within the Unix software world, systems and applications are often programmed in C or C++. The standard C and C++ compiler for Linux is GNU GCC, which is an advanced, modern compiler that supports C++, including ATT 3.0 features, as well as Objective-C, another object-oriented dialect of C.

Besides C and C++, other compiled and interpreted programming languages have been ported to Linux, like Smalltalk, FORTRAN, Java, Pascal, LISP, Scheme, and Ada (if you're masochistic enough to program in Ada, we aren't going to stop you). In addition, various assemblers for writing protected-mode 80386 code are available, as are Unix hacking favorites like Perl (the script language to end all script languages) and Tcl/Tk (a shell-like command-processing system that has support for developing simple X Window System applications).

The advanced gdb debugger can step through a program one line of source code at a time or examine a core dump to find the cause of a crash. The gprof profiling utility provides performance statistics for your program, telling you where your program spends most of its execution time. As mentioned above, the emacs text editor provides interactive editing and compilation environments for various programming languages. Other tools include GNU make and imake, which manage compilation of large applications, and RCS, a system for source code locking and revision control.

Finally, Linux supports dynamically linked, shared libraries (DLLs), which result in much smaller binaries. The common subroutine code is linked at runtime. These DLLs let you override function definitions with your own code. For example, if you wish to write your own version of the malloc() library routine, the linker will use your new routine instead of the one in the libraries.

Introduction to the X Window System

The X Window System, or simply X, is a standard graphical user interface (GUI) for Unix machines and is a powerful environment that supports many applications. Using the X Window System, you can have multiple terminal windows on the screen at once, each having a different login session. A pointing device like a mouse is often used with X, although it isn't required.

Many X-specific applications have been written, including games, graphics and programming utilities, and documentation tools. Linux and X make your system a bona fide workstation. With TCP/IP networking, your Linux machine can display X applications running on other machines.

The X Window System was originally developed at the Massachusetts Institute of Technology and is freely distributable. Many commercial vendors have distributed proprietary enhancements to the original X Window System as well. The version of X for Linux is XFree86, a port of X11R6 that is freely distributable. XFree86 supports a wide range of video hardware, including VGA, Super VGA, and accelerated video adaptors. XFree86 is a complete distribution of the X Windows System software and contains the X server itself, many applications and utilities, programming libraries, and documents.

Standard X applications include xterm, a terminal emulator used for most text-based applications within a window; xdm, which handles logins; xclock, a simple clock display; xman, an X-based manual page reader; and xmore. The many X applications available for Linux are too numerous to mention here, but their number includes spreadsheets, word processors, graphics programs, and Web browsers like Netscape Navigator. Many other applications are available separately. Theoretically, any application written for X should compile cleanly under Linux.

The interface of the X Window System is controlled largely by the window manager. This user-friendly program is in charge of the placement of windows, the user interface for resizing and moving them, changing windows to icons, and the appearance of window frames, among other tasks. XFree86 includes twm, the classic MIT window manager, and advanced window managers like the Open Look Virtual Window Manager (olvwm) are available. Popular among Linux users is fvwm—a small window manager that requires less than half the memory of twm. It provides a three-dimensional appearance for windows and a virtual desktop. The user moves the mouse to the edge of the screen, and the desktop shifts as though the display were much larger than it really is. Fvwm is greatly customizable and allows access to functions from the keyboard as well as the mouse. Many Linux distributions use fvwm as the standard window manager. A version of fvwm called fvwm95-2 offers a Microsoft Windows 95-like look and feel.

The XFree86 distribution includes programming libraries for wily programmers who wish to develop X applications. Widget sets like Athena,

Open Look, and Xaw3D are supported. All of the standard fonts, bitmaps, manual pages, and documentation are included. PEX (a programming interface for three-dimensional graphics) is also supported.

Many X application programmers use the proprietary Motif widget set for development. Several vendors sell single and multiple user licenses for binary versions of Motif. Because Motif itself is relatively expensive, not many Linux users own it. However, binaries statically linked with Motif routines can be freely distributed. If you write a program using Motif, you may provide a binary so users without the Motif libraries can use the program.

A major caveat to using the X Window System is its hardware requirements. An 80386-based CPU with 4 megabytes of RAM is capable of running X, but 16 megabytes or more of physical RAM is needed for comfortable use. A faster processor is nice to have as well, but having enough physical RAM is much more important. In addition, to achieve really slick video performance, we recommend getting an accelerated video card, like a VESA Local Bus (VLB) S3 chipset card. Performance ratings in excess of 300,000 xstones have been achieved with Linux and XFree86. Using adequate hardware, you'll find that running X and Linux is as fast, or faster, than running X on other Unix workstations.

In Chapter 5 we discuss how to install and use X on your system.

Introduction to Networking

Would you like to communicate with the world? Linux supports two primary Unix networking protocols: TCP/IP and UUCP. TCP/IP (Transmission Control Protocol/Internet Protocol) is the networking paradigm that allows systems all over the world to communicate on a single network, the Internet. With Linux, TCP/IP, and a connection to the Internet, you can communicate with users and machines via electronic mail, Usenet news, and FTP file transfer.

Most TCP/IP networks use Ethernet as the physical network transport. Linux supports many popular Ethernet cards and interfaces for personal computers, including pocket and PCMCIA Ethernet adaptors.

However, because not everyone has an Ethernet connection at home, Linux also supports SLIP (Serial Line Internet Protocol) and PPP (Point-to-Point Protocol), which provide Internet access via modem. Many businesses and universities provide SLIP and PPP servers. In fact, if your

Linux system has an Ethernet connection to the Internet and a modem, your system can become a SLIP or PPP server for other hosts.

NFS (Network File System) lets your system seamlessly share file systems with other machines on the network. FTP (File Transfer Protocol) lets you transfer files with other machines. Sendmail sends and receives electronic mail via the SMTP protocol; C-News and INN are NNTP based new systems; and Telnet, rlogin, and rsh let you log in and execute commands on other machines on the network. Finger lets you get information about other Internet users.

Linux also supports Microsoft Windows connectivity via Samba and Macintosh connectivity with AppleTalk and LocalTalk. Support for Novell's IPX protocol is also included.

The full range of mail and news readers is available for Linux, including elm, pine, rn, nn, and tin. Whatever your preference, you can configure a Linux system to send and receive electronic mail and news from all over the world.

The system provides a standard Unix socket programming interface. Virtually any program that uses TCP/IP can be ported to Linux. The Linux X server also supports TCP/IP, and applications running on other systems may use the display of your local system.

In Part III of *Linux Complete*, we discuss the installation of TCP/IP software, including SLIP and PPP.

UUCP (Unix-to-Unix Copy) is an older mechanism to transfer files, electronic mail, and electronic news between Unix machines. Historically, UUCP machines are connected over telephone lines via modem, but UUCP is able to transfer data over a TCP/IP network as well. If you do not have access to a TCP/IP network or a SLIP or PPP server, you can configure your system to send and receive files and electronic mail using UUCP. The UUCP HOWTO provides more information (see `http://metalab.unc.edu/LDP/HOWTO/UUCP-HOWTO.html`).

Telecommunications and BBS Software

If you have a modem, you'll be able to communicate with other machines via telecommunications packages available for Linux. Many people use telecommunications software to access bulletin board systems (BBSs) and commercial, online services like Prodigy, CompuServe, and America Online. People use modems to connect to Unix systems at work or school. Modems can send and receive faxes.

A popular communications package for Linux is seyon, which provides a customizable, ergonomic interface under X and has built-in support for the Kermit and ZModem file transfer protocols. Other telecommunications programs include C-Kermit, pcomm, and minicom. These are similar to communications programs found on other operating systems and are quite easy to use.

If you do not have access to a SLIP or PPP server (see the previous section), you can use term to multiplex your serial line. The term program allows you to open more than one login session over a modem connection. It lets you redirect X client connections to your local X server via a serial line. Another software package, KA9Q, implements a similar, SLIP-like interface.

Operating a Bulletin Board System (BBS) is a favorite hobby and means of income for many people. Linux supports a wide range of BBS software, most of which is more powerful than that available for other operating systems. With a phone line, modem, and Linux, you can turn your system into a BBS and provide dial-in access for users worldwide. BBS software for Linux includes XBBS and UniBoard BBS packages.

Most BBS software locks the user into a menu-based system where only certain functions and applications are available. An alternative to BBS access is full Unix access, which lets users dial into your system and log in normally. This requires a fair amount of maintenance by the system administrator, but providing public Unix access is not difficult. In addition to TCP/IP networking, you can make electronic mail and news access available on your system.

If you do not have access to a TCP/IP network or UUCP feed, Linux lets you communicate with BBS networks like FidoNet, which lets you exchange electronic news and mail over a telephone line. You can find more information on telecommunications and BBS software online.

World Wide Web

It is worth noting that Linux includes Web server software, as well as Web browsers. The most common server is Apache. Thousands of Linux systems run Apache on the Internet today.

Linux distributions include different Web browsers, and other browsers can be downloaded from the Internet. Available browsers include Lynx, Mosaic, Netscape, Arena, and Amaya.

Linux provides complete support for Java and CGI applets, and Perl is a standard tool in the Linux programming environment.

Interfacing and MS-DOS

Various utilities exist to interface with MS-DOS. The most well-known application is the Linux MS-DOS Emulator, which lets you run MS-DOS applications directly from Linux. Although Linux and MS-DOS are completely different operating systems, the 80386 protected-mode environment allows MS-DOS applications to behave as if they were running in their native 8086 environment.

The MS-DOS emulator is still under development, but many popular applications run under it. Understandably, MS-DOS applications that use bizarre or esoteric features of the system may never be supported because of the limitations inherent in any emulator. For example, you shouldn't expect to run programs that use 80386 protected-mode features, like Microsoft Windows (in 386 enhanced mode, that is).

Standard MS-DOS commands and utilities like PKZIP.EXE work under the emulators, as do 4DOS, a COMMAND.COM replacement, FoxPro 2.0, Harvard Graphics, MathCad, Stacker 3.1, Turbo Assembler, Turbo C/C++, Turbo Pascal, Microsoft Windows 3.0 (in real mode), and WordPerfect 5.1.

The MS-DOS Emulator is meant mostly as an ad-hoc solution for those who need MS-DOS for only a few applications and use Linux for everything else. It's not meant to be a complete implementation of MS-DOS. Of course, if the Emulator doesn't satisfy your needs, you can always run MS-DOS and Linux on the same system. Using the LILO boot loader, you can specify at boot time which operating system to start. Linux can also coexist with other operating systems, like OS/2.

Linux provides a seamless interface to transfer files between Linux and MS-DOS. You can mount an MS-DOS partition or floppy under Linux, and directly access MS-DOS files as you would any file.

Currently under development is *WINE*–a Microsoft Windows emulator for the X Window System under Linux. Once WINE is complete, users will be able to run MS-Windows applications directly from Linux. This is similar to the commercial WABI Windows emulator from Sun Microsystems, which is also available for Linux.

Other Applications

A host of miscellaneous programs and utilities exist for Linux, as one would expect of such a hodgepodge operating system. Linux's primary focus is Unix personal computing, but this is not the only field where it excels. The selection of business and scientific software is expanding, and commercial software vendors have begun to contribute to the growing pool of Linux applications.

Several relational databases are available for Linux, including Postgres, Ingres, and Mbase. These are full-featured, professional, client/server database applications, similar to those found on other Unix platforms. Many commercial database systems are available as well.

Scientific computing applications include FELT (finite element analysis); gnuplot (data plotting and analysis); Octave (a symbolic mathematics package similar to MATLAB); xspread (a spreadsheet calculator); xfractint (an X-based port of the popular Fractint fractal generator); and xlispstat (statistics). Other applications include SPICE (circuit design and analysis) and Khoros (image and digital signal processing and visualization). Commercial packages like Maple and MathLab are available.

Many more applications have been ported to Linux. If you absolutely cannot find what you need, you can attempt to port the application from another platform to Linux yourself. Whatever your field, porting standard Unix applications to Linux is straightforward. Linux's complete Unix programming environment is sufficient to serve as the base for any scientific application.

Linux also has its share of games. These include classic text-based dungeon games like Nethack and Moria; MUDs (multi-user dungeons, which allow many users to interact in a text-based adventure) like DikuMUD and TinyMUD; and a slew of X games like xtetris, netrek, and xboard, the X11 version of gnuchess. The popular shoot-em-up, arcade-style game Doom has also been ported to Linux.

For audiophiles, Linux supports various sound cards and related software, like CDplayer, which makes a CD-ROM drive into an audio CD player; MIDI sequencers and editors, which let you compose music for playback through a synthesizer or other MIDI controlled instrument; and sound editors for digitized sounds.

Can't find the application you're looking for? The Linux Software Map lists software packages that have been written or ported to Linux. A more up-to-date, Web-based listing of Linux software is Freshmeat (see `http://www.freshmeat.net/`).

Most freely distributable Unix-based software will compile on Linux with little difficulty. If all else fails, you can write the application yourself. If you're looking for a commercial application, there may be a free clone available, or you can encourage the software company to consider releasing a binary version for Linux. Several individuals have contacted software companies and asked them to port their applications to Linux, with various degrees of success.

Copyright Issues

Linux is covered by what is known as the GNU General Public License, or GPL. The GPL was developed for the GNU project by the Free Software Foundation and specifies several provisions for the distribution and modification of free software. Free, in this sense, refers to distribution, not cost. The GPL has always been subject to misinterpretation. We hope that this summary will help you understand the extent and goals of the GPL and its effect on Linux. A complete copy of the GPL is printed in Appendix D.

Originally, Linus Torvalds released Linux under a license more restrictive than the GPL, which allowed the software to be freely distributed and modified but prevented any money from changing hands for its distribution and use. On the other hand, the GPL allows people to sell and profit from free software but does not allow them to restrict another's right to distribute the software in any way.

First, it should be explained that free software that is covered by the GPL is not in the public domain. Public domain software by definition is not copyrighted and is literally owned by the public. Software covered by the GPL, on the other hand, is copyrighted by the author. The software is protected by standard international copyright laws, and the author is legally defined. The GPL provides for software that may be freely distributed but is not in the public domain.

GPL-licensed software is also not shareware. Generally, shareware is owned and copyrighted by an author who requires users to send in money for its use. Software covered by the GPL may be distributed and used free of charge.

The GPL also lets people take, modify, and distribute their own versions of the software. However, any derived works of GPL software must also be covered by the GPL. In other words, a company may not take Linux, modify it, and sell it under a restrictive license. If the software is derived from Linux, that software must be covered under the GPL also.

The GPL allows free software to be distributed and used free of charge. It also lets a person or organization distribute GPL software for a fee and even make a profit from its sale and distribution. However, a distributor of GPL software cannot take those rights away from a purchaser. If you purchase GPL software from a third-party source, you may distribute the software for free and sell it yourself as well.

This may sound like a contradiction. Why sell software when the GPL allows you to get it for free? Let's say that a company decided to bundle a large amount of free software on a CD-ROM and distribute it. That company would need to charge for the overhead of producing and distributing the CD-ROM and might even decide to profit from the sales of the software. This is allowed by the GPL.

Organizations that sell free software must follow certain restrictions set forth in the GPL. They cannot restrict the rights of users who purchase the software. If you buy a CD-ROM that contains GPL software, you can copy and distribute the CD-ROM free of charge or resell it yourself. Distributors must make obvious to users that the software is covered by the GPL. Distributors must also provide, free of charge, the complete source code to the software distributed. This permits anyone who purchases GPL software to make modifications to that software.

Allowing a company to distribute and sell free software is a good thing. Not everyone has access to the Internet and the ability to download software for free. Many organizations sell Linux on diskette, tape, or CD-ROM via mail order and profit from the sales. Linux developers may never see any of this profit; that is the understanding reached between the developer and the distributor when software is licensed by the GPL. In other words, Linus Torvalds knew that companies might wish to sell Linux and that he might not see a penny of the profits.

In the free software world, the important issue is not money. The goal of free software is always to develop and distribute fantastic software and allow anyone to obtain and use it. In the next section, we'll discuss how this applies to the development of Linux.

The Design and Philosophy of Linux

New users often have a few misconceptions and false expectations about Linux. It is important to understand the philosophy and design of Linux in order to use it effectively. We'll start by describing how Linux is not designed.

In commercial Unix development houses, the entire system is developed under a rigorous quality assurance policy that utilizes source and revision control systems, documentation, and procedures to report and resolve bugs. Developers may not add features or change key sections of code on a whim. They must validate the change as a response to a bug report and subsequently check in all changes to the source control system so that the changes may be reversed if necessary. Each developer is assigned one or more parts of the system code, and only that developer can alter those sections of the code while it is checked out (that is, while the code is under his or her control).

Organizationally, a quality assurance department runs rigorous tests on each new version of the operating system and reports any bugs. The developers fix these bugs as reported. A complex system of statistical analysis is used to ensure that a certain percentage of bugs are fixed before the next release and that the operating system as a whole passes certain release criteria.

The software company, quite reasonably, must have quantitative proof that the next revision of the operating system is ready to be shipped–hence the gathering and analysis of statistics about the performance of the operating system. It is a big job to develop a commercial Unix system, often large enough to employ hundreds, if not thousands, of programmers, testers, documenters, and administrative personnel. Of course, no two commercial Unix vendors are alike, but that is the general picture.

The Linux model of software development discards the entire concept of organized development, source-code control systems, structured bug reporting, and statistical quality control. Linux is, and likely always will be, a hacker's operating system. (By *hacker*, I mean a feverishly dedicated programmer who enjoys exploiting computers and does interesting things with them. This is the original definition of the term, in contrast to the connotation of *hacker* as a computer wrongdoer or outlaw.)

There is no single organization responsible for developing Linux. Anyone with enough know-how has the opportunity to help develop and debug the kernel, port new software, write documentation, and help new users. For the most part, the Linux community communicates via mailing lists and Usenet newsgroups. Several conventions have sprung up around the development effort. Anyone who wishes to have their code included in the official kernel mails it to Linus Torvalds. He will test and include the code in the kernel as long as it doesn't break things or go against the overall design of the system.

The system itself is designed using an open-ended, feature-minded approach. The number of new features and critical changes to the system has recently diminished, and the general rule is that a new version of the kernel will be released every few weeks. Of course, this is a rough figure. New release criteria include the number of bugs to be fixed, feedback from users testing pre-release versions of the code, and the amount of sleep Linus Torvalds has had this week.

Suffice it to say that not every bug is fixed, nor is every problem ironed out between releases. As long as the revision appears to be free of critical or recurring bugs, it is considered to be stable, and the new version is released. The thrust behind Linux development is not to release perfect, bug-free code; it is to develop a free Unix implementation. Linux is for the developers, more than anyone else.

Anyone who has a new feature or software application generally makes it available in an *alpha version*—that is, a test version, for those brave users who want to hash out problems in the initial code. Because the Linux community is largely based on the Internet, alpha software is usually uploaded to one or more Linux FTP sites, and a message is posted to one of the Linux Usenet newsgroups about how to obtain and test the code. Users who download and test alpha software can then mail results, bug fixes, and questions to the author.

After the initial bugs have been fixed, the code enters a *beta test* stage, in which it is usually considered stable but not complete. It works, but not all of the features may be present. The software may also go directly to a final stage, in which the software is considered complete and usable.

Keep in mind that these are only conventions, not rules. Some developers may feel so confident about their software that they decide it isn't necessary to release alpha or test versions. It is always up to the developer to make these decisions.

You might be amazed at how such an unstructured system of volunteers who program and debug a complete Unix system gets anything done at all. As it turns out, this is one of the most efficient and motivated development efforts ever employed. The entire Linux kernel is written from scratch, without code from proprietary sources. It takes a huge amount of work to port all the free software under the sun to Linux. Libraries are written and ported, file systems are developed, and hardware drivers are written for many popular devices—all due to the work of volunteers.

Linux software is generally released as a *distribution*, a set of prepackaged software that comprises an entire system. It would be difficult for most users to build a complete system from the ground up, starting with the kernel, adding utilities, and installing all of the necessary software by hand. Instead, many software distributions are available that include everything necessary to install and run a complete system. There is no single, standard distribution—there are many, and each has its own advantages and disadvantages. We describe installation of the various Linux distributions in Chapter 4.

Differences between Linux and Other Operating Systems

It is important to understand the differences between Linux and other operating systems, like MS-DOS, OS/2, and the other implementations of Unix for personal computers. First of all, Linux coexists happily with other operating systems on the same machine. You can run MS-DOS and OS/2 along with Linux on the same system without problems. There are even ways to interact between various operating systems, as we'll see.

Why Use Linux?

Why use Linux instead of a well-known, well-tested, and well-documented commercial operating system? We could give you a thousand reasons. One of the most important, however, is that Linux is an excellent choice for personal Unix computing. If you're a Unix software developer, why use MS-DOS at home? Linux allows you to develop and test Unix software on your PC, including database and X Window System applications. If you're a student, chances are that your university computing systems run Unix. You can run your own Unix system and tailor it to your needs. Installing and running Linux is also an excellent way to learn Unix if you don't have access to other Unix machines.

But let's not lose sight. Linux isn't only for personal Unix users. It is robust and complete enough to handle large tasks, as well as distributed computing needs. Many businesses—especially small ones—have moved their systems to Linux in lieu of other Unix-based workstation environments. Universities have found that Linux is perfect for teaching courses in operating system design. Large, commercial software vendors have started to realize the opportunities that a free operating system can provide.

Linux vs. MS-DOS

It's not uncommon to run both Linux and MS-DOS on the same system. Many Linux users rely on MS-DOS for applications like word processing. Linux provides its own analogs for these applications, but you might have a good reason to run MS-DOS and Linux. If your dissertation is written using WordPerfect for MS-DOS, you may not be able to convert it easily to TeX or some other format. Many commercial applications for MS-DOS aren't available for Linux yet, but there's no reason that you can't use both.

MS-DOS does not fully utilize the functionality of 80386 and 80486 processors, while Linux runs completely in the processor's protected mode and utilizes all of its features. You can directly access all of your available memory (and beyond, with virtual RAM). Linux provides a complete Unix interface that is not available under MS-DOS. You can easily develop and port Unix applications to Linux, but under MS-DOS you are limited to a subset of Unix functionality.

Linux and MS-DOS are different entities. MS-DOS is inexpensive compared to other commercial operating systems and has a strong foothold in the personal computer world. No other operating system for the personal computer has reached the level of popularity of MS-DOS because justifying spending $1,000 for other operating systems is unrealistic for many users. Linux, however, is free, and you may finally have the chance to decide for yourself.

You can judge Linux vs. MS-DOS based on your expectations and needs. Linux is not for everybody. If you always wanted to run a complete Unix system at home, without the high cost of other Unix implementations for personal computers, Linux may be what you're looking for.

Linux vs. The Other Guys

Several other advanced operating systems have become popular in the PC world. Specifically, IBM's OS/2 and Microsoft Windows have become popular for users upgrading from MS-DOS.

Both OS/2 and Windows NT are full-featured multitasking operating systems, like Linux. OS/2, Windows NT, and Linux support roughly the same user interface, networking, and security features. However, the real difference between Linux and The Other Guys is the fact that Linux is a version of Unix and benefits from contributions of the Unix community at large.

What makes Unix so important? Not only is it the most popular operating system for multiuser machines, it is also a foundation of the free software world. Much of the free software available on the Internet is written specifically for Unix systems.

There are many implementations of Unix from many vendors. No single organization is responsible for its distribution. There is a large push in the Unix community for standardization in the form of open systems, but no single group controls this design. Any vendor (or, as it turns out, any hacker) may develop a standard implementation of Unix.

OS/2 and Microsoft operating systems, on the other hand, are proprietary. The interface and design are controlled by a single corporation, which develops the operating system code. In one sense, this kind of organization is beneficial because it sets strict standards for programming and user-interface design, unlike those found even in the open systems community.

Several organizations have attempted the difficult task of standardizing the Unix programming interface. Linux, in particular, is mostly compliant with the POSIX.1 standard. As time goes by, it is expected that the Linux system will adhere to other standards, but standardization is not the primary goal of Linux development.

Linux vs. Other Implementations of Unix

Several other implementations of Unix exist for 80386 or better personal computers. The 80386 architecture lends itself to Unix, and vendors have taken advantage of this.

Other implementations of Unix for the personal computer are similar to Linux. Almost all commercial versions of Unix support roughly the same software, programming environment, and networking features. However, there are differences between Linux and commercial versions of Unix.

Linux supports a different range of hardware than commercial implementations. In general, Linux supports most well-known hardware devices, but support is still limited to hardware that the developers own. Commercial Unix vendors tend to support more hardware at the outset, but the list of hardware devices that Linux supports is expanding continuously. We'll cover Linux's hardware requirements a little later on in this chapter and in more depth in Part II.

Many users report that Linux is at least as stable as commercial Unix systems. Linux is still under development, but the two-pronged release philosophy has made stable versions available without impeding development.

The most important factor for many users is price. Linux software is free if you can download it from the Internet or another computer network. If you do not have Internet access, you can still purchase Linux inexpensively via mail order on diskette, tape, or CD-ROM.

Of course, you may copy Linux from a friend who already has the software or share the purchase cost with someone else. If you plan to install Linux on a large number of machines, you need only purchase a single copy of the software–Linux is not distributed with a single-machine license.

The value of commercial Unix implementations should not be demeaned. In addition to the price of the software itself, one often pays for documentation, support, and quality assurance. These are very important factors for large institutions, but personal computer users may not require these benefits. In any case, many businesses and universities have found that running Linux in a lab of inexpensive personal computers is preferable to running a commercial version of Unix in a lab of workstations. Linux can provide workstation functionality on a personal computer at a fraction of the cost.

Linux systems have travelled the high seas of the North Pacific and manage telecommunications and data analysis for an oceanographic research vessel. Linux systems are used at research stations in Antarctica. Several hospitals maintain patient records on Linux systems.

Other free or inexpensive implementations of Unix are available for the 80386 and 80486. One of the best known is 386BSD, an implementation of BSD Unix for the 80386. The 386BSD package is comparable to Linux in many ways, but which one is better depends on your needs and expectations. The only strong distinction we can make is that Linux is developed openly, and any volunteer can aid in the development process, while 386BSD is developed by a closed team of programmers. Because of this, serious philosophical and design differences exist between the two projects. The goal of Linux is to develop a complete Unix system from scratch (and have a lot of fun in the process), and the goal of 386BSD is in part to modify the existing BSD code for use on the 80386.

NetBSD is another port of the BSD NET/2 distribution to several machines, including the 80386. NetBSD has a slightly more open development structure and is comparable to 386BSD in many respects.

Another project of note is HURD, an effort by the Free Software Foundation to develop and distribute a free version of Unix for many platforms. Contact the Free Software Foundation (the address is given in Appendix D) for more information about this project. At the time of this writing, HURD is still under development.

Other inexpensive versions of Unix exist as well, like Minix, an academic but useful Unix clone upon which early development of Linux was based. Some of these implementations are mostly of academic interest, while others are full-fledged systems.

Hardware Requirements

You must be convinced by now of how wonderful Linux is and of all the great things it can do for you. However, before you rush out and install Linux, you need to be aware of its hardware requirements and limitations.

Keep in mind that Linux is developed by users. This means, for the most part, that the hardware supported by Linux is that which the users and developers have access to. As it turns out, most popular hardware and peripherals for personal computers are supported. Linux supports more hardware than some commercial implementations of Unix. However, some obscure devices aren't supported yet.

Another drawback of hardware support under Linux is that many companies keep their hardware interfaces proprietary. Volunteer Linux developers can't write drivers for the devices because the manufacturer does not make the technical specifications public. Even if Linux developers could develop drivers for proprietary devices, they would be owned by the company that owns the device interface, which violates the GPL. Manufacturers that maintain proprietary interfaces write their own drivers for operating systems like MS-DOS and Microsoft Windows. Users and third-party developers never need to know the details of the interface.

In some cases, Linux programmers have attempted to write hackish device drivers based on assumptions about the interface. In other cases, developers work with the manufacturer and try to obtain information about the device interface, with varying degrees of success.

In the following sections, we attempt to summarize the hardware requirements for Linux. The Linux Hardware HOWTO (`http://metalab.unc.edu/LDP/HOWTO/Hardware-HOWTO.html`) contains a more complete listing of hardware supported by Linux.

NOTE

Much hardware support for Linux is in the development stage. Some distributions may or may not support experimental features. This section lists hardware that has been supported for some time and is known to be stable. When in doubt, consult the documentation of your Linux distribution. See Chapter 3 for more information about Linux distributions.

Linux is available for many platforms in addition to Intel 80x86 systems. These include Macintosh, Amiga, Sun SparcStation, and Digital Equipment Corporation Alpha-based systems. In this book, however, we focus on garden-variety Intel 80386, 80486, and Pentium processors, and clones by manufacturers like AMD, Cyrix, and IBM.

Motherboard and CPU Requirements

Linux currently supports systems with the Intel 80386, 80486, or Pentium CPU, including all variations like the 80386SX, 80486SX, 80486DX, and 80486DX2. Non-Intel clones work with Linux as well. Linux has also been ported to the DEC Alpha and the Apple PowerMac.

If you have an 80386 or 80486SX, you may also wish to use a math coprocessor, although one isn't required. The Linux kernel can perform FPU emulation if the machine doesn't have a coprocessor. All standard FPU couplings are supported, including IIT, Cyrix FasMath, and Intel.

Most common PC motherboards are based on the PCI bus but also offer ISA slots. This configuration is supported by Linux, as are EISA and VESA-bus systems. IBM's MicroChannel (MCA) bus, found on most IBM PS/2 systems, is significantly different, and support has been recently added.

Memory Requirements

Linux requires very little memory, compared to other advanced operating systems. You should have 4 megabytes of RAM at the very least, and 16 megabytes is strongly recommended. The more memory you have, the faster the system will run. Some distributions require more RAM for installation.

Linux supports the full 32-bit address range of the processor. In other words, it uses all of your RAM automatically.

Linux will run with only 4 megabytes of RAM, including bells and whistles like the X Window System and emacs. However, having more memory is almost as important as having a faster processor. For general use, 16 megabytes is enough, and 32 megabytes, or more, may be needed for systems with a heavy user load.

Most Linux users allocate a portion of their hard drive as swap space, which is used as *virtual RAM*. Even if your machine has more than 16 megabytes of physical RAM, you may wish to use swap space. It is no replacement for physical RAM, but it can let your system run larger applications by swapping inactive portions of code to disk. The amount of swap space that you should allocate depends on several factors; we'll take a closer look at this issue in Chapter 4.

Hard Drive Controller Requirements

It is possible to run Linux from a floppy diskette or, for some distributions, a live file system on CD-ROM, but for good performance, you need hard disk space. Linux can coexist with other operating systems—it only needs one or more disk partitions.

Linux supports all IDE and EIDE controllers, as well as older MFM and RLL controllers. Most, but not all, ESDI controllers are supported. The general rule for non-SCSI hard drive and floppy controllers is that if you can access the drive from MS-DOS or another operating system, you should be able to access it from Linux.

Linux also supports a number of popular SCSI drive controllers. This includes most Adaptec and Buslogic cards, as well as cards based on the NCR chip sets.

Hard Drive Space Requirements

Of course, to install Linux, you need to have some amount of free space on your hard drive. Linux will support more than one hard drive on the same machine; you can allocate space for Linux across multiple drives if necessary.

How much hard drive space depends on your needs and the software you're installing. Linux is relatively small, as Unix implementations go. You could run a system in 20 megabytes of disk space. However, for expansion and larger packages like X, you need more space. If you plan to let more than one person use the machine, you need to allocate storage for their files. Realistic space requirements range from 200 megabytes to one gigabyte or more.

Also, you will likely want to allocate disk space as virtual RAM.

Each Linux distribution comes with literature to help you gauge the precise amount of storage required for your software configuration. Look at the information that comes with your distribution.

Monitor and Video Adaptor Requirements

Linux supports standard Hercules, CGA, EGA, VGA, IBM monochrome, Super VGA, and many accelerated video cards, and monitors for the default, text-based interface. In general, if the video card and monitor work under an operating system like MS-DOS, the combination should work fine under Linux. However, original IBM CGA cards suffer from "snow" under Linux, which is not pleasant to view.

Graphical environments like X have video hardware requirements of their own. Rather than list them here, we relegate that discussion to Chapter 5. Popular video cards are supported and new card support is added regularly.

Miscellaneous Hardware

You may also have devices like a CD-ROM drive, mouse, or sound card and may be interested in whether or not this hardware is supported by Linux.

Mice and Other Pointing Devices

Typically, a mouse is used only in graphical environments like X. However, several Linux applications that are not associated with a graphical environment also use mice.

Linux supports standard serial mice like Logitech, MM series, Mouseman, Microsoft (2-button), and Mouse Systems (3-button). Linux also supports Microsoft, Logitech, and ATIXL bus mice, and the PS/2 mouse interface.

Pointing devices that emulate mice, like trackballs and touchpads, should work also.

CD-ROM Drives

Many common CD-ROM drives attach to standard IDE controllers. Another common interface for CD-ROM is SCSI. SCSI support includes multiple logical units per device, so you can use CD-ROM jukeboxes. Additionally, a few proprietary interfaces, like the NEC CDR-74, Sony CDU-541 and CDU-31a, Texel DM-3024, and Mitsumi are supported.

Linux supports the standard ISO 9660 file system for CD-ROMs and the High Sierra file system extensions.

Tape Drives

Any SCSI tape drive, including quarter inch, DAT, and 8MM are supported, if the SCSI controller is supported. Devices that connect to the floppy controller like floppy tape drives are supported as well, as are some other interfaces, like QIC-02.

Printers

Linux supports the complete range of parallel printers. If MS-DOS or some other operating system can access your printer from the parallel port, Linux should be able to access it, too. Linux printer software includes the Unix standard lp and lpr software. This software allows you to print remotely via a network, if you have one. Linux also includes software that allows most printers to handle PostScript files.

For a list of specific printers supported, see Chapter 7.

Modems

As with printer support, Linux supports the full range of serial modems, both internal and external. A great deal of telecommunications software is available for Linux, including Kermit, pcomm, minicom, and seyon. If your modem is accessible from another operating system on the same machine, you should be able to access it from Linux with no difficulty.

Ethernet Cards

Many popular Ethernet cards and LAN adaptors are supported by Linux. Linux also supports some FDDI, frame relay, and token ring cards, and all Arcnet cards. A list of supported network cards is included in the kernel source of your distribution.

Sources of Linux Information

Many other sources of information about Linux are available. In particular, a number of books about Unix in general will be of use, especially for readers unfamiliar with Unix. We suggest that you peruse one of these books before attempting to brave the jungles of Linux.

Information is also available online in electronic form. You must have access to an online network like the Internet, Usenet, or Fidonet to access the information. A good place to start is `http://MetaLab.unc.edu/LDP/HOWTO/META-FAQ.html`. If you cannot get online, you might be able to find someone who is kind enough to give you hard copies of the documents.

Online Documents

Many Linux documents are available via anonymous FTP from Internet archive sites around the world and networks like Fidonet and CompuServe. Linux CD-ROM distributions also contain the documents mentioned here. If you can send mail to Internet sites, you may be able to retrieve these files using one of the FTP e-mail servers that mail you the documents or files from the FTP sites.

A list of well-known Linux archive sites is given in `http://MetaLab.unc.edu/LDP/HOWTO/META-FAQ.html`. To reduce network traffic, you should use an FTP site that is geographically close to you.

Appendix A contains a partial list of the Linux documents available via anonymous FTP. The filenames vary depending on the site. Most sites keep Linux-related documents in the `docs` subdirectory of their Linux archive. For example, the FTP site `MetaLab.unc.edu`, keeps Linux files in `/pub/Linux`, with Linux-related documentation in `/pub/Linux/docs`.

Examples of available online documents are Linux Frequently Asked Questions with Answers, a collection of frequently asked questions about Linux; Linux HOWTO documents, which describe specific aspects of the system, like the Installation HOWTO, Printing HOWTO, and Ethernet HOWTO; and the Linux META-FAQ, which is a list of information sources on the Internet.

Many of these documents are also regularly posted to one or more Linux-related Usenet newsgroups; see "Usenet Newsgroups" below.

Linux on the World Wide Web

The Linux Documentation Project Home Page is on the World Wide Web at `http://metalab.unc.edu/LDP/`. This Web page lists many

HOWTOs and other documents in HTML format, as well as pointers to other sites of interest to Linux users, like the *Linux Journal*, a monthly magazine. You can find the journal at `http://www.ssc.com/`.

Books and Other Published Works

The books of the Linux Documentation Project are the result of an effort carried out over the Internet to write and distribute a bona fide set of manuals for Linux, analogs of the documentation that comes with commercial Unix versions and covers installation, operation, programming, networking, and kernel development.

Linux Documentation Project manuals are available via anonymous FTP and by mail order. `http://MetaLab.unc.edu/LDP/HOWTO/META-FAQ.html` lists the manuals available and describes how to obtain them.

Many large publishers, including Sybex, MIS:Press, Digital Press, O'Reilly Associates, and SAMS, have jumped onto the Linux bandwagon. Check with computer bookstores or SSC's Web page at `http://www.ssc.com/`, or the book reviews in *Linux Journal*, sometimes made available on their site, `http://www.linuxjournal.com`.

A large number of books about Unix in general are applicable to Linux. In its use and programming interface, Linux does not differ greatly from other implementations of Unix. Almost everything you would like to know about using and programming Linux can be found in general Unix texts. In fact, this book is meant to supplement the library of Unix books currently available. Here, we present the most important Linux-specific details and hope that you will look to other sources for in-depth information.

Armed with good books about Unix, as well as this book, you should be able to tackle just about anything. Appendix B lists several Unix books that are recommended highly for Unix newcomers and wizards.

The *Linux Journal* is distributed worldwide and is an excellent way to keep in touch with the goings-on of the Linux community, especially if you do not have access to Usenet news. See `http://ssc.com/` for information on subscribing to the *Linux Journal*.

Usenet Newsgroups

Usenet is a worldwide electronic news and discussion forum with a diverse selection of *newsgroups*, which are discussion areas devoted to specific topics. Much discussion about Linux development occurs over the Internet and Usenet. Not surprisingly, a number of Usenet newsgroups are dedicated to Linux.

The original Linux newsgroup, `alt.os.linux`, was created to move some of the discussion about Linux from `comp.os.minix` and various mailing lists. Soon, the traffic on `alt.os.linux` grew large enough that a newsgroup in the `comp` hierarchy was warranted. A vote was taken in February 1992, and `comp.os.linux` was created.

`comp.os.linux` quickly became one of the most popular (and loudest) of the Usenet groups, more popular than any other group in the `comp.os` hierarchy. In December 1992, a vote was taken to split the newsgroup to reduce traffic; only `comp.os.linux.announce` passed this vote. In July 1993, the group was finally split into a new hierarchy. Almost 2,000 people voted in the `comp.os.linux` reorganization, making it one of the largest Usenet Calls For Votes ever.

If you do not have Usenet, there are mail-to-news gateways available for many (if not all) of the newsgroups below.

> `comp.os.linux.answers` For posting Linux FAQs, How-To's, READMEs, and other documents that answer questions about Linux. This will help keep the traffic down in other c.o.l.* groups and will leave `comp.os.linux.announce` for true announcements.

> `comp.os.linux.announce` A moderated newsgroup for announcements about Linux, including bug reports and important patches to software. If you read any Linux newsgroup at all, read this one. Often, the important postings in this group are not crossposted. This group also contains many periodic postings about Linux, including the online documents described in Appendix C.

Postings to the above newsgroups must be approved by the moderators, Matt Welsh and Lars Wirzenius. If you wish to submit an article, you simply post the article as you normally would; the news software will forward the article to the moderators for approval. However, if your news system is not set up correctly, you may need to mail the article directly to `linux-announce@tc.cornell.edu`.

> `comp.os.linux.development.apps` An unmoderated newsgroup for questions and discussion regarding the writing of applications for Linux and the porting of applications to Linux.

`comp.os.linux.development.system` An unmoderated newsgroup for discussions about the development of the Linux system related to the kernel, device drivers, and loadable modules.

`comp.os.linux.hardware` This newsgroup is for questions and discussion specific to a particular piece of hardware, for instance, "Can this system run Linux?", "How do I use this disk drive with Linux?", and so forth.

`comp.os.linux.m68k` This is to further interest in and development of the port of Linux to Motorola 680x0 architecture.

`comp.os.linux.misc` All discussion that doesn't quite fit into the other available Linux groups. Any nontechnical or metadiscourse about Linux should occur in `comp.os.linux.misc`.

`comp.os.linux.networking` Discussion relating to networking and communications, including Ethernet boards, SLIP, and PPP.

`comp.os.linux.setup` Questions and discussion relating to Linux installation and system administration.

`comp.os.linux.x` Discussion of X Window System features unique to Linux, including servers, clients, fonts, and libraries.

`comp.os.linux.advocacy` A newsgroup for discussion of the benefits of Linux compared to other operating systems.

`comp.os.linux.alpha` This newsgroup should be used for all discussions relating to buying, installing, running, maintaining, and developing Linux on Digital Alpha processor based systems.

This list is by no means complete. New groups are created when a need for a subdivision of discussion is advisable, and there are Linux groups in other hierarchies as well.

Internet Mailing Lists

If you have access to Internet electronic mail, you can participate in several mailing lists, even if you do not have Usenet access. If you are not directly on the Internet, you can join one of these mailing lists if you can exchange electronic mail with the Internet (for example, through UUCP, Fidonet, CompuServe, or other networks which exchange Internet mail).

For more information about the Linux mailing lists, send e-mail to `majordomo@vger.rutgers.edu`.

Include a line with the word *help* in the body of the message, and a message will be returned to you that describes how to subscribe and unsubscribe to various mailing lists. The word lists on a line by itself will retrieve the names of mailing lists that are accessible through the `majordomo.vger.rutgers.edu` server.

There are several special-purpose mailing lists for Linux as well. The best way to find out about these is to watch the Linux Usenet newsgroups for announcements, as well as to read the list of publicly available mailing lists, which is posted to the Usenet `news.answers` group.

GETTING HELP WITH LINUX

You will undoubtedly need assistance during your adventures in the Linux world. Even Unix wizards are occasionally stumped by some quirk or feature of Linux. It's important to know how, where, and when to find help.

The primary means of obtaining help is through Internet mailing lists and newsgroups. If you don't have access to these sources, you may be able to find comparable Linux discussion forums on online services, like BBSs and CompuServe. Also available online are *Linux Journal*'s Best of Technical Support columns, at `http://www.linuxjournal.com/techsup.html`.

Several businesses provide commercial support for Linux. These services allow you to pay a subscription fee that lets you call consultants for help with your Linux problems.

Keeping the following suggestions in mind will greatly improve your experience with Linux and guarantee more success in finding help.

- Consult all available documentation first! You should do this when you first encounter a problem. Various sources of information are listed in `http://MetaLab.unc.edu/LDP/HOWTO/META-FAQ.html`. These documents are laboriously written for people who need help with the Linux system, like you. As mentioned above, books written for Unix are applicable to Linux, and you should use them, too.

  If you have access to Usenet news, or any of the Linux-related mailing lists, be sure to read the information there before posting. Often, solutions to common problems that are not easy to find in the documentation are well covered in newsgroups and mailing lists. If you only post to these groups but don't read them, you are asking for trouble.

- Learn to appreciate self-reliance. You asked for it by running Linux in the first place. Remember, Linux is all about hacking and fixing problems. It is not a commercial operating system, nor does it try to be one. Hacking won't kill you. In fact, it will be enlightening to investigate and solve problems yourself–you may even one day call yourself a Linux guru. Learn to appreciate the full value of hacking the system and fixing problems yourself. You shouldn't expect to run a complete, homebrew Linux system without some handiwork.
- Remain calm. Nothing is earned by taking an axe–or worse, a powerful electromagnet–to your Linux box. A large punching bag or a long walk is a good way to relieve occasional stress attacks. As Linux matures and distributions become more reliable, we hope this problem will disappear. However, even commercial Unix implementations can be tricky. When all else fails, sit back, take a few deep breaths, and return to the problem when you feel relaxed. Your mind and conscience will be clearer.
- Refrain from posting hastily. Many people make the mistake of posting or mailing messages pleading for help prematurely. When encountering a problem, do not rush immediately to the nearest terminal and post a message to one of the Linux Usenet groups. First try to resolve the problem yourself, and be absolutely certain what the problem is. Does your system not respond when switched on? Perhaps it is unplugged.
- When you post for help, make it worthwhile. Remember that people who read your post are not necessarily there to help you. Therefore, it is important to remain as polite, terse, and informative as possible.

  How does one accomplish this? First, you should include as much relevant information about your system and your problem as possible. Posting the simple request "I cannot seem to get e-mail to work" will probably get you nowhere unless you include information about your system, what software you're using, what you have attempted to do so far, and what the results were. When you include technical information, it is also a good idea to include general information about the version of your software (the Linux kernel version, for example), as well as a brief summary of your hardware configuration. But don't overdo it–your monitor type and brand is probably irrelevant if you're trying to configure network software.

Chapter 2

Unix and Internet Fundamentals

This chapter describes the basics of PC-class computers, Unix-like operating systems, and the Internet in non-technical language. It is reprinted from the Unix and Internet Fundamentals HOWTO, version 1.1 of 3 December 1998, by Eric S. Raymond.

Introduction

This chapter is intended to help Linux and Internet users who are learning by doing. While this is a great way to acquire skills, sometimes it leaves peculiar gaps in one's knowledge of the basics—gaps that can make it hard to think creatively or troubleshoot effectively because of a lack of a clear mental model of what is really going on.

I'll try to describe how it all works in clear, simple language. The presentation will be tuned for people using Unix or Linux on PC-class hardware. Nevertheless I'll usually refer simply to Unix here, as most of what I will describe is constant across platforms and across Unix variants.

I'm going to assume you're using an Intel PC. The details differ slightly if you're running an Alpha or PowerPC or some other Unix box, but the basic concepts are the same.

It's a good idea to just skim when you first read this; you should come back and reread it a few times after you've digested what you have learned. I won't repeat things, so you'll have to pay attention, but that also means you'll learn from every word you read.

Related Resources

If you're reading this to learn how to hack, you should also read the How To Become a Hacker FAQ (see `http://www.tuxedo.org/~esr/faqs/hacker-howto.html`). It has links to some other useful resources.

New Versions of This Document

New versions of the Unix and Internet Fundamentals HOWTO will be periodically posted to `comp.os.linux.help` and `comp.os.linux.announce` and `news.answers`. They will also be uploaded to various Linux WWW and FTP sites, including the LDP home page.

You can view the latest version of this on the World Wide Web via the URL `http://MetaLab.unc.edu/LDP/HOWTO/Fundamentals-HOWTO.html`. If you have questions or comments about this document, please feel free to e-mail Eric S. Raymond at `esr@thyrsus.com`. I welcome any suggestions or criticisms. I especially welcome hyperlinks to more detailed explanations of individual concepts. If you find a mistake with this document, please let me know so I can correct it in the next version.

Basic Anatomy of Your Computer

Your computer has a processor chip inside it that does the actual computing. It has internal memory (what DOS/Windows people call *RAM* and Unix people often call *core*). The processor and memory live on the *motherboard,* which is the heart of your computer.

Your computer has a screen and keyboard. It has hard drives and floppy disks. The screen and your disks have *controller cards* that plug into the motherboard and help the computer drive these outboard devices. (Your keyboard is too simple to need a separate card; the controller is built into the keyboard chassis itself.)

We'll go into some of the details of how these devices work later. For now, here are a few basic things to keep in mind about how they work together.

All the inboard parts of your computer are connected by a *bus*. Physically, the bus is what you plug your controller cards into (the video card, the disk controller, and a sound card, if you have one). The bus is the data highway between your processor, your screen, your disk, and everything else.

The processor, which makes everything else go, can't actually see any of the other pieces directly; it has to talk to them over the bus. The only other subsystem it has really fast, immediate access to is memory (the core). In order for programs to run, then, they have to be *in core*.

When your computer reads a program or data off the disk, the processor uses the bus to send a disk read request to your disk controller. Some time later the disk controller uses the bus to signal the computer that it has read the data and put the data in a certain location in core. The processor can then use the bus to look at that memory.

Your keyboard and screen also communicate with the processor via the bus, but in simpler ways. We'll discuss those later on. For now, you know enough to understand what happens when you turn on your computer.

What Happens When You Switch on a Computer?

A computer without a program running is just an inert hunk of electronics. The first thing a computer has to do when it is turned on is start up a special program called an *operating system*. The operating system's job is to help other computer programs to work by handling the messy details of controlling the computer's hardware.

The process of bringing up the operating system is called *booting* (originally this was *bootstrapping* and alluded to the difficulty of pulling yourself up by your bootstraps). Your computer knows how to boot because instructions for booting are built into one of its chips, the BIOS (or Basic Input/Output System) chip.

The BIOS chip tells it to look in a fixed place on the lowest-numbered hard disk (the *boot disk*) for a special program called a *boot loader* (under Linux the boot loader is called LILO). The boot loader is pulled into core and started. The boot loader's job is to start the real operating system.

The loader does this by looking for a *kernel*, loading it into core, and starting it. When you boot Linux and see *LILO* on the screen followed by a bunch of dots, it is loading the kernel. (Each dot means it has loaded another *disk block* of kernel code.)

NOTE

You may wonder why the BIOS doesn't load the kernel directly—why the two-step process with the boot loader? Well, the BIOS isn't very smart. In fact it's very stupid, and Linux doesn't use it at all after boot time. It was originally written for primitive 8-bit PCs with tiny disks and literally can't access enough of the disk to load the kernel directly. The boot loader step also lets you start one of several operating systems off different places on your disk, in the unlikely event that Unix isn't good enough for you.

Once the kernel starts, it has to look around, find the rest of the hardware, and get ready to run programs. It does this by poking not at ordinary memory locations but rather at *I/O ports*—special bus addresses that are likely to have device controller cards listening at them for commands. The kernel doesn't poke at random; it has a lot of built-in knowledge about what it's likely to find where and how controllers will respond if they're present. This process is called *autoprobing*.

Most of the messages you see at boot time are the kernel autoprobing your hardware through the I/O ports, figuring out what it has available to it and adapting itself to your machine. The Linux kernel is extremely good at this, better than most Unices and much better than DOS or Windows. In fact, many Linux old-timers think the cleverness of Linux's boot-time probes (which made it relatively easy to install) was a major reason it broke out of the pack of free-Unix experiments to attract a critical mass of users.

But getting the kernel fully loaded and running isn't the end of the boot process it's just the first stage (sometimes called *run level 1*).

The kernel's next step is to check to make sure your disks are OK. Disk file systems are fragile things. If they've been damaged by a hardware failure or a sudden power outage, there are good reasons to take recovery steps before your Unix is all the way up. We'll go into some of this later in "How a File Gets Looked Up."

The kernel's next step is to start several *daemons*. A daemon is a program like a print spooler, a mail listener, or a WWW server that lurks in the background, waiting for things to do. These special programs often have to coordinate several requests that could conflict. They are daemons because it's often easier to write one program that runs constantly and knows about all requests than it would be to try to make sure that a flock of copies (each processing one request and all running at the same time) don't step on each other. The particular collection of daemons your system starts may vary, but will almost always include a print spooler (a gatekeeper daemon for your printer).

Once all daemons are started, we're at *run level 2*. The next step is to prepare for users. The kernel starts a copy of a program called `getty` to watch your console (and maybe more copies to watch dial-in serial ports). This program is what issues the `login` prompt to your console. We're now at *run level 3* and ready for you to log in and run programs.

When you log in (give a name and password) you identify yourself to getty and the computer. It then runs a program called (naturally enough) login, which does some housekeeping things and then starts up a command interpreter, the shell. (Yes, getty and login could be one program. They're separate for historical reasons not worth going into here.)

In the next section, we'll talk about what happens when you run programs from the shell.

What Happens When You Run Programs from the Shell?

The normal shell gives you the $ prompt that you see after logging in (unless you've customized it to something else). We won't talk about shell syntax and the easy things you can see on the screen here; instead we'll take a look behind the scenes at what's happening from the computer's point of view.

After boot time and before you run a program, you can think of your computer as containing a zoo of processes that are all waiting for something to do. They're all waiting on *events*. An event can be you pressing a key or moving a mouse. Or, if your machine is hooked to a network, an event can be a data packet coming in over that network.

The kernel is one of these processes. It's a special one because it controls when the other user processes can run, and it is normally the only process with direct access to the machine's hardware. In fact, user processes have to make requests to the kernel when they want to get keyboard input, write to your screen, read from or write to disk, or do just about anything other than crunching bits in memory. These requests are known as *system calls*.

Normally all I/O goes through the kernel so it can schedule the operations and prevent processes from stepping on each other. A few special user processes are allowed to slide around the kernel, usually by being given direct access to I/O ports. X servers (the programs that handle other programs' requests to do screen graphics on most Unix boxes) are the most common example of this. But we haven't gotten to an X server yet; you're looking at a shell prompt on a character console.

The shell is just a user process, and not a particularly special one. It waits on your keystrokes, listening (through the kernel) to the keyboard I/O port. As the kernel sees them, it echoes them to your screen then passes them to the shell. When the kernel sees an Enter, it passes your line of text to the shell. The shell tries to interpret those keystrokes as commands.

Let's say you type **`ls`** and press Enter to invoke the Unix directory lister. The shell applies its built-in rules to figure out that you want to run the executable command in the file `/bin/ls`. It makes a system call asking the kernel to start `/bin/ls` as a new *child process* and gives it access to the screen and keyboard through the kernel. Then the shell goes to sleep, waiting for `ls` to finish.

When `/bin/ls` is done, it tells the kernel it's finished by issuing an *exit system call*. The kernel then wakes up the shell and tells it to continue running. The shell issues another prompt and waits for another line of input.

Other things may be going on while your `ls` is executing (we'll have to suppose that you're listing a very long directory). You might switch to another virtual console, log in there, and start a game of Quake, for example. Or, suppose you're hooked up to the Internet, your machine might be sending or receiving mail while `/bin/ls` runs.

How Do Input Devices and Interrupts Work?

Your keyboard is a very simple input device, simple because it generates small amounts of data very slowly (by a computer's standards). When you press or release a key, that event is signaled up the keyboard cable to raise a *hardware interrupt*.

It's the operating system's job to watch for such interrupts. For each possible kind of interrupt, there will be an interrupt handler, a part of the operating system that stashes away any data associated with it (like your keypress/keyrelease value) until it can be processed.

What the interrupt handler for your keyboard actually does is post the key value into a system area near the bottom of core. There it will be available for inspection when the operating system passes control to whichever program is currently supposed to be reading from the keyboard.

More complex input devices, like disk or network cards, work in a similar way. Above, we referred to a disk controller using the bus to signal that a disk request has been fulfilled. What actually happens is that the disk raises an interrupt. The disk interrupt handler then copies the retrieved data into memory, for later use by the program that made the request.

Every kind of interrupt has an associated *priority level*. Lower-priority interrupts (like keyboard events) have to wait on higher-priority interrupts (like clock ticks or disk events). Unix is designed to give high priority to the kinds of events that need to be processed rapidly in order to keep the machine's response smooth.

In your OS's boot-time messages, you may see references to *IRQ* numbers. You may be aware that one of the common ways to misconfigure hardware is to have two different devices trying to use the same IRQ, without understanding exactly why.

Here's the answer: IRQ is short for *Interrupt Request*. The operating system needs to know at startup time which numbered interrupts each hardware device will use so it can associate the proper handlers with each one. If two different devices try to use the same IRQ, interrupts will sometimes get dispatched to the wrong handler. Usually this will at least lock up the device, and can sometimes confuse the OS badly enough that it will flake out or crash.

How Does My Computer Do Several Things at Once?

It doesn't, actually. Computers can only do one task (or process) at a time. But a computer can change tasks very rapidly and fool slow human beings into thinking it's doing several things at once. This is called *timesharing*.

One of the kernel's jobs is to manage timesharing. It has a part called the *scheduler* that keeps information about all the other (non-kernel) processes in your zoo. Every 1/60th of a second, a timer goes off in the kernel, generating a clock interrupt. The scheduler stops whatever process is currently running, suspends it in place, and hands control to another process.

1/60th of a second may not sound like a lot of time. But on today's microprocessors it's enough to run tens of thousands of machine instructions, which can do a great deal of work. So even if you have many processes, each one can accomplish quite a bit in each of its timeslices.

In practice, a program may not get its entire timeslice. If an interrupt comes in from an I/O device, the kernel effectively stops the current task, runs the interrupt handler, and then returns to the current task. A storm of high-priority interrupts can squeeze out normal processing; this misbehavior is called *thrashing* and is fortunately very hard to induce under modern Unices.

In fact, the speed of programs is only very seldom limited by the amount of machine time they can get (there are a few exceptions to this rule, such as sound or 3-D graphics generation). Much more often, delays are caused when the program has to wait on data from a disk drive or network connection.

An operating system that can routinely support many simultaneous processes is called *multitasking*. The Unix family of operating systems was designed from the ground up for multitasking and is very good at it–much more effective than Windows or the Mac OS, which have had multitasking bolted into them as an afterthought and do it rather poorly. Efficient, reliable multitasking is a large part of what makes Linux superior for networking, communications, and Web service.

How Does My Computer Keep Processes from Stepping On Each Other?

The kernel's scheduler takes care of dividing processes in time. Your operating system also has to divide them in space so that processes don't step on each other's working memory. The things your operating system does to solve this problem are called *memory management*.

Each process in your zoo needs its own area of core memory as a place to run its code from and keep variables and results in. You can think of this set as consisting of a read-only *code segment* (containing the process's instructions) and a writeable *data segment* (containing all the process's variable storage). The data segment is truly unique to each process, but if two processes are running the same code, Unix automatically arranges for them to share a single code segment as an efficiency measure.

Efficiency is important, because core memory is expensive. Sometimes you don't have enough to hold the entirety of programs the machine is running, especially if you are using a large program like an X server. To get around this, Unix uses a strategy called *virtual memory*. It doesn't try to hold all the code and data for a process in core. Instead, it keeps in core only a relatively small working set; the rest of the process's state is left in a special area on your hard disk called a *swap space*.

As the process runs, Unix tries to anticipate how the working set will change and keeps only the pieces that are needed in its core, thereby decreasing processing time. Doing this effectively is both complicated and tricky, so I won't try and describe it all here—but it depends on the fact that code and data references tend to happen in clusters, with each new one likely to refer to somewhere close to an old one. So if Unix keeps around the code or data most frequently (or most recently) used, you will usually succeed in saving time.

Note that, in the past, the size of core was typically small relative to the size of running programs, so swapping was frequent. Memory is far less expensive nowadays and even low-end machines have quite a lot of it. On modern single-user machines with 64MB of core and up, it's possible to run X and a typical mix of jobs without ever swapping.

Even in this happy situation, the part of the operating system called the *memory manager* still has important work to do. It has to make sure that programs can only alter their own data segments—that is, prevent erroneous or malicious code in one program from corrupting the data in another. To do this, Unix keeps a table of data and code segments. The table is updated whenever a process requests more memory or releases memory (the latter usually when it exits).

This table is used to pass commands to a specialized part of the underlying hardware called an MMU or *memory management unit*. Modern processor chips have MMUs built right onto them. The MMU has the special ability to put fences around areas of memory, so an out-of-bound reference will be refused and cause a special interrupt to be raised.

If you ever see a Unix message that says "Segmentation fault", "core dumped", or something similar, this is exactly what has happened; an attempt by the running program to access memory outside its segment has raised a fatal interrupt. This indicates a bug in the program code; the *core dump* it leaves behind is diagnostic information intended to help a programmer track it down.

How Does My Computer Store Things on Disk?

When you look at a hard disk under Unix, you see a tree of named directories and files. Normally you won't need to look any deeper than that, but it does become useful to know what's going on underneath if you have a disk crash and need to try to salvage files. Unfortunately, there's no good way to describe disk organization from the file level downwards, so I'll have to describe it from the hardware up.

Low-Level Disk and File System Structure

The surface area of your disk, where data is stored, is divided up something like a dartboard—into circular tracks that are pie-sliced into sectors. Because tracks near the outer edge have more area than those close to the center of the disk, they have more sector slices. Each sector (or *disk block*) is the same size, which under modern kinds of Unix is generally 1 binary K (1024 8-bit words). Each disk block has a unique address or *disk block number*.

Unix divides the disk into *disk partitions*. Each partition is a continuous span of blocks used separately from any other partition, either as a file system or as swap space. The lowest-numbered partition is often treated specially—as a boot partition where you can put a kernel to be booted.

Each partition is either *swap space* (used to implement virtual memory) or a *file system* used to hold files. Swap-space partitions are treated as a linear sequence of blocks. File systems, on the other hand, need a way to map filenames to sequences of disk blocks. Because files grow, shrink, and change over time, a file's data blocks will not be a linear sequence but may be scattered all over its partition (from wherever the operating system can find a free block when it needs one).

Filenames and Directories

Within each file system, the mapping from names to blocks is handled through a structure called an *i-node*. There's a pool of these things near the bottom (lowest-numbered blocks) of each file system (the very lowest ones are used for housekeeping and labeling purposes we won't describe here). Each i-node describes one file. File data blocks live above the i-nodes.

Every i-node contains a list of the disk block numbers in the file it describes. (Actually this is a half-truth, only correct for small files, but the rest of the details aren't important here.) Note that the i-node does not contain the name of the file.

Names of files live in *directory structures*. A directory structure maps names to i-node numbers. This is why, in Unix, a file can have multiple true names (or hard links); they're simply multiple directory entries that happen to point to the same i-node.

Mount Points

In the simplest case, your entire Unix file system lives in just one disk partition. While you'll see this arrangement on some small personal Unix systems, it's unusual. It is more typical for it to be spread across several disk partitions, possibly on different physical disks. So, for example, your system may have one small partition where the kernel lives, a slightly larger one where OS utilities live, and a much bigger one where user home directories live.

The only partition you'll have access to immediately after system boot is your *root partition*, which is (almost always) the one you booted from. It holds the root directory of the file system, the top node from which everything else hangs.

The other partitions in the system have to be attached to this root in order for your entire, multiple-partition file system to be accessible. About midway through the boot process, your Unix will make these non-root partitions accessible. It will mount each one onto a directory on the root partition.

For example, if you have a Unix directory called `/usr`, it is probably a mount point to a partition that contains many programs installed with your Unix but not required during initial boot.

How a File Gets Looked Up

Now we can look at the file system from the top down. When you open a file (such as, say, `/home/esr/WWW/ldp/fundamentals.sgml`) here is what happens.

Your kernel starts at the root of your Unix file system (in the root partition). It looks for a directory there called `home`. Usually `home` is a mount point to a large user partition elsewhere, so it will go there. In the top-level directory structure of that user partition, it will look for an entry called `esr` and extract an i-node number. It will go to that i-node, notice it is a directory structure, and look up `WWW`. Extracting that i-node, it will go to the corresponding subdirectory and look up `ldp`. That will take it to yet another directory i-node. Opening that one, it will find an i-node number for `fundamentals.sgml`. That i-node is not a directory, but instead holds the list of disk blocks associated with the file.

How Things Can Go Wrong

Earlier I hinted that file systems can be fragile things. Now you know that to get to a file you have to hopscotch through what may be an arbitrarily long chain of directory and i-node references. Now suppose your hard disk develops a bad spot?

If you're lucky, it will only trash some file data. If you're unlucky, it could corrupt a directory structure or i-node number and leave an entire subtree of your system hanging in limbo—or, worse, result in a corrupted structure that points multiple ways at the same disk block or i-node. Such corruption can be spread by normal file operations, trashing data that was not in the original bad spot.

Fortunately, as disk hardware has become more reliable, this kind of contingency has become quite uncommon. Still, it means that your Unix will want to integrity-check the file system periodically to make sure nothing is amiss. Modern kinds of Unix do a fast integrity check on each partition at boot time, just before mounting it. Every few reboots they'll do a much more thorough check that takes a few minutes longer.

If all of this makes Unix sound terribly complex and failure-prone, it may be reassuring to know that these boot-time checks typically catch and correct normal problems before they become really disastrous. Other operating systems don't have these facilities, which speeds up booting but can leave you with more problems when attempting to recover by hand (and that's assuming you have a copy of Norton Utilities or similar software in the first place).

How Do Computer Languages Work?

Earlier, we discussed how programs are run. Every program ultimately has to execute as a stream of bytes that are instructions in your computer's machine language. But human beings don't deal with machine language very well; doing so has become a rare, black art, even among hackers.

Nowadays almost all Unix code, except a small amount of direct hardware-interface support in the kernel itself, is written in a *high-level* language. (*High-level* is a historical term meant to distinguish from low-level assembler languages, which are basically thin wrappers around machine code.)

There are several different kinds of high-level languages. In order to talk about these, you'll find it useful to bear in mind that a program's *source code* (the human-created, editable version) has to go through some kind of translation into machine code that the machine can run.

Compiled Languages

The most conventional kind of language is a *compiled language*. Compiled languages get translated into runnable files of binary machine code by a special program called (logically enough) a *compiler*. Once the binary has been generated, you can run it directly without looking at the source code again. (Most software is delivered as compiled binaries made from code you don't see.)

Compiled languages tend to give excellent performance and have the most complete access to the OS, but also tend to be difficult to program in.

C, the language in which Unix is written, is by far the most important of these (with its variant C++). FORTRAN is another compiled language still used among engineers and scientists but years older and much more primitive. In the Unix world no other compiled languages are in mainstream use. Outside the world of Unix, COBOL is widely used for financial and business software.

There used to be many other compiler languages, but most of them have either become extinct or are strictly research tools. If you are a new Unix developer using a compiled language, it is overwhelmingly likely to be C or C++.

Interpreted Languages

An *interpreted language* depends on an interpreter program that reads the source code and translates it on the fly into computations and system calls. The source has to be reinterpreted (and the interpreter present) each time the code is executed.

Interpreted languages tend to be slower than compiled languages, and often have limited access to the underlying operating system and hardware. On the other hand, they tend to be easier to program and more forgiving of coding errors.

Many Unix utilities, including the shell, bc, sed, and awk, are effectively small interpreted languages. BASICs are usually interpreted. So is Tcl. Historically, the most important interpretive language has been LISP (a major improvement over most of its successors). Today Perl is very widely used and steadily growing more popular.

P-code Languages

Since 1990, *p-code*, a kind of hybrid language that uses both compilation and interpretation, has become increasingly important. P-code languages are like compiled languages in that the source is translated to a compact binary form you actually execute, but which is not machine code. Instead it's *pseudocode* (or p-code), which is usually a lot simpler but more powerful than a real machine language. When you run the program, you interpret the p-code.

P-code can run nearly as fast as a compiled binary (p-code interpreters can be made quite simple, small, and speedy). But p-code languages can keep the flexibility and power of a good interpreter.

Important p-code languages include Python and Java.

How Does the Internet Work?

To help you understand how the Internet works, we'll look at the things that happen when you do a typical Internet operation. What happens when you use a Web browser to access the first page of this document at the Linux Documentation Project site?

NOTE

This document can be found at `http://MetaLab.unc.edu/LDP/HOWTO/Fundamentals.html`**. It lives in the file** `LDP/HOWTO/Fundamentals.html` **under the World Wide Web export directory of the host** `MetaLab.unc.edu`**.**

Names and Locations

The first thing your browser has to do to connect to the online version of this document is to establish a network connection to the machine where the document lives. To do that, it first has to find the network location of the host `MetaLab.unc.edu` (*host* is short for *host machine* or *network host*; `MetaLab.unc.edu` is a typical hostname). The corresponding location is actually a number called an *IP address* (I'll explain the *IP* part of this term later).

To do this, your browser queries a program called a *name server*. The name server may live on your machine, but it's more likely to run on a service machine that yours talks to. When you sign up with an ISP, part of your setup procedure will almost certainly involve telling your Internet software the IP address of a nameserver on the ISP's network.

The name servers on different machines talk to each other, exchanging and keeping up to date all the information needed to resolve hostnames (map them to IP addresses). Your nameserver may query three or four different sites across the network in the process of resolving `MetaLab.unc.edu`, but this usually happens very quickly (as in less than a second).

The nameserver will tell your browser that Metalab's IP address is 152.19.254.81; knowing this, your machine will be able to exchange bits with Metalab directly.

Packets and Routers

What the browser wants to do is send a command to the Web server on Sunsite that looks like this:

```
GET /LDP/HOWTO/Fundamentals.html HTTP/1.0
```

Here's how that happens. The command is made into a *packet*, a block of bits like a telegram that is wrapped with three important things: the *source address* (the IP address of your machine), the *destination address* (152.19.254.81), and a *service number* or *port number* (80 in this case) that indicates that it's a World Wide Web request.

Your machine then ships the packet down the wire (modem connection to your ISP, or local network) until it gets to a specialized machine called a router. The router has a map of the Internet in its memory–not always a complete one, but one that completely describes your network neighborhood and knows how to get to the routers for other neighborhoods on the Internet.

Your packet may pass through several routers on the way to its destination. Routers are smart. They watch how long it takes for other routers to acknowledge receipt of a packet. They use that information to direct traffic over fast links. They use it to notice when other routers (or a cable) have dropped off the network, and compensate if possible by finding another route.

There's an urban legend that the Internet was designed to survive nuclear war. This is not true, but the Internet's design is extremely good at getting reliable performance out of flaky hardware in an uncertain world. This is because its intelligence is distributed through thousands of routers rather than a few massive switches (like the phone network). This means that failures tend to be well localized and the network can route around them.

Once your packet gets to its destination machine, that machine uses the service number to feed the packet to the Web server. The Web server can tell where to reply to by looking at the command packet's source IP address. When the Web server returns this document, it will be broken up into a number of packets. The size of the packets will vary according to the transmission media in the network and the type of service.

TCP and IP

To understand how multiple-packet transmissions are handled, you need to know that the Internet actually uses two protocols, stacked one on top of the other.

The lower level, *IP* (Internet Protocol), knows how to get individual packets from a source address to a destination address (this is why these are called IP addresses). However, IP is not reliable; if a packet gets lost or dropped, the source and destination machines may never know it. In network jargon, IP is a *connectionless* protocol; the sender just fires a packet at the receiver and doesn't expect an acknowledgement.

IP is fast and cheap, though—sometimes fast, cheap, and unreliable is OK. When you play networked Doom or Quake, each bullet is represented by an IP packet. If a few of those get lost, that's OK.

The upper level, *TCP* (Transmission Control Protocol) gives you reliability. When two machines negotiate a TCP connection (which they do using IP), the receiver knows to send acknowledgements of the packets it sees back to the sender. If the sender doesn't see an acknowledgement for a packet within some timeout period, it resends that packet. Furthermore, the sender gives each TCP packet a sequence number that the receiver can use to reassemble packets in case they show up out of order. (This can happen if network links go up or down during a connection.)

TCP/IP packets also contain a checksum to enable detection of data corrupted by bad links. So, from the point of view of anyone using TCP/IP and nameservers, it looks like a reliable way to pass streams of bytes between hostname/service-number pairs. People who write network protocols almost never have to think about all the packetizing, packet reassembly, error checking, checksumming, and retransmission that goes on below that level.

HTTP, an Application Protocol

Now let's get back to our example. Web browsers and servers speak an *application protocol* that runs on top of TCP/IP, using it simply as a way to pass strings of bytes back and forth. This protocol is called *HTTP* (Hypertext Transfer Protocol) and we've already seen one command in it—the GET shown above.

When the GET command goes to `MetaLab.unc.edu`'s Web server with service number 80, it will dispatched to a *server daemon* listening on port 80. Most Internet services are implemented by server daemons that do nothing but wait on ports, watching for and executing incoming commands.

If the design of the Internet has one overall rule, it's that all the parts should be as simple and human accessible as possible. HTTP, and its relatives (like the Simple Mail Transfer Protocol, *SMTP*, that is used to move electronic mail between hosts) tend to use simple printable-text commands that end with a carriage-return/line feed.

This is marginally inefficient; in some circumstances you could get more speed by using a tightly coded binary protocol. But experience has shown that the benefits of making commands easy for human beings to describe and understand outweigh any marginal gain in efficiency that you might get at the cost of making things tricky and opaque.

Therefore, what the server daemon ships back to you via TCP/IP is also text. The beginning of the response will look something like this (a few headers have been suppressed):

```
HTTP/1.1 200 OK
Date: Sat, 10 Oct 1998 18:43:35 GMT
Server: Apache/1.2.6 Red Hat
Last-Modified: Thu, 27 Aug 1998 17:55:15 GMT
Content-Length: 2982
Content-Type: text/html
```

These headers will be followed by a blank line and the text of the Web page (after which the connection is dropped). Your browser just displays that page. The headers tell it how (in particular, the Content-Type header tells it the returned data is really HTML).

Chapter 3

Distributions

This chapter describes some of the most popular Linux distributions, or commercial, pre-packaged offerings of the operating system. Not only do these products eliminate the time it takes to download Linux and good Linux utilities, but many vendors also select software that compliments the entire package, providing you with a relatively complete solution.

This chapter explains the differences and similarities of distribution packages and outlines a handful of the many products available.

What Are Distributions?

A Linux system is actually constructed from thousands of independent parts. You'll need the Linux kernel, the GNU C library, assorted standard GNU utilities, various networking programs, a set of startup scripts, an X Window server, some applications to run, and so forth. It's actually quite a time-consuming task to assemble a complete system from all of these parts (believe me–I've done it!). Luckily, as is often the way of these things, where there's a time-consuming task, there are people who have already done it. They've assembled a complete system for you and provided software to install it in a relatively automated way. These ready-to-install Linux systems are called *distributions*, and there are quite a few to choose from. All you need to do is choose one.

NOTE

Most of the distributions are available on CD for just a few dollars, so you can try more than one to see which you like best.

Similarities

Each distribution contains the Linux kernel, libraries, and software. Most modern distributions have a mechanism to update components as newer versions become available. Many distributions also go to some trouble to make the installation process easy. All distributions draw upon the same set of free software components. They all ship the GNU project's libraries and utilities, the standard Linux kernel, and the XFree86 Project's X Window servers, and most of them ship either or both of the desktops KDE and GNOME, and so on.

Practically all distributions offer a mechanism to upgrade to newer versions of their distribution when one comes along. Generally this process is mostly or fully automated, and great pains are taken not to break old software.

Differences

The biggest difference between the distributions is in their objectives. Some distributions are made by companies who want to sell as many copies as they can; these distributions usually cater to the standard desktop user. Other distributions are made by groups of people as part of the free software movement; these people wish to encourage the growth of free software. Still other distributions are made to simplify the use of Linux for a particular task.

Another difference between distributions is what they include. Some commercial distributions include a few commercial applications for free. The most common thing added is a commercial X Window server. Such servers sometimes support more video cards (and more notebooks) than the free XFree86 Project's servers. This trend has been fading, though, as projects like Red Hat's X Binary Free offer no-cost binary-only servers for some popular but undocumented video hardware.

Commercial distributions often include a small amount of support. They'll let you e-mail them a question or two, or perhaps even provide telephone support. This may sound like a good thing, but in practice you'll get better answers from other users who've had the same problem as you. Usenet is the best way to get in touch with other users; first be sure to search old postings with Dejanews (`http://www.dejanews.com/`), in case your problem has been answered already.

A big difference among distributions is the type of packaging system used. A packaging system makes software installation and removal easier, as well as helping you keep track of what software is installed on your system. Red Hat, SuSE, and a number of other distributions use RPM (Red Hat Package Manager), while Debian, the Linux Router Project, and some others use dpkg. The two are approximately equivalent in functionality; both can add, remove, and upgrade software very easily, and both keep track of interdependencies between software packages. The catch is that RPM cannot install dpkg packages, and dpkg cannot install RPM packages. There is, however, a program to convert packages from one format to the other: alien.

NOTE

One way that Linux distributions do not differ is in software compatibility—Linux distributions all run the same application software.

Red Hat

Red Hat (`http://www.redhat.com/`) is the most popular commercial distribution of Linux. Eric Troan and Marc Ewing wrote the RPM package manager now used by many other distributions, and they have gone to great lengths to simplify installation. Red Hat is also working with big-name manufacturers like Dell, Intel, IBM, and the like to smooth the adoption of Linux by companies.

Red Hat rose to prominence mainly by being the first distribution to clearly spell out an upgrade path. Before RPM, upgrading often meant a complete reinstall of the system from the new CD. Nowadays, although the kinks involved in upgrading are out of most distributions, Red Hat continues to offer new installation features like KickStart (which lets you script identical installations for a flock of computers) and install-time probing (which attempts to identify your hardware automatically).

As one of the first financially successful Linux resellers, Red Hat has been careful to set a clear precedent for other Linux businesses to follow: they contribute back to the Linux community upon which their business is based. Red Hat licenses almost all of its custom-written software under the GPL (see Appendix D) and contributes people, hardware, or money to a number of ongoing Linux community efforts, including the GNOME project (see Part V), Freshmeat (`http://www.freshmeat.net/`), and so forth.

Debian

Debian (`http://www.debian.org/`) is the most popular non-profit Linux distribution. It is organized by a group called Software in the Public Interest, which has close ties to the Free Software Foundation (coordinators of the GNU project). The actual construction work for the Debian Linux distribution is done by volunteers scattered around the world; the Internet and some complex software allows each of them to work on one small program.

Debian is one of the most open of Linux organizations. Anyone can join the Debian project, which has its own constitution and holds periodic elections for project leaders. This is the true spirit of Linux—Debian is software by the people, for the people.

Because of its highly distributed development model, the Debian distribution is one of the most complete—it includes in its core practically all of the available free software, and its "contrib", "non-free", and "non-us" areas include practically everything else legally distributable.

Debian's dpkg-based package system is similar to RPM, but when used with the front-end dselect, it provides some powerful facilities that few other Linux distributions can match. In particular, not only will it tell you about prerequisites to a program you want to install, but it will also suggest companion programs and alternatives. Furthermore, dselect will automatically find and download whatever software you decide upon and install it automatically. Similarly, dselect can survey your system and compare it to the available software in the Debian archives so as to offer a list of programs for which updates are available. These features are not included with most RPM-based distributions and so you must use add-on scripts to help find and upgrade packages.

Another characteristic of Debian is that its development is completely open. Practically all decisions are made on publicly viewable discussion lists. Similarly, all known bugs are tracked in a publicly viewable bug system; everything the developers know is available to everyone. This open development structure means that bugs just can't be swept under the carpet.

One historical flaw of Debian has been that it is not quite so easy to install the first time as other distributions. However, progress has been made on this in recent releases, and once installed, Debian certainly gives you an easily maintainable and upgradable system.

Special Purpose Distributions

Special-purpose distributions are designed to make it easy to build such things as a Linux-based router or to run Linux on unusual hardware like that found in palmtop computers or in massively parallel supercomputers.

These types of distributions are often not as long-lived as the major distributions; sometimes new hardware will create a temporary need for a special distribution, and sometimes mainstream distributions will adopt the special features of a smaller distribution, rendering it obsolete. For example, this was exactly the life history of the UltraPenguin distribution; which served UltraSPARC users until Red Hat offered support for the UltraSPARC architecture.

For the most part, these special purpose distributions will only be of use to you if you have a need for the particular problem they solve.

Linux Router Project

The Linux Router Project (`http://www.linuxrouter.org/`) produces a distribution of Linux that can fit on a single floppy. It's designed to turn a cheap PC into a full-function router without requiring the ongoing use of a hard disk (moving parts are always the first to go).

Trinux

Trinux (`http://www.trinux.org/`) is a compact distribution that includes a large assortment of network management and security tools and not much else. It's designed to be used for network intrusion monitoring, as a firewall, and so forth.

ipfwadm -V your
outgoing -
such as ip masq
define the CONF
/bin:/usr/

Chapter 4

Installing Linux

This chapter describes how to install Linux software. It is the first document a new user should read in order to get started using Linux. It covers hardware and software requirements, preliminary steps to take before installation, and specifics on hard drive repartitioning and booting a Linux system.

This chapter is reprinted from the Linux Installation HOWTO, version 4.15 of November 20, 1998, by Eric S. Raymond.

Introduction

This document assumes that you have heard of and know about Linux and now want to get it running. The document focuses on the Intel base version, which is the most popular, but much of the advice applies on Power PCs, Sparcs, and Alphas, as well.

Other Sources of Information

If you are new to Linux, there are several sources of basic information about the system. The best place to find these is at the Linux Documentation Project home page at `http://MetaLab.unc.edu/LDP/linux.html`. You can find the latest version of this chapter there, as `http://MetaLab.unc.edu/LDP/HOWTO/Installation-HOWTO.html`.

You should probably start by browsing the resources under General Linux Information: the Linux INFO-SHEET (`http://MetaLab.unc.edu/LDP/HOWTO/INFO-SHEET.html`) and the Linux META-FAQ (`http://MetaLab.unc.edu/LDP/HOWTO/META-FAQ.html`). The Linux Frequently Asked Questions document contains many common questions (and answers!) about Linux—it is a must read for new users.

You can find help for common problems on the USENET newsgroups `comp.os.linux.help` and `comp.os.linux.announce`.

The Linux Documentation Project is writing a set of manuals and books about Linux, all of which are freely distributable on the Net and available from the LDP home page.

The book *Linux Installation and Getting Started* is a complete guide to getting and installing Linux, as well as how to use the system once you've installed it. The book contains a complete tutorial to using and running the system and much more information than is contained here. You can browse it, or download a copy, from the LDP home page (`http://MetaLab.unc.edu/LDP/`).

Finally, there is a rather technical Guide to x86 Bootstrapping (`http://www.paranoia.com/~vax/boot.html`). This document is NetBSD, rather than Linux, oriented but contains useful material on disk configuration and boot managers for multi-OS setups.

New Versions of This Document

New versions of the Linux Installation HOWTO will be periodically posted to `comp.os.linux.help`, `comp.os.linux.announce`, and news.answers. They will also be uploaded to various Linux WWW and FTP sites, including the LDP home page.

You can also view the latest version of this on the World Wide Web at http://MetaLab.unc.edu/LDP/HOWTO/Installation-HOWTO.html.

Feedback and Corrections

If you have questions or comments about this document, please feel free to mail Eric S. Raymond at esr@thyrsus.com. I welcome any suggestions or criticisms. If you find a mistake with this document, please let me know so I can correct it in the next version. Thanks.

Please do not mail me questions about how to solve hardware problems encountered during installation. Consult *Linux Installation and Getting Started*, bug your vendor, or consult the Linux newsgroup comp.os.linux.setup. This HOWTO is intended to be a rapid, painless guide to normal installation—a separate HOWTO on hardware problems and diagnosis is in preparation.

The Easiest Option: Buy, Don't Build

Linux has matured enough that there are now system integrators who will assemble a workstation for you, install and configure Linux, and do an intensive burn-in to test it before it's shipped to you. If you have more money than time, or you have stringent reliability or performance requirements, these integrators provide a valuable service by making sure you won't get hardware that's flaky or dies two days out of the box.

There are several firms of this kind. The only such outfit I know about personally is VA Research (http://www.varesearch.com).

These good people build high-end, high-quality Linux workstations with a nifty Tux-the-penguin logo on the front. They have intimate ties to the Linux community (the Debian project, http://www.debian.org, lives on a machine in their back room, Linus owns one of their boxes, and they even throw resources at your humble HOWTO maintainer occasionally).

For those of us without a champagne budget, the rest of this HOWTO is about how to install Linux ourselves.

Before You Begin

Before you can install Linux, you'll need to be sure your machine is Linux-capable, and choose a Linux to install. The Linux Pre-installation checklist (`http://members.tripod.com/~algolog/lnxchk.htm`) may help you organize configuration data before you begin.

Hardware Requirements

What kind of system is needed to run Linux? This is a good question; the actual hardware requirements for the system change periodically. The Linux Hardware-HOWTO, `http://MetaLab.unc.edu/LDP/HOWTO/Hardware-HOWTO.html`, gives a (more or less) complete listing of hardware supported by Linux. The Linux INFO-SHEET, `http://MetaLab.unc.edu/LDP/HOWTO/INFO-SHEET.html`, provides another list.

For the Intel versions of Linux, any 80386, 80486, Pentium or Pentium II processor will do. Non-Intel clones of the 80386 and up will generally work. You do not need a math coprocessor, although it is nice to have one.

The ISA, EISA, VESA Local Bus, and PCI bus architectures are supported. The MCA bus architecture (found on IBM PS/2 machines) is supported in the newest development (2.1.*x*) kernels but may not be ready for prime time yet.

You need at least 4 megabytes of memory in your machine. Technically, Linux will run with only 2 megs, but most installations and software require 4. The more memory you have, the happier you'll be. I suggest 8 or 16 megabytes if you're planning to use X-Windows.

Of course, you'll need a hard drive and an AT-standard drive controller. All MFM, RLL, and IDE drives and controllers should work. Many SCSI drives and adaptors are supported as well; the Linux SCSI-HOWTO contains more information on SCSI. If you are assembling a system from scratch to run Linux, the small additional cost of SCSI is well worth it for the extra performance and reliability it brings.

You will need a 3.5 floppy drive. While 5.25 floppies are supported under Linux, they are so rarely used that you should not count on disk images necessarily fitting on them. (A stripped-down Linux can actually run on a single floppy, but that's only useful for installation and certain troubleshooting tasks.)

You also need an MDA, Hercules, CGA, EGA, VGA, or Super VGA video card and monitor. In general, if your video card and monitor work under MS-DOS, it should work under Linux. However, if you wish to run X-Windows, there are other restrictions on the supported video hardware. The Linux XFree86-HOWTO, `http://MetaLab.unc.edu/LDP/HOWTO/XFree86-HOWTO.html`, contains more information about running X and its requirements.

You'll want a CD-ROM drive. If it's ATAPI, SCSI, or true IDE you should have no problem making it work (but watch for cheap drives advertising "IDE" interfaces that aren't true IDE). If your CD-ROM uses a proprietary interface card, it's possible the installation kernel you're going to boot from a floppy won't be able to see it—and an inaccessible CD-ROM is an installation showstopper. Also, CD-ROMs that attach to your parallel port won't work at all. If you're in doubt, consult the Linux CD-ROM HOWTO, `http://MetaLab.unc.edu/LDP/HOWTO/CDROM-HOWTO.html`, for a list and details of supported hardware.

So-called Plug'n'Play jumperless cards can be a problem. Support for these is under active development but not there yet in the 2.0.25 kernel. Fortunately this is only likely to be a problem with sound or Ethernet cards.

If you're running a box that uses one of the Motorola 68K processors (including pre-PowerPC Macintosh, Amiga, Atari, or VMEbus machines), see the Linux/m68k FAQ at `http://www.clark.net/pub/lawrencc/linux/faq/faq.html` for information on minimum requirements and the state of the port. The FAQ now says m68k Linux is as stable and usable as the Intel versions.

Space Requirements and Coexistence

You'll need free space for Linux on your hard drive. The amount of space needed depends on how much software you plan to install. Most installations require somewhere in the ballpark of 200 to 500 megs. This includes space for the software, swap space (used as virtual RAM on your machine), free space for users, and so on.

It's conceivable that you could run a minimal Linux system in 80 megs or less (this used to be common when Linux distributions were smaller), and it's conceivable that you could use well over 500 megs or more for all of your Linux software. The amount varies greatly depending on the amount of software you install and how much space you require. I'll discuss this in more detail later.

Linux will coexist with other operating systems, such as MS-DOS, Microsoft Windows, or OS/2, on your hard drive. (In fact, you can even access MS-DOS files and run some MS-DOS programs from Linux.) In other words, when partitioning your drive for Linux, MS-DOS or OS/2 live on their own partitions, and Linux exists on its own. We'll go into more detail about such dual-boot systems later.

You do *not* need to be running MS-DOS, OS/2, or any other operating system to use Linux. Linux is a completely different, stand-alone operating system and does not rely on other OSs for installation and use.

In all, the minimal setup for Linux is not much more than is required for most MS-DOS or Windows 3.1 systems sold today (and it's a good deal less than the minimum for Windows 95!). If you have a 386 or 486 with at least 4 megs of RAM, then you'll be happy running Linux. Linux does not require huge amounts of disk space, memory, or processor speed. Matt Welsh, the originator of this HOWTO, used to run Linux on a 386/16 MHz (the slowest machine you can get) with 4 megs of RAM and was quite happy. The more you want to do, the more memory (and faster processor) you'll need. In our experience, a 486 with 16 megabytes of RAM running Linux outdoes several expensive workstation models.

Choosing a Linux Distribution

Before you can install Linux, you need to decide on one of the distributions of Linux that are available. There is no single, standard release of the Linux software—there are many such releases. Each release has its own documentation and installation instructions.

Linux distributions are available both via anonymous FTP and via mail order on disk, tape, and CD-ROM. The Linux Distribution HOWTO, `http://MetaLab.unc.edu/LDP/HOWTO/Distribution-HOWTO.html`, includes descriptions of many Linux distributions available via FTP and mail order.

In the dim and ancient past when this HOWTO was first written (1992–93), most people got Linux by tortuous means, involving long downloads off the Internet or a BBS onto their DOS machines, followed by an elaborate procedure that transferred the downloads onto multiple floppy disks. One of these disks would then be booted and used to install the other dozen. With luck (and no media failures) you'd finish your installation many hours later with a working Linux. Or maybe not.

While this path is still possible (and you can download any one of several distributions from `http://MetaLab.unc.edu/pub/Linux/`

`distributions/`), there are now much less strenuous ways. The easiest is to buy one of the high-quality commercial Linux distributions distributed on CD-ROM, such as Red Hat, Debian, Linux Pro, or WGS. These are typically available for less than $50 at your local bookstore or computer shop and will save you many hours of aggravation.

You can also buy an anthology CD-ROMs such as the InfoMagic Linux Developer's Resource set. These typically include several Linux distributions and a recent dump of major Linux archive sites, such as sunsite or tsx-11.

In the remainder of this HOWTO we will focus on the steps needed to install from an anthology CD-ROM or a lower-end commercial Linux that doesn't include a printed installation manual. If your Linux includes a paper manual some of this HOWTO may provide useful background, but you should consult the manual for detailed installation instructions.

Installation Overview

It's wise to collect configuration information on your hardware before installing. Know the vendor and model number of each card in your machine; collect the IRQs and DMA channel numbers. You probably won't need this information, but if it turns out you do, you'll need it very badly.

If you want to run a dual-boot system (Linux and DOS or Windows both), rearrange (repartition) your disk to make room for Linux. If you're wise, you'll back up everything first!

First Installation Steps: The Easy Way

If you have an EIDE/ATAPI CD-ROM (fairly common these days), check your machine's BIOS settings to see if it has the capability to boot from CD-ROM. Most machines made after mid-1997 can do this.

If yours is among them, change the settings so that the CD-ROM is checked first. This is often in a BIOS FEATURES submenu of the BIOS configuration menus.

Then insert the installation CD-ROM. Reboot. You're started.

If you have a SCSI CD-ROM you can often still boot from it, but it gets a little more motherboard-BIOS dependent. Those who know enough to spend the extra dollars on a SCSI CD-ROM drive probably know enough to figure it out.

First Installation Steps: The Hard Way

1. Make installation floppies.
2. Boot an installation mini-Linux from the floppies in order to get access to the CD-ROM.

Continuing the Installation

1. Prepare the Linux file systems. (If you didn't edit the disk partition table earlier, you will at this stage.)
2. Install a basic production Linux from the CD-ROM.
3. Boot Linux from the hard drive.
4. (Optional) Install more packages from CD-ROM.

Basic Parts of an Installation Kit

Here are the basic parts of an installable distribution:

- The README and FAQ files. These will usually be located in the top-level directory of your CD-ROM and be readable once the hard disk has been mounted under Linux. (Depending on how the CD-ROM was generated, they may even be visible under DOS/Windows.) To become aware of important updates or changes, it is a good idea to read these files as soon as you have access to them.
- A number of boot-disk images (often in a subdirectory). If your CD-ROM is not bootable, one of these is the file that you will write to a floppy to create the boot disk. You'll select one of the above boot-disk images, depending on the type of hardware that you have in your system.

NOTE

The issue here is that some hardware drivers conflict with each other in strange ways, and instead of attempting to debug hardware problems on your system, it's easier to use a boot floppy image with only the drivers you need enabled. (This will have the nice side effect of making your kernel smaller.)

- A root-disk image (or perhaps two). If your CD-ROM is not bootable, you will write one of these to a floppy to create the installation disk(s). Nowadays the root disk or disks is generally independent of your hardware type; it will assume an EGA or better color screen.

- A rescue disk image. This is a disk containing a basic kernel and tools for disaster recovery in case something steps on the kernel or boot block of your hard disk.
- RAWRITE.EXE. This is an MS-DOS program that will write the contents of a file (such as a boot or root-disk image) directly to a floppy, without regard to format. You only need RAWRITE.EXE if you plan to create your boot and root floppies from an MS-DOS system. If you have access to a Unix workstation with a floppy drive instead, you can create the floppies from there, using the `dd(1)` command, or possibly a vendor-provided build script. See the man page for `dd(1)` on the LDP, and ask your local Unix gurus for assistance.
- The CD-ROM itself. The purpose of the boot disk is to get your machine ready to load the root or installation disks, which in turn are just devices for preparing your hard disk and copying portions of the CD-ROM to it. If your CD-ROM is bootable, you can boot it and skip right to preparing your disk.

Installation in Detail

Linux makes more effective use of PC hardware than MS-DOS, Windows, or NT and is accordingly less tolerant of misconfigured hardware. There are a few things you can do before you start that will lessen your chances of being stopped by this kind of problem.

Getting Prepared for Installation

First, collect any manuals you have on your hardware—motherboard, video card, monitor, modem, etc.—and put them within easy reach.

Second, gather detailed information on your hardware configuration. One easy way to do this, if you're running MS-DOS 5.0 or up, is to print a report from the Microsoft diagnostic utility msd.exe (you can leave out the TSR, driver, memory-map, environment-strings and OS-version parts). Among other things, this will guarantee you full and correct information on your video card and mouse type, which will be helpful in configuring X later on.

Third, check your machine for configuration problems with supported hardware that could cause an unrecoverable lockup during Linux installation.

TIP

It is possible for a DOS/Windows system using IDE hard drive(s) and CD-ROM to be functional even with the master/slave jumpers on the drives incorrectly set. Linux won't fly this way. If in doubt, check your master/slave jumpers!

Is any of your peripheral hardware designed with neither configuration jumpers nor non-volatile configuration memory? If so, it may require boot-time initialization via an MS-DOS utility to start up, and may not be easily accessible from Linux. CD-ROMs, sound cards, Ethernet cards and low-end tape drives can have this problem. If so, you may be able to work around this with an argument to the boot prompt; see the Linux Boot Prompt HOWTO, `http://MetaLab.unc.edu/LDP/HOWTO/BootPrompt-HOWTO.html`, for details.

WARNING

Some other operating systems will allow a bus mouse to share an IRQ with other devices. Linux doesn't support this; in fact, trying it may lock up your machine. If you are using a bus mouse, see the Linux Bus Mouse HOWTO, `http://MetaLab.unc.edu/LDP/HOWTO/Busmouse-HOWTO.html`**, for details.**

If possible, get the telephone number of an experienced Linux user you can call in case of emergency. Nine times out of ten, you won't need it, but it's comforting to have.

Budget time for installation. That will be about one hour on a bare system or one being converted to all-Linux operation—or up to three hours for a dual-boot system (they have a much higher incidence of false starts and hangups).

Creating the Boot and Root Floppies

Your Linux CD-ROM may come with installation aids that will take you through the process of building boot, root, and rescue disks with interactive prompts. These may be an MS-DOS installation program (such as the Red Hat redhat.exe program) or a Unix script, or both.

NOTE

This step is only needed if you can't boot from a CD-ROM.

If you have such a program and can use it, you should read the rest of this subsection for information only. Run the program to do actual installation—its authors certainly knew more about the specific distribution than I, and you'll avoid many error-prone hand-entry steps.

TIP

For more detailed information on making boot and root disks, see the Linux Bootdisk HOWTO at `http://MetaLab.unc.edu/LDP/HOWTO/Bootdisk-HOWTO.html`.

Your first step will be to select a boot-disk image to fit your hardware. If you must do this by hand, you'll generally find that either (a) the boot-disk images on your CD-ROM are named in a way that will help you pick a correct one, or (b) there's an index file nearby describing each image.

Next, you must create floppies from the boot-disk image you selected and from the root and rescue disk images. This is where the MS-DOS program RAWRITE.EXE comes into play.

Next, you must have two or three high-density MS-DOS formatted floppies. (They must be of the same type; that is, if your boot floppy drive is a 3.5 drive, both floppies must be high-density 3.5 disks.) You will use RAWRITE.EXE to write the boot and root-disk images to the floppies.

Invoke it with no arguments, like this:

```
C:> RAWRITE
```

Answer the prompts for the name of the file to write and the floppy to write it to (such as `A:`). RAWRITE will copy the file, block-by-block, directly to the floppy. Also use RAWRITE for the root disk image (such as COLOR144). When you're done, you'll have two floppies: one containing the boot disk, the other containing the root disk. Note that these two floppies will no longer be readable by MS-DOS (they are Linux format floppies, in some sense).

You can use the `dd` commands on a Unix system to do the same job. (For this, you will need a Unix workstation with a floppy drive, of course.) For example, on a Sun workstation with the floppy drive on device `/dev/rfd0`, you can use the command:

```
$ dd if=bare of=/dev/rfd0 obs=18k
```

You must provide the appropriate output block size argument (the `obs` argument) on some workstations (e.g., Suns) or this will fail. If you have problems, the man page for `dd(1)` may be instructive.

Be sure that you're using brand-new, error-free floppies. The floppies must have no bad blocks on them.

Note that you do not need to be running Linux or MS-DOS in order to install Linux. However, running Linux or MS-DOS makes it easier to create the boot and root floppies from your CD-ROM. If you don't have an operating system on your machine, you can use someone else's Linux or MS-DOS just to create the floppies and install from there.

Repartitioning Your DOS/Windows Drives

On most used systems, the hard drive is already dedicated to partitions for MS-DOS, OS/2, and so on. You'll need to resize these partitions in order to make space for Linux. If you're going to run a dual-boot system, it's strongly recommended that you read one or more of the following mini-HOWTOS, which describe different dual-boot configurations.

- The DOS-Win95-OS2-Linux mini-HOWTO:
  `http://MetaLab.unc.edu/LDP/HOWTO/mini/Linux+DOS+Win95+OS2.html`
- The Linux+Win95 mini-HOWTO:
  `http://MetaLab.unc.edu/LDP/HOWTO/mini/Linux+Win95.html`
- The Linux+NT-Loader mini-HOWTO:
  `http://MetaLab.unc.edu/LDP/HOWTO/mini/Linux+NT-Loader.html`

Even if they are not directly applicable to your system, they will help you understand the issues involved.

Note that some kinds of Linux will install to a directory on your MS-DOS partition. (This is different from installing *from* an MS-DOS partition.) Instead, you use the UMSDOS filesystem, which allows you to treat a directory of your MS-DOS partition as a Linux filesystem. In this way, you don't have to repartition your drive.

I only suggest using this method if your drive already has four partitions (the maximum supported by DOS) and repartitioning would be more trouble than it's worth (it slows down your Linux due to filename translation overhead). Or, if you want to try out Linux before repartitioning, this is a good way to do so. But in most cases you should repartition, as described here. If you do plan to use UMSDOS, you are on your own–it is not documented in detail here. From now on, we assume that you are not using UMSDOS and that you will be repartitioning.

A *partition* is just a section of the hard drive set aside for a particular operating system to use. If you only have MS-DOS installed, your hard drive probably has just one partition, entirely for MS-DOS. To use Linux, however, you'll need to repartition the drive so that you have one partition for MS-DOS and one (or more) for Linux.

Partitions come in three flavors: *primary*, *extended*, and *logical*. Briefly, primary partitions are one of the four main partitions on your drive. However, if you wish to have more than four partitions per drive, you need to create an extended partition, which can contain many logical partitions. You don't store data directly on an extended partition–it is used only as a container for logical partitions. Data is stored only on either primary or logical partitions.

To put this another way, most people use only primary partitions. However, if you need more than four partitions on a drive, you create an extended partition. Logical partitions are then created on top of the extended partition, and there you have it–more than four partitions per drive.

Note that you can easily install Linux on the second drive on your system (known as D: to MS-DOS). You simply specify the appropriate device name when creating Linux partitions. This is described in detail later in this chapter.

Back to repartitioning your drive. The problem with resizing partitions is that there is no way to do it (easily) without deleting the data on those partitions. Therefore, you will need to make a full backup of your system before repartitioning. In order to resize a partition, we simply delete the partition(s) and re-create them with smaller sizes.

There is a nondestructive disk repartitioner called FIPS available for MS-DOS. Look at `http://MetaLab.unc.edu/pub/Linux/system/install`. With FIPS, a disk optimizer (such as Norton Speed Disk), and a little bit of luck, you should be able to resize MS-DOS partitions without destroying the data on them. It's still suggested that you make a full backup before attempting this.

If you're not using FIPS, however, the classic way to modify partitions is with the program FDISK. For example, let's say that you have an 80 meg hard drive dedicated to MS-DOS. You'd like to split it in half–40 megs for MS-DOS and 40 megs for Linux. In order to do this, you run FDISK under MS-DOS, delete the 80 meg MS-DOS partition, and re-create a 40 meg MS-DOS partition in its place. You can then format the new partition and reinstall your MS-DOS software from backups. 40 megabytes of the drive is left empty. Later, you create Linux partitions on the unused portion of the drive.

In short, you should do the following to resize MS-DOS partitions with FDISK:

1. Make a full backup of your system.
2. Create an MS-DOS bootable floppy, using a command such as

```
C:> FORMAT /S A:
```

3. Copy the files `FDISK.EXE` and `FORMAT.COM` to this floppy, as well as any other utilities that you need (for example, utilities to recover your system from backup).
4. Boot the MS-DOS system floppy.
5. Run FDISK, possibly specifying the drive to modify (such as C: or D:).
6. Use the FDISK menu options to delete the partitions you wish to resize. *This will destroy all data on the affected partitions.*
7. Use the FDISK menu options to re-create those partitions, with smaller sizes.
8. Exit FDISK and re-format the new partitions with the FORMAT command.
9. Restore the original files from backup.

Note that MS-DOS FDISK will give you an option to create a logical DOS drive. A logical DOS drive is just a logical partition on your hard drive. You can install Linux on a logical partition, but you don't want to create that logical partition with MS-DOS FDISK. So, if you're currently using a logical DOS drive and want to install Linux in its place, you should delete the logical drive with MS-DOS FDISK and (later) create a logical partition for Linux in its place.

The mechanism used to repartition for OS/2 and other operating systems is similar. See the documentation for those operating systems for details.

Creating Partitions for Linux

After repartitioning your drive, you need to create partitions for Linux. Before describing how to do that, we'll talk about partitions and filesystems under Linux.

Partition Basics

Linux requires at least one partition for the *root filesystem*, which will hold the Linux kernel itself.

You can think of a *filesystem* as a partition formatted for Linux. Filesystems are used to hold files. Every system must have a root filesystem, at least. However, many users prefer to use multiple filesystems—one for each major part of the directory tree. For example, you may wish to create a separate filesystem to hold all files under the `/usr` directory. (Note that on Unix systems, forward slashes are used to delimit directories, not backslashes as with MS-DOS.) In this case you have both a root filesystem and a `/usr` filesystem.

Each filesystem requires its own partition. Therefore, if you're using both root and `/usr` filesystems, you'll need to create two Linux partitions.

In addition, most users create a *swap partition*, which is used for virtual RAM. If you have, say, 4 megabytes of memory on your machine and a 10-megabyte swap partition, you have 14 megabytes of virtual memory as far as Linux is concerned.

When using swap space, Linux moves unused pages of memory out to disk, allowing you to run more applications at once on your system. However, because swapping is often slow, it's no replacement for physical RAM. But applications that require a great deal of memory (such as the X Window System) often rely on swap space if you don't have enough physical RAM.

Nearly all Linux users employ a swap partition. If you have 4 megabytes of RAM or less, a swap partition is required to install the software. It is strongly recommended that you have a swap partition anyway, unless you have a great amount of physical RAM.

The size of your swap partition depends on how much virtual memory you need. It's often suggested that you have at least 16 megabytes of virtual memory total. Therefore, if you have 8 megs of physical RAM, you might want to create an 8-megabyte swap partition. Note that swap partitions can be no larger than 128 megabytes in size. Therefore, if you need more than 128 megs of swap, you must create multiple swap partitions. You may have up to 16 swap partitions in all.

You can find more on the theory of swap space layout and disk partitioning in the Linux Partition mini-HOWTO (`http://MetaLab.unc.edu/LDP/HOWTO/mini/Partition.html`).

NOTE

It is possible, though a bit tricky, to share swap partitions between Linux and Windows 95 in a dual-boot system. For details, see the Linux Swap Space Mini-HOWTO, `http://MetaLab.unc.edu/LDP/HOWTO/unmaintained/Swap-Space`.

WARNING

Gotcha 1: If you have an EIDE drive with a partition that goes above 504MB, your BIOS may not allow you to boot to a Linux installed there. So keep your root partition below 504MB. This shouldn't be a problem for SCSI drive controllers, which normally have their own drive BIOS firmware. For technical details, see the Large Disk Mini-HOWTO, `http://MetaLab.unc.edu/LDP/HOWTO/mini/Large-Disk.html`.

WARNING

Gotcha 2: Are you mixing IDE and SCSI drives? Then watch out. Your BIOS may not allow you to boot directly to a SCSI drive.

Sizing Partitions

Besides your root and swap partitions, you'll want to set up one or more partitions to hold your software and home directories.

While, in theory, you could run everything off a single huge root partition, almost nobody does this. Having multiple partitions has several advantages:

- It often cuts down the time required for boot-time file-system checks.
- Files can't grow across partition boundaries. Therefore you can use partition boundaries as firebreaks against programs (like Usenet news) that want to eat huge amounts of disk, to prevent them from crowding out file space needed by your kernel and the rest of your applications.
- If you ever develop a bad spot on your disk, formatting and restoring a single partition is less painful than having to redo everything from scratch.

On today's large disks, a good basic setup is to have a small root partition (less than 80 megs), a medium-sized `/usr` partition (up to 300 megs or so) to hold system software, and a /home partition occupying the rest of your available space for home directories.

You can get more elaborate. If you know you're going to run Usenet news, for example, you may want to give it a partition of its own to control its maximum possible disk usage. Or create a /var partition for mail, news, and temporary files all together. But in today's regime of very cheap, very large hard disks, these complications seem less and less necessary for your first Linux installation. For your first time, especially, keep it simple.

Booting the Installation Disk

The first step is to boot the boot disk you generated. Normally you'll be able to boot hands-off; the boot kernel prompt will fill itself in after 10 seconds. This is how you'll normally boot from an IDE disk.

By giving arguments after the kernel name, you can specify various hardware parameters, such as your SCSI controller IRQ and address, or drive geometry, before booting the Linux kernel. This may be necessary if Linux does not detect your SCSI controller or hard drive geometry, for example.

In particular, many BIOS-less SCSI controllers require you to specify the port address and IRQ at boot time. Likewise, IBM PS/1, ThinkPad, and ValuePoint machines do not store drive geometry in the CMOS, and you must specify it at boot time. (Later on, you'll be able to configure your production system to supply such parameters itself.)

Watch the messages as the system boots. They will list and describe the hardware your installation Linux detects. In particular, if you have a SCSI controller, you should see a listing of the SCSI hosts detected. If you see the message

```
SCSI: 0 hosts
```

your SCSI controller was not detected, and you will have to figure out how to tell the kernel where it is.

Also, the system will display information on the drive partitions and devices detected. If any of this information is incorrect or missing, you will have to force hardware detection.

On the other hand, if all goes well and your hardware seems to be detected, you can skip to the section "Using the Root Disk."

To force hardware detection, you must enter the appropriate parameters at the boot prompt, using the following syntax:

```
linux <parameters...>
```

There are a number of such parameters available; we list some of the most common here.

TIP

Modern Linux boot disks will often give you the option to look at a help screen, describing kernel parameters, before you boot.

`hd=cylinders,heads,sectors` Specify the drive geometry. Required for systems such as the IBM PS/1, ValuePoint, and ThinkPad. For example, if your drive has 683 cylinders, 16 heads, and 32 sectors per track, enter

```
linux hd=683,16,32
```

`tmc8xx=memaddr,irq` Specify address and IRQ for BIOS-less Future Domain TMC-8xx SCSI controller. For example,

```
linux tmc8xx=0xca000,5
```

NOTE

Note that the ox prefix must be used for all values given in hex. This is true for all of the following options.

`st0x=memaddr,irq` Specify address and IRQ for BIOS-less Seagate ST02 controller.

`t128=memaddr,irq` Specify address and IRQ for BIOS-less Trantor T128B controller.

`ncr5380=port,irq,dma` Specify port, IRQ, and DMA channel for generic NCR5380 controller.

`aha152x=port,irq,scsiid,1` Specify port, IRQ, and SCSI ID for BIOS-less AIC-6260 controllers. This includes Adaptec 1510, 152x, and Soundblaster-SCSI controllers.

NOTE

If you have questions about these boot-time options, please read the Linux SCSI HOWTO, which should be available on any Linux FTP archive site . The SCSI HOWTO explains Linux SCSI compatibility in much more detail.

Using the Root Disk

After booting the boot disk, you will be prompted to enter the root disk or disks. At this point you should remove the boot disk from the drive and insert the root disk. Then press Enter to go on. You may have to load a second root disk.

What's actually happening here is this: the boot disk provides a miniature operating system that (because the hard drive isn't prepared) uses a portion of your RAM as a virtual disk (called, logically enough, a *ram disk*).

The root disk loads onto the ram disk a small set of files and installation tools, which you'll use to prepare your hard drive and install a production Linux on it from your CD-ROM.

Choosing EGA or X Installation

Older kinds of Linux (including Slackware) gave you a shell at this point and required you to enter installation commands by hand in a prescribed sequence. This is still possible, but newer ones start by running a screen-oriented installation program that tries to interactively walk you through these steps, giving lots of help.

You will probably get the option to try to configure X right away so the installation program can have a graphical look. If you choose this route, the installation program will quiz you about your mouse and monitor type before getting to the installation proper. Once you get your production Linux installed, these settings will be saved for you. You will be able to tune your monitor's performance later, so at this stage it makes sense to settle for a basic 640x480 SVGA mode.

X isn't necessary for installation, but (assuming you can get past the mouse and monitor configuration) many people find the graphical interface easier to use. And you're going to want to bring up X anyway, so trying it early makes some sense.

Just follow the prompts in the program. It will take you through the steps necessary to prepare your disk, create initial user accounts, and install software packages off the CD-ROM.

In the following subsections we'll describe some of the tricky areas in the installation sequence as if you were doing them by hand. This should help you understand what the installation program is doing and why.

Using Fdisk and Cfdisk

Your first installation step once the root-disk Linux is booted will be to create or edit the partition tables on your disks. Even if you used FDISK to set up partitions earlier, you'll need to go back to the partition table and insert some Linux-specific information.

To create or edit Linux partitions, we'll use the Linux version of the fdisk program or its screen-oriented sibling cfdisk.

Generally the installation program will look for a preexisting partition table and offer to run fdisk or cfdisk on it for you. Of the two, cfdisk is definitely easier to use, but current versions of it are also less tolerant of a nonexistent or garbled partition table.

Therefore you may find (especially if you're installing on virgin hardware) that you need to start with fdisk to get to a state that cfdisk can deal with. Try running cfdisk; if it complains, run fdisk. (A good way to proceed if you're building an all-Linux system and cfdisk complains is to use fdisk to delete all the existing partitions and then fire up cfdisk to edit the empty table.)

A few notes apply to both fdisk and cfdisk. Both take an argument that is the name of the drive on which you wish to create Linux partitions. Hard drive device names are

- `/dev/hda` First IDE drive
- `/dev/hdb` Second IDE drive
- `/dev/sda` First SCSI drive
- `/dev/sdb` Second SCSI drive

For example, to create Linux partitions on the first SCSI drive in your system, you will use (or your installation program might generate from a menu choice) the command

```
cfdisk /dev/sda
```

If you use fdisk or cfdisk without an argument, it will assume `/dev/hda`.

To create Linux partitions on the second drive on your system, simply specify either `/dev/hdb` (for IDE drives) or `/dev/sdb` (for SCSI drives) when running fdisk.

Your Linux partitions don't all have to be on the same drive. You might want to create your root filesystem partition on `/dev/hda` and your swap partition on `/dev/hdb`, for example. In order to do so just run fdisk or cfdisk once for each drive.

In Linux, partitions are given a name based on the drive which they belong to. For example, the first partition on the drive /dev/hda is /dev/hda1, the second is /dev/hda2, and so on. If you have any logical partitions, they are numbered starting with /dev/hda5, /dev/hda6, and so on.

WARNING

With Linux fdisk or cfdisk, you should not create or delete partitions for operating systems other than Linux. That is, don't create or delete MS-DOS partitions with this version of fdisk; use MS-DOS's version of FDISK instead. If you try to create MS-DOS partitions with Linux fdisk, chances are MS-DOS will not recognize the partition and not boot correctly.

Here's an example of using fdisk. Assume you have a single MS-DOS partition using 61693 blocks on the drive, and the rest of the drive is free for Linux. (Under Linux, one block is 1024 bytes. Therefore, 61693 blocks is about 61 megabytes.) You'll create just two partitions in this tutorial example, swap and root. You should probably extend this to four Linux partitions in line with the recommendations above: one for swap, one for the root filesystem, one for system software, and a home directory area.

First, use the p command to display the current partition table. As you can see, /dev/hda1 (the first partition on /dev/hda) is a DOS partition of 61693 blocks.

```
Command (m for help):  p
Disk /dev/hda: 16 heads, 38 sectors, 683 cylinders
Units = cylinders of 608 * 512 bytes

Device  Boot Begin Start End Blocks Id System
/dev/hda1 *  1  1   203  61693 6 DOS 16-bit >=32M

Command (m for help):
```

Next, use the n command to create a new partition. The Linux root partition will be 80 megs in size.

```
Command (m for help): n
Command action
  e  extended
  p  primary partition (1-4)
p
```

Here the system is asking if you want to create an extended or primary partition. In most cases you want to use primary partitions, unless you need more than four partitions on a drive. See the section "Repartitioning Your DOS/Windows Drives" for more information.

The first cylinder should be the cylinder *after* where the last partition left off. In the following case, /dev/hda1 ends on cylinder 203, so we start the new partition at cylinder 204.

```
Partition number (1-4): 2
First cylinder (204-683): 204
Last cylinder or +size or +sizeM or +sizeK (204-683): +80M
```

As you can see, if we use the notation +80M, it specifies a partition 80 megs in size. Likewise, the notation +80K would specify an 80 kilobyte partition, and +80 would specify just an 80 byte partition.

If you see this warning, you can ignore it:

```
Warning: Linux cannot currently use 33090 sectors of this
partition
```

It is left over from an old restriction that Linux filesystems could only be 64 megs in size. However, with newer filesystem types, that is no longer the case—partitions can now be up to 4 terabytes in size.

Next, create your 10 megabyte swap partition, /dev/hda3.

```
Command (m for help): n
Command action
   e  extended
   p  primary partition (1-4)
p

Partition number (1-4): 3
First cylinder (474-683): 474
Last cylinder or +size or +sizeM or +sizeK (474-683): +10M
```

Again, display the contents of the partition table. Be sure to write down the information here, especially the size of each partition in blocks. You need this information later.

```
Command (m for help): p
Disk /dev/hda: 16 heads, 38 sectors, 683 cylinders
Units = cylinders of 608 * 512 bytes

   Device Boot Begin   Start End Blocks   Id System
/dev/hda1   *     1      1 203  61693  6 DOS 16-bit >=32M
/dev/hda2       204    204 473  82080  83 Linux native
/dev/hda3       474    474 507  10336  83 Linux native
```

Note that the Linux swap partition (here, /dev/hda3) has type `Linux native`. We need to change the type of the swap partition to

`Linux swap` so that the installation program will recognize it as such. In order to do this, use the fdisk `t` command:

```
Command (m for help): t
Partition number (1-4): 3
Hex code (type L to list codes): 82
```

If you use L to list the type codes, you'll find that 82 is the type corresponding to Linux swap.

To quit fdisk and save the changes to the partition table, use the `w` command. To quit fdisk without saving changes, use the `q` command.

After quitting fdisk, the system may tell you to reboot to make sure that the changes took effect. In general, there is no reason to reboot after using fdisk—modern versions of fdisk and cfdisk are smart enough to update the partitions without rebooting.

Post-partition Steps

After you've edited the partition tables, your installation program asks you if it should look at them and offer to enable your swap partition for you. (The install program does not do this automatically, on the off chance that you're running a dual-boot system and one of your non-Linux partitions might happen to look like a swap volume.) Go ahead and have the install program do this.

Next the program will ask you to associate Linux filesystem names (such as `/`, `/usr`, `/var`, `/tmp`, `/home`, `/home2`, etc.) with each of the non-swap partitions you're going to use.

There is only one hard and fast rule for this. There must be a root filesystem, named `/`, and it must be bootable. You can name your other Linux partitions anything you like. But there are some conventions about how to name them which will probably simplify your life later on.

Earlier on I recommended a basic three-partition setup including a small root, a medium-sized system-software partition, and a large home-directory partition. Traditionally, these would be called `/`, `/usr`, and `/home`. The counterintuitive `/usr` name is an historical carryover from the days when (much smaller) Unix systems carried system software and user home directories on a single non-root partition. Some software depends on it.

If you have more than one home-directory area, it's conventional to name them `/home`, `/home2`, `/home3`, etc. This may come up if you have two physical disks. On my personal system, for example, the layout currently looks like this:

```
Filesystem  1024-blocks Used Available Capacity Mounted on
/dev/sda1      30719  22337    6796    77%  /
/dev/sda3     595663 327608  237284     58%  /usr
/dev/sda4    1371370   1174 1299336      0%  /home
/dev/sdb1    1000949 643108  306130     68%  /home2
```

The second disk (`sdb1`) isn't really all `/home2`; the swap partitions on `sda` and `sdb` aren't shown in this display. But you can see that `/home` is the large free area on `sda` and `/home2` is the user area of `sdb`.

If you want to create a partition for scratch, spool, temporary, mail, and news files, call it `/var`. Otherwise you'll probably want to create a `/usr/var` and create a symbolic link named `/var` that points back to it (the installation program may offer to do this for you).

Installing Software Packages

Once you've gotten past preparing your partitions, the remainder of the installation should be almost automatic. Your installation program (whether EGA or X-based) will guide you through a series of menus that allow you to specify the CD-ROM to install from, the partitions to use, and so forth.

Here we're not going to document many of the specifics of this stage of installation. It's one of the parts that varies most between Linux distributions (vendors traditionally compete to add value here) but also the simplest part. And the installation programs are pretty much self-explanatory, with good on-screen help.

After Package Installations

After installation is complete, and if all goes well, the installation program will walk you through a few options for configuring your system before its first boot from a hard drive.

LILO, the LInux LOader

LILO (which stands for LInux LOader) is a program that will allow you to boot Linux (as well as other operating systems, such as MS-DOS) from your hard drive.

You may be given the option of installing LILO on your hard drive. Unless you're running OS/2, answer "yes." OS/2 has special requirements; see the section "Custom LILO Configuration." Installing LILO as your primary loader makes a separate boot disk unnecessary; instead, you can tell LILO at each boot time which OS to boot.

Making a Production Boot Disk (Optional)

You may also be given the chance to create a *standard boot disk*, which you can use to boot your newly installed Linux system. (This is an older and slightly less convenient method, which assumes that you will normally boot DOS but use the boot disk to start Linux.)

For this you will need a blank, high-density MS-DOS formatted disk of the type that you boot your system with. Simply insert the disk when prompted and a boot disk will be created.

WARNING

This is not the same as an installation boot disk, and you can't substitute one for the other!

Miscellaneous System Configuration

The post-installation procedure may also take you through several menu items allowing you to configure your system. This includes specifying your modem and mouse device, as well as your time zone. Follow the menu options.

It may also prompt you to create user accounts or put a password on the root (administration) account. This is not complicated and you can usually just walk through the screen instructions.

Booting Your New System

If everything went as planned, you should now be able to boot Linux from the hard drive using LILO. Alternatively, you should be able to boot your Linux boot floppy (not the original boot disk floppy, but the floppy created after installing the software). After booting, log in as root.

If you are booting using LILO, try holding down Shift or Ctrl during boot. This will present you with a boot prompt; press Tab to see a list of options. In this way you can boot Linux, MS-DOS, and so forth directly from LILO.

After Your First Boot

You should now be looking at the login prompt of a new Linux, just booted from your hard drive. Congratulations!

Beginning System Administration

Depending on how the installation phase went, you may need to create accounts, change your hostname, or (re)configure X at this stage. There are many more things you could set up and configure, including backup devices, SLIP/PPP links to an Internet Service Provider, and so forth.

TIP

A good book on Unix systems administration should help. (I suggest *Essential Systems Administration* from O'Reilly and Associates.) You should also read various other Linux HOWTOs, such as the NET-3-HOWTO and Printing-HOWTO, for information on other configuration tasks.

Custom LILO Configuration

LILO is a boot loader, which can be used to select either Linux, MS-DOS, or some other operating system at boot time. Chances are your distribution automatically configured LILO for you during the installation phase (unless you're using OS/2, this is what you should have done). If so, you can skip the rest of this section.

If you installed LILO as the primary boot loader, it will handle the first-stage booting process for all operating systems on your drive. This works well if MS-DOS is the only other operating system that you have installed. However, you might be running OS/2, which has its own Boot Manager. In this case, you want OS/2's Boot Manager to be the primary boot loader and use LILO just to boot Linux (as the secondary boot loader).

WARNING

An important gotcha for people using EIDE systems: due to a BIOS limitation, your boot sectors for any OS have to live on one of the first two physical disks. Otherwise LILO will hang after writing "LI," no matter where you run it from.

If you have to configure LILO manually, this will involve editing the file `/etc/lilo.conf`. Below we present an example of a LILO configuration file, where the Linux root partition is on /dev/hda2, and MS-DOS is installed on /dev/hdb1 (on the second hard drive).

Tell LILO to install itself as the primary boot loader on /dev/had:

```
boot = /dev/hda
# The boot image to install; you probably shouldn't change this
install = /boot/boot.b
```

The stanza for booting Linux:

```
image = /vmlinuz    # The kernel is in /vmlinuz
 label = linux    # Give it the name "linux"
 root = /dev/hda2   # Use /dev/hda2 as the root filesystem
 vga = ask      # Prompt for VGA mode
 append = "aha152x=0x340,11,7,1" # Add this to the boot options,
  # for detecting the SCSI controller
```

The stanza for booting MS-DOS:

```
other = /dev/hdb1   # This is the MS-DOS partition
 label = msdos     # Give it the name "msdos"
 table = /dev/hdb   # The partition table for the second drive
```

Once you have edited the /etc/lilo.conf file, run /sbin/lilo as root. This will install LILO on your drive. Note that you must rerun /sbin/lilo anytime that you recompile your kernel in order to point the boot loader at it properly (something that you don't need to worry about just now, but keep it in mind).

Note how we use the append option in /etc/lilo.conf to specify boot parameters as we did when booting the boot disk.

You can now reboot your system from the hard drive. By default LILO will boot the operating system listed first in the configuration file, which in this case is Linux. In order to bring up a boot menu, in order to select another operating system, hold down Shift or Ctrl while the system boots; you should see a prompt such as

```
Boot:
```

Here, enter either the name of the operating system to boot (given by the label line in the configuration file–in this case, either linux or msdos), or press Tab to get a list.

Now let's say that you want to use LILO as the secondary boot loader–if you want to boot Linux from OS/2's Boot Manager, for example. In order to boot a Linux partition from OS/2's Boot Manager, unfortunately, you must create the partition using OS/2's FDISK (not Linux's) and format the partition as FAT or HPFS so that OS/2 knows about it. (That's IBM for you.)

In order to have LILO boot Linux from OS/2's Boot Manager, you only want to install LILO on your Linux root filesystem (in the above example, /dev/hda2). In this case, your LILO config file should look something like the following:

```
boot = /dev/hda2
install = /boot/boot.b
compact

image = /vmlinuz
 label = linux
 root = /dev/hda2
 vga = ask
```

Note the change in the boot line. After running /sbin/lilo you should be able to add the Linux partition to Boot Manager. This mechanism should work for boot loaders used by other operating systems as well.

Terms of Use

Acknowledgements

My grateful acknowledgement to Matt D. Welsh, who originated this HOWTO. I removed much of the Slackware-specific content and refocused the remainder of the document on CD-ROM installation, but a substantial part of the content is still his.

The 4.1 version was substantially improved by some suggestions from David Shao <dshao@best.com>.

PART ii

HARDWARE

-s your
masquera
ipfwadm -o -f deny
V your static
outgoing
ipfwadm
such as ip masq
, define the
/bin:/usr/sb
CONFIG

Chapter 5

XFree86

In this chapter, you'll learn how to obtain, install, and configure version 3.3 of the XFree86 version of the X Window System (X11R6) for Linux systems.

This chapter contains the complete text of the Linux XFree86 HOWTO, version 5.10, of 2 January 1999 by Eric S. Raymond.

INTRODUCTION

Understanding XFree86 requires a little background: XFree86 is a relative of the *X Window System*, a large and powerful (some might say excessively large and overly complex) graphics environment for Unix systems. The original X Window System code was developed at MIT; commercial vendors have since made X the industry standard for Unix platforms. Virtually every Unix workstation in the world runs some variant of the X Window system.

A freely redistributable port of the MIT X Window System version 11, release 6 (X11R6) for 80386/80486/Pentium Unix systems has been developed by a team of programmers originally headed by David Wexelblat `<dwex@XFree86.org>`. The release, known as *XFree86*, is available for System V/386, 386BSD, and other x86 Unix implementations, including Linux. It includes all of the required binaries, support files, libraries, and tools.

Complete information on XFree86 is available at the XFree86 Web site, `http://www.XFree86.org/`.

In this document, we'll give a step-by-step description of how to install and configure XFree86 for Linux, but you will have to fill in some of the details yourself by reading the documentation released with XFree86 itself. (This documentation is discussed below.) However, using and customizing the X Window System is far beyond the scope of this book–for this purpose you should obtain one of the many good books on using the X Window System.

Other Sources of Information

If you have never heard of Linux before, there are several sources of basic information about the system. The best place to find these is at the Linux Documentation Project home page at `http://metalab.unc.edu/LDP/`. You can find the latest, up-to-date version of this document there, at `http://metalab.unc.edu/LDP/HOWTO/XFree86-HOWTO.html`.

New Versions of This Chapter

New versions of the Linux XFree86 HOWTO will be periodically posted to `comp.os.linux.help` and `comp.os.linux.announce` and `news.answers`. They will also be uploaded to various Linux WWW and FTP sites, including the LDP home page.

Feedback and Corrections

If you have questions or comments about this chapter, please feel free to mail Eric S. Raymond, at esr@thyrsus.com. I welcome any suggestions or criticisms. If you find a mistake with this chapter, please let me know so I can correct it in the next version. Thanks.

Please do not mail me questions about how to make your video card and monitor work with X. This HOWTO is intended to be a rapid, painless guide to normal installation using the new interactive configurator.

If you run into problems, browse the XFree86 Video Timings HOWTO, http://metalab.unc.edu/LDP/HOWTO/XFree86-Video-Timings-HOWTO.html. (This is the up-to-date HTML version of XFree86's Videomodes.doc file.) That document has everything I know about configuration troubleshooting. If it can't help you, neither can I.

Hardware Requirements

The documentation included with your video adaptor should specify the chipset used. If you are in the market for a new video card or are buying a new machine that comes with a video card, have the vendor find out exactly what the make, model, and chipset of the video card is. This may require the vendor to call technical support on your behalf; in general vendors will be happy to do this. Many PC hardware vendors will state that the video card is a standard SVGA card which should work on your system. Explain that your software (mention Linux and XFree86!) does not support all video chipsets and that you must have detailed information.

You can also determine your video card chipset by running the SuperProbe program included with the XFree86 distribution. This is covered in more detail later in this chapter. XFree86 3.3.3 presently supports the chipsets listed in Table 5.1.

TABLE 5.1: Chipsets Supported by XFree86 3.3.3

Manufacturer	Chipset
Ark Logic	ARK1000PV, ARK1000VL, ARK2000PV, ARK2000MT
Alliance	AP6422, AT24

TABLE 5.1 continued: Chipsets Supported by XFree86 3.3.3

Manufacturer	Chipset
ATI	18800, 18800-1, 28800-2, 28800-4, 28800-5, 28800-6, 68800-3, 68800-6, 68800AX, 68800LX, 88800GX-C, 88800GX-D, 88800GX-E, 88800GX-F, 88800CX, 264CT, 264ET, 264VT, 264GT, 264VT-B, 264VT3, 264GT-B, 264GT3 (this list includes the Mach8, Mach32, Mach64, 3D Rage, 3D Rage II, and 3D Rage Pro)
Avance Logic	ALG2101, ALG2228, ALG2301, ALG2302, ALG2308, ALG2401
Chips Technologies	65520, 65525, 65530, 65535, 65540, 65545, 65546, 65548, 65550, 65554, 65555, 68554, 69000, 64200, 64300
Cirrus Logic	CLGD5420, CLGD5422, CLGD5424, CLGD5426, CLGD5428, CLGD5429, CLGD5430, CLGD5434, CLGD5436, CLGD5440, CLGD5446, CLGD5462, CLGD5464, CLGD5465, CLGD5480, CLGD6205, CLGD6215, CLGD6225, CLGD6235, CLGD6410, CLGD6412, CLGD6420, CLGD6440, CLGD7541(*), CLGD7543(*), CLGD7548(*), CLGD7555(*)
Cyrix	MediaGX, MediaGXm
Compaq	AVGA
Digital Equipment Corporation	TGA
Epson	SPC8110
Genoa	GVGA
IBM	8514/A (and true clones), XGA-2
IIT	AGX-014, AGX-015, AGX-016
Matrox	MGA2064W (Millennium), MGA1064SG (Mystique and Mystique 220), MGA2164W (Millennium II PCI and AGP), G100, G200
MX	MX68000(*), MX680010(*)
NCR	77C22(*), 77C22E(*), 77C22E+(*)
NeoMagic	2200, 2160, 2097, 2093, 2090, 2070
Number Nine	I128 (series I and II), Revolution 3D (T2R)
NVidia/SGS Thomson	NV1, STG2000, RIVA128, Riva TNT
OAK	OTI067, OTI077, OTI087
RealTek	RTG3106(*)
Rendition	V1000, V2x00

TABLE 5.1 continued: Chipsets Supported by XFree86 3.3.3

Manufacturer	Chipset
S3	86C911, 86C924, 86C801, 86C805, 86C805i, 86C928, 86C864, 86C964, 86C732, 86C764, 86C765, 86C767, 86C775, 86C785, 86C868, 86C968, 86C325, 86C357, 86C375, 86C385, 86C988, 86CM65, 86C260
SiS	86C201, 86C202, 86C205, 86C215, 86C225, 5597, 5598, 6326
3Dlabs	GLINT 500TX, GLINT MX, Permedia, Permedia 2, Permedia 2v
Tseng	ET3000, ET4000AX, ET4000/W32, ET4000/W32i, ET4000/W32p, ET6000, ET6100
Trident	TVGA8800CS, TVGA8900B, TVGA8900C, TVGA8900CL, TVGA9000, TVGA9000i, TVGA9100B, TVGA9200CXR, Cyber9320(*), TVGA9400CXi, TVGA9420, TGUI9420DGi, TGUI9430DGi, TGUI9440AGi, TGUI9660XGi, TGUI9680, Pro Vidia 9682, Pro Vidia 9685(*), Cyber 9382, Cyber 9385, Cyber 9388, 3DImage975, 3DImage985, Cyber 9397, Cyber 9520
Video 7/Headland Technologies	HT216-32(*)
Weitek	P9000, P9100
Western Digital/Paradise	PVGA1
Western Digital	WD90C00, WD90C10, WD90C11, WD90C24, WD90C24A, WD90C30, WD90C31, WD90C33

(*) Note, chips marked in this way have either limited support or the drivers for them are not actively maintained.

All of the chips listed in Table 5.1 are supported in 256 color, some are supported in mono and 16 color modes, and some are supported in higher color depths.

The monochrome server also supports generic VGA cards, using 64K of video memory in a single bank, the Hercules monochrome card, the Hyundai HGC1280, Sigma LaserView, Visa, and Apollo monochrome cards.

The VGA16 server supports memory banking with the ET4000, Trident, ATI, NCR, OAK, and Cirrus 6420 chipsets allowing virtual display sizes up to about 1600 × 1200 (with 1MB of video memory). For other chipsets the display size is limited to approximately 800 × 600.

Video cards using these chipsets are supported on all bus types, including VLB and PCI.

TIP

You can find an up-to-date list of supported cards at `http://www.xfree86.org/3.3.3/README3.html`.

One problem faced by XFree86 developers is that some video card manufacturers use non-standard mechanisms for determining clock frequencies used to drive the card. Some of these manufacturers either don't release specifications describing how to program the card or they require developers to sign a non-disclosure statement to obtain the information. This would obviously restrict the free distribution of the XFree86 software, something that the XFree86 development team is not willing to do. For a long time, this has been a problem with certain video cards manufactured by Diamond, but as of release 3.1 of XFree86, Diamond has started to work with the development team to release free drivers for these cards.

The suggested setup for XFree86 under Linux is a 486 or better with at least 8 megabytes of RAM, and a video card with a chipset listed above. For optimal performance, we suggest using an accelerated card, such as an S3-chipset card. You should check the documentation for XFree86 and verify that your particular card is supported before taking the plunge and purchasing expensive hardware.

NOTE

As a side note, the personal Linux system of Matt Welsh (this FAQ's originator) was a 486DX2-66, 20 megabytes of RAM, equipped with a VLB S3-864 chipset card with 2 megabytes of DRAM. He ran X benchmarks on this machine as well as on Sun Sparc IPX workstations. The Linux system was roughly seven times faster than the Sparc IPX (for the curious, XFree86-3.1 under Linux, with this video card, runs at around 171,000 xstones; the Sparc IPX at around 24,000). In general, XFree86 on a Linux system with an accelerated SVGA card will give you much greater performance than that found on commercial Unix workstations (which usually employ simple framebuffers for graphics).

Your machine will need at least 4 megabytes of physical RAM, and 16 megabytes of virtual RAM (for example, 8 megs physical and 8 megs swap). Remember that the more physical RAM you have, the less the system will swap to and from disk when memory is low. Because swapping is inherently slow (disks are very slow compared to memory), having 8 megabytes of RAM or more is necessary to run XFree86 comfortably. 16 is better. A system with 4 megabytes of physical RAM could run much (up to 10 times) more slowly than one with 8 megs or more.

Installing XFree86

It's quite likely that you obtained XFree86 as part of a Linux distribution, in which case downloading the software separately is not necessary. Or you may be able to get RPM binary packages built for your machine, in which case you can just install those using rpm(1). In either case you can skip this the rest of this section.

The Linux binary distribution of XFree86 can be found on a number of FTP sites. On the XFree86 site it's at `ftp://ftp.xfree86.org/pub/XFree86/current/binaries/Linux-ix86`. (At the time of writing, the current version is 3.2A; newer versions are released periodically.)

Before doing anything else, download and run the `preinst.sh` shell script first. This may tell you about prerequisites you'll need to have in place before continuing your installation.

If you are downloading XFree86 directly, Table 5.2 lists the files in the XFree86-3.3 distribution, and the required server.

TABLE 5.2: XFree86-3.3 Files and Required Servers

XFree86-3.3 File	Required Server
`X338514.tgz`	Server for 8514-based boards
`X33AGX.tgz`	Server for AGX-based boards
`X33I128.tgz`	Server for the Number Nine Imagine 128
`X33Mach32.tgz`	Server for Mach32-based boards
`X33Mach64.tgz`	Server for Mach64-based boards
`X33Mach8.tgz`	Server for Mach8-based boards
`X33Mono.tgz`	Server for monochrome video modes
`X33P9K.tgz`	Server for P9000-based boards
`X33S3.tgz`	Server for S3-based boards
`X33S3V.tgz`	Server for the S3 ViRGE and ViRGE/VX (considered beta)
`X33SVGA.tgz`	Server for Super VGA-based boards
`X33W32.tgz`	Server for ET4000/W32-based boards

If you don't know which one to use, choose the VGA16 server, X33VGA16.tgz. You want to download this one anyway, because you'll need it to run the auto-configuration utility in the next step.

Table 5.3 lists the required files.

TABLE 5.3: Required XFree86-3.3 Distribution Files

Filename	File Contents
preinst.sh	Pre-installation script
postinst.sh	Post-installation script
X33bin.tgz	The rest of the X11R6 binaries
X33cfg.tgz	Config files for xdm, xinit, and fs
X33doc.tgz	Documentation
X33man.tgz	Manual pages
X33fnts.tgz	75dpi, misc, and PEX fonts
X33lib.tgz	Shared X libraries and support files
X33set.tgz	XF86Setup utility
X33VG16.tgz	Server for VGA/EGA-based boards

Table 5.4 lists the optional files.

TABLE 5.4: Optional XFree86-3.3 Distribution Files

Filename	Contents
X33f100.tgz	100dpi fonts
X33fcyr.tgz	Cyrillic fonts
X33fnon.tgz	Other fonts (Chinese, Japanese, Korean, Hebrew)
X33fscl.tgz	Scalable fonts (Speedo and Type1)
X33fsrv.tgz	Font server and config files
X33prog.tgz	X header files, config files, and compile-time libs
X33lkit.tgz	X server LinkKit
X33lk98.tgz	PC98 X server LinkKit
X33nest.tgz	Nested X server
X33prt.tgz	X print server
X33vfb.tgz	Virtual framebuffer X server
X33ps.tgz	PostScript version of the documentation
X33html.tgz	HTML version of the documentation

The XFree86 directory should contain release notes for the current version in RELNOTES. Consult those for installation details.

To install XFree86 you just need to obtain the above files, create the directory `/usr/X11R6` (as root) and unpack the files from `/usr/X11R6` with a command such as:

```
gzip -dc X33bin.tgz | tar xfB -
```

Remember that these tar files are packed relative to `/usr/X11R6`, so it's important to unpack the files there.

You need to make sure that `/usr/X11R6/bin` is on your path. This can be done by editing your system default `/etc/profile` or `/etc/csh.login` (based on the shell that you, or other users on your system, use). Or you can simply add the directory to your personal path by modifying `.bashrc` or `.cshrc`, based on your shell.

You also need to make sure that `/usr/X11R6/lib` can be located by `ld.so`, the runtime linker. To do this, add the line

```
/usr/X11R6/lib
```

to the file `/etc/ld.so.conf`, and run `/sbin/ldconfig`, as root.

Configuring XFree86

This section discusses standard configuration of XFree86, then moves onto troubleshooting, custom configuration, and configuring XFree86 for 16-bit color.

Normal Configuration

Configuring XFree86 to use your mouse, keyboard, monitor, and video card correctly used to be something of a black art—requiring extensive hand-hacking of a complex configuration file. No more—the 3.2/3.3 release made the process nearly trivial. All you do is fire up the program XF86Setup.

This program depends on the fact that all new PC hardware these days ships with EGA/VGA capable monitors. It invokes the VGA16 server and uses it to bring up X in a lowest-common-denominator 640 × 480 mode. Then it runs an interactive program that walks you through a series of five configuration panels—mouse, keyboard, (video) card, monitor, and other (miscellaneous server options). The whole process is quite painless.

NOTE

If you're running Red Hat Linux, you may see a different program called xf86config. This works fairly similarly to XF86Setup but does not itself use an X interface and the VGA16 server.

One minor point to keep in mind is that, if you're like most people using a current PC, your keyboard is actually what XF86Setup calls *Generic 102-key PC (intl)* rather than the default *Generic 101-key PC.* If you pick the default (101) the key cluster on the extreme right of your keyboard (numeric keypad and friends) may stop working.

If you're not sure of your monitor type, you can try the listed ones in succession. Work your way from the top down (upper choices involve lower dot-clock speeds and are less demanding on the hardware). Change back to default if you get hash or a seriously distorted picture. Minor distortions (picture slightly too large, slightly too small, or slightly off-center) are no problem; you'll get a chance to correct those immediately by fine-tuning the mode.

And, when the program brings up xvidtune to allow you to tweak your video mode, don't let the initial warning box make you nervous. Modern multisync monitors (unlike their fixed-frequency predecessors) are not easy to damage this way.

XF86Config may assume that your mouse device is `/dev/mouse`. If you find this doesn't work, you may need to link `/dev/mouse` to whatever `/dev/ca[01]` the mouse is on. If you find that XFree86 gives you a "mouse busy" error when gpm is running, you may need to link to `/dev/ttyS[01]` instead.

The configuration process operates by selecting a server corresponding to the general type of your video card (such as XF86VGA16, XF86Mach64, or XF86S3) and configuring an XF86Config that the server will read on startup to get specific parameters for your installation. The location of XF86Config varies depending on your OS, but one place to look for it is `/etc/X11`.

On older versions of XFree86, XF86Setup links the X command directly to the chosen server. In recent versions, X is instead linked to a set-user-id wrapper program called Xwrapper. The idea is that all the `setuid` root stuff gets localized in Xwrapper so the server doesn't have to run `setuid` root.

Troubleshooting

Occasionally, when you first fire up the X server something will not be quite right. This is almost always caused by a problem in your configuration file. Usually, the monitor timing values are off or the video card dot clocks are set incorrectly. Minor problems can be fixed with xvidtune; a really garbled screen usually means you need to go back into XF86Setup and choose a less capable monitor type.

If your display seems to roll, or the edges are fuzzy, this is a clear indication that the monitor timing values or dot clocks are wrong. Also be sure that you are correctly specifying your video card chipset, as well as other options for the Device section of XF86Config. Be absolutely certain that you are using the right X server and that `/usr/X11R6/bin/X` is a symbolic link to this server.

If all else fails, try to start X *bare*; that is, use a command such as:

```
X > /tmp/x.out 2>1
```

You can then kill the X server (using the Ctrl+Alt+Backspace key combination) and examine the contents of `/tmp/x.out`. The X server will report any warnings or errors—for example, if your video card doesn't have a dot clock corresponding to a mode supported by your monitor.

Remember that you can use Ctrl+Alt+numeric + and Ctrl+Alt+numeric – to switch between the video modes listed on the Modes line of the Screen section of XF86Config. If the highest resolution mode doesn't look right, try switching to lower resolutions. This will let you know, at least, that those parts of your X configuration are working correctly.

Also, check the vertical and horizontal size/hold knobs on your monitor. In many cases it is necessary to adjust these when starting up X. For example, if the display seems to be shifted slightly to one side, you can usually correct this using the monitor controls.

TIP

The Usenet newsgroup `comp.windows.x.i386unix` is devoted to discussions about XFree86, as is `comp.os.linux.x`. It might be a good idea to watch that newsgroup for postings relating to your video configuration—you might run across someone with the same problems as your own.

Custom Configuration

You will need to hand-hack your X configuration to get optimal performance if your monitor can support 1600 × 1200—the highest canned resolution XF86Setup supports is 1280 × 1024.

If you want to hand-hack your video configuration for this or any other reason, go see the LDP's XFree86 Video Timings HOWTO, `http://metalab.unc.edu/LDP/HOWTO/XFree86-Video-Timings-HOWTO.html`. (This is the up-to-date HTML version of XFree86's `Videomodes.doc` file.)

Using 16-bit Color

By default, X uses 8-bit color depth giving 256 colors. To circumvent this restriction, many applications allocate their own color maps, resulting in sudden color jumps when the cursor moves between two windows each having a color map of its own. The Arena WWW browser does it this way.

If you want to use advanced graphic applications, 256 colors may be not sufficient. You may need to go to 16-bit color depth (65,536 colors). But beware, not all applications will work with 16-bit colors.

You can use 16-bit color depth with 65K different colors simply by starting X with

```
startx -- -bpp 16
```

or putting

```
exec X :0 -bpp 16
```

into your `.xserverrc` file. In order for this to work, however, you need to have a screen section in your XF86Config with `DefaultColorDepth 16`.

If you're using xdm, you may need to change the Xservers file, which is probably located in `/etc/X11/xdm/`. A typical configuration has just one uncommented line, looking something like

```
:0 local /usr/X11R6/bin/X
```

Add

```
-bpp 16
```

to the startup options:

```
:0 local /usr/X11R6/bin/X -bpp 16
```

Also, you'll need to add a Display part with a Depth value of 16 to the screen section of your X configuration. Generally you can just duplicate the 8-bit Display section and change the Depth field.

More colors make your video card transfer more data during the same time. If your video card cannot cope, then either the resolution or the refresh rate has to be reduced. By default, XFree reduces the resolution. If you want to keep the resolution and reduce the refresh rate, you must insert a new appropriate Modeline into your XF86Config file. This defines that resolution with a lower refresh rate. For instance replace the old value

```
Modeline "1024x768" 75 1024 1048 1184 1328 768 771 777 _
806 -hsync -vsync
```

with the following value:

```
Modeline "1024x768" 65 1024 1032 1176 1344 768 771 777 _
806 -hsync -vsync.
```

The magic numbers 75 and 65 are the respective clock rates that you find reported by X in your `.X.err` file. Consult the monitor's file in the XF86 documentation for Modelines suitable for the maximum clock rate your video card can deliver under 16-bit color depth.

Running XFree86

With your XF86Config file configured, you're ready to fire up the X server and give it a spin. First, be sure that `/usr/X11R6/bin` is on your path.

The command to start up XFree86 is

```
startx
```

This is a front-end to xinit (in case you're used to using xinit on other Unix systems).

This command will start the X server and run the commands found in the file `.xinitrc` in your home directory. `.xinitrc` is just a shell script containing X clients to run. If this file does not exist, the system default `/usr/X11R6/lib/X11/xinit/xinitrc` will be used.

A standard `.xinitrc` file looks like this:

```
#!/bin/sh

xterm -fn 7x13bold -geometry 80x32+10+50 &
xterm -fn 9x15bold -geometry 80x34+30-10 &
oclock -geometry 70x70-7+7 &
xsetroot -solid midnightblue &

exec fvwm2
```

This script will start up two xterm clients, an oclock, and set the root window (background) color to midnightblue. It will then start up fvwm2, the window manager. Note that fvwm2 is executed with the shell's `exec` statement; this causes the xinit process to be replaced with fvwm2. Once the fvwm2 process exits, the X server will shut down. You can cause fvwm2 to exit by using the root menus: depress mouse button 1 on the desktop background—this will display a pop-up menu that will allow you to exit fvwm2.

Be sure that the last command in `.xinitrc` is started with `exec`, and that it is not placed into the background (no ampersand on the end of the line). Otherwise the X server will shut down as soon as it has started the clients in the `.xinitrc` file.

Alternately, you can exit X by pressing Ctrl+Alt+Backspace in combination. This will kill the X server directly, exiting the window system.

The above is a very, very simple desktop configuration. Many wonderful programs and configurations are available with a bit of work on your `.xinitrc` file.

TIP

If you are new to the X Window System environment, we strongly suggest picking up a book such as *The Joy of X: An Overview of the X Window System* by Niall Manfield (Addison-Wesley 1993, ISBN 0201-565129). Using and configuring X is far too in-depth to cover here. See the man pages for xterm, oclock, and fvwm2 for clues on getting started.

Terms of Use

This document is copyright ©1996 by Eric S. Raymond. You may use, disseminate, and reproduce it freely, provided you

- Do not omit or alter this copyright notice.
- Do not omit or alter the version number and date.
- Do not omit or alter the document's pointer to the current WWW version.
- Clearly mark any condensed or altered versions as such.

These restrictions are intended to protect potential readers from stale or mangled versions. If you think you have a good case for an exception, ask me.

Acknowledgements

This document was originated by Matt Welsh in the dim and backward abysm of time. Thanks, Matt!

Translations

Italian: `http://www.pluto.linux.it/ildp/HOWTO/XFree86-HOWTO.html`

Slovenian: `http://www.lugos.si/delo/slo/HOWTO-sl/XFree86-HOWTO-sl.html`

Croatian: `http://meta.mioc.hr/XFree86-KAKO.html`

Chapter 6

PRINTERS

This chapter comprises the Linux Printing HOWTO, a collection of information on how to generate, preview, print, and fax anything under Linux (and other kinds of Unix).

This is the complete text of the Linux Printing HOWTO, version 3.29 of 9 March 1999, by Grant Taylor <gtaylor+pht@picante.com>.

INTRODUCTION

The Printing HOWTO should contain everything you need to know to set up printing services on your Linux box(en). As life would have it, it's a bit more complicated than in the point-and-click world of Microsoft and Apple, but it's also a bit more flexible and certainly easier to administer for large LANs.

This document is structured so that most people will only need to read the first half or so. Most of the more obscure and situation-dependent information in here is in the last half and can be easily located in the Table of Contents, whereas most of the information through the "Vendor Solutions" or "Ghostscript" sections is probably needed by most people.

Since version *3.x* is a complete rewrite, much information from previous editions has been lost. This is by design, as the previous HOWTOs were so large as to be 60 typeset pages and had the narrative flow of a dead turtle. If you do not find the answer here, you are encouraged to (a) scan the previous version at the Printing HOWTO Home Page (`http://www.picante.com/~gtaylor/pht/`) and (b) drop me a note saying what ought to be here but isn't.

The Printing HOWTO Home Page is a good place to find the latest version; it is also, of course, distributed from Metalab <`metalab.unc.edu`> and your friendly local LDP mirror.

History

This is the third generation, which is to say the third complete rewrite, of the Printing HOWTO. The history of the PHT may be chronicled thusly:

1. I wrote the Printing HOWTO in 1992, in response to too many printing questions in `comp.os.linux`, and posted it. This predated the HOWTO project by a few months and was the first FAQlet called a HOWTO. This edition was in plain ASCII.
2. After joining the HOWTO project, the Printing HOWTO was merged with an lpd FAQ by Brian McCauley <`B.A.McCauley@bham.ac.uk`>; we continued to coauthor the PHT for two years or so. At some point we incorporated the work of Karl Auer <`Karl.Auer@anu.edu.au`>. This generation of the PHT was in TeXinfo and available in PS, HTML, ASCII, and Info.
3. After letting the PHT rot and decay for over a year and an unsuccessful attempt at getting someone else to maintain it,

this rewrite happened. This generation of the PHT is written in SGML using the LinuxDoc DTD and the SGML-Tools-1 package. Beginning with version 3.27, it incorporates a summary of a companion printer support database; before 3.27 there was never a printer compatibility list in this HOWTO (!).

Copyright

This chapter is Copyright ©1992-1999 by Grant Taylor. Feel free to copy and redistribute it according to the terms of the GNU General Public License, revision 2 or later.

How to Print

If you've already got lpd set up to print to your printer, your system administrator already did so, or your vendor did so for you, then all you need to do is learn how to use the `lpr` command. The Printing Usage HOWTO (`http://metalab.unc.edu/LDP/HOWTO/Printing-Usage-HOWTO.html`) covers this and a few other queue manipulation commands you should probably know.

If, however, you have a new system or new printer, then you'll have to set up printing services one way or another before you can print. Read on!

Kernel Printer Devices

There are two completely different device drivers for the parallel port; which one you are using depends on your kernel version. The driver changed in Linux 2.1.33.

A few details are the same for both styles of driver. Most notably, many people have found that Linux will not detect their parallel port unless they disable Plug and Play in their PC BIOS. (This is no surprise; the track record for PnP of non-PCI devices with Windows and elsewhere has been something of a disaster).

The lp Device (Kernels =2.1.32)

The Linux kernel (=2.1.32), assuming you have compiled in or loaded the lp device (the output of `cat/proc/devices` should include the device lp if it is loaded), provides one or more of /dev/lp0, /dev/lp1, and /dev/lp2. These are *not* assigned dynamically; rather, each corresponds to a specific hardware I/O address. This means that your first printer may be lp0 or lp1 depending on your hardware. Just try both.

A few users have reported that their bidirectional lp ports aren't detected if they use an older unidirectional printer cable. Check that you've got a decent cable.

One cannot run the plip and lp drivers at the same time on any given port (under 2.0, anyway). You can, however, have one or the other driver loaded at any given time either manually, or by kerneld with version 2.x (and later 1.3.x) kernels. By carefully setting the interrupts and such, you can supposedly run plip on one port and lp on the other. One person did so by editing the drivers; I eagerly await a success report of someone doing so with only a clever command line.

There is a little utility called tunelp floating about with which you, as root, can tune the Linux 2.0 lp device's interrupt usage, polling rate, and other options.

When the lp driver is built into the kernel, the kernel will accept an lp= option to set interrupts and IO addresses.

When the lp driver is built into the kernel, you may use the LILO/LOADLIN command line to set the port addresses and interrupts that the driver will use. The syntax is

```
lp=port0[,irq0[,port1[,irq1[,port2[,irq2]]]]]
```

For example,

```
lp=0x378,0  or  lp=0x278,5,0x378,7
```

NOTE

For those of you who (like me) can never find the standard port numbers when you need them, they are as in the second example above. The other port (lpo) is at ox3bc. I've no idea what interrupt it usually uses.

Note that if this feature is used, you must specify *all* the ports you want considered; there are no defaults. You can disable a built-in driver with lp=0.

When loaded as a module, it is possible to specify IO addresses and interrupt lines on the insmod command line (or in /etc/conf.modules so as to affect kerneld) using the usual module argument syntax. The parameters are io=port0,port1,port2 and irq=irq0,irq1,irq2.

The source code for the Linux 2.0 parallel port driver is in `/usr/src/linux/drivers/char/lp.c`.

The parport Device (Kernels = 2.1.33)

Beginning with kernel 2.1.33 (and available as a patch for kernel 2.0.30), the lp device is merely a client of the new parport device. The addition of the parport device corrects a number of the problems that plague the old lp device driver–it can share the port with other drivers, it dynamically assigns available parallel ports to device numbers rather than enforcing a fixed correspondence between I/O addresses and port numbers, and so forth.

The advent of the parport device has enabled a whole flock of new parallel-port drivers for things like Zip drives, Backpack CD-ROMs and disks, and so forth. Some of these are also available in versions for 2.0 kernels; look around on the Web.

The main difference that you will notice, so far as printing goes, is that parport-based kernels dynamically assign lp devices to parallel ports. So what was lp1 under Linux 2.0 may well be lp0 under Linux 2.2. Be sure to check this if you upgrade from an lp-driver kernel to a parport-driver kernel.

I'll cover the parport driver more completely when I find myself using one, but in the meantime you can read the file `Documentation/parport.txt` in your kernel sources, or look at the parport Web site (`http://www.cyberelk.demon.co.uk/parport.html`).

Serial Devices

Serial devices are usually called something like */dev/ttyS1* under Linux. The utility stty will allow you to interactively view or set the settings for a serial port; setserial will allow you to control a few extended attributes and configure IRQs and I/O addresses for nonstandard ports. Further discussion of serial ports under Linux may be found in the Serial HOWTO (`http://metalab.unc.edu/mdw/HOWTO/Serial-HOWTO.html`).

When using a slow serial printer with flow control, you may find that some of your print jobs get truncated. This may be due to the serial port, whose default behavior is to purge any untransmitted characters from its buffer 30 seconds after the port device is closed. The buffer can hold up to 4,096 characters, and if your printer uses flow control and is slow enough that it can't accept all the data from the buffer within 30 seconds after printing software has closed the serial port, the tail end of the buffer's contents will be lost. If the command `cat file /dev/ttyS2` produces complete printouts for short files but truncated ones for longer files, you may have this condition.

The 30-second interval can be adjusted through the closingwait commandline option of setserial (version 2.12 and later). A machine's serial ports are usually initialized by a call to setserial in the `rc.serial` boot file. The call for the printing serial port can be modified to set the closingwait at the same time as it sets that port's other parameters.

Supported Printers

The Linux kernel mostly supports any printer that you can plug into a serial or parallel port, but there are things to look out for, and printers that you won't be able to use, even though they can (electrically speaking) communicate with Linux. Primary among these incompatible printers are those referred to as Windows or GDI printers. They are called this because part or all of the printer control language and the design details of the printing mechanism are not documented. Typically the vendor will provide a Windows driver and happily sell only to Windows users; this is why they are called Winprinters. In some cases the vendor also provides drivers for NT, OS/2, or other operating systems.

Many of these printers *do not work* with Linux. A few of them do, and some of them only work a little bit (usually because someone has reverse engineered the details needed to write a driver). See the printer support list later in this chapter for details on specific printers.

A few printers are in-between. Some of NEC's models, for example, implement a simple form of the standard printer language PCL that allows PCL-speaking software to print at up to 300dpi, but only NEC knows how to get the full 600dpi out of these printers.

Note that if you already have one of these Winprinters, there are roundabout ways to get Linux to print to one, but they're rather awkward and I've never tried it myself. See the "Windows-Only Printers" section of this chapter for more discussion of Windows-only printers.

PostScript

As for what printers *do* work with Linux, the best choice is to buy a printer with native PostScript support. Nearly all Unix software that produces printable output produces it in PostScript, so obviously it'd be nice to get a printer that supports PostScript directly. Unfortunately, PostScript support is scarce outside the laser printer domain and is sometimes a costly add-on.

Unix software, and the publishing industry in general, have standardized upon PostScript as the printer control language of choice. This happened for several reasons:

Timing PostScript arrived as part of the Apple LaserWriter, a perfect companion to the Macintosh, the system largely responsible for the desktop publishing revolution of the 80s.

It's device-independent PostScript programs can be run to generate output on a pixel screen, a vector screen, a fax machine, or almost any sort of printer mechanism, without the original program needing to be changed. PostScript output will look the same on any PostScript device, at least within the limits of the device's capabilities. Before the creation of PDF, people exchanged complex documents online as PostScript files. The only reason this standard didn't stick was because Windows machines didn't usually include a PostScript previewer, so Adobe specified hyperlinks and compression for PostScript, called the result PDF, distributed previewers for it, and invented a market for their distiller tools (the functionality of which is also provided by Ghostscript's ps2pdf and pdf2ps programs).

It's a real programming language PostScript is a complete programming language; you can write software to do most anything in it. This is mostly useful for defining subroutines at the start of your program to reproduce complex things over and over throughout your document, like a logo or a big *DRAFT* in the background.

It's open PostScript is fully specified in a publicly available series of books, which you can find at any good bookstore. Although Adobe invented it and provides the dominant commercial implementation, other vendors like Aladdin produce independently coded implementations as well.

Non-PostScript

Failing the (larger) budget necessary to buy a PostScript printer, you can use any printer supported by Ghostscript, the free PostScript interpreter used in lieu of actual printer PostScript support. The Ghostscript Home Page (`http://www.cs.wisc.edu/~ghost/`) has a list of supported printers and information on the status of new and experimental drivers. Note that this page lists supported printers in the latest version of Ghostscript, while most Linux distributions can only ship a somewhat outdated version of Ghostscript because of the license. Fortunately, there is usually a prepackaged, up-to-date Ghostscript made available in each distribution's contrib area. Please help improve the Ghostscript printer support page by reporting your successes and failures as it asks.

Adobe now has a new printer language called PrintGear. I think it's a greatly simplified binary format language with some PostScript heritage but no PostScript compatibility. And I haven't heard of Ghostscript supporting it. But some PrintGear printers seem to support another language like PCL, and these printers will work with Linux (if and only if the PCL is implemented in the printer and not in a Windows driver).

What Printers Work?

If you want to buy a printer, you can look in several places to see if it will work. The cooperatively maintained Printing HOWTO printer database (`http://www.picante.com/~gtaylor/pht/printer_list.cgi`) aims to be a comprehensive listing of the state of Linux printer support. A summary of it is below; be sure to check online for more details and information on what driver to use.

Ghostscript's printer compatibility page (`http://www.cs.wisc.edu/~ghost/printer.html`) has a list of some working printers, as well as links to other pages. And Dejanews contains hundreds of "it works" and "it doesn't work" testimonials. Try all three, and when you're done, check that your printer is present and correct in the database (`http://www.picante.com/~gtaylor/pht/printer_list.cgi`) so that it will be listed properly in this document in the future.

Printer Compatibility List

This section is a summary of the online version. The online version includes basic specifications, notes, links to driver information, user-maintained documentation, manufacturer Web pages, and so forth. The online version of this list is also interactive; people can and do add printers all the time, so be sure to check it as well. Finally, if your printer isn't listed, add it!

Printers here are categorized into four types:

Perfectly Perfect printers work perfectly–you can print to the full ability of the printer, including color, full resolution, etc. In a few cases, printers with undocumented resolution enhancement modes that don't work are listed as perfect; generally the difference in print quality is small enough that it isn't worth worrying about.

Mostly You can print fine, but there may be minor limitations of one sort or another in either printing or other features.

Partially You can print but maybe not in color or only at a poor resolution. See the online listing's notes column for information on the limitation.

Paperweight You can't print a darned thing; typically this will be due to lack of a driver and/or documentation on how to write one.

In all cases, since this information is provided by dozens of people, none of it is guaranteed to be correct. It should, however, be easy to corroborate from the driver Web pages and manufacturer Web sites.

And without further ado, here is the printer compatibility list:

Brother

Perfectly: HL-10V, HL-660, HL-720, HL-760.

Mostly: HL-1050.

Canon

Perfectly: BJ-10e, BJ-20, BJ-200, BJC-210, BJC-240, BJC-250, BJC-610, BJC-620, BJC-70, BJC-800, LBP-8II, LIPS-III.

Mostly: BJ-300, BJC-4000, BJC-4100, BJC-4200, BJC-4300, BJC-4400, BJC-7000, BJC-7004.

Partially: BJC-4550, MultiPASS C2500, MultiPASS C3500.

Paperweight: BJC-5000, LBP-460, LBP-660.

Epson

Perfectly: ActionLaser 1100, LP 8000, LQ 850, Stylus Color, Stylus Color 400, Stylus Color 500, Stylus Color 600, Stylus Color 640, Stylus Color 850, Stylus Color II, Stylus Color IIs, Stylus Pro XL.

Mostly: Stylus Color 800, Stylus Photo 750.

Partially: Stylus Color 740.

HP

Perfectly: 2000Cse, 2500C, DesignJet 650C, DeskJet 1200C, DeskJet 1600C, DeskJet 1600Cm, DeskJet 400, DeskJet 420C, DeskJet 500, DeskJet 550C, DeskJet 600, DeskJet 660Cse, DeskJet 690C, DeskJet 850C, DeskJet 855C, DeskJet 870, DeskJet 870Cxi, DeskJet 890, LaserJet 1100, LaserJet 2100, LaserJet 2100M, LaserJet 4000N, LaserJet 4L, LaserJet 5, LaserJet 5L, LaserJet 5MP, LaserJet 6L, LaserJet 6MP, LaserJet 8000, LaserJet 8100, Laserjet 5000, Mopier 320, PaintJet XL300.

Mostly: HP 660C.

Partially: DeskJet 1000C, DeskJet 670C, DeskJet 710, DeskJet 720C, DeskJet 722C, DeskJet 820C.

Paperweight: LaserJet 3100.

IBM

Perfectly: Jetprinter 3852.

Lexmark

Perfectly: Optra Color 1200, Optra Color 1275, Optra Color 40, Optra Color 45, Optra E, Optra E+, Optra Ep, Optra S 1250.

Partially: 1020 Business, 3000, 5700, 7000.

Paperweight: 1000, 1020, 1100, 2030, 2050, 2070, 5000, 7200, Winwriter 100, Winwriter 150c, Winwriter 200.

Minolta

Perfectly: PagePro 6, PagePro 8.

NEC

Perfectly: P2X.

Partially: SuperScript 100C, SuperScript 1260, SuperScript 150C, SuperScript 650C, SuperScript 750C, SuperScript 860, SuperScript 870.

Paperweight: SuperScript 660i, SuperScript 660plus.

Okidata

Perfectly: OL 410e, OL 610e/PS, OL 810e/PS, Okipage 6e, Okipage 6ex, Okipage 8c.

Mostly: Okipage 4w.

Paperweight: Okipage 8w, Okijet 2010.

Olivetti

Perfectly: JP350S.

Panasonic

Perfectly: KX-P1123, KX-P4440, KX-P5400, KX-P8420, KX-P8475.

Partially: KX-P6500.

Paperweight: KX-P6100, KX-P8410.

QMS

Perfectly: 2425 Turbo EX.

Ricoh

Perfectly: 4801, 6000.

Xerox

Perfectly: DocuPrint C55, DocuPrint N17, DocuPrint N32.

Which Spooling Software?

Until recently, the choice for Linux users was simple—everyone ran the same old lpd (Line Printer Daemon), lifted mostly verbatim out of BSD's Net-2 code. The term lpd refers in different contexts to both the daemon and the whole collection of programs which run print spooling. Even today, most vendors ship this software. But this is beginning to change. SVR4-like systems, including Sun's Solaris, come with a completely different print spooling package, centered around lpsched. And there are signs that some Linux vendors will shift to providing LPRng, a far less ancient print spooling implementation that is freely available. LPRng is far easier to administer for large installations (read: more than one printer, any serial printers, or any peculiar non-lpd network printers) and has a less frightfully haphazard codebase than does stock lpd. It can even honestly claim to be secure—there are no SUID binaries, and it supports authentication via PGP or Kerberos.

For the moment, even in light of the new options, lpd is probably fine for most Linux users. While it isn't the snazziest system, it works fine once set up, and it is well understood and extensively documented in third-party Unix books.

If you'd like more information on LPRng, check out the LPRng Web page (`http://www.astart.com/lprng/LPRng.html`). Future versions of this HOWTO will include information on using both LPRng and regular lpd.

How It Works: Basic

In order to get printing working well, you need to understand how the lpd system works.

lpd refers in different contexts to both the daemon and the whole collection of programs which run print spooling. These are

lpd The spooling daemon. One of these runs to control everything on a machine, AND one is run per printer while the printer is printing.

`lpr` The user spooling command. It contacts lpd and injects a new print job into the spool.

`lpq` Lists the jobs in a print queue.

`lpc` The lpd system control command. With `lpc` you can stop, start, reorder, etc. the print queues.

`lprm` This will remove a job from the print spool.

So how does it fit together? Well, when the system boots, lpd is run. It scans the file `/etc/printcap` to learn which printers it will be managing spools for. Each time someone runs `lpr`, it contacts lpd through the named socket `/dev/printer` and feeds lpd both the file to print and some information about who is printing and how to print it. lpd then prints the file on the appropriate printer.

The lp system was originally designed when most printers were line printers—that is, people mostly printed plain ASCII. As it turns out, only a little extra scripting is needed to make lpd work quite well for today's print jobs, which are often in PostScript, or text, or dvi, or...

How to Set Up the Basics

This section discusses the minimal requirements for setting up your Linux system. You'll learn how to add a print queue and print documents.

Traditional lpd Configuration

The minimal setup for lpd results in a system that can queue files and print them. It will not pay any attention to whether or not your printer will understand them and will probably not let you produce attractive output. Nevertheless, it is the first step to understanding, so read on!

Basically, to add a print queue to lpd, you must add an entry in `/etc/printcap` and make the new spool directory under `/var/spool/lpd`.

An entry in `/etc/printcap` looks like the following:

```
# LOCAL djet500
lp|dj|deskjet:\
      :sd=/var/spool/lpd/dj:\
      :mx#0:\
      :lp=/dev/lp0:\
      :sh:
```

This defines a spool called lp, dj, or deskjet, spooled in the directory `/var/spool/lpd/dj`, with no per-job maximum size limit, which prints to the device `/dev/lp0` and which does not have a banner page (with the name of the person who printed etc.) added to the front of the print job.

TIP

At this point, it would behoove you to read the man page for printcap.

The above looks very simple, but there is a catch—unless I send in files a DeskJet 500 can understand, this DeskJet will print strange things. For example, sending an ordinary Unix text file to a DeskJet results in literally interpreted new lines and gets me the following ad nauseam:

```
This is line one.
         This is line two.
                 This is line three.
```

Printing a PostScript file to this spool would get a beautiful listing of the PostScript commands, printed out with this staircase effect but no useful output.

Clearly more is needed, and this is the purpose of filtering. The more observant of you who read the printcap man page might have noticed the spool attributes `if` and `of`. Well, `if`, or the input filter, is just what is needed here.

If you write a small shell script called filter that adds carriage returns before new lines, the staircasing can be eliminated. So, you have to add in an `if` line to your printcap entry above:

```
lp|dj|deskjet:\
    :sd=/var/spool/lpd/dj:\
    :mx#0:\
    :lp=/dev/lp0:\
    :if=/var/spool/lpd/dj/filter:\
    :sh:
```

A simple filter script might be

```
#!perl
# The above line should really have the whole path to perl
# This script must be executable: chmod 755 filter
while(<STDIN>){chop $_; print "$_\r\n";};
# You might also want to end with a form feed: print "\f";
```

If you were to do the above, you'd have a spool to which you could print regular Unix text files and get meaningful results. (Yes, there are four million better ways to write this filter, but few are so illustrative. You are encouraged to do this more efficiently.)

The only remaining problem is that printing plain text is really not too hot—surely it would be better to be able to print PostScript and other formatted or graphic types of output. Well, yes, it would, and it's easy to do. The method is simply an extension of the above linefeed-fixing filter. If you write a filter that can accept arbitrary file types as input and produce DeskJet-kosher output for each case, then you've got a clever print spooler indeed!

Such a filter is called a magic filter. Don't bother writing one yourself unless you print strange things—there are a good many written for you already on the Net. APS Filter is among the best, or your Linux distribution may have a printer setup tool that makes this all really easy.

File Permissions

By popular demand, I include below a listing of the permissions on interesting files on my system. There are a number of better ways to do this, ideally using only SGID binaries and not making everything SUID root, but this is how my system came out of the box, and it works for me. (Quite frankly, if your vendor can't even ship a working lpd, you're in for a rough ride).

```
-r-sr-sr-x  1 root   lp  /usr/bin/lpr*
-r-sr-sr-x  1 root   lp  /usr/bin/lprm*
-rwxr--r--  1 root   root /usr/sbin/lpd*
-r-xr-sr-x  1 root   lp  /usr/sbin/lpc*
drwxrwxr-x  4 root   lp  /var/spool/lpd/
drwxr-xr-x  2 root   lp  /var/spool/lpd/lp/
```

lpd must currently be run as root so that it can bind to the low-numbered lp service port. It should probably become UID lp.lp or something after binding, but I don't think it does. Bummer.

Getting Printing Software

Many prewritten filter packages (and other printer-related software) are available from Metalab (`ftp://metalab.unc.edu/pub/Linux/system/printing/`). Such utilities as psutils, a2ps, mpage, dvitodvi, and rlpr can be found there.

For a while, there were several packages out there all trying to make printer configuration easier. They probably all still exist, but one of the best and most up-to-date is Andreas Klemm's APS Filter package, which has a menu-driven printcap configurator and handles practically any type of input imaginable. If your vendor doesn't ship a nice printer setup tool, APS Filter is the way to go.

VENDOR SOLUTIONS

This section is, by definition, incomplete. Feel free to send in details of your favorite distribution.

Red Hat

Red Hat has a GUI printer administration tool (in the control panel) which can add remote printers and printers on local devices. It lets you choose a Ghostscript-supported printer type and Unix device file to print to, then installs a print queue in `/etc/printcap` and writes a short PostScript-and-ASCII magic filter based around gs and nenscript. This solution works fairly well and is trivial to setup for common cases.

Where Red Hat fails is when you have a printer which isn't supported by their standard Ghostscript (which is GNU rather than Aladdin Ghostscript and which supports fewer printers). Check in the printer compatibility list above (or online at `http://www.picante.com/~gtaylor/pht/printer_list.cgi`) if you find that you can't print properly with the stock Red Hat software. If your printer isn't supported by Red Hat's tools, you may need to install a contributed version of Aladdin Ghostscript and will probably also be better off if you use the apsfilter package, which knows all about the printers supported by late-model Ghostscripts.

Debian

Debian offers a choice between plain lpd and LPRng; LPRng is probably a better choice. I believe Debian also offers a choice of printer configuration tools; apsfilter version 5 or later is probably your best bet, since that version adds support for LPRng and Ghostscript's uniprint driver scheme.

Other Distributions

Please send me info on what other distributions do!

GHOSTSCRIPT

Ghostscript (`http://www.cs.wisc.edu/~ghost/`) is an incredibly significant program for Linux printing. Most printing software under Unix generates PostScript, which is typically a $100 option on a printer.

Ghostscript, however, is free and will generate the language of your printer from PostScript. When tied in with your lpd input filter, it gives you a virtual PostScript printer and simplifies life immensely.

Ghostscript is available in two forms. The commercial version of Ghostscript, called Aladdin Ghostscript, may be used freely for personal use but may not be distributed by commercial Linux distributions. It is generally a year or so ahead of the free Ghostscript; at the moment, for example, it supports many color inkjets that the older Ghostscripts do not.

The free version of Ghostscript is GNU Ghostscript and is simply an aged version of Aladdin Ghostscript kindly given to GNU. (Kudos to Aladdin for this arrangement; more software vendors should support free software in this way, if they can't handle full-blown GPL distribution of their code.)

Whatever you do with gs (see http://www.picante.com/~gtaylor/pht/man/gs.1.html), be very sure to run it with the option for disabling file access (-dSAFER). PostScript is a fully functional language, and a bad PostScript program could give you quite a headache.

Speaking of PDF, Adobe's Portable Document Format is actually little more than organized PostScript in a compressed file. Ghostscript can handle PDF input just as it does PostScript. So you can be the first on your block with a PDF-capable printer.

Invoking Ghostscript

Typically, Ghostscript will be run by whatever magic filter you settle upon (I recommend apsfilter if your vendor didn't supply anything that suits you), but for debugging purposes it's often handy to run it directly.

Gs -help will give a brief informative listing of options and available drivers (note that this list is the list of drivers compiled in, not the master list of all available drivers).

You might run gs for testing purposes, like the following: gs <options> -q -dSAFER -sOutputFile=/dev/lp1 test.ps.

Ghostscript Output Tuning

There are a number of things one can do if gs's output is not satisfactory (actually, you can do anything you darn well please, since you have the source).

Output Location and Size

The location, size, and aspect ratio of the image on a page is controlled by the printer-specific driver in Ghostscript. If you find that your pages are coming out too short, too long, or too big by a factor of two, you might want to look in your driver's source module and adjust whatever parameters jump out at you. Unfortunately, each driver is different, so I can't really tell you what to adjust, but most of them are reasonably well commented.

Gamma, Dotsizes, Etc.

Most non-laser printers suffer from the fact that their dots are rather large. This results in pictures coming out too dark. If you experience this problem you should use your own transfer function. Simply create the following file in the Ghostscript lib-dir and add its name to the gs call just before the actual file. You may need to tweak the actual values to fit your printer. Lower values result in a brighter print. Especially if your driver uses a Floyd-Steinberg algorithm to rasterize colors, lower values (0.2 - 0.15) are probably a good choice.

```
---8<---- gamma.ps ----8<---
%!
%transfer functions for cyan magenta yellow black
{0.3 exp} {0.3 exp} {0.3 exp} {0.3 exp} setcolortransfer
---8<------------------8<---
```

It is also possible to mend printers that have some kind of color fault by tweaking these values. If you do that kind of thing, I recommend using the file `colorcir.ps`, which comes with Ghostscript (in the `examples/` subdir) as a test page.

For many of the newer color inkjet drivers, there are command-line options, or different upp driver files, which implement gamma and other changes to adapt the printer to different paper types. You should look into this before playing with PostScript to fix things.

How to Print to a Printer over the Network

One of the features of lpd is that it supports printing over the network to printers physically connected to a different machine. With the careful combination of filter scripts and assorted utilities, you can make lpr print transparently to printers on all sorts of networks.

To a Unix/lpd Host

To allow remote machines to print to your printer, you must list the machines in `/etc/hosts.equiv` or `/etc/hosts.lpd`. (Note that `hosts.equiv` has a host of other effects; be sure you know what you are doing if you list any machine there.) You can allow only certain users on the other machines to print to your printer by using the rs attribute; read the lpd man page for information on this.

With lpd

To print to another machine, you make an `/etc/printcap` entry like this:

```
# REMOTE djet500
lp|dj|deskjet:\
        :sd=/var/spool/lpd/dj:\
        :rm=machine.out.there.com:\
        :rp=printername:\
        :lp=/dev/null:\
        :sh:
```

Note that there is still a spool directory on the local machine managed by lpd. If the remote machine is busy or offline, print jobs from the local machine wait in the spool area until they can be sent.

With rlpr

You can also use rlpr to send a print job directly to a queue on a remote machine without going through the hassle of configuring lpd to handle it. This is mostly useful in situations where you print to a variety of printers only occasionally. From the announcement for rlpr,

> **Rlpr uses TCP/IP to send print jobs to lpd servers anywhere on a network.**

Unlike lpr, it *does not* require that the remote printers be explicitly known to the machine you wish to print from (e.g., through `/etc/printcap`) and thus is considerably more flexible and requires less administration.

Rlpr can be used anywhere a traditional lpr might be used and is backward compatible with traditional BSD lpr.

The main power gained by rlpr is the power to print remotely *from anywhere to anywhere* without regard for how the system you wish to print from was configured. Rlpr can work as a filter just like traditional lpr so that clients executing on a remote machine like netscape, xemacs, and others can print to your local machine with little effort.

Rlpr is available from Metalab (`ftp://metalab.unc.edu/pub/Linux/system/printing/`).

To a Win95, WinNT, LANManager, or Samba Printer

There is a Printing to Windows mini-HOWTO out there which has more info than there is here.

It is possible to direct an lpd queue through the smbclient program (part of the samba suite) to a TCP/IP based SMB print service. Samba includes a script to do this called smbprint. In short, you put a configuration file for the specific printer in question in the spool directory and install the smbprint script as the if.

The `/etc/printcap` entry goes like this:

```
lp|remote-smbprinter:\
    :lp=/dev/null:sh:\
    :sd=/var/spool/lpd/lp:\
    :if=/usr/local/sbin/smbprint:
```

You should read the documentation inside the smbprint script for more information on how to set this up.

You can also use smbclient to submit a file directly to an SMB printing service without involving lpd. See the man page for smbclient(1).

To a NetWare Printer

The ncpfs suite includes a utility called nprint, which provides the same functionality as smbprint but for NetWare. You can get ncpfs from Metalab (`ftp://metalab.unc.edu/pub/Linux/system/filesystems/ncpfs/`). The following is from the LSM entry for version 0.16:

With ncpfs you can mount volumes of your netware server under Linux. You can also print to netware print queues and spool netware print queues to the Linux printing system. You need kernel 1.2.*x* or 1.3.54 and above. ncpfs does NOT work with any 1.3.*x* kernel below 1.3.54.

To make nprint work via lpd, you write a little shell script to print stdin on the NetWare printer and install that as the if for an lpd print queue. You'll get something like this:

```
sub2|remote-NWprinter:\
    :lp=/dev/null:sh:\
    :sd=/var/spool/lpd/sub2:\
    :if=/var/spool/lpd/nprint-script:
```

The nprint-script might look approximately like the following:

```
#! /bin/sh
# You should try the guest account with no password first!
/usr/local/bin/nprint -S net -U name -P passwd -q _
    printq-name -
```


To an EtherTalk (Apple) Printer

The netatalk package includes something like nprint and smbclient. Others have documented the procedure for printing to and from an Apple network far better than I ever will; see the Linux Netatalk-HOWTO (`http://thehamptons.com/anders/netatalk/`).

To an HP or Other Ethernet Printer

HPs and some other printers come with an Ethernet interface which you can print to directly using lpd. You should follow the instructions that came with your printer or its network adaptor, but in general, such printers are running lpd and provide one or more queues which you can print to. An HP, for example, might work with a printcap like this:

```
lj-5|remote-hplj:\
    :lp=/dev/null:sh:\
    :sd=/var/spool/lpd/lj-5:\
    :rm=printer.name.com:rp=raw:
```

HP LaserJet printers with Jet Direct interfaces generally support two built-in lpd queues—raw, which accepts PCL (and possibly PostScript), and text, which accepts straight ASCII (and copes automatically with the staircase effect). If you've got a JetDirect Plus3 three-port box, the queues are named raw1, text2, and so forth.

WARNING

Note that the ISS company has identified an assortment of denial of service attacks which hang HP JetDirect interfaces. Most of these have been addressed beginning in Fall 98.

In a large-scale environment, especially a large environment where some printers do not support PostScript, it may be useful to establish a dedicated print server to which all machines print and on which all Ghostscript jobs are run.

This also allows your Linux box to act as a spool server for the printer so that your network users can complete their print jobs quickly and get on with things without waiting for the printer to print any other job that someone else has sent. This is suggested too if you have unfixable older HP JetDirects; it reduces the likelihood of the printers wedging.

To do this, set up a queue on your Linux box that points at the Ethernet equipped HP LJ (as above). Now set up all the clients on your LAN to point at the Linux queue (e.g., lj-5 in the example above).

Some HP network printers apparently don't heed the banner page setting sent by clients; you can turn off their internally generated banner page by telnetting to the printer, hitting return twice, typing **banner: 0** followed by **quit**. There are other settings you can change this way, as well; type **?** to see a list.

The full range of settings can be controlled with HP's WebJet33 software (`http://www.hp.com/go/webjetadmin`). This package runs as a daemon and accepts HTTP requests on a designated port. It serves up forms and Java applets which can control HP printers on the network. In theory, it can also control Unix print queues, but it does so using the rexec service, which is completely insecure. I don't advise using that feature.

To Older HPs

Some printers (and printer networking black boxes) support only a cheesy little non-protocol involving plain TCP connections. Notable in this category are early-model JetDirect (including some JetDirectEx) cards. Basically, to print to the printer, you must open a TCP connection to the printer on a specified port (typically 9100 or 9100, 9101, and 9102 for three-port boxes) and stuff your print job into it. LPRng (which you really should be using instead, if you're reading this section) has built-in support for stuffing print jobs into random TCP ports, but with BSD lpd it's not so easy. This can be implemented, among other ways, in Perl:

```
#!/usr/bin/perl
# Thanks to Dan McLaughlin for writing the original version
# of this script (And to Jim W. Jones for sitting next to Dan
# when writing me for help ;)

$fileName = @ARGV[0];
```

```
open(IN,"$fileName") || die "Can't open file $fileName";

$dpi300   = "\x1B*t300R";
$dosCr   = "\x1Bk3G";
$ends = "\x0A";

$port = 9100 unless $port;
$them = "bach.sr.hp.com" unless $them;

$AF_INET = 2;
$SOCK_STREAM = 1;
$SIG{'INT'} = 'dokill';
$sockaddr = 'S n a4 x8';

chop($hostname = `hostname`);
($name,$aliases,$proto) = getprotobyname('tcp');
($name,$aliases,$port) = getservbyname($port,'tcp')
  unless $port =~ /^\d+$/;;
($name,$aliases,$type,$len,$thisaddr) = gethostbyname($hostname);
($name,$aliases,$type,$len,$thataddr) = gethostbyname($them);
$this = pack($sockaddr, $AF_INET, 0, $thisaddr);
$that = pack($sockaddr, $AF_INET, $port, $thataddr);

if (socket(S, $AF_INET, $SOCK_STREAM, $proto)) {
#  print "socket ok\n";
}
else {
  die $!;
}
# Give the socket an address.
if (bind(S, $this)) {
#  print "bind ok\n";
}
else {
  die $!;
}

# Call up the server.

if (connect(S,$that)) {
#  print "connect ok\n";
}
else {
  die $!;
}
```

```
# Set socket to be command buffered.

select(S); $| = 1; select(STDOUT);

#  print S "@PJL ECHO Hi $hostname! $ends";
#  print S "@PJL OPMSG DISPLAY=\"Job $whoami\" $ends";
#  print S $dpi300;

# Avoid deadlock by forking.

if($child = fork) {
  print S $dosCr;
  print S $TimesNewR;

  while (<IN>) {
    print S;
  }
  sleep 3;
  do dokill();
} else {
  while(<S>) {
    print;
  }
}

sub dokill {
  kill 9,$child if $child;
}
```

Running an If for Remote Printers

One oddity of lpd is that the if is not run for remote printers. If you find that you need to run an if, you can do so by setting up a double queue and requeueing the job. As an example, consider this printcap

```
lj-5:\
    :lp=/dev/null:sh:\
    :sd=/var/spool/lpd/lj-5:\
    :if=/usr/lib/lpd/filter-lj-5:
lj-5-remote:lp=/dev/null:sh:rm=printer.name.com:\
    :rp=raw:sd=/var/spool/lpd/lj-5-raw:
```

in light of this filter-lj-5 script:

```
#!/bin/sh
gs <options> -q -dSAFER -sOutputFile=- - | \
    lpr -Plj-5-remote -U$5
```

The -U option to lpr only works if lpr is run as daemon, and it sets the submitter's name for the job in the resubmitted queue correctly. You should probably use a more robust method of getting the username, since in some cases it is not argument 5. See the man page for printcap (5).

From Windows

Printing from a Windows (or presumably, OS/2) client to a Linux server is directly supported over SMB through the use of the SAMBA package, which also supports file sharing of your Linux filesystem to Windows clients.

Samba includes fairly complete documentation, and there is a good Samba FAQ which covers it, too. You can either configure a magic filter on the Linux box and print PostScript to it or run around installing printer-specific drivers on all the Windows machines and having a queue for them with no filters at all. Relying on the Windows drivers may in some cases produce better output but is a bit more of an administrative hassle if there are many Windows boxes. So try PostScript first.

From an Apple

Netatalk supports printing from Apple clients over EtherTalk. See the Netatalk HOWTO Page (`http://thehamptons.com/anders/netatalk/`) for more information.

From Netware

The ncpfs package includes a daemon named pserver, which can be used to provide service to a NetWare print queue. From what I understand, this system requires a Bindery-based NetWare, i.e., 2.x, 3.x, or 4.x with bindery access enabled.

For more information on ncpfs and its pserver program, see the ncpfs FTP site (`ftp://ftp.gwdg.de/pub/linux/misc/ncpfs/`).

Windows-Only Printers

As I discussed earlier, some printers are inherently unsupported because they don't speak a normal printer language, instead using the computer's CPU to render a bitmap which is then piped to the printer at a fixed speed. In a few cases, these printers also speak something normal like PCL, but often they do not. In some (really low-end) cases, the printer doesn't even use a normal parallel connection but relies on the vendor's driver to emulate what should be hardware behavior (most importantly flow control).

In any case, there are a few possible workarounds if you find yourself stuck with such a lemon.

The Ghostscript Windows Redirector

There is now a Windows printer driver available (called mswinpr2) that will run a print job through Ghostscript before finally printing it. (Rather like an if filter in Unix's lpd). There is also a new Ghostscript driver which will print using Windows GDI calls. Taken all together, this should allow a Windows machine to print PostScript to a Windows-only printer through the vendor's driver.

If you get that working, you can then follow the instructions above for printing to a Windows printer over the network from Linux to let Unix (and other Windows, Mac, etc.) hosts print to your lemon printer.

The Pbm2ppa Program

Some HP printers use Printing Performance Architecture (marketing-speak for "we were too cheap to implement PCL"). This is supported in a roundabout way via the pbm2ppa translator written by Tim Norman. Basically, you use Ghostscript to render PostScript into a bitmapped image in pbm format and then use pbm2ppa to translate this into a printer-specific ppa format bitmap ready to be dumped to the printer. This program may also come in Ghostscript-driver format by now.

The ppa software can be had from the ppa home page (`http://www.httptech.com`); pbm2ppa supports some models of the HP 720, 820, and 1000; read the documentation that comes with the package for more details on ppa printer support.

The Pbm2l7k Program

Most of the cheap Lexmark inkjets use a proprietary language and are therefore Winprinters. However, Henryk Paluch has written a program which can print in black and white on a Lexmark 7000. Hopefully he'll be able to figure out color and expand support to other Lexmark inkjets. See `http://bimbo.fjfi.cvut.cz/~paluch/l7kdriver/` for more info.

How to Print to a Fax Machine

This section lists fax programs and provides information on how to send an e-mail message to a fax machine.

Using a Faxmodem

There are a number of fax programs out there that will let you fax and receive documents. One of the most complex is Sam Leffler's HylaFax, available from `ftp.sgi.com`. It supports all sorts of things, from multiple modems to broadcasting.

SuSE ships a Java HylaFax client which allegedly works on any Java platform (including Windows and Linux). There are also non-Java fax clients for most platforms; Linux can almost certainly handle your network faxing needs.

Also available, and a better choice for most Linux boxes, is efax, a simple program that sends faxes. The getty program mgetty can receive faxes (and even do voicemail on some modems!).

Using the Remote Printing Service

There is an experimental service offered that lets you send an e-mail message containing something you'd like printed on a fax machine elsewhere. Nice formats like PostScript are supported, so even though global coverage is spotty, this can still be a very useful service. For more information on printing via the remote printing service, see the Remote Printing Web site (`http://www.tpc.int/`).

How to Generate Something Worth Printing

Here we get into a real rat's nest of software. Basically, Linux can run many types of binaries with varying degrees of success: Linux/x86, Linux/Alpha, Linux/Sparc, Linux/foo, iBCS, Win16/Win32s (with dosemu and, someday, with Wine), Mac/68k (with Executor), and Java. I'll just discuss native Linux and common Unix software.

For Linux itself, choices are mostly limited to those available for Unix in general.

Markup Languages

Most markup languages are more suitable for large or repetitive projects, where you want the computer to control the layout of the text to make things uniform.

Nroff This was one of the first Unix markup languages. Man pages are the most common examples of things formatted in roff macros; many people swear by them, but nroff has, to me at least, a more arcane syntax than needed and probably makes a poor choice for new works. It is worth knowing, though, that you can typeset a man page directly into PostScript with groff. Most man commands will do this for you with `man -t foo | lpr`.

TeX TeX, and the macro package LaTeX, is one of the most widely used markup languages on Unix. Technical works are frequently written in LaTeX because it greatly simplifies layout issues and is still one of the few text processing systems to support mathematics both completely and well. TeX's output format is dvi and is converted to PostScript or Hewlett Packard's PCL with dvips or dvilj. If you wish to install TeX or LaTeX, install the whole teTeX group of packages; it contains everything.

SGML There is at least one free SGML parser available for Unix and Linux; it forms the basis of Linuxdoc-SGML's homegrown document system. It can support other DTD's, as well.

HTML Someone suggested that for simple projects, it may suffice to write it in HTML and print it out using Netscape. I disagree, but YMMV.

WYSIWYG Word Processors

There is no longer any shortage of WYSIWYG word processing software. Several complete office suites are available, including one that's free for personal use: StarOffice.

StarOffice A German company is distributing StarOffice on the Net free for Linux. This full-blown office suite has all the features you'd expect, and you can't beat the price. There's a mini-HOWTO out there which describes how to obtain and install it. It generates PostScript or PCL, so it should work with most any printer that works otherwise on Linux. Apparently it's an Office clone and is rather bloated.

WordPerfect Corel distributes a basic version of Word Perfect 8 free for Linux and has suggested that they will distribute Corel Draw and Quattro Pro as well, once they are ported. This is probably the best option if you have an ARM machine; Corel makes the ARM-based Netwinder Linux computers and is almost certain to offer ARM Linux versions of everything. You can also buy the full-blown version and support, together or separately. The Linux WordPerfect Fonts and Printers (`http://www.channel1.com/users/rodsmith/wpfonts.html`) page has information about configuring WordPerfect for use with either Ghostscript or its built-in printer drivers (which are apparently identical to the DOS WordPerfect drivers, if your printer's driver isn't included in the WP8 distribution).

Applix Applix is a cross-platform (i.e., various versions of Unix, Windows, and others) office suite sold by the Applix company. Red Hat and SuSE sold it themselves when it was the only game in town; now sales have reverted to Applix.

LyX LyX is a front end to LaTeX, which looks very promising. See the LyX home page (`http://www.lyx.org/`) for more information. There is a KDE-styled version of LyX, called Klyx; the author of LyX and the instigator of KDE are the same person.

Maxwell Maxwell is a simple MS RTF-format based word processor which started as a commercial product but is now distributed under the GPL.

The Andrew User Interface System AUIS includes ez, a WYSIWYG-style editor with the most basic word processor features, HTML capabilities, and full MIME e-mail and newsgroup support. Unfortunately, AUIS is no longer maintained.

Koffice The KDE project is working toward a whole office suite. I don't think it's ready for prime time yet. The word processor will apparently be a descendant of LyX.

GNOME The GNOME project also is working toward various GNU-licensed Office-like tools. None are available yet, though.

Jeff Phillips <jeff@IRATUS.org> uses Caldera's WordPerfect 7 for Linux (on Slackware, of all things) and says that it works well. It apparently includes built-in printer support, as one would expect. Caldera should have info at http://www.caldera.com/. You can also buy a newer version of WordPerfect directly from Corel's chosen Unix port company.

Other vendors should feel free to drop me a line with your offerings.

On-Screen Previewing of Printable Things

In this section you'll learn that nearly anything you can print can be viewed on the screen, too.

PostScript

Ghostscript has an X11 driver best used under the management of the PostScript previewer gv. The latest versions of these programs should be able to view PDF files, as well. Note that gv has replaced the older previewer Ghostview; the new user interface is much prettier and more full of features than Ghostview's plain old Athena GUI.

TeX DVI

TeX DeVice Independent files may be previewed under X11 with xdvi. Modern versions of xdvi call Ghostscript to render PostScript specials.

A VT100 driver exists as well. It's called dgvt. Tmview works with Linux and svgalib, if that's all you can do.

Adobe PDF

Adobe's Acrobat Reader is available for Linux; just download it from their Web site at http://www.adobe.com/.

You can also use xpdf, which is freeware and comes with source, and I should think Ghostview supports viewing PDF files with gs under X11 by now.

SERIAL PRINTERS UNDER LPD

This section discusses how to set up and use a serial printer with lpd.

Setting Up in Printcap

lpd provides five attributes which you can set in `/etc/printcap` to control all the settings of the serial port a printer is on. Read the printcap man page and note the meanings of br, fc, xc, fs, and xs. The last four of these attributes are bitmaps indicating the settings for using the port. The br atrribute is simply the baud rate, i.e., br9600.

It is very easy to translate from stty (`http://www.picante.com/~gtaylor/pht/man/stty.1.html`) settings to printcap flag settings. If you need to, see the man page for stty now.

Use stty to set up the printer port so that you can cat a file to it and have it print correctly. Here's what `stty -a` looks like for my printer port:

```
dina:/usr/users/andy/work/lpd/lpd# stty -a < /dev/ttyS2
speed 9600 baud; rows 0; columns 0; line = 0;
intr = ^C; quit = ^\; erase = ^?; kill = ^U; eof = ^D;
eol = <undef>; eol2 = <undef>; start = ^Q; stop = ^S;
susp = ^Z; rprnt = ^R; werase = ^W; lnext = ^V; min = 1;
time = 0;
-parenb -parodd cs8 hupcl -cstopb cread -clocal -crtscts
-ignbrk -brkint -ignpar -parmrk -inpck -istrip -inlcr
-igncr -icrnl ixon -ixoff -iuclc -ixany -imaxbel
-opost -olcuc -ocrnl -onlcr -onocr -onlret -ofill -ofdel
nl0 cr0 tab0 bs0 vt0 ff0 -isig -icanon -iexten -echo -echoe
-echok -echonl -noflsh -xcase -tostop -echoprt -echoctl
-echoke
```

The only changes between this and the way the port is initialized at bootup are -clocal, -crtscts, and ixon. Your port may well be different depending on how your printer does flow control.

You actually use stty in a somewhat odd way. Since stty operates on the terminal connected to its standard input, you use it to manipulate a given serial port by using the < character as above.

Once you have your stty settings right, so that `cat file > /dev/ttyS2` (in my case) sends the file to the printer, look at the file `/usr/src/linux/include/asm-i386/termbits.h`. This contains a lot of defines and a few structs (You may wish to cat this file to the printer [you do have that working, right?] and use it as scratch paper). Go to the section that starts out

```
/* c_cflag bit meaning */
#define CBAUD  0000017
```

This section lists the meaning of the fc and fs bits. You will notice that the names there (after the baud rates) match up with one of the lines of stty output. Didn't I say this was going to be easy?

Note which of those settings are preceded with a - in your stty output. Sum up all those numbers (they are octal). This represents the bits you want to clear, so the result is your fc capability. Of course, remember that you will be setting bits directly after you clear, so you can just use fc0177777 (I do).

Now do the same for those settings (listed in this section) which do not have a - before them in your stty output. In my example the important ones are CS8 (0000060), HUPCL (0002000), and CREAD (0000200). Also note the flags for your baud rate (mine is 0000015). Add those all up, and in my example you get 0002275. This goes in your fs capability (fs02275 works fine in my example).

Do the same with set and clear for the next section of the include file, `clflag bits`. In my case I didn't have to set anything, so I just use xc0157777 and xs0.

Older Serial Printers that Drop Characters

Jon Luckey points out that some older serial printers with ten-cent serial interfaces and small buffers really mean stop when they say so with flow control. He found that disabling the FIFO in his Linux box's 16550 serial port with setserial corrected the problem of dropped characters (you apparently just specify the uart type as an 8250 to do this).

CREDITS

The smbprint information is from an article by Marcel Roelofs <marcel@paragon.nl>.

The nprint information for using NetWare printers was provided by Michael Smith <mikes@bioch.ox.ac.uk>.

The serial printers under lpd section is from Andrew Tefft <teffta@engr.dnet.ge.com>.

The blurb about gammas and such for gs was sent in by Andreas <quasi@hub-fue.franken.de>.

The two paragraphs about the 30-second closingwait of the serial driver was contributed by Chris Johnson <cdj@netcom.com>.

Robert Hart sent a few excellent paragraphs about setting up a print server to networked HPs, which I used verbatim.

And special thanks to the dozens upon dozens of you who've pointed out typos, bad URLs, and errors in the document over the years.

PART iii

NETWORKING

Chapter 7
Networking Overview

This chapter provides a complete overview of Linux's networking capabilities. Each feature or available package is briefly described and pointers to more information, as well as the tools themselves, are given.

You can use this chapter as a reference each time you have a new networking-related problem to solve. So many people use Linux these days that someone is bound to have had the same problem already, and, thanks to the spirit of the Linux community, it's quite likely that they've shared their solution with everyone. If so, it'll probably be described here.

"Networking Overview" is reprinted from the Linux Networking Overview HOWTO, version 0.2 of 10 July 1998, by Daniel López Ridruejo.

INTRODUCTION

The purpose of this document is to give an overview of the networking capabilities of the Linux Operating System. Although one of the strengths of Linux is that there is plenty of information available for nearly every topic, most of it is focused on implementation. Most new Linux users, particularly those coming from a Windows environment, are unaware of the networking possibilities of Linux. This document aims to show a general picture of such possibilities with a brief description of each one and pointers for further information. The information has been gathered from many sources: HOWTOs, FAQs, projects' Web pages and my own hands-on experience. Full credit is given to the authors. Without them and their programs, this document would have not been possible or necessary.

WHAT IS LINUX?

The primary author of Linux is Linus Torvalds. Since his original version, it has been improved by countless numbers of people. It is a clone, written entirely from scratch, of the Unix operating system. One of the more interesting facts about Linux is that development occurs simultaneously around the world.

Linux has been copyrighted under the terms of the GNU General Public License (see Appendix D). This is a license written by the Free Software Foundation (FSF) that is designed to prevent people from restricting the distribution of software. In brief, it says that although money can be charged for a copy, the person who receivs the copy cannot be prevented from giving it away for free. It also means that the source code must be available. This is useful for programmers. Anybody can modify Linux and even distribute his/her modifications, provided that they keep the code under the same copyright.

WHAT MAKES LINUX DIFFERENT?

Why work on Linux? Linux is generally cheaper (or at least no more expensive) than other operating systems and is frequently less problematic than many commercial systems. But what makes Linux different is not its price (after all, why would anyone want an OS—even if it is free—if it is not good enough?) but its outstanding capabilities:

- Linux is a true 32-bit multitasking operating aystem, robust and capable enough to be used by organizations from universities to large corporations.
- It runs from low-end 386 boxes to massive ultra-parallel machines in research centers.
- There are out-of-the-box available versions for Intel/Sparc/Alpha architectures, and experimental support for Power PC and embedded systems among others (SGI, Ultra Sparc, AP1000+, Strong ARM, MIPS R3000/R4000, etc.)
- Finally, when it comes networking, Linux is the choice. Not only because networking is tightly integrated with the OS itself and a plethora of applications is freely available, but for the robustness under heavy load that can only be achieved after years of debugging and testing in an Open Source project.

NETWORKING PROTOCOLS

Linux supports many different networking protocols.

TCP/IP

The Internet Protocol was originally developed two decades ago for the United States Department of Defense (DoD), mainly for the purpose of interconnecting different brand computers. The TCP/IP suite of protocols provided, through its layered structure, for the insulation of applications from networking hardware.

Although it is based in a layered model, it is focused more on delivering interconnectivity than on rigidly adhering to functional layers. This is one of the reasons why TCP/IP has become the de facto standard internetworking protocol, as opposed to OSI.

TCP/IP networking has been present in Linux since its beginnings. It has been implemented from scratch. It is one of the most robust, fast, and reliable implementations and is one of the key factors for Linux success.

The related HOWTO can be found at `http://MetaLab.unc.edu/mdw/HOWTO/NET-3-HOWTO.html`.

TCP/IP Version 6

IPv6, sometimes also referred to as IPng (IP Next Generation) is an upgrade of the IPv4 protocol that addresses many issues. These issues include: shortage of available IP addresses, lack of mechanisms to handle time-sensitive traffic, lack of network layer security, etc.

The increase in address space will be accompanied by an expanded addressing scheme, which will have a great impact on routing performance. A beta implementation already exists for Linux, and a production version is expected for the 2.2.0 Linux kernel release. The Linux IPv6 HOWTO can be found at `http://www.terra.net/ipv6/linux-ipv6.faq.htm` and the IPv6 home page can be found at `http://playground.sun.com/pub/ipng/html/ipng-main.html`.

IPX/SPX

IPX/SPX (Internet Packet Exchange/Sequenced Packet Exchange) is a proprietary protocol stack developed by Novell and based on Xerox Network Systems (XNS) protocol. IPX/SPX became prominent during the early 1980s as an integral part of Novell Inc.'s NetWare. NetWare became the de facto standard network operating system (NOS) of first generation LANs. Novell complemented its NOS with a business-oriented application suite and client-side connection utilities.

Linux has a very clean IPX/SPX implementation, allowing it to be configured as an:

- IPX router
- IPX bridge
- NCP client and/or NCP Server (for sharing files)
- Novell Print Client, Novell Print Server

It also has the capability to enable

- PPP/IPX, allowing a Linux box to act as a PPP server/client
- IPX tunnelling through IP, allowing the connection of two IPX networks through an IP only link

Additionally, Caldera (`http://www.caldera.com`) offers commercial support for Novell NetWare under Linux. Caldera provides a fully featured Novell NetWare client built on technology licensed from Novell Corporation.

The client provides full client access to Novell 3.*x* and 4.*x* fileservers and includes features such as NetWare Directory Service (NDS) and RSA encryption. See the IPX HOWTO at `http://MetaLab.unc.edu/mdw/HOWTO/IPX-HOWTO.html`.

AppleTalk Protocol Suite

AppleTalk is the name of Apple's internetworking stack. It allows a peer-to-peer network model that provides basic functionality such as file and printer sharing. Each machine can simultaneously act as a client and a server, and the software and hardware necessary are included with every Apple computer.

Linux provides full AppleTalk networking. Netatalk is a kernel-level implementation of the AppleTalk Protocol Suite, originally for BSD-derived systems. It includes support for routing AppleTalk, serving Unix and AFS filesystems over AFP (AppleShare), and serving Unix printers and accessing AppleTalk printers over PAP.

WAN Networking: X.25, Frame-Relay, Etc.

Several third parties provide T-1, T-3, X.25, and Frame Relay products for Linux. Generally special hardware is required for these types of connections. Vendors that provide the hardware also provide the drivers with protocol support. You can find WAN resources for Linux at `http://www.secretagent.com/networking/wan.html`.

ISDN

Linux kernel has built-in ISDN capabilities. Isdn4linux controls ISDN PC cards and can emulate a modem with the Hayes command set ("AT" commands). The possibilities range from using a terminal program to connections via HDLC (using included devices) to full connection to the Internet with PPP to audio applications. You can find FAQ for isdn4linux at `http://tsikora.tiac.net/i4l-faq/eng-i4l-faq.html`.

PPP, SLIP, PLIP

The Linux kernel has built-in support for PPP (Point-to-Point-Protocol), SLIP (Serial Line IP) and PLIP (Parallel Line IP). PPP is the most popular way individual users access their ISP (Internet Service Provider). PLIP allows cheap connection of two machines. It uses a parallel port and a special cable, achieving speeds of 10-20kBps.

- The Linux PPP HOWTO can be found in Chapter 10 of this book.
- The PPP/SLIP emulator can be found at `http://MetaLab.unc.edu/mdw/HOWTO/mini/SLIP-PPP-Emulator.html`.
- PLIP information can be found in The Network Administrator Guide at `http://MetaLab.unc.edu/mdw/LDP/nag/nag.html`.

Amateur Radio

Linux kernel has built-in support for amateur radio protocols. Especially interesting is the AX.25 support. The AX.25 protocol offers both connected and connectionless modes of operation and is used either by itself for point-to-point links or to carry other protocols such as TCP/IP and NetRom.

It is similar to X.25 level 2 in structure, with some extensions to make it more useful in the amateur radio environment. The amateur radio HOWTO can be found at `http://MetaLab.unc.edu/mdw/HOWTO/HAM-HOWTO.html`.

ATM

ATM support for Linux is currently in the pre-alpha stage. There is an experimental release, which supports raw ATM connections (PVCs and SVCs), IP over ATM, and LAN emulation. You can find it at the Linux ATM-Linux home page at `http://lrcwww.epfl.ch/linux-atm/`.

Networking Hardware Supported

Linux supports a great variety of networking hardware, including obsolete ones. Some interesting documents can be found at `http://MetaLab.unc.edu/mdw/HOWTO/Hardware-HOWTO.html` (Hardware HOWTO) and `http://MetaLab.unc.edu/mdw/HOWTO/Ethernet-HOWTO.html` (Ethernet HOWTO).

File Sharing and Printing

The primary purpose of many PC-based Local Area Networks is to provide file and printer sharing services to the users. Linux as a corporate file and print server turns out to be a great solution.

Apple Environment

As outlined in previous sections, Linux supports the AppleTalk family of protocols. Linux netatalk allows Macintosh clients to see Linux Systems as another Macintosh on the network, share files, and use printers connected to Linux servers.

Netatalk FAQ and HOWTO can be found at:

- `http://thehamptons.com/anders/netatalk/`
- `http://www.umich.edu/~rsug/netatalk/`
- `http://www.umich.edu/~rsug/netatalk/faq.html`

Windows Environment

Samba is a suite of applications that allows most Unices (and Linux in particular) to integrate into a Microsoft network both as a client and a server. Acting as a server it allows Windows 95, Windows for Workgroups, DOS, and Windows NT clients to access Linux files and printing services. It can completely replace Windows NT for file and printing services, including the automatic downloading of printer drivers to clients. Acting as a client allows the Linux workstation to mount locally exported windows file shares. According to the SAMBA Meta-FAQ:

> **"Many users report that compared to other SMB implementations Samba is more stable, faster, and compatible with more clients. Administrators of some large installations say that Samba is the only SMB server available which will scale to many tens of thousands of users without crashing."**

The Samba project home page can be found at `http://samba.anu.edu.au/samba/`. The Samba HOWTO can be found at `http://MetaLab.unc.edu/mdw/HOWTO/SMB-HOWTO.html`. The printing HOWTO can be found in Chapter 6 of this book.

Novell Environment

As stated in previous sections, Linux can be configured to act as an NCP client or server, thus allowing file and printing services over a Novell network for both Novell and Unix clients. The IPX HOWTO can be found at `http://MetaLab.unc.edu/mdw/HOWTO/IPX-HOWTO.html`.

Unix Environment

The preferred way of sharing files in an Unix networking environment is through NFS. NFS stands for Network File Sharing and it is a protocol originally developed by Sun Microsystems.It is a way to share files between machines as if they were local. A client "mounts" a filesystem "exported" by an NFS server. The mounted filesystem will appear to the client machine as if it was part of the local filesystem.

It is possible to mount the root filesystem at startup time, thus allowing diskless clients to boot up and access all files from a server. More clearly, it is possible to have a fully functional computer without a hard disk.

Here are the locations of some NFS-related documents:

- `http://MetaLab.unc.edu/mdw/HOWTO/mini/NFS-Root.html`
- `http://MetaLab.unc.edu/mdw/HOWTO/mini/Diskless.html`
- `http://MetaLab.unc.edu/mdw/HOWTO/mini/NFS-Root-Client.html`
- `http://www.redhat.com/support/docs/rhl/NFS-Tips/NFS-Tips.html`
- `http://MetaLab.unc.edu/mdw/HOWTO/NFS-HOWTO.html`

INTERNET/INTRANET

Linux is a great platform to act as an Internet/Intranet Server. The term Intranet refers to the application of Internet technologies inside an organization mainly for the purpose of distributing and making available information inside the company. Internet and Intranet services offered by Linux include Mail, News, WWW servers, and many more that will be outlined in the next sections.

Mail

The following section deals with mail servers, remote access to mail, mail user agents, mailing list software, and fetchmail.

Mail Servers

Sendmail is the de facto standard mail server program for Unix platforms. It is robust, scalable, and, properly configured and with the necessary hardware, can handle thousands of users without blinking. Other mail servers (MTA Mail Transport Agents) exist as smail and qmail, which are designed as replacements for sendmail. The sendmail Web site is `http://www.sendmail.org/`. The Smail faq can be found at `http://www.sbay.org/smail-faq.html`. And the Qmail Web site is `http://www.qmail.org`.

Mail HOWTOs can be found at

- `http://MetaLab.unc.edu/mdw/HOWTO/Mail-HOWTO.html`
- `http://MetaLab.unc.edu/mdw/HOWTO/mini/Qmail+MH.html`
- `http://MetaLab.unc.edu/mdw/HOWTO/mini/Sendmail+UUCP.html`
- `http://MetaLab.unc.edu/mdw/HOWTO/mini/Mail-Queue.html`

Remote Access to Mail

In an organization or ISP, users will likely access their mail remotely from their desktops. Several alternatives exist in Linux, including POP (Post Office Protocol) and IMAP (Internet Message Access Protocol) servers. POP protocol is usually used to transfer messages from the server to the client. IMAP also admits manipulation of the messages in the server, remote creation and deletion of folders in the server, concurrent access to shared mail folders, etc.

A brief comparison between IMAP and POP can be found at `http://www.imap.org/imap.vs.pop.brief.html`. Mail-related HOWTOs can be found at `http://MetaLab.unc.edu/mdw/HOWTO/Mail-HOWTO.html` and `http://MetaLab.unc.edu/mdw/HOWTO/mini/Cyrus-IMAP.html`.

Mail User Agents

There are a number of MUA (Mail User Agents) in Linux, both graphical and in text mode. Those most widely used include: pine, elm, mutt, and Netscape. For a list of mail-related software, go to `http://www.linuxlinks.com/Software/Internet/Mail/` or `http://MetaLab.unc.edu/mdw/HOWTO/mini/TkRat.html`.

Mailing List Software

There are many MLM (Mail List Management) programs available for Unix in general and for Linux in particular. Comparison of existing MLMs may be found at:

- `ftp://ftp.uu.net/usenet/news.answers/mail/list-admin/`
- Listserv at `http://www.lsoft.com/`
- The Majordomo home page at `http://www.greatcircle.com/majordomo/`

Fetchmail

One useful mail-related utility is fetchmail. Fetchmail is a free, full-featured, robust, well-documented, remote-mail retrieval and forwarding utility intended to be used over on-demand TCP/IP links (such as SLIP or PPP connections). It supports every remote-mail protocol now in use on the Internet. It can even support IPv6 and IPSEC.

Fetchmail retrieves mail from remote mail servers and forwards it via SMTP, so it can then be be read by normal mail user agents such as mutt, elm, or BSD Mail. It allows all of the system MTA's filtering, forwarding, and aliasing facilities to work just as they would on normal mail.

Fetchmail can be used as a POP/IMAP-to-SMTP gateway for an entire DNS domain, collecting mail from a single drop box on an ISP and SMTP-forwarding it based on header addresses.

A small company may centralize its mail in a single mailbox, programming fetchmail to collect all the outgoing mail, send it to the Internet, and retrieve all incoming mail.

Fetchmail's home page can be found at `http://sagan.earthspace.net/~esr/fetchmail/`.

Web Servers

Most Linux distribution includes Apache (http://www.apache.org). Apache is the number one server on the Internet (http://www.netcraft.co.uk/survey/); more than a half of all Internet sites are running Apache or one of it derivatives. Apache advantages include its modular design, stability, and speed. Given the appropriate hardware and configuration, it can support the highest loads. Yahoo, Altavista, GeoCities, and Hotmail are based on customized versions of this server.

Optional support for SSL (which enables secure transactions) is also available at:

- http://www.apache-ssl.org/
- http://raven.covalent.net/
- http://www.c2.net/

Related HOWTOs can be found at:

- http://MetaLab.unc.edu/mdw/HOWTO/WWW-HOWTO.html
- http://MetaLab.unc.edu/mdw/HOWTO/Virtual-Services-HOWTO.html
- http://MetaLab.unc.edu/mdw/HOWTO/Intranet-Server-HOWTO.html

Web servers for Linux can be found at http://www.linuxlinks.com/Software/Internet/WebServers/.

Web Browsers

A number of Web browsers exist for the Linux platform. Netscape Navigator is one of the choices, available from the very beginning, and the upcoming Mozilla (http://www.mozilla.org) will have a Linux version. Another popular text-based Web browser is Lynx. It is fast and handy when no graphical environment is available.

Browser software for Linux can be found at http://www.linuxlinks.com/Software/Internet/WebBrowsers/. and at http://MetaLab.unc.edu/mdw/HOWTO/mini/Public-Web-Browser.html.

FTP Servers and Clients

FTP stands for File Transfer Protocol. An FTP server allows clients to connect to it and retrieve (download) files. Many FTP servers and clients exist for Linux and are usually included with most distributions. There are text-based clients as well as GUI-based ones. FTP-related software (servers and clients) for Linux may be found at `http://MetaLab.unc.edu/pub/Linux/system/network/file-transfer/`.

News Service

Usenet (also known as news) is a big bulletin board system that covers all kind of topics and is organized hierarchically. A network of computers across the Internet (Usenet) exchange articles through the NNTP protocol. Several implementations exist for Linux; either for heavily loaded sites or small sites receiving only a few newsgroups.

The INN home page can be found at `http://www.isc.org/`. Linux news-related software can be found at `http://www.linuxlinks.com/Software/Internet/News/`.

Domain Name System

A DNS server has the job of translating names (readable by humans) to an IP address. A DNS server does not know all the IP addresses in the world; rather, it is able to request other servers for the unknown addresses. The DNS server will either return the wanted IP address to the user or report that the name cannot be found in the tables.

Name serving on Unix (and on the vast majority of the Internet) is done by a program called `named`. This is a part of the bind package of The Internet Software Consortium.

The BIND home page can be found at `http://www.isc.org/`.The DNS HOWTO can be found at `http://www.MetaLab.unc.edu/LDP/HOWTO/DNS-HOWTO.html`.

DHCP, Bootp

DHCP and bootp are protocols that allow a client machine to obtain network information (such as their IP number) from a server. Many organizations are starting to use it because it eases network administration, especially in large networks or networks that have lots of mobile users.

Related documents can be found in the DHCP HOWTO at `http://MetaLab.unc.edu/mdw/HOWTO/mini/DHCP.html`.

NIS

The Network Information Service (NIS) provides a simple network lookup service consisting of databases and processes. Its purpose is to provide information, which has to be known throughout the network, to all machines on the network. It allows, for example, for one person to log on to any machine in the network running NIS without the need for the administrator to add a password entry for him in all the machines, only in the main database.

The NIS HOWTO can be found at `http://MetaLab.unc.edu/mdw/HOWTO/NIS-HOWTO.html`.

Authentication

There are also various ways of authenticating users in mixed networks. For Linux/Windows NT, go to `http://www.mindware.com.au/ftp/smb-NT-verify.1.1.tar.gz`. For the PAM (pluggable authentication module), which is a flexible method of Unix authentication, go to the PAM library at `http://www.kernel.org/pub/linux/libs/pam/index.html`. For LDAP in Linux, go to `http://www.umich.edu/~dirsvcs/ldap/index.html`.

Remote Execution of Applications

One of the most amazing features of Unix (yet one of the most unknown to new users) is the great support it provides for the remote and distributed execution of applications.

Telnet

Telnet is a program that allows a person to use a remote computer as if that person was actually at that site. Telnet is one of the most powerful tools for Unix, allowing for true remote administration. It is also an interesting program from a user's point of view, because it allows remote access to all their files and programs from anywhere in the Internet. Combined with an X server, there is no difference (apart from the delay) between being at the console or on the other side of the planet. Telnet daemons and clients are available with most Linux distributions.

Encrypted remote shell sessions are available through SSH (`http://www.cs.hut.fi/ssh/`), thus effectively allowing secure remote administration. For Telnet-related software, go to `http://MetaLab.unc.edu/pub/Linux/system/network/telnet/`.

Remote Commands

In Unix, and Linux in particular, remote commands exist that allow for interaction with other computers from the shell prompt. Two examples are rlogin, which allows for login from a remote machine in a similar way to telnet and rcp, which allows for remote transfer of files among machines. Finally, the remote shell command `rsh` allows the execution of a command on a remote machine without actually logging onto that machine.

X Window

The X Window system was developed at MIT in the late 1980s and is rapidly becoming the industry standard windowing system for Unix graphics workstations. The software is freely available, very versatile, and suitable for a wide range of hardware platforms.Any X Window system consists of 2 distinct parts: the X server and 1 or more X clients. It is important to realize the distinction between the server and the clients. The server controls the display directly and is responsible for all input/output via the keyboard, mouse, or display. The clients, on the other hand, do not access the screen directly—they communicate with the server, which handles all input and output. It is the clients that do the "real" computing work—running applications or whatever. The clients communicate with the server, causing the server to open one or more windows to handle input and output for that client.

In short, the X Window system allows a user to log in to a remote machine, execute a process (for example open a Web browser), and have the output displayed on his own machine. Because the process is actually being executed on the server, very little CPU power is needed by the client. Indeed it is possible to have computers whose primary purpose is to act as a pure X Windows servers and they are known as X terminals.

A free port of the X Window system exists for Linux and can be found at Xfree at `http://www.xfree86.org/`. It is usually included in most Linux distributions.

The related remote X Apps HOWTO can be found at `http://MetaLab.unc.edu/mdw/HOWTO/mini/Remote-X-Apps.html`.

VNC

VNC stands for Virtual Network Computing. It is, in essence, a remote display system that allows you to view a computing "desktop" environment not only on the machine where it is running but also from anywhere on the Internet and from a wide variety of machine architectures. Both client and server exist for Linux as well as for many other platforms. It is possible to execute MS Word in a Windows NT or 95 machine and have the output displayed on a Linux machine. The opposite is also true. It is possible to execute an application on a Linux machine and have the output displayed on any other Linux or Windows machine. A Java client exists, which allows you to run the remote display inside a Web browser. Finally a port for Linux using the SVGAlib graphics library allows 386s with as little as 4 Mb of RAM to become fully functional X Terminals. The VNC Web site can be found at `http://www.orl.co.uk/vnc/`.

Network Interconnection

Linux networking is rich in features. A Linux box can be configured to act as a router, a bridge, etc. Some of the available options are described below.

Router

The Linux kernel has built-in support for routing functions. A Linux box can act either as an IP or an IPX router for a fraction of the cost of a commercial router. Recent kernels include special options for machines acting primarily as routers:

Multicasting Allows the Linux machine to act as a router for IP packets that have several destination addresses. It is needed on the MBONE, a high bandwidth network on top of the Internet which carries audio and video broadcasts

IP policy routing Normally, a router decides what to do with a received packet based solely on the packet's final destination address, but routing can also take into account the originating address and the network device from which the packet reached it.

There are some related projects, including one aimed at building a complete running Linux router on a floppy disk, which can be found at `http://www.psychosis.com/linux-router/`.

Bridge

The Linux kernel has built-in support to act as an ethernet bridge, which means that the different ethernet segments it is connected to will appear as one ethernet to the participants. Several bridges can work together to create even larger networks of ethernets using the IEEE802.1 spanning tree algorithm. Because this is a standard, Linux bridges will interwork properly with other third-party bridge products. Additional packages allow filtering based on IP, IPX, or MAC addresses.

Related HOWTOs can be found at Bridge+Firewall at `http://MetaLab.unc.edu/mdw/HOWTO/mini/Bridge+Firewall.html` and at Bridge at `http://MetaLab.unc.edu/mdw/HOWTO/mini/Bridge.html`.

IP Masquerading

IP Masquerade is a developing networking function in Linux. If a Linux host is connected to the Internet with IP Masquerade enabled, then computers connecting to it (either on the same LAN or connected with modems) can reach the Internet as well, even though they have no official assigned IP addresses. This allows for reduction of costs, since many people may be able to access the Internet using a single modem connection, as well as contributes to increased security (in some way the machine is acting as a firewall, since unofficial assigned addresses cannot be accessed out of that network).

IP masquerade-related pages and documents can be found at:

- `http://www.tor.shaw.wave.ca/~ambrose/`
- `http://www.indyramp.com/masq/links.pfhtml`
- `http://MetaLab.unc.edu/mdw/HOWTO/mini/IP-Masquerade.html`

IP Accounting

This option of the Linux kernel keeps track of IP network traffic, packet logging, and the production of some statistics. A series of rules may be defined so when a certain packet matches a pattern a counter is increased and it is accepted/rejected, etc.

IP Aliasing

This feature of the Linux kernel provides the possibility of setting multiple network addresses on the same low-level network device driver (e.g. two IP addresses in one Ethernet card). This is typically used for services that act differently based on the address they listen on (e.g. "multihosting," "virtual domains," or "virtual hosting services").

A related IP Aliasing HOWTO can be found at `http://MetaLab.unc.edu/mdw/HOWTO/mini/IP-Alias.html`.

Traffic Shaping

The traffic shaper is a virtual network device that makes it possible to limit the rate of outgoing data flow over another network device. This is specially useful in scenarios (as ISPs) in which it is desirable to control and enforce policies regarding how much bandwidth is used by each client. Another alternative (for web services only) may be certain Apache modules that restrict the number of IP connections by client or the bandwith used.

Firewall

A firewall is a device that protects a private network from the public part (the Internet as a whole). It is designed to control the flow of packets based on the source, destination, port, and packet type information contained in each packet.

Different firewall toolkits exist for Linux as well as built-in support in the kernel. Other firewalls are TIS and SOCKS. These firewall toolkits are very complete and combined with other tools allow blocking/redirection of all kinds of traffic and protocols. Different policies can be implemented via configuration files or GUI programs.

The TIS home page can be found at `http://www.tis.com`. SOCKS can be found at `http://www.socks.nec.com/socksfaq.html`. And the firewall HOWTO can be found at `http://metalab.unc.edu/LDP/`.

Port Forwarding

An increasing number of Web sites are becoming interactive by having cgi-bins or Java applets that access some database or other service. Since this access may pose a security problem, the machine containing the database should not be directly connected to the Internet.

Port forwarding can provide an almost ideal solution to this access problem. On the firewall, IP packets that come in to a specific port number can be re-written and forwarded to the internal server providing the actual service. The reply packets from the internal server are re-written to make it appear as if they came from the firewall.

Port forwarding information may be found at `http://www.ox.compsoc.net/~steve/portforwarding.html`.

Load Balancing

Demand for load balancing arises usually in database/Web access when many clients make simultaneous requests to a server. It would be desirable to have multiple identical servers and redirect requests to the less loaded server. This can be achieved through Network Address Translation techniques (NAT), of which IP Masquerading is a subset. Network administrators can replace a single server providing Web services—or any other application—with a logical pool of servers sharing a common IP address. Incoming connections are directed to a particular server using one load-balancing algorithm. The virtual server rewrites incoming and outgoing packets so clients have transparent access to the server as if only one existed.

Linux IP NAT information may be found at `http://www.csn.tu-chemnitz.de/~mha/linux-ip-nat/diplom/`.

EQL

EQL is integrated into the Linux kernel. If two serial connections exist to some other computer (this usually requires two modems and two telephone lines) and SLIP or PPP (protocols for sending Internet traffic over telephone lines) are used on them, it is possible to make them behave like one double speed connection using this driver. Naturally, this has to be supported at the other end as well.

The EQL HOWTO can be found at `http://www.abies.com/eql-howto.mhtml`.

Proxy Server

The term *proxy* means to do something on behalf of someone else. In networking terms, a proxy server computer can act on the behalf of several clients. An HTTP proxy is a machine that receives requests for Web pages from another machine (machine A). The proxy gets the page requested and returns the result to machine A. The proxy may have a cache with the requested pages, so if another machine asks for the same page the copy in the cache will be returned instead. This allows efficient use of bandwidth resources and a quicker response time. As a side effect, as client machines are not directly connected to the outside world this is a way of securing the internal network. A well-configured proxy can be as effective as a good firewall.

Several proxy servers exist for Linux. One popular solution is the Apache proxy module, which can be found at `http://www.apache.org`. A more complete and robust implementation of an HTTP proxy is SQUID, which can be found at `http://squid.nlanr.net/`.

Dial on Demand

The purpose of dial on demand is to make it transparently appear that the users have a permanent connection to a remote site. Usually, there is a daemon who monitors the traffic of packets and when an interesting packet (interesting is defined usually by a set of rules/priorities/permissions) arrives it establishes a connection with the remote end. When the channel is idle for a certain period of time, it drops the connection.

The Diald HOWTO can be found at `http://MetaLab.unc.edu/mdw/HOWTO/mini/Diald.html`.

Tunnelling, Mobile IP, and Virtual Private Networks

The Linux kernel allows the tunnelling (encapsulation) of protocols. It can do IPX tunnelling through IP, allowing the connection of two IPX networks through an IP only link. It can also do IP-IP tunnelling (which is essential for mobile IP support), multicast support, and amateur radio (see `http://MetaLab.unc.edu/mdw/HOWTO/NET-3-HOWTO-6.html#ss6.13`).

Mobile IP specifies enhancements that allow transparent routing of IP datagrams to mobile nodes in the Internet. Each mobile node is identified by its home address, regardless of its current point of attachment to the Internet. While situated away from its home, a mobile node is also associated with a care-of address, which provides information about its current point of attachment to the Internet. The protocol provides for registering the care-of address with a home agent. The home agent sends datagrams destined for the mobile node through a tunnel to the care-of address. After arriving at the end of the tunnel, each datagram is then delivered to the mobile node.

Point-to-Point Tunneling Protocol (PPTP) is a networking technology that allows the use of the Internet as a secure virtual private network (VPN). PPTP is integrated with the Remote Access Services (RAS) server which is built into the Windows NT server. With PPTP, users can dial into a local ISP, or connect directly to the Internet, and access their network as if they were at their desks. PPTP is a closed protocol and its security has recently been compromised. It is highly recomended to use other Linux-based alternatives, since they rely on open standards that have been carefully examined and tested.

A client implementation of the PPTP for Linux is available at `http://www.pdos.lcs.mit.edu/~cananian/Projects/PPTP/`.

Mobile Ips can be found at `http://www-uk.hpl.hp.com/people/jt/mip.html` and `http://anchor.cs.binghamton.edu/~mobileip/`.

Virtual Private Network-related documents can be found at `http://MetaLab.unc.edu/mdw/HOWTO/mini/VPN.html` and `http://sites.inka.de/sites/bigred/devel/cipe.html`.

NETWORK MANAGEMENT

This section describes network management applications and SNMP.

Network Management Applications

There is an impressive number of tools focused on network management and remote administration. Some interesting remote administration projects are linuxconf–which can be found at `http://solucor.solucorp.qc.ca/linuxconf/` and webmin–which can be found at `http://www.webmin.com/webmin/`.

Other tools include network traffic analysis tools, network security tools, monitoring tools, configuration tools, etc. An archive of many of these tools may be found at Sunsite at `http://www.MetaLab.unc.edu/pub/Linux/system/network/`.

SNMP

The Simple Network Management Protocol is a protocol for Internet network management services. It allows for remote monitoring and configuration of routers, bridges, network cards, switches, etc. There are a large number of libraries, clients, daemons, and SNMP-based monitoring programs available for Linux. A good page dealing with SNMP and Linux software may be found at `http://linas.org/linux/NMS.html`.

Enterprise Linux Networking

In certain situations it is necessary for the networking infrastructure to have proper mechanisms to guarantee network availability near 100 percent of the time. Some related techniques are described in the following sections. Most of the following material can be found at Linas' excellent Web site at `http://linas.org/linux/index.html` and in the Linux High-Availability HOWTO at `http://MetaLab.unc.edu/pub/Linux/ALPHA/linux-ha/High-Availability-HOWTO.html`.

High Availability

Redundancy is used to prevent the overall IT system from having single points of failure. A server with only one network card or a single SCSI disk has two single points of failure. The objective is to mask unplanned outages from users to let users continue to work quickly. High availability software is a set of scripts and tools that automatically monitor and detect failures, taking the appropriate steps to restore normal operation and to notify system administrators.

RAID

RAID, short for Redundant Array of Inexpensive Disks, is a method whereby information is spread across several disks using techniques such as disk striping (RAID Level 0) and disk mirroring (RAID level 1) to achieve redundancy, lower latency, and/or higher bandwidth for reading and/or writing and recoverability from hard-disk crashes. Over six different types of RAID configurations have been defined.There are three types of RAID solution options available to Linux users: software RAID, outboard DASD boxes, and RAID disk controllers.

Software RAID Pure software RAID implements the various RAID levels in the kernel disk (block device) code.

Outboard DASD Solutions DASD (Direct Access Storage Device) are separate boxes that come with their own power supply, provide a cabinet/chassis for holding the hard drives, and appear to Linux as just another SCSI device. In many ways, these offer the most robust RAID solution.

RAID Disk Controllers Disk Controllers are adapter cards that plug into the ISA/EISA/PCI bus. Just like regular disk controller cards, a cable attaches them to the disk drives. Unlike regular disk controllers, the RAID controllers will implement RAID on the card itself, performing all necessary operations to provide various RAID levels.

Related HOWTOs can be found at:

- `http://MetaLab.unc.edu/mdw/HOWTO/mini/DPT-Hardware-RAID.html`
- `http://MetaLab.unc.edu/mdw/HOWTO/Root-RAID-HOWTO.html`
- `http://MetaLab.unc.edu/mdw/HOWTO/mini/Software-RAID.html`

RAID at `linas.org`:

- `http://linas.org/linux/raid.html`

Redundant Networking

IP Address Takeover (IPAT) When a network adapter card fails, its IP address should be taken by a working network card in the same node or in another node.

MAC Address Takeover When an IP takeover occurs, it should be made sure that all the nodes in the network update their ARP caches (the mapping between IP and MAC addresses).

See the High-Availability HOWTO for more details at `http://MetaLab.unc.edu/pub/Linux/ALPHA/linux-ha/High-Availability-HOWTO.html`.

Sources of Information

You can get further information at

- Linux: `http://www.linux.org`
- Linux Documentation Project at `http://MetaLab.unc.edu/mdw/linux.html` (check out the *Linux Network Administrator Guide*)
- Freshmeat: The latest releases of Linux Software at `http://www.freshmeat.net`
- Linux links at `http://www.linuxlinks.com/Networking/`

Acknowledgements and Disclaimer

This document is based on the work of many other people who have made it possible for Linux to be what it is now: one of the best network operating systems. All credit is theirs. A lot of effort has been put into this document to make it simple but accurate and complete and not excessively long. Nevertheless, no liability will be assumed by the author under any circumstance. Use the information contained here at your own risk. Please feel free to e-mail me with suggestions, corrections, or general comments about the document so I can improve it. Other topics that will probably be included in futures revisions of this document may include radius, Web/ftp mirroring tools such as wget, traffic analyzers, CORBA, and many others that may be suggested and suitable. You can reach me at `ridruejo@esi.us.es`.

Finally I would like to thank FinnBjørn av Teilgum <`efat@kampsax.dtu.dk`> for his careful "beta-testing" of this HOWTO.

Chapter 8

Linux Networking

The Linux Operating System boasts kernel-based networking support written almost entirely from scratch. The performance of the TCP/IP implementation in recent kernels makes it a worthy alternative to even the best of its peers. This document aims to describe how to install and configure the Linux networking software and associated tools.

This chapter is a good read for everyone. Even though most Linux distributions today provide point-and-click tools for the configuration of common network types like Ethernet and PPP, there will always be a time when something unusual comes up. In these odd situations, even the most basic background in how it's really working under the hood will be useful. That's what this chapter provides: a description of how all the little user programs and all the kernel code work together to provide your Linux system with its powerful networking capabilities.

Linux Networking is reprinted from the Linux NET-3 HOWTO version 1.4 of August 1998 by Terry Dawson and Alessandro Rubini.

Introduction

The original NET-FAQ was written by Matt Welsh and Terry Dawson to answer frequently asked questions about networking for Linux at a time before the Linux Documentation Project had formally started. It covered the very early development versions of the Linux Networking Kernel. The NET-2-HOWTO superceded the NET-FAQ and was one of the original LDP HOWTO documents. It covered what was called version 2 and later version 3 of the Linux kernel Networking software. This document in turn supercedes it and relates only to version 3 of the Linux Networking Kernel.

Previous versions of this document became quite large because of the enormous amount of material that fell within its scope. To help reduce this problem a number of HOWTO's dealing with specific networking topics have been produced. This document will provide pointers to them where relevant and cover those areas not yet covered by other documents.

In April 1998 Terry left as NET-3 maintainer, due to his high load. Alessandro Rubini is the new maintainer and would like to keep the document as good as before, although he's new to this kind of stuff.

Feedback

I always appreciate feedback and especially value contributions. Please direct any feedback or contributions to me by e-mail `<rubini@linux.it>`.

How to Use This HOWTO Document (NET-3-HOWTO howto?)

This document is organized top-down. The first sections include informative material and can be skipped if you are not interested; what follows is a generic discussion of networking issues, and you must ensure you understand this before proceeding to more specific parts. The rest, "technology-specific" information, is grouped in three main sections: Ethernet and IP-related information, technologies pertaining to widespread PC hardware, and seldom-used technologies.

The suggested path through the document is thus the following:

Read the generic sections These sections apply to every, or nearly every, technology described later and so are very important for you to understand. On the other hand, I expect many of the readers to be already confident with this material.

Consider your network You should know how your network is, or will be, designed and exactly what hardware and technology types you will be implementing.

Read the "Ethernet and IP" section if you are directly connected to a LAN or the Internet This section describes basic Ethernet configuration and the various features that Linux offers for IP networks, like firewalling, advanced routing, and so on.

Read the next section if you are interested in low-cost local networks or dial-up connections The section describes PLIP, PPP, SLIP, and ISDN, the widespread technologies used on personal workstations.

Read the technology-specific sections related to your requirements If your needs differ from IP and/or common hardware, the final section covers details specific to non-IP protocols and peculiar communication hardware.

Do the configuration work You should actually try to configure your network and take careful note of any problems you have.

Look for further help if needed If you experience problems that this document does not help you to resolve, then read the section related to where to get help or where to report bugs.

Have fun! Networking is fun. Enjoy it.

Conventions Used in This Document

No special convention is used here, but you must be warned about the way commands are shown. Following the classic Unix documentation, any command you should type to your shell is prefixed by a prompt. This howto shows "user%" as the prompt for commands that do not require superuser privileges, and "root#" as the prompt for commands that need to run as root. I chose to use "root#" instead of a plain "#" to prevent confusion with snapshots from shell scripts, where the hash mark is used to define comment lines.

When "Kernel Compile Options" are shown, they are represented in the format used by *menuconfig*. They should be understandable even if you (like me) are not used to *menuconfig*. If you are in doubt about the options' nesting, running the program once can't but help.

Note that any link to other HOWTOs is local to help you browse your local copy of the LDP documents, in case you are using the HTML version of this document. If you don't have a complete set of documents, every HOWTO can be retrieved from `MetaLab.unc.edu` (directory `/pub/Linux/HOWTO`) and its countless mirrors.

General Information About Linux Networking

A Brief History of Linux Networking Kernel Development

Developing a brand new kernel implementation of the tcp/ip protocol stack that would perform as well as existing implementations was not an easy task. The decision not to port one of the existing implementations was made at a time when there was some uncertainty as to whether the existing implementations may become encumbered by restrictive copyrights because of the court case put by U.S.L., and when there was a lot of fresh enthusiasm for doing it differently, and perhaps even better than had already been done.

The original volunteer to lead development of the kernel network code was Ross Biro `<biro@yggdrasil.com>`. Ross produced a simple and incomplete but mostly usable implementation set of routines that was complemented by an Ethernet driver for the WD-8003 network interface card. This was enough to get many people testing and experimenting with the software, and some people even managed to connect machines in this configuration to live Internet connections. The pressure within the Linux community driving development for networking support was building, and eventually the cost of a combination of some unfair pressure applied to Ross and his own personal commitments outweighed the benefit he was deriving, and he stepped down as lead developer. Ross's efforts in getting the project started and accepting the responsibility for actually producing something useful in such controversial circumstances were what catalyzed all future work and were therefore an essential component of the success of the current product.

Orest Zborowski <obz@Kodak.COM> produced the original BSD socket programming interface for the Linux kernel. This was a big step forward as it allowed many of the existing network applications to be ported to Linux without serious modification.

Somewhere about this time Laurence Culhane <loz@holmes.demon.co.uk> developed the first drivers for Linux to support the SLIP protocol. These enabled many people who did not have access to Ethernet networking to experiment with the new networking software. Again, some people took this driver and pressed it into service to connect them to the Internet. This gave many more people a taste of the possibilities that could be realized if Linux had full networking support and grew the number of users actively using and experimenting with the networking software that existed.

One of the people that had also been actively working on the task of building networking support was Fred van Kempen <waltje@uwalt.nl.mugnet.org>. After a period of some uncertainty following Ross's resignation from the lead developer position, Fred offered his time and effort and accepted the role essentially unopposed. Fred had some ambitious plans for the direction that he wanted to take the Linux networking software and he set about progressing in those directions. Fred produced a series of networking code called the "NET-2" kernel code (the "NET" code being Ross's) which many people were able to use pretty much usefully. Fred formally put a number of innovations on the development agenda, such as the dynamic device interface, Amateur Radio AX.25 protocol support and a more modularly designed networking implementation. Fred's NET-2 code was used by a fairly large number of enthusiasts, the number increasing all the time as word spread that the software was working. The networking software at this time was still a large number of patches to the standard release of kernel code and was not included in the normal release. The NET-FAQ and subsequent NET-2-HOWTOs described the then fairly complex procedure to get it all working. Fred's focus was on developing innovations to the standard network implementations and this was taking time. The community of users was growing impatient for something that worked reliably and satisfied 80% of the users, and, as with Ross, the pressure on Fred as lead developer rose.

Alan Cox <iialan@www.uk.linux.org> proposed a solution to the problem designed to resolve the situation. He proposed that he would take

Fred's NET-2 code and debug it, making it reliable and stable so that it would satisfy the impatient user base while relieving that pressure from Fred, allowing him to continue his work. Alan set about doing this, with some good success, and his first version of Linux networking code was called "Net-2D(ebugged)." The code worked reliably in many typical configurations and the user base was happy. Alan clearly had ideas and skills of his own to contribute to the project, and many discussions relating to the direction the NET-2 code was heading ensued. There developed two distinct schools within the Linux networking community, one that had the philosophy of "make it work first, then make it better" and the other of "make it better first." Linus ultimately arbitrated and offered his support to Alan's development efforts and included Alan's code in the standard kernel source distribution. This placed Fred in a difficult position. Any continued development would lack the large user base actively using and testing the code, and this would mean progress would be slow and difficult. Fred continued to work for a short time and eventually stood down and Alan came to be the new leader of the Linux networking kernel development effort.

Donald Becker `<becker@cesdis.gsfc.nasa.gov>` soon revealed his talents in the low-level aspects of networking and produced a huge range of Ethernet drivers; nearly all of those included in the current kernels were developed by Donald. There have been other people who have made significant contributions, but Donald's work is prolific and so warrants special mention.

Alan continued refining the NET-2-Debugged code for some time while working on progressing some of the matters that remained unaddressed on the "TODO" list. By the time the Linux `1.3.*` kernel source had grown its teeth, the kernel networking code had migrated to the NET-3 release on which current versions are based. Alan worked on many different aspects of the networking code and with the assistance of a range of other talented people from the Linux networking community grew the code in all sorts of directions. Alan produced dynamic network devices and the first standard AX.25 and IPX implementations. Alan has continued tinkering with the code, slowly restructuring and enhancing it to the state it is in today.

PPP support was added by Michael Callahan `<callahan@maths.ox.ac.uk>` and Al Longyear `<longyear@netcom.com>`. This too was critical to increasing the number of people actively using Linux for networking.

Jonathan Naylor `<jsn@cs.nott.ac.uk>` has contributed by significantly enhancing Alan's AX.25 code, adding NetRom and Rose protocol support. The AX.25/NetRom/Rose support itself is quite significant, because no other operating system can boast standard native support for these protocols beside Linux.

There have of course been hundreds of other people who have made significant contributions to the development of the Linux networking software. Some of these you will encounter later in the technology-specific sections; other people have contributed modules, drivers, bug-fixes, suggestions, test reports, and moral support. In all cases each can claim to have played a part and offered what they could. The Linux kernel networking code is an excellent example of the results that can be obtained from the Linux style of anarchic development; if it hasn't yet surprised you, it is bound to soon enough. The development hasn't stopped.

Where to Get Other Information About Linux Networking

There are a number of places where you can find good information about Linux networking.

Alan Cox, the current maintainer of the Linux kernel networking code maintains a World Wide Web page that contains highlights of current and new developments in Linux Networking at: `www.uk.linux.org`.

Another good place is a book written by Olaf Kirch entitled the *Network Administrators Guide*. It is a work of the Linux Documentation Project (see `http://MetaLab.unc.edu/LDP/`), and you can read it interactively at Network Administrators Guide HTML version (see `http://MetaLab.unc.edu/LDP/LDP/nag/nag.html`) or you can obtain it in various formats by ftp from the MetaLab.unc.edu LDP ftp archive (see `ftp://MetaLab.unc.edu/pub/Linus/docs/LDP/network-guide/`). Olaf's book is quite comprehensive and provides a good high level overview of network configuration under Linux.

There is a newsgroup in the Linux news hierarchy dedicated to networking and related matters (see `news:comp.os.linux.networking`).

There is a mailing list to which you can subscribe where you may ask questions relating to Linux networking. To subscribe you should send a mail message:

```
To: majordomo@vger.rutgers.edu
Subject: anything at all
Message:

subscribe linux-net
```

On the various IRC networks there are often `#linux` channels on which people will be able to answer questions on Linux networking.

Please remember when reporting any problem to include as much relevant detail about the problem as you can. Specifically you should specify the versions of software that you are using, especially the kernel version, the version of tools such as *pppd* or *dip*, and the exact nature of the problem you are experiencing. This means taking note of the exact syntax of any error messages you receive and of any commands that you are issuing.

Where to Get Some Non-Linux-Specific Network Information

If you are after some basic tutorial information on TCP/IP networking generally, then I recommend you take a look at the following documents:

TCP/IP Introduction This document comes as both a text version (see `ftp://athos.rutgers.edu/runet/tcp-ip-intro.doc`) and a postscript version (see `ftp://athos.rutgers.edu/runet/tcp-ip-intro.ps`).

TCP/IP Administration This document comes as both a text version (see `ftp://athos.rutgers.edu/runet/tcp-ip-admin.doc`) and a postscript version (see `ftp://athos.rutgers.edu/runet/tcp-ip-admin.ps`).

If you are after some more detailed information on TCP/IP networking, then I highly recommend:

Internetworking with TCP/IP, Volume 1: principles, protocols and architecture, by Douglas E. Comer, ISBN 0-13-227836-7, Prentice Hall, Third Edition, 1995.

If you are wanting to learn about how to write network applications in a Unix compatible environment then I also highly recommend:

Unix Network Programming, by W. Richard Stevens, ISBN 0-13-949876-1, Prentice Hall, 1990.

A second edition of this book is appearing on the bookshelves; the new book is made up of three volumes: check Prentice-Hall's Web site (`http://www.phptr.com/`) to probe further.

You might also try the comp.protocols.tcp-ip newsgroup (see `news:comp.protocols.tcp-ip`).

An important source of specific technical information relating to the Internet and the TCP/IP suite of protocols are RFCs. RFC is an acronym for "Request For Comment" and is the standard means of submitting and documenting Internet protocol standards. There are many RFC repositories. Many of these sites are ftp sites and others provide World Wide Web access with an associated search engine that allows you to search the RFC database for particular keywords.

One possible source for RFCs is at Nexor RFC database (see `http://pubweb.nexor.co.uk/public/rfc/index/rfc.html`).

Generic Network Configuration Information

The following subsections you will pretty much need to know and understand before you actually try to configure your network. They are fundamental principles that apply regardless of the exact nature of the network you wish to deploy.

What Do I Need to Start?

Before you start building or configuring your network you will need some things. The most important of these are:

Current Kernel Source

Because the kernel you are running now might not yet have support for the network types or cards that you wish to use you will probably need the kernel source so that you can recompile the kernel with the appropriate options.

You can always obtain the latest kernel source from ftp.kernel.org (see `ftp://ftp.kernel.org/pub/linux/kernel`). Please remember that ftp.kernel.org is seriously overloaded: the preferred way to get current sources is by downloading patches instead of whole tar files; moreover, you should first try to reach mirrors of the main ftp site, like ftp.funet.fi (see `ftp://ftp.funet.fi//mirrors/ftp.kernel.org/pub/linux/kernel`); also remember that every Linux site usually carries updated kernel sources).

Normally the kernel source will be untarred into the `/usr/src/linux` directory. For information on how to apply patches and build the kernel you should read the Kernel-HOWTO (see "Kernel-HOWTO.html"). For information on how to configure kernel modules you should read the "Modules mini-HOWTO." Also, the README file found in the kernel sources and the `Documentation` directory are very informative for the brave reader.

Unless specifically stated otherwise, I recommend you stick with the standard kernel release (the one with the even number as the second digit in the version number). Development release kernels (the ones with the odd second digit) may have structural or other changes that may cause problems working with the other software on your system. If you are uncertain that you could resolve those sorts of problems, then don't use them.

On the other hand, some of the features described here have been introduced during the development of 2.1 kernels, so you must take your choice: you can stick to 2.0 while waiting for 2.2 and an updated distribution with every new tool, or you can get 2.1 and look around for the various support programs needed to exploit the new features. As I write this paragraph, in August 1998, 2.1.115 is current and 2.2 is expected to appear pretty soon.

Current Network Tools

The network tools are the programs that you use to configure Linux network devices. These tools allow you to assign addresses to devices and configure routes, for example.

Most modern Linux distributions are supplied with the network tools, so if you have installed from a distribution and haven't yet installed the network tools, then you should do so.

If you haven't installed from a distribution, then you will need to source and compile the tools yourself. This isn't difficult.

The network tools are now maintained by Bernd Eckenfels and are available at: `ftp.inka.de` (see `ftp://ftp.inka.de/pub/comp/Linux/networking/NetTools/`) and are mirrored at: `ftp.uk.linux.org` (see `ftp://ftp.uk.linux.org/pub/linux/Networking/base/`).

Be sure to choose the version that is most appropriate for the kernel you wish to use and follow the instructions in the package to install.

To install and configure the version current at the time of this writing, you need do the following:

```
user% tar xvfz net-tools-1.33.tar.gz
user% cd net-tools-1.33
```

```
user% make config
user% make
root# make install
```

Additionally, if you plan on configuring a firewall or using the IP masquerade feature you will require the *ipfwadm* command. The latest version of it may be obtained from: ftp.xos.nl (see `ftp:/ftp.xos.nl/pub/linux/ipfwadm`). Again, there are a number of versions available. Be sure to pick the version that most closely matches your kernel. Note that the firewalling features of Linux changed during 2.1 development. This only applies to version 2.0 of the kernel.

To install and configure the version current at the time of this writing, you need do the following:

```
user% tar xvfz ipfwadm-2.3.0.tar.gz
user% cd ipfwadm-2.3.0
user% make
root# make install
```

Note that if you run version 2.2 (or late 2.1) of the kernel, *ipfwadm* is not the right tool to configure firewalling. This version of the NET-3-HOWTO currently doesn't deal with the new firewalling setup.

Network Application Programs

The network application programs are programs such as *telnet* and *ftp* and their respective server programs. David Holland has been managing a distribution of the most common of these, which is now maintained by `netbug@ftp.uk.linux.org`. You may obtain the distribution from: `ftp.uk.linux.org` (see `ftp://ftp.uk.linux.org/pub/linux/Networking/base`).

In March 1997 the package was split to several smaller packages, but in May 1997 the most basic programs were merged into a package called `netkit-base-0.10`. You might need to get the base package and/or additional packages.

To install and configure the version current at the time of this writing, you need do the following:

```
user% tar xvfz netkit-base-0.10
user% cd netkit-base-0.10
user% more README
user% vi MCONFIG
user% make
root# make install
```

Addresses

Internet Protocol Addresses are composed of four bytes. The convention is to write addresses in what is called "dotted decimal notation." In this form each byte is converted to a decimal number (0–255), dropping any leading zeroes unless the number is zero and written with each byte separated by a "." character. By convention each interface of a host or router has an IP address. It is legal for the same IP address to be used on each interface of a single machine in some circumstances, but usually each interface will have its own address.

Internet Protocol Networks are contiguous sequences of IP addresses. All addresses within a network have a number of digits within the address in common. The portion of the address that is common amongst all addresses within the network is called the "network portion" of the address. The remaining digits are called the "host portion." The number of bits that are shared by all addresses within a network is called the netmask, and it is role of the netmask to determine which addresses belong to the network it is applied to and which don't. For example, consider the following:

Host Address	192.168.110.23
Network Mask	255.255.255.0
Network Portion	192.168.110.
Host portion	.23
Network Address	192.168.110.0
Broadcast Address	192.168.110.255

Any address that is "bitwise anded" with its netmask will reveal the address of the network it belongs to. The network address is therefore always the lowest numbered address within the range of addresses on the network and always has the host portion of the address coded all zeroes.

The broadcast address is a special address that every host on the network listens to in addition to its own unique address. This address is the one that a datagram is sent to if every host on the network is meant to receive it. Certain types of data like routing information and warning messages are transmitted to the broadcast address, so that every host on the network can receive them simultaneously. There are two commonly used standards for what the broadcast address should be. The most widely accepted one is to use the highest possible address on the network as the broadcast address. In the example above this would be `192.168.110.255`. For some reason other sites have adopted the convention of using the network address as the broadcast address. In practice it doesn't matter very much which you use, but you must make sure that every host on the network is configured with the same broadcast address.

For administrative reasons some time early in the development of the IP protocol some arbitrary groups of addresses were formed into networks, and these networks were grouped into what are called classes. These classes provide a number of standard-size networks that could be allocated. The ranges allocated are:

Network Class	Netmask	Network Addresses
A	255.0.0.0	0.0.0.0–127.255.255.255
B	255.255.0.0	128.0.0.0–191.255.255.255
C	255.255.255.0	192.0.0.0–223.255.255.255
Multicast	240.0.0.0	224.0.0.0–239.255.255.255

What addresses you should use depends on exactly what it is that you are doing. You may have to use a combination of the following activities to get all the addresses you need:

Installing a Linux machine on an existing IP network If you wish to install a Linux machine onto an existing IP network, then you should contact whoever administers the network, and ask them for the following information:

- Host IP Address
- IP network address
- IP broadcast address
- IP netmask
- Router address
- Domain Name Server Address

You should then configure your Linux network device with those details. You can not make them up and expect your configuration to work.

Building a brand new network that will never connect to the Internet If you are building a private network and you never intend that network to be connected to the Internet then you can choose whatever addresses you like. However, for safety and consistency reasons there have been some IP network addresses that have been reserved specifically for this purpose. These are specified in RFC1597 and are as follows in Table 8.1:

TABLE 8.1 Reserved private network allocations

Network Class	Netmask	Network Addresses
A	255.0.0.0	10.0.0.0–10.255.255.255
B	255.255.0.0	172.16.0.0–172.31.255.255
C	255.255.255.0	192.168.0.0–192.168.255.255

You should first decide how large you want your network to be and then choose as many of the addresses as you require.

Where Should I Put the Configuration Commands?

There are a few different approaches to Linux system boot procedures. After the kernel boots, it always executes a program called "*init.*" The *init* program then reads its configuration file called `/etc/inittab` and commences the boot process. There are a few different flavors of *init* around, although everyone is now converging to the System V (Five) flavor, developed by Miguel van Smoorenburg.

Despite the fact that the *init* program is always the same, the setup of system boot is organized in a different way by each distribution.

Usually the `/etc/inittab` file contains an entry looking something like:

```
si::sysinit:/etc/init.d/boot
```

This line specifies the name of the shell script file that actually manages the boot sequence. This file is somewhat equivalent to the `AUTOEXEC.BAT` file in MS-DOS.

There are usually other scripts that are called by the boot script and often the network is configured within one of many of these.

The following table may be used as a guide for your system:

Distribution	Interface Config/Routing	Server Initialization
Debian	`/etc/init.d/network`	`/etc/rc2.d/*`
Slackware	`/etc/rc.d/rc.inet1`	`/etc/rc.d/rc.inet2`
Red Hat	`/etc/rc.d/init.d/network`	`/etc/rc.d/rc3.d/*`

Note that Debian and Red Hat use a whole directory to host scripts that fire up system services, and usually information does not lie within these files. For example Red Hat systems store all of system configuration in files under `/etc/sysconfig`, whence it is retrieved by boot scripts. If you want to grasp the details of the boot process, my suggestion is to check */etc/inittab* and the documentation that accompanies *init*. Linux Journal is also going to publish an article about system initialization, and this document will point to it as soon as it is available on the Web.

Most modern distributions include a program that will allow you to configure many of the common sorts of network interfaces. If you have one of these then you should see if it will do what you want before attempting a manual configuration.

Distribution	Network configuration program
Red Hat	/usr/bin/netcfg
Slackware	/sbin/netconfig

Creating Your Network Interfaces

In many Unix operating systems the network devices have appearances in the */dev* directory. This is not so in Linux. In Linux the network devices are created dynamically in software and do not require device files to be present.

In the majority of cases the network device is automatically created by the device driver while it is initializing and has located your hardware. For example, the Ethernet device driver creates `eth[0..n]` interfaces sequentially as it locates your Ethernet hardware. The first Ethernet card found becomes `eth0`, the second `eth1`, etc.

In some cases though, notably SLIP and PPP, the network devices are created through the action of some user program. The same sequential device numbering applies, but the devices are not created automatically at boot time. The reason for this is that unlike Ethernet devices, the number of active SLIP or PPP devices may vary during the uptime of the machine. These cases will be covered in more detail in later sections.

Configuring a Network Interface

When you have all of the programs you need and your address and network information, you can configure your network interfaces. When we talk about configuring a network interface we are talking about the process of assigning appropriate addresses to a network device and setting appropriate values for other configurable parameters of a network device. The program most commonly used to do this is the *ifconfig* (interface configure) command.

Typically you would use a command similar to the following:

```
root# ifconfig eth0 192.168.0.1 netmask 255.255.255.0 up
```

In this case I'm configuring an Ethernet interface "`eth0`" with the IP address "`192.168.0.1`" and a network mask of "`255.255.255.0`." The "*u*" that trails the command tells the interface that it should become active, but can usually be omitted, as it is the default. To shutdown an interface, you can just call "`ifconfig eth0 down`."

The kernel assumes certain defaults when configuring interfaces. For example, you may specify the network address and broadcast address for an interface, but if you don't, as in my example above, then the kernel will make reasonable guesses as to what they should be based on the netmask you supply, and if you don't supply a netmask, then on the network class of the IP address configured. In my example the kernel would assume that it is a class-C network being configured on the interface and configure a network address of "`192.168.0.0`" and a broadcast address of "`192.168.0.255`" for the interface.

There are many other options to the *ifconfig* command. The most important of these are:

up This option activates an interface (and is the default).

down This option deactivates an interface.

[-]arp This option enables or disables use of the address resolution protocol on this interface.

[-]allmulti This option enables or disables the reception of all hardware multicast packets. Hardware multicast enables groups of hosts to receive packets addressed to special destinations. This may be of importance if you are using applications like desktop videoconferencing that are normally not used.

mtu N This parameter allows you to set the *MTU* of this device.

netmask <addr> This parameter allows you to set the network mask of the network this device belongs to.

irq <addr> This parameter only works on certain types of hardware and allows you to set the IRQ of the hardware of this device.

broadcast addr This parameter allows you to enable and set the accepting of datagrams destined to the broadcast address, or to disable reception of these datagrams.

pointopoint addr This parameter allows you to set the address of the machine at the remote end of a point-to-point link, such as for *SLIP* or *PPP*.

hw <type> <addr> This parameter allows you to set the hardware address of certain types of network devices. This is not often useful for Ethernet, but is useful for other network types such as AX.25.

You may use the *ifconfig* command on any network interface. Some user programs such as *pppd* and *dip* automatically configure the network devices as they create them, so manual use of *ifconfig* is unnecessary.

Configuring Your Name Resolver

The "*Name Resolver*" is a part of the Linux standard library. Its prime function is to provide a service to convert human-friendly hostnames like "`ftp.funet.fi`" into machine friendly IP addresses such as `128.214.248.6`.

What's In a Name?

You will probably be familiar with the appearance of Internet host names, but may not understand how they are constructed, or deconstructed. Internet domain names are hierarchical in nature, that is, they have a tree-like structure. A *"domain"* is a family, or group of names. A domain may be broken down into *"subdomain."* A *"top level domain"* is a domain that is not a subdomain. The Top Level Domains are specified in RFC-920. Some examples of the most common top level domains are:

COM Commercial Organizations

EDU Educational Organizations

GOV Government Organizations

MIL Military Organizations

ORG Other organizations

NET Internet-Related Organizations

Country Designator These are two-letter codes that represent a particular country.

For historical reasons most domains belonging to one of the non-country based top level domains were used by organizations within the United States, although the United States also has its own country code "`.us`." This is not true any more for `.com` and `.org` domains, which are commonly used by non-U.S. companies.

Each of these top level domains has subdomains. The top level domains based on country name are often next broken down into subdomains based on the `com`, `edu`, `gov`, `mil` and `org` domains. So, for example, you end up with `com.au` and `gov.au` for commercial and government organizations in Australia; note that this is not a general rule, as actual policies depend on the naming authority for each domain.

The next level of division usually represents the name of the organization. Further subdomains vary in nature, often the next level of subdomain is based on the departmental structure of the organization, but it may be based on any criterion considered reasonable and meaningful by the network administrators for the organization.

The very left-most portion of the name is always the unique name assigned to the host machine and is called the *"hostname"*; the portion of the name to the right of the hostname is called the *"domainname"*; and the complete name is called the *"Fully Qualified Domain Name."* To use Terry's host as an example, the fully qualified domain name is "`perf.no.itg.telstra.com.au`." This means that the hostname is "`perf`" and the domain name is "`no.itg.telstra.com.au`." The domain name is based on a top-level domain based on Terry's country, Australia, and as

Terry's e-mail address belongs to a commercial organization, "`.com`" is there as the next level domain. The name of the company is (was) "`telstra`," whose internal naming structure is based on organizational structure; in this case the machine belongs to the Information Technology Group, Network Operations section.

Usually, the names are fairly short; for example, my ISP is called "`systemy.it`" and my nonprofit organization is called "`linux.it`," without any `com` and `org` subdomain, so that my own host is just called "`morgana.systemy.it`" and `rubini@linux.it` is a valid e-mail address. Note that the owner of a domain has the rights to register hostnames as well as subdomains; for example, the LUG I belong to uses the domain `pluto.linux.it`, because the owners of `linux.it` agreed to open a subdomain for the LUG.

What Information You Will Need

You will need to know what domain your hosts name will belong to. The name resolver software provides this name translation service by making requests to a "*Domain Name Server*," so you will need to know the IP address of a local nameserver that you can use.

There are three files you need to edit, I'll cover each of these in turn.

/etc/resolv.conf

The `/etc/resolv.conf` is the main configuration file for the name resolver code. Its format is quite simple. It is a text file with one keyword per line. There are three keywords typically used; they are:

domain This keyword specifies the local domain name.

search This keyword specifies a list of alternate domain names to search for a hostname.

nameserver This keyword, which may be used many times, specifies an IP address of a domain name server to query when resolving names.

An example `/etc/resolv.conf` might look something like:

```
domain maths.wu.edu.au
search maths.wu.edu.au wu.edu.au
nameserver 192.168.10.1
nameserver 192.168.12.1
```

This example specifies that the default domain name to append to unqualified names (i.e., hostnames supplied without a domain) is `maths.wu.edu.au` and that if the host is not found in that domain to also try the `wu.edu.au` domain directly. Two nameservers entry are supplied, each of which may be called upon by the name resolver code to resolve the name.

/etc/host.conf

The `/etc/host.conf` file is where you configure some items that govern the behavior of the name resolver code. The format of this file is described in detail in the "`resolv+`" man page. In nearly all circumstances the following example will work for you:

```
order hosts,bind
multi on
```

This configuration tells the name resolver to check the `/etc/hosts` file before attempting to query a nameserver and to return all valid addresses for a host found in the `/etc/hosts` file instead of just the first.

/etc/hosts

The `/etc/hosts` file is where you put the name and IP address of local hosts. If you place a host in this file, then you do not need to query the domain name server to get its IP Address. The disadvantage of doing this is that you must keep this file up-to-date yourself if the IP address for that host changes. In a well-managed system the only hostnames that usually appear in this file are an entry for the loopback interface and the local host name.

```
# /etc/hosts
127.0.0.1    localhost loopback
192.168.0.1  this.host.name
```

You may specify more than one hostname per line as demonstrated by the first entry, which is a standard entry for the loopback interface.

Running a Name Server

If you want to run a local nameserver, you can do it easily. Please refer to the DNS-HOWTO and to any documents included in your version of *BIND* (Berkeley Internet Name Domain).

Configuring Your Loopback Interface

The "`loopback`" interface is a special type of interface that allows you to make connections to yourself. There are various reasons why you might want to do this; for example, you may wish to test some network software without interfering with anybody else on your network. By convention the IP address "`127.0.0.1`" has been assigned specifically for loopback. So no matter what machine you go to, if you open a telnet connection to `127.0.0.1` you will always reach the local host.

Configuring the loopback interface is simple and you should ensure you do (but note that this task is usually performed by the standard initialization scripts).

```
root# ifconfig lo 127.0.0.1
root# route add -host 127.0.0.1 lo
```

We'll talk more about the *route* command in the next section.

Routing

Routing is a big topic. It is easily possible to write large volumes of text about it. Most of you will have fairly simple routing requirements, some of you will not. I will cover some basic fundamentals of routing only. If you are interested in more detailed information, then I suggest you refer to the references provided at the start of the document.

Let's start with a definition. What is IP routing ? Here is one that I'm using:

> IP Routing is the process by which a host with multiple network connections decides where to deliver IP datagrams it has received.

It might be useful to illustrate this with an example. Imagine a typical office router; it might have a PPP link off the Internet, a number of Ethernet segments feeding the workstations, and another PPP link off to another office. When the router receives a datagram on any of its network connections, routing is the mechanism that it uses to determine which interface it should send the datagram to next. Simple hosts also need to route; all Internet hosts have two network devices, one is the loopback interface described above and the other is the one it uses to talk to the rest of the network, perhaps an Ethernet, perhaps a PPP or SLIP serial interface.

Ok, so how does routing work ? Each host keeps a special list of routing rules, called a routing table. This table contains rows that typically contain at least three fields: the first is a destination address, the second is the name of the interface to which the datagram is to be routed, and the third is optionally the IP address of another machine which will carry the datagram on its next step through the network. In Linux you can see this table by using the following command:

```
user% cat /proc/net/route
```

or by using either of the following commands:

```
user% /sbin/route -n
user% netstat -r
```

The routing process is fairly simple: an incoming datagram is received, the destination address (who it is for) is examined and compared with each entry in the table. The entry that best matches that address is selected and the datagram is forwarded to the specified interface. If the gateway field is filled, then the datagram is forwarded to that host via the specified interface; otherwise the destination address is assumed to be on the network supported by the interface.

To manipulate this table a special command is used. This command takes command line arguments and converts them into kernel system calls that request the kernel to add, delete, or modify entries in the routing table. The command is called "*route*."

A simple example. Imagine you have an Ethernet network. You've been told it is a class-C network with an address of `192.168.1.0`. You've been supplied with an IP address of `192.168.1.10` for your use and have been told that `192.168.1.1` is a router connected to the Internet.

The first step is to configure the interface as described earlier. You would use a command like:

```
root# ifconfig eth0 192.168.1.10 netmask 255.255.255.0 up
```

You now need to add an entry into the routing table to tell the kernel that datagrams for all hosts with addresses that match `192.168.1.*` should be sent to the Ethernet device. You would use a command similar to:

```
root# route add -net 192.168.1.0 netmask 255.255.255.0 eth0
```

Note the use of the "`-net`" argument to tell the route program that this entry is a network route. Your other choice here is a "`-host`" route, which is a route that is specific to one IP address.

This route will enable you to establish IP connections with all of the hosts on your Ethernet segment. But what about all of the IP hosts that aren't on your Ethernet segment?

It would be a very difficult job to have to add routes to every possible destination network, so there is a special trick that is used to simplify this task. The trick is called the "`default`" route. The `default` route matches every possible destination, but poorly, so that if any other entry exists that matches the required address it will be used instead of the `default` route. The idea of the `default` route is simply to enable you to say "and everything else should go here." In the example I've contrived you would use an entry like:

```
root# route add default gw 192.168.1.1 eth0
```

The "`gw`" argument tells the route command that the next argument is the IP address, or name, of a gateway or router machine which all datagrams matching this entry should be directed to for further routing.

So, your complete configuration would look like:

```
root# ifconfig eth0 192.168.1.10 netmask 255.255.255.0 up
root# route add -net 192.168.1.0 netmask 255.255.255.0 eth0
root# route add default gw 192.168.1.1 eth0
```

If you take a close look at your network "`rc`" files you will find that at least one of them looks very similar to this. This is a very common configuration.

Let's now look at a slightly more complicated routing configuration. Let's imagine we are configuring the router we looked at earlier, the one supporting the PPP link to the Internet and the lan segments feeding the workstations in the office. Lets imagine the router has three Ethernet segments and one PPP link. Our routing configuration would look something like:

```
root# route add -net 192.168.1.0 netmask 255.255.255.0 eth0
root# route add -net 192.168.2.0 netmask 255.255.255.0 eth1
root# route add -net 192.168.3.0 netmask 255.255.255.0 eth2
root# route add default ppp0
```

Each of the workstations would use the simpler form presented above, only the router needs to specify each of the network routes separately because for the workstations the `default` route mechanism will capture all of them letting the router worry about splitting them up appropriately. You may be wondering why the default route presented doesn't specify a "gw." The reason for this is simple, serial link protocols such as PPP and SLIP only ever have two hosts on their network, one at each end. To specify the host at the other end of the link as the gateway is pointless and redundant as there is no other choice, so you do not need to specify a gateway for these types of network connections. Other network types such as Ethernet, arcnet or Token Ring do require the gateway to be specified as these networks support large numbers of hosts on them.

So What Does the *Routed* Program Do?

The routing configuration described above is best suited to simple network arrangements where there are only ever single possible paths to destinations. When you have a more complex network arrangement things get a little more complicated. Fortunately for most of you this won't be an issue.

The big problem with "manual routing" or "static routing," as described, is that if a machine or link fails in your network, then the only way you can direct your datagrams another way, if another way exists, is by manually intervening and executing the appropriate commands. Naturally this is clumsy, slow, impractical, and hazard prone. Various techniques have been developed to automatically adjust routing tables in the event of network failures where there are alternate routes; all of these techniques are loosely grouped by the term "dynamic routing protocols."

You may have heard of some of the more common dynamic routing protocols. The most common are probably RIP (Routing Information Protocol) and OSPF (Open Shortest Path First Protocol). The Routing Information Protocol is very common on small networks such as small-medium sized corporate networks or building networks. OSPF is more modern and more capable at handling large network configurations and better suited to environments where there is a large number of possible paths through the network. Common implementations of these protocols are: "*routed*" - RIP and "*gated*" - RIP, OSPF, and others. The "*routed*" program is normally supplied with your Linux distribution or is included in the "NetKit" package detailed above.

An example of where and how you might use a dynamic routing protocol might look something like the diagram on the following page:

We have three routers A, B, and C. Each supports one Ethernet segment with a Class C IP network (netmask 255.255.255.0). Each router also has a PPP link to each of the other routers. The network forms a triangle.

It should be clear that the routing table at router A could look like:

```
root# route add -net 192.168.1.0 netmask 255.255.255.0 eth0
root# route add -net 192.168.2.0 netmask 255.255.255.0 ppp0
root# route add -net 192.168.3.0 netmask 255.255.255.0 ppp1
```

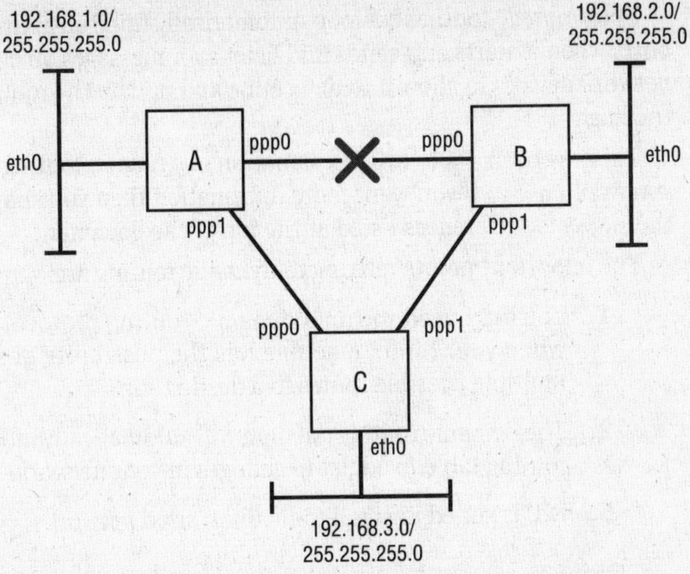

This would work just fine until the link between router A and B should fail. If that link failed then with the routing entry shown above hosts on the Ethernet segment of A could not reach hosts on the Ethernet segment on B because their datagram would be directed to router A's ppp0 link, which is broken. They could still continue to talk to hosts on the Ethernet segment of C, and hosts on the C's Ethernet segment could still talk to hosts on B's Ethernet segment because the link between B and C is still intact.

But wait, if A can talk to C and C can still talk to B, why shouldn't A route its datagrams for B via C and let C send them to B? This is exactly the sort of problem that dynamic routing protocols like RIP were designed to solve. If each of the routers A, B, and C were running a routing daemon, then their routing tables would be automatically adjusted to reflect the new state of the network should any one of the links in the network fail. To configure such a network is simple: at each router you need only do two things. In this case for Router A:

```
root# route add -net 192.168.1.0 netmask 255.255.255.0 eth0
root# /usr/sbin/routed
```

The *"routed"* routing daemon automatically finds all active network ports when it starts and sends and listens for messages on each of the network devices to allow it to determine and update the routing table on the host.

This has been a very brief explanation of dynamic routing and where you would use it. If you want more information then you should refer to the suggested references listed at the top of the document.

The important points relating to dynamic routing are:

1. You only need to run a dynamic routing protocol daemon when your Linux machine has the possibility of selecting multiple possible routes to a destination.
2. The dynamic routing daemon will automatically modify your routing table to adjust to changes in your network.
3. RIP is suited to small-to-medium sized networks.

Configuring Your Network Servers and Services

Network servers and services are those programs that allow a remote user to make user of your Linux machine. Server programs listen on network ports. Network ports are a means of addressing a particular service on any particular host and are how a server knows the difference between an incoming telnet connection and an incoming ftp connection. The remote user establishes a network connection to your machine and the server program, the network daemon program, listening on that port accepts the connection and executes. There are two ways that network daemons may operate. Both are commonly employed in practice. The two ways are:

standalone The network daemon program listens on the designated network port and when an incoming connection is made it manages the network connection itself to provide the service.

slave to the *inetd* server The *inetd* server is a special network daemon program that specializes in managing incoming network connections. It has a configuration file that tells it what program needs to be run when an incoming connection is received. Any service port may be configured for either of the tcp or udp protcols. The ports are described in another file that we will talk about soon.

There are two important files that we need to configure. They are the `/etc/services` file which assigns names to port numbers and the `/etc/inetd.conf` file which is the configuration file for the *inetd* network daemon.

/etc/services

The `/etc/services` file is a simple database that associates a human-friendly name to a machine-friendly service port. Its format is quite simple. The file is a text file with each line representing and entry in the database. Each entry is comprised of three fields separated by any number of white-space (tab or space) characters. The fields are: name port/protocol aliases # comment

name A single word name that represents the service being described.

port/protocol This field is split into two subfields.

port A number that specifies the port number the named service will be available on. Most of the common services have assigned service numbers. These are described in `RFC-1340`.

protocol This subfield may be set to either `tcp` or `udp`.

It is important to note that an entry of `18/tcp` is very different from an entry of `18/udp` and that there is no technical reason why the same service needs to exist on both. Normally common sense prevails and it is only if a particular service is available via both `tcp` and `udp` that you will see an entry for both.

aliases Other names that may be used to refer to this service entry.

Any text appearing in a line after a "#" character is ignored and treated as a comment.

An Example /Etc/Services File

All modern Linux distributions provide a good `/etc/services` file. Just in case you happen to be building a machine from the ground up, here is a copy of the `/etc/services` file supplied with an old Debian distribution (see `http://www.debian.org/`).

```
# /etc/services:
# $Id: services,v 1.3 1996/05/06 21:42:37 tobias Exp $
#
```

```
# Network services, Internet style
#
# Note that it is presently the policy of IANA to assign a
# single well-known port number for both TCP and UDP; hence,
# most entries here have two entries even if the protocol
# doesn't support UDP operations.
# Updated from RFC 1340, ``Assigned Numbers'' (July 1992).
# Not all ports are included, only the more common ones.

tcpmux          1/tcp                   # TCP port service multiplexer
echo            7/tcp
echo            7/udp
discard         9/tcp   sink null
discard         9/udp   sink null
systat          11/tcp  users
daytime         13/tcp
daytime         13/udp
netstat         15/tcp
qotd            17/tcp  quote
msp             18/tcp                  # message send protocol
msp             18/udp                  # message send protocol
chargen         19/tcp  ttytst source
chargen         19/udp  ttytst source
ftp-data        20/tcp
ftp             21/tcp
ssh             22/tcp                  # SSH Remote Login Protocol
ssh             22/udp                  # SSH Remote Login Protocol
telnet          23/tcp
# 24 - private
smtp            25/tcp  mail
# 26 - unassigned
time            37/tcp  timserver
time            37/udp  timserver
rlp             39/udp  resource        # resource location
nameserver      42/tcp  name            # IEN 116
whois           43/tcp  nicname
re-mail-ck      50/tcp                  # Remote Mail Checking Protocol
re-mail-ck      50/udp                  # Remote Mail Checking Protocol
domain          53/tcp  nameserver      # name-domain server
domain          53/udp  nameserver
mtp             57/tcp                  # deprecated
bootps          67/tcp                  # BOOTP server
bootps          67/udp
bootpc          68/tcp                  # BOOTP client
```

```
bootpc          68/udp
tftp            69/udp
gopher          70/tcp              # Internet Gopher
gopher          70/udp
rje             77/tcp  netrjs
finger          79/tcp
www             80/tcp  http        # WorldWideWeb HTTP
www             80/udp              # HyperText Transfer Prot
link            87/tcp  ttylink
kerberos        88/tcp  kerberos5 krb5  # Kerberos v5
kerberos        88/udp  kerberos5 krb5  # Kerberos v5
supdup          95/tcp
# 100 - reserved
hostnames       101/tcp hostname    # usually from sri-nic
iso-tsap        102/tcp tsap        # part of ISODE.
csnet-ns        105/tcp cso-ns      # also used by CSO name srvr
csnet-ns        105/udp cso-ns
rtelnet         107/tcp             # Remote Telnet
rtelnet         107/udp
pop-2           109/tcp postoffice  # POP version 2
pop-2           109/udp
pop-3           110/tcp             # POP version 3
pop-3           110/udp
sunrpc          111/tcp portmapper  # RPC 4.0 portmapper TCP
sunrpc          111/udp portmapper  # RPC 4.0 portmapper UDP
auth            113/tcp authentication tap ident
sftp            115/tcp
uucp-path       117/tcp
nntp            119/tcp readnews untp   # USENET
ntp             123/tcp
ntp             123/udp         # Network Time Protocol
netbios-ns      137/tcp         # NETBIOS Name Service
netbios-ns      137/udp
netbios-dgm     138/tcp         # NETBIOS Datagram Service
netbios-dgm     138/udp
netbios-ssn     139/tcp         # NETBIOS session service
netbios-ssn     139/udp
imap2           143/tcp         # Interim Mail Access Proto v2
imap2           143/udp
snmp            161/udp         # Simple Net Mgmt Proto
snmp-trap       162/udp snmptrap        # Traps for SNMP
cmip-man        163/tcp         # ISO mgmt over IP (CMOT)
cmip-man        163/udp
cmip-agent      164/tcp
cmip-agent      164/udp
xdmcp           177/tcp         # X Disp Mgr. Control Proto
xdmcp           177/udp
```

```
nextstep        178/tcp              # NeXTStep window
nextstep        178/udp              # server
bgp             179/tcp              # Border Gateway Proto.
bgp             179/udp
prospero        191/tcp              # Cliff Neuman's Prospero
prospero        191/udp
irc             194/tcp              # Internet Relay Chat
irc             194/udp
smux            199/tcp              # SNMP Unix Multiplexer
smux            199/udp
at-rtmp         201/tcp              # AppleTalk routing
at-rtmp         201/udp
at-nbp          202/tcp              # AppleTalk name binding
at-nbp          202/udp
at-echo         204/tcp              # AppleTalk echo
at-echo         204/udp
at-zis          206/tcp              # AppleTalk zone information
at-zis          206/udp
z3950           210/tcp wais         # NISO Z39.50 database
z3950           210/udp wais
ipx             213/tcp              # IPX
ipx             213/udp
imap3           220/tcp              # Interactive Mail Access
imap3           220/udp              # Protocol v3
ulistserv       372/tcp              # UNIX Listserv
ulistserv       372/udp
#
# UNIX specific services
#
exec            512/tcp
biff            512/udp comsat
login           513/tcp
who             513/udp whod
shell           514/tcp cmd          # no passwords used
syslog          514/udp
printer         515/tcp spooler # line printer spooler
talk            517/udp
ntalk           518/udp
route           520/udp router routed   # RIP
timed           525/udp timeserver
tempo           526/tcp newdate
courier         530/tcp rpc
conference      531/tcp chat
netnews         532/tcp readnews
netwall         533/udp              # -for emergency broadcasts
uucp            540/tcp uucpd        # uucp daemon
remotefs        556/tcp              # Brunhoff remote filesystem
```

```
klogin          543/tcp          # Kerberized `rlogin' (v5)
kshell          544/tcp krcmd    # Kerberized `rsh' (v5)
kerberos-adm    749/tcp          # Kerberos `kadmin' (v5)
#
webster         765/tcp          # Network dictionary
webster         765/udp
#
# From ``Assigned Numbers'':
#
#> The Registered Ports are not controlled by the IANA and
#> on most systems can be used by ordinary user processes or
#> programs executed by ordinary users.
#
#> Ports are used in the TCP [45,106] to name the ends of
#> logical connections which carry long term conversations.
#> For the purpose of providing services to unknown callers,
#> a service contact port is defined.  This list specifies
#> the port used by the server process as its contact port.
#> While the IANA can not control uses of these ports it does
#> register or list uses of these ports as a convenience to
#> the community.
#
ingreslock      1524/tcp
ingreslock      1524/udp
prospero-np     1525/tcp         # Prospero non-privileged
prospero-np     1525/udp
rfe             5002/tcp         # Radio Free Ethernet
rfe             5002/udp         # Actually uses UDP only
bbs             7000/tcp         # BBS service
#
#
# Kerberos (Project Athena/MIT) services
# Note that these are for Kerberos v4 and are unofficial.
# Sites running v4 should uncomment these and comment out
# the v5 entries above.
#
kerberos4       750/udp kdc      # Kerberos (server) udp
kerberos4       750/tcp kdc      # Kerberos (server) tcp
kerberos_master 751/udp          # Kerberos authentication
kerberos_master 751/tcp          # Kerberos authentication
passwd_server   752/udp          # Kerberos passwd server
krb_prop        754/tcp          # Kerberos slave propagation
krbupdate       760/tcp kreg     # Kerberos registration
kpasswd         761/tcp kpwd     # Kerberos "passwd"
kpop            1109/tcp         # Pop with Kerberos
knetd           2053/tcp         # Kerberos de-multiplexor
zephyr-srv      2102/udp         # Zephyr server
```

```
zephyr-clt      2103/udp        # Zephyr serv-hm connection
zephyr-hm       2104/udp        # Zephyr hostmanager
eklogin         2105/tcp        # Kerberos encrypted rlogin
#
# Unofficial but necessary (for NetBSD) services
#
supfilesrv      871/tcp         # SUP server
supfiledbg      1127/tcp        # SUP debugging
#
# Datagram Delivery Protocol services
#
rtmp            1/ddp   # Routing Table Maintenance Protocol
nbp             2/ddp   # Name Binding Protocol
echo            4/ddp   # AppleTalk Echo Protocol
zip             6/ddp   # Zone Information Protocol
#
# Debian GNU/Linux services
rmtcfg          1236/tcp # Gracilis Packeten rmt cfg server
xtel            1313/tcp # french minitel
cfinger         2003/tcp # GNU Finger
postgres        4321/tcp # POSTGRES
mandelspawn     9359/udp # network mandelbrot

# Local services
```

In the real world, the actual file is always growing as new services are being created. If you fear your own copy is incomplete, I'd suggest to copy a new `/etc/services` from a recent distribution.

/etc/inetd.conf

The `/etc/inetd.conf` file is the configuration file for the *inetd* server daemon. Its function is to tell *inetd* what to do when it receives a connection request for a particular service. For each service that you wish to accept connections for, you must tell *inetd* what network server daemon to run and how to run it.

Its format is also fairly simple. It is a text file with each line describing a service that you wish to provide. Any text in a line following a "#" is ignored and considered a comment. Each line contains seven fields separated by any number of whitespace (tab or space) characters. The general format is as follows:

```
service socket_type proto flags user server_path server_args
```

service is the service relevant to this configuration as taken from the `/etc/services` file.

socket_type This field describes the type of socket that this entry will consider relevant; allowable values are: `stream`, `dgram`, `raw`, `rdm`, or `seqpacket`. This is a little technical in nature, but as a rule of thumb nearly all `tcp`-based services use `stream`, and nearly all `udp`-based services use `dgram`. It is only very special types of server daemons that would use any of the other values.

proto The protocol to considered valid for this entry. This should match the appropriate entry in the `/etc/services` file and will typically be either `tcp` or `udp`. Sun RPC (Remote Procedure Call)-based servers will use `rpc/tcp` or `rpc/udp`.

flags There are really only two possible settings for this field. This field setting tells *inetd* whether the network server program frees the socket after it has been started and therefore whether *inetd* can start another one on the next connection request, or whether *inetd* should wait and assume that any server daemon already running will handle the new connection request. Again, this is a little tricky to work out, but as a rule of thumb all `tcp` servers should have this entry set to `nowait` and most `udp` servers should have this entry set to `wait`. Be warned there are some notable exceptions to this, so let the example guide you if you are not sure.

user This field describes which user account from `/etc/passwd` will be set as the owner of the network daemon when it is started. This is often useful if you want to safeguard against security risks. You can set the user of an entry to the `nobody` user so that if the network server security is breached the possible damage is minimized. Typically this field is set to `root`, though, because many servers require root privileges in order to function correctly.

server_path This field is pathname to the actual server program to execute for this entry.

server_args This field comprises the rest of the line and is optional. This field is where you place any command line arguments that you wish to pass to the server daemon program when it is launched.

An Example /etc/inetd.conf As for the `/etc/services` file all modern distributions will include a good `/etc/inetd.conf` file for you to work with. Here, for completeness is, the `/etc/inetd.conf` file from the Debian distribution (see `http://www.debian.org/`).

```
# /etc/inetd.conf:  see inetd(8) for further informations.
#
# Internet server configuration database
#
#
# Modified for Debian by Peter Tobias
# <tobias@et-inf.fho-emden.de>
#
# service_name sock_type proto flags user path args
#
# Internal services
#
#echo      stream   tcp   nowait   root   internal
#echo      dgram    udp   wait     root   internal
discard    stream   tcp   nowait   root   internal
discard    dgram    udp   wait     root   internal
daytime    stream   tcp   nowait   root   internal
daytime    dgram    udp   wait     root   internal
#chargen   stream   tcp   nowait   root   internal
#chargen   dgram    udp   wait     root   internal
time       stream   tcp   nowait   root   internal
time       dgram    udp   wait     root   internal
#
# These are standard services.
#
telnet     stream   tcp   nowait   root   tcpd   in.telnetd
ftp        stream   tcp   nowait   root   tcpd   in.ftpd
#fsp       dgram    udp   wait     root   tcpd   in.fspd
#
# Shell, login, exec and talk are BSD protocols.
#
shell      stream   tcp   nowait   root   tcpd   in.rshd
login      stream   tcp   nowait   root   tcpd   in.rlogind
#exec      stream   tcp   nowait   root   tcpd   in.rexecd
talk       dgram    udp   wait     root   tcpd   in.talkd
ntalk      dgram    udp   wait     root   tcpd   in.ntalkd
#
# Mail, news and uucp services.
#
smtp       stream   tcp   nowait   root   tcpd   in.smtpd
```

```
#nntp       stream  tcp     nowait  news    tcpd    in.nntpd
#comsat     dgram   udp     wait    root    tcpd    in.comsat
#
# Pop et al
#
#pop-2      stream  tcp     nowait  root    tcpd    in.pop2d
#pop-3      stream  tcp     nowait  root    tcpd    in.pop3d
#
# `cfinger' is for the GNU finger server available for
# Debian.  (NOTE: The current implementation of the `finger'
# daemon allows it to be run as `root'.)
#
#cfinger    stream  tcp     nowait  root    tcpd in.cfingerd
#finger     stream  tcp     nowait  root    tcpd in.fingerd
#netstat    stream  tcp     nowait  nobody  tcpd /bin/netstat
#systat     stream  tcp     nowait  nobody  tcpd /bin/ps -auwwx
#
# Tftp service is provided primarily for booting.  Most sites
# run this only on machines acting as "boot servers."
#
#tftp       dgram   udp  wait  nobody tcpd   in.tftpd
#bootps     dgram   udp  wait  root   bootpd bootpd -i -t 120
#
# Kerberos authenticated services (these probably need to
# be corrected)
#
#klogin   stream tcp nowait root   tcpd   in.rlogind -k
#eklogin  stream tcp nowait root   tcpd   in.rlogind -k -x
#kshell   stream tcp nowait root   tcpd   in.rshd -k
#
# Services run ONLY on the Kerberos server (these probably
# need to be corrected)
#
#krbupdate stream tcp     nowait root   tcpd   registerd
#kpasswd   stream tcp     nowait root   tcpd   kpasswdd
#
# RPC based services
#
#mountd/1    dgram   rpc/udp  wait  root  tcpd   rpc.mountd
#rstatd/1-3  dgram   rpc/udp  wait  root  tcpd   rpc.rstatd
#rusersd/2-3 dgram   rpc/udp  wait  root  tcpd   rpc.rusersd
#walld/1     dgram   rpc/udp  wait  root  tcpd   rpc.rwalld
#
# End of inetd.conf.
ident        stream   tcp   nowait   nobody   identd  identd -I
```

Other Miscellaneous Network-Related Configuration Files

There are a number of miscellaneous files relating to network configuration under Linux that you might be interested in. You may never have to modify these files, but it is worth describing them so you know what they contain and what they are for.

/etc/protocols

The `/etc/protocols` file is a database that maps protocol ID numbers against protocol names. This is used by programmers to allow them to specify protocols by name in their programs and also by some programs, such as *tcpdump*,to allow them to display names instead of numbers in their output. The general syntax of the file is:

```
protocolname number aliases
```

The `/etc/protocols` file supplied with the Debian distribution (see `http://www.debian.org/`) is as follows:

```
# /etc/protocols:
# $Id: protocols,v 1.1 1995/02/24 01:09:41 imurdock Exp $
#
# Internet (IP) protocols
#
#     from: @(#)protocols     5.1 (Berkeley) 4/17/89
#
# Updated for NetBSD based on RFC 1340, Assigned
# Numbers (July 1992).

ip       0  IP          # internet protocol, pseudo protocol number
icmp     1  ICMP        # internet control message protocol
igmp     2  IGMP        # Internet Group Management
ggp      3  GGP         # gateway-gateway protocol
ipencap  4  IP-ENCAP    # IP encaps in IP (officially "IP")
st       5  ST          # ST datagram mode
tcp      6  TCP         # transmission control protocol
egp      8  EGP         # exterior gateway protocol
pup      12 PUP         # PARC universal packet protocol
udp      17 UDP         # user datagram protocol
hmp      20 HMP         # host monitoring protocol
xns-idp  22 XNS-IDP     # Xerox NS IDP
rdp      27 RDP         # "reliable datagram" protocol
```

```
iso-tp4   29 ISO-TP4      # ISO Transport Protocol class 4
xtp       36 XTP          # Xpress Tranfer Protocol
ddp       37 DDP          # Datagram Delivery Protocol
idpr-cmtp 39 IDPR-CMTP    # IDPR Control Message Transport
rspf      73 RSPF         # Radio Shortest Path First.
vmtp      81 VMTP         # Versatile Message Transport
ospf      89 OSPFIGP      # Open Shortest Path First IGP
ipip      94 IPIP         # Yet Another IP encapsulation
encap     98 ENCAP        # Yet Another IP encapsulation
```

/etc/networks

The /etc/networks file has a similar function to that of the /etc/hosts file. It provides a simple database of network names against network addresses. Its format differs in that there may be only two fields per line and that the fields are coded as:

```
networkname networkaddress
```

An example might look like:

```
loopnet  127.0.0.0
localnet  192.168.0.0
amprnet  44.0.0.0
```

When you use commands like the *route* command, if a destination is a network and that network has an entry in the /etc/networks file, then the route command will display that network name instead of its address.

Network Security and Access Control

Let me start this section by warning you that securing your machine and network against malicious attack is a complex art. I do not consider myself an expert in this field at all, and while the following mechanisms I describe will help, if you are serious about security, then I recommend you do some research of your own into the subject. There are many good references on the Internet relating to the subject, including the Security-HOWTO.

An important rule of thumb is: *"Don't run servers you don't intend to use."* Many distributions come with all sorts of services configured and automatically started. To ensure even a minimum level of safety, you should go through your /etc/inetd.conf file and comment out (place a "#" at the start of the line) any entries for services you don't intend to use. Good candidates are services such as: `shell`, `login`, `exec`, `uucp`, `ftp`, and informational services such as `finger`, `netstat`, and `systat`.

There are all sorts of security and access control mechanisms. I'll describe the most elementary of them.

/etc/ftpusers

The `/etc/ftpusers` file is a simple mechanism that allows you to deny certain users from logging into your machine via ftp. The `/etc/ftpusers` file is read by the ftp daemon program (*ftpd*) when an incoming ftp connection is received. The file is a simple list of those users who are disallowed from logging in. It might looks something like:

```
# /etc/ftpusers - users not allowed to login via ftp
root
uucp
bin
mail
```

/etc/securetty

The `/etc/securetty` file allows you to specify which `tty` devices `root` is allowed to login on. The `/etc/securetty` file is read by the login program (usually */bin/login*). Its format is a list of the tty devices names allowed; on all others `root` login is disallowed:

```
# /etc/securetty - tty's on which root is allowed to login
tty1
tty2
tty3
tty4
```

The *Tcpd* Hosts Access Control Mechanism

The *tcpd* program you will have seen listed in the same `/etc/inetd.conf` provides logging and access control mechanisms to services it is configured to protect.

When it is invoked by the *inetd*, program, it reads two files containing access rules and either allows or denies access to the server it is protecting ,accordingly.

It will search the rules files until the first match is found. If no match is found, then it assumes that access should be allowed to anyone. The files it searches in sequence are: `/etc/hosts.allow`, `/etc/hosts.deny`. I'll describe each of these in turn. For a complete description of this facility, you should refer to the appropriate *man* pages (`hosts_access(5)` is a good starting point).

/etc/hosts.allow The `/etc/hosts.allow` file is a configuration file of the */usr/sbin/tcpd* program. The `hosts.allow` file contains rules describing which hosts are *allowed* access to a service on your machine.

The file format is quite simple:

```
# /etc/hosts.allow
#
# <service list>: <host list> [: command]
```

`service list` is a comma-delimited list of server names that this rule applies to. Example server names are: `ftpd`, `telnetd` and `fingerd`.

`host list` is a comma-delimited list of hostnames. You may also use IP addresses here. You may additionally specify host names or addresses using wildcard characters to match groups of hosts. Examples include: `gw.vk2ktj.ampr.org` to match a specific host; `.uts.edu.au` to match any host name ending in that string; and `44.` to match any IP address commencing with those digits. There are some special tokens to simplify configuration. Some of these are: `ALL` matches every host; `LOCAL` matches any host whose name does not contain a "`.`" (i.e., is in the same domain as your machine); and `PARANOID` matches any host whose name does not match its address (name spoofing). There is one last token that is also useful. The `EXCEPT` token allows you to provide a list with exceptions. This will be covered in an example later.

`command` is an optional parameter. This parameter is the full pathname of a command that would be executed every time this rule is matched. It could, for example, run a command that would attempt to identify who is logged onto the connecting host, or attempt to generate a mail message or some other warning to a system administrator that someone is attempting to connect. There are a number of expansions that may be included. Some common examples are: `%h` expands to the name of the connecting host or address if it doesn't have a name, and %d is the daemon name being called.

An example:

```
# /etc/hosts.allow
#
# Allow mail to anyone
in.smtpd: ALL
# All telnet and ftp to only hosts within my domain and my
# host at home.
telnetd, ftpd: LOCAL, myhost.athome.org.au
# Allow finger to anyone but keep a record of who they are.
fingerd: ALL: (finger @%h | mail -s "finger from %h" root)
```

/etc/hosts.deny The `/etc/hosts.deny` file is a configuration file of the */usr/sbin/tcpd* program. The `hosts.deny` file contains rules describing which hosts are *disallowed* access to a service on your machine.

A simple sample would look something like this:

```
# /etc/hosts.deny
#
# Disallow all hosts with suspect hostnames
ALL: PARANOID
#
# Disallow all hosts.
ALL: ALL
```

The `PARANOID` entry is really redundant because the other entry traps everything in any case. Either of these entries would make a reasonable default, depending on your particular requirement.

Having an `ALL: ALL` default in the `/etc/hosts.deny`, and then specifically enabling those services and hosts that you want in the `/etc/hosts.allow` file is the safest configuration.

/etc/hosts.equiv The `hosts.equiv` file is used to grant certain hosts and users access rights to accounts on your machine without having to supply a password. This is useful in a secure environment where you control all machines, but is a security hazard otherwise. Your machine is only as secure as the least secure of the trusted hosts. To maximize security, don't use this mechanism and encourage your users not to use the `.rhosts` file as well.

Configure Your *ftp* Daemon Properly

Many sites will be interested in running an anonymous `ftp` server to allow other people to upload and download files without requiring a specific user ID. If you decide to offer this facility, make sure you configure the `ftp` daemon properly for anonymous access. Most *man* pages for `ftpd(8)` describe in some length how to go about this. You should always ensure that you follow these instructions. An important tip is to not use a copy of your `/etc/passwd` file in the anonymous account `/etc` directory. Make sure you strip out all account details except those that you must have, otherwise you will be vulnerable to brute force password-cracking techniques.

Network Firewalling

Not allowing datagrams to even reach your machine or servers is an excellent means of security. This is covered in depth in the Firewall HOWTO (see `http://metalab.unc.edu/LDP/`).

Other Suggestions

Here are some other, potentially religious, suggestions for you to consider.

sendmail Despite its popularity, the *sendmail* daemon appears with frightening regularity on security warning announcements. It's up to you, but I choose not to run it.

NFS and other Sun RPC services Be wary of these. There are all sorts of possible exploits for these services. It is difficult finding an option to services like NFS, but if you configure them, make sure you are careful about whom you allow mount rights to.

IP- and Ethernet-Related Information

This section covers information specific to Ethernet and IP. These subsections have been grouped together because I think they are the most interesting ones in the section formerly called "Technology Specific." Anyone with a LAN should be able to benefit from these goodies.

Ethernet

Ethernet device names are "eth0," "eth1," "eth2," etc. The first card detected by the kernel is assigned "eth0," and the rest are assigned sequentially in the order they are detected.

By default, the Linux kernel only probes for one Ethernet device, you need to pass command line arguments to the kernel in order to force detection of furter boards.

To learn how to make your Ethernet card(s) work under Linux, you should refer to the Ethernet-HOWTO (see http://metalab.unc.edu/LDP/).

Once you have your kernel properly built to support your Ethernet card, then configuration of the card is easy.

Typically you would use something like the following (which most distributions already do for you, if you configured them to support your Ethernet):

```
root# ifconfig eth0 192.168.0.1 netmask 255.255.255.0 up
root# route add -net 192.168.0.0 netmask 255.255.255.0 eth0
```

Most of the Ethernet drivers were developed by Donald Becker <becker@CESDIS.gsfc.nasa.gov>.

EQL—Multiple Line Traffic Equalizer

The EQL device name is "eql." With the standard kernel source you may have only one EQL device per machine. EQL provides a means of utilizing multiple point-to-point lines such as PPP, SLIP, or PLIP as a single logical link to carry TCP/IP. Often it is cheaper to use multiple lower-speed lines than to have one high-speed line installed.

Kernel Compile Options:

```
Network device support --->
  [*] Network device support
  <*> EQL (serial line load balancing) support
```

To support this mechanism the machine at the other end of the lines must also support EQL. Linux, Livingstone Portmasters, and newer dial-in servers support compatible facilities.

To configure EQL you will need the EQL tools which are available from: MetaLab.unc.edu (see ftp://MetaLab.unc.edu/pub/linux/system/Serial/eql-1.2.tar.gz).

Configuration is fairly straightforward. You start by configuring the EQL interface. The EQL interface is just like any other network device. You configure the IP address and MTU using the *ifconfig* utility. This would look something like

```
root# ifconfig eql 192.168.10.1 mtu 1006
```

Next you need to manually initiate each of the lines you will use. These may be any combination of point-to-point network devices. How you initiate the connections will depend on what sort of link they are; refer to the appropriate sections for further information.

Lastly you need to associate the serial link with the EQL device. This is called "enslaving" and is done with the *eql_enslave* command as shown:

```
root# eql_enslave eql sl0 28800
root# eql_enslave eql ppp0 14400
```

The *"estimated speed"* parameter you supply *eql_enslave* doesn't do anything directly. It is used by the EQL driver to determine what share of the datagrams that device should receive. So you can fine tune the balancing of the lines by playing with this value.

To disassociate a line from an EQL device, you use the *eql_emancipate* command as shown:

```
root# eql_emancipate eql sl0
```

You add routing as you would for any other point-to-point link, except your routes should refer to the `eql` device, rather than the actual serial devices themselves. Typically you would use

```
root# route add default eql
```

The EQL driver was developed by Simon Janes `<simon@ncm.com>`.

Part iii

IP Accounting (for Linux-2)

The IP accounting features of the Linux kernel allow you to collect and analyze some network usage data. The data collected comprise the number of packets and the number of bytes accumulated since the figures were last reset. You may specify a variety of rules to categorize the figures to suit whatever purpose you may have. This option has been removed in kernel 2.1.102, because the old ipfwadm-based firewalling was replaced by "ipfwchains."

Kernel Compile Options:

```
Networking options --->
  [*] IP: accounting
```

After you have compiled and installed the kernel, you need to use the *ipfwadm* command to configure IP accounting. There are many different ways of breaking down the accounting information that you might choose. I've picked a simple example of what might be useful to use. You should read the *ipfwadm* man page for more information.

Scenario: You have a Ethernet network that is linked to the Internet via a PPP link. On the Ethernet you have a machine that offers a number of services and you are interested in knowing how much traffic is generated by each of FTP and World Wide Web traffic, as well as total TCP and UDP traffic.

You might use a command set that looks like the following, which is shown as a shell script:

```
#!/bin/sh
#
# Flush the accounting rules
ipfwadm -A -f
#
# Set shortcuts
localnet=44.136.8.96/29
any=0/0
# Add rules for local Ethernet segment
ipfwadm -A in -a -P tcp -D $localnet ftp-data
ipfwadm -A out -a -P tcp -S $localnet ftp-data
ipfwadm -A in -a -P tcp -D $localnet www
ipfwadm -A out -a -P tcp -S $localnet www
ipfwadm -A in -a -P tcp -D $localnet
ipfwadm -A out -a -P tcp -S $localnet
ipfwadm -A in -a -P udp -D $localnet
ipfwadm -A out -a -P udp -S $localnet
#
# Rules for default
ipfwadm -A in -a -P tcp -D $any ftp-data
ipfwadm -A out -a -P tcp -S $any ftp-data
ipfwadm -A in -a -P tcp -D $any www
ipfwadm -A out -a -P tcp -S $any www
ipfwadm -A in -a -P tcp -D $any
ipfwadm -A out -a -P tcp -S $any
ipfwadm -A in -a -P udp -D $any
ipfwadm -A out -a -P udp -S $any
#
# List the rules
ipfwadm -A -l -n
#
```

The names "ftp-data" and "www" refer to lines in `/etc/services`. The last command lists each of the Accounting rules and displays the collected totals.

An important point to note when analyzing IP accounting is that *totals for all rules that match will be incremented*, so that to obtain differential figures you need to perform appropriate maths. For example, if I wanted to know how much data was not `ftp` nor www, I would substract the individual totals from the rule that matches all ports.

```
root# ipfwadm -A -l -n
IP accounting rules
 pkts bytes  dir  prot source          destination       ports
   0  0      in   tcp  0.0.0.0/0       44.136.8.96/29     * -> 20
   0  0      out  tcp  44.136.8.96/29  0.0.0.0/0         20 -> *
  10  1166   in   tcp  0.0.0.0/0       44.136.8.96/29     * -> 80
  10  572    out  tcp  44.136.8.96/29  0.0.0.0/0         80 -> *
 252  10943  in   tcp  0.0.0.0/0       44.136.8.96/29     * -> *
 231  18831  out  tcp  44.136.8.96/29  0.0.0.0/0          * -> *
  0   0      in   udp  0.0.0.0/0       44.136.8.96/29     * -> *
  0   0      out  udp  44.136.8.96/29  0.0.0.0/0          * -> *
  0   0      in   tcp  0.0.0.0/0       0.0.0.0/0          * -> 20
  0   0      out  tcp  0.0.0.0/0       0.0.0.0/0         20 -> *
  10  1166   in   tcp  0.0.0.0/0       0.0.0.0/0          * -> 80
  10  572    out  tcp  0.0.0.0/0       0.0.0.0/0         80 -> *
 253  10983  in   tcp  0.0.0.0/0       0.0.0.0/0          * -> *
 231  18831  out  tcp  0.0.0.0/0       0.0.0.0/0          * -> *
   0  0      in   udp  0.0.0.0/0           0.0.0.0/0       * -> *
   0  0      out  udp  0.0.0.0/0           0.0.0.0/0       * -> *
```

Part iii

IP Accounting (for Linux 2.2)

The new accounting code is accessed via "IP Firewall Chains." See the IP chanins home page (`http://www.adelaide.net.au/~rustcorp/ipfwchains/ipfwchains.html`) for more information. Among other things, you'll now need to use *ipchains* instead of `ipfwadm` to configure your filters. (See `Documentation/Changes` in the latest kernel sources).

IP Aliasing

There are some applications where being able to configure multiple IP addresses to a single network device is useful. Internet Service Providers often use this facility to provide a "customized" domain name to their

World Wide Web and FTP offerings for their customers. You can refer to the "IP-Alias mini-HOWTO" for more information.

Kernel Compile Options:

```
Networking options --->
  ....
  [*] Network aliasing
  ....
  <*> IP: aliasing support
```

After compiling and installing your kernel with IP_Alias, support configuration is very simple. The aliases are added to virtual network devices associated with the actual network device. A simple naming convention applies to these devices: `<devname>:<virtual dev num>`, e.g., `eth0:0`, `ppp0:10`, etc. Note that the the ifname:number device can only be configured *after* the main interface has been set up.

For example, if you have an Ethernet network that supports two different IP subnetworks simultaneously and you wish your machine to have direct access to both, you could use something like:

```
root# ifconfig eth0 192.168.1.1 netmask 255.255.255.0 up
root# route add -net 192.168.1.0 netmask 255.255.255.0 eth0

root# ifconfig eth0:0 192.168.10.1 netmask 255.255.255.0 up
root# route add -net 192.168.10.0 netmask 255.255.255.0 eth0:0
```

To delete an alias you simply add a "-" to the end of its name and refer to it and is as simple as:

```
root# ifconfig eth0:0- 0
```

All routes associated with that alias will also be deleted automatically.

IP Firewall (for Linux 2)

IP Firewall and Firewalling issues are covered in more depth in the Firewall-HOWTO (see `http://metalab.unc.edu`). IP Firewalling allows you to secure your machine against unauthorized network access by filtering or allowing datagrams from or to IP addresses that you nominate. There are three different classes of rules: incoming filtering, outgoing filtering, and forwarding filtering. Incoming rules are applied to datagrams that are received by a network device. Outgoing rules are applied to datagrams that are to be transmitted by a network device. Forwarding rules are applied to datagrams that are received and are not for this machine, i.e., datagrams that would be routed.

Kernel Compile Options:

```
Networking options --->
  [*] Network firewalls
  ....
  [*] IP: forwarding/gatewaying
  ....
  [*] IP: firewalling
  [ ] IP: firewall packet logging
```

Configuration of the IP firewall rules is performed using the *ipfwadm* command. As I mentioned earlier, security is not something I am expert at, so while I will present an example you can use, you should do your own research and develop your own rules if security is important to you.

Probably the most common use of the IP firewall is when you are using your Linux machine as a router and firewall gateway to protect your local network from unauthorized access from outside your network.

The following configuration is based on a contribution from Arnt Gulbrandsen <agulbra@troll.no>.

The example describes the configuration of the firewall rules on the Linux firewall/router machine illustrated in this diagram:

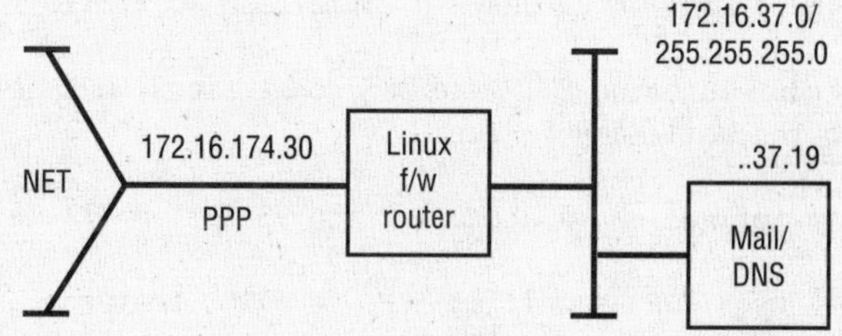

The following commands would normally be placed in an `rc` file so that they are automatically started each time the system boots. For maximum security, they would be performed after the network interfaces are configured, but before the interfaces are actually brought up, to prevent anyone gaining access while the firewall machine is rebooting.

```
#!/bin/sh

# Flush the 'Forwarding' rules table
# Change the default policy to 'accept'
#
/sbin/ipfwadm -F -f
/sbin/ipfwadm -F -p accept
```

```
#
# .. and for 'Incoming'
#
/sbin/ipfwadm -I -f
/sbin/ipfwadm -I -p accept

# First off, seal off the PPP interface
# I'd love to use '-a deny' instead of '-a reject -y' but then it
# would be impossible to originate connections on that interface
# too. The -o causes all rejected datagrams to be logged. This
# trades disk space against knowledge of an attack of configuration
# error.
#
/sbin/ipfwadm -I -a reject -y -o -P tcp -S 0/0 -D 172.16.174.30

# Throw away certain kinds of obviously forged packets right away:
# Nothing should come from multicast/anycast/broadcast addresses
#
/sbin/ipfwadm -F -a deny -o -S 224.0/3 -D 172.16.37.0/24
#
# and nothing coming from the loopback network should ever be
# seen on a wire
#
/sbin/ipfwadm -F -a deny -o -S 127.0/8 -D 172.16.37.0/24

# accept incoming SMTP and DNS connections, but only
# to the Mail/Name Server
#
/sbin/ipfwadm -F -a accept -P tcp -S 0/0 -D 172.16.37.19 25 53
#
# DNS uses UDP as well as TCP, so allow that too
# for questions to our name server
#
/sbin/ipfwadm -F -a accept -P udp -S 0/0 -D 172.16.37.19 53
#
# but not "answers" coming to dangerous ports like NFS and
# Larry McVoy's NFS extension. If you run squid, add its port here.
#
/sbin/ipfwadm -F -a deny -o -P udp -S 0/0 53 \
    -D 172.16.37.0/24 2049 2050

# answers to other user ports are okay
#
/sbin/ipfwadm -F -a accept -P udp -S 0/0 53 \
    -D 172.16.37.0/24 53 1024:65535
```

```
# Reject incoming connections to identd
# We use 'reject' here so that the connecting host is told
# straight away not to bother continuing, otherwise we'd experience
# delays while ident timed out.
#
/sbin/ipfwadm -F -a reject -o -P tcp -S 0/0 -D 172.16.37.0/24 113

# Accept some common service connections from the 192.168.64 and
# 192.168.65 networks, they are friends that we trust.
#
/sbin/ipfwadm -F -a accept -P tcp -S 192.168.64.0/23 \
   -D 172.16.37.0/24 20:23

# accept and pass through anything originating inside
#
/sbin/ipfwadm -F -a accept -P tcp -S 172.16.37.0/24 -D 0/0

# deny most other incoming TCP connections and log them
# (append 1:1023 if you have problems with ftp not working)
#
/sbin/ipfwadm -F -a deny -o -y -P tcp -S 0/0 -D 172.16.37.0/24

# ... for UDP too
#
/sbin/ipfwadm -F -a deny -o -P udp -S 0/0 -D 172.16.37.0/24
```

Good firewall configurations are a little tricky. This example should be a reasonable starting point for you. The *ipfwadm* man page offers some assistance in how to use the tool. If you intend to configure a firewall, be sure to ask around and get as much advice from sources you consider reliable, and get someone to test/sanity check your configuration from the outside.

IP Firewall (for Linux 2.2)

The new firewalling code is accessed via "IP Firewall Chains." See Chapter 14, "IP Chains," for more information. Among other things, you'll now need to use *ipchains* instead of `ipfwadm` to configure your filters (see `Documentation/Changes` in the latest kernel sources).

IPIP Encapsulation

Why would you want to encapsulate IP datagrams within IP datagrams? It must seem an odd thing to do if you've never seen an application of it before. Ok, here are a couple of common places where it is used: Mobile-IP and IP-Multicast. Amateur Radio is perhaps the most widespread use of it though it is also the least well known.

Kernel Compile Options:

```
Networking options --->
  [*] TCP/IP networking
  [*] IP: forwarding/gatewaying
  ....
  <*> IP: tunneling
```

IP tunnel devices are called "`tunl0`," "`tunl1`," etc.

"But why ?" Ok, ok. Conventional IP routing rules mandate that an IP network comprises a network address and a network mask. This produces a series of contiguous addresses that may all be routed via a single routing entry. This is very convenient, but it means that you may only use any particular IP address while you are connected to the particular piece of network to which it belongs. In most instances this is ok, but if you are a mobile netizen, then you may not be able to stay connected to one place all the time. IP/IP encapsulation (IP tunneling) allows you to overcome this restriction by allowing datagrams destined for your IP address to be wrapped up and redirected to another IP address. If you know that you're going to be operating from some other IP network for some time, you can set up a machine on your home network to accept datagrams to your IP address and redirect them to the address that you will actually be using temporarily.

A Tunneled Network Configuration

As always, I believe a diagram will save me lots of confusing text, so here is one:

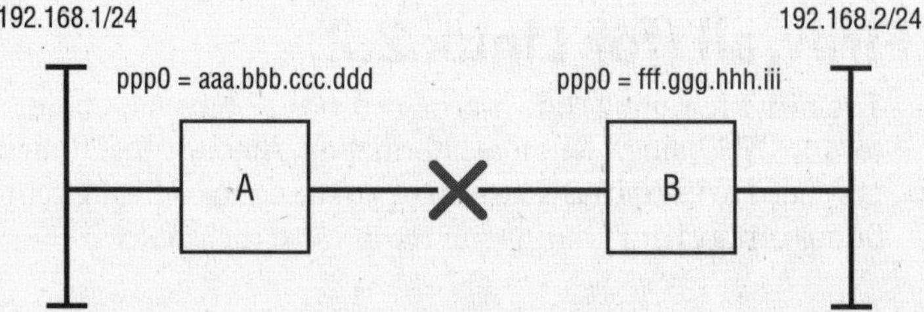

The diagram illustrates another possible reason to use IPIP encapsulation: virtual private networking. This example presupposes that you have two machines each with a simple dial-up Internet connection. Each host is allocated just a single IP address. Behind each of these machines are some private local area networks configured with reserved IP network addresses. Suppose that you want to allow any host on network A to connect to any host on network B, just as if they were properly connected to the Internet with a network route. IPIP encapsulation will allow you to do this. Note, encapsulation does not solve the problem of how you get the hosts on networks A and B to talk to others on the Internet–you still need tricks like IP Masquerade for that. Encapsulation is normally performed by machine functioning as routers.

Linux router "A" would be configured with a script like the following:

```
#!/bin/sh
PATH=/sbin:/usr/sbin
mask=255.255.255.0
remotegw=fff.ggg.hhh.iii
#
# Ethernet configuration
ifconfig eth0 192.168.1.1 netmask $mask up
route add -net 192.168.1.0 netmask $mask eth0
#
# ppp0 configuration (start ppp link, set default route)
pppd
route add default ppp0
#
# Tunnel device configuration
ifconfig tunl0 192.168.1.1 up
route add -net 192.168.2.0 netmask $mask gw $remotegw tunl0
```

Linux router "B" would be configured with a similar script:

```
#!/bin/sh
PATH=/sbin:/usr/sbin
mask=255.255.255.0
remotegw=aaa.bbb.ccc.ddd
#
# Ethernet configuration
ifconfig eth0 192.168.2.1 netmask $mask up
route add -net 192.168.2.0 netmask $mask eth0
#
# ppp0 configuration (start ppp link, set default route)
pppd
route add default ppp0
#
# Tunnel device configuration
ifconfig tunl0 192.168.2.1 up
route add -net 192.168.1.0 netmask $mask gw $remotegw tunl0
```

The command:

```
route add -net 192.168.1.0 netmask $mask gw $remotegw tunl0
```

reads: "Send any datagrams destined for `192.168.1.0/24` inside an IPIP encap datagram with a destination address of `aaa.bbb.ccc.ddd`."

Note that the configurations are reciprocated at either end. The tunnel device uses the "`gw`" in the route as the *destination* of the IP datagram in which it will place the datagram it has received to route. That machine must know how to decapsulate IPIP datagrams; that is, it must also be configured with a tunnel device.

A Tunneled Host Configuration

It doesn't have to be a whole network you route. You could, for example, route just a single IP address. In that instance you might configure the `tunl` device on the "remote" machine with its home IP address and at the A end just use a host route (and Proxy Arp), rather than a network route via the tunnel device. Let's redraw and modify our configuration appropriately. Now we have just host "B," which you want to act and behave as if it is both fully connected to the Internet and also part of the remote network supported by host "A":

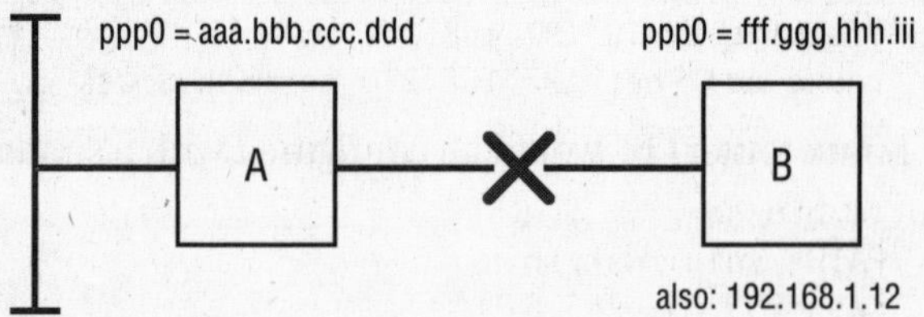

Linux router "A" would be configured with:

```
#!/bin/sh
PATH=/sbin:/usr/sbin
mask=255.255.255.0
remotegw=fff.ggg.hhh.iii
#
# Ethernet configuration
ifconfig eth0 192.168.1.1 netmask $mask up
route add -net 192.168.1.0 netmask $mask eth0
#
```

```
# ppp0 configuration (start ppp link, set default route)
pppd
route add default ppp0
#
# Tunnel device configuration
ifconfig tunl0 192.168.1.1 up
route add -host 192.168.1.12 gw $remotegw tunl0
#
# Proxy ARP for the remote host
arp -s 192.168.1.12 xx:xx:xx:xx:xx:xx pub
```

Linux host "B" would be configured with:

```
#!/bin/sh
PATH=/sbin:/usr/sbin
mask=255.255.255.0
remotegw=aaa.bbb.ccc.ddd
#
# ppp0 configuration (start ppp link, set default route)
pppd
route add default ppp0
#
# Tunnel device configuration
ifconfig tunl0 192.168.1.12 up
route add -net 192.168.1.0 netmask $mask gw $remotegwtunl0
```

This sort of configuration is more typical of a Mobile-IP application. Where a single host wants to roam around the Internet and maintain a single usable IP address the whole time. You should refer to the Mobile-IP section for more information on how that is handled in practice.

Masquerade (for Linux 2)

Many people have a simple dial-up account to connect to the Internet. Nearly everybody using this sort of configuration is allocated a single IP address by the Internet Service Provider. This is normally enough to allow only one host full access to the network. IP Masquerade is a clever trick that enables you to have many machines make use of that one IP address, by causing the other hosts to look like the machine supporting the dial-up connection–hence the term masquerade. There is a small caveat: the masquerade function nearly always works only in one direction. That is, the masqueraded hosts can make calls out, but they cannot accept or receive network connections from remote hosts. This means that some network services such as *talk*, do not work, and others such as *ftp* must be configured in passive (PASV) mode to operate. Fortunately the most common network services such as *telnet*, World Wide Web, and *irc* do work just fine.

Kernel Compile Options:

```
Code maturity level options --->
  [*] Prompt for development and/or incomplete code/drivers
Networking options --->
  [*] Network firewalls
  ....
  [*] TCP/IP networking
  [*] IP: forwarding/gatewaying
  ....
  [*] IP: masquerading (EXPERIMENTAL)
```

Normally you have your Linux machine supporting an SLIP or PPP dial-up line, just as it would if it were a standalone machine. Additionally it would have another network device, perhaps an Ethernet, configured with one of the reserved network addresses. The hosts to be masqueraded would be on this second network. Each of these hosts would have the IP address of the Ethernet port of the Linux machine set as their default gateway or router.

A typical configuration might look something like this:

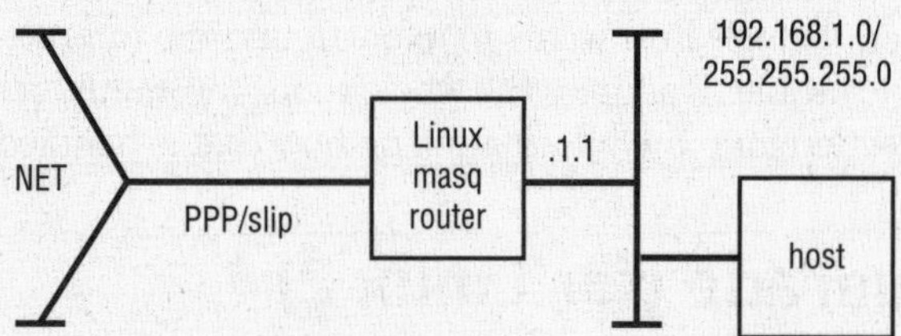

The most relevant commands for this configuration are:

```
# Network route for Ethernet
route add -net 192.168.1.0 netmask 255.255.255.0 eth0
#
# Default route to the rest of the internet.
route add default ppp0
#
# Cause all hosts on the 192.168.1/24 network to be masqueraded.
ipfwadm -F -a m -S 192.168.1.0/24 -D 0.0.0.0/0
```

If you are minimalist and a lazy typist, like me, and your masquerading host has only two interfaces (so that every packet being forwarded must be masqueraded), the following command will suffice:

```
root# /sbin/ipfwadm -F -a accept -m
```

You can get more information on the Linux IP Masquerade feature from the IP Masquerade Resource Page (see `http://www.hwy401.com/achau/ipmasq/`). Also, a *very* detailed document about masquerading is the "IP-Masquerade mini-HOWTO" (which also explains how to configure other OSs to run with a Linux masquerade server).

IP Transparent Proxy

IP transparent proxy is a feature that enables you to redirect servers or services destined for another machine to those services on this machine. Typically this would be useful where you have a Linux machine as a router and also provides a proxy server. You would redirect all connections destined for that service remotely to the local proxy server.

Kernel Compile Options:

```
Code maturity level options --->
    [*] Prompt for development and/or incomplete code/drivers
Networking options --->
    [*] Network firewalls
    ....
    [*] TCP/IP networking
    ....
    [*] IP: firewalling
    ....
    [*] IP: transparent proxy support (EXPERIMENTAL)
```

Configuration of the transparent proxy feature is performed using the *ipfwadm* command.

An example that might be useful is as follows:

```
root# ipfwadm -I -a accept -D 0/0 telnet -r 2323
```

This example will cause any connection attempts to port `telnet` (23) on any host to be redirected to port 2323 on this host. If you run a service on that port, you can forward telnet connections, log them, or do whatever fits your needs.

A more interesting example is redirecting all `http` traffic through a local cache. However, the protocol used by proxy servers is different from native `http`, where a client connects to `www.server.com:80` and asks for /path/page. When it connects to the local cache, it contacts proxy .local.domain:8080 and asks for www.server.com/path/page.

To filter an http request through the local proxy, you need to adapt the protocol by inserting a small server, called transproxy (you can find it on the World Wide Web). You can choose to run transproxy on port 8081, and issue this command:

```
root# ipfwadm -I -a accept -D 0/0 80 -r 8081
```

The transproxy program, then, will receive all connections meant to reach external servers and will pass them to the local proxy after fixing protocol differences.

IPv6

Just when you thought you were beginning to understand IP networking the rules get changed! IPv6 is the shorthand notation for version 6 of the Internet Protocol. IPv6 was developed primarily to overcome the concerns in the Internet community that there would soon be a shortage of IP addresses to allocate. IPv6 addresses are 16 bytes long (128 bits). IPv6 incorporates a number of other changes, mostly simplifications, that will make IPv6 networks more managable than IPv4 networks.

Linux already has a working, but not complete, IPv6 implementation in the 2.1.* series kernels.

If you wish to experiment with this next-generation Internet technology, or have a requirement for it, then you should read the IPv6-FAQ which is available from www.terra.net (see http://www.terra.net/ipv6/).

Mobile IP

The term "IP mobility" describes the ability of a host to move its network connection from one point on the Internet to another without changing its IP address or losing connectivity. Usually when an IP host changes its point of connectivity it must also change its IP address. IP Mobility overcomes this problem by allocating a fixed IP address to the mobile host and using IP encapsulation (tunneling) with automatic routing to ensure that datagrams destined for it are routed to the actual IP address it is currently using.

A project is underway to provide a complete set of IP mobility tools for Linux. The status of the project and tools may be obtained from the: Linux Mobile IP Home Page (see http://anchor.cs.binghamton.edu/~mobileip/).

Multicast

IP Multicast allows an arbitrary number of IP hosts on disparate IP networks to have IP datagrams simultaneously routed to them. This mechanism is exploited to provide Internet-wide "broadcast" material, such as audio and video transmissions and other novel applications.

Kernel Compile Options:

```
Networking options --->
  [*] TCP/IP networking
  ....
  [*] IP: multicasting
```

A suite of tools and some minor network configurations are required. Please check the Multicast-HOWTO (see `Multicast-HOWTO.html`) for more information on Multicast support in Linux.

NAT—Network Address Translation

The IP Network Address Translation facility is pretty much the standardized big brother of the Linux IP Masquerade facility. It is specified in some detail in RFC-1631 at your nearest RFC archive. NAT provides features that IP Masquerade does not that make it eminently more suitable for use in corporate firewall router designs and larger-scale installations.

An alpha implementation of NAT for Linux 2.0.29 kernel has been developed by Michael.Hasenstein <`Michael.Hasenstein@informatik.tu-chemnitz.de`>. Michael's documentation and implementation are available from: Linux IP Network Address Web Page (see `http://www.csn.tu-chemnitz.de/HyperNews/get/linux-ip-nat.html`).

Newer Linux 2.1.* kernels also include some NAT functionality in the routing algorithm.

Traffic Shaper—Changing Allowed Bandwidth

The traffic shaper is a driver that creates new interface devices, which are traffic-limited in a user-defined way. They rely on physical network devices for actual transmission and can be used as outgoing routed for network traffic.

The shaper was introduced in Linux-2.1.15 and was backported to Linux-2.0.36. (It appeared in `2.0.36-pre-patch-2` distributed by Alan Cox, the author of the shaper device and maintainer of Linux 2.)

The traffic shaper can only be compiled as a module and is configured by the *shapecfg* program with commands like the following:

```
shapecfg attach shaper0 eth1
shapecfg speed shaper0 64000
```

The shaper device can only control the bandwidth of outgoing traffic, as packets are transmitted via the shaper only according to the routing tables; therefore, a "route by source address" functionality could help in limiting the overall bandwidth of specific hosts using a Linux router.

Linux-2.1 already has support for such routing, if you need it for Linux 2 please check the patch by Mike McLagan at `ftp.invlogic.com`. Refer to `Documentationnetworking/shaper.txt` for further information about the shaper.

If you want to try out a (tentative) shaping for incoming packets, try out `rshaper-1.01` (or newer), from `ftp.systemy.it` (see `ftp://ftp.systemy.it/pub/develop`).

Routing in Linux-2.2

The latest versions of Linux-2.1 offer a lot of flexibility in routing policy. Unfortunately, you will have to wait for the next version of this HOWTO, or read the kernel sources.

Using Common PC Hardware

ISDN

The Integrated Services Digital Network (ISDN) is a series of standards that specify a general purpose switched digital data network. An ISDN "call" creates a synchronous point-to-point data service to the destination. ISDN is generally delivered on a high-speed link that is broken down into a number of discrete channels. There are two different types of channels: the "B Channels," which will actually carry the user data, and a single channel called the "D channel," which is used to send control information to the ISDN exchange to establish calls and other functions. In Australia for example, ISDN may be delivered on a 2Mbps link that is broken into 30 discrete 64kbps B channels with one 64kbps D channel. Any number of channels may be used at a time and in any combination. You could, for example, establish 30 separate calls to 30 different destinations at 64kbps each, or you could establish 15 calls to 15 different destinations at 128kbps each (two channels used per call), or just a small number of calls and leave the rest idle. A channel may be used for either incoming or outgoing calls. The original intention of ISDN was to allow telecommunications companies to provide a single data service that could deliver either telephone (via digitized voice) or data services to your home or business without requiring you to make any special configuration changes.

There are a few different ways to connect your computer to an ISDN service. One way is to use a device called a "Terminal Adaptor," which plugs into the Network Terminating Unit that your telecommunications carrier installed when you got your ISDN service and which presents a number of serial interfaces. One of those interfaces is used to enter commands to establish calls and configuration, and the others are actually connected to the network devices that will use the data circuits when they are established. Linux will work in this sort of configuration without modification; you just treat the port on the Terminal Adaptor like you would treat any other serial device. Another way, which is what the kernel ISDN support is designed for, allows you to install an ISDN card into your Linux machine and then has your Linux software handle the protocols and make the calls itself.

Kernel Compile Options:

```
ISDN subsystem --->
    <*> ISDN support
    [ ] Support synchronous PPP
    [ ] Support audio via ISDN
    < > ICN 2B and 4B support
    < > PCBIT-D support
    < > Teles/NICCY1016PC/Creatix support
```

The Linux implementation of ISDN supports a number of different types of internal ISDN cards. These are those listed in the kernel configuration options:

- ICN 2B and 4B
- Octal PCBIT-D
- Teles ISDN-cards and compatibles

Some of these cards require software to be downloaded to them to make them operational. There is a separate utility to do this with.

Full details on how to configure the Linux ISDN support are available from the `/usr/src/linux/Documentation/isdn/` directory, and a FAQ dedicated to *isdn4linux* is available at `www.lrz-muenchen.de` (see `http://www.lrz-muenchen.de/~ui161ab/www/isdn/`). (You can click the English flag to get an English version.)

A note about PPP. The PPP suite of protocols will operate over either asynchronous or synchronous serial lines. The commonly distributed PPP daemon for Linux "*pppd*" supports only asynchronous mode. If you wish to run the PPP protocols over your ISDN service you need a specially modified version. Details of where to find it are available in the documentation referred to above.

PLIP for Linux 2

PLIP device names are "`plip0`," "`plip1`," and "`plip2`."

Kernel Compile Options:

```
Network device support --->
  <*> PLIP (parallel port) support
```

PLIP (Parallel Line IP), is like SLIP, in that it is used for providing a *point-to-point* network connection between two machines. However, it is designed to use the parallel printer ports on your machine instead of the serial ports (a cabling diagram is included in the cabling diagram section later in this document). Because it is possible to transfer more than one bit at a time with a parallel port, it is possible to attain higher speeds with the PLIP interface than with a standard serial device. In addition, even the simplest of parallel ports, printer ports, can be used in lieu of you having to purchase comparatively expensive 16550AFN UARTs for your serial ports. PLIP uses a lot of CPU compared to a serial link and is most certainly not a good option if you can obtain some cheap Ethernet cards. But it will work when nothing else is available and will work quite well. You should expect a data transfer rate of about 20 kilobytes per second when a link is running well.

The PLIP device driver competes with the parallel device driver for the parallel port hardware. If you wish to use both drivers, then you should compile them both as modules to ensure that you are able to select which port you want to use for PLIP and which ports you want for the printer driver. Refer to the "Mudules mini-HOWTO" for more information on kernel module configuration.

Please note that some laptops use chipsets that will not work with PLIP because they do not allow some combinations of signals that PLIP relies on, that printers don't use.

The Linux PLIP interface is compatible with the *Crynwyr Packet Driver PLIP,* and this will mean that you can connect your Linux machine to a DOS machine running any other sort of tcp/ip software via PLIP.

In the 2.0.* series kernel the PLIP devices are mapped to i/o port and IRQ as follows:

device	i/o	IRQ
plip0	0x3bc	5
plip1	0x378	7
plip2	0x278	2

If your parallel ports don't match any of the above combinations, then you can change the IRQ of a port using the *ifconfig* command and the "`irq`" parameter (be sure to enable IRQs on your printer ports in your ROM BIOS if it supports this option). As an alternative, you can specify "`io=`" and "`irq=`" options on the *insmod* command line, if you use modules. For example:

```
root# insmod plip.o io=0x288 irq=5
```

PLIP operation is controlled by two timeouts, whose default values are probably ok in most cases. You will probably need to increase them if you have an especially slow computer, in which case the timers to increase are actually on the *other* computer. A program called *plipconfig* exists that allows you to change these timer settings without recompiling your kernel. It is supplied with many Linux distributions.

To configure a PLIP interface, you will need to invoke the following commands (or *add* them to your initialization scripts):

```
root# /sbin/ifconfig plip1 localplip pointopoint remoteplip
root# /sbin/route add remoteplip plip1
```

Here, the port being used is the one at I/O address 0x378; *localplip* amd *remoteplip* are the names or IP addresses used over the PLIP cable. I personally keep them in my `/etc/hosts` database:

```
# plip entries
192.168.3.1  localplip
192.168.3.2  remoteplip
```

The *pointopoint* parameter has the same meaning as for SLIP, in that it specifies the address of the machine at the other end of the link.

In almost all respects you can treat a PLIP interface as though it were a *SLIP* interface, except that neither *dip* nor *slattach* need be, nor can be, used.

Further information on PLIP may be obtained from the "PLIP mini-HOWTO."

PLIP for Linux-2.2

During development of the 2.1 kernel versions, support for the parallel port was changed to a better setup.

Kernel Compile Options:

```
General setup --->
  [*] Parallel port support
Network device support --->
  <*> PLIP (parallel port) support
```

The new code for PLIP behaves like the old one. Use the same *ifconfig* and *route* commands as in the previous section, but initialization of the device is different due to the advanced parallel port support.

The "first" PLIP device is always called "plip0," where first is the first device detected by the system, similar to what happens for Ethernet devices. The actual parallel port being used is one of the available ports, as shown in `/proc/parport`. For example, if you have only one parallel port, you'll only have a directory called `/proc/parport/0`.

If your kernel didn't detect the IRQ number used by your port, "`insmod plip`" will fail; in this case just write the right number to `/proc/parport/0/irq` and reinvoke *insmod*.

Complete information about parallel port management is available in the file `Documentation/parport.txt`, part of your kernel sources.

PPP

PPP devices names are "`ppp0`," "`ppp1`," etc. Devices are numbered sequentially with the first device configured receiving "`0`."

Kernel Compile Options:

```
Networking options --->
  <*> PPP (point-to-point) support
```

PPP configuration is covered in detail in the PPP-HOWTO (see `PPP-HOWTO.html`).

Maintaining a Permanent Connection to the Net with *pppd*

If you are fortunate enough to have a semi-permanent connection to the Net and would like to have your machine automatically redial your PPP connection if it is lost, then here is a simple trick to do so.

Configure PPP such that it can be started by the `root` user by issuing the command:

```
# pppd
```

Be sure that you have the "`-detach`" option configured in your `/etc/ppp/options` file. Then insert the following line into your `/etc/inittab` file, down with the *getty* definitions:

```
pd:23:respawn:/usr/sbin/pppd
```

This will cause the *init* program to spawn and monitor the *pppd* program and automatically restart it if it dies.

slip Client

slip devices are named "`sl0`," "`sl1`," etc. with the first device configured being assigned "`0`" and the rest incrementing sequentially as they are configured.

Kernel Compile Options:

```
Network device support --->
  [*] Network device support
  <*> SLIP (serial line) support
  [ ] CSLIP compressed headers
  [ ] Keepalive and linefill
  [ ] Six bit SLIP encapsulation
```

slip (Serial Line Internet Protocol) allows you to use TCP/IP over a serial line, be that a phone line with a dial-up modem, or a leased line of some sort. Of course to use slip you need access to a *slip-server* in your area. Many universities and businesses provide slip access all over the world.

slip uses the serial ports on your machine to carry IP datagrams. To do this it must take control of the serial device. slip device names are named *sl0*, *sl1*, etc. How do these correspond to your serial devices? The networking code uses what is called an *ioctl* (i/o control) call to change the serial devices into slip devices. There are two programs supplied that can do this: *dip* and *slattach*

dip

dip (Dial-up IP) is a smart program that is able to set the speed of the serial device; command your modem to dial the remote end of the link; automatically log you into the remote server; search for messages sent to you by the server and extract information for them, such as your IP address; and perform the *ioctl* necessary to switch your serial port into SLIP mode. *dip* has a powerful scripting ability and you can exploit this to automate your logon procedure.

You can find it at: MetaLab.unc.edu (see `ftp://MetaLab.unc.edu/pub/Linux/system/Network/serial/dip/dip337o-uri.tgz`).

To install it, try the following:

```
user% tar xvzf dip337o-uri.tgz
user% cd dip-3.3.7o
user% vi Makefile
root# make install
```

The `Makefile` assumes the existence of a group called *uucp*, but you might like to change this to either *dip* or *SLIP*, depending on your configuration.

slattach

slattach, as contrasted with *dip*, is a very simple program, that is very easy to use, but it does not have the sophistication of *dip*. It does not have the scripting ability; all it does is configure your serial device as a SLIP device. It assumes you have all the information you need and the serial line is established before you invoke it. *slattach* is ideal to use where you have a permanent connection to your server, such as a physical cable, or a leased line.

When Do I Use Which?

You would use *dip* when your link to the machine that is your SLIP server is a dial-up modem, or some other temporary link. You would use *slattach* when you have a leased line, perhaps a cable, between your machine and the server and there is no special action needed to get the link working. See section "Permanent SLIP connection" for more information.

Configuring SLIP is much like configuring an Ethernet interface (read section "Configuring an Ethernet device" above). However there are a few key differences.

First of all, SLIP links are unlike Ethernet networks in that there are only two hosts on the network, one at each end of the link. Unlike an

Ethernet which is available for use as soon are you are cabled, with SLIP, depending on the type of link you have, you may have to initialize your network connection in some special way.

If you are using *dip*, then this would not normally be done at boot time, but at some time later, when you were ready to use the link. It is possible to automate this procedure. If you are using *slattach* then you will probably want to add a section to your *rc.inet1* file. This will be described soon.

There are two major types of SLIP servers: Dynamic IP address servers and static IP address servers. Almost every SLIP server will prompt you to log in using a username and password when dialing in. *dip* can handle logging you in automatically.

Static SLIP Server with a Dial-Up Line and dip

A static SLIP server is one in which you have been supplied an IP address that is exclusively yours. Each time you connect to the server, you will configure your SLIP port with that address. The static SLIP server will answer your modem call, possibly prompt you for a username and password, and then route any datagrams destined for your address to you via that connection. If you have a static server, then you may want to put entries for your hostname and IP address (since you know what it will be) into your `/etc/hosts`. You should also configure some other files such as: `rc.inet2`, `host.conf`, `resolv.conf`, `/etc/HOSTNAME` and `rc.local`. Remember that when configuring `rc.inet1`, you don't need to add any special commands for your SLIP connection since it is *dip* that does all of the hard work for you in configuring your interface. You will need to give *dip* the appropriate information, and it will configure the interface for you after commanding the modem to establish the call and logging you into your SLIP server.

If this is how your SLIP server works then you can move to the "Using dip" section to learn how to configure *dip* appropriately.

Dynamic SLIP Server with a Dial-Up Line and dip.

A *dynamic* SLIP server is one which allocates you an IP address randomly, from a pool of addresses, each time you log on. This means that there is no guarantee that you will have any particular address each time, and that your address may well be used by someone else after you have logged off. The network administrator who configured the SLIP server will have assigned a pool of address for the SLIP server to use. When the server receives a new incoming call, it finds the first unused address, guides the caller through the login process, and then prints a welcome message that contains the IP address it has allocated. It will proceed to use that IP address for the duration of that call.

Configuring for this type of server is similar to configuring for a static server, except that you must add a step where you obtain the IP address that the server has allocated for you and configure your SLIP device with that.

Again, *dip* does the hard work and new versions are smart enough to not only log you in, but to also be able to automatically read the IP address printed in the welcome message and store it so that you can have it configure your SLIP device with it.

If this is how your SLIP server works then you can move to the, "Using dip" section to learn how to configure *dip* appropriately.

Using dip

As explained earlier, *dip* is a powerful program that can simplify and automate the process of dialing into the SLIP server, logging you in, starting the connection, and configuring your SLIP devices with the appropriate *ifconfig* and *route* commands.

Essentially, to use *dip* you'll write a "dip script," which is basically a list of commands that tell *dip* how to perform each of the actions you want it to perform. See `sample.dip` that comes supplied with *dip* to get an idea of how it works. *dip* is quite a powerful program, with many options. Instead of going into all of them here, you should look at the *man* page, README, and sample files that will have come with your version of *dip*.

You may notice that the `sample.dip` script assumes that you're using a static SLIP server, so you know what your IP address is beforehand. For dynamic SLIP servers, the newer versions of *dip* include a command you can use to automatically read and configure your SLIP device with the IP address that the dynamic server allocates for you. The following sample is a modified version of the `sample.dip` that came supplied with *dip337j-uri.tgz* and is probably a good starting point for you. You might like to save it as `/etc/dipscript` and edit it to suit your configuration:

```
#
# sample.dip  Dialup IP connection support program.
#
#        This file (should show) shows how to use the DIP
#    This file should work for Annex type dynamic servers, if you
#    use a static address server then use the sample.dip file that
```

```
#    comes as part of the dip337-uri.tgz package.
#
#
# Version:   @(#)sample.dip 1.40  07/20/93
#
# Author:    Fred N. van Kempen, <waltje@uWalt.NL.Mugnet.ORG>
#

main:
# Next, set up the other side's name and address.
# My dialin machine is called 'xs4all.hacktic.nl' (== 193.78.33.42)
get $remote xs4all.hacktic.nl
# Set netmask on sl0 to 255.255.255.0
netmask 255.255.255.0
# Set the desired serial port and speed.
port cua02
speed 38400

# Reset the modem and terminal line.
# This seems to cause trouble for some people!
reset

# Note! "Standard" pre-defined "errlevel" values:
# 0 - OK
# 1 - CONNECT
# 2 - ERROR
#
# You can change those grep'ping for "addchat()" in *.c...

# Prepare for dialing.
send ATQ0V1E1X4\r
wait OK 2
if $errlvl != 0 goto modem_trouble
dial 555-1234567
if $errlvl != 1 goto modem_trouble

# We are connected. Login to the system.
login:
sleep 2
wait ogin: 20
if $errlvl != 0 goto login_trouble
send MYLOGIN\n
wait ord: 20
if $errlvl != 0 goto password_error
send MYPASSWD\n
loggedin:
```

```
# We are now logged in.
wait SOMEPROMPT 30
if $errlvl != 0 goto prompt_error

# Command the server into SLIP mode
send SLIP\n
wait SLIP 30
if $errlvl != 0 goto prompt_error

# Get and Set your IP address from the server.
#  Here we assume that after commanding the SLIP server into SLIP
#  mode that it prints your IP address
get $locip remote 30
if $errlvl != 0 goto prompt_error

# Set up the SLIP operating parameters.
get $mtu 296
# Ensure "route add -net default xs4all.hacktic.nl" will be done
default

# Say hello and fire up!
done:
print CONNECTED $locip ---> $rmtip
mode CSLIP
goto exit

prompt_error:
print TIME-OUT waiting for sliplogin to fire up...
goto error

login_trouble:
print Trouble waiting for the Login: prompt...
goto error

password:error:
print Trouble waiting for the Password: prompt...
goto error

modem_trouble:
print Trouble occurred with the modem...
error:
print CONNECT FAILED to $remote
quit

exit:
exit
```

The above example assumes you are calling a *dynamic* SLIP server. If you are calling a *static* SLIP server, then the `sample.dip` file that comes with *dip337j-uri.tgz* should work for you.

When *dip* is given the *get local* command—it searches the incoming text from the remote end for a string that looks like an IP address—i.e., string numbers separated by "." characters. This modification was put in place specifically for *dynamic* SLIP servers, so that the process of reading the IP address granted by the server could be automated.

The example above will automatically create a default route via your SLIP link, if this is not what you want. Instead you should remove the *default* command from the script.

After this script has finished running, if you do an *ifconfig* command, you will see that you have a device *sl0*. This is your SLIP device. Should you need to, you can modify its configuration manually, after the *dip* command has finished, using the *ifconfig* and *route* commands. Please note that *dip* allows you to select a number of different protocols to use with the `mode` command. The most common example is *cSLIP* for SLIP with compression. Please note that both ends of the link must agree, so you should ensure that whatever you select agrees with what your server is set to. The above example is fairly robust and should cope with most errors. Please refer to the *dip* man page for more information. Naturally you could, for example, code the script to do such things as redial the server if it doesn't get a connection within a prescribed period of time, or even try a series of servers if you have access to more than one.

Permanent SLIP Connection Using a Leased Line and slattach

If you have a cable between two machines, or are fortunate enough to have a leased line or some other permanent serial connection between your machine and another, then you don't need to go to all the trouble of using *dip* to set up your serial link. *slattach* is a very simple-to-use utility that will allow you just enough functionality to configure your connection. Since your connection will be a permanent one, you will want to add some commands to your `rc.inet1` file. In essence all you need to do for a permanent connection is ensure that you configure the serial device to the correct speed and switch the serial device into SLIP mode. *slattach* allows you to do this with one command. Add the following to your `rc.inet1` file:

```
#
# Attach a leased line static SLIP connection
#
```

```
# configure /dev/cua0 for 19.2kbps and cslip
/sbin/slattach -p cslip -s 19200 /dev/cua0 &
/sbin/ifconfig sl0 IPA.IPA.IPA.IPA pointopoint\
      IPR.IPR.IPR.IPR up
#
# End static SLIP.
```

Where:

IPA.IPA.IPA.IPA represents your IP address.

IPR.IPR.IPR.IPR represents the IP address of the remote end.

slattach allocates the first unallocated SLIP device to the serial device specified. *slattach* starts with *sl0*. Therefore the first *slattach* command attaches SLIP device *sl0* to the serial device specified, and *sl1* the next time, etc.

slattach allows you to configure a number of different protocols with the `-p` argument. In your case you will use either *SLIP* or *cSLIP*, depending on whether you want to use compression or not. Note: both ends must agree on whether you want compression or not.

SLIP Server

If you have a machine that is perhaps network connected, that you'd like other people be able to dial into and provide network services, then you will need to configure your machine as a server. If you want to use SLIP as the serial line protocol, then currently you have three options as to how to configure your Linux machine as a SLIP server. My preference would be to use the first presented, *sliplogin*, as it seems the easiest to configure and understand. But I will present a summary of each, so you can make your own decision.

SLIP Server Using *sliplogin*

sliplogin is a program that you can use in place of the normal login shell for SLIP users that converts the terminal line into a SLIP line. It allows you to configure your Linux machine as either a *static address server*, where users get the same address everytime they call in, or a *dynamic address server*, where users get an address allocated for them that will not necessarily be the same as the last time they called.

The caller will log in as per the standard login process, entering their username and password, but instead of being presented with a shell after their login, *sliplogin* is executed. The *sliplogin* then searches its configuration file (`/etc/slip.hosts`) for an entry with a login name that matches that of the caller. If it locates one, it configures the line as an 8-bit clean line, and uses an *ioctl* call to convert the line discipline to SLIP. When this process is complete, the last stage of configuration takes place, where *sliplogin* invokes a shell script that configures the SLIP interface with the relevant IP address, netmask, and sets appropriate routing in place. This script is usually called `/etc/slip.login`, but in a similar manner to *getty*, if you have certain callers who require special initialization, then you can create configuration scripts called `/etc/slip.login.loginname` that will be run instead of the default specifically for them.

There are either three or four files that you need to configure to get *sliplogin* working for you. I will detail how and where to get the software and how each is configured in detail. The files are:

- `/etc/passwd`, for the dial-in user accounts.
- `/etc/slip.hosts`, to contain the information unique to each dial-in user.
- `/etc/slip.login`, which manages the configuration of the routing that needs to be performed for the user.
- `/etc/slip.tty`, which is required only if you are configuring your server for *dynamic address allocation* and contains a table of addresses to allocate
- `/etc/slip.logout`, which contains commands to clean up after the user has hung up or logged out.

Where to Get *sliplogin* You may already have the *sliplogin* package installed as part of your distribution, if not then *sliplogin* can be obtained from: `MetaLab.unc.edu` (see `ftp://MetaLab.unc.edu/pub/linux/system/Network/serial/sliplogin-2.1.1.tar.gz`). The tar file contains both source, precompiled binaries, and a *man* page.

To ensure that only authorized users will be able to run *sliplogin* program, you should add an entry to your `/etc/group` file similar to the following:

```
..
slip::13:radio,fred
..
```

When you install the *sliplogin* package, the `Makefile` will change the group ownership of the *sliplogin* program to `slip`, and this will mean that only users who belong to that group will be able to execute it. The example above will allow only users `radio` and `fred` to execute *sliplogin*.

To install the binaries into your `/sbin` directory and the *man* page into section 8, do the following:

```
# cd /usr/src
# gzip -dc .../sliplogin-2.1.1.tar.gz | tar xvf -
# cd sliplogin-2.1.1
# <..edit the Makefile if you don't use shadow passwords..>
# make install
```

If you want to recompile the binaries before installation, add a `make clean` before the `make install`. If you want to install the binaries somewhere else, you will need to edit the `Makefile` *install* rule.

Please read the README files that come with the package for more information.

Configuring /etc/passwd for SLIP Hosts Normally you would create some special logins for SLIP callers in your `/etc/passwd` file. A convention commonly followed is to use the *hostname* of the calling host with a capital "S" prefixing it. So, for example, if the calling host is called `radio` then you could create a `/etc/passwd` entry that looked like:

```
Sradio:FvKurok73:1427:1:radio SLIP login:/tmp:/sbin/sliplogin
```

It doesn't really matter what the account is called, so long as it is meaningful to you.

Note: the caller doesn't need any special home directory, as they will not be presented with a shell from this machine. So `/tmp` is a good choice. Also note that *sliplogin* is used in place of the normal login shell.

Configuring /etc/slip.hosts The `/etc/slip.hosts` file is the file that *sliplogin* searches for entries matching the login name to obtain configuration details for this caller. It is this file where you specify the IP address and netmask that will be assigned to the caller and configured for their use. Sample entries for two hosts, one a static configuration for host `radio`, and another, a dynamic configuration for user host `albert`, might look like:

```
#
Sradio  44.136.8.99  44.136.8.100 255.255.255.0 normal     -1
Salbert 44.136.8.99  DYNAMIC      255.255.255.0 compressed 60
#
```

The /etc/slip.hosts file entries are:

1. The login name of the caller.
2. IP address of the server machine, i.e., this machine.
3. IP address that the caller will be assigned. If this field is coded DYNAMIC, then an IP address will be allocated based on the information contained in your /etc/slip.tty file discussed later. *Note:* you must be using at least version 1.3 of *sliplogin* for this to work.
4. The netmask assigned to the calling machine in dotted decimal notation, e.g., 255.255.255.0 for a Class C network mask.
5. The SLIP mode setting, which allows you to enable/disable compression and SLIP other features. Allowable values here are "normal" or "compressed."
6. A timeout parameter that specifies how long the line can remain idle (no datagrams received) before the line is automatically disconnected. A negative value disables this feature.
7. Optional arguments.

Note: You can use either hostnames or IP addresses in dotted decimal notation for fields 2 and 3. If you use hostnames then those hosts must be resolvable. That is, your machine must be able to locate an ip address for those hostnames; otherwise the script will fail when it is called. You can test this by trying to telnet to the hostname. If you get the *"Trying nnn.nnn.nnn..."* message, then your machine has been able to find an IP address for that name. If you get the message *"Unknown host,"* then it has not. If not, either use IP addresses in dotted decimal notation, or fix up your name resolver configuration (see the "Name Resolution" section).

The most common SLIP modes are:

normal to enable normal uncompressed SLIP.

compressed to enable van Jacobsen header compression (cSLIP).

Naturally these are mutually exclusive; you can use one or the other. For more information on the other options available, refer to the *man* pages.

Configuring the /etc/slip.login File After *sliplogin* has searched the /etc/slip.hosts and found a matching entry, it will attempt to execute the /etc/slip.login file to actually configure the SLIP interface with its IP address and netmask. The sample /etc/slip.login file supplied with the *sliplogin* package looks like this:

```
#!/bin/sh -
#
#    @(#)slip.login 5.1 (Berkeley) 7/1/90
#
# generic login file for a SLIP line. sliplogin invokes this
# with the parameters:
#   $1     $2     $3  $4, $5, $6 ...
#  SLIPunit ttyspeed  pid  the arguments from the slip.host
#  entry
#
/sbin/ifconfig $1 $5 pointopoint $6 mtu 1500 -trailers up
/sbin/route add $6
arp -s $6 <hw_addr> pub
exit 0
#
```

You will note that this script simply uses the *ifconfig* and *route* commands to configure the SLIP device with its IP address, remote IP address and netmask, and creates a route for the remote address via the SLIP device. Just the same as you would if you were using the *slattach* command.

Note also the use of *Proxy ARP* to ensure that other hosts on the same Ethernet as the server machine will know how to reach the dial-in host. The <hw_addr> field should be the hardware address of the Ethernet card in the machine. If your server machine isn't on an Ethernet network, then you can leave this line out completely.

Configuring the /etc/slip.logout File When the call drops out, you want to ensure that the serial device is restored to its normal state so that future callers will be able to log in correctly. This is achieved with the use of the /etc/slip.logout file. It is quite simple in format and is called with the same argument as the /etc/slip.login file.

```
#!/bin/sh -
#
#        slip.logout
#
/sbin/ifconfig $1 down
arp -d $6
exit 0
#
```

All it does is "down" the interface, which will delete the manual route previously created. It also uses the *arp* command to delete any proxy arp put in place. Again, you don't need the *arp* command in the script if your server machine does not have an Ethernet port.

Configuring the /etc/slip.tty File If you are using dynamic IP address allocation (i.e., have any hosts configured with the DYNAMIC keyword in the `/etc/slip.hosts` file), then you must configure the `/etc/slip.tty` file to list which addresses are assigned to which port. You only need this file if you wish your server to dynamically allocate addresses to users.

The file is a table that lists the *tty* devices that will support dial-in SLIP connections and the IP address that should be assigned to users who call in on that port. Its format is as follows:

```
# slip.tty  tty -> IP address mappings for dynamic SLIP
# format: /dev/tty?? xxx.xxx.xxx.xxx
#
/dev/ttyS0   192.168.0.100
/dev/ttyS1   192.168.0.101
#
```

What this table says is that callers dialing in on port `/dev/ttyS0` who have their remote address field in the `/etc/slip.hosts` file set to DYNAMIC will be assigned an address of `192.168.0.100`.

In this way you need only allocate one address per port for all users who do not require a dedicated address for themselves. This helps you keep the number of addresses you need down to a minimum to avoid wastage.

Part iii

SLIP Server Using *dip*

Let me start by saying that some of the information below came from the *dip* man pages, where how to run Linux as a SLIP server is briefly documented. Please also beware that the following has been based on the *dip337o-uri.tgz* package and probably will not apply to other versions of *dip*. *dip* has an input mode of operation, where it automatically locates an entry for the user who invoked it and configures the serial line as a SLIP link according to information it finds in the `/etc/diphosts` file. This input mode of operation is activated by invoking *dip* as *diplogin*. This therefore is how you use *dip* as a SLIP server, by creating special accounts where *diplogin* is used as the login shell. The first thing you will need to do is to make a symbolic link as follows:

```
# ln -sf /usr/sbin/dip /usr/sbin/diplogin
```

You then need to add entries to both your `/etc/passwd` and your `/etc/diphosts` files. The entries you need to make are formatted as follows: To configure Linux as a SLIP server with *dip*, you need to create some special SLIP accounts for users, where *dip* (in input mode) is used as the login shell. A suggested convention is to have all SLIP accounts begin with a capital "S," e.g. "Sfredm." A sample `/etc/passwd` entry for a SLIP user looks like:

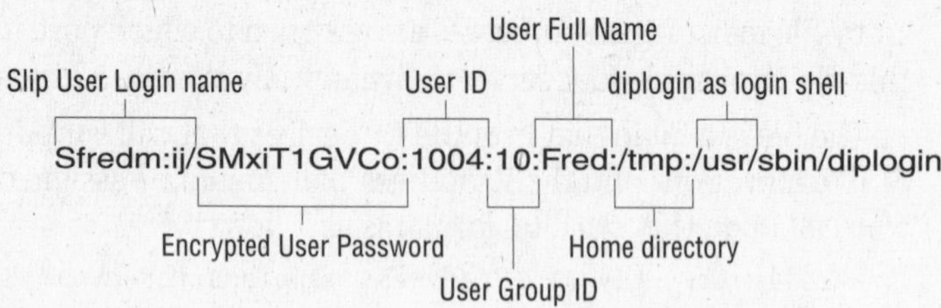

After the user logs in, the *login* program, if it finds and verifies the user ok, will execute the *diplogin* command. *dip*, when invoked as *diplogin*, knows that it should automatically assume that it is being used a login shell. When it is started as *diplogin* the first thing it does is use the *getuid()* function call to get the user ID of whomever has invoked it. It then searches the `/etc/diphosts` file for the first entry that matches either the user ID or the name of the `tty` device that the call has come in on and configures itself appropriately. By judicious decision as to whether to give a user an entry in the `diphosts` file, or whether to let the user be given the default configuration you can build your server in such a way that you can have a mix of static and dynamically assigned address users. *dip* will automatically add a "Proxy-ARP" entry if invoked in input mode, so you do not need to worry about manually adding such entries.

Configuring /etc/diphosts `/etc/diphosts` is used by *dip* to lookup preset configurations for remote hosts. These remote hosts might be users dialing into your Linux machine, or they might be for machines that you dial into with your Linux machine. The general format for `/etc/diphosts` is as follows:

```
..
Suwalt::145.71.34.1:145.71.34.2:255.255.255.0:SLIP uwalt:CSLIP,1006
ttyS1::145.71.34.3:145.71.34.2:255.255.255.0:Dynamic ttyS1:CSLIP,296
..
```

The fields are:

1. `login name`: as returned by getpwuid(getuid()) or tty name.
2. `unused`: compat. with passwd.
3. `Remote Address`: IP address of the calling host, either numeric or by name.
4. `Local Address`: IP address of this machine, again numeric or by name.
5. `Netmask`: in dotted decimal notation.
6. `Comment field`: put whatever you want here.
7. `protocol`: SLIP, CSLIP, etc.
8. MTU: decimal number.

An example `/etc/net/diphosts` entry for a remote SLIP user might be:

```
Sfredm::145.71.34.1:145.71.34.2:255.255.255.0:SLIP uwalt:SLIP,296
```

which specifies a SLIP link with remote address of 145.71.34.1 and MTU of 296, or:

```
Sfredm::145.71.34.1:145.71.34.2:255.255.255.0:SLIP uwalt:CSLIP,1006
```

which specifies a cSLIP-capable link with remote address 145.71.34.1 and MTU of 1006.

Therefore, all users who you wish to be allowed a statically allocated dial-up IP access should have an entry in the `/etc/diphosts`. If you want users who call a particular port to have their details dynamically allocated, then you must have an entry for the `tty` device, and you must not configure a user-based entry. You should remember to configure at least one entry for each `tty` device that your dial-up users use, to ensure that a suitable configuration is available for them, regardless of which modem they call in on.

When a user logs in they will receive a normal login and password prompt, at which they should enter their SLIP-login user ID and password. If these verify ok, then the user will see no special messages and they should just change into SLIP mode at their end. The user should then be able to connect ok and be configured with the relevant parameters from the `diphosts` file.

SLIP Server Using the dSLIP Package

Matt Dillon <dillon@apollo.west.oic.com> has written a package that does not only dial-in but also dials-out SLIP. Matt's package is a combination of small programs and scripts that manage your connections for you. You will need to have *tcsh* installed, as at least one of the scripts requires it. Matt supplies a binary copy of the *expect* utility, as it too is needed by one of the scripts. You will most likely need some experience with *expect* to get this package working to your liking, but don't let that put you off.

Matt has written a good set of installation instructions in the README file, so I won't bother repeating them.

You can get the *dSLIP* package from its home site at: *apollo.west.oic.com*

```
/pub/linux/dillon_src/dSLIP203.tgz
```

or from: MetaLab.unc.edu

```
/pub/Linux/system/Network/serial/dSLIP203.tgz
```

Read the README file and create the `/etc/passwd` and `/etc/group` entries *before* doing a `make install`.

OTHER NETWORK TECHNOLOGIES

The following subsections are specific to particular network technologies. The information contained in these sections does not necessarily apply to any other type of network technology. The topics are sorted alphabetically.

ARCNet

ARCNet device names are "`arc0e`," "`arc1e`," "`arc2e`," etc., or "`arc0s`," "`arc1s`," "`arc2s`," etc. The first card detected by the kernel is assigned "`arc0e`" or "`arc0s`" and the rest are assigned sequentially in the order they are detected. The letter at the end signifies whether you've selected Ethernet encapsulation packet format or RFC1051 packet format.

Kernel Compile Options:

```
Network device support --->
  [*] Network device support
  <*> ARCnet support
  [ ]  Enable arc0e (ARCnet "Ether-Encap" packet format)
  [ ]  Enable arc0s (ARCnet RFC1051 packet format)
```

Once you have your kernel properly built to support your Ethernet card then configuration of the card is easy.

Typically you would use something like:

```
root# ifconfig arc0e 192.168.0.1 netmask 255.255.255.0 up
root# route add -net 192.168.0.0 netmask 255.255.255.0 arc0e
```

Please refer to the `/usr/src/linux/Documentation/networking/arcnet.txt` and `/usr/src/linux/Documentation/networking/arcnet-hardware.txt` files for further information.

ARCNet support was developed by Avery Pennarun <apenwarr@foxnet.net>.

Appletalk (AF_APPLETALK)

The Appletalk support has no special device names, as it uses existing network devices.

Kernel Compile Options:

```
Networking options --->
  <*> Appletalk DDP
```

Appletalk support allows your Linux machine to interwork with Apple networks. An important use for this is to share resources such as printers and disks between both your Linux and Apple computers. Additional software is required. This is called *netatalk*. Wesley Craig <netatalk@umich.edu> represents a team called the "Research Systems Unix Group" at the University of Michigan, and they have produced the *netatalk* package which provides software that implements the Appletalk protocol stack and some useful utilities. The *netatalk* package will either have been supplied with your Linux distribution, or you will have to FTP it from its home site at the University of Michigan (see `ftp://terminator.rs.itd.umich.edu/unix/netatalk/`).

To build and install the package, do something like:

```
user% tar xvfz .../netatalk-1.4b2.tar.Z
user% make
root# make install
```

You may want to edit the "Makefile" before calling *make* to actually compile the software. Specifically, you might want to change the DESTDIR variable which defines where the files will be installed later. The default of /usr/local/atalk is fairly safe.

Configuring the Appletalk Software

The first thing you need to do to make it all work is to ensure that the appropriate entries in the `/etc/services` file are present. The entries you need are:

```
rtmp  1/ddp  # Routing Table Maintenance Protocol
nbp   2/ddp  # Name Binding Protocol
echo  4/ddp  # AppleTalk Echo Protocol
zip   6/ddp  # Zone Information Protocol
```

The next step is to create the Appletalk configuration files in the `/usr/local/atalk/etc` directory (or wherever you installed the package).

The first file to create is the `/usr/local/atalk/etc/atalkd.conf` file. Initially this file needs only one line that gives the name of the network device that supports the network that your Apple machines are on:

```
eth0
```

The Appletalk daemon program will add extra details after it is run.

Exporting a Linux Filesystems via Appletalk

You can export filesystems from your Linux machine to the network so that Apple machine on the network can share them.

To do this you must configure the `/usr/local/atalk/etc/AppleVolumes.system` file. There is another configuration file called `/usr/local/atalk/etc/AppleVolumes.default` which has exactly the same format and describes which filesystems users connecting with guest privileges will receive.

Full details on how to configure these files and what the various options are can be found in the *afpd* man page.

A simple example might look like:

```
/tmp Scratch
/home/ftp/pub "Public Area"
```

which would export your `/tmp` filesystem as AppleShare Volume "Scratch" and your FTP public directory as AppleShare Volume "Public Area." The volume names are not mandatory. The daemon will choose some for you, but it won't hurt to specify them anyway.

Sharing Your Linux Printer Across Appletalk

You can share your Linux printer with your Apple machines quite simply. You need to run the *papd* program, which is the Appletalk Printer Access

Protocol Daemon. When you run this program it will accept requests from your Apple machines and spool the print job to your local line printer daemon for printing.

You need to edit the `/usr/local/atalk/etc/papd.conf` file to configure the daemon. The syntax of this file is the same as that of your usual `/etc/printcap` file. The name you give to the definition is registered with the Appletalk naming protocol, NBP.

A sample configuration might look like:

```
TricWriter:\
    :pr=lp:op=cg:
```

which would make a printer named "TricWriter" available to your Appletalk network, and all accepted jobs would be printed to the Linux printer "`lp`" (as defined in the `/etc/printcap` file) using *lpd*. The entry "`op=cg`" says that the Linux user "`cg`" is the operator of the printer.

Starting the Appletalk Software

Ok, you should now be ready to test this basic configuration. There is an *rc.atalk* file supplied with the *netatalk* package that should work ok for you, so all you should have to do is:

```
root# /usr/local/atalk/etc/rc.atalk
```

and all should startup and run ok. You should see no error messages and the software will send messages to the console indicating each stage as it starts.

Testing the Appletalk Software

To test that the software is functioning properly, go to one of your Apple machines, pull down the Apple menu, select the Chooser, click AppleShare, and your Linux box should appear.

Caveats of the Appletalk Software

- You may need to start the Appletalk support before you configure your IP network. If you have problems starting the Appletalk programs, or if after you start them you have trouble with your IP network, then try starting the Appletalk software before you run your `/etc/rc.d/rc.inet1` file.
- The *afpd* (Apple Filing Protocol Daemon) severely messes up your hard disk. Below the mount points it creates a couple of directories

called "AppleDesktop" and Network Trash Folder. Then, for each directory you access it will create a .AppleDouble below it so it can store resource forks, etc. So think twice before exporting /. You will have a great time cleaning up afterwards.

- The *afpd* program expects clear text passwords from the Macs. Security could be a problem, so be very careful when you run this daemon on a machine connected to the Internet. You have yourself to blame if somebody nasty does something bad.
- The existing diagnostic tools such as *netstat* and *ifconfig* don't support Appletalk. The raw information is available in the /proc/net/ directory if you need it.

More Information

For a much more detailed description of how to configure Appletalk for Linux, refer to Anders Brownworth *Linux Netatalk-HOWTO* page at thehamptons.com (see http://thehamptons.com/anders/netatalk/).

ATM

Werner Almesberger <werner.almesberger@lrc.di.epfl.ch> is managing a project to provide Asynchronous Transfer Mode support for Linux. Current information on the status of the project may be obtained from lrcwww.epfl.ch (see http://lrcwww.epfl.ch/linux-atm/).

AX25 (AF_AX25)

AX.25 device names are "sl0," "sl1," etc. in 2.0.* kernels or "ax0," "ax1," etc. in 2.1.* kernels.

Kernel Compile Options:

```
Networking options --->
  [*] Amateur Radio AX.25 Level 2
```

The AX25, Netrom and, Rose protocols are covered by the AX25-HOWTO (see http://metalab.unc.edu/LAP/). These protocols are used by Amateur Radio Operators worldwide in packet radio experimentation.

Most of the work for implementation of these protocols has been done by Jonathan Naylor <jsn@cs.nott.ac.uk>.

DECNet

Support for DECNet is currently being worked on. You should expect it to appear in a late `2.1.*` kernel.

FDDI

FDDI device names are "`fddi0`," "`fddi1`," "`fddi2`," etc. The first card detected by the kernel is assigned "`fddi0`," and the rest are assigned sequentially in the order they are detected.

Larry Stefani <`lstefani@ultranet.com`> has developed a driver for the Digital Equipment Corporation FDDI EISA and PCI cards.

Kernel Compile Options:

```
Network device support --->
  [*] FDDI driver support
  [*] Digital DEFEA and DEFPA adapter support
```

When you have your kernel built to support the FDDI driver and installed, configuration of the FDDI interface is almost identical to that of an Ethernet interface. You just specify the appropriate FDDI interface name in the *ifconfig* and *route* commands.

Frame Relay

The Frame Relay device names are "`dlci00`," "`dlci01`," etc. for the DLCI encapsulation devices, and "`sdla0`," "`sdla1`," etc. for the FRAD(s).

Frame Relay is a new networking technology that is designed to suit data communications traffic that is of a "bursty" or intermittent nature. You connect to a Frame Relay network using a Frame Relay Access Device (FRAD). The Linux Frame Relay supports IP over Frame Relay as described in RFC-1490.

Kernel Compile Options:

```
Network device support --->
  <*> Frame relay DLCI support (EXPERIMENTAL)
  (24)  Max open DLCI
  (8)  Max DLCI per device
  <*>  SDLA (Sangoma S502/S508) support
```

Mike McLagan <`mike.mclagan@linux.org`> developed the Frame Relay support and configuration tools.

Currently the only FRADs supported are the Sangoma Technologies (see `http://www.sangoma.com/`) S502A, S502E and S508.

To configure the FRAD and DLCI devices after you have rebuilt your kernel, you will need the Frame Relay configuration tools. These are available from `ftp.invlogic.com` (see `ftp://ftp.invlogic.com/pub/linux/fr/frad-0.15.tgz`). Compiling and installing the tools is straightforward, but the lack of a top level Makefile makes it a fairly manual process:

```
user% tar xvfz .../frad-0.15.tgz
user% cd frad-0.15
user% for i in common dlci frad; make -C $i clean; make -C $i; done
root# mkdir /etc/frad
root# install -m 644 -o root -g root bin/*.sfm /etc/frad
root# install -m 700 -o root -g root frad/fradcfg /sbin
rppt# install -m 700 -o root -g root dlci/dlcicfg /sbin
```

Note that the previous commands use *sh* syntax. If you use a *csh* flavor instead (like *tcsh*), the *for* loop will look different.

After installing the tools you need to create an `/etc/frad/router.conf` file, you can use this template, which is a modified version of one of the example files:

```
# /etc/frad/router.conf
# This is a template configuration for frame relay.
# All tags are included. The default values are based on the code
# supplied with the DOS drivers for the Sangoma S502A card.
#
# A '#' anywhere in a line constitutes a comment
# Blanks are ignored (you can indent with tabs too)
# Unknown [] entries and unknown keys are ignored
#

[Devices]
Count=1          # number of devices to configure
Dev_1=sdla0      # the name of a device
#Dev_2=sdla1     # the name of a device

# Specified here, these are applied to all devices and can be
# overridden for each individual board.
#
Access=CPE
Clock=Internal
KBaud=64
Flags=TX
#
```

```
# MTU=1500        # Maximum transmit IFrame length, default is 4096
# T391=10         # T391 value  5 - 30, default is 10
# T392=15         # T392 value  5 - 30, default is 15
# N391=6          # N391 value  1 - 255, default is 6
# N392=3          # N392 value  1 - 10, default is 3
# N393=4          # N393 value  1 - 10, default is 4

# Specified here, these set the defaults for all boards
# CIRfwd=16        # CIR forward  1 - 64
# Bc_fwd=16        # Bc forward  1 - 512
# Be_fwd=0         # Be forward  0 - 511
# CIRbak=16        # CIR backward 1 - 64
# Bc_bak=16        # Bc backward  1 - 512
# Be_bak=0         # Be backward  0 - 511


#
#
# Device specific configuration
#
#

#
# The first device is a Sangoma S502E
#
[sdla0]
Type=Sangoma       # Type of the device to configure, currently only
                   # SANGOMA is recognized
#
# These keys are specific to the 'Sangoma' type
#
# The type of Sangoma board - S502A, S502E, S508
Board=S502E
#
# The name of the test firmware for the Sangoma board
# Testware=/usr/src/frad-0.10/bin/sdla_tst.502
#
# The name of the FR firmware
# Firmware=/usr/src/frad-0.10/bin/frm_rel.502
#
Port=360        # Port for this particular card
Mem=C8          # Address of memory window, A0-EE, depending on card
IRQ=5           # IRQ number, do not supply for S502A
DLCIs=1         # Number of DLCI's attached to this device
DLCI_1=16       # DLCI #1's number, 16 - 991
# DLCI_2=17
```

Part iii

```
# DLCI_3=18
# DLCI_4=19
# DLCI_5=20
#
# Specified here, these apply to this device only,
# and override defaults from above
#
# Access=CPE      # CPE or NODE, default is CPE
#
Flags=TXIgnore,RXIgnore,BufferFrames,DropAborted,Stats,MCI,AutoDLCI
# Clock=Internal # External or Internal, default is Internal
# Baud=128       # Specified baud rate of attached CSU/DSU
# MTU=2048       # Maximum transmit IFrame length, default is 4096
# T391=10        # T391 value  5 - 30, default is 10
# T392=15        # T392 value  5 - 30, default is 15
# N391=6         # N391 value  1 - 255, default is 6
# N392=3         # N392 value  1 - 10, default is 3
# N393=4         # N393 value  1 - 10, default is 4

#
# The second device is some other card
#
# [sdla1]
# Type=FancyCard    # Type of the device to configure.
# Board=            # Type of Sangoma board
# Key=Value         # values specific to this type of device


#
# DLCI Default configuration parameters
# These may be overridden in the DLCI specific configurations
#
CIRfwd=64         # CIR forward  1 - 64
# Bc_fwd=16       # Bc forward  1 - 512
# Be_fwd=0        # Be forward  0 - 511
# CIRbak=16       # CIR backward 1 - 64
# Bc_bak=16       # Bc backward  1 - 512
# Be_bak=0        # Be backward  0 - 511

#
# DLCI Configuration
# These are all optional. The naming convention is
# [DLCI_D<devicenum>_<DLCI_Num>]
#

[DLCI_D1_16]
# IP=
```

```
# Net=
# Mask=
# Flags defined by Sangoma: TXIgnore,RXIgnore,BufferFrames
# DLCIFlags=TXIgnore,RXIgnore,BufferFrames
# CIRfwd=64
# Bc_fwd=512
# Be_fwd=0
# CIRbak=64
# Bc_bak=512
# Be_bak=0

[DLCI_D2_16]
# IP=
# Net=
# Mask=
# Flags defined by Sangoma: TXIgnore,RXIgnore,BufferFrames
# DLCIFlags=TXIgnore,RXIgnore,BufferFrames
# CIRfwd=16
# Bc_fwd=16
# Be_fwd=0
# CIRbak=16
# Bc_bak=16
# Be_bak=0
```

When you've built your `/etc/frad/router.conf` file, the only step remaining is to configure the actual devices themselves. This is only a little trickier than a normal network device configuration. You need to remember to bring up the FRAD device before the DLCI encapsulation devices. These commands are best hosted in a shell script, due to their number:

```
#!/bin/sh
# Configure the frad hardware and the DLCI parameters
/sbin/fradcfg /etc/frad/router.conf || exit 1
/sbin/dlcicfg file /etc/frad/router.conf
#
# Bring up the FRAD device
ifconfig sdla0 up
#
# Configure the DLCI encapsulation interfaces and routing
ifconfig dlci00 192.168.10.1 pointopoint 192.168.10.2 up
route add -net 192.168.10.0 netmask 255.255.255.0 dlci00
#
ifconfig dlci01 192.168.11.1 pointopoint 192.168.11.2 up
route add -net 192.168.11.0 netmask 255.255.255.0 dlci00
#
route add default dev dlci00
#
```

IPX (AF_IPX)

The IPX protocol is most commonly utilized in Novell NetWare(tm) local area network environments. Linux includes support for this protocol and may be configured to act as a network endpoint, or as a router for IPX.

Kernel Compile Options:

```
Networking options --->
  [*] The IPX protocol
  [ ] Full internal IPX network
```

The IPX protocol and the NCPFS are covered in greater depth in the IPX-HOWTO (see `IPX-HOWTO.html`).

NetRom (AF_NETROM)

NetRom device names are "`nr0`," "`nr1`," etc.

Kernel Compile Options:

```
Networking options --->
  [*] Amateur Radio AX.25 Level 2
  [*] Amateur Radio NET/ROM
```

The AX25, Netrom, and Rose protocols are covered by the AX25-HOWTO (see `http://metalab.unc.edu/LDP/`). These protocols are used by Amateur Radio Operators worldwide in packet radio experimentation.

Most of the work for implementation of these protocols has been done by Jonathan Naylor `<jsn@cs.nott.ac.uk>`.

Rose Protocol (AF_ROSE)

Rose device names are "`rs0`," "`rs1`," etc. in `2.1.*` kernels. Rose is available in the `2.1.*` kernels.

Kernel Compile Options:

```
Networking options --->
  [*] Amateur Radio AX.25 Level 2
  <*> Amateur Radio X.25 PLP (Rose)
```

The AX25, Netrom, and Rose protocols are covered by the AX25-HOWTO (see `http://metalab.unc.edu/LDP/`). These protocols are used by Amateur Radio Operators worldwide in packet radio experimentation.

Most of the work for implementation of these protocols has been done by Jonathan Naylor <jsn@cs.nott.ac.uk>.

SAMBA—"NetBEUI," "NetBios" Support

SAMBA is an implementation of the Session Management Block protocol. Samba allows Microsoft and other systems to mount and use your disks and printers.

SAMBA and its configuration are covered in detail in the SMB-HOWTO (see `http://metalab.unc.edu/LDP/`).

STRIP Support (Starmode Radio IP)

STRIP device names are "`st0`," "`st1`," etc.

Kernel Compile Options:

```
Network device support --->
    [*] Network device support
    ....
    [*] Radio network interfaces
    < > STRIP (Metricom starmode radio IP)
```

STRIP is a protocol designed specifically for a range of Metricom radio modems for a research project being conducted by Stanford University called the MosquitoNet Project (see `http://mosquitonet.Stanford.EDU/mosquitonet.html`). There is a lot of interesting reading here, even if you aren't directly interested in the project.

The Metricom radios connect to a serial port, employ spread spectrum technology, and are typically capable of about 100kbps. Information on the Metricom radios is available from the Metricom Web Server (see `http://www.metricom.com/`).

At present the standard network tools and utilities do not support the STRIP driver, so you will have to download some customized tools from the MosquitoNet Web server. Details on what software you need are available at the MosquitoNet STRIP Page (see `http://mosquitonet.Stanford.EDU/strip.html`).

A summary of configuration is that you use a modified *slattach* program to set the line discipline of a serial `tty` device to STRIP, and then configure the resulting "st[0-9]" device as you would for Ethernet with one important exception: for technical reasons, STRIP does not support the ARP protocol, so you must manually configure the ARP entries for each of the hosts on your subnet. This shouldn't prove too onerous.

Token Ring

Token Ring device names are "tr0," "tr1," etc. Token Ring is an IBM standard LAN protocol that avoids collisions by providing a mechanism that allows only one station on the LAN the right to transmit at a time. A "token" is held by one station at a time, and the station holding the token is the only station allowed to transmit. When it has transmitted its data, it passes the token onto the next station. The token loops amongst all active stations–hence the name "Token Ring."

Kernel Compile Options:

```
Network device support --->
     [*] Network device support
     ....
     [*] Token Ring driver support
     < > IBM Tropic chipset based adaptor support
```

Configuration of Token Ring is identical to that of Ethernet with the exception of the network device name to configure.

X.25

X.25 is a circuit-based packet switching protocol defined by the C.C.I.T.T. (a standards body recognized by telecommunications companies in most parts of the world). An implementation of X.25 and LAPB is being worked on and recent 2.1.* kernels include the work in progress.

Jonathan Naylor <jsn@cs.nott.ac.uk> is leading the development, and a mailing list has been established to discuss Linux X.25-related matters. To subscribe send a message to majordomo@vger.rutgers.edu with the text "subscribe linux-x25" in the body of the message.

Early versions of the configuration tools may be obtained from Jonathan's FTP site at ftp.cs.nott.ac.uk (see ftp://ftp.cs.nott.ac.uk/jsn/).

WaveLAN Card

WaveLAN device names are "eth0," "eth1," etc.

Kernel Compile Options:

```
Network device support --->
    [*] Network device support
    ....
    [*] Radio network interfaces
    ....
    <*> WaveLAN support
```

The WaveLAN card is a spread spectrum wireless LAN card. The card looks very like an Ethernet card in practice and is configured in much the same way.

You can get information on the WaveLAN card from Wavelan.com (see http://www.wavelan.com/).

Cables and Cabling

Those of you handy with a soldering iron may want to build your own cables to interconnect two Linux machines. The following cabling instructions should assist you in this.

Serial NULL Modem Cable

Not all NULL modem cables are alike. Many null modem cables do little more than trick your computer into thinking all the appropriate signals are present and swap transmit and receive data. This is ok but means that you must use software flow control (XON/XOFF), which is less efficient than hardware flow control. The following cable provides the best possible signalling between machines and allows you to use hardware (RTS/CTS) flow control.

```
Pin Name  Pin                              Pin
Tx Data    2 ----------------------------- 3
Rx Data    3 ----------------------------- 2
RTS        4 ----------------------------- 5
CTS        5 ----------------------------- 4
Ground     7 ----------------------------- 7
DTR        20 -\-------------------------- 8
DSR        6 -/
RLSD/DCD   8 ---------------------------/- 20
                                        \- 6
```

Parallel Port Cable (PLIP Cable)

If you intend to use the PLIP protocol between two machines, then this cable will work for you irrespective of what sort of parallel ports you have installed.

```
Pin Name      pin              pin
STROBE        1*
D0->ERROR     2  ----------- 15
D1->SLCT      3  ----------- 13
D2->PAPOUT    4  ----------- 12
D3->ACK       5  ----------- 10
D4->BUSY      6  ----------- 11
D5            7*
D6            8*
D7            9*
ACK->D3       10 ----------- 5
BUSY->D4      11 ----------- 6
PAPOUT->D2    12 ----------- 4
SLCT->D1      13 ----------- 3
FEED          14*
ERROR->D0     15 ----------- 2
INIT          16*
SLCTIN        17*
GROUND        25 ----------- 25
```

Notes:

- Do not connect the pins marked with an asterisk "*."
- Extra grounds are 18,19,20,21,22,23, and 24.
- If the cable you are using has a metallic shield, it should be connected to the metallic DB-25 shell at *one end only*.

Warning: A miswired PLIP cable can destroy your controller card. Be very careful and double-check every connection to ensure you don't cause yourself any unnecessary work or heartache.

While you may be able to run PLIP cables for long distances, you should avoid it if you can. The specifications for the cable allow for a cable length of about 1 meter or so. Please be very careful when running long PLIP cables, as sources of strong electromagnetic fields, such as lightning, power lines, and radio transmitters can interfere with and sometimes even damage your controller. If you really want to connect two of your computers over a large distance, you really should be looking at obtaining a pair of thin-net Ethernet cards and running some coaxial cable.

10base2 (Thin Coax) Ethernet Cabling

10base2 is an Ethernet cabling standard that specifies the use of 52 ohm coaxial cable with a diameter of about 5 millimeters. There are a couple of important rules to remember when interconnecting machines with 10base2 cabling. The first is that you must use terminators at *both ends* of the cabling. A terminator is a 52 ohm resistor that helps to ensure that the signal is absorbed and not reflected when it reaches the end of the cable. Without a terminator at each end of the cabling, you may find that the Ethernet is unreliable or doesn't work at all. Normally you'd use "T pieces" to interconnect the machines, so that you end up with something that looks like:

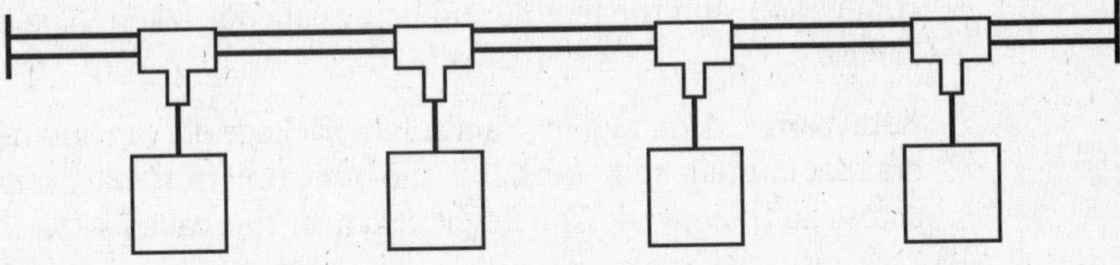

where the bars at either end represents a terminator, the parallel lines represents a length of coaxial cable with BNC plugs at either end, and the "T" represents a "T piece" connector. You should keep the length of cable between the "T piece" and the actual Ethernet card in the PC as short as possible. Ideally the "T piece" will be plugged directly into the Ethernet card.

Twisted Pair Ethernet Cable

If you have only two twisted pair Ethernet cards and you wish to connect them, you do not require a hub. You can cable the two cards directly together. A diagram showing how to do this is included in the Ethernet-HOWTO (see `Ethernet-HOWTO.html`).

Glossary of Terms Used in This Document

The following is a list of some of the most important terms used in this document.

ARP This is an acronym for the *Address Resolution Protocol,* and this is how a network machine associates an IP Address with a hardware address.

ATM This is an acronym for *Asynchronous Transfer Mode*. An ATM network packages data into standard-size blocks which it can convey efficiently from point to point. ATM is a circuit-switched packet network technology.

client This is usually the piece of software at the end of a system where the user is. There are exceptions to this. For example, in the X11 window system it is actually the server with the user, and the client runs on the remote machine. The client is the program or end of a system that is receiving the service provided by the server. In the case of *peer-to-peer* systems such as *SLIP* or *PPP* the client is taken to be the end that initiates the connection, and the remote end being called is taken to be the server.

datagram A datagram is a discrete package of data and headers that contain addresses. It is the basic unit of transmission across an IP network. You might also hear this called a "packet."

DLCI The DLCI is the Data Link Connection Identifier and is used to identify a unique virtual point-to-point connection via a Frame Relay network. The DLCIs are normally assigned by the Frame Relay network provider.

Frame Relay Frame Relay is a network technology ideally suited to carrying traffic that is of a bursty or sporadic nature. Network costs are reduced by having many Frame Relay customers sharing the same network capacity and relying on them wanting to make use of the network at slightly different times.

Hardware address This is a number that uniquely identifies a host in a physical network at the media access layer. Examples of this are *Ethernet Addresses* and *AX.25 Addresses*.

ISDN This is an acronym for *Integrated Services Digital Network*. ISDN provides a standardized means by which Telecommunications companies may deliver either voice or data information to a customers premises. Technically ISDN is a circuit-switched data network.

ISP This is an acronym of Internet Service Provider. These are organizations or companies that provide people with network connectivity to the Internet.

IP address This is a number that uniquely identifies a TCP/IP host on the network. The address is 4 bytes long and is usually represented in what is called the "dotted decimal notation," where each byte is represented in decimal from with dots (".") between them.

MSS The Maximum Segment Size (*MSS*) is the largest quantity of data that can be transmitted at one time. If you want to prevent local fragmentation, MSS would equal MTU-IP header.

MTU The Maximum Transmission Unit (*MTU*) is a parameter that determines the largest datagram that can be transmitted by an IP interface without it needing to be broken down into smaller units. The MTU should be larger than the largest datagram you wish to transmit unfragmented. Note, this only prevents fragmentation locally; some other link in the path may have a smaller MTU and the datagram will be fragmented there. Typical values are 1500 bytes for an Ethernet interface, or 576 bytes for a SLIP interface.

route The *route* is the path that your datagrams take through the network to reach their destination.

server This is usually the piece of software or end of a system remote from the user. The server provides some service to one or many clients. Examples of servers include *ftp*, *Networked File System*, or *Domain Name Server*. In the case of *peer-to-peer* systems such as SLIP or PPP, the server is taken to be the end of the link that is called, and the end calling is taken to be the client.

window The *window* is the largest amount of data that the receiving end can accept at a given point in time.

Linux for an ISP?

If you are interested in using Linux for ISP purposes, I recommend you take a look at the Linux ISP homepage (see `http://www.anime.net/linuxisp/`) for a good list of pointers to information you might need and use.

Administrava

I'd like to thank the following people for their contributions to this document (in no particular order): Terry Dawson, Axel Boldt, Arnt Gulbrandsen, Gary Allpike, Cees de Groot, Alan Cox, Jonathan Naylor, Claes Ensson, Ron Nessim, John Minack, Jean-Pierre Cocatrix, and Erez Strauss.

Copyright

Chapter 9
PPP

This document shows how to connect your Linux PC to a PPP server, how to use PPP to link two LANs together, and it provides one method of setting up your Linux computer as a PPP server. The document also provides help in debugging nonfunctional PPP connections.

If your Internet Service Provider is telephone-line and modem-based, then they are almost certainly providing you with PPP service. You'll definitely want to read this chapter to learn all about how PPP works under Linux. In some cases, it'll be a little tricky to get going, but everything you need to know should be here, and you'll only have to do it once, so don't give up!

PPP is reprinted from the Linux PPP HOWTO by Robert Hart, version 3 of 31 March 1997.

Copyright

Distribution

This document will be posted to `comp.os.linux.answers` as new versions of the document are produced. It is also available in HTML format at

- Linux HOWTO Index (see `http://MetaLab.unc.edu/mdw/linux.html#howto`)
- PPP-HOWTO (see `http://www.interweft.com.au/other/ppp-howto/ppp-howto.html`)

Other formats (SGML, ASCII, PostScript, DVI) are available from "HOWTOs–other formats" (see `ftp://MetaLab.unc.edu/pub/Linux/docs/HOWTO/other-formats`).

As MetaLab.unc.edu carries a very heavy load, please use an appropriate mirror site close to you.

Acknowledgements

A growing number of people have provided me with assistance in preparing this document. Special thanks go to Al Longyear for the guidance on PPP itself (if there are mistakes here, they are mine not his), Greg Hankins (maintainer of the Linux Howto system), and Debi Tackett (of MaximumAccess.com) for many helpful suggestions on style, content order, logic, and clarity of explanations.

Finally, to the many people who have contacted me by e-mail offering comments–my thanks. As with all HOWTO authors, the satisfaction of helping is all the payment we receive and it is enough. By writing this HOWTO I am repaying in a small way the debt I–and all other Linux users–owe to the people who write and maintain our OS of choice.

Introduction

PPP (the Point to Point Protocol) is a mechanism for creating and running IP (the Internet Protocol) and other network protocols over a serial link–be that a direct serial connection (using a null-modem cable), over a telnet established link, or a link made using modems and telephone lines (and of course using digital lines such as ISDN).

Using PPP, you can connect your Linux PC to a PPP server and access the resources of the network to which the server is connected (almost) as if you were directly connected to that network.

You can also set up your Linux PC as a PPP server, so that other computers can dial into your computer and access the resources on your local PC and/or network.

As PPP is a peer-to-peer system, you can also use PPP on two Linux PCs to link together two networks (or a local network to the Internet), creating a Wide Area Network (WAN).

One major difference between PPP and an Ethernet connection is, of course, speed—a standard Ethernet connection operates at 10 Mbs (Megabits [million bits] per second) maximum theoretical throughput, whereas an analogue modem operates at speeds up to 56 kbps (kilobits [thousand bits] per second).

Also, depending on the type of PPP connection, there may be some limitations in usage of some applications and services.

Clients and Servers

PPP is strictly a *peer–to–peer* protocol; there is (technically) no difference between the machine that dials in and the machine that is dialed into. However, for clarity's sake, it is useful to think in terms of *servers* and *clients*.

When you dial into a site to establish a PPP connection, you are a *client*. The machine to which you connect is the *server*.

When you are setting up a Linux box to receive and handle dial-in PPP connections, you are setting up a PPP *server*.

Any Linux box can be both a PPP server and client—even simultaneously if you have more than one serial port (and modem if necessary). As stated above, there is no real difference between clients and servers as far as PPP is concerned, once the connection is made.

This document refers to the machine that initiates the call (that dials in) as the *client*, while the machine that answers the telephone, checks the authentication of the dial-in request (using user names, passwords, and possibly other mechanisms) is referred to as the *server*.

The use of PPP as a client to link one or more machines at a location into the Internet is, probably, the one in which most people are interested—that is using their Linux box as a client.

The procedure described in this document will allow you to establish and automate your Internet connection.

This document will also give you guidance in setting up your Linux PC as a PPP *server* and in linking two LANs together (with full routing) using PPP. (This is frequently characterized as establishing a WAN [wide area network] link.)

Differences between Linux Distributions

There are many different Linux distributions and they all have their own idiosyncrasies and ways of doing things.

In particular, there are two different ways a Linux (and Unix) computer actually starts up, configures its interfaces, and so forth.

These two ways are *BSD system initialization* and *System V system initialization*. If you dip into some of the Unix news groups, you will find occasional religious wars between proponents of these two systems. If that sort of thing amuses you, have fun burning bandwidth and join in!

Possibly the most widely used distributions are:

- Slackware, which uses BSD style system initialization
- Red Hat (and its former associate, Caldera), which use SysV system initialization (although in a slightly modified form)
- Debian, which uses SysV system initialization

BSD style initialization typically keeps its initialization files in `/etc/....`These files are

```
/etc/rc
    /etc/rc.local
    /etc/rc.serial
        (and possibly other files)
```

Of recent times, some BSD system initialization schemes use a `/etc/rc.d...` directory to hold the startup file rather than putting everything into `/etc`.

System V initialization keeps its initialization files in directories under `/etc/...` or `/etc/rc.d/...` and a number of subdirectories under there:

```
drwxr-xr-x  2 root   root     1024 Jul 6 15:12 init.d
-rwxr-xr-x  1 root   root     1776 Feb 9 05:01 rc
-rwxr-xr-x  1 root   root     820 Jan 2 1996 rc.local
-rwxr-xr-x  1 root   root     2567 Jul 5 20:30 rc.sysinit
drwxr-xr-x  2 root   root     1024 Jul 6 15:12 rc0.d
drwxr-xr-x  2 root   root     1024 Jul 6 15:12 rc1.d
drwxr-xr-x  2 root   root     1024 Jul 6 15:12 rc2.d
```

```
drwxr-xr-x  2 root   root      1024 Jul 18 18:07 rc3.d
drwxr-xr-x  2 root   root      1024 May 27 1995 rc4.d
drwxr-xr-x  2 root   root      1024 Jul 6 15:12 rc5.d
drwxr-xr-x  2 root   root      1024 Jul 6 15:12 rc6.d
```

If you are trying to track down where your Ethernet interface and associated network routes are actually configured, you will need to track through these files to find where the commands are that do this.

Distribution-Specific PPP Configuration Tools

On some installations (for example Red Hat and Caldera), there is a X Windows configured PPP dial-up system. This HOWTO does not cover these distribution-specific tools. If you are having problems with them, contact the distributors directly.

For Red Hat 4.*x* users, there is now a Red Hat PPP-TIP (see `http://www.interweft.com.au`) in the Linux resources area and also from Red Hat Software (see `http://www.redhat.com`) in the support area.

IP Numbers

Every device that connects to the Internet must have its own, unique IP number. These are assigned centrally by a designated authority for each country.

If you are connecting a local area network (LAN) to the Internet, you *must* use an IP number from your own assigned network range for all the computers and devices you have on your LAN. You *must not* pick IP numbers out of the air and use these while connecting to another LAN (let alone the Internet). At worst this will simply not work at all and could cause total havoc as your "stolen" IP number starts interfering with the communications of another computer that is already using the IP number you have picked out of the air.

Please note that the IP numbers used throughout this document (with some exceptions) are from the "unconnected network numbers" series that are reserved for use by networks that are not (ever) connected to the Internet.

There are IP numbers that are specifically dedicated to LANs that do not connect to the Internet. The IP number sequences are

- One A Class Network Address 10.0.0.0 (netmask 255.0.0.0)

- 16 B Class Network Addresses 172.16.0.0–172.31.0.0 (netmask 255.255.0.0)
- 256 C Class Network Addresses 192.168.0.0–192.168.255.0 (netmask 255.255.255.0)

If you have a LAN for which you have *not* been allocated IP numbers by the responsible authority in your country, you should use one of the network numbers from the above sequences for your machines.

These numbers should *never* be used on the Internet.

However, they can be used for the local Ethernet on a machine that is connecting to the Internet. This is because IP numbers are actually allocated to a network interface, not to a computer. So while your Ethernet interface may use 10.0.0.1 (for example), when you hook onto the Internet using PPP, your PPP interface will be given another (and valid) IP number by the server. Your PC will have Internet connectivity, but the other computers on your LAN will not.

However, using Linux and the IP Masquerade (also known as NAT–Network Address Translation) capabilities of Linux and the *ipfwadm* software, you can connect your LAN to the Internet (with some restriction of services), even if you do not have valid IP numbers for the machines on your Ethernet.

For more information on how to do this see the IP Masquerade mini-HOWTO at Linux IP Masquerade mini HOWTO (see `http://MetaLab.unc.edu/mdw/HOWTO/mini/IP-Masquerade`).

For most users, who are connecting a single machine to an Internet service provider via PPP, obtaining an IP number (or more accurately, a network number) will not be necessary.

If you wish to connect a small LAN to the Internet, many Internet Service Providers (ISPs) can provide you with a dedicated subnet (a specific sequence of IP numbers) from their existing IP address space. Alternatively, use IP Masquerading.

For users, who are connecting a single PC to the Internet via an ISP, most providers use *dynamic* IP number assignment. That is, as part of the connection process, the PPP service you contact will tell your machine what IP number to use for the PPP interface during the current session. This number will not be the same every time you connect to your ISP.

With dynamic IP numbers, you are *not* given the same IP number each time you connect. This has implications for server-type applications on your Linux machine such as *Sendmail*, *ftpd*, *httpd*, and so forth. These services are based on the premise that the computer offering the service is accessible at the same IP number all the time (or at least the same fully qualified domain name–FQDN–and that DNS resolution of the name to IP address is available).

The limitations of service due to dynamic IP number assignment (and ways to work around these, where possible) are discussed later in the document.

AIMS OF THIS DOCUMENT

Setting up a PPP Client

This document provides guidance to people who wish to use Linux and PPP to dial into a PPP server and set up an IP connection using PPP. It assumes that PPP has been compiled and installed on your Linux machine (but does briefly cover reconfiguring/recompiling your kernel to include PPP support).

While DIP (the standard way of creating a SLIP connection) can be used to set up a PPP connection, DIP scripts are generally quite complex. For this reason, this document does NOT cover using DIP to set up a PPP connection.

Instead, this document describes the standard Linux PPP software (*chat/pppd*).

Linking Two LANs, Or a LAN to the Internet, Using PPP

This document provides (basic) information on linking two LANs, or a LAN to the Internet, using PPP.

Setting up a PPP Server

This document provides guidance on how to configure your Linux PC as a PPP server (allowing other people to dial into your Linux PC and establish a PPP connection).

You should note that there are a myriad of ways of setting up Linux as a PPP server. This document gives one method–that used by the author to set up several small PPP servers (each of 16 modems).

This method is known to work well. However, it is not necessarily the best method.

Using PPP Over a Direct Null Modem Connection

This document provides a brief overview of using PPP to link two Linux PCs via a null-modem cable. It is possible to link other OSes to Linux this way as well. To do so, you will need to consult the documentation for the operating system you are interested in.

This Document at Present Does Not Cover...

- Compiling the PPP daemon software. See the documentation that comes with the version of pppd you are using.
- Connecting and configuring a modem to Linux (in detail). See the Serial-HOWTO and for modem specific initialization, see Modem Setup Information (`http://www.in.net/info/modems/index.html`) for information that may help you to configure your modem.
- Using DIP to make PPP connections. Use *chat* instead.
- Using *socks* or IP Masquerade. There are perfectly good documents already covering these two packages.
- Using *diald* to set up an automated connection. See the diald documentation for information on this.
- Using EQL to gang together two modems into a single PPP link.
- Distribution-specific PPP connection methods (such as the Red Hat 4.*x* network configuration tool). See the distribution for documentation on the methods used.
- The growing number of tools available to automate PPP setup. See the appropriate documentation.

Software Versions Covered

This HOWTO assumes that you are using a Linux 1.2.*x* kernel with the PPP 2.1.2 software or Linux 1.3.*x*/2.0.*x* and PPP 2.2.

At the time of writing, the latest official version of PPP available for Linux is ppp-2.2f. The new version (ppp-2.3) is still in beta.

It is possible to use PPP 2.2.0 with kernel 1.2.13. This requires kernel patches. It is recommended that version 1.2.13 kernel users move up to ppp-2.2 as it includes several bug fixes and enhancements.

Also, you should particularly note that you cannot use the PPP 2.1.2 software with Linux kernel version 2.0.x.

Please note that this document does *not* cover problems arising from the use of loadable modules for Linux kernel 2.0.*x*. Please see the *kerneld* mini-HOWTO and the kernel/module 2.0.*x* documentation (in the Linux 2.0.*x* source tree at `/usr/src/linux/Documentation/...`).

As this document is designed to assist new users, it is highly recommended that you use a version of the Linux kernel and the appropriate PPP version that are known to be stable together.

Other Useful/Important Documents

Users are advised to read

- The documentation that comes with the PPP package.
- The pppd and chat man pages (use `man chat` and `man pppd` to explore these).
- The Linux Network Administration Guide (NAG); see *The Network Administrators' Guide (*`http://MetaLab.unc.edu/mdw/LDP-books/nag-1.0/nag.html`*)*.
- The Net-2/3 HOWTO; see Linux NET-2/3-HOWTO (`http://MetaLab.unc.edu/mdw/HOWTO/NET-2-HOWTO.html`).
- Linux kernel documentation installed in `/usr/src/linux/Documentation` when you install the Linux source code.
- The modem setup information page—see Modem Setup Information (`http://www.in.net/info/modems/index.html`).
- The excellent Unix/Linux books published by O'Reilly and Associates. See O'Reilly and Associates' On-Line Catalog (`http://www.ora.com/`). If you are new to Unix/Linux, *run* (don't walk) to your nearest computer book shop and invest in a number of these immediately!

- The PPP-FAQ maintained by Al Longyear, available from Linux PPP-FAQ (`ftp://MetaLab.unc.edu/pub/Linux/docs/faqs`); this contains a great deal of useful information in question/answer format that is very useful when working out why PPP is not working (properly).
- The growing number of Linux books from various publishing houses and authors; you are actively encouraged to check the currency of these books. Linux development and distributions tend to evolve fairly rapidly, while the revision of books moves (generally) much more slowly! Buying an excellent book (and there are many) that is now out of date will cause new users considerable confusion and frustration.

The best general starting point for Linux documentation is The Linux Documentation Project Home Page (`http://MetaLab.unc.edu/mdw/`). The HOWTOs tend to be revised reasonably regularly.

While you can use this document to create your PPP link without reading any of these documents, you will have a far better understanding of what is going on if you do so! You will also be able to address problems yourself (or at least ask more intelligent questions on the `comp.os.linux`... newsgroups or Linux mailing lists).

These documents (as well as various others, including the relevant RFCs) provide additional and more detailed explanation than is possible in this HOWTO.

If you are connecting a LAN to the Internet using PPP, you will need to know a reasonable amount about TCP/IP networking. In addition to the documents above, you will find the O'Reilly books *TCP/IP Network Administration* and *Building Internet Firewalls* of considerable benefit!

Useful Linux Mailing Lists

There are many Linux mailing lists that operate as a means of communication between users of many levels of ability. By all means subscribe to those that interest you, and contribute your expertise and views.

A word to the wise: some lists are specifically aimed at "high powered" users and/or specific topics. While no one will complain if you *lurk* (subscribe but don't post messages), you are likely to earn heated comments (if not outright flames) if you post "newbie" questions to inappropriate lists. This is not because guru level users hate new users, but because these lists are there to handle the specific issues at particular levels of difficulty.

By all means join the lists that offer open subscription, but keep your comments relevant to the subject of the list!

A good starting point for Linux mailing lists is Linux Mailing List Directory (see `http://summer.snu.ac.kr/~djshin/linux/mail-list/index.shtml`).

OVERVIEW OF WHAT HAS TO BE DONE TO GET PPP WORKING AS A CLIENT

This document contains a great deal of information—and with each version it grows!

As a consequence, this section aims to provide a concise overview of the actions you will need to take to get your Linux system connected as a client to a PPP server.

Obtaining/Installing the Software

If your Linux distribution does not include the PPP software, you will need to obtain this from the Linux PPP daemon (see `ftp://MetaLab.unc.edu/pub/Linux/system/Network/serial/ppp/ppp-2.2.0f.tar.gz`).

This is the latest official version at the time of writing. However, choose the latest version available from this site (ppp-2.3 is in beta at the time of writing and should be released soon).

The PPP package contains instructions on how to compile and install the software *so this HOWTO does not*!

Part iii

Compiling PPP Support into the Kernel

Linux PPP operations come in two parts:

- the PPP daemon mentioned above
- kernel support for PPP

Many distributions seem to provide PPP kernel support in their default installation kernels, but others do not.

If at boot your kernel reports messages like

```
PPP Dynamic channel allocation code copyright 1995 Caldera, Inc.
PPP line discipline registered.
```

your kernel does have PPP support compiled in.

That said, you will probably want to compile your own kernel whatever your distribution to provide the most efficient use of system resources given your particular hardware configuration. It is worth remembering that the kernel cannot be swapped out of memory and so keeping the kernel as small as possible has advantages on a memory limited machine.

This document provides minimal kernel recompilation instructions in the section, "Configuring Your Linux Kernel."

For greater detail, see the Kernel-HOWTO at The Linux Kernel HOWTO (`http://MetaLab.unc.edu/mdw/HOWTO/Kernel-HOWTO.html`).

Obtaining Information from Your ISP

There are an almost infinite number of ways in which a PPP server can be set up. In order to connect to your ISP (or corporate PPP server to access your intranet), you will need to obtain information on how the PPP server operates.

Because you are using Linux, you may have some difficulty with some ISP help-desks (and work-site-based PPP intranet servers) which know only about MS Windows clients.

However, a rapidly growing number of ISPs use Linux to provide their service–and Linux is also penetrating the corporate environment as well, so you may be lucky if you *do* strike problems.

The section, "Getting the Information You Need about the PPP Server," tells you what you need to know about the PPP server to which you are going to connect–and how to find out the information you need to know.

Configuring Your Modem and Serial Port

In order to connect to a PPP server and to obtain the best possible data transfer rate, your modem needs to be configured correctly.

Similarly, the serial ports on your modem and computer need to be set up correctly.

The section, "Configuring Your Modem and Serial Port," provides information on this.

Setting up Name to Address Resolution (DNS)

In addition to the files that run PPP and perform the automated login to the PPP server, there are a number of text configuration files that have to be set up for your computer to be able to resolve names like `www.interweft.com.au` to the IP address that is actually used to contact that computer. These are

- `/etc/resolv.conf`
- `/etc/host.conf`

See the section, "Setting up Name to Address Resolution (DNS)," for details on setting this up.

In particular, you do *not* need to run a name server on your Linux box in order to connect to the Internet (although you may wish to). All you need is to know the IP number of at least one name server that you can use (preferably one at your ISP's site).

PPP and root Privileges

As establishing a PPP link between your Linux computer and another PPP server requires manipulation of network devices (the PPP interface is a network interface) and the kernel routing table, pppd requires root privileges.

For details, see the section, "Using PPP and Root Privileges."

Part iii

Checking Your Distribution PPP Files and Setting up the PPP Options

There are a number of configuration and dialer files that need to be set up to get PPP operational. There are examples as part of the PPP distribution and this section shows what files you should have:

```
/etc/ppp/options
/etc/ppp/scripts/ppp-on
/etc/ppp/scripts/ppp-on-dialer
/etc/ppp/options.tpl
```

You may need to create some additional files depending on exactly what you are aiming to achieve with PPP:

```
/etc/ppp/options.ttyXX
/etc/ppp/ip-up
/etc/ppp/pap-secrets
/etc/ppp/chap-secrets
```

In addition, the PPP daemon can use a large number of command line options and it is important to use the right ones; so this section takes you through the standard PPP options and helps you choose the options you should use.

For details on this, see the section, "Setting up the PPP Connection Files."

If Your PPP Server Uses PAP (Password Authentication Protocol)

Many ISPs and corporate PPP servers use PAP. If your server does *not* require you to use PAP (if you can log in manually and receive the standard user name/password text based prompts it does not use PAP), you can safely ignore this section.

Instead of logging into such a server using a user name and password when prompted to enter them by the server, a PPP server using PAP does not require a text-based login.

The user authentication information instead is exchanged as part of the link control protocol (LCP), which is the first part of establishing a PPP link.

The section, "If Your PPP Server Uses PAP (Password Authentication Protocol)," provides information on the files you need to set up to establish a PPP link using PAP.

Connecting to the PPP Server by Hand

Having set up the basic files, it is a good idea to test these by connecting (using minicom or seyon) and starting pppd on your Linux PC by hand.

See the section, "Setting up the PPP Connection Manually," for full details of setting this up.

Automating Your PPP Connection

Once you are able to log in by hand, you can now move to setting up a set of scripts that will automate the establishment of the connection.

The section entitled "Automating Your Connections–Creating the Connection Scripts" covers setting up the necessary scripts, with considerable attention paid to *chat* and scripting the login process to the PPP server.

This section discusses scripts for user name/password authentication as well as scripts for PAP/CHAP authenticating servers.

Shutting down the Link

Once your link is up and working, you need to be able to deactivate the link.

This is covered in the section, "Shutting down the PPP Link."

If You Have Problems

Many people have problems getting PPP to work straightaway. The variation in PPP servers and how they require you to set up the connection is enormous. Similarly, there are many options to PPP—and some combinations of these just do not work together, ever.

In addition to the problems of logging in and starting the PPP service, there are problems with the modems and the actual telephone lines as well!

The section entitled "Debugging" provides some basic information about common errors, how to isolate these and fix them.

This is *NOT* intended to provide more than just the basics. Al Longyear maintains the PPP-FAQ which contains much more information on this topic!

After the Link Comes Up

Once a PPP link is operational (specifically, once the IP layer is operational) Linux PPP can automatically run (as the root user) a script to perform *any* function you can write a script to accomplish.

The section, "After the Link Comes Up—the `/etc/ppp/ip-up` Script," provides information on the `/etc/ppp/ip-up` script, the parameters it receives from PPP, and how to use it to do things like acquire your e-mail from your ISP account and send any queued e-mail awaiting transmission on your machine and such.

Problems with Standard IP Services on a Dynamic IP Number PPP Link

As noted in the introduction, dynamic IP numbers affect the ability of your Linux PC to act as a server on the Internet.

The section, "Using Internet Services with Dynamic IP Numbers," provides information on the (main) services affected and what you can do (if anything) to overcome this.

Configuring Your Linux Kernel

In order to use PPP, your Linux kernel must be compiled to include PPP support. Obtain the Linux source code for your kernel if you do not already have this–it belongs in `/usr/src/linux` on Linux's standard file system.

Check out this directory–many Linux distributions install the source tree (the files and subdirectories) as part of their installation process.

At bootup, your Linux kernel prints out a great deal of information. Among this is information about PPP support if the kernel includes it. To view this information, look at your *syslog* file or use *dmesg less* to display the information to the screen. If your kernel includes PPP support, you will see lines like

```
PPP Dynamic channel allocation code copyright 1995 Caldera, Inc.
PPP line discipline registered.
```

(this is for the Linux 2.0.*x* kernel series).

Linux kernel sources can be obtained by ftp from `MetaLab.unc.edu` or its mirror sites.

Installing the Linux Kernel Source

The following are brief instructions for obtaining and installing the Linux kernel sources. Full information can be obtained from the Linux Kernel HOWTO (see `http://MetaLab.unc.edu/mdw/HOWTO/Kernel-HOWTO.html`).

In order to install and compile the Linux kernel, you need to be logged in as root.

1. Change directory to the `/usr/src` directory `cd /usr/src.`
2. Check in `/usr/src/linux` to see if you already have the sources installed.
3. If you don't have the sources, get them from the Linux kernel source directory (`ftp://MetaLab.unc.edu/pub/Linux/kernel/v2.0`) or your nearest mirror. If you are looking for

earlier versions of the kernel (such as 1.2.*x*), these are kept in Old Linux kernel source directory (`ftp://MetaLab.unc.edu/pub/Linux/kernel/old`).

4. Choose the appropriate kernel—usually the most recent one available is what you are looking for. Retrieve this and put the source *tar* file in `/usr/src`.

NOTE

A *tar* file is an archive—possibly compressed (as are the Linux kernel source *tar* files) containing many files in a number of directories. It is the Linux equivalent of a DOS multi-directory zip file.

5. If you already have the Linux sources installed but are upgrading to a new kernel, you must remove the old sources. Use the command `rm -rf /usr/src/linux`

6. Now uncompress and extract the sources using the command `tar xzf linux-2.0.XX.tar.gz`.

7. Now, `cd/usr/src/linux` and read the README file. This contains an excellent explanation of how to go about configuring and compiling a new kernel. Read this file. (It's a good idea to print it out and have a copy handy while you are compiling until you have done this enough times to know your way around.)

Knowing Your Hardware

You *must* know what cards/devices you have inside your PC if you are going to recompile your kernel!!! For some devices (such as sound cards) you will also need to know various settings (such as IRQs, I/O addresses and such).

Kernel Compilation—the Linux 1.2.13 Kernel

To start the configuration process, follow the instructions in the README file to properly install the sources. You start the kernel configuration process with

```
make config
```

In order to use PPP, you must configure the kernel to include PPP support (PPP requires BOTH pppd AND kernel support for PPP).

```
PPP (point-to-point) support (CONFIG_PPP) [n] y
```

Answer the other make config questions according to the hardware in your PC and the features of the Linux operating system you want. Then continue to follow the README to compile and install your new kernel.

The 1.2.13 kernel creates only 4 PPP devices. For multiport serial cards, you will need to edit the kernel PPP sources to obtain more ports. (See the `README.linux` file that comes as part of the PPP-2.1.2 distribution for full details of the simple edits you need to make.)

NOTE

The 1.2.13 configuration dialogue does NOT allow you to go backwards—so if you make a mistake in answering one of the questions in the `make config` dialogue, exit by typing CTRL+C and start again.

Kernel Compilation—the Linux 1.3.*x* and 2.0.*x* Kernels

For Linux 1.3.*x* and 2.0.*x*, you can use a similar process as for Linux 1.2.13. Again, follow the instructions in the README file to properly install the sources. You start the kernel configuration process with

```
make config
```

However, you also have the choice of

```
make menuconfig
```

This provides a menu-based configuration system with online help that allows you to move backwards and forwards in the configuration process.

There is also a highly recommended X Windows based configuration interface

```
make xconfig
```

You can compile PPP support directly into your kernel or as a loadable module.

If you only use PPP some of the time that your Linux machine is operating, then compiling PPP support as a loadable module is recommended. Using *kerneld*, your kernel will automatically load the module(s) required to provide PPP support when you start your PPP link process. This saves valuable memory space: No part of the kernel can be swapped out of memory, but loadable modules are automatically removed if they are not in use.

To do this, you need to enable loadable module support:

```
Enable loadable module support (CONFIG_MODULES) [Y/n/?] y
```

To add PPP kernel support, answer the following question:

```
PPP (point-to-point) support (CONFIG_PPP) [M/n/y/?]
```

For a PPP loadable module, answer *M*, otherwise for PPP compiled in as part of the kernel, answer *Y*.

Unlike kernel 1.2.13, kernel 2.0.*x* creates PPP devices on the fly as needed and it is not necessary to hack the sources to increase the available PPP device numbers at all.

Note on PPP-2.2 and */proc/net/dev*

If you are using PPP-2.2, you will find that a side effect of the "on the fly" creation of the PPP devices is that no devices show up if you look in the `/proc/net` file system until a device is created by starting up pppd:

```
[hartr@archenland hartr]$ cat /proc/net/dev
Inter-|  Receive              | Transmit
 face |packets errs drop fifo frame|packets errs drop fifo
 colls carrier
  lo: 92792  0  0  0  0  92792  0  0  0    0  0
 eth0: 621737  13  13  0  23  501621  0  0  0 1309  0
```

Once you have one (or more) PPP services started, you will see entries such as this (from a PPP server):

```
[root@kepler /root]# cat /proc/net/dev
Inter-|   Receive                         | Transmit
 face |packets errs drop fifo frame|packets errs drop fifo colls carrier
   lo: 428021    0    0    0    0   428021    0    0    0    0    0
 eth0:4788257  648  648  319  650  1423836    0    0    0 4623    5
 ppp0:   2103    3    3    0    0     2017    0    0    0    0    0
 ppp1:  10008    0    0    0    0     8782    0    0    0    0    0
 ppp2:    305    0    0    0    0      297    0    0    0    0    0
 ppp3:   6720    7    7    0    0     7498    0    0    0    0    0
 ppp4: 118231  725  725    0    0   117791    0    0    0    0    0
 ppp5:  38915    5    5    0    0    28309    0    0    0    0    0
```

General Kernel Config Considerations for PPP

If you are setting up your Linux PC as a PPP server, you must compile in IP forwarding support. This is also necessary if you want to use Linux to link two LANs together, or link your LAN to the Internet.

If you are linking a LAN to the Internet (or linking together two LANs), you should be concerned about security. Adding support for IP firewalls to the kernel is probably a must!

You will also need this if you want to use IP masquerade to connect a LAN that uses any of the above mentioned "unconnected" IP network numbers.

To enable IP Masquerade and IP firewalling, you *MUST* answer *yes* to the first question in the `make config` process:

```
Prompt for development and/or incomplete code/drivers _
(CONFIG_EXPERIMENTAL)?
```

While this may sound a bit off-putting to new users, many users are actively using the IP Masquerade and IP firewalling features of the Linux 2.0.*XX* kernel with no problems.

Once you have installed and rebooted your new kernel, you can start configuring and testing your PPP link(s).

Getting the Information You Need about the PPP Server

Before you can establish a PPP connection with a server, you need to obtain the following information (from the sysadmin/user-support people of the PPP server):

- The telephone number(s) to dial for the service. If you are behind a PABX, you also need the PABX number that gives you an outside dial tone–this is frequently digit zero (0) or nine (9).
- Does the server use dynamic or static IP numbers? If the server uses static IP numbers, then you may need to know what IP number to use for your end of the PPP connection. If your ISP is providing you with a subnet of valid IP numbers, you will need to know the IP numbers you can use and the network mask (netmask). Most Internet Service Providers use dynamic IP numbers. As mentioned above, this has some implications in terms of the services you can use. However, even if you are using static IP numbers, most PPP servers will never (for security reasons) allow the client to specify an IP number. You *do* still need to know this information!
- What are the IP numbers of the ISPs Domain Name Servers? There should be at least two, although only one is needed. There could be

a problem here. The MS Windows 95 PPP setup allows the DNS address to be passed to the client as part of its connection process. So your ISP (or corporate help desk) may well tell you you don't need the IP address of the DNS server(s). For Linux, you *DO* need the address of at least one DNS. The linux implementation of PPP does not allow the setting of the DNS IP number dynamically at connection time–and quite possibly will never do so.

NOTE

While Linux (as a PPP client) cannot accept the DNS address from a server, it can, when acting as a server, pass this information to clients using the `dns-addr` pppd option.

- Does the server require the use of PAP/CHAP? If this is the case, you need to know the "id" and "secret" you are to use in connecting. (These are probably your user name and password at your ISP.)
- Does the server automatically start PPP or do you need to issue any commands to start PPP on the server once you are logged in? If you must issue a command to start PPP, what is it?
- Is the server a Microsoft Windows NT system and, if so, is it using the MS PAP/CHAP system? Many corporate LANs seem to use MS Windows NT this way for increased security.

Carefully note down this information–you are going to use it!

Configuring Your Modem and Serial Port

You should make sure that your modem is correctly set up and that you know which serial port it is connected to.

Remember:

- DOS com1: = Linux /dev/cua0 (and /dev/ttyS0)
- DOS com2: = Linux /dev/cua1 (and /dev/ttyS1) et cetera

It is also worth remembering that if you have four serial ports, the standard PC set up is to have com1 and com3 share IRQ4 and com2 and com4 share IRQ3.

If you have devices on standard serial ports that share an IRQ with your modem you are going to have problems. You need to make sure that your modem serial port is on its own, unique IRQ. Many modern serial cards (and better quality motherboard serial ports) allow you to move the IRQ of the serial ports around.

If you are running Linux kernel 2, you can check the in-use IRQs using `cat/proc/interrupts`, which will produce output like

```
 0:  6766283  timer
 1:    91545  keyboard
 2:        0  cascade
 4:   156944 + serial
 7:   101764  WD8013
10:   134365 + BusLogic BT-958
13:        1  math error
15:  3671702 + serial
```

This shows a serial port on IRQ4 (a mouse) and a serial port on IRQ15 (the permanent modem based PPP link to the Internet). (There is also a serial port on com2, IRQ3, and com4 is on IRQ14, but as they are not in use, they do not show up.)

Be warned—you need to know what you are doing if you are going to play with your IRQs! Not only do you have to open up you computer, pull out cards and play with jumpers, but you need to know what is on which IRQ. In my case, this is a totally SCSI-based PC, and so I can disable the on motherboard IDE interfaces that normally use IRQ14 and 15!

You should also remember that if your PC boots other operating systems, moving IRQs around may well mean that OS cannot boot properly—or at all!

If you do move your serial ports to nonstandard IRQs, then you need to tell Linux which IRQ each port is using. This is done using `setserial` and is best done as part of the boot process in `rc.local` or `rc.serial` which is called from `rc.local` or as part of the SysV initialization. For the machine illustrated above, the commands used are

```
/bin/setserial -b /dev/ttyS2 IRQ 11
/bin/setserial -b /dev/ttyS3 IRQ 15
```

However, if `kerneld` is loading your serial modules on doamins then, you cannot set and forget the IRQ, etc., once at boot time. This is because if the serial module is unloaded, Linux forgets the special settings.

So, if you are loading the serial module on demand, you will need to reconfigure the IRQs, etc., each time the module is loaded.

A Note About Serial Ports and Speed Capabilities

If you are using a high speed (external) modem (14,400 Baud or above), your serial port needs to be capable of handling the throughput that such a modem is capable of producing, particularly when the modems are compressing the data.

This requires your serial port to use a modern UART (Universal Asynchronous Receiver Transmitter) such as a 16550(A). If you are using an old machine (or old serial card), it is quite possible that your serial port has only an 8250 UART, which will cause you considerable problems when used with a high speed modem.

Use the command

```
setserial -a /dev/ttySx
```

to get Linux to report to you the type of UART you have. If you do not have a 16550A type UART, invest in a new serial card (available for under $50). When you purchase a new card, make sure you can move the IRQs around on it!

NOTE

The first versions of the 16550 UART chip had an error. This was rapidly discovered and a revision of the chip was released—the 16550A UART. A relatively small number of the faulty chips did however get into circulation. It is unlikely that you will encounter one of these but you should look for a response that says 16550A, particularly on serial cards of some vintage.

Serial Port Names

Historically, Linux used `cuaX` devices for dial-out and `ttySx` devices for dial-in.

The kernel code that required this was changed in kernel version 2.0.*x* and you should now use `ttySx` for both dial-in and dial-out. I understand that the `cuaX` device names may well disappear in future kernel versions.

Configuring Your Modem

You will need to configure your modem correctly for PPP—to do this *read your manual*! Most modems come with a *factory default* setting that selects the options required for PPP. The minimum configuration specifies

- Hardware flow control (RTS/CTS) (K3 on many Hayes modems)

- Other settings (in standard Hayes commands) you should investigate are

E1	Command/usr/src/linux-2.0.27/include/linux/serial.h Echo ON (required for chat to operate)
Q0	Report result codes (required for chat to operate)
S0=0	Auto Answer OFF (unless you want your modem to answer the phone)
C1	Carrier Detect ON only after connect
S0	Data Set Ready (DSR) always ON
(depends)	Data Terminal Ready

There is a site offering modem setups for a growing variety of modem makes and models at `modem setup information` (see `http://www.in.net/info/modems/index.html`), which may assist you in this.

It is also worthwhile investigating how the modem's serial interface between your computer and modem operates. Most modern modems allow you to run the serial interface at a fixed speed while allowing the telephone line interface to change its speed to the highest speed it and the remote modem can both handle.

This is known as split speed operation. If your modem supports this, lock the modem's serial interface to its highest available speed (usually 115,200 baud but maybe 38,400 baud for 14,400 baud modems).

Use your communications software (e.g. *minicom* or *seyon*) to find out about your modem configuration and set it to what is required for PPP. Many modems report their current settings in response to ATV, but you should consult your modem manual.

If you completely mess up the settings, you can return to sanity (usually) by issuing an ATF—return to factory settings. (For most modems I have encountered, the factory settings include all you need for PPP—but you should check.)

Once you have worked out the modem setup string required, write it down. You now have a decision: You can store these settings in your modem nonvolatile memory so they can be recalled by issuing the appropriate AT command. Alternatively you can pass the correct settings to your modem as part of the PPP dialing process.

If you only use your modem from Linux to call into your ISP or corporate server, the simplest set up will have you save your modem configuration in nonvolatile RAM.

If on the other hand, you modem is used by other applications and operating systems, it is safest to pass this information to the modem as each call is made so that the modem is guaranteed to be in the correct state for the call. (This has the added advantage also of recording the modem setup string in case the modem loses the contents of its NV-RAM, which can indeed happen).

Note on Serial Flow Control

When data is traveling on serial communication lines, it can happen that data arrives faster than a computer can handle it (the computer may be busy doing something else–remember, Linux is a multi-user, multi-tasking operating system). In order to ensure that data is not lost (if the input buffer is overrun with data, it will be dropped), some method of controlling the flow of data is necessary.

There are two ways of doing this on serial lines:

- Using hardware signals (Clear To Send/Request to Send–CTS/RTS)
- Using software signals (control S and control Q, also known as XON/XOFF)

While the latter may be fine for a terminal (text) link, data on a PPP link uses all 8 bits–and it is quite probable that somewhere in the data there will be data bytes that translate as Ctrl-S and Ctrl-Q. So, if a modem is set up to use software flow control, things can rapidly go berserk!

For high speed links using PPP (which uses 8 bits of data) hardware flow control is vital.

Testing Your Modem for Dial Out

Now that you have sorted out the serial port and modem settings it is a good idea to make sure that these setting do indeed work by dialing your ISP and seeing if you can connect.

Using you terminal communications package (such as *minicom*), set up the modem initialization required for PPP and dial into the PPP server you want to connect to with a PPP session.

NOTE

At this stage we are *not* trying to make a PPP connection—just establishing that we have the right phone number and also to find out *exactly* what the server sends to us in order to get logged in and start PPP.

During this process, either capture (log to a file) the entire login process or carefully (*very carefully*) write down *exactly* what prompts the server gives to let you know it is time to enter your user name and password (and any other commands needed to establish the PPP connection).

If your server uses PAP, you should not see a login prompt, but should instead see the text representation of the link control protocol (which looks like garbage) starting on your screen.

A few words of warning:

- Some servers are quite intelligent: you can log in using text-based user name/passwords or using PAP. So if your ISP or corporate site uses PAP but you do not see the garbage start up immediately, this may not mean you have done something wrong.
- Some servers require you to enter some text initially and *then* start a standard PAP sequence.
- Some PPP servers are passive–that is, they simply sit there sending nothing until the client that is dialing in sends them a valid LCP packet. If the PPP server you are connecting to operates in passive mode, you will never see the garbage!
- Some servers do not start PPP until you press *Enter*–so it is worth trying this if you correctly log in and do not see the garbage!

It is worth dialing in at least twice–some servers change their prompts (e.g. with the time!) every time you log in. The two critical prompts your Linux box needs to be able to identify every time you dial in are:

- the prompt that requests you to enter your user name
- the prompt that requests you to enter your password

If you have to issue a command to start PPP on the server, you will also need to find out the prompt the server gives you once you are logged in to tell you that you can now enter the command to start PPP.

If your server automatically starts PPP, once you have logged in, you will start to see garbage on your screen–this is the PPP server sending your machine information to start up and configure the PPP connection.

This should look something like this:

```
~y}#.!}!}!} }8}!}$}%U}"}&} } } } }%}& ...}'}"}(}"} .~~y}
```

(and it just keeps on coming!)

On some systems PPP must be explicitly started on the server. This is usually because the server has been set up to allow PPP logins and shell logins using the same user name/password pair. If this is the case, issue this command once you have logged in. Again, you will see the garbage as the server end of the PPP connection starts up.

If you do not see this immediately after connecting (and logging in and starting the PPP server if required), press *Enter* to see if this starts the PPP server.

At this point, you can hang up your modem (usually, type +++ quickly and then issue the *ATHO* command once your modem responds with *OK*).

If you can't get your modem to work, read your modem manual, the man pages for your communications software, and the Serial HOWTO! Once you have this sorted out, carry on as above.

Setting up Name to Address Resolution (DNS)

While we humans like to give names to things, computers really like numbers. On a TCP/IP network (which is what the Internet is), we call machines by a particular name—and every machine lives in a particular domain. For example, my Linux workstation is called *archenland* and it resides in the *interweft.com.au* domain. Its human readable address is thus `archenland.interweft.com.au` (which is known as the FQDN—fully qualified domain name).

However, for this machine to be found by other computers on the Internet, it is actually known by its IP number when computers are communicating across the Internet.

Translating (resolving) machine (and domain) names into the numbers actually used on the Internet is the business of machines that offer the Domain Name Service.

What happens is this:

- Your machine needs to know the IP address of a particular computer; the application requiring this information asks the resolver on your Linux PC to provide this information.
- The resolver queries the local host file (`/etc/hosts` and/or the domain name servers it knows about); the exact behavior of the resolver is determined by `/etc/host.conf`.

- If the answer is found in the host file, this answer is returned.
- If a domain name server is specified, your PC queries this machine.
- If the DNS machine already knows the IP number for the required name, it returns it. If it does not, it queries other name servers across the Internet to find the information. The name server then passes this information back to the requesting resolver—which gives the information to the requesting application.

When you make a PPP connection, you need to tell your Linux machine where it can get host name to IP number (address resolution) information so that *you* can use the machine names but your *computer* can translate these to the IP numbers it needs to do its work.

One way is to enter every host that you want to talk to into the `/etc/hosts` file (which is in reality totally impossible if you are connecting to the Internet); another is to use the machine IP numbers as opposed to the names (an impossible memory task for all but the smallest LANs).

The best way is to set up Linux so that it knows where to go to get this name-to-number information—automatically. This service is provided by the Domain Name Server (DNS) system. All that is necessary is to enter the IP number(s) for the domain name servers into your `/etc/resolv.conf` file.

The */etc/resolv.conf* File

Your PPP server sysadmin/user-support people should provide you with two DNS IP numbers. (Only one is necessary—but two gives some redundancy in the event of failure.)

As previously mentioned, Linux cannot set its name server IP number in the way that MS Windows 95 does. So you must *insist* (politely) that your ISP provide you with this information!

Your `/etc/resolv.conf` should look something like

```
domain your.isp.domain.name
nameserver 10.25.0.1
nameserver 10.25.1.2
```

Edit this file (creating it if necessary) to represent the information that your ISP has provided. It should have ownership and permissions as follows:

```
-rw-r--r--  1 root   root      73 Feb 19 01:46 /etc/resolv.conf
```

If you have already set up a `/etc/resolv.conf` because you are on a LAN, simply add the IP numbers of the PPP DNS servers to your existing file.

The */etc/host.conf* File

You should also check that your `/etc/host.conf` file is correctly set up. This should look like

```
order hosts,bind
multi on
```

This tells the resolver to use information in the host file before it sends queries to the DNS for resolution.

Using PPP and Root Privileges

Because PPP needs to set up networking devices, change the kernel routing table, and so forth, it requires root privileges.

If users other than root are to set up PPP connections, the pppd program should be set uid root:

```
-rwsr-xr-x  1 root   root    95225 Jul 11 00:27 /usr/sbin/pppd
```

If `/usr/sbin/pppd` is not set up this way, then *as root* issue the command:

```
chmod u+s /usr/sbin/pppd
```

What this does is make pppd run with root privileges *even if* the binary is run by an ordinary user. This allows a normal user to run pppd with the necessary privileges to set up the network interfaces and the kernel routing table.

Programs that run as root are potential security holes and you should be extremely cautious about making programs "set uid root." A number of programs (including pppd) have been carefully written to minimize the danger of running suid root, so you should be safe with this one (but no guarantees).

Depending on how you want your system to operate–specifically if you want *any* user on your system to be able to initiate a PPP link, you should make your ppp-on/off scripts world read/execute. (This is probably fine if your PC is used ONLY by you.)

However, if you do NOT want just anyone to be able to start up a PPP connection (for example, your children have accounts on your Linux PC and you do not want them hooking into the Internet without your supervision), you will need to establish a PPP group (as root, edit /etc/group) and

- Make pppd set uid root, owned by user root and group PPP, with the "other" permissions on this file empty. It should then look like

```
-rwsr-x---  1 root   PPP    95225 Jul 11 00:27 /usr/sbin/pppd
```

- Make the ppp-on/off scripts owned by user root and group PPP
- Make the ppp-on/off scripts read/executable by group PPP

```
-rwxr-x---  1 root   PPP       587 Mar 14 1995 /usr/sbin/ppp-on
-rwxr-x---  1 root   PPP       631 Mar 14 1995 /usr/sbin/ppp-off
```

- Make the other access rights for ppp-on/off nill
- Add the users who will be firing up PPP to the PPP group in /etc/group

Even if you do this, ordinary users will still not be able to shut down the link under software control. Running the `ppp-off` script requires root privileges. However, any user can just turn off the modem (or disconnect the telephone line from an internal modem).

An alternative (and better method) to this setup is to use the `sudo` program. This offers superior security and will allow you to set things up so that any (authorized) user can activate/deactivate the link using the scripts. Using `sudo` will allow an authorized user to activate/deactivate the PPP link cleanly and securely.

Setting up the PPP Connection Files

You now need to be logged in as *root* to create the directories and edit the files needed to set up PPP, even if you want PPP to be accessible to all users.

PPP uses a number of files to connect and set up a PPP connection. These differ in name and location between PPP 2.1.2 and 2.2.

For PPP 2.1.2 the files are

```
/usr/sbin/pppd               # the PPP binary
/usr/sbin/ppp-on             # the dialer/connection script
/usr/sbin/ppp-off            # the disconnection script
/etc/ppp/options             # the options pppd uses for all
                             connections
/etc/ppp/options.ttyXX       # the options specific to a
                             connection on this port
```

For PPP 2.2 the files are

```
/usr/sbin/pppd                     # the PPP binary
/etc/ppp/scripts/ppp-on            # the dialer/connection
                                   script
/etc/ppp/scripts/ppp-on-dialer     # part 1 of the dialer
                                   script
```

```
/etc/ppp/scripts/ppp-off        # the actual chat script
                                itself
/etc/ppp/options                # the options pppd uses for
                                all connections
/etc/ppp/options.ttyXX          # the options specific to a
                                connection on this port
```

Red Hat Linux users should note that the standard Red Hat 4.*x* installation places these scripts in `/usr/doc/ppp-2.2.0f-2/scripts`.

In your /etc directory there should be a PPP directory:

```
drwxrwxr-x  2 root   root      1024 Oct 9 11:01 ppp
```

If it does not exist, create it with these ownerships and permissions.

If the directory already existed, it should contain a template options file called `options.tpl`. This file is included below in case it does not.

Print it out as it contains an explanation of nearly all the PPP options. (These are useful to read in conjunction with the pppd man pages.) While you can use this file as the basis of your `/etc/ppp/options` file, it is probably better to create your own options file that does not include all the comments in the template—it will be much shorter and easier to read/maintain.

If you have multiple serial lines/modems (typically the case for PPP servers), create a general `/etc/ppp/options` file containing the options that are common for all the serial ports on which you are supporting dial-in/out and set up individual option files for each serial line on which you will be establishing a PPP connection with the individual settings required for each port.

These port specific option files are named `options.ttyx1`, `options.ttyx2`, and so forth (where *x* is the appropriate letter for your serial ports).

However, for a single PPP connection, you can happily use the `/etc/ppp/options` file. Alternatively, you can put all the options as arguments in the pppd command itself.

It is easier to maintain a setup that uses `/etc/ppp/options.ttySx` files. If you use PPP to connect to a number of different sites, you can create option files for each site in `/etc/ppp/options.site` and then specify the option file as a parameter to the PPP command as you connect (using the `file option-file` pppd option to pppd on the command line).

The Supplied *Options.tpl* File

Some distributions of PPP seem to have lost the `options.tpl` file, so here is the complete file. I suggest that you do *not* edit this file to create

Part iii

your `/etc/ppp/options` file(s). Rather, copy this to a new file and then edit that. If you mess up your edits, you can then go back to the original and start again.

```
# /etc/ppp/options -*- sh -*- general options for pppd
# created 13-Jul-1995 jmk
# autodate: 01-Aug-1995
# autotime: 19:45

# Use the executable or shell command specified to set up the serial
# line. This script would typically use the "chat" program to dial
# the modem and start the remote ppp session.
#connect "echo You need to install a connect command."

# Run the executable or shell command specified after pppd has
# terminated the link. This script could, for example, issue commands
# to the modem to cause it to hang up if hardware modem control
# the signals were not available.
#disconnect "chat -- \d+++\d\c OK ath0 OK"

# async character map -- 32-bit hex; each bit is a character
# that needs to be escaped for pppd to receive it. 0x00000001
# represents '\x01', and 0x80000000 represents '\x1f'.
#asyncmap 0

# Require the peer to authenticate itself before allowing network
# packets to be sent or received.
#auth

# Use hardware flow control (i.e. RTS/CTS) to control the flow of
# data on the serial port.
#crtscts

# Use software flow control (i.e. XON/XOFF) to control the flow of
# data on the serial port.
#xonxoff

# Add a default route to the system routing tables, using the peer
# as the gateway, when IPCP negotiation is successfully completed.
# This entry is removed when the PPP connection is broken.
#defaultroute

# Specifies that certain characters should be escaped on transmission
# (regardless of whether the peer requests them to be escaped with
# its async control character map). The characters to be escaped are
# specified as a list of hex numbers separated by commas. Note that
# almost any character can be specified for the escape option, unlike
```

```
# the asyncmap option which only allows control characters to be
# specified. The characters which may not be escaped are those with
# hex values 0x200x3f or 0x5e.
#escape 11,13,ff

# Don't use the modem control lines.
#local

# Specifies that pppd should use a UUCP-style lock on the serial
# device to ensure exclusive access to the device.
#lock

# Use the modem control lines. On Ultrix, this option implies
# hardware flow control, as for the crtscts option. (This option is
# not fully implemented.)
#modem

# Set the MRU [Maximum Receive Unit] value to <n> for negotiation.
# pppd will ask the peer to send packets of no more than <n> bytes.
# The minimum MRU value is 128. The default MRU value is 1500. A
# value of 296 is recommended for slow links (40 bytes for TCP/IP
# header + 256 bytes of data).
#mru 542

# Set the interface netmask to <n>, a 32 bit netmask in "decimal dot"
# notation (e.g. 255.255.255.0).
#netmask 255.255.255.0

# Disables the default behaviour when no local IP address is
# specified, which is to determine (if possible) the local IP address
# from the hostname. With this option, the peer will have to supply
# the local IP address during IPCP negotiation (unless it specified
# explicitly on the command line or in an options file).
#noipdefault

# Enables the "passive" option in the LCP. With this option, pppd
# will attempt to initiate a connection; if no reply is received from
# the peer, pppd will then just wait passively for a valid LCP packet
# from the peer (instead of exiting, as it does without this option).
#passive

# With this option, pppd will not transmit LCP packets to initiate a
# connection until a valid LCP packet is received from the peer (as
# for the "passive" option with old versions of pppd).
#silent
```

```
# Don't request or allow negotiation of any options for LCP and IPCP
# (use default values).
#-all

# Disable Address/Control compression negotiation (use default, i.e.
# address/control field disabled).
#-ac

# Disable asyncmap negotiation (use the default asyncmap, i.e. escape
# all control characters).
#-am

# Don't fork to become a background process (otherwise pppd will do
# so if a serial device is specified).
#-detach

# Disable IP address negotiation (with this option, the remote IP
# address must be specified with an option on the command line or in
# an options file).
#-ip

# Disable magic number negotiation. With this option, pppd cannot
# detect a looped-back line.
#-mn

# Disable MRU [Maximum Receive Unit] negotiation (use default, i.e.
# 1500).
#-mru

# Disable protocol field compression negotiation (use default, i.e.
# protocol field compression disabled).
#-pc

# Require the peer to authenticate itself using PAP.
# This requires TWO WAY authentication - do NOT use this for a
# standard PAP authenticated link to an ISP as this will require the
# ISP machine to authenticate itself to your machine (and it will
# not be able to).
#+pap

# Don't agree to authenticate using PAP.
#-pap

# Require the peer to authenticate itself using CHAP [Cryptographic
# Handshake Authentication Protocol] authentication.
# This requires TWO WAY authentication - do NOT use this for a
```

```
# standard CHAP authenticated link to an ISP as this will require the
# ISP machine to authenticate itself to your machine (and it will not
# be able to).
#+chap

# Don't agree to authenticate using CHAP.
#-chap

# Disable negotiation of Van Jacobson style IP header compression
# (use default, i.e. no compression).
#-vj

# Increase debugging level (same as -d). If this option is given,
# pppd will log the contents of all control packets sent or received
# in a readable form. The packets are logged through syslog with
# facility daemon and level debug. This information can be directed
# to a file by setting up /etc/syslog.conf appropriately (see
#  syslog.conf(5)). (If pppd is compiled with extra debugging
# enabled, it will log messages using facility local2 instead of
# daemon).
#debug

# Append the domain name <d> to the local host name for
# authentication purposes. For example, if gethostname() returns
# the name porsche, but the fully qualified domain name is
# porsche.Quotron.COM, you would use the domain option to set the
# domain name to Quotron.COM.
#domain <d>

# Enable debugging code in the kernel-level PPP driver. The argument
# n is a number which is the sum of the following values: 1 to enable
# general debug messages, 2 to request that the contents of received
# packets be printed, and 4 to request that the contents of
# transmitted packets be printed.
#kdebug n

# Set the MTU [Maximum Transmit Unit] value to <n>. Unless the peer
# requests a smaller value via MRU negotiation, pppd will request
# that the kernel networking code send data packets of no more than n
# bytes through the PPP network interface.
#mtu <n>

# Set the name of the local system for authentication purposes to
# <n>. This will probably have to be set to your ISP user name if you
# are using PAP/CHAP.
#name <n>
```

```
# Set the user name to use for authenticating this machine with the
# peer using PAP to <u>.
# Do NOT use this if you are using 'name' above!
#user <u>

# Enforce the use of the host name as the name of the local system
# for authentication purposes (overrides the name option).
#usehostname

# Set the assumed name of the remote system for authentication
# purposes to <n>.
#remotename <n>

# Add an entry to this system's ARP [Address Resolution Protocol]
# table with the IP address of the peer and the Ethernet address of
# this system.
#proxyarp

# Use the system password database for authenticating the peer using
# PAP.
#login

# If this option is given, pppd will send an LCP echo-request frame
# to the peer every n seconds. Under Linux, the echo-request is sent
# when no packets have been received from the peer for n seconds.
# Normally the peer should respond to the echo-request by sending an
# echo-reply. This option can be used with the lcp-echo-failure
# option to detect that the peer is no longer connected.
#lcp-echo-interval <n>

# If this option is given, pppd will presume the peer to be dead if
# n LCP echo-requests are sent without receiving a valid LCP
# echo-reply. If this happens, pppd will terminate the connection.
# Use of this option requires a non-zero value for the lcp-echo-
# interval parameter. This option can be used to enable pppd to
# terminate after the physical connection has been broken (e.g., the
# modem has hung up) in situations where no hardware modem control
# lines are available.
#lcp-echo-failure <n>

# Set the LCP restart interval (retransmission timeout) to <n>
# seconds (default 3).
#lcp-restart <n>

# Set the maximum number of LCP terminate-request transmissions to
# <n> (default 3).
#lcp-max-terminate <n>
```

```
# Set the maximum number of LCP configure-request transmissions to
# <n> (default 10).
# Some PPP servers are slow to start up. You may need to increase
# this if you keep getting 'serial line looped back' errors and your
# are SURE that you have logged in correctly and PPP should be
# starting on the server.
#lcp-max-configure <n>

# Set the maximum number of LCP configure-NAKs returned before
# starting to send configure-Rejects instead to <n> (default 10).
#lcp-max-failure <n>

# Set the IPCP restart interval (retransmission timeout) to <n>
# seconds (default 3).
#ipcp-restart <n>

# Set the maximum number of IPCP terminate-request transmissions to
# <n> (default 3).
#ipcp-max-terminate <n>

# Set the maximum number of IPCP configure-request transmissions to
# <n> (default 10).
#ipcp-max-configure <n>

# Set the maximum number of IPCP configure-NAKs returned before
# starting to send configure-Rejects instead to <n> (default 10).
#ipcp-max-failure <n>

# Set the PAP restart interval (retransmission timeout) to <n>
# seconds (default 3).
#pap-restart <n>

# Set the maximum number of PAP authenticate-request transmissions to
# <n> (default 10).
#pap-max-authreq <n>

# Set the CHAP restart interval (retransmission timeout for
# challenges) to <n> seconds (default 3).
#chap-restart <n>

# Set the maximum number of CHAP challenge transmissions to <n>
# (default 10).
#chap-max-challenge

# If this option is given, pppd will re-challenge the peer every <n>
```

Part iii

```
# seconds.
#chap-interval <n>

# With this option, pppd will accept the peer's idea of our local IP
# address, even if the local IP address was specified in an option.
#ipcp-accept-local

# With this option, pppd will accept the peer's idea of its (remote)
# IP address, even if the remote IP address was specified in an
# option.
#ipcp-accept-remote
```

What Options Should I Use? (No PAP/CHAP)

Well, as in all things, that depends (sigh). The options specified here should work with most servers.

However, if it does *not* work, read the template file (`/etc/ppp/options.tpl`) *and* the pppd man pages *and* speak to the sysadmin/user support people who run the server to which you are connecting.

You should also note that the connect scripts presented here also use some command line options to pppd to make things a bit easier to change.

```
# /etc/ppp/options (NO PAP/CHAP)
#
# Prevent pppd from forking into the background
   -detach
#
# use the modem control lines
   modem
# use uucp style locks to ensure exclusive access to the serial
# device
   lock
# use hardware flow control
   crtscts
# create a default route for this connection in the routing table
   defaultroute
# do NOT set up any "escaped" control sequences
   asyncmap 0
# use a maximum transmission packet size of 552 bytes
   mtu 552
# use a maximum receive packet size of 552 bytes
   mru 552
#
#-------END OF SAMPLE /etc/ppp/options (no PAP/CHAP)
```

If Your PPP Server Uses PAP (Password Authentication Protocol)

If the server to which you are connecting requires PAP or CHAP authentication, you have a little bit more work.

To the above options file, add the following lines:

```
#
# force pppd to use your ISP user name as your 'host name'
# during the authentication process
name <your ISP user name>    # you need to edit this line
#
# If you are running a PPP *server* and need to force PAP or
# CHAP uncomment the appropriate one of the following lines.
# Do NOT use these is you are a client connecting to a PPP
# server (even if it uses PAP or CHAP) as this tells the
# SERVER to authenticate itself to your machine (which almost
# certainly can't do - and the link will fail).
#+chap
#+pap
#
# If you are using ENCRYPTED secrets in the /etc/ppp/pap-secrets
# file, then uncomment the following line.
# Note: this is NOT the same as using MS encrypted passwords as
# can be set up in MS RAS on Windows NT.
#+papcrypt
```


Using MSCHAP

Microsoft Windows NT RAS can be set up to use a variation on CHAP (Challenge/Handshake Authentication Protocol). In your PPP sources tar ball, you will find a file called README.MSCHAP80 that discusses this.

You can determine if the server is requesting authentication using this protocol by enabling debugging for pppd. If the server is requesting MS CHAP authentication, you will see lines like

```
rcvd [LCP ConfReq id=0x2 <asyncmap 0x0> <auth chap 80> _
<magic 0x46a3>]
```

The critical information here is *auth chap 80*.

In order to use MS CHAP, you will need to recompile pppd to support this. Please see the instructions in the README.MSCHAP80 file in the PPP source file for instructions on how to compile and use this variation.

You should note that at present this code supports only Linux PPP clients connecting to an MS Windows NT server. It does *NOT* support setting up a Linux PPP server to use MSCHAP80 authentication from clients.

The PAP/CHAP Secrets File

If you are using PAP or CHAP authentication, then you also need to create the secrets file. These are

```
/etc/ppp/pap-secrets
/etc/ppp/chap-secrets
```

They must be owned by user root, group root, and have file permissions 740 for security.

The first point to note about PAP and CHAP is that they are designed to authenticate *computer systems* not *users*.

Huh? What's the difference? I hear you ask.

Well now, once your computer has made its PPP connection to the server, *any* user on your system can use that connection—not just you. This is why you can set up a WAN (wide area network) link that joins two LANs (local area networks) using PPP.

PAP can (and for CHAP *does*) require *bidirectional* authentication—that is, a valid name and secret is required on each computer for the other computer involved. However, this is *not* the way most PPP servers offering dial-up PPP PAP-authenticated connections operate.

That being said, your ISP will probably have given you a user name and password to allow you to connect to their system and thence the Internet. Your ISP is not interested in your computer's name at all, so you will probably need to use the user name at your ISP as the name for your computer.

This is done using the *name user name* option to pppd. So, if you are to use the user name given you by your ISP, add the line

```
name your_user name_at_your_ISP
```

to your `/etc/ppp/options` file.

Technically, you should really use `user ouruser nameatyourISP` for PAP, but pppd is sufficiently intelligent to interpret *name* as *user* if it is required to use PAP. The advantage of using the *name* option is that this is also valid for CHAP.

As PAP is for authenticating *computers*, technically you need also to specify a remote computer name. However, as most people only have one ISP, you can use a wild card (*) for the remote host name in the secrets file.

It is also worth noting that many ISPs operate multiple modem banks connected to different terminal servers—each with a different name, but accessed from a single (rotary) dial-in number. It can therefore be quite difficult in some circumstances to know ahead of time what the name of the remote computer is, as this depends on which terminal server you connect to!

The PAP Secrets File

The /etc/ppp/pap-secrets file looks like

```
# Secrets for authentication using PAP
# client    server    secret    acceptable_local_IP_addresses
```

The four fields are white space delimited and the last one can be blank (which is what you want for a dynamic and probably static IP allocation from your ISP).

Suppose your ISP gave you a user name of *fred* and a password of *flintstone* you would set the *name fred* option in /etc/ppp/options [.ttySx] and set up your /etc/ppp/pap-secrets file as follows:

```
# Secrets for authentication using PAP
# client    server secret     acceptable_local_IP_addresses
fred        *    flintstone
```

This says for the local machine name *fred* (which we have told pppd to use even though it is not our local machine name) and for *any* server, use the password (secret) of *flintstone*.

Note that we do not need to specify a local IP address, unless we are required to force a particular local, static IP address. Even if you try this, it is unlikely to work as most PPP servers (for security reasons) do not allow the remote system to set the IP number they are to be given.

The CHAP Secrets File

This requires that you have mutual authentication methods—that is you must allow for both your machine to authenticate the remote server *and* the remote server to authenticate your machine.

So, if your machine is `fred` and the remote machine is `barney`, your machine would set `name fred remotename barney` and the remote machine would set `name barney remotename fred` in their respective `/etc/ppp/options.ttySx` files.

The `/etc/chap-secrets` file for fred would look like

```
# Secrets for authentication using CHAP
# client    server secret      acceptable local IP addresses
fred       barney flintstone
barney      fred  wilma
```

and for barney

```
# Secrets for authentication using CHAP
# client    server secret      acceptable local IP addresses
barney      fred  flintstone
fred       barney wilma
```

Note in particular that both machines must have entries for bidirectional authentication. This allows the local machine to authenticate itself to the remote *and* the remote machine to authenticate itself to the local machine.

Handling Multiple PAP-Authenticated Connections

Some users have more than one server to which they connect that use PAP. Provided that your user name is different on each machine to which you want to connect, this is not a problem.

However, many users have the same user name on two (or more—even all) systems to which they connect. This then presents a problem in correctly selecting the appropriate line from `/etc/ppp/pap-secrets`.

As you might expect, PPP provides a mechanism for overcoming this. PPP allows you to set an "assumed name" for the remote (server) end of the connection using the *remotename* option to pppd.

Let us suppose that you connect to two PPP servers using the username *fred*. You set up your `/etc/ppp/pap-secrets` something like

```
fred pppserver1   barney
fred  pppserver2   wilma
```

Now, to set connect to pppserver1 you would use `name fred remotename pppserver1` in your ppp-options and for pppserver2 `name fred remotename pppserver2`.

As you can select the PPP options file to use with pppd using the `file filename` option, you can set up a script to connect to each of your PPP servers, correctly picking the options file to use and hence selecting the right `remotename` option.

Setting up the PPP Connection Manually

Now that you have created your `/etc/ppp/options` and `/etc/resolv.conf` files (and, if necessary, the `/etc/ppp/papchap-secrets` file), you can test the settings by manually establishing a PPP connection. (Once we have the manual connection working, we will automate the process.)

To do this, your communications software must be capable of quitting without resetting the modem. Minicom can do this with Alt-Q (or in older version of minicom Ctrl-Alt-Q).

Make sure you are logged in as root.

Fire up your communications software (such as minicom), dial into the PPP server, and log in as normal. If you need to issue a command to start up PPP on the server, do so. You will now see the garbage you saw before.

If you are using PAP or CHAP, then merely connecting to the remote system should start PPP on the remote and you will see the garbage without logging in (although this may not happen for some servers–try pressing *Enter* and see if the garbage starts up).

Now quit the communications software *without resetting the modem* (Alt-Q or Ctrl-Alt-Q in minicom) and at the Linux prompt (as root) type

```
pppd -d -detach /dev/ttySx 38400 &
```

The -d option turns on debugging–the PPP connection start up conversation will be logged to your system log–which is useful if you are having trouble.

Your modem lights should now flash as the PPP connection is established. It will take a short while for the PPP connection to be made.

At this point you can look at the PPP interface, by issuing the command

```
ifconfig
```

In addition to any Ethernet and loop back devices you have, you should see something like

```
ppp0    Link encap:Point-Point Protocol
        inet addr:10.144.153.104 P-t-P:10.144.153.51
        Mask:255.255.255.0
        UP POINTOPOINT RUNNING MTU:552 Metric:1
        RX packets:0 errors:0 dropped:0 overruns:0
        TX packets:0 errors:0 dropped:0 overruns:0
```

Where

- inet addr:10.144.153.10 is the IP number of your end of the link
- P-t-P:10.144.153.5 is the SERVER's IP number

(Naturally, ifconfig will not report these IP numbers, but the ones used by your PPP server.)

NOTE

ifconfig also tells you that the link is UP and RUNNING!

If you get no PPP device listed or something like

```
ppp0    Link encap:Point-Point Protocol
        inet addr:0.0.0.0 P-t-P:0.0.0.0 Mask:0.0.0.0
        POINTOPOINT MTU:1500 Metric:1
        RX packets:0 errors:0 dropped:0 overruns:0
        TX packets:0 errors:0 dropped:0 overruns:0
```

your PPP connection has not been made...see the later section on debugging!

You should also be able to see a route to the the remote host (and beyond). To do this, issue the command

```
route -n
```

You should see something like

```
Kernel routing table
Destination   Gateway       Genmask          Flags MSS   Window Use Iface
10.144.153.3  *             255.255.255.255  UH    1500  0        1 ppp0
127.0.0.0     *             255.0.0.0        U     3584  0       11 lo
10.0.0.0      *             255.0.0.0        U     1500  0       35 eth0
default       10.144.153.3  *                UG    1500  0        5 ppp0
```

Of particular importance here, notice we have *two* entries pointing to our PPP interface.

The first is a HOST route (indicated by the H flag) and that allows us to see the host we are connected to—but no further.

The second is the default route (established by giving pppd the option `defaultroute`). This is the route that tells our Linux box to send any packets *not* destined for the local Ethernet(s)—to which we have specific network routes—to the PPP server itself. The PPP server then is responsible for routing our packets out onto the Internet and routing the return packets back to us.

If you do not see a routing table with two entries, something is wrong. In particular if your syslog shows a message telling you pppd is not replacing an existing default route, then you have a default route pointing at your Ethernet interface—which *MUST* be replaced by a specific network route: *YOU CAN ONLY HAVE ONE DEFAULT ROUTE!!!*

You will need to explore your system initialization files to find out where this default route is being set up (it will use a `route add default`... command). Change this command to something like `route add net`....

Now test the link by *pinging* the server at its IP number as reported by the ifconfig output, i.e.

```
ping 10.144.153.51
```

You should receive output like

```
PING 10.144.153.51 (10.144.153.51): 56 data bytes
64 bytes from 10.144.153.51: icmp_seq=0 ttl=255 time=328.3 ms
64 bytes from 10.144.153.51: icmp_seq=1 ttl=255 time=190.5 ms
64 bytes from 10.144.153.51: icmp_seq=2 ttl=255 time=187.5 ms
64 bytes from 10.144.153.51: icmp_seq=3 ttl=255 time=170.7 ms
```

This listing will go on forever—to stop it press Ctrl-C, at which point you will receive some more information:

```
--- 10.144.153.51 ping statistics ---
4 packets transmitted, 4 packets received, 0% packet loss
round-trip min/avg/max = 170.7/219.2/328.3 ms
```

So far so good.

Now try pinging a host by name (not the name of the PPP server itself but a host at another site that you *know* is probably going to be up and running...). For example:

```
ping MetaLab.unc.edu
```

This time there will be a bit of a pause as Linux obtains the IP number for the fully qualified host name you have pinged from the DNS you specified in `/etc/resolv.conf`—so don't worry (but you will see your modem lights flash). Shortly you will receive output like

```
 PING MetaLab.unc.edu (152.2.254.81): 56 data bytes
64 bytes from 152.2.254.81: icmp_seq=0 ttl=254 time=190.1 ms
64 bytes from 152.2.254.81: icmp_seq=1 ttl=254 time=180.6 ms
```

```
64 bytes from 152.2.254.81: icmp_seq=2 ttl=254 time=169.8 ms
64 bytes from 152.2.254.81: icmp_seq=3 ttl=254 time=170.6 ms
64 bytes from 152.2.254.81: icmp_seq=4 ttl=254 time=170.6 ms
```

Again, stop the output by pressing Ctrl-C and get the statistics.

```
--- MetaLab.unc.edu ping statistics ---
5 packets transmitted, 5 packets received, 0% packet loss
round-trip min/avg/max = 169.8/176.3/190.1 ms
```

If you don't get any response, try pinging the IP address of the DNS server at your ISP's site. If you get a result from this, then it looks like you have a problem with `/etc/resolv.conf`.

If this doesn't work, you have a routing problem, or your ISP has a problem routing packets back to you. Check your routing table as shown above and if that is OK, contact your ISP. A good test of the ISP is to use another operating system to connect. If you can get beyond your ISP with that, then the problem is at your end.

If everything works, shut down the connection by typing:

```
ppp-off
```

After a short pause, the modem should hang itself up.

If that does not work, either turn off your modem or fire up your communications software and interrupt the modem with +++ and then hang up with ATH0 when you receive the modem's OK prompt.

You may also need to clean up the lock file created by pppd

```
rm -f /var/lock/LCK..ttySx
```

Automating Your Connections— Creating the Connection Scripts

While you can continue to log in by hand as shown above, it is much neater to set up some scripts to do this automatically for you.

A set of scripts automates the log in and PPP start up so all you have to do (as root or as a member of the PPP group) is issue a single command to fire up your connection.

Connection Scripts for User Name/Password Authentication

If your ISP does NOT require the use of PAP/CHAP, these are the scripts for you!

If the PPP package installed correctly, you should have two example files. For PPP 2.1.2 they are in `/usr/sbin` and for PPP 2.2 they are in `/etc/ppp/scripts`. They are called:

for PPP-2.1.2

```
ppp-on
ppp-off
```

for PPP-2.2.2

```
ppp-off
ppp-on
ppp-on-dialer
```

Now, if you are using PPP 2.1.2, I strongly urge you to delete the sample files. There are potential problems with these—and don't tell me they work fine—I used them for ages too (and recommended them in the first version of this HOWTO)!

For the benefit of PPP 2.1.2 users, here are *better* template versions, taken from the PPP 2.2 distribution. I suggest you copy and use these scripts *instead of* the old PPP-2.1.2 scripts.

The ppp-on Script

This is the first of a *pair* of scripts that actually fire up the connection.

```
#!/bin/sh
#
# Script to initiate a PPP connection. This is the first part of the
# pair of scripts. This is not a secure pair of scripts as the codes
# are visible with the 'ps' command. However, it is simple.
#
# These are the parameters. Change as needed.
TELEPHONE=555-1212   # The telephone number for the connection
ACCOUNT=george      # The account name for logon (as in 'George
                    # Burns')
PASSWORD=gracie      # The password for this account (and 'Gracie
                     # Allen')
LOCAL_IP=0.0.0.0     # Local IP address if known. Dynamic = 0.0.0.0
REMOTE_IP=0.0.0.0    # Remote IP address if desired. Normally 0.0.0.0
NETMASK=255.255.255.0  # The proper netmask if needed
#
# Export them so that they will be available to 'ppp-on-dialer'
export TELEPHONE ACCOUNT PASSWORD
#
# This is the location of the script which dials the phone and logs
# in. Please use the absolute file name as the $PATH variable is not
```

Part iii

```
# used on the connect option. (To do so on a 'root' account would be
# a security hole so don't ask.)
#
DIALER_SCRIPT=/etc/ppp/ppp-on-dialer
#
# Initiate the connection
#
#
exec /usr/sbin/pppd debug /dev/ttySx 38400 \
    $LOCAL_IP:$REMOTE_IP \
    connect $DIALER_SCRIPT
```

Here is the ppp-on-dialer script:

```
#!/bin/sh
#
# This is part 2 of the ppp-on script. It will perform the
# connection protocol for the desired connection.
#
/usr/sbin/chat -v                                   \
    TIMEOUT       3                     \
    ABORT         '\nBUSY\r'                \
    ABORT         '\nNO ANSWER\r'               \
    ABORT         '\nRINGING\r\n\r\nRINGING\r'   \
    ''         \rAT                         \
    'OK-+++\c-OK'  ATH0                         \
    TIMEOUT       30                    \
    OK         ATDT$TELEPHONE               \
    CONNECT       ''                    \
    ogin:--ogin:  $ACCOUNT                  \
    assword:      $PASSWORD
```

For PPP-2.2, the `ppp-off` script looks like

```
#!/bin/sh
######################################################################
#
# Determine the device to be terminated.
#
if [ "$1" = "" ]; then
    DEVICE=ppp0
else
    DEVICE=$1
fi

######################################################################
#
# If the ppp0 pid file is present then the program is running.
```

```
# Stop it.
if [ -r /var/run/$DEVICE.pid ]; then
    kill -INT `cat /var/run/$DEVICE.pid`
#
# If the kill did not work then there is no process running for
# this pid. It may also mean that the lock file will be left. You
# may wish to delete the lock file at the same time.
    if [ ! "$?" = "0" ]; then
        rm -f /var/run/$DEVICE.pid
        echo "ERROR: Removed stale pid file"
        exit 1
    fi
#
# Success. Let pppd clean up its own junk.
    echo "PPP link to $DEVICE terminated."
    exit 0
fi
#
# The ppp process is not running for ppp0
echo "ERROR: PPP link is not active on $DEVICE"
exit 1
```

Editing the Supplied PPP Startup Scripts

As the new scripts come in two parts, we will edit them in turn.

The ppp-on script

You will need to edit the script to reflect *your* user name at your ISP, *your* password at your ISP, and the telephone number of your ISP.

Each of the lines like TELEPHONE= actually sets up shell variables that contain the information to the right of the "=" (excluding the comments, of course). So edit each of these lines so it is correct for your ISP and connection.

Also, as you are setting the IP number (if you need to) in the /etc/ppp/options file, *delete* the line that says

```
$LOCAL_IP:$REMOTE_IP \
```

Also, make sure that the shell variable *DIALERSCRIPT* points at the full path and name of the dialer script that you are actually going to use. So, if you have moved this or renamed the script, make sure you edit this line correctly in the ppp-on script!

Part iii

The ppp-on-dialer script

This is the second of the scripts that actually brings up our PPP link.

NOTE

A chat script is normally all on one line; the backslashes are used to allow line continuations across several physical lines (for human readability) and do not form part of the script itself. However, it is very useful to look at it in detail so that we understand what it is actually (supposed) to be doing!

What a Chat Script Means

A chat script is a sequence of *expect string send string* pairs. In particular, note that we *always* expect *something* before we send something.

If we are to send something *without* receiving anything first, we must use an empty expect string (indicated by "") and similarly for expecting something without sending anything! Also, if a string consists of several words (e.g. NO CARRIER), you must quote the string so that it is seen as a single entity by chat.

The chat line in our template is

```
exec /usr/sbin/chat -v
```

Invoke chat, the -v tells chat to copy *all* its I/O into the system log (usually `/var/log/messages`). Once you are happy that the chat script is working reliably, edit this line to remove the -v to save unnecessary clutter in your syslog.

```
TIMEOUT      3
```

This sets the timeout for the receipt of expected input to three seconds. You may need to increase this to say five or ten seconds if you are using a really slow modem!

```
ABORT        '\nBUSY\r'
```

If the string *BUSY* is received, abort the operation.

```
ABORT        '\nNO ANSWER\r'
```

If the string *NO ANSWER* is received, abort the operation

```
ABORT        '\nRINGING\r\n\r\nRINGING\r'
```

If the (repeated) string *RINGING* is received, abort the operation. This is because someone is ringing your phone line!

```
""       \rAT
```

Expect nothing from the modem and send the string AT.

```
OK-+++\c-OK  ATH0
```

This one is a bit more complicated as it uses some of chat's error recovery capabilities.

What is says is...Expect *OK*; if it is *not* received (because the modem is not in command mode) then send +++ (the standard Hayes-compatible modem string that returns the modem to command mode) and expect *OK*. Then send ATH0 (the modem hangup string). This allows your script to cope with the situation of your modem being stuck online.

```
TIMEOUT     30
```

Set the timeout to 30 seconds for the remainder of the script. If you experience trouble with the chat script aborting due to timeouts, increase this to 45 seconds or more.

```
OK          ATDT$TELEPHONE
```

Expect *OK* (the modem's response to the ATH0 command) and dial the number we want to call.

```
CONNECT     ''
```

Expect *CONNECT* (which our modem sends when the remote modem answers) and send nothing in reply.

```
ogin:--ogin:  $ACCOUNT
```

Again, we have some error recovery built in here. Expect the login prompt (...ogin:) but if we don't receive it by the timeout, send a return and then look for the login prompt again. When the prompt is received, send the user name (stored in the shell variable *ACCOUNT*).

```
assword:     $PASSWORD
```

Expect the password prompt and send our password (again, stored in a shell variable).

This chat script has reasonable error recovery capability. Chat has considerably more features than demonstrated here. For more information consult the chat manual page (`man 8 chat`).

Starting PPP at the Server End

While the ppp-on-dialer script is fine for servers that automatically start pppd at the server end once you have logged in, some servers require that you explicitly start PPP on the server.

If you need to issue a command to start up PPP on the server, you *do* need to edit the ppp-on-dialer script.

At the END of the script (after the password line) add an additional *expect send* pair—this one would look for your login prompt (beware of characters that have a special meaning in the Bourne shell—such as [and or] (open and close square brackets).

Once chat has found the shell prompt, chat must issue the PPP startup command required for your ISP's PPP server.

In my case, my PPP server uses the standard Linux Bash prompt

```
[hartr@kepler hartr]$
```

and requires that I type

```
ppp
```

to start up PPP on the server.

It is a good idea to allow for a bit of error recovery here, so in my case I use

```
hartr--hartr  ppp
```

This says, if we don't receive the prompt within the timeout, send a carriage return and look for the prompt again.

Once the prompt is received, then send the string ppp.

NOTE

Don't forget to add a \ to the end of the previous line so chat still thinks the entire chat script is on one line.

Unfortunately, some servers produce a very variable set of prompts. You may need to log in several times using minicom to understand what is going on and pick the stable *expect* strings.

A Chat Script for PAP/CHAP Authenticated Connections

If your ISP is using PAP/CHAP, then your chat script is much simpler. All your chat script needs to do is dial the telephone, wait for a connect, and then let pppd handle the logging in.

```
#!/bin/sh
#
# This is part 2 of the ppp-on script. It will perform the
# connection protocol for the desired connection.
#
exec /usr/sbin/chat -v                    \
    TIMEOUT     3                    \
```

```
ABORT       '\nBUSY\r'              \
ABORT       '\nNO ANSWER\r'         \
ABORT       '\nRINGING\r\n\r\nRINGING\r'  \
''      \rAT                        \
'OK-+++\c-OK'  ATH0                 \
TIMEOUT    30                       \
OK      ATDT$TELEPHONE              \
CONNECT    ''                       \
```

The pppd *debug* and *file optionfile* Options

As we have already seen, you can turn on debug information logging with the *-d* option to pppd. The *debug* option is equivalent to this.

As we are establishing a new connection with a new script, leave in the debug option for now.

WARNING

If your disk space is tight, logging pppd exchanges can rapidly extend your syslog file and run you into trouble—but to do this you must fail to connect and keep on trying for quite a few minutes).

Once you are happy that all is working properly, then you can remove this option.

If you have called your PPP options file anything other than `/etc/ppp/options` or `/etc/ppp/options.ttySx`, specify the file name with the *file* option to pppd–for example

```
exec /usr/sbin/pppd debug file options.myserver /dev/ttyS0\ 38400
```

Part iii

Testing Your Connection Script

Open a new root Xterm (if you are in X) or open a new virtual console and log in as root.

In this new session, issue the command

```
tail -f /var/log/messages
```

(or whatever your system log file is).

In the first window (or virtual console) issue the command

```
ppp-on
```

(or whatever name you have called your edited version of /usr/sbin/ppp-on). If you do not put the script into the background by specifying at the end of the command, you will not get your terminal prompt back until PPP exits (when the link terminates).

Now switch back to the window that is tracking your system log.

You will see something like the following (provided you specified *-v* to chat and *-d* to pppd) this is the chat script and responses being logged to the system log file followed by the startup information for pppd:

```
Oct 21 16:09:58 hwin chat[19868]: abort on (NO CARRIER)
Oct 21 16:09:59 hwin chat[19868]: abort on (BUSY)
Oct 21 16:09:59 hwin chat[19868]: send (ATZ^M)
Oct 21 16:09:59 hwin chat[19868]: expect (OK)
Oct 21 16:10:00 hwin chat[19868]: ATZ^M^M
Oct 21 16:10:00 hwin chat[19868]: OK -- got it
Oct 21 16:10:00 hwin chat[19868]: send (ATDT722298^M)
Oct 21 16:10:00 hwin chat[19868]: expect (CONNECT)
Oct 21 16:10:00 hwin chat[19868]: ^M
Oct 21 16:10:22 hwin chat[19868]: ATDT722298^M^M
Oct 21 16:10:22 hwin chat[19868]: CONNECT -- got it
Oct 21 16:10:22 hwin chat[19868]: send (^M)
Oct 21 16:10:22 hwin chat[19868]: expect (ogin:)
Oct 21 16:10:23 hwin chat[19868]: kepler login: -- got it
Oct 21 16:10:23 hwin chat[19868]: send (hartr^M)
Oct 21 16:10:23 hwin chat[19868]: expect (ssword:)
Oct 21 16:10:23 hwin chat[19868]: hartr^M
Oct 21 16:10:23 hwin chat[19868]: Password: -- got it
Oct 21 16:10:23 hwin chat[19868]: send (??????^M)
Oct 21 16:10:23 hwin chat[19868]: expect (hartr)
Oct 21 16:10:24 hwin chat[19868]: [hartr -- got it
Oct 21 16:10:24 hwin chat[19868]: send (ppp^M)
Oct 21 16:10:27 hwin pppd[19872]: pppd 2.1.2 started by root, uid 0
Oct 21 16:10:27 hwin pppd[19873]: Using interface ppp0
Oct 21 16:10:27 hwin pppd[19873]: Connect: ppp0 <--> /dev/cua1
Oct 21 16:10:27 hwin pppd[19873]: fsm_sdata(LCP): Sent code 1, id 1.
Oct 21 16:10:27 hwin pppd[19873]: LCP: sending Configure-Request, id 1
Oct 21 16:10:27 hwin pppd[19873]: fsm_rconfreq(LCP): Rcvd id 1.
Oct 21 16:10:27 hwin pppd[19873]: lcp_reqci: rcvd MRU
Oct 21 16:10:27 hwin pppd[19873]: (1500)
Oct 21 16:10:27 hwin pppd[19873]: (ACK)
Oct 21 16:10:27 hwin pppd[19873]: lcp_reqci: rcvd ASYNCMAP
Oct 21 16:10:27 hwin pppd[19873]: (0)
Oct 21 16:10:27 hwin pppd[19873]: (ACK)
Oct 21 16:10:27 hwin pppd[19873]: lcp_reqci: rcvd MAGICNUMBER
Oct 21 16:10:27 hwin pppd[19873]: (a098b898)
Oct 21 16:10:27 hwin pppd[19873]: (ACK)
```

```
Oct 21 16:10:27 hwin pppd[19873]: lcp_reqci: rcvd PCOMPRESSION
Oct 21 16:10:27 hwin pppd[19873]: (ACK)
Oct 21 16:10:27 hwin pppd[19873]: lcp_reqci: rcvd ACCOMPRESSION
Oct 21 16:10:27 hwin pppd[19873]: (ACK)
Oct 21 16:10:27 hwin pppd[19873]: lcp_reqci: returning CONFACK.
Oct 21 16:10:27 hwin pppd[19873]: fsm_sdata(LCP): Sent code 2, id 1.
Oct 21 16:10:27 hwin pppd[19873]: fsm_rconfack(LCP): Rcvd id 1.
Oct 21 16:10:27 hwin pppd[19873]: fsm_sdata(IPCP): Sent code 1, id 1.
Oct 21 16:10:27 hwin pppd[19873]: IPCP: sending Configure-Request, id 1
Oct 21 16:10:27 hwin pppd[19873]: fsm_rconfreq(IPCP): Rcvd id 1.
Oct 21 16:10:27 hwin pppd[19873]: ipcp: received ADDR
Oct 21 16:10:27 hwin pppd[19873]: (10.144.153.51)
Oct 21 16:10:27 hwin pppd[19873]: (ACK)
Oct 21 16:10:27 hwin pppd[19873]: ipcp: received COMPRESSTYPE
Oct 21 16:10:27 hwin pppd[19873]: (45)
Oct 21 16:10:27 hwin pppd[19873]: (ACK)
Oct 21 16:10:27 hwin pppd[19873]: ipcp: returning Configure-ACK
Oct 21 16:10:28 hwin pppd[19873]: fsm_sdata(IPCP): Sent code 2, id 1.
Oct 21 16:10:30 hwin pppd[19873]: fsm_sdata(IPCP): Sent code 1, id 1.
Oct 21 16:10:30 hwin pppd[19873]: IPCP: sending Configure-Request, id 1
Oct 21 16:10:30 hwin pppd[19873]: fsm_rconfreq(IPCP): Rcvd id 255.
Oct 21 16:10:31 hwin pppd[19873]: ipcp: received ADDR
Oct 21 16:10:31 hwin pppd[19873]: (10.144.153.51)
Oct 21 16:10:31 hwin pppd[19873]: (ACK)
Oct 21 16:10:31 hwin pppd[19873]: ipcp: received COMPRESSTYPE
Oct 21 16:10:31 hwin pppd[19873]: (45)
Oct 21 16:10:31 hwin pppd[19873]: (ACK)
Oct 21 16:10:31 hwin pppd[19873]: ipcp: returning Configure-ACK
Oct 21 16:10:31 hwin pppd[19873]: fsm_sdata(IPCP): Sent code 2, id 255.
Oct 21 16:10:31 hwin pppd[19873]: fsm_rconfack(IPCP): Rcvd id 1.
Oct 21 16:10:31 hwin pppd[19873]: ipcp: up
Oct 21 16:10:31 hwin pppd[19873]: local IP address 10.144.153.104
Oct 21 16:10:31 hwin pppd[19873]: remote IP address 10.144.153.51
```

NOTE

I am using static IP numbers—hence my machine sent that to the PPP server; you won't see this if you are using dynamic IP numbers. Also, this server requires a specific command to start PPP at its end.

This looks OK–so test it out as before with pings to IP numbers and host names.

Fire up you Web browser or whatever and go surfing–you are connected.

Shutting down the PPP Link

When you have finished with the PPP link, use the standard ppp-off command to shut it down (remember—you need to be root or a member of the PPP group).

In your system log you will see something like

```
Oct 21 16:10:45 hwin pppd[19873]: Interrupt received: ↵
terminating link
Oct 21 16:10:45 hwin pppd[19873]: ipcp: down
Oct 21 16:10:45 hwin pppd[19873]: default route
ioctl(SIOCDELRT): Bad address
Oct 21 16:10:45 hwin pppd[19873]: fsm_sdata(LCP): ↵
Sent code 5, id 2.
Oct 21 16:10:46 hwin pppd[19873]: fsm_rtermack(LCP).
Oct 21 16:10:46 hwin pppd[19873]: Connection terminated.
Oct 21 16:10:46 hwin pppd[19873]: Exit.
```

Don't worry about the `SIOCDELRT`—this is just pppd noting that it is terminating and is nothing to worry about.

Debugging

There are any number of reasons that your connection does not work—chat has failed to complete correctly, you have a dirty line, etc. So check your syslog for indications.

I Have Compiled PPP Support into the Kernel, But...

A very common problem is that people compile PPP support into the kernel and yet when they try to run pppd, the kernel complains that it does not support PPP! There are a variety of reasons this can occur.

Are You Booting the Right Kernel? While you *have* recompiled your kernel to support PPP, you are not booting the new kernel. This can happen if you do not update `/etc/lilo.conf` and rerun lilo.

A good check on the kernel can be obtained by issuing the command `uname -a`, which should produce a line like

```
Linux archenland 2.0.28 #2 Thu Feb 13 12:31:37 EST 1997 i586
```

This gives the kernel version and the date on which this kernel was compiled—which should give you a pretty good idea of what is going on.

Did You Compile PPP Kernel Support as a Module? If you compiled your kernel PPP support as a module, but did not make and install the modules, then you can get this error. Check the kernel-HOWTO and the README file in `/usr/src/linux`.

Another module-connected possibility is that you are expecting required modules to be automatically loaded, but are not running the `kerneld` daemon (which auto-loads and unloads modules on the fly). Check the kerneld mini-HOWTO for information on setting up kerneld.

Are You Using the Correct Version of PPP for Your Kernel? You *must* use ppp-2.2 with kernel version 2.0.*x*. You can use ppp-2.2 with kernel version 1.2.*x* (if you patch the kernel); otherwise you must use ppp-2.1.2.

Are You Running pppd as Root? If you are not running pppd as the root user (and pppd is not suid to root), you can receive this message.

My Modem Connects but PPP Never Starts Up

There are innumerable variations on this (take a look in `comp.os.linux`...).

A *very* common mistake is that you have mistyped something in your scripts. The only thing to do here is to make sure you are logging the chat conversation between your Linux box and the server into your syslog (`/var/log/messages`) and then go through this *line by line*. You may need to dial into the PPP server manually to check things out again.

You need to check the log against the actual prompts very carefully—and bear in mind that we humans have a tendency to read what we *think* we have typed—not what is actually there.

The syslog Says *Serial Line Is Not 8 Bit Clean...*

There are variations on this too—such as `serial line looped back`, etc., and the cause can be one (or a sequence) of a number of things.

To understand what is going on here, it is necessary to grasp a bit of what is going on behind the scenes in pppd itself.

When pppd starts up, it sends LCP (Link Control Protocol) packets to the remote machine. If it receives a valid response it then goes on to the next stage (using IPCP -IP control protocol packets) and only when this negotiation completes is the actual IP layer started so that you can use the PPP link.

If there is no PPP server operating at the remote end when your PC sends LCP packets, these get reflected by the login process at the far end. As these packets use 8 bits, reflecting them strips the 8th bit (remember, ASCII is a 7 bit code). PPP sees this and complains accordingly.

There are several reasons this reflection can occur:

You Are Not Correctly Logging into the Server When your chat script completes, pppd starts on your PC. However, if you have not completed the login process to the server (including sending any command required to start PPP on the server), PPP will not start.

So, the LCP packets are reflected and you receive this error.

You need to carefully check and correct (if necessary) your chat script (see above).

You Are Not Starting PPP on the Server Some PPP servers require you to enter a command and/or a *return* after completing the login process before the remote end starts PPP.

Check your chat script (see above).

If you log in manually and find you need to send a RETURN after this to start PPP, simply add a blank expect/send pair to the end of your chat script (an empty *send* string actually sends a *return*).

The Remote PPP Process Is Slow to Start This one is a bit tricky!

By default, your Linux pppd is compiled to send a maximum of 10 LCP configuration requests. If the server is a bit slow to start up, all 10 such requests can be sent before the remote PPP is ready to receive them.

On your machine, pppd sees all 10 requests reflected back (with the 8th bit stripped) and exits.

There are two ways round this:

- Add `lcp-max-configure 30` to your PPP options. This increases the maximum number of LCP configure packets pppd sends before giving up. For a really slow server, you may need even more than this.

- Alternatively, you can get a bit tricky in return. You may have noticed that when you logged in by hand to the PPP server and PPP started there, the *first* character of the PPP garbage that appears was always the tilde character (~). Using this knowledge we can add a new `expect/send` pair to the end of the chat script which expects a tilde and sends nothing. This would look like:

```
\~      ''
```

NOTE

As the tilde character has a special meaning in the shell, it must be escaped (and hence the leading backslash).

Default Route Not Set

If pppd refuses to set up a default route, it is because (quite correctly) it refuses *remove/replace an existing default route.*

The usual reason that this error occurs is that some distributions set up a default route via your Ethernet card as opposed to setting up a specific network route.

See the Linux NAG and the Net2/3 HOWTOs for information on correctly setting up your Ethernet card and associated routes.

An alternative to this is that your LAN uses a gateway/router already and your routing table has been set up to point the default route at this.

Fixing up this last situation can require a fair bit of IP networking knowledge and is beyond the scope of this HOWTO. It is suggested you obtain some expert advice (via the news groups or from someone locally you can ask).

Other Problems

There are many reasons apart from these that PPP fails to connect and/or operate properly.

Look in the PPP FAQ (which is really a series of questions and answers). This is a very comprehensive document and the answers *are* there. From my own (sad) experience, if the answer to your problems is not there, the problem is not PPP's fault! In my case I was using an ELF kernel that I had not upgraded to the appropriate kernel modules. I only wasted about two days (and most of one night) cursing what had been a perfect PPP server before the light dawned!

Getting Help When Totally Stuck

If you can't get your PPP link to work, go back through this document and check everything—in conjunction with the output created by *chat-v...* and *pppd -d* in your system log.

Also consult the PPP documentation and FAQ plus the other documents mentioned herein.

If you are still stuck, try the `comp.os.linux.misc`, `comp.os.linux.networking`, and `comp.protocols.ppp` newsgroups, which are reasonably regularly scanned by people that can help you with PPP.

You can try sending me personal e-mail, but I do have a day job (and a life) and I do not guarantee a response quickly (if at all) as this depends on my current workload and the state of my private life.

In particular—do not post reams of debugging output to the news groups nor send it to me by e-mail—the former wastes huge amounts of network bandwidth and the latter will be consigned to `/dev/null` (unless I have specifically requested it).

Common Problems Once the Link Is Working

One problem you will find is that many service providers will only support the connection software package that they distribute to new accounts. This is (typically) for Microsoft Windows and many service provider help-desks seem to know nothing about Unix (or Linux). So, be prepared for limited assistance from them.

You could of course do the individual a favour and educate them about Linux. (Any ISP help-desk person should be reasonably "with it" in Internet terms and that means they should have a home Linux box—of course it does.)

I Can't See Beyond the PPP Server I Connect To

OK—your PPP connection is up and running and you can ping the PPP server by IP number (the second or *remote* IP number shown by `ifconfig ppp0`), but you can't reach anything beyond this.

First of all, try pinging the IP numbers you have specified in `/etc/resolv.conf` as name servers. If this works, you *can* see beyond your PPP server (unless this has the same IP number as the *remote* IP number of your connection). So now try pinging the full Internet name of your service provider, for example

```
ping my.provider.net.au
```

If this does *not* work, you have a problem with the name resolution. This is probably because of a typo in your `/etc/resolv.conf` file. Check this carefully against the information you acquired by ringing your service provider. If all looks OK, ring your service provider and check that you wrote down the IP numbers correctly.

If it *still* doesn't work (and your service provider confirms that their name servers are up and running), you have a problem somewhere else—and I suggest you check carefully through your Linux installation (looking particularly for file permissions).

If you *still* can't ping your service provider's IP name servers by IP number, either they are down (give them a voice call and check) or there is a routing problem at your service provider's end. Again, ring them and check this out.

One possibility is that the *remote end* is a Linux PPP server where the IP forwarding option has not been specified in the kernel!

A good general test is to try connecting to your service provider using the software that most supply for (gulp) Microsoft Windows. If everything works from another operating system to exactly the same account, then the problem is with your Linux system and *not* your service provider.

I Can Send E-Mail, but Not Receive It

If you are using dynamic IP numbers, this is perfectly normal. See the "Setting up Services" section.

Why Can't People Finger, WWW, Gopher, Talk, Etc., to My Machine?

Again, if you are using dynamic IP numbers, this is perfectly normal. See the "Setting up Services" section.

Using Internet Services with Dynamic IP Numbers

If you are using dynamic IP numbers (and many service providers will only give you a dynamic IP number unless you pay significantly more for your connection), then you have to recognize the limitations this imposes.

First of all, outbound service requests will work just fine. That is, you can send e-mail using Sendmail (provided you have correctly set up Sendmail), ftp files from remote sites, finger users on other machines, browse the Web, etc.

In particular, you can answer e-mail that you have brought down to your machine while you are offline. Mail will simply sit in your mail queue until you dial back into your ISP.

However, your machine is *not* connected to the Internet 24 hours a day, nor does it have the same IP number every time it is connected. So it is impossible for you to receive e-mail directed to your machine, and very difficult to set up a Web or ftp server that your friends can access! As far as the Internet is concerned your machine does not exist as a unique, permanently contactable machine as it does not have a unique IP number (remember—other machines will be using the IP number when they are allocated it on dial-in).

If you set up a WWW (or any other server), it is totally unknown by any user on the Internet *unless* they know that your machine is connected *and* its actual (current) IP number. There are a number of ways they can get this info, ranging from you ringing them, sending them e-mail to tell, or cunning use of *.plan* files on a shell account at your service provider (assuming that your provider allows shell and finger access).

Now, for most users, this is not a problem—all that most people want is to send and receive e-mail (using your account on your service provider) and make outbound connections to WWW, ftp, and other servers on the

Internet. If you *must* have inbound connections to your server, you should really get a static IP number. Alternatively you can explore the methods hinted at above.

Setting up E-mail

Even for dynamic IP numbers, you can certainly configure Sendmail on your machine to send out any e-mail that you compose locally. Configuration of Sendmail can be obscure and difficult—so this document does not attempt to tell you how to do this. However, you should probably configure Sendmail so that your Internet service provider is designated as your *smart relay* host (the `sendmail.cf` *DS* option). (For more Sendmail configuration info, see the Sendmail documents—and look at the m4 configurations that come with Sendmail. There is almost certain to be one there that will meet your needs.)

There are also excellent books on Sendmail (notably the "bible" from O'Reilly and Associates), but these are almost certainly overkill for most users.

Once you have Sendmail configured, you will probably want to have Sendmail dispatch any messages that have been sitting in the outbound mail queue as soon as the PPP connection comes up. To do this, add the command

```
sendmail -q &
```

to your `/etc/ppp/ip-up` script (see the following).

Inbound e-mail is a problem for dynamic IP numbers. The way to handle this is to

- configure your mail user agent so that all mail is sent out with a *reply to* header giving your e-mail address at your Internet Service Provider. If you can, you should also set your *from* address to be your e-mail address at your ISP as well.
- use the popclient, fetchmail programs to retrieve your e-mail from your service provider. Alternatively, if your ISP is using IMAP, use an IMAP enabled mail user agent (such as pine).

You can automate this process at dial-up time by putting the necessary commands in the `/etc/ppp/ip-up` script (see the following).

Setting Up a Local Name Server

While you can quite happily use the domain name servers located at your ISP, you can also set up a local caching-only (secondary) name server that is brought up by the `ip-up` script. The advantage of running a local (caching only) name server is that it will save you time (and bandwidth) if you frequently contact the same sites during a long online session.

DNS configuration for a caching only name server (that uses a *forwarders'* line in the `named.boot` file pointing at your ISPs DNS) is relatively simple. The O'Reilly book (*DNS and Bind*) explains all you want to know about this.

There is also a DNS-HOWTO available.

If you are running a small LAN that can access the Internet through your Linux box (using IP Masquerade for example), it is probably a good idea to run a local name server (with a forwarders' directive) while the link is up as this will minimize the bandwidth and delays associated with name resolution.

One point of Nettiquette: Ask permission from your ISP before you start using a secondary, caching-only name server in your ISP's domain. Properly configured, your DNS will not cause any problems to your ISP at all, but if you get things wrong, it can cause problems.

Linking Two Networks Using PPP

There is basically no difference between linking a single Linux box to a PPP server and linking two LANs using PPP on a machine on each LAN. Remember, PPP is a *peer to peer* protocol.

However, you *definitely* need to understand how routing is established. Read the NET-2 HOWTO and the Linux Network Administrator Guide (NAG). You will also find *TCP/IP Network Administration* (published by O'Reilly and Assoc., ISBN 0-937175-82-X) to be of invaluable assistance.

If you are going to be subnetworking an IP network number on either side of the link, you will also find the Linux (draft) subnetworking mini-HOWTO) to be of use. This is available at `http://www.interweft.com.au/other/`.

In order to link two LANs, you *must* be using different IP network numbers (or subnets of the same network number) and you will need to use static IP numbers–or use IP masquerade. If you want to use IP masquerade, see the IP masquerade mini-HOWTO for instructions on setting that up.

Setting up the IP Numbers

Arrange with the network administrator of the other LAN the IP numbers that will be used for each end of the PPP interface. If you are using static IP numbers, this will also probably require you to dial into a specific telephone number.

Now edit the appropriate `/etc/ppp/options[.ttyXX]` file–it's a good idea to have a specific modem and port at your end for this connection. This may well require you to change your `/etc/ppp/options` file–and create appropriate `options.ttyXX` files for any other connections!

Specify the IP numbers for your end of the PPP link in the appropriate options file exactly as shown above for static IP numbers.

Setting up the Routing

You must arrange that packets on your local LAN are routed across the interface that the PPP link establishes. This is a two stage process.

First of all, you need to establish a route from the machine running the PPP link to the network(s) at the far end of the link. If the link is to the Internet, this can be handled by a default route established by pppd itself at your end of the connection using the *defaultroute* option to pppd.

If however, the link is only linking two LANs, then a specific network route must be added for each network that is accessible across the link. This is done using a *route* command for each network in the `/etc/ppp/ip-up` script (see the section, "After the Link Comes up–the `/etc/ppp/ip-up` Script," for instructions on doing this).

The second thing you need to do is to tell the other computers on your LAN that your Linux computer is actually the *gateway* for the network(s) at the far end of the PPP link.

Of course, the network administrator at the other end of the link has to do all this too. However, as s/he will be routing packets to your specific networks, a *specific network route* will be required, not a default route (unless the LANs at the far end of the link are linking into you to access the Internet across your connection).

Network Security

If you are linking you LAN to the Internet using PPP—or even just to a foreign LAN, you need to think about security issues. I strongly urge you to think about setting up a firewall!

You should also speak to the LAN administrator at your site *before* you start linking to foreign LANs or the Internet this way. Failure to do so could earn you anything from no reaction to really serious trouble.

After the Link Comes up—the /etc/ppp/ip-up Script

Once the PPP link is established, pppd looks for `/etc/ppp/ip-up`. If this script exists and is executable, the PPP daemon executes the script. This allows you to automate any special routing commands that may be necessary and any other actions that you want to occur every time the PPP link is activated.

This is just a shell script and can do anything that a shell script can do (i.e. virtually anything you want).

For example, you can get Sendmail to dispatch any waiting outbound messages in the mail queue.

Similarly, you can insert the commands into *ip-up* to collect (using pop) any e-mail waiting for you at your ISP.

There are restrictions on `/etc/ppp/ip-up`:

- It runs in a deliberately restricted environment to enhance security. This means you must give a full path to binaries, etc.
- Technically, `/etc/ppp/ip-up` is a *program* not a script. This means it can be directly executed—and hence it requires the standard file magic (`#!/bin/bash`) at the start of the first line and must be readable and executable by root.

Special Routing

If you are linking two LANs, you will need to set up specific routes to the "foreign" LANs. This is easily done using the `/etc/ppp/ip-up` script. The only difficulty arises if your machine handles multiple PPP links.

This is because the `/etc/ppp/ip-up` is executed for *every* PPP connection that comes up, so you need to carefully execute the correct routing commands for the particular link that comes up—and not when any other link comes up!

Handling E-mail Queues

When the link between two LANs comes up, you may well want to make sure that e-mail that is queued at either end is *flushed*—sent out to its destination. This is done by adding the appropriate `sendmail` invocation.

Using the bash *case* statement on an appropriate parameter that pppd passes into the script accomplishes this. For example, this is the `/etc/ppp/ip-up` script I use to handle our WAN links and the link to my home Ethernet (also handled on the same PPP server).

A Sample */etc/ppp/ip-up* Script

The following example provides a variety of example uses.

```
#!/bin/bash
#
# Script which handles the routing issues as necessary for pppd
# Only the link to Newman requires this handling.
#
# When the ppp link comes up, this script is called with the
# following parameters
#     $1    the interface name used by pppd (e.g. ppp3)
#     $2    the tty device name
#     $3    the tty device speed
#     $4    the local IP address for the interface
#     $5    the remote IP address
#     $6    the parameter specified by the 'ipparam' option to pppd
#
case "$5" in
# Handle the routing to the Newman Campus server
    202.12.126.1)
         /sbin/route add -net 202.12.126.0 gw 202.12.126.1
# and flush the mail queue to get their email there asap!
         /usr/sbin/sendmail -q &
         ;;
    139.130.177.2)
# Our Internet link
# When the link comes up, start the time server and synchronise
# to the world provided it is not already running
```

Part iii

```
        if [ ! -f /var/lock/subsys/xntpd ]; then
            /etc/rc.d/init.d/xntpd.init start &
        fi
# Start the news server (if not already running)
        if [ ! -f /var/lock/subsys/news ]; then
            /etc/rc.d/init.d/news start &
        fi
        ;;
    203.18.8.104)
# Get the email down to my home machine as soon as the link comes
# up No routing is required as my home Ethernet is handled by IP
# masquerade and proxyarp routing.
        /usr/sbin/sendmail -q &
        ;;
    *)
esac
exit 0
```

As a result of bringing up the PPP link to our Newman campus and this script, we end up with the following routing table entries. (This machine also is our general dial-up PPP server *and* handles our Internet link.) I have interspersed comments in the output to help explain what each entry is:

```
[root@kepler /root]# route -n
Kernel routing table
Destination     Gateway         Genmask         Flags MSS    Window Use Iface
# the HOST route to our remote internet gateway
139.130.177.2   *               255.255.255.255 UH    1500   0       134 ppp4
# the HOST route to our Newman campus server
202.12.126.1    *               255.255.255.255 UH    1500   0        82 ppp5
# the HOST route to my home ethernet
203.18.8.104    *               255.255.255.255 UH    1500   0        74 ppp3
# two of our general dial up PPP lines
203.18.8.64     *               255.255.255.255 UH    552    0         0 ppp2
203.18.8.62     *               255.255.255.255 UH    552    0         1 ppp1
# the specific network route to the Newman campus LAN
202.12.126.0    202.12.126.1    255.255.255.0   UG    1500   0         0 ppp5
# the route to our local Ethernet (super-netting two adjacent C classes)
203.18.8.0      *               255.255.254.0   U     1500   0      1683 eth0
# the route to the loop back device
127.0.0.0       *               255.0.0.0       U     3584   0       483 lo
# the default route to the Internet
default         139.130.177.2   *               UG    1500   0      3633 ppp4
```

Handling E-mail

The previous section shows how to handle the outgoing mail—simply by flushing the mail queue once the link is up.

If you are running a WAN link, you can arrange with the network administrator of the remote LAN to do exactly the same thing. For example, at the Newman Campus end of our WAN link, the `/etc/ppp/ip-up` script looks like

```
#!/bin/bash
#
# Script which handles the routing issues as necessary for
# pppd Only the link to Hedland requires this handling.
#
# When the ppp link comes up, this script is called with the
# following parameters
#     $1    the interface name used by pppd (e.g. ppp3)
#     $2    the tty device name
#     $3    the tty device speed
#     $4    the local IP address for the interface
#     $5    the remote IP address
#     $6    the parameter specified by the 'ipparam' option to pppd
#
case "$5" in
    203.18.8.4)
        /usr/sbin/sendmail -q
        ;;
    *)
esac
exit 0
```

If however you have only a dynamic IP PPP link to your ISP, you need to get your e-mail from the account on your ISPs machine. This is usually done using the POP (Post Office Protocol). This process can be handled using the *popclient* program—and the `ip-up` script can automate this process for you too.

Simply create a `/etc/ppp/ip-up` script that contains the appropriate invocation of popclient. For my laptop that runs Red Hat Linux (which I take on any travels), this is

```
popclient -3 -c -u hartr -p <password> kepler.hedland.edu. _
au |formail -s procmail
```

You could use *slurp* or whatever to do the same for news, and so forth. Remember, the `ip-up` script is just a standard bash script and so can be used to automate *any* function that needs to be accomplished every time the appropriate PPP link comes up.

USING /ETC/PPP/IP-DOWN

You can create a script that will be executed once the link has been terminated. This is stored in `/etc/ppp/ip-down`. It can be used to undo anything special that you did in the corresponding `/etc/ppp/ip-up` script.

ROUTING ISSUES ON A LAN

If you are connected to a LAN but still want to use PPP on your personal Linux machine , you need to address some issues of the routes packets need to take from your machine to reach your LAN (through your Ethernet interface) and also to the remote PPP server and beyond.

This section does *not* attempt to teach you about routing–it deals only with a simple, special case of (static) routing.

I strongly urge you to read the Linux Network Administrator Guide (NAG) if you are *not* familiar with routing. Also the O'Reilly book *TCP/IP Network Administration* covers this topic in a very understandable form.

The basic rule of static routing is that the *default* route should be the one that points to the *most* number of network addresses. For other networks, enter specific routes to the routing table.

The *only* situation I am going to cover here is where your Linux box is on a LAN that is not connected to the Internet–and you want to dial out to the Internet for personal use while still connected to the LAN.

First of all, make sure that your Ethernet route is set up to the specific network addresses available across your LAN–*not* set to the default route.

Check this by issuing a route command; you should see something like the following:

```
[root@hwin /root]# route -n
Kernel routing table
Destination   Gateway     Genmask       Flags MSS  Window Use Iface
loopback      *         255.255.255.0  U   1936  0    50 lo
10.0.0.0      *         255.255.255.0  U   1436  0   565 eth0
```

If your Ethernet interface (eth0) is pointing at the default route (the first column will show *default* in the eth0 line) you need to change your Ethernet initialization scripts to make it point at the specific network numbers rather than the default route (consult the Net2 HOWTO and NAG).

This will allow pppd to set up your default route as shown below:

```
[root@hwin /root]# route -n
Kernel routing table

Destination     Gateway  Genmask          Flags  MSS   Window   Use Iface
10.144.153.51   *        255.255.255.255  UH     488   0        0 ppp0
127.0.0.0       *        255.255.255.0    U      1936  0        50 lo
10.1.0.0        *        255.255.255.0    U      1436  0        569 eth0
default                  10.144.153.51    *      UG    488      0 3 ppp0
```

As you can see, we have a host route to the PPP server (10.144.153.51) via ppp0 and also a default network route that uses the PPP server as its gateway.

If your setup needs to be more complex than this, read the routing documents already mentioned and consult an expert at your site.

If your LAN already has routers on it, you will already have gateways established to the wider networks available at your site. You should *still* point your default route at the PPP interface–and make the other routes specific to the networks they serve.

Note on Security

When you set up a Linux box on an existing LAN to link into the Internet, you are potentially opening your entire LAN to the Internet–and the hackers that reside there. Before you do this, I strongly urge you to consult your network administrator and site security policy. If your PPP connection to the Internet is used to successfully attack your site, you will at the very least earn the intense anger of your fellow users and network and system administrators. You may also find yourself in much more serious trouble!

Before you connect a LAN to the Internet, you should consider the security implications of even a dynamic connection–hence the earlier reference to the O'Reilly *Building Internet Firewalls*.

Setting up a PPP Server

As already mentioned, there are many ways to do this. What I present here is the way I do it (using a Cyclades multiport serial card) and a rotary dial-in set of telephone lines.

If you don't like the method I present here, please feel free to go your own way. I would, however, be pleased to include additional methods in future versions of the HOWTO. So, please send me your comments and methods.

Please note, this section only concerns setting up Linux as a PPP server. I do not (ever) intend to include information on setting up special terminal servers and such.

Also, I have yet to experiment with shadow passwords (but will be doing so sometime). Information currently presented does *not* therefore include any bells and whistles that are required by the shadow suite.

Kernel Compilation

All the earlier comments regarding kernel compilation and kernel versions versus pppd versions apply. This section assumes that you have read the earlier sections of this document!

For a PPP server, you *must* include IP forwarding in your kernel. You may also wish to include other capabilities (such as IP firewalls, accounting, etc.).

If you are using a multiport serial card, then you must obviously include the necessary drivers in your kernel too.

Overview of the Server System

We offer dial-up PPP (and SLIP) accounts and shell accounts using the same user name/password pair. This has the advantages (for us) that a user requires only one account and can use it for all types of connectivity.

As we are an educational organization, we do not charge our staff and students for access, and so do not have to worry about accounting and charging issues.

We operate a firewall between our site and the Internet, and this restricts some user access as the dial-up lines are inside our (Internet) firewall (for fairly obvious reasons, details of our other internal firewalls are not presented here and are irrelevant in any case).

The process a user goes through to establish a PPP link to our site (once they have a valid account of course) is

- Dial into our rotary dialer (this is a single phone number that connects to a bank of modems—the first free modem is then used).

- Log in using a valid user name and password pair.
- At the shell prompt, issue the command ppp to start PPP on the server.
- Start PPP on their PC (be it running Windows, DOS, Linux, Mac OS or whatever—that is their problem).

The server uses individual `/etc/ppp/options.ttyXX` files for each dial-in port that sets the remote IP number for dynamic IP allocation. The server users proxyarp routing for the remote clients (set via the appropriate option to pppd). This obviates the need for *routed* or *gated*.

When the user hangs up at their end, pppd detects this and tells the modem to hang up, bringing down the PPP link at the same time.

Getting the Software Together

You will need the following software:

- Linux, properly compiled to include the necessary options.
- The appropriate version of pppd for your kernel.
- A *getty* program that intelligently handles modem communications. We use gettyps2.0.7h, but mgetty is highly thought of. I understand that mgetty can detect a call that is using PAP/CHAP (PAP is the standard for Windows 95) and invoke pppd automatically, but I have yet to explore this.
- An operational domain name server (DNS) that is accessible to your dial-up users. You should really be running your own DNS if possible...

Setting up Standard (Shell Access) Dialup

Before you can set up your PPP server, your Linux box must be capable of handling standard dial-up access.

This howto does *not* cover setting this up. Please see the documentation of the getty of your choice and serial HOWTO for information on this.

Setting up the PPP Options Files

You will need to set up the overall `/etc/ppp/options` with the common options for all dial-up ports. The options we use are

```
asyncmap 0
netmask 255.255.254.0
proxyarp
lock
crtscts
modem
```

NOTE

We do *not* use any (obvious) routing—and in particular there is no *defaultroute* option. The reason for this is that all you (as a PPP server) are required to do is to route packets *from* the PPP client out across your LAN/Internet, and route packets *to* the client from your LAN and beyond.

All that is necessary for this is a host route to the client machine and the use of the *proxyarp* option to pppd.

The *proxyarp* option sets up (surprise) a proxy ARP entry in the PPP server's ARP table that basically says "send all packets destined for the PPP client to me." This is the easiest way to set up routing to a single PPP client, but you cannot use this if you are routing between two LANs–you must add proper network routes, which can't use proxy ARP.

You will almost certainly wish to provide dynamic IP number allocation to your dial-up users. You can accomplish this by allocating an IP number to each dial-up port. Now, create a `/etc/ppp/options.ttyXX` for each dial-up port.

In this, simply put the local (server) IP number and the IP number that is to be used for that port. For example

```
kepler:slip01
```

In particular, note that you can use valid host names in this file. (I find that I only remember the IP numbers of critical machines and devices on my networks–names are more meaningful.)

Setting pppd up to Allow Users to (Successfully) Run It

As starting a PPP link implies configuring a kernel device (a network interface) and manipulating the kernel routing tables, special privileges are required–in fact full root privileges.

Fortunately, pppd has been designed to be "safe" to run set uid to root. So you will need to

```
chmod u+s /usr/sbin/pppd
```

When you list the file, it should then appear as

```
-rwsr-xr-x  1 root   root    74224 Apr 28 07:17 /usr/sbin/pppd
```

If you do not do this, users will be unable to set up their PPP link.

Setting up the Global Alias for pppd

In order to simplify things for our dial-up PPP users, we create a global alias (in `/etc/bashrc`) so that one simple command will start PPP on the server once they are logged in.

This looks like

```
alias ppp="exec /usr/sbin/pppd -detach"
```

What this does is

- **exec** this means replace the running program (in this case the shell) with the program that is run.
- **pppd-detach** start up pppd and do *not* fork into the background. This ensures that when pppd exits there is no process hanging around.

When a user logs in like this, they will appear in the output of *w* as

```
  6:24pm up 3 days, 7:00, 4 users, load average: 0.05, 0.03, 0.00
User   tty    login@ idle  JCPU  PCPU what
hartr  ttyC0   3:05am 9:14          -
```

And that is it...I told you this was a simple, basic PPP server system.

Part iii

Using PPP Across a Null-Modem (Direct Serial) Connection

This is very simple—there is no modem in the way so things are much simpler.

First of all, choose one of the machines as a "server," setting up a getty on the serial port so you can test that you do have connectivity using minicom to access the serial port on the "client."

Once you have this functioning, you can remove the getty *unless* you want to make sure that the connection is validated using user name/password pairs as for a dial-up connection. As you have physical control of both machines, I will presume that you do *not* want to do this.

Now, on the server, remove the getty and make sure that you have the serial ports on both machines configured correctly using *setserial*.

All you need to do now is to start pppd on both systems. I will assume that the connection uses `/dev/ttyS3` on both machines. So, on both machines execute the command

```
pppd -detach crtscts lock <local IP>:<remote IP> /dev/ttyS3
38400 &
```

This will bring up the link—but as yet you have no routing specified. You can test the link by pinging to and fro to each machine. If this works, bring down the link by killing one of the pppd processes.

The routing you need will of course depend on exactly what you are trying to do. Generally, one of the machines will be connected to an Ethernet (and beyond) and so the routing required is exactly the same as for a PPP server and client.

So on the Ethernet equipped machine, the pppd command would be

```
pppd -detach crtscts lock proxyarp <local IP>:<remote IP> _
    /dev/ttyS3 38400 &
```

and on the other machine

```
pppd -detach crtscts lock defaultroute <local IP>:<remote IP> _
    /dev/ttyS3 38400 &
```

If you are linking two networks (using a serial link) or have more complex routing requirements, you can use `/etc/ppp/ip-up` in exactly the same way as mentioned earlier in this document.

Chapter 10

Cable Modems

This chapter attempts to answer basic questions on how to connect your Linux box to a cable modem or cable Internet provider.

If you live in an area where two-way (as opposed to telco-return) cable modems are available, then you should give serious consideration to getting one. Cable modems can offer faster service than DSL, are more uniformly available, and in many cases cost less than other services. Cable modems are certainly much faster than plain old dial-up Internet access.

Linux can take full advantage of a cable modem, and this chapter describes how. It includes specific information on many of the current cable modem systems around the world and general information on how to set things up. You'll also want to read the DHCP chapter of this book (Chapter 11 for more information on related topics.

This chapter is reprinted from the Cable Modem mini-HOWTO by Vladimir Vuskan <`vuksan@veus.hr`>, version 3.15 of 6 December 1998.

INTRODUCTION

The main goal of this document is to get your system running with your cable modem and cable Internet provider. Unfortunately, many ISPs that provide cable modem services give you Windows and Macintosh software only.

This document attempts to explain how to set up some cable modems and Internet providers in Linux, the tricks to get them working correctly, and the traps not to fall down. It is hoped that this document will assist you; however, we make no claims for the validity of the information contained within.

New Versions of This Document

New versions of this document will be periodically posted to comp.os.linux.answers. They will also be added to the various anonymous FTP sites that archive such information, including ftp://MetaLab.unc.edu/pub/Linux/docs/HOWTO.

In addition, you should generally be able to find this document on the Linux Documentation Project page at http://MetaLab.unc.edu/LDP/.

Feedback

Feedback is most certaintly welcome for this document. Without your submissions and input, this document wouldn't exist. So, please post your additions, comments, and criticisms to vuksan@veus.hr.

Contributors

The following people have contributed to this mini-HOWTO.

- Dan Sullivan <dsulli@home.com>
- Andrew Novick
- Michael Strates

Standard Disclaimer

No liability for the content of this chapter can be accepted. Use the concepts, examples and other content at your own risk. As this is a new edition of this document, there may be errors and inaccuracies, which may be damaging to your system. Proceed with caution, and although damage is highly unlikely, I won't take any responsibility for it if it does occur.

Also bear in mind that this is *not* official information. Obtaining official information is usually an impossibility with many ISPs. Much of the content in this chapter is based on assumptions, which appears to work for people. Use the information at your own risk.

Copyright Information

This document is copyrighted ©1998 Vladimir Vuksan and distributed under the following terms:

- Linux HOWTO documents may be reproduced and distributed in whole or in part, in any medium physical or electronic, as long as this copyright notice is retained on all copies. Commercial redistribution is allowed and encouraged; however, the author would like to be notified of any such distributions.
- All translations, derivative works, or aggregate works incorporating any Linux HOWTO documents must be covered under this copyright notice. That is, you may not produce a derivative work from a HOWTO and impose additional restrictions on its distribution. Exceptions to these rules may be granted under certain conditions; please contact the Linux HOWTO coordinator at `linux-howto@MetaLab.unc.edu`.

Setting Up Your Ethernet Card

All of the setups below use Ethernet cards (network cards) to connect you somehow to the Internet. That is why we need first to check if your Ethernet card is working and most importantly can be used (read "is supported") in Linux. There is a comprehensive Ethernet HOWTO at `http://MetaLab.unc.edu/LDP/HOWTO/Ethernet-HOWTO.html` if you would like to read it; otherwise, try the following steps.

Boot into Linux. During boot up a message like this should appear:

```
eth0: 3c509 at 0x300 tag 1, 10baseT port, address 00 20 af ee
01 23, IRQ 10. 3c509.c:1.07 6/15/95 becker@cesdis.gsfc.nasa.gov
```

If you missed it, type **dmesg**.

If you see a message like that, you are set and you can go to the next section. If you don't see a message like that, there are two possible explanations. The first is that your Ethernet card is PnP (Plug and Play) and you need to use tools, such as isapnptools, to get it recognized. (I am not quite sure on this because I don't have a single PnP card, so correct me if I am wrong.) The other explanation is that you need to set up your card.

Most cards today come with DOS programs that are used to set up your card. For example, to get my 3COM 3c509 to work, all I need to do is boot into DOS and use a utility to configure my card. There is usually a Auto Configure option. If that does not solve your problem, try changing the IRQ for the card using the same utility. I find that usually IRQs 10, 11, and 12 work well. If none of this solves your problem, please read the Ethernet HOWTO referenced above or post to a newsgroup such as `comp.os.linux.setup` or `comp.os.linux.networking`.

Your ISP

If you think you have the card recognized, you now have to look at the entry for your ISP. I have sorted the information according to provider because setups are mostly ISP specific.

MediaOne Express

MediaOne Express is an Internet cable service provided by MediaOne. The hardware setup consists of a cable modem produced by LanCity or General Instruments, which plugs into an Ethernet card using a 10BaseT (UTP-45) cable. Assignment of IP addresses and other networking information is done using DHCP, which stands for Dynamic Host Configuration Protocol. The only thing you need to do is read the DHCP mini-HOWTO and configure your system appropriately. There is no other necessary configuration. The DHCP mini-HOWTO is Chapter 11 of this book, or you can find it at `http://MetaLab.unc.edu/LDP/HOWTO/mini/DHCP.html`.

Information about MediaOne Service can be found at `http://www.mediaone.com`.

@Home

@Home uses a similar setup to MediaOne Express. However, there are a few fundamental differences outlined by contributors. Since @Home spans different geographic locations, you might get assigned different kinds of equipment and have slightly different kinds of setups.

Before you try anything, go to Control Panel ➢ Network ➢ Properties for your network card. Write down all of the information. You will need it later.

TCI, the company that runs @Home, issues an Etherlink III 3c509b NIC for all of their customers. What TCI does not tell you is that when they install your Ethernet card, it is in PnP mode. Now in Slackware, if you uncomment the proper line for this card, everything will appear to be working fine. There will be no system problems, but the 'PC' light on your CyberSURFR modem will never turn on. If you are using Slackware, and are having this problem, reboot in DOS and skip the next paragraph.

In RedHat5, your system will have some trouble autodetecting the card. If you try to pass the paramaters manually, the system will hang. It should be obvious that your card was not set up properly. Before wasting anymore time, reboot in DOS. (This is a must because, as of 12/25/97, there is no utility written for Linux to turn off PnP and turn on ISA.)

TCI does not give out a utility disk for your Ethernet card, so you must download the utility from one of 3Com's sites. Here is a link to 3COM's page for driver download:

```
http://support.3com.com/infodeli/tools/nic/index.htm
```

Once you have downloaded your driver files, you will need to run them and disable the PnP mode of your network card.

What you've now done will make your Ethernet card broken in Windows 95. You'll need to go to Control Panel ➢ Network and remove the network card and the adapter. Reboot your computer, and again go back to Control Panel. Go to Add/Remove New Hardware and have it autodetect. It will automatically set up the correct I/O address for you. You will most likely need to reboot again. Now you should be in Windows 95, with the PC light on your cable modem on. You will also notice that none of your Internet applications seem to work–you can't ping, and you can't resolve DNS. You now must go back to Control Panel ➢ Network, and click on Properties for your network card (not the adapter). Re-enter all the data you wrote down, and reboot.

With a little luck, your Ethernet card should be working in Windows 95 and ready to rock in Linux.

If you live in Hampton Roads, VA, you should read a little note from Mark Solomon:

> **With the @Home service in Hampton Roads, VA, it is absolutly neccessary to run dhcpcd-0.70 (or higher) that supports the "-h" option to specify the hostname of your computer. Without this switch the @Home dhcpcd server will not assign addresses.**

More information on setting up dhcpcd-0.70 and @Home service with Intel Ether Express cards can be found at `http://www.monmouth.com/~jay/Linux/`.

In Baltimore and Colleyville, Texas, subscribers are issued Intel Ether Express Pro 10 nics and a static IP number.

Information about @Home service can be found at `http://www.home.com`.

RoadRunner

RoadRunner is an Internet cable service provided by Excalibur Group (Time Warner). The hardware setup consists of a cable modem produced by Motorola and Toshiba, which plugs into an Ethernet card using a 10BaseT (UTP-45) cable. From what I can gather, RR uses DHCP for IP assignment. In order to set up Linux to use DHCP, you need to read the DHCP mini-HOWTO and configure your system appropriately. The DHCP mini-HOWTO is Chapter 11 or can be found at `http://MetaLab.unc.edu/LDP/HOWTO/mini/DHCP.html`.

If this doesn't work out for you, you should check out `http://www.math.uakron.edu/RoadRunner/` for Akron, Ohio, and `http://people.qualcomm.com/karn/rr/index.html` for San Diego, California. It might help solve your problem.

Information about the RoadRunner service can be found at `http://www.rr.com`.

Rogers Wave

The hardware setup consists of a cable modem produced by LanCity, which plugs into an Ethernet card using a 10BaseT (UTP-45) cable.

When the cable modem is installed by Rogers Wave technicians you are assigned a static IP address. They should also provide you with information on your subnet mask, router (gateway) numbers, and DNS numbers. For additional info, please visit `http://home.on.rogers.wave.ca/mreid/rogwave/index.html`.

Other information about Rogers Wave Service can be found at `http://www.rogerswave.ca`.

Sunflower Cablevision

This information was provided by Andrew Novick:

> **I recently saw your cable modem howto and I have an addition. Sunflower Cable is a company stricly in Lawrence, KS, however we have a rather large Linux community because of the University of Kansas. On our local LUG mailing list, we are starting to get more and more questions on how to configure their Linux machine for the cable modem. It is just regular static addressing, and the modem is made by Zenith.**

To configure your Linux box, make sure you get all the pertinent information from the Cablevision tech support or use these settings.

- IP address: Assigned by SunFlower Cablevision
- Subnet mask: 255.255.255.0
- Gateway (router) address: 24.124.11.254
- Hostname: Assigned by SunFlower Cablevision
- Domain name: `lawrence.ks.us`
- Primary DNS server (nameserver): 24.124.0.1
- Secondary DNS server (nameserver): 24.124.0.6

Have all those numbers written down before you proceed. To register, visit `http://www.sunflower.com`.

To register in the `lawrence.ks.us` domain, contact Stephen Spencer at `gladiatr@artorius.sunflower.com`.

Under Red Hat use Control Panel and Network Configuration to put in these numbers. Just say Add Interface, Device type=Ethernet, Device name=eth0 (this is zero, not O in eth0), and fill out all the fields. Then click Activate.

In Slackware, type **netconfig**. When you are finished, reboot and you should be up and running.

If this doesn't work, make sure you do network card troubleshooting from the beginning of this document.

Jones Intercable

This information was provided by Bob Kimble:

> Jones Internet Cable supplies a Hybrid cable modem that connects to your machine/network via 10BaseT Ethernet. They provide you with a static IP address for your machine and another static IP address for the modem. The modem acts as a gateway to their network. Your IP address and the modem IP address are on the same network and have the same network mask (in my case 255.255.255.0—24 bits). They also provide two DNS IP addresses, which you enter into your configuration. I just entered the numbers when I installed Red Hat Linux 5 and it worked like a champ from the beginning. Since then I have configured my Linux machine to enable IP masquerading and domain name services, and it now acts as a router for my entire private network. My other machines are connected via a private network using the addresses 192.168.0.x. They are running Windows 95, Windows NT (Intel and Alpha), and OS/2. My Linux machine has two IP addresses—the one from the cable company and one from the 192.168.0.x private network. Everything works like a champ. All six machines can browse the Web simultaneously. My kids are even able to connect to their favorite game site, *The Realm* from Sierra.

GTE Worldwind

This information was provided by Mike Hughes:

> The information you provided for Rogers Wave works for GTE WorldWind cable modem services also. However, GTE's service is *extremely* slow, barely faster than ISDN. More information at `http://www.psilord.com`.

SpeedChoice, Phoenix, Arizona

This information is from Micah <peenchee@asu.edu>:

> Just thought I'd let you know that in my area (Phoenix, AZ, USA) there is a company called SpeedChoice that provides cable modem service. The service uses a hybrid cable modem and the setup is almost identical to that of Jones intercable described in the HOWTO.

See "@Home" above. For any other issues, e-mail Micah.

Cedar Falls Cybernet, Iowa

This information was provided thanks to Joe Breu <breu@cfu.net>.

> We are an ISP in Cedar Falls, Iowa, that uses the Zenith HomeWorks Universal over our own Hybrid Fiber/Coax system. Our system uses no proprietary connection software and is straight TCP/IP connections. We do use DHCP, but will offer static IP addresses to customers requesting them because they cannot use DHCP.

Telstra Bigpond Cable, Australia

This information was provided by Geoff Conway <gconway@vic.bigpond.net.au>.

WARNING

The information contained herein is in no way the responsibility of Big Pond Cable, Telstra Multimedia, Telstra, IBM Global Services Australia, or any related company. Any loss or consequential damage associated with the attempted installation of the Big Pond Cable Linux software is the *personal* responsibility of whomsoever follows these instructions.

Big Pond Cable does not currently support Linux, so do not report faults to them regarding any aspect of the Linux installation and/or operation.

Big Pond Cable Linux Installation Notes. V 1.1 (12/03/98)

NOTE

Change Note 1.1 12/3/98—Corrected spelling of *dhcpcd* and *rrdhcpcd*

Linux is not officially supported by Big Pond Cable. However, the TMM cable infrastructure does allow Linux to be used—with the appropriate login client. The following installation notes should allow you to install the Linux software without too many difficulties.

The full client distribution of rrclientd was obtained from `ftp://ftp.vortech.net/pub/rrlinux/rrclientd-1.3.tar.gz`

I am running Red Hat version 5 of Linux, but the documentation indicates that it will work with other releases.

Note that there is also more information in the rrclientd release than is documented here.

Here are the installation procedures:

1. Copy the distribution file `rrclientd-1.3.tar.gz` to your Linux PC.
2. Login as root for all of the following.
3. Expand the distribution (with gunzip) and then untar it.
4. In directory `rrclientd-1.3/bin` you will find all the executables that you need: fetchmail (not used), kdestroy, kinit, rdate, rrclientd, rrdhcpcd, and rrpasswd.
5. Rename `/sbin/dhcpcd` to `/sbin/dhcpcd.orig`. Copy and rename `rrdhcpcd` to `/sbin/dhcpcd`.
6. Copy kdestroy, kinit, rdate, rrclientd, rrdhcpd, and rrpasswd to `/usr/local/bin`.
7. Set up your Ethernet card to use DHCP and restart the system. If the DHCP configuration is OK, an IP address will be assigned, with the details being placed in `/etc/dhcpc/hostinfo-eth0` and `/etc/dhcpc/resolv.conf`.

NOTE

You may see a startup warning about not finding dhcp.conf**—this doesn't seem to matter.**

8. At this point you should be able to ping proxy-server successfully. (If you can't, you won't be able to login later.)
9. Copy the `krb5.ini` file (from your Win95 `\netmanag` directory) to `/etc/krb5.conf`.

   You will need to make the following changes (adding 2 new sections)

   The example shown is for the Melbourne `krb5.ini` file–Sydney users will need to substitute appropriately.

   This is also documented in the distribution's examples/ sub-directories.

```
[libdefaults]
    ticket_lifetime = 600
    default_realm = c3.telstra-mm.net.au

** new *1
    kdc_req_checksum_type = 2
    ap_req_checksum_type = 2
    safe_req_checksum_type = 3
    ccache_type = 2
** end of new *1

[realms]
c3.telstra-mm.net.au = {
    kdc = dce-server
    admin_server = dce-server
    default_domain = c3.telstra-mm.net.au
    }

wfh.c3.telstra-mm.net.au = {
    kdc = wfh.c3.telstra-mm.net.au
    admin_server = wfh.c3.telstra-mm.net.au
    default_domain = c3.telstra-mm.net.au
    }

wfh1.c3.telstra-mm.net.au = {
    kdc = wfh1.c3.telstra-mm.net.au
    admin_server = wfh1.c3.telstra-mm.net.au
    default_domain = c3.telstra-mm.net.au
    }
```

```
wfh2.c3.telstra-mm.net.au = {
     kdc = wfh2.c3.telstra-mm.net.au
     admin_server = wfh2.c3.telstra-mm.net.au
     default_domain = c3.telstra-mm.net.au
     }

wfh3.c3.telstra-mm.net.au = {
     kdc = wfh3.c3.telstra-mm.net.au
     admin_server = wfh3.c3.telstra-mm.net.au
     default_domain = c3.telstra-mm.net.au
     }

wfh4.c3.telstra-mm.net.au = {
     kdc = wfh4.c3.telstra-mm.net.au
     admin_server = wfh4.c3.telstra-mm.net.au
     default_domain = c3.telstra-mm.net.au
     }

wfh5.c3.telstra-mm.net.au = {
     kdc = wfh5.c3.telstra-mm.net.au
     admin_server = wfh5.c3.telstra-mm.net.au
     default_domain = c3.telstra-mm.net.au
     }

** new *2

[domain_realm]
  .c3.telstra-mm.net.au = c3.telstra-mm.net.au

** end *2
```

10. Save your existing services file `/etc/services` to `/etc/services.orig`.

11. Copy the services file from `examples/Nassau/services` to `/etc/services`.

12. Create a new file `/etc/rrpasswd`, with the contents being your current BPC password.

13. Change the PATH environment variable as follows: `PATH=$PATH:/usr/local/bin ; export PATH`. (This is most likely not necessary.)

14. Login to BPC as follows: `rrclientd -u username /etc/rrpasswd dce-server`. So if you're username jsmith,

```
rrclientd -u jsmith /etc/rrpasswd dce-server
```

If this is successful, you'll see a message in `/var/log/messages` indicating it was OK. `tail /var/log/messages` will display the end of the file.

15. Logout of BPC by entering `rrclientd -k`.
16. To make this automatic, you'll need to set the PATH and invoke rrclientd each time the system boots.
17. The `rrpasswd` command has *not* been tried.
18. That's it. Set up your Linux Netscape proxies and go for it!

NOTE

According to the documentation, the client will logout and then log in automatically at 3 am. This has not been checked.

Problems

If you don't set up the PATH properly, then the login will fail with GSS-API complaints about non-supported checksum type.

If you don't make the needed changes to `krb5.conf`, you'll also get a similar error.

If you are using your PC to dual/triple boot between W95/NT/Linux, the PC's CMOS clock will be altered by Linux, giving continual Kerberos errors if you try to log in using NT. You need to log in using Win95 first (which will fix the CMOS clock settings); then you can get in via NT.

Make sure you set up you PC time/timezone correctly in Linux. Note also that the `/var/log/messages` timestamps are a bit strange (possibly referenced to GMT).

Fibertel, Buenos Aires, Argentina

This information was provided by Pablo Godel.

My name is Pablo Godel and want report that I'm using the cable service of Fibertel in Buenos Aires, Argentina, and it works perfectly with Linux.

They gave me a static IP. The brand of the cablemodem is COM21 and the model is ComPort.

I connect it to the nic properly, configured in Linux, and it worked perfectly.

More information about Fibertel can be found at `http://www.fibertel.com.ar`.

Videotron, Canada

I don't have much information about Videotron except the fact that they use DHCP for the assignment of IP addresses and other networking information. Just read the DHCP mini-HOWTO (see Chapter 11) and configure your system appropriately. There is no other necessary configuration.

Here is additional information from Mihai Petre <mihaip@videotron.ca>:

> **Yes, they are using DHCP for the TCP settings. They have also included DHCPcd on their FTP server at `ftp://ftp.videotron.ca/pub/linux/`. Of course, the tech support cannot help you with the Linux-related stuff.**
>
> **They don't allow setup of any kind of servers on your machine (on ports 80, 21, 110, 25) so the only thing is to use some exotic ports.**

Information about Videotron can be found at `http://www.videotron.ca`.

Telekabel (Teleweb), Austria

The following information is from Andreas Kostyrka.

> **The Austrian Telekabel (Teleweb) ISP works with Linux. It seems quite similiar to MediaOne Express (3c509+dhcp, etc.).**
>
> **There are 3COM configuration utilities for Linux (but don't fool around with them on a busy system; 3c509 may lock the bus if touched the wrong way):**
>
> ```
> ftp://ftp.redhat.com/pub/contrib/hurricane/SRPMS/ _
> 3c5x9utils-1.0-3.src.rpm
>  ftp://ftp.redhat.com/pub/contrib/readmes/ _
> 3c5x9utils-1.0-1.README
> ```
>
> **Information about Telekabel can be found at `http://www.telekabel.at/`.**

Tebecai, Netherlands

According to Frodo Looijaard, Tebecai is yet another provider that uses a LANcity cable modem connected to a 10BaseT Ethernet card. DHCP is used for configuration (see Chapter 11). A step-by-step guide to install the cable modem under Linux can be found at `http://huizen.dds.nl/~frodol`. It is in Dutch, but it is really very straightforward. You must only remember that your IP-address is not visible from the Internet (it is on the private 10.x.y.z subnet), so you cannot set up a publicly available server.

Information about Tebecai can be found at `http://www.tebenet.nl` (in Dutch only).

A2000, Netherlands

This information was provided by Johan List <`J.A.List@speed.A2000.nl`>.

> **Basically, the way to go is the same as with Tebecai. A2000 provides cable Internet access by means of a LANCity cable modem, connected to a 10BaseT Ethernet card. This also works well for the Vortex/Boomerang cards by 3COM (I've got a 3COM Boomerang Fast Etherlink XL 10/100Mb TX Ethernet Adapter), providing you compile the Vortex/Boomerang drivers. (See the Linux Ethernet-HOWTO.)**
>
> **Setting up access can be done with DHCP (see Chapter 11). A Dutch guide to setting up Internet access for A2000 is available at** `http://agvk.a2000.nl/LINUX/index.html`.
>
> **Contrary to Tebecai, your IP-number *is* visible from the Internet, so take your precautions regarding security and safety when setting up a Linux machine using A2000 Internet access!**

Part iii

Shaw Cable, Canada

This is from Peng F. Mok <pmok@shaw.wave.ca>:

I recently signed up for a cable modem service from Shaw Cable here in Canada, which they have christened Shaw Wave. They also appear to have another service called Shaw@Home, which they are using in some locations. Shaw has been upgrading their cable network for about a year and a half now and now offer cable-modem service to a number of locations across Canada. Information about the Shaw Wave service can be found at `http://www.shaw.wave.ca`, while information about the Shaw@Home service can be found at `http://shaw.home.com`. General information about Shaw Cable can be found at `http://www.shaw.ca`.

I thought I'd just drop you a line to inform you that your DHCP mini-HOWTO (`http://MetaLab.unc.edu/LDP/HOWTO/mini/DHCP.html`) was very useful in helping me set up Linux to work with my cable-modem service and that you might want to add Shaw Wave (and perhaps Shaw@Home) to your Cable-Modem mini-HOWTO as another entry explaining how to set up Linux with the service. I don't have specific information on the Shaw@Home service yet, but from conversations I've had with Shaw technical support, it seems that Shaw@Home involves the same features and setup procedure as that described in the "@Home" section in the Cable-Modem mini-HOWTO document.

In both services, Shaw Cable techs will come over and bring you two pieces of hardware: a Motorola CyberSURFR cable modem and either a 3Com EtherLink III 16-Bit ISA 3C509B-TPO NIC or an EtherLink XL PCI 3C900-TPO NIC. You have your choice of either an ISA or a PCI card, depending on your needs, and these models only have the RJ-45 (UTP) connectors. The ISA cards come with PnP-mode enabled by default, so it may be necessary to boot into DOS, disable PnP operation, and configure the card to some base I/O address and IRQ setting that is available. Once this is done, Linux should have no problems detecting the NIC at boot-time. I'm not sure about what needs to be done in the case of a PCI card since I don't currently have a PC which supports either PCI or PnP.

Here's a note from another user:

Shaw now also issues SMC PCI Ethernet cards. They give these out without boxes or manuals. I found out that these are the SMC Ether-Power PCI RJ45 card (model 8432T). They use the DEC 21041 chip so the tulip Ethernet driver is needed for it.

If you need to set up your POP3 mailboxes you can do that at `https://profile.home.net/Users/menu.htm`, and you can log in and set up the POP3 mailboxes that way.

Oh, and for the record, Shaw's technical support is horrendous. The best place to go for information is the `athome.users-unix` newsgroup (which is not even mentioned by any of the documentation) or please consult `http://www.ee.ualberta.ca/~pmok/linux/`.

Cogeco Cable, Canada

This information was provided thanks to Terry O'Grady `<togrady@cgocable.net>`.

I have a Cable Modem through a company called Cogeco Cable, located in various parts of Canada. They are part of the Wave system, which includes Rogers Cable and Shaw Cable. The technical setup is different for each provider, though. They supplied me with a D-Link Ethernet card (the version of that has changed since then but I believe are still using D-Link) and a Zenith modem. The IP setup is easy since they use DHCP, so all I did was install the DHCP daemon [see Chapter 11] and that was that. If you like, you can list my e-mail address `<togrady@cgocable.net>` for anyone with questions.

Optimum Online, New York and Connecticut

This information was provided by Seth Greenfield <islesfan@nassau.cv.net>.

> Optimum Online uses DHCP and rrclientd in Linux, by John Clark. Check out `http://www.netaxis.com/~wharris/optimum/index.html` for instructions on how to set up your service with Linux.
>
> People who had private IPs but have public IPs now should change their `/etc/resolv.conf` to look like this: domain `nassau.cv.net` (or `optonline.net`, depending on the user's mood), nameserver 167.206.112.3, nameserver 167.206.112.4. Other than that, it's the same setup procedure.

NOTE

The rrclientd software will work if you tell it `dce-server`, and you specify the domain as `optonline.net`.

Singapore Cable Vision, Singapore

This information was provided by Jieyao <jieyao@letterbox.com>:

> SCV provides a Motorola Cybersurfer modem connected to the network card via UTP cable. The IP setup is easy, since they use DHCP, so all you need to do is install the DHCP daemon. If you can't make access the first time, turn the modem off then on again.

Cable Wanadoo, France

This information was provided by Jerome Sautret <Jerome.Sautret@wanadoo.fr>:

> I just read your Cable Modem HOWTO. I live in France, and I use Cable Wanadoo, the cable service of France Telecom, which is the main telecom operator in France. It is available in a few cities in France at the moment, like Angers and Metz. This service provides a dynamic IP address via DHCP. It uses a COM 21 modem plugged in a 10BaseT Ethernet card. The IP setup is easy; just read the DHCP mini HOWTO [see Chapter 11].

Prime Cable Expressnet, Las Vegas, NV

This information is provided by jedi <jedi@penguin.lcvm.com>:

They use the Com21, which can either be connected directly to your 10BaseT input or inserted into the downlink input on your router. Static IPs are available for $10 per month and the usual address assignment is through DHCP.

More information can be obtained from http://penguin.lvcm.com.

TVD, Belgium

This information was provided by Pierre-Yves Keldermans <pykeldermans@usa.net>:

At home, my cable TV company is TVD. It is the first company to offer the Internet on cable in Belgium.

Hardware: LanCity cable modem and 10BaseT NIC (DLink ISA, if you buy it from TVD)

Config: DHCP

Prices:

> **Cheap:** for home use, real IP address but dynamic, DHCP expires every 10 min, 1 user only (theorically), no problems with firewall. The Web server on my computer is even reachable from the outside, full speed from the Internet, low speed to the Internet
>
> **Not so cheap:** for small office use, same as Cheap but not limited to 1 user and more speed to the Internet
>
> **Expensive:** for Web servers and Static IP addresses and reserved bandwidth to the Internet

Speed :

> **From TVD's mirror site:** up to 250Kbytes/sec—very nice (and yes, they have some Linux mirrors like Redhat)
>
> **From the Internet:** variable but rather good if the remote server isn't overloaded

---

For more info, go to http://www.tvd.be and http://www.tvd.net.

ipfwadm -O -a deny
masquera
V your static
outgoing
ipfwadm
such as ip masq
define the
bin:/usr/
CONFIG

Chapter 11

DHCP

This document attempts to answer basic questions on how to set up your Linux box to serve as a DHCP server or a DHCP client.

DHCP, the Dynamic Host Configuration Protocol, is commonly used on Ethernet and Ethernet-like networks to automatically give hosts an IP address and network address information at startup (a host needs this information to communicate over an Internet). Typically, the assigned IP address will expire after a time, and the host will have to request a new address when its current IP address expires; hence the *dynamic* in DHCP.

Very small networks seldom bother with DHCP, but larger networks in offices and towns often do use it. If your Linux host is part of a corporate network or you'll be plugging into a cable modem network, you may need to run a DHCP client. This chapter will tell you how.

Similarly, if you operate a medium- or large-sized network yourself, you may want to run a DHCP *server* to assign IP addresses to your hosts. This will save you some legwork, especially when hosts move around. This chapter will tell you how to do so.

This chapter is reprinted from the DHCP mini-HOWTO, version 2.6 of 14 November 1998, by Vladimir Vuskan.

INTRODUCTION

This introductory section contains general information about this chapter and contact information for the author.

Standard Disclaimer

No liability for the content of this chapter can be accepted. Use the concepts, examples, and other content at your own risk. As this is a new edition of this document, there may be errors and inaccuracies, which may, of course, be damaging to your system. Proceed with caution, and although damage is highly unlikely, I won't take any responsibility for it if it does occur.

Also bear in mind that this is *not* official information. Much of the content in this chapter is based on assumptions, which appear to work for people. Use the information at your own risk.

New Versions of This Document

New versions of this document will be periodically posted to `comp.os.linux.answers`. They will also be added to the various anonymous FTP sites that archive such information, including

`ftp://MetaLab.unc.edu/pub/Linux/docs/HOWTO`

In addition, you should generally be able to find this document on the Linux Documentation Project page via `http://MetaLab.unc.edu/LDP/`.

Feedback

Feedback is most certaintly welcome for this document. Without your submissions and input, this document wouldn't exist. So, please post your additions, comments, and criticisms to vuksan@veus.hr.

Contributors

This chapter has been modified from the original version by Paul Makeev.

The following people have contributed to this mini-HOWTO.

- Heiko Schlittermann
- Jonathan Smith
- Dan Khabaza
- Hal Sadofsky
- Henrik Stoerner
- Paul Rossington

Copyright Information

This document is copyrighted ©1998 Vladimir Vuksan and distributed under the following terms:

- Linux HOWTO documents may be reproduced and distributed in whole or in part, in any medium—physical or electronic, as long as this copyright notice is retained on all copies. Commercial redistribution is allowed and encouraged; however, the author would like to be notified of any such distributions.
- All translations, derivative works, or aggregate works incorporating any Linux HOWTO documents must be covered under this copyright notice. That is, you may not produce a derivative work from a HOWTO and impose additional restrictions on its distribution. Exceptions to these rules may be granted under certain conditions; please contact the Linux HOWTO coordinator at the address given below.
- If you have questions, please contact the Linux HOWTO coordinator at linux-howto@MetaLab.unc.edu.

DHCP

DHCP is Dynamic Host Configuration Protocol. It is used to control vital networking parameters of hosts (running clients) with the help of a server. DHCP is backward compatible with BOOTP. For more information, see RFC 2131 (old RFC 1531). (See Internet Resources section at the end of the document). You can also read DHCP FAQ (`http://web.syr.edu/~jmwobus/comfaqs/dhcp.faq.html`).

This mini-HOWTO covers both the DHCP server daemon as well as DHCP client daemon. Most people need the client daemon, which is used by workstations to obtain network information from a remote server. The server daemon is used by system administrators to distribute network information to clients, so if you are just a regular user, you need the client daemon.

Client Setup

This section details setting up and troubleshooting the DHCP client daemon on different distributions of Linux.

Downloading the Client Daemon

2.0.x kernels No matter what distribution you are using, you will need to download the DHCP client daemon for Linux. The package you need to download is called dhcpcd and the current version is 0.70. You can read the description of the package at `ftp://MetaLab.unc.edu/pub/Linux/system/network/daemons/dhcpcd-0.70.lsm`.

2.1.x kernels Because of changes in the IPV4 network package in 2.1.x kernels (e.g., the way it sets the defaults for several fields) dhcpcd doesn't work properly. Most users don't run experimental kernels, so this shouldn't be a problem. If you do, you should try dhcpcd 1.3.16, which is a modified version written by Sergei Viznyuk <`sergei@phystech.com`>. You can fetch it at:

- `ftp://phystech.dyn.ml.org/pub/`
- `http://www.cps.msu.edu/~dunham/out/dhcpcd-1.3.6.tar.gz`

Slackware

You can download the latest copy of the dhcpcd from any Sunsite mirror or the following:

- `ftp://ftp.cdrom.com/pub/linux/sunsite/system/network/daemons/`
- `ftp://MetaLab.unc.edu/pub/Linux/system/network/daemons`
- `ftp://ftp.kobe-u.ac.jp/pub/PC-UNIX/Linux/network/dhcp` (Primary site in Japan)

Once you've downloaded the latest version of `dhcpcd.tar.gz`, follow these steps:

1. Unpack it: `tar -zxvf dhcpcd-0.70.tar.gz`.
2. Cd into the directory and make dhcpcd: `cd dhcpcd-0.70 make`
3. Install it (you have to run the following command as root): `make install`

This will create the directory `/etc/dhcpc`, where dhcpcd will store the DHCP information, and the `dhcpcd` file will be copied into `/usr/sbin`.

In order to make the system initialize using DHCP during boot, type the following:

```
cd /etc/rc.d
mv rc.inet1 rc.inet1.OLD
```

This will move the old network initialization script into `rc.inet1.OLD`. You now need to create the new rc.inet1 script. The following code is all you need:

```
#!/bin/sh
#
# rc.inet1   This shell script boots up the base INET system.

HOSTNAME=`cat /etc/HOSTNAME` #This is probably not necessary
                             #but I will leave it in anyways


# Attach the loopback device.
/sbin/ifconfig lo 127.0.0.1
/sbin/route add -net 127.0.0.0 netmask 255.0.0.0 lo
```

Part iii

```
# IF YOU HAVE AN ETHERNET CONNECTION, use these lines below
# to configure the eth0 interface. If you're only using
# loopback or SLIP, don't include therest of the lines in
# this file.

/usr/sbin/dhcpcd
```

Save it and reboot your computer.

When you are finished, go to the "Tying It All Together" section.

Red Hat 5.x

dhcpcd configuration under Red Hat 5.0+ is really easy. All you need to do is start the Control Panel by typing **`control-panel`**. Then follow these steps:

1. Select "Network Configuration".
2. Click Interfaces.
3. Click Add.
4. Select Ethernet.
5. In the Edit Ethernet/Bus Interface select "Activate interface at boot time", as well as DHCP as "Interface configuration protocol".

When you are finished, go the "Tying It All Together" section.

Red Hat 4.x and Caldera OpenLinux 1.1/1.2

dhcpcd is included in the standard Red Hat distribution as an RPM, and you can find it on your distribution's CD-ROM in the RPMS directory or you can download it from

```
ftp://ftp.redhat.com/pub/redhat/redhat-4.2/i386/RedHat/RPMS/
    dhcpcd-0.6-2.i386.rpm
```

and install it with `rpm -i dhcpcd-0.6-2.i386.rpm`.

Alternatively you can compile your own version by following the steps outlined in the Slackware.

The following information was provided to me by Nothing <nothing@cc.gatech.edu>. I removed my static ip and name from /etc/resolv.conf. However, I did leave in the search line and my two nameserver lines (for some reason my dhcpcd never creates a /etc/dhcpc/resolv.conf, so I have to use a static /etc/resolv.conf).

In /etc/sysconfig/network, I removed the HOSTNAME and GATEWAY entries. I left the other entries as is (NETWORKING, DOMAINNAME, GATEWAYDEV).

In /etc/sysconfig/network-scripts/ifcfg-eth0, I removed the IPADDR, NETMASK, NETWORK, and BROADCAST entries. I left DEVICE and ONBOOT as is.

I changed the BOOTPROTO line to BOOTPROTO=dhcp.

Save the file. Reboot your computer.

When you are finished, go the "Tying It All Together" section.

Debian

There is a Deb package of dhcpcd at ftp://ftp.debian.org/debian/dists/slink/main/binary-i386/net/dhcpcd_0.70-4.deb or you can follow the Slackware installation instructions. To unpack the deb package, type

```
dpkg -i /where/ever/your/debian/packages/are/dhcpd*deb
```

It appears that there isn't a need for any dhcpcd configuration.

From: Heiko Schlittermann (heiko@os.inf.tu-dresden.de)

The dhcpcd package installs it's startup script as usual for Debian packages in /etc/init.d/packagename, here as /etc/init.d/dhcpcd, and links this to the various /etc/rc?.d/directories.

The contents of the /etc/rc?.d/ dirs are then executed at boot time.

If you don't reboot after installing, you should consider starting the daemon manually:

```
/etc/init.d/dhcpcd start
```

When you are finished, go to the "Tying It All Together" section.

LinuxPPC and MkLinux

The following section was written by R. Shapiro.

Versions 0.65 and 0.70 of Yoichi Hariguchi's dhcpcd should work properly in MkLinux and in LinuxPPC kernel 2.1.24, with the following caveats:

- If you want, or need, to build the executable from sources, note that the LinuxPPC compilers assume that 'char' is 'unsigned char', while the Hariguchi sources assume 'char' is 'signed char'. To build from sources you must edit the Makefile so that CFLAGS includes the option "-fsigned-char".
- The current stable release of LinuxPPC, (a k a linux-pmac), is 2.1.24 and requires the 2.1 patch (`http://www.cro.net/vuksan/dhcppatch`). Both the DR2.1 and DR3.0 releases of MkLinux use a 2.0 kernel (2.0.33) and do not require this patch, although it's harmless to apply it. Note that the dhcpcd rpm on the LinuxPPC CD-ROM does not include the 2.1 patch and therefore will not work with the Linux on that CD! It will work with MkLinux, however.
- In LinuxPPC 2.1.24, you'll see a router warning shortly after dhcpcd starts up. You can ignore this.
- The Hariguchi dhcpcd takes a while, about 30 seconds, to make its initial connection to the server and to set up routing. In LinuxPPC 2.1.24, the warning mentioned above is an indication that the routing is ready.

For later LinuxPPC kernels, no version of the Hariguchi dhcpcd will work: you *must* use Sergei Viznyuk's version instead (the current release is 1.3.9; see the above for URL). Unfortunately the Viznyuk dhcpcd is written for glibc 2, which LinuxPPC 2.1.1xx isn't. As a result, compiling it is a bit tricky—contact me for details. Once compiled, however, it works fine on late kernels (and not at all in MkLinux or LinuxPPC 2.1.24).

As far as Viznyuk's version of dhcpcd is concerned, I have a Viznyuk dhcpcd (v1.3.7) executable that works in recent LinuxPPC kernels; 2.1.102, 103, 115, and 119 have been tested. It's possible to build this from sources, but I don't know the details. The Viznyuk dhcpcd doesn't work in 2.1.24, but in that kernel the patched Hariguchi dhcpcd works. The Hariguchi dhcpcd can be built easily from sources.

Short summary:

Linux Version	Hariguch	Viznyuk
MkLinux	Yes	No
2.1.24	With patch	No
2.1.102	No	Yes

Note that the Viznyuk dhcpcd writes into /etc/resolv.conf directly (after renaming the existing one), so there's no need to copy or link it from /etc/dhcpc. Also note that it's typically installed into /sbin, not /usr/sbin, and that the command lines options are slightly different from the Hariguchi version. These differences may require small changes to ifup, if you're starting dhcpcd that way.

If you want a precompiled dhcpcd for LinuxPPC, send mail to reshapiro@mediaone.net.

I've also made binary RPMs available in

```
ftp://ftp.linuxppc.org//pub/linuxppc/contrib/linuxppc-R4/RPMS/
```

Don't use dhcpcd-1.3.8-2.ppc.rpm in that directory; it's broken. The reliable versions here are dhcpcd-0.70-0.ppc.rpm (for LinuxPPC 2.1.24), and dhcpcd-1.3.8-3.ppc.rpm (LinuxPPC 2.1.102 and up). An RPM for 1.3.9 should show up shortly. I also have a modified 1.3.9, which includes the -c command-file option, as in 0.65 and 0.70 (the standard Viznyuk dhcpcd doesn't include this).

Token Ring Networks

If you are trying to run dhcpcd on the Token Ring Network, it will not work. This is the solution provided to me by Henrik Stoerner <henrikstoerner@olicom.dk>.

The problem is that dhcpcd only knows about Ethernet cards. If it finds a Token Ring card, it refuses to do anything with it and reports "interface is not ethernet".

The solution is to apply a simple patch to the dhcpcd sources. I have put up a small Web page with the patch, Red Hat RPM-files, and a precompiled binary at http://eolicom.olicom.dk/~storner/dhcp/.

The patch has been sent to the dhcpcd maintainer, so hopefully it will be included in a future release of dhcpcd.

Tying It All Together

After your machine reboots, your network interface should be configured. Type

```
ifconfig
```

You should get something like this:

```
lo    Link encap:Local Loopback
      inet addr:127.0.0.1 Bcast:127.255.255.255 Mask:255.0.0.0
      UP BROADCAST LOOPBACK RUNNING MTU:3584 Metric:1
      RX packets:302 errors:0 dropped:0 overruns:0 frame:0
      TX packets:302 errors:0 dropped:0 overruns:0 carrier:0
      coll:0

eth0  Link encap:Ethernet HWaddr 00:20:AF:EE:05:45
      inet addr:24.128.53.102 Bcast:24.128.53.255
      ^^^^^^^^^^^^^^^^^^^^^^^
      UP BROADCAST NOTRAILERS RUNNING MULTICAST MTU:1500
      Metric:1
      RX packets:24783 errors:1 dropped:1 overruns:0 frame:1
      TX packets:11598 errors:0 dropped:0 overruns:0 carrier:0
      coll:96
      Interrupt:10 Base address:0x300
```

If you have some normal number under `inet addr`, you are set. If you see 0.0.0.0, don't despair; it is a temporary setting before dhcpcd acquires the IP address. If even after few minutes you are seeing 0.0.0.0, please check out the "Troubleshooting" section. dhcpcd is a daemon and will stay running as long as you have your machine on. Every three hours it will contact the DHCP server and try to renew the IP address lease. It will log all the messages in the syslog (on `Slackware /var/adm/syslog`, `RedHat/OpenLinux /var/log/syslog`).

One final thing. You need to specify your nameservers. There are two ways to do it. You can either ask your provider to provide you with the addresses of your name server and then put those in the `/etc/resolv.conf`, or dhcpcd will obtain the list from the DHCP server and build a `resolv.conf` in `/etc/dhcpc`. I decided to use dhcpcd's `resolv.conf` by doing the following:

1. Back up your old `/etc/resolv.conf`:

   ```
   mv /etc/resolv.conf /etc/resolv.conf.OLD
   ```

2. If directory /etc/dhcpc doesn't exist, create it:

   ```
   mkdir /etc/dhcpc
   ```

3. Make a link from /etc/dhcpc/resolv.conf to /etc/resolv.conf:

   ```
   ln -s /etc/dhcpc/resolv.conf /etc/resolv.conf
   ```

If that doesn't work, try this (fix suggested by Nothing <nothing@cc.gatech.edu>, with a little amendment by Henrik Stoerner).

This last step I had to perform only because my dhcpcd didn't create an /etc/dhcpc/resolv.conf. In /etc/sysconfig/network-scripts/ifup; I made the following changes (which are a very poor hack, but they work for me):

```
elif [ "$BOOTPROTO" = dhcp -a "$ISALIAS" = no ]; then
   echo -n "Using DHCP for ${DEVICE}... "
   /sbin/dhcpcd -c /etc/sysconfig/.........
   echo "echo \$$ ........

   if [ -f /var/run/dhcp-wait-${DEVICE}.pid ]; then
        ^^
      echo "failed."
      exit 1
```

I changed this to:

```
elif [ "$BOOTPROTO" = dhcp -a "$ISALIAS" = no ]; then
   echo -n "Using DHCP for ${DEVICE}... "
   /sbin/dhcpcd
   echo "echo \$$ ............

   if [ ! -f /var/run/dhcp-wait-${DEVICE}.pid ]; then
       ^^^^^^
      echo "failed."
      exit 1
```

Notice the ! (bang) in if [! -f /var/run/dhcp-wait-$DEVICE.pid];

Now sit back and enjoy.

Part iii

Various Notes

The following steps are not necessary but might be useful to some people.

- If you need network connectivity only occasionally you can start dhcpcd from the command line (you have to be root to do this) with

  ```
  /usr/sbin/dhcpcd
  ```

- When you need to down (turn off) the network, type

  ```
  /usr/sbin/dhcpcd -k
  ```

Troubleshooting

If you have followed the steps outlined above and you are unable to access the network, there are several possible explanations.

Your Network Card Is Not Configured Properly During the boot up process, your Linux will probe your network card and should say something along these lines:

```
eth0: 3c509 at 0x300 tag 1, 10baseT port, address 00 20 af ee
11 11, IRQ 10.
3c509.c:1.07 6/15/95 becker@cesdis.gsfc.nasa.gov
```

If a message like this doesn't appear, your Ethernet card might not be recognized by your Linux system. If you have a generic Ethernet card (a NE2000 clone), you should have received a disk with DOS utilities that you can use to set up the card. Try playing with IRQs until Linux recognizes your card (IRQ 9,10,12 are usually good).

Your DHCP Server Supports RFC 1541 Try running dhcpcd by typing

```
dhcpcd -r
```

Use ifconfig to check if your network interface is configured (wait a few seconds for the configuration process; initally it will say Inet.addr=0.0.0.0)

If this solves your problem, add the "-r" flag to the boot up scripts—i.e., instead of `/sbin/dhcpcd`, you will have `/sbin/dhcpcd -r`.

During Bootup I Get the Error Message "Using DHCP for eth0 ... failed" but My System Works Fine You are most likely using Red Hat and you haven't followed instructions carefully. You are missing the ! (bang) in one of the if statements. See the last part of "Tying It All Together" for the script change needed.

My Network Works for a Few Minutes and Then Stops Responding
There are some reports of gated (gateway daemon) screwing up routing on Linux boxes, which results in the problem described above. Check if gated is running:

```
ps -auxww grep gate
```

If it is, try removing it with Red Hat's RPM manager or removing the entry in `/etc/rc.d/`.

My Ethernet Card Is Recognized during Boot Up but I Still Get a "NO DHCPOFFER" Message in My Logs; I Also Happen to Have a PCMCIA Ethernet Card You need to make sure that you have the 10BaseT port ("phone" plug) on your network card activated. The best way to verify it is to check what kind of connector your card is configured for during boot up, for example,

```
eth0: 3c509 at 0x300 tag 1, 10baseT port, address  00 20 af
                            ^^^^^^^^^^^^
ee 11 11, IRQ 10.  3c509.c:1.07 6/15/95
becker@cesdis.gsfc.nasa.gov
```

I have received reports of laptop users having this kind of problem because of the PCMCIA utilities (specifically ifport) that would set the connector type to 10Base2 (thinnet). You have to make sure you use 10BaseT for your connection. If you haven't, reconfigure the card and restart the computer.

My DHCP Client Broadcasts Requests but No One Answers (Contributed By Peter Amstutz) On some systems, you need to include some hostname for your machine as part of the request. With dhcpcd, do this with 'dhcpcd -h foohost'. Probably the hostname wanted will be your account username on the network.

I Have Followed All the Steps but Still My Machine Is Not Able to Connect The cable modem will usually memorize the Ethernet address of your network card, so if you connect a new computer or switch network cards, you will somehow have to teach your cable modem to recognize the new computer/card. Usually you can turn off the modem and bring it back up while the computer is on, or you will have to call tech support to tell them that you have changed a network card in the computer. You have firewall rules (ipfwadm rules) that disallow port 67/68 traffic used by DHCP to distribute configuration info. Check your firewall rules carefully.

I Have MediaOne Express Service and I Still Can't Connect It appears that MediaOne has been adding some things to DHCP that shouldn't be there. Supposedly this is not a problem anymore, but if you experience outages, check for these things. If you are (un)lucky to have Windows NT on your machine, you will see a warning like this if you go into Event Viewer:

DHCP received an unknown option 067 of length 005. The raw option data is given below.

```
0000: 62 61 73 69 63 basic
```

If this is the problem go to `ftp://vanbuer.ddns.org/pub/` and either download a binary or get the source for the change.

DHCP Server Setup

This section concentrates on setting up the DHCP server.

DHCP Server for Unix

There are several DHCP servers available for Unix-like OSes, both commercial and free. One of the more popular free DHCP servers is Paul Vixie/ISC dhcpd. The latest version is 1.0 (suggested for most users), but 2.0 is in beta testing. You can get them from

```
ftp://ftp.isc.org/isc/dhcp/
```

After you download one of them, you need to unpack it. After you do cd into the distribution directory and type

```
./configure
```

it will take some time to configure the settings. After it is done, type

```
make
```

and

```
make install
```

Network Configuration

When done with installation, type **ifconfig -a**. You should see something like this:

```
eth0 Link encap:10Mbps Ethernet HWaddr 00:C0:4F:D3:C4:62
     inet addr:183.217.19.43 Bcast:183.217.19.255
     Mask:255.255.255.0
     UP BROADCAST RUNNING MULTICAST MTU:1500 Metric:1
     RX packets:2875542 errors:0 dropped:0 overruns:0
     TX packets:218647 errors:0 dropped:0 overruns:0
     Interrupt:11 Base address:0x210
```

If it doesn't say MULTICAST, you should reconfigure your kernel and add multicast support. On most systems you will not need to do this.

The next step is to add route for 255.255.255.255. The following is quoted from the dhcpd Readme:

> **In order for dhcpd to work correctly with picky DHCP clients (e.g., Windows 95), it must be able to send packets with an IP destination address of 255.255.255.255. Unfortunately, Linux insists on changing 255.255.255.255 into the local subnet broadcast address (here, that's 192.5.5.223). This results in a DHCP protocol violation, and while many DHCP clients don't notice the problem, some (e.g., all Microsoft DHCP clients) do. Clients that have this problem will appear not to see DHCP-OFFER messages from the server.**

Type

```
route add -host 255.255.255.255 dev eth0
```

If you get the message

```
"255.255.255.255: Unknown host"
```

you should try adding the following entry to your `/etc/hosts file`:

```
255.255.255.255 all-ones
```

Then, try

```
route add -host all-ones dev eth0
```

or

```
route add -net 255.255.255.0 dev eth0
```

`eth0` is of course the name of the network device you are using. If it differs change appropriately.

Options for dhcpd

Now you need to configure dhcpd. In order to do this, you will have to create or edit `/etc/dhcpd.conf`.

Most commonly what you want to do is assign IP addresses randomly. This can be done with settings as follows:

```
default-lease-time 600;
max-lease-time 7200;
option subnet-mask 255.255.255.0;
option broadcast-address 192.168.1.255;
option routers 192.168.1.254;
option domain-name-servers 192.168.1.1, 192.168.1.2;
option domain-name "mydomain.org";

subnet 192.168.1.0 netmask 255.255.255.0 {
  range 192.168.1.10 192.168.1.100;
  range 192.168.1.150 192.168.1.200;
}
```

This will result in the DHCP server giving a client an IP address from the range 192.168.1.10-192.168.1.100 or 192.168.1.150-192.168.1.200. It will lease an IP address for 600 seconds if the client doesn't ask for a specific time frame. Otherwise the maximum allowed lease will be 7200 seconds. The server will also advise the client that it should use 255.255.255.0 as its subnet mask, 192.168.1.255 as its broadcast address, 192.168.1.254 as the router/gateway, and 192.168.1.1 and 192.168.1.2 as its DNS servers.

You can also assign specific IP addresses based on clients' Ethernet addresses, e.g.,

```
host haagen {
  hardware ethernet 08:00:2b:4c:59:23;
  fixed-address 192.168.1.222;
}
```

This will assign IP address 192.168.1.222 to a client with Ethernet address 08:00:2b:4c:59:23.

You can also mix and match, e.g., you can have certain clients getting static IP addresses (e.g., servers) and others being alloted dynamic IPs (e.g., mobile users with laptops). There are a number of other options, e.g., wins server addresses, time server, etc. If you need any of those options, please read the `dhcpd.conf` man page.

Starting the Server

You can now invoke the DHCP server. Simply type (or include in the bootup scripts)

```
/usr/sbin/dhcpd
```

If you want to verify that everything is working fine, you should first turn on the debugging mode and put the server in the foreground. You can do this by typing

```
/usr/sbin/dhcpd -d -f
```

Then boot up one of your clients and check out the console of your server. You will see a number of debugging messages coming up.

Chapter 12

IP Masquerading

This document describes how to enable the IP masquerade feature on a Linux host, allowing connected computers that do not have registered Internet IP addresses to connect to the Internet through your Linux box.

If you have one Internet connection but many computers, IP Masquerading (also called Network Address Translation, or NAT) may be for you. It will make all of your hosts connect through one IP address used by your Internet-connected Linux box. (In the Windows world, products to do this refer to the sharing of an Internet connection. With Linux, it's a standard part of the OS, and it works much faster.)

"IP Masquerading" is reprinted from the Linux IP Masquerade mini-HOWTO, v1.50 of 7 February 1999, by Ambrose Au <ambrose@writeme.com> and David Ranch <dranch@trinnet.net>.

INTRODUCTION

This document describes how to enable the IP masquerade feature on a Linux host, allowing connected computers that do not have registered Internet IP addresses to connect to the Internet through your Linux box. It is possible to connect your machines to the Linux host with Ethernet, as well as other kinds of connection such as a dialup PPP link. This document will focus on Ethernet connections, since they should be the most likely case.

This document is intended for users using stable kernels 2.2.x and 2.0.x. Older kernels such as 1.2.x are *not* covered.

Foreword and Feedback Credits

I found it very confusing as a new user setting up IP masquerade on a newer kernel, i.e., 2.x kernel. Although there is a FAQ and a mailing list about it, there is no document dedicated to it. There have been some requests on the mailing list for such a HOWTO, so I decided to write this up as a starting point for new users and possibly a foundation for knowledgeable users to build on for documentation. If you think I'm not doing a good job, feel free to tell me so that I can make it better.

This document is heavily based on the original FAQ by Ken Eves and numerous helpful messages in the IP Masquerade mailing list. A special thanks to Mr. Matthew Driver, whose mailing list message inspired me to set up IP Masquerade and eventually write this.

Please feel free to send any feedback or comments to ambrose@writeme.com and dranch@trinnet.net if we're mistaken on any information or if any information is missing. Your invaluable feedback will certainly influence the future of this HOWTO!

NOTE

This HOWTO is meant to be a quick guide to get your IP Masquerade working in the shortest time possible. As I am not a technical writer, you may find the information in this document not as general and objective as it could be. The latest news and information can be found at the IP Masquerade Resource Web page (`http://ipmasq.cjb.net/`), which we maintain. If you have any technical questions on IP Masquerade, please join the IP Masquerade Mailing List instead of sending e-mail to me, as I have limited time and the developers of IPMasq are more capable of answering your questions.

The latest version of this document can be found at the IP Masquerade Resource Page, which also contains the HTML and PostScript versions. The URLs for the page are

```
http://ipmasq.cjb.net/
```

and

```
http://ipmasq2.cjb.net/
```

Please refer to the IP Masquerade Resource Mirror Sites Listing for other mirror sites available:

```
http://ipmasq.cjb.net/index.html#mirror
```

Copyright & Disclaimer

This document is Copyright ©1999 Ambrose Au and is free. You can redistribute it under the terms of the GNU General Public License.

The information and other contents in this document are correct to the best of my knowledge. However, IP Masquerade is *experimental*, and there is a chance that I have made mistakes; so you should determine if you want to follow the information in this document.

None of us are responsible for any damage on your computers or any other losses resulting from using the information in this document that is, the author and maintainers are not responsible for any damages incurred due to actions taken based on the information in this document.

What Is IP Masquerade?

IP Masquerade is a networking function in Linux. If a Linux host is connected to the Internet with IP Masquerade enabled, then computers connecting to it (either on the same LAN or connected with modems) can reach the Internet as well, even though they have *no official assigned IP addresses*.

This allows a set of machines to *invisibly* access the Internet, hidden behind a gateway system, which appears to be the only system using the Internet. Breaking the security of a well set-up masquerading system should be considerably more difficult than breaking a good packet-filter-based firewall (assuming there are no bugs in either).

Current Status

IP Masquerade had been out for several years and is maturing as Linux heads into the 2.2.*x* stage. Kernels since 1.3.*x* have built-in support. Many individuals and even busnesses are using it with satisfactory results.

Browsing Web pages and Telnet are reported to work well over IP Masquerade. FTP, IRC, and listening to Real Audio are working with certain modules loaded. Streaming audio, such as True Speech and Internet Wave, work too. Some fellow users on the mailing list even tried videoconferencing software. Ping is now working with the newly available ICMP patch.

NOTE

Please refer to the "Before You Begin" section in Chapter 4 for a more complete listing of software supported.

IP Masquerade works well with 'client machines' on several different OSes and platforms. There are successful cases with systems using Unix, Windows 95, Windows NT, Windows for Workgroups (with the TCP/IP package), OS/2, the Macintosh OS with Mac TCP, Mac Open Transport, DOS with the NCSA Telnet package, VAX, Alpha with Linux, and even Amiga with AmiTCP or AS225-stack. The list goes on and on; the point is, if your OS talks TCP/IP, it should work with IP Masquerade.

Who Can Benefit from IP Masquerade?

You can benefit from IP Masquerade if the following criteria are met:

- You have a Linux host connected to the Internet.
- You have some computers running TCP/IP connected to that Linux box on a local subnet, and/or
- Your Linux host has more than one modem and acts as a PPP or SLIP server connecting to others.
- Those other machines do not have official assigned IP addresses. (These machines are represented by *other machines* hereinafter.)
- You want those other machines to make it onto the Internet without spending extra bucks.

Who Doesn't Need IP Masquerade?

You don't need IP Masquerade if

- Your machine is a stand-alone Linux host connected to the Internet.
- You already have assigned addresses for your other machines.
- You don't like the idea of a free ride.

How Does IP Masquerade Work?

The following is from the IP Masquerade FAQ by Ken Eves.

Here is a drawing of the most simple setup.

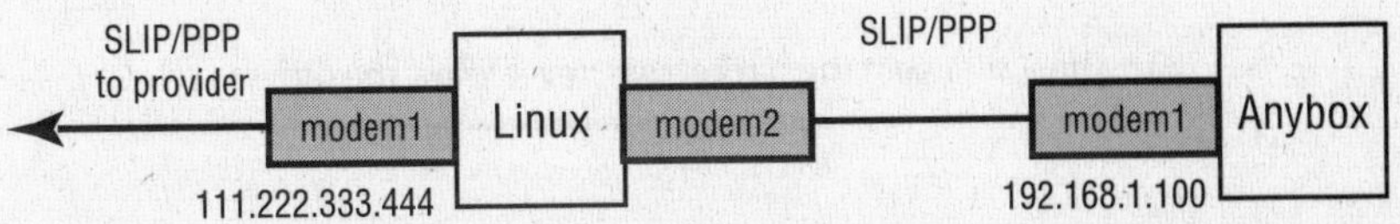

In the above drawing, a Linux box with IP Masquerade installed and running is connected to the Internet via SLIP or PPP using modem1. It has an assigned IP address of 111.222.333.444. It is set up so that modem2 allows callers to log in and start a SLIP or PPP connection.

The second system (which doesn't have to be running Linux) calls into the Linux box and starts a SLIP or PPP connection. It does *not* have an assigned IP address on the Internet, so it uses 192.168.1.100 (see below).

With IP Masquerade and the routing configured properly, the machine Anybox can interact with the Internet as if it were really connected (with a few exceptions).

Quoting Pauline Middelink:

> **Do not forget to mention that Anybox should have the Linux box as its gateway (whether it's the default route or just a subnet is no matter). If Anybox cannot do this, the Linux machine should do a proxy arp for all routed addresses, but the setup of proxy arp is beyond the scope of the document.**

The following is an excerpt from a post on `comp.os.linux.networking`, which has been edited to match the names used in the above example:

> **I tell machine Anybox that my slipped Linux box is its gateway.**
>
> **When a packet comes into the Linux box from Anybox, it will assign it a new source port number and slap its own IP address in the packet header, saving the originals. It will then send the modified packet out over the SLIP or PPP interface to the Internet.**
>
> **When a packet comes from the Internet to the Linux box, if the port number is one of those assigned above, it will get the original port and IP address, put them back in the packet header, and send the packet to Anybox.**
>
> **The host that sent the packet will never know the difference.**

An IP Masquerading Example

A typical example is given in the diagram that follows.

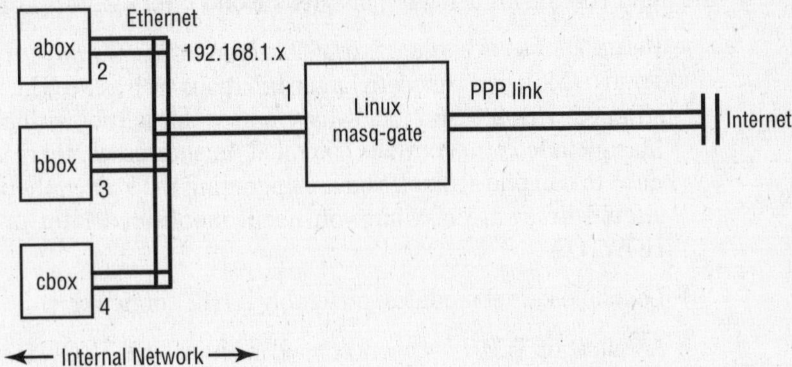

In this example there are four computer systems that we are concerned about. (There is presumably also something on the far right that your IP connection to the Internet comes through, and there is something—far off the page—on the Internet that you are interested in exchanging information with.) The Linux system masq-gate is the masquerading gateway for the internal network of machines abox, bbox, and cbox to get to the Internet. The internal network uses one of the assigned private network addresses, in this case the class C network 192.168.1.0, with the Linux box having address 192.168.1.1 and the other systems having addresses on that network.

The three machines abox, bbox, and cbox (which can, by the way, be running any operating system, as long as they can speak IP—such as Windows 95, the Macintosh OS, or even another Linux box) can connect to other machines on the Internet; however, the masquerading system masq-gate converts all of their connections so that they appear to originate from masq-gate and arranges the data coming back into a masqueraded connection and relays it back to the originating system. The systems on the internal network therefore see a direct route to the Internet and are unaware that their data is being masqueraded.

Requirements for Using IP Masquerade on Linux 2.2.*x*

The requirements for using IP masquerade on Linux 2.2.*x* are as follows:

- Kernel 2.2.*x* source, which is available from `http://www.kernel.org/`. (Most of the modern Linux dributions such as Red Hat 5.2—shipped with 2.0.36 kernel—have a modular kernel with all IP Masquerade kernel options compiled. In such cases, there is no need to compile again. If you are upgrading the kernel, then you should be aware of what you need, mentioned later in the HOWTO.)
- Loadable kernel modules, preferably 2.1.121 or newer.
- A well set up TCP/IP network covered in Linux NET-3 HOWTO (see Chapter 8) and the Network Administrator's Guide (`http://metalab.unc.edu/mdw/LDP/nag/nag.html`). Also check out the Trinity OS Doc (`http://www.ecst.csuchico.edu/~dranch/LINUX/TrinityOS.wri`), a very compreshensive guide on Linux networking.
- Connectivity to the Internet for your Linux host covered in Linux ISP Hookup HOWTO (`http://metalab.unc.edu/mdw/HOWTO/ISP-Hookup-HOWTO.html`), Linux PPP HOWTO (see Chapter 9), Linux DHCP mini-HOWTO (see Chapter 11), and Linux Cable Modem mini-HOWTO (see Chapter 10).
- IP Chains 1.3.8 or newer available from `http://www.rustcorp.com/linux/ipchains/`. More information on version requirements is on the Linux IP Firewalling Chains page.

NOTE

For other options and the latest information, please see the Linux IP Masquerade Resource at `http://ipmasq.cjb.net/`.

Requirements for Using IP Masquerade on Linux 2.0.*x*

The requirements for using IP Masquerade on Linux 2.0.*x* are as follows:

- Kernel 2.0.*x* source, available from `http://www.kernel.org/`. (Most of the modern Linux dributions, such as Red Hat 5.2, have a modular kernel with all IP Masquerade kernel options compiled. In such cases, there is no need to compile again. If you are upgrading your kernel, then you should be aware of what you need, mentioned later in the HOWTO.)
- Loadable kernel modules, preferably 2.0.0 or newer, available from `http://www.pi.se/blox/modules/modules-2.0.0.tar.gz` (modules-1.3.57 is the minimal requirement).
- A well set up TCP/IP network, covered in Linux NET-3 HOWTO (see Chapter 8) and the Network Administrator's Guide (`http://metalab.unc.edu/mdw/LDP/nag/nag.html`). Also check out the Trinity OS Doc (`http://www.ecst.csuchico.edu/~dranch/LINUX/TrinityOS.wri`), a very compreshensive guide on Linux networking.
- Connectivity to the Internet for your Linux host, covered in Linux ISP Hookup HOWTO (`http://metalab.unc.edu/mdw/HOWTO/ISP-Hookup-HOWTO.html`), Linux PPP HOWTO (see Chapter 9), Linux DHCP mini-HOWTO (see Chapter 11), and Linux Cable Modem mini-HOWTO (see Chapter 10).
- Ipfwadm 2.3 or newer, available from `ftp://ftp.xos.nl/pub/linux/ipfwadm/ipfwadm-2.3.tar.gz`. More information on version requirements is on the Linux IPFWADM page `http://www.xos.nl/linux/ipfwadm/`.

You can optionally apply some IP Masquerade patches to enable other functionality. More information is available at the IP Masquerade Resource at `http://ipmasq.cjb.net/`. (These patches apply to all 2.0.*x* kernels.)

Setting Up IP Masquerade

If your private network contains any vital information, think carefully before using IP Masquerade. This may be a gateway for you to get to the

Internet and, vice versa—for someone on the other side of the world to get into your network.

Compiling the Kernel for IP Masquerade Support

If your Linux distribution already has the required features and modules compiled (most modular kernels will have all you need) mentioned below, then you do not have to recompile the kernel. Reading this section is still highly recommended as it contains other useful informaiton.

Linux 2.2.x Kernels

1. First of all, you need the kernel source for 2.2.*x*.

TIP

If this is your first time compiling the kernel, don't be scared. It's rather easy and it's covered in the Linux Kernel HOWTO: `http://metalab.unc.edu/mdw/HOWTO/Kernel-HOWTO.html`.

2. Unpack the kernel source to `/usr/src/` with the command `tar xvzf linux-2.2.x.tar.gz -C /usr/src`, where *x* is the patch level beyond 2.0 (make sure there is a directory or symbolic link called `linux`).
3. Apply appropriate patches. Since new patches are coming out, details will not be included here. Please refer to the IP Masquerade Resource (`http://ipmasq.cjb.net/`) for up-to-date information.
4. Refer to the Kernel HOWTO and the README file in the kernel source directory for further instructions on compiling a kernel.

Here are the options that you need to compile in. Say *YES* to the following:

```
* Prompt for development and/or incomplete code/drivers
  CONFIG_EXPERIMENTAL
  - this will allow you to select experimental IP
  Masquerade code compiled into the kernel
```

```
* Enable loadable module support
  CONFIG_MODULES
  - allows you to load ipmasq modules such as ip_masq_ftp.o

* Networking support
  CONFIG_NET

* Network firewalls
  CONFIG_FIREWALL

* TCP/IP networking
  CONFIG_INET

* IP: forwarding/gatewaying
  CONFIG_IP_FORWARD

* IP: firewalling
  CONFIG_IP_FIREWALL

* IP: masquerading
  CONFIG_IP_MASQUERADE

* IP: ipportfw masq support
  CONFIG_IP_MASQUERADE_IPPORTFW
  - recommended

* IP: ipautofw masquerade support
  CONFIG_IP_MASQUERADE_IPAUTOFW
  - optional

* IP: ICMP masquerading
  CONFIG_IP_MASQUERADE_ICMP
  - support for masquerading ICMP packets, recommended.

* IP: always defragment
  CONFIG_IP_ALWAYS_DEFRAG
  - highly recommended

* Dummy net driver support
  CONFIG_DUMMY
  - recommended

* IP: ip fwmark masq-forwarding support
  CONFIG_IP_MASQUERADE_MFW
  - optional
```

NOTE

These are just the components you need for IP Masquerade; select whatever other options you need for your specific setup.

5. After compiling the kernel, you should compile and install the modules:

```
make modules; make modules_install
```

6. Then you should add a few lines into your `/etc/rc.d/rc.local` file (or any file you think is appropriate) to load the required modules, which reside in `/lib/modules/2.2.x/ipv4/` automatically during each reboot:

```
/sbin/depmod -a
/sbin/modprobe ip_masq_ftp
/sbin/modprobe ip_masq_raudio
/sbin/modprobe ip_masq_irc
# (and other modules such as ip_masq_cuseeme, ip_masq_
# vdolive if you have applied the patches)
```

WARNING

IP forwarding is disabled by default in 2.2.*x* kernels. Please make sure you enable it by running `echo "1" > /proc/sys/net/ipv4/ipforwarding`**. For Red Hat users, you may try changing** `FORWARDIPV4=false` **to** `FORWARDIPV4=true` **in** `/etc/sysconfig/network`.

7. Reboot the Linux box.

Linux 2.0.x Kernels

1. First of all, you need the kernel source (preferably the latest kernel version 2.0.36 or above).

TIP

If this is your first time compiling the kernel, don't be scared. It's rather easy and it's covered in Linux Kernel HOWTO: `http://metalab.unc.edu/mdw/HOWTO/Kernel-HOWTO.html`.

2. Unpack the kernel source to `/usr/src/` with the command `tar xvzf linux-2.0.x.tar.gz -C /usr/src`, where

x is the patch level beyond 2.0 (make sure there is a directory or symbolic link called `linux`).

3. Apply appropriate patches. Since new patches are coming out, details will not be included here. Please refer to the IP Masquerade Resource (`http://ipmasq.cjb.net/`) for up-to-date information.

4. Refer to the Kernel HOWTO and the README file in the kernel source directory for further instructions on compiling a kernel.

Here are the options that you need to compile in. Say *YES* to the following:

```
* Prompt for development and/or incomplete code/drivers
  CONFIG_EXPERIMENTAL
  - this will allow you to select experimental IP
   Masquerade code compiled into the kernel

* Enable loadable module support
  CONFIG_MODULES
  - allows you to load modules

* Networking support
  CONFIG_NET

* Network firewalls
  CONFIG_FIREWALL

* TCP/IP networking
  CONFIG_INET

* IP: forwarding/gatewaying
  CONFIG_IP_FORWARD

* IP: firewalling
  CONFIG_IP_FIREWALL

* IP: masquerading (EXPERIMENTAL)
  CONFIG_IP_MASQUERADE
  - although it is experimental, it is a *MUST*

* IP: ipautofw masquerade support (EXPERIMENTAL)
  CONFIG_IP_MASQUERADE_IPAUTOFW
  -recommended
```

```
* IP: ICMP masquerading
  CONFIG_IP_MASQUERADE_ICMP
  - support for masquerading ICMP packets, optional.

* IP: always defragment
  CONFIG_IP_ALWAYS_DEFRAG
  - highly recommended

* Dummy net driver support
  CONFIG_DUMMY
  - recommended
```

NOTE

These are just the components you need for IP Masquerade. Select whatever other options you need for your specific setup.

5. After compiling the kernel, you should compile and install the modules:

   ```
   make modules; make modules_install
   ```

6. Then you should add a few lines into your `/etc/rc.d/rc.local` file (or any file you think is appropriate) to load the required modules, which reside in `/lib/modules/2.0.x/ipv4/`, automatically during each reboot:

   ```
   /sbin/depmod -a
   /sbin/modprobe ip_masq_ftp
   /sbin/modprobe ip_masq_raudio
   /sbin/modprobe ip_masq_irc
   # (and other modules such as ip_masq_cuseeme, ip_masq_
   # vdolive if you have applied the patches)
   ```

WARNING

IP forwarding is disabled by default since 2.0.34 kernels. Please make sure you enable it by running `echo "1" > /proc/sys/net/ipv4/ipforward`**. Red Hat users, you may try changing** `FORWARDIPV4=false` **to** `FORWARDIPV4=true` **in** `/etc/sysconfig/network`.

7. Reboot the Linux box.

Assigning a Private Network IP Addresses

Since all other machines do not have official assigned addresses, there must be a right way to allocate addresses to those machines.

The following information is from the IP Masquerade FAQ. There is an RFC (1597, probably obsolete by now) on which IP addresses are to be used on a non-connected network. There are three blocks of numbers set aside specifically for this purpose. One which I use is 255 Class C subnets at 192.168.1.n to 192.168.255.n.

The following is from RCF 1597:

Section 3: Private Address Space

The Internet Assigned Numbers Authority (IANA) has reserved the following three blocks of the IP address space for private networks:

```
10.0.0.0      -  10.255.255.255
  172.16.0.0    -  172.31.255.255
  192.168.0.0    -  192.168.255.255
```

We will refer to the first block as "24-bit block", the second as "20-bit block", and to the third as "16-bit" block". Note that the first block is nothing but a single class A network number, while the second block is a set of 16 contiguous class B network numbers, and the third block is a set of 255 contiguous class C network numbers.

So, if you're using a class C network, you should name your machines as 192.168.1.1, 1.92.168.1.2, 1.92.168.1.3, ..., 192.168.1.*x*.

192.168.1.1 is usually the gateway machine, which is your Linux host connecting to the Internet. Notice that 192.168.1.0 and 192.168.1.255 are the Network and Broadcast address respectively, which are reserved. Avoid using these addresses on your machines.

Configuring the Other Machines

Besides setting the appropriate IP address for each machine, you should also set the appropriate gateway. In general, it is rather straightforward. You simply enter the address of your Linux host (usually 192.168.1.1) as the gateway address.

For the Domain Name Service, you can add in any DNS available. The most apparent one should be the one that your Linux is using. You can optionally add any domain search suffix, as well.

After you have reconfigured those IP addresses, remember to restart the appropriate services or reboot your systems.

The following configuration instructions assume that you are using a Class C network with 192.168.1.1 as your Linux host's address. Please note that 192.168.1.0 and 192.168.1.255 are reserved.

Configuring Windows 95

1. If you haven't installed your network card and adapter driver, do so now.
2. Go to Control Panel/Network.
3. Add TCP/IP protocol if you don't already have it.
4. In TCP/IP properties, go to IP Address and set IP Address to 192.168.1.*x*, (1 x 255), and then set Subnet Mask to 255 .255.255.0.
5. Add 192.168.1.1 as your gateway under Gateway.
6. Under DNS Configuration/DNS Server search order add the DNS that your Linux host uses (usually found in `/etc/resolv.conf`). Optionally, you can add the appropriate domain search suffix.
7. Leave all the other settings as they are, unless you know what you're doing.
8. Click OK in all dialog boxes and restart your system.
9. Ping the Linux box to test the network connection: Start/Run, type **`ping 192.168.1.1`**. (This is only a LAN connection testing, you can't ping the outside world yet.)
10. You can optionally create a HOSTS file in the windows directory so that you can use the hostname of the machines on your LAN. There is an example called `HOSTS.SAM` in the Windows directory.

Configuring Windows for Workgroup 3.11

1. If you haven't installed your network card and adapter driver, do so now.
2. Install the TCP/IP 32b package if you don't have it already.
3. In Main/Windows Setup/Network Setup, click Drivers.
4. Highlight Microsoft TCP/IP-32 3.11b in the Network Drivers section, and click Setup.
5. Set the IP Address to 192.168.1.*x* (1 x 255), then set Subnet Mask to 255.255.255.0 and Default Gateway to 192.168.1.1
6. Do not enable Automatic DHCP Configuration or put anything in those WINS Server input areas, unless you're in a Windows NT domain and you know what you're doing.
7. Click DNS, fill in the appropriate information mentioned in step 6 of the previous section, then click OK when you're done.
8. Click Advanced, and check Enable DNS for Windows Name Resolution and Enable LMHOSTS lookup if you're using a lookup host file, similar to the one mentioned in step 10 of the previous section.
9. Click OK in all dialog boxes and restart your system.
10. Ping the Linux box to test the network connection: File/Run, type **`ping 192.168.1.1`**. (This is only a LAN connection testing; you can't ping the outside world yet.)

Configuring Windows NT

1. If you haven't installed your network card and adapter driver, do so now.
2. Go to Main/Control Panel/Network.
3. Add the TCP/IP Protocol and Related Component from the Add Software menu if you don't have TCP/IP service installed already.

4. Under the Network Software and Adapter Cards section, highlight TCP/IP Protocol in the Installed Network Software selection box.
5. In TCP/IP Configuration, select the appropriate adapter, for example, `[1]Novell NE2000 Adapter`. Then set the IP Address to 192.168.1.*x* (1 x 255), then set Subnet Mask to 255.255.255.0 and Default Gateway to 192.168.1.1
6. Do not enable Automatic DHCP Configuration or put anything in those WINS Server input areas unless you're in a Windows NT domain and you know what you're doing.
7. Click DNS, fill in the appropriate information mentioned in step 6 of the "Configuring Windows 95" section, then click OK when you're done.
8. Click Advanced, and check Enable DNS for Windows Name Resolution and Enable LMHOSTS lookup if you're using a lookup host file, similar to the one mentioned in step 10 of the "Configuring Windows 95" section.
9. Click OK in all dialog boxes and restart your system.
10. Ping the Linux box to test the network connection: File/Run, type **`ping 192.168.1.1`**. (This is only a LAN connection testing; you can't ping the outside world yet.)

Configuring Unix Based Systems

1. If you haven't installed your network card and recompiled your kernel with the appropriate adapter driver, do so now.
2. Install TCP/IP networking, such as the nettools package, if you don't have it already.
3. Set IPADDR to 192.168.1.*x* (1 x 255), then set NETMASK to 255.255.255.0, GATEWAY to 192.168.1.1, and BROADCAST to 192.168.1.255. For example, you can edit the `/etc/sysconfig/network-scripts/ifcfg-eth0` file on a Red Hat Linux system, or simply do it through the Control Panel. (It's different in SunOS, BSDi, Slackware Linux, etc.)
4. Add your domain name service (DNS) and domain search suffix in `/etc/resolv.conf`.

5. You may want to update your `/etc/networks` file, depending on your settings.
6. Restart the appropriate services, or simply restart your system.
7. Issue a ping command (`ping 192.168.1.1`) to test the connection to your gateway machine. (This is only a LAN connection testing; you can't ping the outside world yet.)

Configuring DOS Using the NCSA Telnet Package

1. If you haven't installed your network card, do so now.
2. Load the appropriate packet driver. For an NE2000 card, issue `nwpd 0x60 10 0x300`, with your network card set to IRQ 10 and hardware address at 0x300
3. Make a new directory, and then unpack the NCSA Telnet package: `pkunzip tel2308b.zip`.
4. Use a text editor to open the `config.tel` file.
5. Set `myip=192.168.1.`*x* (1 x 255) and `netmask=255.255.255.0`
6. In this example, you should set `hardware=packet`, `interrupt=10`, and `ioaddr=60`.
7. You should have at least one individual machine specification set as the gateway, that is, the Linux host:

```
name=default
host=yourlinuxhostname
hostip=192.168.1.1
gateway=1
```

8. Have another specification for a domain name service:

```
name=dns.domain.com ; hostip=123.123.123.123;
nameserver=1
```

   Substitute the appropriate information about the DNS that your Linux host uses.

9. Save your `config.tel` file.
10. Telnet to the Linux box to test the network connection: `telnet 192.168.1.1`.

Part iii

Configuring a Macintosh Running MacTCP

1. If you haven't installed the appropriate driver software for your Ethernet adapter, now would be a very good time to do so.
2. Open the MacTCP Control Panel. Select the appropriate network driver (Ethernet, *not* EtherTalk) and click on the More... button.
3. Under Obtain Address click Manually.
4. Under IP Address select class C from the pop-up menu. Ignore the rest of this section of the dialog box.
5. Fill in the appropriate information under Domain Name Server Information:.
6. Under Gateway Address enter **192.168.1.1**.
7. Click OK to save the settings. In the main window of the MacTCP control panel, enter the IP address of your Mac (192.168.1.x, 1 < x < 255) in the IP Address: box.
8. Close the MacTCP control panel. If a dialog box pops up notifying you to do so, restart the system.
9. You may optionally ping the Linux box to test the network connection. If you have the freeware program MacTCP Watcher, click the Ping button, and enter the address of your Linux box (192.168.1.1) in the dialog box that pops up. (This is only a LAN connection testing; you can't ping the outside world yet.)
10. You can optionally create a `Hosts` file in your System Folder so that you can use the hostnames of the machines on your LAN. The file should already exist in your System Folder and should contain some (commented-out) sample entries, which you can modify according to your needs.

Configuring a Macintosh Running Open Transport

1. If you haven't installed the appropriate driver software for your Ethernet adapter, now would be a very good time to do so.
2. Open the TCP/IP Control Panel and choose User Mode... from the Edit menu. Make sure the user mode is set to at least Advanced and click the OK button.

3. Choose Configurations... from the File menu. Select your Default configuration and click the Duplicate... button. Enter **IP Masq** (or something to let you know that this is a special configuration) in the Duplicate Configuration dialog; it will probably say something like Default copy. Then click the OK button and the Make Active button.

4. Select Ethernet from the Connect via: pop-up.

5. Select the appropriate item from the Configure: pop-up. If you don't know which option to choose, you probably should re-select your Default configuration and quit. I use Manually.

6. Enter the IP address of your Mac (192.168.1.x, 1 < x < 255) in the IP Address: box.

7. Enter 255.255.255.0 in the Subnet mask box.

8. Enter 192.168.1.1 in the Router address box.

9. Enter the IP addresses of your domain name servers in the Name server addr. box.

10. Enter the name of your Internet domain (for example, `microsoft.com`) in the Starting domain name box under Implicit Search Path.

11. The following procedures are optional. Incorrect values may cause erratic behavior. If you're not sure, it's probably better to leave them blank, unchecked, and/or unselected. Remove any information from those fields, if necessary. As far as I know, there is no way in the TCP/IP dialogs to tell the system not to use a previously selected alternate `Hosts` file. If you know, I would be interested. Check the 802.3 if your network requires 802.3 frame types.

12. Click the Options... button to make sure that the TCP/IP is active. I use the Load only when needed option. If you run and quit TCP/IP applications many times without rebooting your machine, you may find that unchecking the Load only when needed option will prevent/reduce the effects on your machine's memory management. With the item unchecked, the TCP/IP protocol stacks are always loaded and available for use. If checked, the TCP/IP stacks are automatically loaded when needed and unloaded when not. It's the loading

and unloading process that can cause your machine's memory to become fragmented.

13. You may ping the Linux box to test the network connection. If you have the freeware program MacTCP Watcher, click the Ping button, and enter the address of your Linux box (192.168.1.1) in the dialog box that pops up. (This is only a LAN connection testing; you can't ping the outside world yet.)

14. You can create a `Hosts` file in your System Folder so that you can use the hostnames of the machines on your LAN. The file may or may not already exist in your System Folder. If so, it should contain some (commented-out) sample entries, which you can modify according to your needs. If not, you can get a copy of the file from a system running MacTCP, or just create your own (it follows a subset of the Unix `/etc/hosts` file format, described on RFC952). Once you've created the file, open the TCP/IP Control Panel, click the Select Hosts File... button, and open the `Hosts` file.

15. Click the close box or choose Close or Quit from the File menu, and then click the Save button to save the changes you have made.

16. The changes take effect immediately, but rebooting the system won't hurt.

Configuring a Novell Network Using DNS

1. If you haven't installed the appropriate driver software for your Ethernet adapter, now would be a very good time to do so.

2. Download `tcpip16.exe` from `ftp.novell.com/pub/updates/unixconn/lwp5`.

3. Edit `c:\nwclient\startnet.bat`. (Here is a copy of mine.)

```
SET NWLANGUAGE=ENGLISH
LH LSL.COM
LH KTC2000.COM
LH IPXODI.COM
LH tcpip
LH VLM.EXE
F:
```

4. Edit `c:\nwclient\net.cfg`. (Change the link driver to yours, that is, NE2000.)

```
Link Driver KTC2000
    Protocol IPX 0 ETHERNET_802.3
    Frame ETHERNET_802.3
    Frame Ethernet_II
    FRAME Ethernet_802.2

NetWare DOS Requester
     FIRST NETWORK DRIVE = F
     USE DEFAULTS = OFF
     VLM = CONN.VLM
     VLM = IPXNCP.VLM
     VLM = TRAN.VLM
     VLM = SECURITY.VLM
     VLM = NDS.VLM
     VLM = BIND.VLM
     VLM = NWP.VLM
     VLM = FIO.VLM
     VLM = GENERAL.VLM
     VLM = REDIR.VLM
     VLM = PRINT.VLM
     VLM = NETX.VLM

Link Support
    Buffers 8 1500
    MemPool 4096

Protocol TCPIP
    PATH SCRIPT   C:\NET\SCRIPT
    PATH PROFILE  C:\NET\PROFILE
    PATH LWP_CFG  C:\NET\HSTACC
    PATH TCP_CFG  C:\NET\TCP
    ip_address   xxx.xxx.xxx.xxx
    ip_router    xxx.xxx.xxx.xxx
```

5. Finally, create `c:\bin\resolv.cfg`:

```
SEARCH DNS HOSTS SEQUENTIAL
NAMESERVER 207.103.0.2
NAMESERVER 207.103.11.9
```

6. I hope this helps some people get their Novell Nets online; this can be done using NetWare 3.1*x* or 4.*x*.

Configuring OS/2 Warp

1. If you haven't installed the appropriate driver software for your Ethernet adapter, now would be a very good time to do so.
2. Install the TCP/IP protocol if you don't have it already.
3. Go to Programms / TCP/IP (LAN) / TCP/IP Settings
4. In Network, add your TCP/IP address and set your Netmask (255.255.255.0).
5. Under Routing press Add. Set the Type to default and type the IP Address of your Linux Box in the Field Router Address (192.168.1.1).
6. Set the same DNS (Nameserver) Address that your Linux host uses in Hosts.
7. Close the TCP/IP control panel. Say Yes to the following question(s).
8. Reboot your system.
9. You may ping the Linux box to test the network configuration. Type **`ping 192.168.1.1`** in a OS/2 Command prompt Window. When ping packets are received, all is ok.

Configuring Other Systems

The same logic should apply to setting up other platforms. Consult the sections above. If you're interested in writing about any systems that have not been covered yet, please send detailed setup instructions to `ambrose@writeme.com` and `dranch@trinnet.net`.

Configuring IP Forwarding Policies

At this point, you should have your kernel and other required packages installed, as well as your modules loaded. Also, the IP addresses, gateway, and DNS should be all set on the other machines.

Now, the only thing left to do is to use the IP firewalling tools to forward appropriate packets to the appropriate machine.

This can be accomplished in many different ways. The following suggestions and examples worked for me, but you may have different ideas; please refer to "IP Firewall Administration Cipfwadm") in this chapter and the ipchains(2.2.*x*) and ipfwadm(2.0.*x*) man pages for details.

NOTE

This section only provides you with the bare minimum rules set to get IP Masquerade working while security issues are not being considered. It is highly recomended that you spend some time to apply appropriate firewall rules to tighten security.

Linux 2.2.*x* Kernels

Ipfwadm is no longer the tool for manipulating ipmasq rules for 2.2.*x* kernels; please use ipchains,

```
ipchains -P forward DENY
ipchains -A forward -s yyy.yyy.yyy.yyy/x -j MASQ
```

where *x* is one of the following numbers, according to the class of your subnet, and *yyy.yyy.yyy.yyy* is your network address.

Netmask	*x*	Subnet
255.0.0.0	8	Class A
255.255.0.0	16	Class B
255.255.255.0	24	Class C
255.255.255.255	32	Point-to-point

You may also use the format yyy.yyy.yyy.yyy/xxx.xxx.xxx.xxx, where *xxx.xxx.xxx.xxx* specfies your subnet mask, such as 255.255.255.0.

For example, if I'm on a class C subnet, I would have entered

```
ipchains -P forward DENY
ipchains -A forward -s 192.168.1.0/24 -j MASQ
```

or

```
ipchains -P forward DENY
ipchains -A forward -s 192.168.1.0/255.255.255.0 -j MASQ
```

You can also do it on a per machine basis. For example, if I want 192.168.1.2 and 192.168.1.8 to have access to the Internet, but not the other machines, I would have entered

```
ipchains -P forward DENY
ipchains -A forward -s 192.168.1.2/32 -j MASQ
ipchains -A forward -s 192.168.1.8/32 -j MASQ
```

Do *not* make your default policy masquerading—otherwise someone who can manipulate their routing will be able to tunnel straight back through your gateway, using it to masquerade their identity!

Again, you can add these lines to the `/etc/rc.local` files, one of the rc files you prefer, or do it manually every time you need IP Masquerade.

For detailed ipchains usage, please refer to the Linux IPCHAINS HOWTO in Chapter 14.

Linux 2.0.*x* Kernels

```
ipfwadm -F -p deny
ipfwadm -F -a m -S yyy.yyy.yyy.yyy/x -D 0.0.0.0/0
```

or

```
ipfwadm -F -p deny
ipfwadm -F -a masquerade -S yyy.yyy.yyy.yyy/x -D 0.0.0.0/0
```

where *x* is one of the following numbers, according to the class of your subnet, and *yyy.yyy.yyy.yyy* is your network address.

Netmask	***x***	**Subnet**
255.0.0.0	8	Class A
255.255.0.0	16	Class B
255.255.255.0	24	Class C
255.255.255.255	32	Point-to-point

You may also use the format yyy.yyy.yyy.yyy/xxx.xxx.xxx.xxx, where *xxx.xxx.xxx.xxx* specfies your subnet mask, such as 255.255.255.0.

For example, if I'm on a class C subnet, I would have entered

```
ipfwadm -F -p deny
ipfwadm -F -a m -S 192.168.1.0/24 -D 0.0.0.0/0
```

Since bootp request packets come without valid IPs once the client knows nothing about them, people with a bootp server in the masquerade/firewall machine need to use the following before the `deny` command:

```
ipfwadm -I -a accept -S 0/0 68 -D 0/0 67 \
                         -W bootp_clients_net_if_name -P udp
```

You can also do it on a per machine basis. For example, if I want 192.168.1.2 and 192.168.1.8 to have access to the Internet, but not the other machines, I would have entered

```
ipfwadm -F -p deny
ipfwadm -F -a m -S 192.168.1.2/32 -D 0.0.0.0/0
ipfwadm -F -a m -S 192.168.1.8/32 -D 0.0.0.0/0
```

What appears to be a common mistake is to make the first command be this `ipfwadm -F -p masquerade`. Do *not* make your default policy masquerading—otherwise someone who can manipulate their routing will be able to tunnel straight back through your gateway, using it to masquerade their identity!

Again, you can add these lines to the `/etc/rc.local` files, one of the rc files you prefer, or do it manually every time you need IP Masquerade.

Please read "Installation Overview" in Chapter 4 for a detailed guide to ipfwadm.

Testing IP Masquerade

It's time to give it a try, after all this hard work. Make sure the connection of your Linux hosts to the Internet is OK.

You can try browsing some Web sites on your other machines to see if you get it. I recommend using an IP address rather than a hostname on your first try because your DNS setup may not be correct.

For example, you can access the Linux Documentation Project site, `http://metalab.unc.edu/mdw/linux.html`, with an entry of `http://152.19.254.81/mdw/linux.html`.

If you see the Linux Documentation Project home page, then congratulations! It's working! You may then try one with hostname entry, and then ping, Telnet, ssh, FTP, Real Audio, True Speech, whatever is supported by IP Masquerade.

So far, I have had no trouble with the above settings, and it's full credit to the people who spend their time making this wonderful feature work.

Other IP Masquerade Issues and Software Support

This section touches on a variety of issues surrounding IP Masquerade.

Problems with IP Masquerade

Some protocols will not currently work with masquerading because they either assume things about port numbers or encode data in their data stream about addresses and ports—these latter protocols need specific proxies built into the masquerading code to make them work.

Incoming Services

Masquerading cannot handle incoming services at all. There are a few ways of allowing them, but they are completely separate from masquerading and are really part of standard firewall practice.

If you do not require high levels of security, you can simply redirect ports. There are various ways of doing this. I use a modified redir program (which I hope will be available from sunsite and mirrors soon). If you wish to have some level of authorization on incoming connections, you can either use TCP wrappers or Xinetd on top of redir (0.7 or above) to allow only specific IP addresses through, or use some other tools. The TIS Firewall Toolkit is a good place to look for tools and information.

More details can be found at the IP Masquerade Resource (`http://ipmasq.cjb.net`).

Supported Client Software and Other Setup Notes

The following list is not being maintained anymore. Please refer to `http://dijon.nais.com/~nevo/masq/` for information on applications that work through Linux IP masquerading and the IP Masquerade Resource (`http://ipmasq.cjb.net/`) for more details.

Generally, applications that use TCP and UDP should work. If you have any suggestions, hints, or questions about applications with IP Masquerade, please visit `http://dijon.nais.com/~nevo/masq/` by Lee Nevo.

Clients that Work

General Clients

HTTP All supported platforms, surfing the Web

POP SMTP All supported platforms, e-mail client

Telnet All supported platforms, remote session

FTP All supported platforms, with ipmasqftp.o module (not all sites work with certain clients; for example, some sites cannot be reached using wsftp32 but works with Netscape)

Archie All supported platforms, file searching client (not all archie clients are supported)

NNTP (USENET) All supported platforms, USENET news client

VRML Windows (possibly all supported platforms), virtual reality surfing

traceroute Mainly Unix based platforms, some variations may not work

ping All platforms, with ICMP patch

anything based on IRC All supported platforms, with ipmasqirc.o modules

Gopher client All supported platforms

WAIS client All supported platforms

Multimedia Clients

Real Audio Player Windows, network streaming audio, with ipmasqraudio module loaded

True Speech Player 1.1b Windows, network streaming audio

Internet Wave Player Windows, network streaming audio

Worlds Chat 0.9a Windows, Client-Server 3-D chat program

Alpha Worlds Windows, Client-Server 3-D chat program

Internet Phone 3.2 Windows, Peer-to-peer audio communications, people can reach you only if you initiate the call, but people cannot call you

Powwow Windows, Peer-to-peer Text audio whiteboard communications, people can reach you only if you initiate the call, but people cannot call you

CU-SeeMe All supported platforms, with cuseeme modules loaded, please see the IP Masquerade Resource (`http://ipmasq.cjb.net/`) for details

VDOLive Windows, with vdolive patch

NOTE

Some clients, such as IPhone and Powwow, may work even if you're not the one who initiated the call by using ipautofw package (refer to "Booting Your New System" in Chapter 4.)

Other Clients

NCSA Telnet 2.3.08 DOS, a suite containing Telnet, FTP, Ping, etc.

PC-anywhere for windows 2.0 MS-Windows, Remotely controls a PC over TCP/IP, only works if it is a client but not a host

Socket Watch Uses NTP –(Network Time Protocol)

Linux net-acct package Linux, network administration-account package

Clients that Do Not Work

Intel Internet Phone Beta 2 Connects but voice travels one way (out) traffic only

Intel Streaming Media Viewer Beta 1 Cannot connect to server

Netscape CoolTalk Cannot connect to opposite side

talk,ntalk Will not work–requires a kernel proxy to be written.

WebPhone Cannot work at present (it makes invalid assumptions about addresses)

X Untested, but I think it cannot work unless someone builds an X proxy, which is probably an external program to the masquerading code. One way of making this work is to use *ssh* as the link and use the internal X proxy.

Platforms/OSes Tested as on Other Machines

- Linux
- Solaris
- Windows 95
- Windows NT (both workstation and server)
- Windows For Workgroup 3.11 (with TCP/IP package)
- Windows 3.1 (with Chameleon package)
- Novel 4.01 Server
- OS/2 (including Warp v3)
- Macintosh OS (with MacTCP or Open Transport)
- DOS (with NCSA Telnet package, DOS Trumpet works partially)
- Amiga (with AmiTCP or AS225-stack)
- VAX Stations 3520 and 3100 with UCX (TCP/IP stack for VMS)
- Alpha/AXP with Linux/Redhat
- SCO Openserver (v3.2.4.2 and 5)
- IBM RS/6000 running AIX

Basically all OS platforms support TCP/IP and give you the option to specify how the gateway/router should work with IP Masquerade.

IP Firewall Administration (ipfwadm)

This section provides a more in-depth guide on using ipfwadm.

The setup for a firewall/masquerade system behind a PPP link with a static PPP address follows. A trusted interface is 192.168.255.1; the PPP interface has been changed to protect the guilty. I listed each incoming and outgoing interface individually to catch IP spoofing as well as stuffed routing and/or masquerading. Also, anything not explicitly allowed is forbidden!

```
#!/bin/sh
#
# /etc/rc.d/rc.firewall, define the firewall configuration
# invoked from rc.local.
#
```

```
PATH=/sbin:/bin:/usr/sbin:/usr/bin

# testing, wait a bit then clear all firewall rules.
# uncomment following lines if you want the firewall to
# automatically disable after 10 minutes.
# (sleep 600; \
# ipfwadm -I -f; \
# ipfwadm -I -p accept; \
# ipfwadm -O -f; \
# ipfwadm -O -p accept; \
# ipfwadm -F -f; \
# ipfwadm -F -p accept; \
# ) &

# Incoming, flush and set default policy of deny. Actually
# the default policy is irrelevant because there is a catch
# all rule with deny and log.

ipfwadm -I -f
ipfwadm -I -p deny
# local interface, local machines, going anywhere is valid
ipfwadm -I -a accept -V 192.168.255.1 -S 192.168.0.0/16 \
                         -D 0.0.0.0/0
# remote interface, claiming to be local machines,
# IP spoofing, get lost
ipfwadm -I -a deny -V your.static.PPP.address \
              -S 192.168.0.0/16 -D 0.0.0.0/0 -o
# remote interface, any source, going to permanent
# PPP address is valid
ipfwadm -I -a accept -V your.static.PPP.address \
          -S 0.0.0.0/0 -D your.static.PPP.address/32
# loopback interface is valid.
ipfwadm -I -a accept -V 127.0.0.1 -S 0.0.0.0/0 -D 0.0.0.0/0
# catch all rule, all other incoming is denied and logged.
# pity there is no log option on the policy but this does
# the job instead.
ipfwadm -I -a deny -S 0.0.0.0/0 -D 0.0.0.0/0 -o

# Outgoing flush and set default policy of deny. Actually the
# default policy is irrelevant because there is a catch all
# rule with deny and log.
ipfwadm -O -f
ipfwadm -O -p deny
# local interface, any source going to local net is valid
ipfwadm -O -a accept -V 192.168.255.1 -S 0.0.0.0/0 \
                      -D 192.168.0.0/16
```

```
# outgoing to local net on remote interface, stuffed routing,
# deny
ipfwadm -O -a deny -V your.static.PPP.address -S 0.0.0.0/0 \
                    -D 192.168.0.0/16 -o
# outgoing from local net on remote interface, stuffed
# masquerading, deny
ipfwadm -O -a deny -V your.static.PPP.address \
              -S 192.168.0.0/16 -D 0.0.0.0/0 -o
# outgoing from local net on remote interface, stuffed
# masquerading, deny
ipfwadm -O -a deny -V your.static.PPP.address -S 0.0.0.0/0 \
                    -D 192.168.0.0/16 -o
# anything else outgoing on remote interface is valid
ipfwadm -O -a accept -V your.static.PPP.address \
          -S your.static.PPP.address/32 -D 0.0.0.0/0
# loopback interface is valid.
ipfwadm -O -a accept -V 127.0.0.1 -S 0.0.0.0/0 -D 0.0.0.0/0
# catch all rule, all other outgoing is denied and logged.
# pity there is no log option on the policy but this does the
# job instead.
ipfwadm -O -a deny -S 0.0.0.0/0 -D 0.0.0.0/0 -o

# Forwarding, flush and set default policy of deny. Actually
# the default policy is irrelevant because there is a catch
# all rule with deny and log.
ipfwadm -F -f
ipfwadm -F -p deny
# Masquerade from local net on local interface to anywhere.
ipfwadm -F -a masquerade -W ppp0 -S 192.168.0.0/16 \
                        -D 0.0.0.0/0
# catch all rule, all other forwarding is denied and logged.
# pity there is no log option on the policy but this does the
# job instead.
ipfwadm -F -a deny -S 0.0.0.0/0 -D 0.0.0.0/0 -o
```

You can block traffic to a particular site using the -I, -O, or -F. Remember that the set of rules are scanned top to bottom and -a means "append" to the existing set of rules, so any restrictions need to come before global rules. Here are some (untested) examples:

Using -I rules Probably the fastest, but it only stops the local machines; the firewall itself can still access the forbidden site. Of course you might want to allow that combination.

```
… start of -I rules …
# reject and log local interface, local machines going
# to 204.50.10.13
```

Part iii

```
ipfwadm -I -a reject -V 192.168.255.1 -S 192.168.0.0/16 \
                    -D 204.50.10.13/32 -o
# local interface, local machines, going anywhere is valid
ipfwadm -I -a accept -V 192.168.255.1 -S 192.168.0.0/16 \
                        -D 0.0.0.0/0
... end of -I rules ...
```

Using -O rules Slowest because the packets go through masquerading first, but this rule even stops the firewall accessing the forbidden site.

```
... start of -O rules ...
# reject and log outgoing to 204.50.10.13
ipfwadm -O -a reject -V your.static.PPP.address \
     -S your.static.PPP.address/32 -D 204.50.10.13/32 -o
# anything else outgoing on remote interface is valid
ipfwadm -O -a accept -V your.static.PPP.address \
         -S your.static.PPP.address/32 -D 0.0.0.0/0
... end of -O rules ...
```

Using -F rules Probably slower than -I and this still only stops masqueraded machines (i.e., internal); firewall can still get to the forbidden site.

```
... start of -F rules ...
# Reject and log from local net on PPP interface
# to 204.50.10.13.
ipfwadm -F -a reject -W ppp0 -S 192.168.0.0/16 \
                    -D 204.50.10.13/32 -o
# Masquerade from local net on local interface to anywhere.
ipfwadm -F -a masquerade -W ppp0 -S 192.168.0.0/16 \
                        -D 0.0.0.0/0
... end of -F rules ...
```

No need for a special rule to allow 192.168.0.0/16 to go to 204.50.11.0; it is covered by the global rules.

There is more than one way of coding the interfaces in the above rules. For example, instead of -V 192.168.255.1, you can code -W eth0; instead of -V your.static.PPP.address, you can use -W ppp0. Personal choice and documentation are more important than anything.

IP Firewalling Chains (ipchains)

This is the firewall ruleset manipulation tool primarily intended for 2.2.*x* kernels (there is a patch for this to work on 2.0.*x*).

We will update this section to give several examples on ipchains usage soon.

See the Linux IP Firewalling Chains page (`http://www.rustcorp.com/linux/ipchains/`) and the Linux IPCHAINS HOWTO (see Chapter 14) for details.

IP Masquerade and Demand-Dial-Up

If you would like to set up your network to automatically dial up the Internet, the diald demand dial-up package will be of great utility.

1. To set up the diald, please check out the Setting Up Diald for Linux page (`http://home.pacific.net.sg/~harish/diald.config.html`).
2. Once diald and IP Masquerade have been set up, you can go to any of the client machines and initiate a Web, Telnet, or FTP session.
3. Diald will detect the incoming request, then dial up your ISP and establish the connection.
4. There is a timeout that will occur with the first connection. This is inevitable if you are using analog modems. The time taken to establish the modem link and the PPP connections will cause your client program to timeout. This can be avoided if you are using an ISDN connection. All you need to do is to terminate the current process on the client and restart it.

IPautofw Packet Forwarder

IPautofw (`ftp://ftp.netis.com/pub/members/rlynch/ipautofw.tar.gz`) is a generic forwarder of TCP and UDP for Linux masquerading. Generally, to utilize a package which requires UDP, a specific ipmasq module needs to be loaded: ipmasqraudio, ipmasqcuseeme, and so on. Ipautofw acts in a more generic manner; it will forward any type of traffic, including those which the application-specific modules will not forward. This may create a security hole if not administered correctly.

CU-SeeMe and Linux IP-Masquerade Teeny How-To

The following was provided by Michael Owings <mikey@swampgas.com>.

Introduction

This section will explain the necessary steps to get CU-SeeMe (both the Cornell and White Pine versions) working together with Linux's IP Masquerade.

CU-SeeMe is a desktop video-conferencing package available for both Windows and Macintosh clients. A free version is available from Cornell University (`http://cu-seeme.cornell.edu`). A significantly enhanced commercial version can be obtained from White Pine Software (`http://www.wpine.com`).

IP Masquerading allows one or more workstations on a LAN to masquerade behind a single Linux machine connected to the Internet. The workstations on the LAN can access the Internet almost transparently, even without valid IP addresses. The Linux box rewrites outgoing packets from the LAN to the Internet in such a way that they appear to originate from the Linux machine. Response packets coming back in are rewritten and routed back to the correct workstations on the LAN. This arrangement allows many Internet applications to run transparently from the LAN workstations. For some other applications (such as CU-SeeMe), however, the Linux masquerade code needs a little help to route packets properly. This help usually comes in the form of special kernel loadable modules. For more information on IP Masquerading, see the Linux IP Masquerading Web site (`http://www.indyramp.com/masq/`).

Getting It Running

First, you will need a properly configured kernel. You should have full support compiled in for both IP Masquerading and IP AutoForwarding. IP Autoforwarding is available as a config option on kernels 2.0.30 and later—you will need to patch earlier kernels. See the Linux IP Masquerade Resource (`http://ipmasq.cjb.net`) for pointers to the IP Autoforwarding material.

Next, you will need to get the latest version of `ipmasqcuseeme.c`. The latest version is available via anonymous FTP from `ftp://ftp.swampgas.com/pub/cuseeme/ip_masq_cuseeme.c`. This new module will also be rolled up into the kernel 2.0.31 distribution. You should replace the version in your kernel distribution with this new version. `ipmasqcuseeme.c` normally resides in `net/ipv4` off of the Linux source tree. You should compile and install this module.

Now, you should set up IP Autoforwarding for UDP ports 7648–7649 as follows:

```
ipautofw -A -r udp 7648 7649 -c udp 7648 -u
```

or

```
ipautofw -A -r udp 7648 7649 -h www.xxx.yyy.zzz
```

The first form will allow calls to/from the last workstation to use port 7648 (the primary CU-SeeMe port) . The second invocation of ipautofw will allow CU-SeeMe calls only to/from www.xxx.yyy.zzz. I prefer the former invocation, as it is more flexible because there is no need to specify a fixed workstation IP. However, this invocation also requires a workstation to have previously placed an outgoing call in order to receive incoming calls.

Note that both invocations leave UDP ports 7648–7649 on the client machines open to the outside world–and while this does not pose an enormous security hazard, you should use appropriate caution.

Finally, load up the new ipmasqcuseeme module as follows:

```
modprobe ip_masq_cuseeme
```

You should now be able to fire up CU-SeeMe from a masqueraded machine on your LAN and connect to a remote reflector or another CU-SeeMe user. You should also be able to get incoming calls. Note that outside callers should call using the IP of your Linux gateway, *not* the masqueraded workstation.

Restrictions/Caveats

Password Protected Reflectors No way, no how. Uh-uh. Negatory. White Pine uses the source IP (as computed by the client program) to encrypt the password prior to transmission. Since we have to rewrite this address, the reflector ends up using the wrong source IP to decrypt it, which yields an invalid password. This will only be fixed if White Pine changes their password encryption scheme (which I have suggested), or if they would be willing to make their password encryption routines public so I could add in a fix to ipmasqcuseeme. While chances for the latter solution are vanishingly small, I would encourage anyone reading this to contact White Pine and suggest the former approach. As the traffic on this page is relatively high, I suspect we could generate enough e-mail to get this problem moved up on White Pine's list of priorities.

Thanks to Thomas Griwenka for bringing this to my attention.

Running a Reflector You should not attempt to run a reflector on the same machine where you have ipmasqcuseeme and ipautoforwarding for port 7648 loaded. It simply won't work, as both setups require port 7648. Either run the reflector on another Internet-reachable host, or unload CU-SeeMe client support prior to running the reflector.

Multiple CU-SeeMe Users You cannnot have multiple simultaneous CU-SeeMe users on the LAN at this time. This is due largely to CU-SeeMe's stubborn insistence on always sending to port 7648, which can only be redirected (easily) to one LAN workstation at a time.

Using the -c (control port) invocation of ipautofw above, you can avoid having to specify a fixed workstation address allowed to use CU-SeeMe–the first workstation to send anything out on control port 7648 will be designated to receive traffic on 7648-7649. Five minutes or so after this workstation has been inactive on port 7648, another workstation can come along and use CU-SeeMe.

Help on Setting up CU-SeeMe Feel free to e-mail any comments or questions to `<mikey@swampgas.com>`. Or if you wish, you can call me up via CU-SeeMe (`http://www.swampgas.com/vc/vc.htm`).

Other Related Tools

We will be updating this section soon to cover more ipmasq related tools, such as ipportfw and masqadmin.

Frequently Asked Questions

If you can think of any useful FAQ, please send them to `ambrose@writeme.com` and `dranch@trinnet.net`. Please clearly state the question and an appropriate answer. Thank you!

Does IP Masquerade Work with Dynamically Assigned IP?

Yes, it works with dynamic IP assigned by your ISP, usually by a DHCP server. As long as you have an valid Internet IP address, it should work. Of course, static IP works, too.

Can I Use Cable Modem, DSL, Satellite Link, etc. to Connect to the Internet and Use IP Masquerade?

Sure, as long as Linux supports that network interface, it should work.

What Applications Are Supported with IP Masquerade?

It is very difficult to keep track of a list of working applications. However, most of the normal Internet applications are supported, such as browsing the Internet (Netscape, MSIE, etc.), FTP (such as WSFTP), Real Audio, Telnet, SSH, POP3 (incoming e-mail–Pine, Outlook), SMTP (outgoing e-mail) and so on.

Applications involving more complicated protocols or special connection methods, such as video conferencing software, need special helper tools.

For more details, please see Lee Nevo's `http://dijon.nais.com/~nevo/masq/`, which is about applications that work through Linux IP masquerading.

How Can I Get IP Masquerade Running on Red Hat, Debian, Slackware, Etc.?

No matter what Linux distribution you've got, the procedures for setting up IP Masquerade mentioned in this HOWTO should apply. Some distributions may have GUI or special configuration files that make the setup easier. We try our best to write the HOWTO as general as possible.

I've Just Upgraded to the 2.2.x Kernels; Why Is IP Masquerade Not Working?

There are several things you should check, assuming your Linux ipmasq box already has a proper connection to the Internet and your LAN:

- Make sure you have the necessary features and modules compiled and loaded. See earlier sections for details.
- Check `/usr/src/linux/Documentation/Changes` and make sure you have the minimal requirements for the network tools installed.

- Make sure you have enabled IP forwarding. Try running `echo 1 > /proc/sys/net/ipv4/ipforwarding`.
- You should use ipchains (`http://www.rustcorp.com/linux/ipchains/`) to manipulate ipmasq and firewalling rules.
- Go through all setup and configuration steps again! Many times it's just a typo or a stupid mistake you overlook.

I've Just Upgraded to the Kernels 2.0.30 or Later; Why Is IP Masquerade Not Working?

There are several things you should check, assuming your Linux ipmasq box already has a proper connection to the Internet and your LAN:

- Make sure you have the necessary features and modules compiled and loaded. See earlier sections for details.
- Check `/usr/src/linux/Documentation/Changes` and make sure you have the minimal requirements for the network tools installed.
- Make sure you have enabled IP forwarding. Try running `echo 1 > /proc/sys/net/ipv4/ipforward`.
- You should use ipfwadm (`http://www.xos.nl/`) to manipulate ipmasq and firewalling rules. You need to patch the 2.0.*x* kernels to use ipchains.
- Go through all setup and configuration steps again! Many times it's just a typo or a stupid mistake you overlook.

I Can't Get IP Masquerade to Work! What Options Do I Have for the Windows Platform?

Giving up a free, reliable, high performance solution that works on minimal hardware to pay a fortune for something that needs more hardware, lower performance, and is less reliable? (Yes, I have real life experience with these.)

OK, it's your call. Do a Web search on MS Proxy Server, Wingate, or see `www.winfiles.com`. Don't tell anyone I sent you.

I've Checked All My Configurations and I Still Can't Get IP Masquerade to Work. What Should I Do?

- Stay calm. Get yourself a cup of tea and have a rest, then try the suggestions mentioned below.
- Check the IP Masquerade Mailing List Archive (`http://home.indyramp.com/lists/masq/`); most likely your answer is there waiting for you.
- Post your question to the IP Masquerade Mailing List; next, see the FAQ for details. Please only try this if you cannot find the answer in the mailing list archive.
- Post your question to a related Linux networking newsgroup.
- Send e-mail to `ambrose@writeme.com` and `dranch@trinnet.net`. You have a better chance of getting a reply if you send to both of us. David is usually pretty good about replying, and I do not want to comment on my response time.
- Check your configurations again.

How Do I Join the IP Masquerade Mailing List?

Join the Linux IP Masquerading mailing list by sending an e-mail to `masq-subscribe@indyramp.com`.

The subject and body of the message are ignored. This gives you every message on the list as it comes out. You are welcome to use this form if you need it, but if you can stand the digest, please choose it instead. The digest puts less of a load on the list servers. Note that you can only post from an account/address you are subscribed from.

For more commands, e-mail `masq-help@tori.indyramp.com`.

I Want to Help with IP Masquerade Development. What Can I Do?

Join the Linux IP Masquerading DEVELOPERS list and ask the great developers there, by sending an e-mail to `masq-dev-subscribe@tori`

`.indyramp.com` (or for a digest format, use `masq-dev-digest-|subscribe@tori.indyramp.com`).

Don't ask non-IP-Masquerade development related questions there.

Where Can I Find More Information on IP Masquerade?

You can find more information on IP Masquerade at the Linux IP Masquerade Resource that David and I also maintain. See section 6.2 for availability.

You may also find more information at the Semi-Original Linux IP Masquerading Web site (`http://www.indyramp.com/masq/`) maintained by Indyramp Consulting, which also provides the ipmasq mailing lists.

I Want to Translate This HOWTO into Another Language. What Should I Do?

Make sure the lanaguage you want to translate to is not already covered by someone else. A list of available HOWTO translations is available at the Linux IP Masquerade Resource (http://ipmasq.cjb.net/).

Send an e-mail to `ambrose@writeme.com`, and I will send you the SGML source of the latest version of the HOWTO.

This HOWTO Seems Out-of-Date. Are You Still Maintaining It?

Yes, this HOWTO is still being maintained. I'm guilty of being too busy working on two jobs and don't have much time to work on this; my apologies. However, with the addition of David Ranch as the HOWTO maintainer, things should improve.

If you think of a topic that could be included in the HOWTO, please send e-mail to David and I. It will be even better if you can provide that information. David and I will include the information in the HOWTO if it is appropriate. And many thanks for your contributions.

We have a lot of new ideas and plans for improving the HOWTO, such as case studies that will cover different network setups involving IP Masquerade, more on security, ipchains usage, ipfwadm/ipchains ruleset examples, more FAQs, more coverage on protocol and port forwarding utilities like masqadmin, and so on. If you think you can help, please do. Thanks.

I Got IP Masquerade Working; It's Great! I Want to Thank You Guys. What Can I Do?

Thank the developers and appreciate the time and effort they spent on this. Send an e-mail to us and let us know how happy you are. Introduce other people to Linux and help them when they have problems.

MISCELLANEOUS

This section contains a list of useful resources, information about the IP Masquerade Resource page, and acknowledgements.

Useful Resources

- IP Masquerade Resource page should have enough information for setting up IP Masquerade: `http://ipmasq.cjb.net/`.
- IP masquerade mailing list archive contains some of the recent messages sent to the mailing list: `http://www.indyramp.com/masq/list/`.
- This Linux IP Masquerade mini-HOWTO for kernel 2.2.*x* and 2.0.*x*: `http://ipmasq.cjb.net/ipmasq-HOWTO.html`.
- IP Masquerade HOWTO for kernel 1.2.*x* if you're using an older kernel: `http://ipmasq.cjb.net/ipmasq-HOWTO-1.2.x.txt`.
- IP masquerade FAQ has some general information: `http://www.indyramp.com/masq/ip_masquerade.txt`.
- Linux IPCHAINS HOWTO (see Chapter 14) and `http://www.rustcorp.com/linux/ipchains/` have lots of information for ipchains usage, as well as source and binaries for the ipchains.
- X/OS Ipfwadm page contains sources, binaries, documentation, and other information about the `ipfwadm` package: `http://www.xos.nl/linux/ipfwadm/`.
- A page on applications that work through Linux IP masquerading by Lee Nevo provides tips and tricks on getting applications

Part iii

to work with IP Masquerade: `http://dijon.nais.com/~nevo/masq/`.

- The LDP Network Administrator's Guide is a must for beginners trying to set up a network: `http://metalab.unc.edu/mdw/LDP/nag/nag.html`.
- Trinity OS Doc, a very compreshensive guide on Linux networking: `http://www.ecst.csuchico.edu/~dranch/LINUX/TrinityOS.wri`.
- Linux NET-3 HOWTO also has lots of useful information about Linux networking (see Chapter 8 of this book): `http://metalab.unc.edu/mdw/HOWTO/NET-3-HOWTO.html`.
- Linux ISP Hookup HOWTO and Linux PPP HOWTO (see Chapter 9) gives you information on how to connect your Linux host to the Internet: `http://metalab.unc.edu/mdw/HOWTO/ISP-Hookup-HOWTO.html`.
- You may also be interested in Linux Firewalling and Proxy Server HOWTO: `http://metalab.unc.edu/LDP/`.
- Linux Kernel HOWTO will guide you through the kernel compilation process: `http://metalab.unc.edu/mdw/HOWTO/Kernel-HOWTO.html`.
- Other Linux HOWTOs; see Appendix C for a list of every HOWTO.
- Posting to the USENET newsgroup: `comp.os.linux.networking`.

Linux IP Masquerade Resource

The Linux IP Masquerade Resource is a Web site dedicated to Linux IP Masquerade information and is maintained by David Ranch and I. It usually has the latest information related to IP Masquerade and may have information that is not being included in the HOWTO.

You may find the Linux IP Masquerade Resource at the following locations:

- `http://ipmasq.cjb.net/`, Primary Site, redirected to `http://www.tor.shaw.wave.ca/~ambrose/`

- http://ipmasq2.cjb.net/, Secondary Site, redirected to http://www.geocities.com/SiliconValley/Heights/2288/

Thanks To

- David Ranch, <dranch@trinnet.net> for help maintaining this HOWTO, the Linux IP Masquerade Resource page, and too many other sites to list here
- Michael Owings, <mikey@swampgas.com> for providing a section for CU-SeeMe and Linux IP-Masquerade Teeny How-To
- Gabriel Beitler, <gbeitler@aciscorp.com> for providing the "Configuring a Novell Network Using DNS" section
- Ed Doolittle, <dolittle@math.toronto.edu> for his suggestion to -V option in ipfwadm command for improved security
- Matthew Driver, <mdriver@cfmeu.asn.au> for helping extensively on this HOWTO and providing the "Configuring Windows 95" section
- Ken Eves, <ken@eves.com> for the FAQ that provides invaluable information for this HOWTO
- Ed Lott, <edlott@neosoft.com> for a long list of tested systems and software
- Nigel Metheringham, <Nigel.Metheringham@theplanet.net> for contributing his version of the IP Packet Filtering and IP Masquerading HOWTO, which make this HOWTO a more in-depth document
- Keith Owens, <kaos@ocs.com.au> for providing an excellent guide on ipfwadm, a correction to the ipfwadm -deny option, which avoids a security hole, and clarified the status of ping over IP Masquerade
- Rob Pelkey, <rpelkey@abacus.bates.edu> for providing two sections: "Configuring a Macintosh Running MacTCP" and "Configuring a Macintosh Running Open Transport"
- Harish Pillay, <h.pillay@ieee.org> for providing the "IP Masquerade and Demand-Dial-Up" section

Part iii

- Mark Purcell, <purcell@rmcs.cranfield.ac.uk> for providing the "IPautofw Packet Forwarder" section
- Ueli Rutishauser, <rutish@ibm.net> for providing the "Configuring OS/2 Warp" section
- John B. (Brent) Williams, <forerunner@mercury.net> for providing the "Configuring a Macintosh Running Open Transport" section
- Enrique Pessoa Xavier, <enrique@labma.ufrj.br> for the bootp setup suggestion
- Developers of IP Masquerade, for this great feature:

  Delian Delchev <delian@wfpa.acad.bg>

  Nigel Metheringham <Nigel.Metheringham@theplanet.net>

  Keith Owens <kaos@ocs.com.au>

  Jeanette Pauline Middelink <middelin@polyware.iaf.nl>

  David A. Ranch <trinity@value.net>

  Miquel van Smoorenburg <miquels@q.cistron.nl>

  Jos Vos <jos@xos.nl>

  Paul Russell <Paul.Russell@rustcorp.com.au>

And others whom I may have failed to mention here (please let me know).

- All users sending feedback and suggestions to the mailing list, especially the ones who reported errors in the document and the clients that are supported and not supported
- I apologize if I have not included information that some fellow users sent me. There are many suggestions and ideas sent to me, but I just do not have enough time to verify all of them, and I lose track of some of them. I am trying my best to incorporate into the HOWTO all the information sent to me. I thank you for the effort, and I hope you understand my situation.

Reference

- IP masquerade FAQ by Ken Eves
- IP masquerade mailing list archive by Indyramp Consulting
- Ipfwadm page by X/OS
- Various networking related Linux HOWTOs

PART IV

SECURITY

Chapter 13

Security

This document is a general overview of security issues that face the administrator of Linux systems. It covers general security philosophy and a number of specific examples of how to better secure your Linux system from intruders. Also included are pointers to security-related material and programs. Improvements, constructive criticism, additions, and corrections are gratefully accepted. Please mail your feedback to both authors, with "Security HOWTO" in the subject.

Security is reprinted from *The Linux Security HOWTO* version 1.0.2 of 25 April 1999 by Kevin Fenzi <`kevin@scrye.com`> and Dave Wreski <`dave@nic.com`>.

INTRODUCTION

This document covers some of the main issues that affect Linux security. General philosophy and Net-born resources are discussed.

A number of other HOWTO documents overlap with security issues, and those documents have been pointed to wherever appropriate.

This document is *not* meant to be an up-to-date exploits document. Large numbers of new exploits happen all the time. This document will tell you where to look for such up-to-date information, and will give some general methods to prevent such exploits from taking place.

New Versions of this Document

New versions of this document will be periodically posted to `comp.os.linux.answers`. They will also be added to the various anonymous ftp sites that archive such information, including `ftp://metalab.unc.edu/pub/Linux/docs/HOWTO`.

In addition, you should generally be able to find this document on the Linux World Wide Web home page via `http://metalab.unc.edu/mdw/linux.html`.

Finally, the very latest version of this document should also be available in various formats from `http://scrye.com/~kevin/lsh/`.

Feedback

All comments, error reports, additional information, and criticism of all sorts should be directed to `kevin@scrye.com` and `dave@nic.com`.

NOTE

Please send your feedback to *both* authors. Also, be sure and include *Linux*, *security*, or *HOWTO* in your subject to avoid Kevin's spam filter.

Disclaimer

No liability for the contents of this document can be accepted. Use the concepts, examples, and other content at your own risk. Additionally, this is an early version, possibly with many inaccuracies or errors.

A number of the examples and descriptions use the Red Hat package layout and system setup. Your mileage may vary.

As far as we know, only programs that, under certain terms, may be used or evaluated for personal purposes will be described. Most of the programs will be available, complete with source, under GNU terms. (See Appendix D for more information about the GNU Public License.)

Copyright Information

Overview

This document will attempt to explain some procedures and commonly-used software to help your Linux system be more secure. It is important to discuss some of the basic concepts first, and create a security foundation, before we get started.

Why Do We Need Security?

In the ever-changing world of global data communications, inexpensive Internet connections, and fast-paced software development, security is becoming more and more of an issue. Security is now a basic requirement because global computing is inherently insecure. As your data goes from point A to point B on the Internet, for example, it may pass through several other points along the way, giving other users the opportunity to intercept, and even alter, it. Even other users on your system may maliciously transform your data into something you did not intend. Unauthorized access to your system may be obtained by intruders, also known as *crackers*, who then use advanced knowledge to impersonate you, steal information from you, or even deny you access to your own resources. If you're wondering what the difference is between a h*acker* and a *cracker*, see Eric Raymond's document, "How to Become A Hacker," available at `http://sagan.earthspace.net/~esr/faqs/hacker-howto.html`.

How Secure Is Secure?

First, keep in mind that no computer system can ever be completely secure. All you can do is make it increasingly difficult for someone to compromise your system. For the average home Linux user, not much is required to keep the casual cracker at bay. For high profile Linux users (banks, telecommunications companies, etc), much more work is required.

Another factor to take into account is that the more secure your system is, the more intrusive your security becomes. You need to decide where in this balancing act your system will still be usable, and yet secure for your purposes. For instance, you could require everyone dialing into your system to use a call-back modem to call them back at their home number. This is more secure, but if someone is not at home, it makes it difficult for them to login. You could also setup your Linux system with no network or connection to the Internet, but this limits its usefulness.

If you are a large- to medium-sized site, you should establish a security policy stating how much security is required by your site and what auditing is in place to check it. You can find a well-known security policy example at `http://ds.internic.net/rfc/rfc2196.txt`. It has been recently updated, and contains a great framework for establishing a security policy for your company.

What Are You Trying to Protect?

Before you attempt to secure your system, you should determine what level of threat you have to protect against, what risks you should or should not take, and how vulnerable your system is as a result. You should analyze your system to know what you're protecting, why you're protecting it, what value it has, and who has responsibility for your data and other assets.

- Risk is the possibility that an intruder may be successful in attempting to access your computer. Can an intruder read or write files, or execute programs that could cause damage? Can they delete critical data? Can they prevent you or your company from getting important work done? Don't forget, someone gaining access to your account or your system can also impersonate you.

Additionally, having one insecure account on your system can result in your entire network being compromised. If you allow a single user to log in using a `.rhosts` file, or to use an insecure service, such as `tftp`, you risk an intruder getting "his foot in the door." Once the intruder has a user account on your system, or someone else's system, it can be used to gain access to another system, or another account.

- Threat is typically from someone with motivation to gain unauthorized access to your network or computer. You must decide who you trust to have access to your system, and what threat they could pose.

  There are several types of intruders, and it is useful to keep their different characteristics in mind as you are securing your systems.

  The Curious This type of intruder is basically interested in finding out what type of system and data you have.

  The Malicious This type of intruder is out to either bring down your systems, deface your Web page, or otherwise force you to spend time and money recovering from the damage he has caused.

  The High-Profile Intruder This type of intruder is trying to use your system to gain popularity and infamy. He might use your high-profile system to advertise his abilities.

  The Competition This type of intruder is interested in what data you have on your system. It might be someone who thinks you have something that could benefit him, financially or otherwise.

  The Borrowers This type of intruder is interested in setting up shop on your system and using its resources for their own purposes. They typically will run CHAT or IRC servers, porn archive sites, or even DNS servers.

The Leapfrogger This type of intruder is only interested in your system to use it to get into other systems. If your system is well connected or a gateway to a number of internal hosts, you may well see this type trying to compromise your system.

Vulnerability describes how well-protected your computer is from another network, and the potential for someone to gain unauthorized access.

What's at stake if someone breaks into your system? Of course the concerns of a dynamic PPP home user will be different from those of a company connecting their machine to the Internet, or another large network.

How much time would it take to retrieve/recreate any data that was lost? An initial time investment now can save ten times more time later if you have to recreate data that was lost. Have you checked your backup strategy, and verified your data lately?

Developing a Security Policy

Create a simple, generic policy for your system that your users can readily understand and follow. It should protect the data you're safeguarding as well as the privacy of the users. Some things to consider adding are: who has access to the system (can my friend use my account?), who is allowed to install software on the system, who owns what data, disaster recovery, and appropriate use of the system.

A generally accepted security policy starts with the phrase "that which is not permitted is prohibited."

This means that unless you grant access to a service for a user, that user shouldn't be using that service until you do grant access. Make sure the policies work on your regular user account. Saying, "Ah, I can't figure this permissions problem out, I'll just do it as root" can lead to security holes that are very obvious, and even ones that haven't been exploited yet.

rfc1244 is a document that describes how to create your own network security policy (see `ftp://ds.internic.net/rfc/rfc1244.txt`).

rfc1281 is a document that shows an example security policy with detailed descriptions of each step (see `ftp://ds.internic.net/rfc/rfc1281.txt`).

Finally, you might want to look at the COAST policy archive at `ftp://coast.cs.purdue.edu/pub/doc/policy` to see what some real life security policies look like.

Means of Securing Your Site

This document will discuss various means with which you can secure the assets you have worked hard for: your local machine, your data, your users, your network, even your reputation. What would happen to your reputation if an intruder deleted some of your users' data? Or defaced your Web site? Or published your company's corporate project plan for next quarter? If you are planning a network installation, there are many factors you must take into account before adding a single machine to your network.

Even if you have a single dial-up PPP account, or just a small site, this does not mean intruders won't be interested in your systems. Large, high profile sites are not the only targets–many intruders simply want to exploit as many sites as possible, regardless of their size. Additionally, they may use a security hole in your site to gain access to other sites you're connected to.

Intruders have a lot of time on their hands, and can avoid guessing how you've obscured your system just by trying all the possibilities. There are also a number of reasons an intruder may be interested in your systems, which we will discuss later.

Host Security

Perhaps the area of security on which administrators concentrate most is host-based security. This typically involves making sure your own system is secure, and hoping everyone else on your network does the same. Choosing good passwords, securing your host's local network services, keeping good accounting records, and upgrading programs with known security exploits are among the things the local security administrator is responsible for doing. Although this is absolutely necessary, it can become a daunting task once your network becomes larger than a few machines.

Network Security

Network security is as necessary as local host security. With hundreds, thousands, or more computers on the same network, you can't rely on each one of those systems being secure. Ensuring that only authorized users can use your network, building firewalls, using strong encryption, and ensuring there are no *rogue* (that is, unsecured) machines on your network are all part of the network security administrator's duties.

This document will discuss some of the techniques used to secure your site, and hopefully show you some of the ways to prevent an intruder from gaining access to what you are trying to protect.

Security through Obscurity

One type of security that must be discussed is "security through obscurity." This means, for example, moving a service that has known security vulnerabilities to a nonstandard port in hopes that attackers won't notice it's there and thus won't exploit it. Rest assured that they can determine that it is there and will exploit it. Security through obscurity is no security at all. Simply because you may have a small site, or a relatively low profile, does not mean an intruder won't be interested in what you have. We'll discuss what you're protecting in the next sections.

Organization of This Document

This document has been divided into a number of sections. They cover several broad security issues. The first, "Physical Security," covers how you need to protect your physical machine from tampering. The second, "Local Security," describes how to protect your system from tampering by local users. The third, "Files and Filesystem Security," shows you how to set up your filesystems and premissions on your files. The next, "Password Security and Encryption," discusses how to use encryption to better secure your machine and network. "Kernel Security" discusses what kernel options you should set or be aware of for a more secure system. The "Network Security" section describes how to better secure your Linux system from network attacks. The section "Security Preparation (Before You Go Online)" discusses how to prepare your machine(s) before bringing them online. Next, the section "What to Do during and after a Break-in" discusses what to do when you detect a system compromise in progress or detect one that has recently happened. In "Security Sources," some primary security resources are enumerated. The Q and A section, "Frequently Asked Questions," answers some frequently asked questions, and finally you will find "Conclusion."

The two main points to realize when reading this document are

- Be aware of your system. Check system logs such as `/var/log/messages` and keep an eye on your system, and
- Keep your system up-to-date by making sure you have installed the current versions of software and have upgraded per security alerts. Just doing this will help make your system markedly more secure.

PHYSICAL SECURITY

The first layer of security you need to take into account is the physical security of your computer systems. Who has direct physical access to your machine? Should they? Can you protect your machine from their tampering? Should you?

How much physical security you need on your system is very dependent on your situation, and/or budget.

If you are a home user, you probably don't need a lot (although you might need to protect your machine from tampering by children or annoying relatives). If you are in a lab, you need considerably more, but users will still need to be able to get work done on the machines. Many of the following sections will help out. If you are in an office, you may or may not need to secure your machine off hours or while you are away. At some companies, leaving your console unsecured is a termination offense.

Obvious physical security methods such as locks on doors, cables, locked cabinets, and video surveillance are all good ideas, but beyond the scope of this document.

Computer Locks

Many modern PC cases include a "locking" feature. Usually this will be a socket on the front of the case that allows you to turn an included key to a locked or unlocked position. Case locks can help prevent someone from stealing your PC, or opening up the case and directly manipulating/stealing your hardware. They can also sometimes prevent someone from rebooting your computer on their own floppy or other hardware.

These case locks do different things according to the support in the motherboard and how the case is constructed. On many PCs they make it so you have to break the case to get the case open. On some others, they make it so that it will not let you plug in new keyboards and mice. Check your motherboard or case instructions for more information. This can sometimes be a very useful feature, even though the locks are usually very low quality and can easily be defeated by attackers with locksmithing.

Some cases (most notably SPARCs and Macs) have a dongle on the back that, if you put a cable through attackers would have to cut the cable or break the case to get into it. Just putting a padlock or combo lock through these can be a good deterrent to someone stealing your machine.

BIOS Security

The BIOS is the lowest level of software that configures or manipulates your x86-based hardware. LILO and other Linux boot methods access the BIOS to determine how to boot up your Linux machine. Other hardware that Linux runs on has similar software (OpenFirmware on Macs and new Suns, Sun boot PROM, etc.). You can use your BIOS to prevent attackers from rebooting your machine and manipulating your Linux system.

Many PC BIOSs let you set a boot password. This doesn't provide all that much security (the BIOS can be reset, or removed if someone can get into the case), but might be a good deterrent (i.e. it will take time and leave traces of tampering). Similarly, on S/Linux (Linux for SPARC processor machines), your EEPROM can be set to require a boot-up password. This might slow attackers down.

Many x86 BIOSs also allow you to specify various other good security settings. Check your BIOS manual or look at it the next time you boot up. For example, some BIOSs disallow booting from floppy drives and some require passwords to access some BIOS features.

NOTE

If you have a server machine, and you set up a boot password, your machine will not boot up unattended. Keep in mind that you will need to come in and supply the password in the event of a power failure.

Boot Loader Security

The various Linux boot loaders also can have a boot password set. LILO, for example, has *password* and *restricted* settings; `password` always requires password at boot time, whereas `restricted` requires a boot-time password only if you specify options (such as *single*) at the `LILO` prompt.

Keep in mind when setting all these passwords that you need to remember them. Also remember that these passwords will merely slow the determined attacker. They won't prevent someone from booting from a floppy, and mounting your root partition. If you are using security in conjunction with a boot loader, you might as well disable booting from a floppy in your computer's BIOS, and password-protect the BIOS.

If anyone has security-related information from a different boot loader, we would love to hear it (*grub*, *silo*, *milo*, *linload*, etc).

NOTE

If you have a server machine, and you set up a boot password, your machine will *not* boot up unattended. Keep in mind that you will need to come in and supply the password in the event of a power failure.

xlock and vlock

If you wander away from your machine from time to time, it is nice to be able to "lock" your console so that no one tampers with or looks at your work. Two programs that do this are *xlock* and *vlock*.

xlock is an X display locker. It should be included in any Linux distributions that support X. Check out the man page for it for more options, but in general you can run *xlock* from any xterm on your console and it will lock the display and require your password to unlock.

vlock is a simple little program that allows you to lock some or all of the virtual consoles on your Linux box. You can lock just the one you are working in or all of them. If you just lock one, others can come in and use the console; they will just not be able to use your virtual console until you unlock it. *vlock* ships with Red Hat Linux, but your mileage may vary.

Of course, locking your console will prevent someone from tampering with your work, but won't prevent them from rebooting your machine or otherwise disrupting your work. It also does not prevent them from accessing your machine from another machine on the network and causing problems.

More importantly, it does not prevent someone from switching out of the X Window System entirely, and going to a normal virtual console login prompt, or to the VC that X11 was started from, and suspending it, thus obtaining your privileges. For this reason, you might consider only using it while under control of *xdm*.

Detecting Physical Security Compromises

The first thing to always note is when your machine was rebooted. Since Linux is a robust and stable OS, the only times your machine should reboot is when *you* take it down for OS upgrades, hardware swapping, or the like. If your machine has rebooted without your doing it, that may be a sign that an intruder has compromised it. Many of the ways that your machine can be compromised require the intruder to reboot or power off your machine.

Check for signs of tampering on the case and computer area. Although many intruders clean traces of their presence out of logs, it's a good idea to check through them all and note any discrepancy.

It is also a good idea to store log data at a secure location, such as a dedicated log server within your well-protected network. Once a machine has been compromised, log data becomes of little use as it most likely has also been modified by the intruder.

The syslog daemon can be configured to automatically send log data to a central syslog server, but this is typically sent in cleartext data, allowing an intruder to view data as it is being transferred. This may reveal information about your network that is not intended to be public. There are syslog daemons available that encrypt the data as it is being sent.

Also be aware that faking syslog messages is easy—with an *exploit* program having been published. Syslog even accepts net log entries claiming to come from the local host without indicating their true origin.

Some things to check for in your logs:

- Short or incomplete logs
- Logs containing strange timestamps
- Logs with incorrect permissions or ownership
- Records of reboots or restarting of services
- Missing logs
- `su` entries or logins from strange places

We discuss system log data in the section, "Keep Track of Your System Accounting Data."

Local Security

The next thing to take a look at is the security in your system against attacks from local users. Did we just say *local* users? Yes!

Getting access to a local user account is one of the first things that system intruders attempt while on their way to exploiting the root account. With lax local security, they can then "upgrade" their normal user access to root access using a variety of bugs and poorly set up local services. If you make sure your local security is tight, then the intruder will have another hurdle to jump.

Local users can also cause a lot of havoc with your system even (especially) if they really are who they say they are. Providing accounts to people you don't know or have no contact information for is a very bad idea.

Creating New Accounts

You should make sure to provide user accounts with only the minimal requirements for the task they need to do. If you provide your child (age 10) with an account, you might want that child to have access to a word processor or drawing program, but be unable to delete data that is not theirs.

Several good rules of thumb when allowing other people legitimate access to your Linux machine:

- Give them the minimal amount of privileges they need.
- Be aware when/where they log in from, or should be logging in from.
- Make sure to remove inactive accounts.
- The use of the same user ID on all computers and networks is advisable to ease account maintence, as well as permit easier analysis of log data.
- The creation of group user IDs should be absolutely prohibited. User accounts also provide accountability, and this is not possible with group accounts.

Many local user accounts that are used in security compromises are ones that have not been used in months or years. Since no one is using them they provide the ideal attack vehicle.

Root Security

The most sought-after account on your machine is the root (superuser) account. This account has authority over the entire machine, which may also include authority over other machines on the network. Remember that you should only use the root account for very short, specific tasks, and should mostly run as a normal user. Even small mistakes made while logged in as the root user can cause problems. The less time you are on with root privileges, the safer you will be.

Several tricks to avoid messing up your own box as root:

- When doing some complex command, try running it first in a nondestructive way—especially commands that use globbing: e.g., if you want to do `rm foo*.bak`, first do `ls foo*.bak` and make sure you are going to delete the files you think you are. Using `echo` in place of destructive commands also sometimes works.

- Provide your users with a default alias to the *rm* command to ask for confirmation for deletion of files.
- Only become root to do single specific tasks. If you find yourself trying to figure out how to do something, go back to a normal user shell until you are *sure* what needs to be done by root.
- The command path for the root user is very important. The command path (that is, the *PATH* environment variable) specifies the directories in which the shell searches for programs. Try to limit the command path for the root user as much as possible, and never include `.` (which means "the current directory") in your PATH. Additionally, never have writable directories in your search path, as this can allow attackers to modify or place new binaries in your search path, allowing them to run as root the next time you run that command.
- Never use the `rlogin/rsh/rexec` suite of tools (called the r-utilities) as root. They are subject to many sorts of attacks, and are downright dangerous run as root. Never create a `.rhosts` file for root.
- The `/etc/securetty` file contains a list of terminals that root can log in from. By default (on Red Hat Linux) this is set to only the local virtual consoles (*vtys*). Be very careful when adding anything else to this file. You should be able to log in remotely as your regular user account and then `su` if you need to (hopefully over Section 15.6.4 or other encrypted channel), so there is no need to be able to log in directly as root.
- Always be slow and deliberate running as root. Your actions could affect a lot of things. Think before you type!

If you absolutely positively need to allow someone (hopefully very trusted) to have root access to your machine, there are a few tools that can help. `sudo` allows users to use their password to access a limited set of commands as root. This would allow you to, for instance, let a user be able to eject and mount removable media on your Linux box, but have no other root privileges. `sudo` also keeps a log of all successful and unsuccessful *sudo* attempts, allowing you to track down who used what command to do what. For this reason sudo works well even in places where a number of people have root access, because it helps you keep track of changes made.

Although sudo can be used to give specific users specific privileges for specific tasks, it does have several shortcomings. It should be used only for a limited set of tasks, like restarting a server, or adding new users. Any program that offers a shell escape will give root access to a user invoking it via sudo. This includes most editors, for example. Also, a program as innocuous as /bin/cat can be used to overwrite files, which could allow root to be exploited. Consider sudo as a means for accountability, and don't expect it to replace the root user and still be secure.

Files and Filesystem Security

A few minutes of preparation and planning ahead before putting your systems online can help to protect them and the data stored on them.

- There should never be a reason for users' home directories to allow SUID/SGID programs to be run from there. Use the nosuid option in /etc/fstab for partitions that are writable by others than root. You may also wish to use nodev and noexec on users' home partitions, as well as /var, thus prohibiting execution of programs, and creation of character or block devices, which should never be necessary anyway.
- If you are exporting filesystems using NFS, be sure to configure /etc/exports with the most restrictive access possible. This means not using wildcards, not allowing root write access, and exporting read-only wherever possible.
- Configure your users' file-creation umask to be as restrictive as possible. See the section, "Umask Settings."
- If you are mounting filesystems using a network filesystem such as NFS, be sure to configure /etc/exports with suitable restrictions. Typically, using *nodev*, *nosuid*, and perhaps *noexec*, are desirable.
- Set filesystem limits instead of allowing *unlimited* as is the default. You can control the per-user limits using the resource-limits PAM module and /etc/pam.d/limits.conf. For example, limits for group users might look like this:

```
@users   hard core  0
@users   hard nproc  50
@users   hard rss   5000
```

This says to prohibit the creation of core files, restrict the number of processes to 50, and restrict memory usage per user to 5M.

- The /var/log/wtmp and /var/run/utmp files contain the login records for all users on your system. Their integrity must be maintained because it can be used to determine when and from where a user (or potential intruder) has entered your system. These files should also have 644 permissions, without affecting normal system operation.
- The immutable bit can be used to prevent accidentally deleting or overwriting a file that must be protected. It also prevents someone from creating a symbolic link to the file (such symbolic links have been the source of attacks involving deleting /etc/passwd or /etc/shadow). See the chattr(1) man page for information on the immutable bit.
- SUID and SGID files on your system are a potential security risk, and should be monitored closely. Because these programs grant special privileges to the user who is executing them, it is necessary to ensure that insecure programs are not installed. A favorite trick of crackers is to exploit SUID-root programs, then leave a SUID program as a "back door" to get in the next time, even if the original hole is plugged.

Find all SUID/SGID programs on your system, and keep track of what they are, so you are aware of any changes which could indicate a potential intruder. Use the following command to find all SUID/SGID programs on your system:

```
root# find / -type f \( -perm -04000 -o -perm -02000 \)
```

The Debian distribution runs a job each night to determine what SUID files exist. It then compares this to the previous night's run. You can look in /var/log/suid* for this log.

You can remove the SUID or SGID permissions on a suspicious program with chmod, then change it back if you feel it is absolutely necessary.

- World-writable files, particularly system files, can be a security hole if a cracker gains access to your system and modifies them. Additionally, world-writable directories are dangerous, since they allow a cracker to add or delete files as he wishes. To locate all world-writable files on your system, use the following command:

  ```
  root# find / -perm -2 ! -type l -ls
  ```

and be sure you know why those files are writable. In the normal course of operation, several files will be world-writable, including some from `/dev`, and symbolic links, thus the `! -type l` which excludes these from the previous `find` command.

- Unowned files may also be an indication an intruder has accessed your system. You can locate files on your system that have no owner, or belong to no group with the command

  ```
  root# find / -nouser -o -nogroup -print
  ```

- Finding `.rhosts` files should be a part of your regular system administration duties, as these files should not be permitted on your system. Remember, a cracker only needs one insecure account to potentially gain access to your entire network. You can locate all `.rhosts` files on your system with the following command

  ```
  root# find /home -name .rhosts -print
  ```

- Finally, before changing permissions on any system files, make sure you understand what you are doing. Never change permissions on a file because it seems like the easy way to get things working. Always determine why the file has that permission before changing it.

Umask Settings

The `umask` command can be used to determine the default file creation mode on your system. It is the octal complement of the desired file mode. If files are created without any regard to their permissions settings, the user could inadvertently give read or write permission to someone that should not have this permission. Typically `umask` settings include `022`, `027`, and `077` (which is the most restrictive). Normally the umask is set in `/etc/profile`, so it applies to all users on the system. The file creation mask can be calculated by subtracting the desired value from 777. In other words, a umask of 777 would cause newly-created files to contain no read, write, or execute permission for anyone. A mask of 666 would cause newly-created files to have a mask of 111. For example, you may have a line that looks like this:

```
# Set the user's default umask
umask 033
```

Be sure to make root's umask `077`, which will disable read, write, and execute permission for other users, unless explicitly changed using chmod. In this case, newly-created directories would have 744 permissions, obtained by subtracting 033 from 777. Newly-created files using the 033 umask would have permissions of 644.

If you are using Red Hat, and adhere to their user and group ID creation scheme (User Private Groups), it is only necessary to use 002 for a umask. This is due to the fact that the default configuration is one user per group.

File Permissions

It's important to ensure that your system files are not open for casual editing by users and groups who shouldn't be doing such system maintenance.

Unix separates access control on files and directories according to three characteristics: owner, group, and other. There is always exactly one owner, any number of members of the group, and everyone else.

A quick explanation of Unix permissions:

Ownership–Which user(s) and group(s) retain(s) control of the permission settings of the node and parent of the node

Permissions–Bits capable of being set or reset to allow certain types of access to it. Permissions for directories may have a different meaning than the same set of permissions on files.

Read

- To be able to view contents of a file
- To be able to read a directory

Write

- To be able to add to or change a file
- To be able to delete or move files in a directory

Execute

- To be able to run a binary program or shell script
- To be able to search in a directory, combined with read permission

Save Text Attribute (For directories) The *sticky bit* also has a different meaning when applied to directories than when applied to files. If the sticky bit is set on a directory, then a user may only delete files that the he owns or for which he has explicit write permission granted, even when he has write access to the directory. This is designed for directories like /tmp, which are world-writable, but where it may not be desirable to allow any user to delete files at will. The sticky bit is seen as a *t* in a long directory listing.

SUID Attribute (For Files) This describes set user id permissions on the file. When the set user ID access mode is set in the owner permissions, and the file is executable, processes which run it are granted access to system resources based on the user who owns the file, as opposed to the user who created the process. This is the cause of many "buffer overflow" exploits.

SGID Attribute (For Files) If set in the group permissions, this bit controls the *set group id* status of a file. This behaves the same way as SUID, except the group is affected instead. The file must be executable for this to have any effect.

SGID Attribute (For directories) If you set the SGID bit on a directory (with `chmod g+s directory`), files created in that directory will have their group set to the directory's group.

- You—The owner of the file
- Group—The group you belong to
- Everyone—Anyone on the system that is not the owner or a member of the group

File Example:

```
-rw-r--r-- 1 kevin users     114 Aug 28 1997 .zlogin
1st bit - directory?         (no)
 2nd bit - read by owner?      (yes, by kevin)
  3rd bit - write by owner?      (yes, by kevin)
   4th bit - execute by owner?     (no)
    5th bit - read by group?         (yes, by users)
     6th bit - write by group?        (no)
      7th bit - execute by group?      (no)
       8th bit - read by everyone?       (yes, by everyone)
        9th bit - write by everyone?      (no)
         10th bit - execute by everyone?  (no)
```

The following lines are examples of the minimum sets of permissions that are required to perform the access described. You may want to give more permission than what's listed here, but this should describe what these minimum permissions on files do:

```
-r-------- Allow read access to the file by owner
--w------- Allows the owner to modify or delete the file
      (Note that anyone with write permission to the directory
       the file is in can overwrite it and thus delete it)
---x------ The owner can execute this program, but not shell
       scripts, which still need read permission
---s------ Will execute with effective User ID = to owner
--------s- Will execute with effective Group ID = to group
-rw------T No update of "last modified time". Usually used for
       swap files
---t------ No effect. (formerly sticky bit)
```

Directory Example:

```
    drwxr-xr-x 3 kevin users     512 Sep 19 13:47
.public_html/
1st bit - directory?          (yes, it contains many files)
  2nd bit - read by owner?      (yes, by kevin)
   3rd bit - write by owner?     (yes, by kevin)
    4th bit - execute by owner?    (yes, by kevin)
     5th bit - read by group?       (yes, by users)
      6th bit - write by group?       (no)
       7th bit - execute by group?     (yes, by users)
        8th bit - read by everyone?      (yes, by everyone)
         9th bit - write by everyone?     (no)
          10th bit - execute by everyone?  (yes, by everyone)
```

The following lines are examples of the minimum sets of permissions that are required to perform the access described. You may want to give more permission than what's listed, but this should describe what these minimum permissions on directories do:

```
dr-------- The contents can be listed, but file attributes
       can't be read
d--x------ The directory can be entered, and used in full
       execution paths
dr-x------ File attributes can be read by owner
d-wx------ Files can be created/deleted, even if the
       directory isn't the current one
d------x-t Prevents files from deletion by others with write
       access. Used on /tmp
d---s--s-- No effect
```

System configuration files (usually in `/etc`) are usually mode 640 (`-rw-r-----`), and owned by root. Depending on your site's security requirements, you might adjust this. Never leave any system files writable by a group or everyone. Some configuration files, including `/etc/shadow`, should only be readable by root, and directories in `/etc` should at least not be accessible by others.

> **SUID Shell Scripts** SUID shell scripts are a serious security risk, and for this reason the kernel will not honor them. Regardless of how secure you think the shell script is, it can be exploited to give the cracker a root shell.

Integrity Checking with *Tripwire*

Another very good way to detect local (and also network) attacks on your system is to run an integrity checker like *Tripwire*. *Tripwire* runs a number of checksums on all your important binaries and config files and compares them against a database of former, known-good values as a reference. Thus, any changes in the files will be flagged.

It's a good idea to install Tripwire onto a floppy, and then physically set the write protect on the floppy. This way intruders can't tamper with *Tripwire* itself or change the database. Once you have *Tripwire* set up, it's a good idea to run it as part of your normal security administration duties to see if anything has changed.

You can even add a `crontab` entry to run *Tripwire* from your floppy every night and mail you the results in the morning. Something like

```
# set mailto
MAILTO=kevin
# run Tripwire
15 05 * * * root /usr/local/adm/tcheck/tripwire
```

will mail you a report each morning at 5:15AM.

Tripwire can be a godsend to detecting intruders before you would otherwise notice them. Since a lot of files change on the average system, you have to be careful what is cracker activity and what is your own doing.

You can find *Tripwire* at `http://www.tripwiresecurity.com`, free of charge. Manuals and support can be purchased.

Trojan Horses

"Trojan Horses" are named after the fabled ploy in Homer's *Iliad*. The idea is that a cracker distributes a program or binary that sounds great, and encourages other people to download it and run it as root. Then the program can compromise their system while they are not paying attention. While they think the binary they just pulled down does one thing (and it might very well), it also compromises their security.

You should take care of what programs you install on your machine. Red Hat provides MD5 checksums and PGP signatures on its RPM files so you can verify you are installing the real thing. Other distributions have similar methods. You should never run any unfamiliar binary, for which you don't have the source, as root! Few attackers are willing to release source code to public scrutiny.

Although it can be complex, make sure you are getting the source for a program from its real distribution site. If the program is going to run as root, make sure either you or someone you trust has looked over the source and verified it.

Password Security and Encryption

One of the most important security features used today are passwords. It is important for both you and all your users to have secure, unguessable passwords. Most of the more recent Linux distributions include *passwd* programs that do not allow you to set a easily guessable password. Make sure your *passwd* program is up-to-date and has these features.

In-depth discussion of encryption is beyond the scope of this document, but an introduction is in order. Encryption is very useful, possibly even necessary in this day and age. There are all sorts of methods of encrypting data, each with its own set of characteristics.

Most versions of Unix (and Linux is no exception) primarily use a one-way encryption algorithm, called DES (Data Encryption Standard) to encrypt your passwords. This encrypted password is then stored in (typically) `/etc/passwd` (or less commonly) `/etc/shadow`. When you attempt to login, the password you type in is encrypted again and compared with the entry in the file that stores your passwords. If they match, it must be the same password, and you are allowed access. Although DES is a two-way encryption algorithm (you can code and then decode a message, given the right keys), the variant that versions of Unix use is one-way. This means that it should not be possible to reverse the encryption to get the password from the contents of `/etc/passwd` (or `/etc/shadow`).

Brute force attacks, such as *Crack* or *John the Ripper* can often guess passwords unless your password is sufficiently random (see the section, "*Crack* and *John the Ripper*"). PAM modules (see below) allow you to use a different encryption routine with your passwords (MD5 or the like). You can use Crack to your advantage, as well. Consider periodically running Crack against your own password database, to find insecure passwords. Then contact the offending user, and instruct him to change his password.

You can go to `http://consult.cern.ch/writeup/security/security_3.html` for information on how to choose a good password.

PGP and Public-Key Cryptography

Public-key cryptography, such as that used for PGP, uses one key for encryption, and one key for decryption. Traditional cryptography, however, uses the same key for encryption and decryption; this key must be known to both parties, and thus somehow transferred from one to the other securely.

To alleviate the need to securely transmit the encryption key, public-key encryption uses two separate keys: a public key and a private key. Each person's public key is available by anyone to do the encryption, while at the same time each person keeps his or her private key to decrypt messages encrypted with the correct public key.

There are advantages to both public-key and private-key cryptography, and you can read about those differences in the RSA Cryptography FAQ (see `http://www.rsa.com/rsalabs/newfaq/`).

PGP (Pretty Good Privacy) is well-supported on Linux. Versions 2.6.2 and 5 are known to work well. For a good primer on PGP and how to use it, take a look at the PGP FAQ (`http://www.pgp.com/service/export/faq/55faq.cgi`).

Be sure to use the version that is applicable to your country. Due to export restrictions by the U.S. Government, strong-encryption is prohibited from being transferred in electronic form outside the country.

U.S. export controls are now managed by EAR (Export Administration Regulations). They are no longer governed by ITAR.

There is also a step-by-step guide for configuring PGP on Linux available at `http://mercury.chem.pitt.edu/~angel/LinuxFocus/English/November1997/article7.html`. It was written for the international version of PGP, but is easily adaptable to the United States version. You may also need a patch for some of the latest versions of Linux; the patch is available at `ftp://metalab.unc.edu/pub/Linux/apps/crypto`.

There is a project working on a free re-implementation of PGP with open source. GnuPG is a complete and free replacement for PGP. Because it does not use IDEA or RSA it can be used without any restrictions. GnuPG is nearly in compliance with RFC2440 (OpenPGP). See the GNU Privacy Guard Web page for more information (`http://www.gpg.org/`).

More information on cryptography can be found in the RSA cryptography FAQ, available at `http://www.rsa.com/rsalabs/newfaq/`. Here you will find information on such terms as *Diffie-Hellman, public-key cryptography, digital certificates*, etc.

SSL, S-HTTP, HTTPS and S/MIME

Often users ask about the differences between the various security and encryption protocols, and how to use them. While this isn't an encryption document, it is a good idea to explain briefly what each protocol is, and where to find more information.

SSL SSL, or Secure Sockets Layer, is an encryption method developed by Netscape to provide security over the Internet. It supports several different encryption protocols, and provides client and server authentication. SSL operates at the transport layer, creates a secure encrypted channel of data, and thus can seamlessly encrypt data of many types. This is most commonly seen when going to a secure site to view a secure online document with Communicator, and serves as the basis for secure communications with Communicator, as well as many other Netscape Communications data encryption. More information can be found at `http://www.consensus.com/security/ssl-talk-faq.html`. Information on Netscape's other security implementations, and a good starting point for these protocols is available at `http://home.netscape.com/info/security-doc.html`.

S-HTTP S-HTTP is another protocol that provides security services across the Internet. It was designed to provide confidentiality, authentication, integrity, and non-repudiability (cannot be mistaken for someone else) while supporting multiple key-management mechanisms and cryptographic algorithms via option negotiation between the parties involved in each transaction. S-HTTP is limited to the specific software that is implementing it, and encrypts each message individually (From RSA Cryptography FAQ, page 138).

S/MIME S/MIME, or Secure Multipurpose Internet Mail Extension, is an encryption standard used to encrypt electronic mail and other types of messages on the Internet. It is an open standard developed by RSA, so it is likely we will see it on Linux one day soon. More information on S/MIME can be found at `http://home.netscape.com/assist/security/smime/overview.html`.

Linux IPSEC Implementations

Along with CIPE, and other forms of data encryption, there are also several other implementations of IPSEC for Linux. IPSEC is an effort by the IETF to create cryptographically-secure communications at the IP network level, and to provide authentication, integrity, access control, and confidentiality. Information on IPSEC and Internet draft can be found at `http://www.ietf.org/html.charters/ipsec-charter.html`. You can also find links to other protocols involving key management, and an IPSEC mailing list and archives.

The x-kernel Linux implementation, which is being developed at the University of Arizona, uses an object-based framework for implementing network protocols called *x-kernel*, and can be found at `http://www.cs.arizona.edu/xkernel/hpcc-blue/linux.html`. Most simply, the x-kernel is a method of passing messages at the kernel level, which makes for an easier implementation.

Another freely-available IPSEC implementation is the Linux FreeS/WAN IPSEC. Their Web page states:

> **These services allow you to build secure tunnels through untrusted networks. Everything passing through the untrusted net is encrypted by the IPSEC gateway machine and decrypted by the gateway at the other end. The result is Virtual Private Network or VPN. This is a network which is effectively private even though it includes machines at several different sites connected by the insecure Internet.**

It's available for download from `http://www.xs4all.nl/~freeswan/`, and has just reached 1.0 at the time of this writing.

As with other forms of cryptography, it is not distributed with the kernel by default due to export restrictions.

ssh (Secure Shell) and *stelnet*

ssh and *stelnet* are programs that allow you to log in to remote systems and have a encrypted connection.

ssh is a suite of programs used as a secure replacement for *rlogin*, *rsh* and *rcp*. It uses public-key cryptography to encrypt communications between two hosts, as well as to authenticate users. It can be used to securely log in to a remote host or copy data between hosts, while preventing man-in-the-middle attacks (session hijacking) and DNS spoofing. It will perform data compression on your connections, and secure X11 communications between hosts. The *ssh* home page can be found at `http://www.cs.hut.fi/ssh/`.

You can also use *ssh* from your Windows workstation to your Linux *ssh* server. There are several freely available Windows client implementations, including the one at `http://guardian.htu.tuwien.ac.at/therapy/ssh/` as well as a commercial implementation from DataFellows, at `http://www.datafellows.com`. There is also a open source project to re-implement *ssh* called *psst....* For more information see `http://www.net.lut.ac.uk/psst/`.

SSLeay is a free implementation of Netscape's Secure Sockets Layer protocol, developed by Eric Young. It includes several applications, such as Secure telnet, a module for Apache, several databases, as well as several algorithms including *DES*, *IDEA* and *Blowfish*.

Using this library, a secure telnet replacement has been created that does encryption over a telnet connection. Unlike *ssh*, *stelnet* uses SSL, the Secure Sockets Layer protocol developed by Netscape. You can find Secure telnet and Secure ftp by starting with the SSLeay FAQ, available at `http://www.psy.uq.oz.au/~ftp/Crypto/`.

SRP is another secure telnet/ftp implementation. The following paragraph is a quote from their Web page:

> **The SRP project is developing secure Internet software for free worldwide use. Starting with a fully-secure Telnet and ftp distribution, we hope to supplant weak networked authentication systems with strong replacements that do not sacrifice user-friendliness for security. Security should be the default, not an option!**

For more information, go to `http://srp.stanford.edu/srp`.

PAM—Pluggable Authentication Modules

Newer versions of the Red Hat Linux distribution ship with a unified authentication scheme called *PAM*. PAM allows you to change your authentication methods and requirements on the fly, and encapsulate all local authentication methods without recompiling any of your binaries. Configuration of PAM is beyond the scope of this document, but be sure to take a look at the PAM Web site for more information (`http://www.kernel.org/pub/linux/libs/pam/index.html`).

Just a few of the things you can do with PAM:

- Use encryption other than DES for your passwords (making them harder to brute-force decode).
- Set resource limits on all your users so they can't perform denial-of-service attacks (number of processes, amount of memory, etc).
- Enable shadow passwords (see below) on the fly.
- allow specific users to login only at specific times from specific places.

Within a few hours of installing and configuring your system, you can prevent many attacks before they even occur. For example, use PAM to disable the system-wide usage of `.rhosts` files in users' home directories by adding these lines to `/etc/pam.d/rlogin`:

```
#
# Disable rsh/rlogin/rexec for users
#
login auth required pam_rhosts_auth.so no_rhosts
```

Cryptographic IP Encapsulation (CIPE)

The primary goal of this software is to provide a facility for secure (against eavesdropping, including traffic analysis, and faked message injection) subnetwork interconnection across an insecure packet network such as the Internet.

CIPE encrypts the data at the network level. Packets traveling between hosts on the network are encrypted. The encryption engine is placed near the driver which sends and receives packets.

This is unlike *ssh*, which encrypts the data by connection, at the socket level. A logical connection between programs running on different hosts is encrypted.

CIPE can be used in tunnelling, in order to create a Virtual Private Network. Low-level encryption has the advantage that it can be made to work transparently between the two networks connected in the VPN, without any change to application software.

Summarized from the CIPE documentation:

> The IPSEC standards define a set of protocols which can be used (among other things) to build encrypted VPNs. However, IPSEC is a rather heavy-weight and complicated protocol set with a lot of options, implementations of the full protocol set are still rarely used, and some issues (such as key management) are still not fully resolved. CIPE uses a simpler approach, in which many things which can be parameterized (such as the choice of the actual encryption algorithm used) are an install-time fixed choice. This limits flexibility, but allows for a simple (and therefore efficient, easy to debug) implementation.

Further information can be found at `http://www.inka.de/~bigred/devel/cipe.html`.

As with other forms of cryptography, it is not distributed with the kernel by default due to export restrictions.

Kerberos

Kerberos is an authentication system developed by the Athena Project at MIT. When a user logs in, Kerberos authenticates that user (using a password), and provides the user with a way to prove her identity to other servers and hosts scattered around the network.

This authentication is then used by programs such as *rlogin* to allow the user to login to other hosts without a password (in place of the `.rhosts` file). This authentication method can also used by the mail system in order to guarantee that mail is delivered to the correct person, as well as to guarantee that the sender is who he claims to be.

Kerberos and the other programs that come with it prevent users from "spoofing" the system into believing they are someone else. Unfortunately, installing Kerberos is very intrusive, requiring the modification or replacement of numerous standard programs.

You can find more information about Kerberos by looking at the Kerberos FAQ (`http://www.cis.ohio-state.edu/hypertext/faq/usenet/kerberos-faq/general/faq.html`), and the code can be found at `http://nii.isi.edu/info/kerberos/`.

From: Stein, Jennifer G., Clifford Neuman, and Jeffrey L. Schiller. "Kerberos: An Authentication Service for Open Network Systems." USENIX Conference Proceedings, Dallas, Texas, Winter 1998.

Kerberos should not be your first step in improving security of your host. It is quite involved, and not as widely used as, say, *ssh*.

Shadow Passwords

Shadow passwords are a means of keeping your encrypted password information secret from normal users. Normally, these encrypted passwords are stored in `/etc/passwd` file for all to read. Anyone can then run password guesser programs on them and attempt to determine what they are. Shadow passwords, by contrast, are saved in `/etc/shadow`, which only privileged users can read. In order to use shadow passwords, you need to make sure all your utilities that need access to password information are recompiled to support them. PAM (above) also allows you to just plug in a shadow module; it doesn't require recompilation of executables. You can refer to the Shadow-Password HOWTO for further information if necessary. It is available at `http://metalab.unc.edu/LDP/HOWTO/Shadow-Password-HOWTO.html`. It is rather dated now, and will not be required for distributions supporting PAM.

Crack and *John the Ripper*

If for some reason your *passwd* program is not enforcing hard-to-guess passwords, you might want to run a password-cracking program and make sure your users' passwords are secure.

Password cracking programs work on a simple idea: they try every word in the dictionary, and then variations on those words, encrypting each one and checking it against your encrypted password. If they get a match they know what your password is.

There are a number of programs out there—the two most notable of which are *Crack* and *John the Ripper* (`http://www.false.com/security/john/index.html`). They will take up a lot of your cpu time, but you should be able to tell if an attacker could get in using them by running them first yourself and notifying users with weak passwords. Note that an attacker would have to use some other hole first in order to read your `/etc/passwd` file, but such holes are more common than you might think.

Because security is only as strong as the most insecure host, it is worth mentioning that if you have any Windows machines on your network, you should check out *L0phtCrack*, a *Crack* implementation for Windows. It's available from `http://www.l0pht.com`.

CFS—Cryptographic File System and TCFS—Transparent Cryptographic File System

CFS is a way of encrypting entire directory trees and allowing users to store encrypted files on them. It uses a NFS server running on the local machine. RPMS are available at `http://www.replay.com/redhat/`, and more information on how it all works is at `ftp://ftp.research.att.com/dist/mab/`.

TCFS improves on CFS by adding more integration with the file system, so that it's transparent to users that the file system that is encrypted. More information can be found at `http://edu-gw.dia.unisa.it/tcfs/`.

It also need not be used on entire filesystems. It works on directory trees as well.

X11, SVGA, and Display Security

The following three sections discuss components of video security.

X11

It's important for you to secure your graphical display to prevent attackers from grabbing your passwords as you type them, reading documents or information you are reading on your screen, or even using a hole to gain root access. Running remote X applications over a network also can be fraught with peril, allowing sniffers to see all your interaction with the remote system.

X has a number of access-control mechanisms. The simplest of them is host-based: you use *xhost* to specify what hosts are allowed access to your display. This is not very secure at all, because if someone has access to your machine, they can `xhost + their machine` and get in easily.

Also, if you have to allow access from an untrusted machine, anyone there can compromise your display.

When using *xdm* (X Display Manager) to log in, you get a much better access method: MIT-MAGIC-COOKIE-1. A 128-bit *cookie* is generated and stored in your `.Xauthority` file. If you need to allow a remote machine access to your display, you can use the `xauth` command and the information in your `.Xauthority` file to provide access to only that connection. See the Remote-X-Apps mini-HOWTO, available at `http://metalab.unc.edu/LDP/HOWTO/mini/Remote-X-Apps.html`.

You can also use *ssh* to allow secure X connections. This has the advantage of also being transparent to the end user, and means that no unencrypted data flows across the network (see the section, "*ssh* [Secure Shell] and *stelnet*").

Take a look at the `Xsecurity` man page for more information on X security. The safe bet is to use *xdm* to log in to your console and then use *ssh* to go to remote sites on which you wish to run X programs.

SVGA

SVGAlib programs are typically SUID-root in order to access all your Linux machine's video hardware. This makes them very dangerous. If they crash, you typically need to reboot your machine to get a usable console back. Make sure any SVGA programs you are running are authentic, and can at least be somewhat trusted. Even better, don't run them at all.

GGI (Generic Graphics Interface project)

The Linux GGI project is trying to solve several of the problems with video interfaces on Linux. GGI will move a small piece of the video code into the Linux kernel, and then control access to the video system. This means GGI will be able to restore your console at any time to a known good state. They will also allow a secure attention key, so you can be sure that there is no Trojan horse *login* program running on your console (see `http://synergy.caltech.edu/~ggi/`).

KERNEL SECURITY

This is a description of the kernel configuration options that relate to security, and an explanation of what they do, and how to use them.

As the kernel controls your computer's networking, it is important that it be very secure, and not be compromised. To prevent some of the latest networking attacks, you should try to keep your kernel version current. You can find new kernels at `ftp://ftp.kernel.org` or from your distribution vendor.

There is also a international group providing a single unified crypto patch to the mainstream Linux kernel. This patch provides support for a number of cyrptographic subsystems and things that cannot be included in the mainstream kernel due to export restrictions. For more information, visit their Web page (`http://www.kerneli.org`).

2.0.*x* Kernel Compile Options

For 2.0.*x* kernels, the following options apply. You should see these options during the kernel configuration process. Many of the comments here are from `./linux/Documentation/Configure.help`, which is the same document that is referenced while using the Help facility during the `make config` stage of compiling the kernel.

Network Firewalls (CONFIG_FIREWALL) This option should be on if you intend to run any firewalling or masquerading on your Linux machine. If it's just going to be a regular client machine, it's safe to say no.

IP: forwarding/gatewaying (CONFIG_IP_FORWARD) If you enable IP forwarding, your Linux box essentially becomes a router. If your machine is on a network, you could be forwarding data from one network to another, and perhaps subverting a firewall that was put there to prevent this from happening. Normal dial-up users will want to disable this, and other users should concentrate on the security implications of doing this. Firewall machines will want this enabled, and used in conjunction with firewall software.

You can enable IP forwarding dynamically using the following command:

```
root# echo 1 > /proc/sys/net/ipv4/ip_forward
```

and disable it with the command

```
root# echo 0 > /proc/sys/net/ipv4/ip_forward
```

Keep in mind the files, and their sizes, do not reflect their actual sizes, and despite being zero-length, may or may not be.

IP: SYN cookies (CONFIG_SYN_COOKIES) A *SYN Attack* is a denial of service (DoS) attack that consumes all the resources on your machine, forcing you to reboot. We can't think of a reason you wouldn't normally enable this. In the 2.1 kernel series this config option mearly allows syn cookies, but does not enable them. To enable them, you have to do

```
root# echo 1 > /proc/sys/net/ipv4/tcp_syncookies
```

IP: Firewalling (CONFIG_IP_FIREWALL) This option is necessary if you are going to configure your machine as a firewall, do masquerading, or wish to protect your dial-up workstation from someone entering via your PPP dial-up interface.

IP: firewall packet logging (CONFIG_IP_FIREWALL_VERBOSE) This option gives you information about packets your firewall received, like sender, recipient, port, etc.

IP: Drop source routed frames (CONFIG_IP_NOSR) This option should be enabled. Source routed frames contain the entire path to their destination inside of the packet. This means that routers through which the packet goes do not need to inspect it, and just forward it on. This could lead to data entering your system that may be a potential exploit.

IP: masquerading (CONFIG_IP_MASQUERADE) If one of the computers on your local network for which your Linux box acts as a firewall wants to send something to the outside, your box can "masquerade" as that host, i.e., it forwards the traffic to the intended destination, but makes it look like it came from the firewall box itself. See `http://www.indyramp.com/masq` for more information.

IP: ICMP masquerading (CONFIG_IP_MASQUERADE_ICMP) This option adds ICMP masquerading to the previous option of only masquerading TCP or UDP traffic.

IP: transparent proxy support (CONFIG_IP_TRANSPARENT_PROXY) This enables your Linux firewall to transparently redirect any network traffic originating from the local network and destined for a remote host to a local server, called a "transparent proxy server." This makes the local computers think they are talking to the remote end, while in fact they are connected to the local proxy. See the IP-Masquerading HOWTO and `http://www.indyramp.com/masq` for more information.

IP: always defragment (CONFIG_IP_ALWAYS_DEFRAG) Generally this option is disabled, but if you are building a firewall or a masquerading host, you will want to enable it. When data is sent from one host to another, it does not always get sent as a single packet of data, but rather it is fragmented into several pieces. The problem with this is that the port numbers are only stored in the first fragment. This means that someone can insert information into the remaining packets that isn't supposed to be there. It could also prevent a teardrop attack against an internal host that is not yet itself patched against it.

Packet Signatures (CONFIG_NCPFS_PACKET_SIGNING) This is an option that is available in the 2.1 kernel series that will sign NCP packets for stronger security. Normally you can leave it off, but it is there if you do need it.

IP: Firewall packet netlink device (CONFIG_IP_FIREWALL_NETLINK) This is a really neat option that allows you to analyze the first 128 bytes of the packets in a user-space program, to determine if you would like to accept or deny the packet, based on its validity.

2.2 Kernel Compile Options

For 2.2.*x* kernels, many of the options are the same, but a few new ones have been developed. Many of the comments here are from `./linux/Documentation/Configure.help`, which is the same document that is referenced while using the Help facility during the `make config` stage of compiling the kernel. Only the newly added options are listed below. Consult the 2.0 description for a list of other necessary options. The most signficant change in the 2.2 kernel series is the IP firewalling code. The `ipchains` program is now used to install IP firewalling, instead of the `ipfwadm` program used in the 2.0 kernel.

Socket Filtering (CONFIG_FILTER) For most people, it's safe to say no to this option. This option allows you to connect a userspace filter to any socket and determine if packets should be allowed or denied. Unless you have a very specific need and are capable of programming such a filter, you should say no. Also note that as of this writing, all protocols were supported except TCP.

Port Forwarding Port Forwarding is an addition to IP Masquerading which allows some forwarding of packets from outside to inside a firewall on given ports. This could be useful if, for example, you want to run a Web server behind the firewall or masquerading host and that Web server should be accessible from the outside world. An external client sends a request to port 80 of the firewall, the firewall forwards this request to the Web server, the Web server handles the request and the results are sent through the firewall to the original client. The client thinks that the firewall machine itself is running the Web server. This can also be used for load balancing if you have a farm of identical Web servers behind the firewall. Information about this feature is available from `http://www.monmouth.demon.co.uk/ipsubs/portforwarding.html`. For general info, please see `ftp://ftp.compsoc.net/users/steve/ipportfw/linux21/`.

Socket Filtering (CONFIG_FILTER) Using this option, userspace programs can attach a filter to any socket and thereby tell the kernel that it should allow or disallow certain types of data to get through the socket. Linux socket filtering works on all socket types except TCP for now. See the text file `./linux/Documentation/networking/filter.txt` for more information.

IP: Masquerading The 2.2 kernel masquerading has been improved. It provides additional support for masquerading special protocols, etc. Be sure to read the IP Chains HOWTO for more information.

Kernel Devices

There are a few block and character devices available on Linux that will also help you with security.

The two devices `/dev/random` and `/dev/urandom` are provided by the kernel to provide random data at any time.

Both `/dev/random` and `/dev/urandom` should be secure enough to use in generating PGP keys, `ssh` challenges, and other applications where secure random numbers are requisite. Attackers should be unable to predict the next number given any initial sequence of numbers from these sources. There has been a lot of effort put in to ensuring that the numbers you get from these sources are random in every sense of the word.

The only difference is that `/dev/random` runs out of random bytes and it makes you wait for more to be accumulated. Note that on some systems, it can block for a long time waiting for new user-generated entry to be entered into the system. So you have to use care before using `/dev/random`. (Perhaps the best thing to do is to use it when you're generating sensitive keying information, and you tell the user to pound on the keyboard repeatedly until you print out "OK, enough.")

`/dev/random` is high quality entropy, generated from measuring the inter-interrupt times, etc. It blocks until enough bits of random data are available.

`/dev/urandom` is similar, but when the store of entropy is running low, it'll return a cryptographically strong hash of what there is. This isn't as secure, but it's enough for most applications.

You might read from the devices using something like

```
root# head -c 6 /dev/urandom | mmencode
```

This will print six random characters on the console, suitable for password generation. You can find `mmencode` in the `metamail` package.

See `/usr/src/linux/drivers/char/random.c` for a description of the algorithm.

Thanks to Theodore Y. Ts'o, Jon Lewis, and others from Linux-kernel for helping me (Dave) with this.

Network Security

Network security is becoming more and more important as people spend more and more time connected. Compromising network security is often much easier than compromising physical or local security, and is much more common.

There are a number of good tools to assist with network security, and more and more of them are shipping with Linux distributions.

Packet Sniffers

One of the most common ways intruders gain access to more systems on your network is by employing a packet sniffer on an already compromised host. This *sniffer* just listens on the Ethernet port for things like passwd and login and su in the packet stream and then logs the traffic after that. This way, attackers gain passwords for systems they are not even attempting to break into. Clear-text passwords are very vulnerable to this attack.

Example: Host A has been compromised. Attacker installs a sniffer. Sniffer picks up admin logging into Host B from Host C. It gets the admin's personal password as they log in to B. Then, the admin does a su to fix a problem. They now have the root password for Host B. Later the admin lets someone telnet from his account to Host Z on another site. Now the attacker has a password/login on Host Z.

In this day and age, the attacker doesn't even need to compromise a system to do this: they could also bring a laptop or pc into a building and tap into your net.

Using ssh or other encrypted password methods thwarts this attack. Things like APOP for POP accounts also prevents this attack. (Normal POP logins are very vulnerable to this, as is anything that sends clear-text passwords over the network.)

System Services and tcpwrappers

Before you put your Linux system on *any* network the first thing to look at is what services you need to offer. Services that you do not need to offer should be disabled so that you have one less thing to worry about and attackers have one less place to look for a hole.

There are a number of ways to disable services under Linux. You can look at your /etc/inetd.conf file and see what services are being offered by your inetd. Disable any that you do not need by commenting them out (# at the beginning of the line), and then sending your inetd process a SIGHUP.

You can also remove (or comment out) services in your /etc/services file. This will mean that local clients will also be unable to find the service (i.e., if you remove ftp, and try and ftp to a remote site from that machine it will fail with an "unknown service" message). It's usually not worth the trouble to remove services, since it provides no additional security. If a local person wanted to use ftp even though you had commented it out, they would make their own client that used the common ftp port and it would still work fine.

Some of the services you might want to leave enabled are

- ftp
- telnet (or ssh)
- mail, such as pop-3 or imap
- identd

If you know you are not going to use some particular package, you can also delete it entirely. rpm -e packagename under the Red Hat distribution will erase an entire package. Under Debian dpkg --remove does the same thing.

Additionally, you really want to disable the rsh/rlogin/rcp utilities, including login (used by rlogin), shell (used by rcp), and exec (used by rsh) from being started in /etc/inetd.conf. These protocols are extremely insecure and have been the cause of exploits in the past.

You should check your /etc/rc.d/rc*N*.d, (where *N* is your systems run level) and see if any of the servers started in that directory are not needed. The files in /etc/rc.d/rc*N*.d are actually symbolic links to the directory /etc/rc.d/init.d. Renaming the files in the init.d directory has the effect of disabling all the symbolic links in /etc/rc.d/rc*N*.d. If you only wish to disable a service for a particular run level, rename the appropriate file by replacing the uppercase *S* with a lowercase s, like this:

```
root# cd /etc/rc6.d
root# mv S45dhcpd s45dhcpd
```

If you have BSD style rc files, you will want to check /etc/rc* for programs you don't need.

Most Linux distributions ship with tcpwrappers "wrapping" all your TCP services. A tcpwrapper (tcpd) is invoked from inetd instead of the real server. tcpd then checks the host that is requesting the service, and either executes the real server, or denies access from that host. tcpd allows you to restrict access to your TCP services. You should make a /etc/hosts.allow and add in only those hosts that need to have access to your machine's services.

If you are a home dial-up user, we suggest you deny *all*. tcpd also logs failed attempts to access services, so this can give alert you if you are under attack. If you add new services, you should be sure to configure them to use tcpwrappers if they are TCP based. For example, a normal dial-up user can prevent outsiders from connecting to his machine, yet still have the ability to retrieve mail, and make network connections to the Internet. To do this, you might add the following to your `/etc/hosts.allow`:

```
ALL: 127.
```

And of course `/etc/hosts.deny` would contain

```
ALL: ALL
```

which will prevent external connections to your machine, yet still allow you from the inside to connect to servers on the Internet.

Keep in mind that tcpwrappers only protect services executed from `inetd`, and a select few others. There very well may be other services running on your machine. You can use `netstat -ta` to find a list of all the services your machine is offering.

Verify Your DNS Information

Keeping up-to-date DNS information about all hosts on your network can help to increase security. If an unauthorized host becomes connected to your network, you can recognize it by its lack of a DNS entry. Many services can be configured to not accept connections from hosts that do not have valid DNS entries.

identd

`identd` is a small program that typically runs out of your `inetd` server. It keeps track of what user is running what TCP service, and then reports this to whoever requests it.

Many people misunderstand the usefulness of `identd`, and so disable it or block all off-site requests for it. `identd` is not there to help out remote sites. There is no way of knowing if the data you get from the remote `identd` is correct or not. There is no authentication in `identd` requests.

Why would you want to run it then? Because it helps *you* out, and is another data-point in tracking. If your `identd` is uncompromised, then you know it's telling remote sites the user name or uid of people using TCP services. If the admin at a remote site comes back to you and tells you user so-and-so was trying to hack into their site, you can easily take action against that user. If you are not running `identd`, you will have to look at lots and lots of logs, figure out who was on at the time, and in general take a lot more time to track down the user.

The identd that ships with most distributions is more configurable than many people think. You can disable it for specific users (they can make a .noident file), you can log all identd requests (we recommend it), you can even have identd return a uid instead of a user name or even NO-USER.

SATAN, ISS, and Other Network Scanners

There are a number of different software packages out there that do port- and service-based scanning of machines or networks. SATAN, ISS, SAINT, and Nessus are some of the more well-known ones. This software connects to the target machine (or all the target machines on a network) on all the ports they can, and tries to determine what service is running there. Based on this information, you can tell if the machine is vulnerable to a specific exploit on that server.

SATAN (Security Administrator's Tool for Analyzing Networks) is a port scanner with a Web interface. It can be configured to do light, medium, or strong checks on a machine or a network of machines. It's a good idea to get SATAN and scan your machine or network, and fix the problems it finds. Make sure you get the copy of SATAN from metalab (http://metalab.unc.edu/pub/packages/security/Satan-for-Linux/) or a reputable ftp or Web site. There was a Trojan copy of SATAN that was distributed out on the net (http://www.trouble.org/~zen/satan/satan.html). Note that SATAN has not been updated in quite a while, and some of the other tools below might do a better job.

ISS (Internet Security Scanner) is another port-based scanner. It is faster than SATAN, and thus might be better for large networks. However, SATAN tends to provide more information.

Abacus is a suite of tools to provide host-based security and intrusion detection. Look at its home page on the Web for more information (http://www.psionic.com/abacus/).

SAINT is an updated version of SATAN. It is Web based and has many more up-to-date tests than SATAN. You can find out more about it at: http://www.wwdsi.com/~saint.

Nessus is a free security scanner. It has a GTK graphical interface for ease of use. It is also designed with a very nice plugin setup for new port scanning tests. For more information, take a look at: http://www.nessus.org.

Detecting Port Scans

There are some tools designed to alert you to probes by SATAN and ISS and other scanning software. However, if you make liberal use of tcpwrappers, and make sure to look over your log files regularly, you should be able to notice such probes. Even on the lowest setting, SATAN still leaves traces in the logs on a stock Red Hat system.

There are also *stealth* port scanners. A packet with the TCP ACK bit set (as is done with established connections) will likely get through a packet-filtering firewall. The returned RST packet from a port that *had no established session* can be taken as proof of life on that port. I don't think tcpwrappers will detect this.

sendmail, *qmail*, and MTAs

One of the most important services you can provide is a mail server. Unfortunately, it is also one of the most vulnerable to attack, simply due to the number of tasks it must perform and the privileges it typically needs.

If you are using `sendmail` it is very important to keep up on current versions. `sendmail` has a long, long history of security exploits. Always make sure you are running the most recent version from `http://www.sendmail.org`.

Keep in mind that `sendmail` does not have to be running in order for you to send mail. If you are a home user, you can disable `sendmail` entirely, and simply use your mail client to send mail. You might also choose to remove the *-bd* flag from the `sendmail` startup file, thereby disabling incoming requests for mail. In other words, you can execute `sendmail` from your startup script using the following instead:

```
# /usr/lib/sendmail -q15m
```

This will cause `sendmail` to flush the mail queue every 15 minutes for any messages that could not be successfully delivered on the first attempt.

Many administrators choose not to use `sendmail`, and instead choose one of the other mail transport agents. You might consider switching over to `qmail`. `qmail` was designed with security in mind from the ground up. It's fast, stable, and secure. `qmail` can be found at `http://www.qmail.org`.

In direct competition to `qmail` is *postfix*, written by Wietse Venema, the author of tcpwrappers and other security tools. Formerly called *vmailer*, and sponsored by IBM, this is also a mail transport agent written from the ground up with security in mind. You can find more information about vmailer at `http://www.postfix.org`.

Denial of Service Attacks

A "Denial of Service" (DoS) attack is one where the attacker tries to make some resource too busy to answer legitimate requests, or to deny legitimate users access to your machine.

Denial of service attacks have increased greatly in recent years. Some of the more popular and recent ones are listed below. Note that new ones show up all the time, so this is just a few examples. Read the Linux security lists and the *bugtraq* list and archives for more current information.

SYN Flooding SYN flooding is a network denial of service attack. It takes advantage of a loophole in the way TCP connections are created. The newer Linux kernels (2.0.30 and up) have several configurable options to prevent SYN flood attacks from denying people access to your machine or services. See the section on "Kernel Security" for proper kernel protection options.

Pentium "FOOF" Bug It was recently discovered that a series of assembly codes sent to a genuine Intel Pentium processor would reboot the machine. This affects every machine with a Pentium processor (not clones, not Pentium Pro or PII), no matter what operating system it's running. Linux kernels 2.0.32 and up contain a workaround for this bug, preventing it from locking your machine. Kernel 2.0.33 has an improved version of the kernel fix, and is suggested over 2.0.32. If you are running on a Pentium, you should upgrade now!

Ping Flooding Ping flooding is a simple brute-force denial of service attack. The attacker sends a flood of ICMP packets to your machine. If they are doing this from a host with better bandwidth than yours, your machine will be unable to send anything on the network. A variation on this attack, called *smurfing*, sends ICMP packets to a host with *your* machine's return IP, allowing them to flood you less detectably. You can find more information about the "smurf" attack at `http://www.quadrunner.com/~chuegen/smurf.txt`

If you are ever under a ping flood attack, use a tool like `tcpdump` to determine where the packets are coming from (or appear to be coming from), then contact your provider with this information. Ping floods can most easily be stopped at the router level or by using a firewall.

Ping o' Death The Ping o' Death attack sends ICMP ECHO REQUEST packets that are too large to fit in the kernel data structures intended to store them. Because sending a single, large (65,510 bytes) ping packet to many systems will cause them to hang or even crash, this problem was quickly dubbed the "Ping o' Death." This one has long been fixed, and is no longer anything to worry about.

Teardrop / New Tear One of the most recent exploits involves a bug present in the IP fragmentation code on Linux and Windows platforms. It is fixed in kernel version 2.0.33, and does not require selecting any kernel compile-time options to utilize the fix. Linux is apparently not vulnerable to the *newtear* exploit.

You can find code for most exploits, and a more in-depth description of how they work, at `http://www.rootshell.com` using their search engine.

NFS (Network File System) Security

NFS is a very widely-used file-sharing protocol. It allows servers running `nfsd` and `mountd` to "export" entire filesystems to other machines using NFS filesystem support built into their kernels (or some other client support if they are not Linux machines). `mountd` keeps track of mounted filesystems in `/etc/mtab`, and can display them with `showmount`.

Many sites use NFS to serve home directories to users, so that no matter what machine in the cluster they log in to, they will have all their home files.

There is some small amount of security allowed in exporting filesystems. You can make your `nfsd` map the remote root user (uid=0) to the `nobody` user, denying them total access to the files exported. However, since individual users have access to their own (or at least the same uid) files, the remote root user can login or `su` to their account and have total access to their files. This is only a small hindrance to an attacker that has access to mount your remote filesystems.

If you must use NFS, make sure you export to only those machines that you really need to. Never export your entire root directory; export only directories you need to export.

See the NFS HOWTO for more information on NFS, available at `http://metalab.unc.edu/mdw/HOWTO/NFS-HOWTO.html`.

NIS (Network Information Service) (Formerly YP)

Network Information service (formerly YP) is a means of distributing information to a group of machines. The NIS master holds the information tables and converts them into NIS map files. These maps are then served over the network, allowing NIS client machines to get login, password, home directory, and shell information (all the information in a standard `/etc/passwd` file). This allows users to change their password once and have it take effect on all the machines in the NIS domain.

NIS is not at all secure. It was never meant to be. It was meant to be handy and useful. Anyone that can guess the name of your NIS domain (anywhere on the net) can get a copy of your passwd file, and use *Crack* and *John the Ripper* against your users' passwords. Also, it is possible to spoof NIS and do all sorts of nasty tricks. If you must use NIS, make sure you are aware of the dangers.

There is a much more secure replacement for NIS, called NIS+. Check out the NIS HOWTO for more information `http://metalab.unc.edu/mdw/HOWTO/NIS-HOWTO.html`.

Firewalls

Firewalls are a means of controlling what information is allowed into and out of your local network. Typically the firewall host is connected to the Internet and your local LAN, and the only access from your LAN to the Internet is through the firewall. This way the firewall can control what passes back and forth from the Internet and your LAN.

There are a number of types of firewalls and methods of setting them up. Linux machines make pretty good firewalls. Firewall code can be built right into 2.0 and higher kernels. The `ipfwadm` for 2.0 kernels, or `ipchains` for 2.2 kernels, userspace tools allows you to change, on the fly, the types of network traffic you allow. You can also log particular types of network traffic.

Firewalls are a very useful and important technique in securing your network. However, never think that because you have a firewall, you don't need to secure the machines behind it. This is a fatal mistake. Check out the very good Firewall HOWTO at your latest metalab archive for more information on firewalls and Linux (`http://metalab.unc.edu/mdw/HOWTO/Firewall-HOWTO.html`).

More information can also be found in the IP-Masquerade mini-HOWTO: `http://metalab.unc.edu/mdw/HOWTO/mini/IP-Masquerade.html`.

More information on `ipfwadm` (the tool that lets you change settings on your firewall) can be found at its home page: `http://www.xos.nl/linux/ipfwadm/`.

If you have no experience with firewalls, and plan to set up one for more than just a simple security policy, the *Firewalls* book by O'Reilly and Associates or other online firewall document is mandatory reading. Check out `http://www.ora.com` for more information. The National Institute of Standards and Technology have put together an excellent document on firewalls. Although dated 1995, it is still quite good. You can find it at `http://csrc.nist.gov/nistpubs/800-10/main.html`. Also of interest are

The Freefire Project A list of freely-available firewall tools, available at `http://sites.inka.de/sites/lina/freefire-l/index_en.html`.

SunWorld Firewall Design Written by the authors of the O'Reilly book, this provides a rough introduction to the different firewall types. It's available at `http://www.sunworld.com/swol-01-1996/swol-01-firewall.html`.

IP Chains—Linux Kernel 2.2.x Firewalling

Linux IP Firewalling Chains is an update to the 2.0 Linux firewalling code for the 2.2 kernel. It has a great deal more features than previous implementations, including

- more flexible packet manipulations
- more complex accounting
- simple policy changes possible atomically
- fragments can be explicitly blocked, denied, etc.
- logs suspicious packets
- can handle protocols other than ICMP/TCP/UDP

If you are currently using *ipfwadm* on your 2.0 kernel, there are scripts available to convert the *ipfwadm* command format to the format *ipchains* uses.

Be sure to read the IP Chains HOWTO for further information. It is available at `http://www.rustcorp.com/linux/ipchains/HOWTO.html`.

VPNs—Virtual Private Networks

VPNs are a way to establish a *virtual* network on top of some already existing network. This virtual network often is encrypted and passes traffic only to and from some known entities that have joined the network. VPNs are often used to connect someone working at home over the public Internet to an internal company network by using a encrypted virtual network.

If you are running a Linux masquerading firewall and need to pass MS PPTP (Microsoft's VPN point-to-point product) packets, there is a Linux kernel patch out to do just that. See `ip-masq-vpn` at `ftp://ftp.rubyriver.com/pub/jhardin/masquerade/ip_masq_upn.html`.

There are several Linux VPN solutions available:

vpnd See `http://www.crosswinds.net/nuremberg/~anstein/unix/vpnd.html`.

Free S/Wan available at `http://www.xs4all.nl/~freeswan/`.

ssh can be used to construct a VPN. See the VPN mini-HOWTO for more information.

vps (virtual private server) At `http://www.strongcrypto.com`.

See also the section on IPSEC for pointers and more information.

Security Preparation (Before You Go Online)

Ok, so you have checked over your system, and determined it's as secure as feasible, and you're ready to put it online. There are a few things you should now do in order to prepare for an intrusion, so you can quickly disable the intruder, and get back up and running.

Make a Full Backup of Your Machine

Discussion of backup methods and storage is beyond the scope of this document, but here are a few words relating to backups and security.

If you have less than 650 megabytes of data to store on a partition, a CD-R copy of your data is a good way to go (as it's hard to tamper with later, and if stored properly can last a long time). Tapes and other rewritable media should be write-protected as soon as your backup is complete, and then verified to prevent tampering. Make sure you store your backups in a secure off-line area. A good backup will ensure that you have a known good point to restore your system from.

Choosing a Good Backup Schedule

A six-tape cycle is easy to maintain. This includes four tapes for during the week, one tape for even Fridays, and one tape for odd Fridays. Perform an incremental backup every day, and a full backup on the appropriate Friday tape. If you make some particularly important changes or add some important data to your system, a full backup might well be in order.

Back up Your RPM or Debian File Database

In the event of an intrusion, you can use your RPM database like you would use `tripwire`, but only if you can be sure it too hasn't been modified. You should copy the RPM database to a floppy, and keep this copy off-line at all times. The Debian distribution likely has something similar.

The files `/var/lib/rpm/fileindex.rpm` and `/var/lib/rpm/packages.rpm` most likely won't fit on a single floppy. But if compressed, each should fit on a separate floppy.

Now, when your system is compromised, you can use the command

```
root# rpm -Va
```

to verify each file on the system. See the `rpm` man page, as there are a few other options that can be included to make it less verbose. Keep in mind you must also be sure your RPM binary has not been compromised.

This means that every time a new RPM is added to the system, the RPM database will need to be rearchived. You will have to decide the advantages versus drawbacks.

Keep Track of Your System Accounting Data

It is very important that the information that comes from `syslog` has not been compromised. Making the files in `/var/log` readable and writable by only a limited number of users is a good start.

Be sure to keep an eye on what gets written there, especially under the auth facility. Multiple login failures, for example, can indicate an attempted break-in.

Where to look for your log file will depend on your distribution. In a Linux system that conforms to the *Linux Filesystem Standard*, such as Red Hat, you will want to look in /var/log and check messages, mail.log, and others.

You can find out where your distribution is logging to by looking at your /etc/syslog.conf file. This is the file that tells syslogd (the system logging daemon) where to log various messages.

You might also want to configure your log-rotating script or daemon to keep logs around longer so you have time to examine them. Take a look at the logrotate package on recent Red Hat distributions. Other distributions likely have a similar process.

If your log files have been tampered with, see if you can determine when the tampering started, and what sort of things appeared to be tampered with. Are there large periods of time that cannot be accounted for? Checking backup tapes (if you have any) for untampered log files is a good idea.

Log files are typically modified by the intruder in order to cover his tracks, but they should still be checked for strange happenings. You may notice the intruder attempting to gain entrance, or exploit a program in order to obtain the root account. You might see log entries before the intruder has time to modify them.

You should also be sure to separate the auth facility from other log data, including attempts to switch users using su, login attempts, and other user accounting information.

If possible, configure syslog to send a copy of the most important data to a secure system. This will prevent an intruder from covering his tracks by deleting his login/su/ftp/etc attempts. See the syslog.conf man page, and refer to the @ option.

There are several more advanced syslogd programs out there. Take a look at http://www.core-sdi.com/ssyslog/ for *Secure Syslog*. Secure Syslog allows you to encrypt your syslog entries and make sure no one has tampered with them.

Another syslogd with more features is syslog-ng. It allows you a lot more flexability in your logging and also can hash your remote syslog streams to prevent tampering.

Finally, log files are much less useful when no one is reading them. Take some time out every once in a while to look over your log files, and get a feeling for what they look like on a normal day. Knowing this can help make unusual things stand out.

Apply All New System Updates

Most Linux users install from a CD-ROM. Due to the fast-paced nature of security fixes, new (fixed) programs are always being released. Before you connect your machine to the network, it's a good idea to check with your distribution's ftp site and get all the updated packages since you received your distribution CD-ROM. Many times these packages contain important security fixes, so it's a good idea to get them installed.

What to Do During and After a Break-In

So you have followed some of the advice here (or elsewhere) and have detected a break-in? The first thing to do is to remain calm. Hasty actions can cause more harm than the attacker would have caused.

Security Compromise Underway

Spotting a security compromise underway can be a tense undertaking. How you react can have large consequences.

If the compromise you are seeing is a physical one, odds are you have spotted someone who has broken into your home, office, or lab. You should notify your local authorities. In a lab, you might have spotted someone trying to open a case or reboot a machine. Depending on your authority and procedures, you might ask them to stop, or contact your local security people.

If you have detected a local user trying to compromise your security, the first thing to do is confirm they are in fact who you think they are. Check the site they are logging in from. Is it the site they normally log in from? No? Then use a nonelectronic means of getting in touch. For instance, call them on the phone or walk over to their office/house and talk to them. If they agree that they are on, you can ask them to explain what they were doing or tell them to cease doing it. If they are not on, and have no idea what you are talking about, odds are this incident requires further investigation. Look into such incidents , and have lots of information before making any accusations.

If you have detected a network compromise, the first thing to do (if you are able) is to disconnect your network. If they are connected via modem, unplug the modem cable; if they are connected via Ethernet, unplug the Ethernet cable. This will prevent them from doing any further damage, and they will probably see it as a network problem rather than detection.

If you are unable to disconnect the network (if you have a busy site, or you do not have physical control of your machines), the next best step is to use something like `tcpwrappers` or `ipfwadm` to deny access from the intruder's site.

If you can't deny all people from the same site as the intruder, locking the user's account will have to do. Note that locking an account is not an easy thing. You have to keep in mind `.rhosts` files, ftp access, and a host of possible backdoors.

After you have done one of the above (disconnected the network, denied access from their site, and/or disabled their account), you need to kill all their user processes and log them off.

You should monitor your site well for the next few minutes, as the attacker will try to get back in—perhaps using a different account, and/or from a different network address.

Security Compromise Has Already Happened

So you have either detected a compromise that has already happened or you have detected it and locked (hopefully) the offending attacker out of your system. Now what?

Closing the Hole

If you are able to determine what means the attacker used to get into your system, you should try to close that hole. For instance, perhaps you see several ftp entries just before the user logged in. Disable the ftp service and check and see if there is an updated version, or if any of the lists know of a fix.

Check all your log files, and make a visit to your security lists and pages and see if there are any new common exploits you can fix. You can find Caldera security fixes at `http://www.caldera.com/tech-ref/security/`. Red Hat has not yet separated their security fixes from bug fixes, but their distribution *errata* is available at `http://www.redhat.com/errata`.

Debian now has a security mailing list and Web page. See `http://www.debian.com/security/` for more information.

It is very likely that if one vendor has released a security update, most other Linux vendors will as well.

There is now a Linux security auditing project. They are methodically going through all the userspace utilities and looking for possible security exploits and overflows. From their announcement:

> **We are attempting a systematic audit of Linux sources with a view to being as secure as OpenBSD. We have already uncovered (and fixed) some problems, but more help is welcome. The list is unmoderated and also a useful resource for general security discussions. The list address is:** `security-audit@ferret.lmh.ox.ac.uk`**. To subscribe, send mail to:** `security-audit-subscribe@ferret.lmh.ox.ac.uk`**.**

If you don't lock the attacker out, they will likely be back. Not just back on your machine, but back somewhere on your network. If they were running a packet sniffer, odds are good they have access to other local machines.

Assessing the Damage

The first thing is to assess the damage. What has been compromised? If you are running an Integrity Checker like `Tripwire`, you can use it to perform an integrity check, and it should help to tell you. If not, you will have to look around at all your important data.

Since Linux systems are getting easier and easier to install, you might consider saving your config files and then wiping your disk(s) and reinstalling, then restoring your user files from backups and your config files. This will ensure that you have a new, clean system. If you have to back up files from the compromised system, be especially cautious of any binaries that you restore, as they may be Trojan horses placed there by the intruder.

Re-installation should be considered mandatory upon an intruder obtaining root access. Additionally, you'd like to keep any evidence there is, so having a spare disk in the safe may make sense.

Then you have to worry about how long ago the compromise happened, and whether the backups hold any damaged work. More on backups later.

Backups, Backups, Backups!

Having regular backups is a godsend for security matters. If your system is compromised, you can restore the data you need from backups. Of course, some data is valuable to the attacker too, and they will not only destroy it, they will steal it and have their own copies; but at least you will still have the data.

You should check several backups back into the past before restoring a file that has been tampered with. The intruder could have compromised your files long ago, and you could have made many successful backups of the compromised file!!!

Of course, there are also a raft of security concerns with backups. Make sure you are storing them in a secure place. Know who has access to them. (If an attacker can get your backups, they can have access to all your data without you ever knowing it.)

Tracking Down the Intruder

Ok, you have locked the intruder out, and recovered your system, but you're not quite done yet. While it is unlikely that most intruders will ever be caught, you should report the attack.

You should report the attack to the admin contact at the site where the attacker attacked your system. You can look up this contact with `whois` or the Internic database. You might send them an e-mail with all applicable log entries and dates and times. If you spotted anything else distinctive about your intruder, you might mention that too. After sending the e-mail, you should (if you are so inclined) follow up with a phone call. If that admin in turn spots your attacker, they might be able to talk to the admin of the site where they are coming from and so on.

Good crackers often use many intermediate systems, some (or many) of which may not even know they have been compromised. Trying to track a cracker back to their home system can be difficult. Being polite to the admins you talk to can go a long way to getting help from them.

You should also notify any security organizations you are a part of (CERT [`http://www.cert.org/`] or similar), as well as your Linux system vendor.

Security Sources

There are a *lot* of good sites out there for Unix security in general and Linux security specifically. It's very important to subscribe to one (or more) of the security mailing lists and keep current on security fixes. Most of these lists are very low volume, and very informative.

ftp Sites

CERT is the Computer Emergency Response Team. They often send out alerts of current attacks and fixes. See `ftp://ftp.cert.org` for more information.

Replay (`http://www.replay.com`) has archives of many security programs. Since they are outside the U.S., they don't need to obey U.S. crypto restrictions.

Matt Blaze is the author of CFS and a great security advocate. Matt's archive is available at `ftp://ftp.research.att.com/pub/mab`.

`tue.nl` is a great security ftp site in the Netherlands (`ftp.win.tue.nl`).

Web Sites

- The Hacker FAQ is a FAQ about hackers: `http://www.solon.com/~seebs/faqs/hacker.html`.
- The COAST archive has a large number of Unix security programs and information: `http://www.cs.purdue.edu/coast/`.
- SuSe Security Page: `http://www.suse.de/security/`.
- Rootshell.com is a great site for seeing what exploits are currently being used by crackers: `http://www.rootshell.com/`.
- BUGTRAQ puts out advisories on security issues: `http://www.netscape.org/lsv-archive/bugtraq.html`.
- CERT, the Computer Emergency Response Team, puts out advisories on common attacks on Unix platforms: CERT home (`http://www.cert.org/`).
- Dan Farmer is the author of SATAN and many other security tools. His home site has some interesting security survey information, as well as security tools: `http://www.trouble.org`.

- The Linux Security WWW is a good site for Linux security information: `http://www.aoy.org/Linux/Security`.
- Infilsec has a vulnerability engine that can tell you what vunerabilities affect a specific platform: `http://www.infilsec.com/vulnerabilities/`.
- CIAC sends out periodic security bulletins on common exploits: `http://ciac.llnl.gov/cgi-bin/index/bulletins`.
- A good starting point for Linux Pluggable Authentication Modules can be found at `http://www.kernel.org/pub/linux/libs/pam/`.
- The Debian project has a Web page for their security fixes and information. It is at `http://www.debian.com/security/`.
- WWW Security FAQ, written by Lincoln Stein, is a great Web security reference. Find it at `http://www.w3.org/Security/Faq/www-security-faq.html`.

Mailing Lists

Here is a sampling of Linux mailing lists.

Bugtraq: To subscribe to *bugtraq*, send mail to `listserv@netspace.org` containing *subscribe bugtraq* in the body (not subject) of the message. (See URLs above for archives).

CIAC: Send e-mail to `majordomo@tholia.llnl.gov`. In the *body* (not subject) of the message put (either or both): *subscribe ciac-bulletin*.

Red Hat has a number of mailing lists, the most important of which is the *redhat-announce* list. You can read about security (and other) fixes as soon as they come out. Send e-mail to `majordomo@redhat.com` and put *subscribe redhat-announce*.

The Debian project has a security mailing list that covers their security fixes. See `http://www.debian.com/security/` for more information.

Books—Printed Reading Material

There are a number of good security books out there. This section lists a few of them. In addition to the security specific books, security is covered in a number of other books on system administration.

Building Internet Firewalls, by D. Brent Chapman & Elizabeth D. Zwicky. 1st Edition September 1995. ISBN: 1-56592-124-0.

Practical UNIX & Internet Security, 2nd Edition, by Simson Garfinkel & Gene Spafford. April 1996. ISBN: 1-56592-148-8.

Computer Security Basics, by Deborah Russell & G.T. Gangemi, Sr. 1st Edition July 1991. ISBN: 0-937175-71-4.

Linux Network Administrator's Guide, by Olaf Kirch. 1st Edition January 1995. ISBN: 1-56592-087-2.

PGP: Pretty Good Privacy, by Simson Garfinkel. 1st Edition December 1994. ISBN: 1-56592-098-8.

Computer Crime A Crimefighter's Handbook, by David Icove, Karl Seger & William VonStorch (Consulting Editor Eugene H. Spafford). 1st Edition August 1995. ISBN: 1-56592-086-4.

GLOSSARY

authentication This is the property of knowing that the data received is the same as the data that was sent, and that the claimed sender is in fact the actual sender.

bastion host A computer system that must be highly secured because it is vulnerable to attack, usually because it is exposed to the Internet and is a main point of contact for users of internal networks. It gets its name from the highly fortified projects on the outer walls of medieval castles. Bastions overlook critical areas of defense, usually having strong walls, room for extra troops, and the occasional useful tub of boiling hot oil for discouraging attackers.

buffer overflow Common coding style is to never allocate large enough buffers, and to not check for overflows. When such buffers overflow, the executing program (daemon or setuid program) can be tricked into doing some other things. Generally this works by overwriting a function's return address on the stack to point to another location.

denial of service A denial of service attack is when an attacker consumes the resources on your computer for things it was not intended to be doing, thus preventing normal use of your network resources for legitimate purposes.

dual-homed host A general-purpose computer system that has at least two network interfaces.

firewall A component or set of components that restricts access between a protected network and the Internet, or between other sets of networks.

host A computer system attached to a network.

IP spoofing IP Spoofing is a complex technical attack that is made up of several components. It is a security exploit that works by tricking computers in a trust-relationship that you are someone that you really aren't. There is an extensive paper written by daemon9, route, and infinity, in Vol. 7, Issue 48 of *Phrack* magazine.

non-repudiation The property of a receiver being able to prove that the sender of some data did in fact send the data even though the sender might later deny ever having sent it.

packet The fundamental unit of communication on the Internet.

packet filtering The action a device takes to selectively control the flow of data to and from a network. Packet filters allow or block packets, usually while routing them from one network to another (most often from the Internet to an internal network, and vice-versa). To accomplish packet filtering, you set up rules that specify what types of packets (those to or from a particular IP address or port) are to be allowed and what types are to be blocked.

perimeter network A network added between a protected network and an external network, in order to provide an additional layer of security. A perimeter network is sometimes called a DMZ.

proxy server A program that deals with external servers on behalf of internal clients. Proxy clients talk to proxy servers, which relay approved client requests to real servers, and relay answers back to clients.

superuser An informal name for `root`.

FREQUENTLY ASKED QUESTIONS

Here are some answers to frequently asked questions.

1. Is it more secure to compile driver support directly into the kernel, instead of making it a module?

Answer: Some people think it is better to disable the ability to load device drivers using modules, because an intruder could load a Trojan module or a module that could affect system security.

However, in order to load modules, you must be root. The module object files are also only writable by root. This means the intruder would need root access to insert a module. If the intruder gains root access, there are more serious things to worry about than whether he will load a module.

Modules are for dynamically loading support for a particular device that may be infrequently used. On server machines, or firewalls for instance, this is very unlikely to happen. For this reason, it would make more sense to compile support directly into the kernel for machines acting as a server. Modules are also slower than support compiled directly in the kernel.

2. Why does logging in as root from a remote machine always fail?

Answer: This is done intentionally to prevent remote users from attempting to connect via `telnet` to your machine as `root`, which is a serious security vulnerability. Don't forget: potential intruders have time on their side, and can run automated programs to find your password. (See the "Root Security" section.)

3. How do I enable shadow passwords on my Red Hat 4.2 or 5.*x* Linux box?

Answer: Shadow passwords is a mechanism for storing your password in a file other than the normal `/etc/passwd` file. This has several advantages. The first one is that the shadow file, `/etc/shadow`, is only readable by root, unlike `/etc/passwd`, which must remain readable by everyone. The other advantage is that as the administrator, you can enable or disable accounts without everyone knowing the status of other users' accounts.

The /etc/passwd file is then used to store user and group names, used by programs like /bin/ls to map the user ID to the proper username in a directory listing.

The /etc/shadow file then only contains the username and his/her password, and perhaps accounting information, like when the account expires, etc.

To enable shadow passwords, run pwconv as root, and /etc/shadow should now exist, and be used by applications. Since you are using RH 4.2 or above, the PAM modules will automatically adapt to the change from using normal /etc/passwd to shadow passwords without any other change.

Since you're interested in securing your passwords, perhaps you would also be interested in generating good passwords to begin with. For this you can use the pamcracklib module, which is part of PAM. It runs your password against the *Crack* libraries to help you decide if it is too easily guessable by password cracking programs.

4. How can I enable the Apache SSL extensions?

Answer:

1. Get SSLeay 0.8.0 or later from ftp://ftp.psy.uq.oz.au/pub/Crypto/SSL.
2. Build and test and install it!
3. Get Apache 1.2.5 source.
4. Get Apache SSLeay extensions from: ftp://ftp.ox.ac.uk/pub/crypto/SSL/apache_1.2.5+ssl_1.13.tar.gz.
5. Unpack it in the apache-1.2.5 source directory and patch Apache as per the README.
6. Configure and build it.

You might also try Replay Associates (http://www.replay.com), which has many prebuilt packages, and is located outside of the United States.

5. How can I manipulate user accounts, and still retain security?

Answer: The Red Hat distribution, especially RH 5.0, contains a great number of tools to change the properties of user accounts.

- The `pwconv` and `unpwconv` programs can be used to convert between shadow and non-shadowed passwords.
- The `pwck` and `grpck` programs can be used to verify proper organization of the `passwd` and `group` files.
- The `useradd`, `usermod`, and `userdel` programs can be used to add, delete, and modify user accounts. The `groupadd`, `groupmod`, and `groupdel` programs will do the same for groups.
- Group passwords can be created using `gpasswd`.

All these programs are *shadow-aware*—that is, if you enable shadow they will use `/etc/shadow` for password information, otherwise it won't.

See the respective man pages for further information.

6. How can I password protect specific HTML documents using Apache?

I bet you didn't know about `http://www.apacheweek.org`, did you?

You can find information on user authentication at `http://www.apacheweek.com/features/userauth` as well as other Web server security tips from `http://www.apache.org/docs/misc/security_tips.html`.

Conclusion

By subscribing to the security alert mailing lists, and keeping current, you can do a lot towards securing your machine. If you pay attention to your log files and run something like `tripwire` regularly, you can do even more.

A reasonable level of computer security is not difficult to maintain on a home machine. More effort is required on business machines, but Linux can indeed be a secure platform. Due to the nature of Linux development, security fixes often come out much faster than they do on commercial operating systems, making Linux an ideal platform when security is a requirement.

ACKNOWLEDGEMENTS

Information here is collected from many sources. Thanks to the following that either indirectly or directly have contributed:

- Rob Riggs <rob@DevilsThumb.com>
- S. Coffin <scoffin@netcom.com>
- Viktor Przebinda <viktor@CRYSTAL.MATH.ou.edu>
- Roelof Osinga <roelof@eboa.com>
- Kyle Hasselbacher <kyle@carefree.quux.soltc.net>
- David S. Jackson <dsj@dsj.net>
- Todd G. Ruskell <ruskell@boulder.nist.gov>
- Rogier Wolff <R.E.Wolff@BitWizard.nl>
- Antonomasia <ant@notatla.demon.co.uk>
- Nic Bellamy <sky@wibble.net>
- Eric Hanchrow <offby1@blarg.net>
- Robert J. Berger <rberger@ibd.com>
- Ulrich Alpers <lurchi@cdrom.uni-stuttgart.de>
- David Noha <dave@c-c-s.com>

The following have translated this HOWTO into various other languages! A special thank you to all of them for help spreading the Linux word.

- Polish: Ziemek Borowski <ziembor@FAQ-bot.ZiemBor.Waw.PL>
- Japanese: FUJIWARA Teruyoshi <fjwr@mtj.biglobe.ne.jp>
- Indonesian: Tedi Heriyanto <22941219@students.ukdw.ac.id>

ipfwadm -O -i deny
V your static
outgoing to
ipfwadm
such as ip mas
define the
bin:/usr/
CONFIG

Chapter 14

IP Chains

Linux's packet firewalling capabilities will be essential if your Linux machine is connected to a dedicated Internet connection like a cable modem, DSL line, or the ethernet in a connected office environment. For such an application, you should almost certainly be using the latest 2.2.*x* Linux kernel, which includes the "ipchains" packet filtering system.

This document aims to describe how to obtain, install, and configure the enhanced IP firewalling chains software for Linux, as well as some ideas on how you might use them.

This document is reprinted from the Linux IPCHAINS HOWTO, version 1.0.6, of Jan 18, 1999 by Paul Russell `<Paul.Russell@rustcorp.com.au>`

Introduction

This is the Linux IPChains-HOWTO. You should also read the Linux NET-3-HOWTO (see Chapter 8), the IP Masquerading HOWTO (see Chapter 12), the PPP HOWTO (see Chapter 9), the Ethernet HOWTO (see `http://metalab.unc.edu/LDP/`), and the Firewall HOWTO (`http://metalab.unc.edu/LDP/`). (Then again, so might the `alt.fan.bigfoot` FAQ.)

If packet filtering is passe to you, read the "Why?" and "How?" sections later in this chapter and scan through the titles in the "IP Firewalling Chains," also later in this chapter.

If you are converting from `ipfwadm`, read the "What," "How," "Differences between `ipchains` and `ipfwadm`," and "Using the `ipfwadm-wrapper` Script" sections later in this chapter.

What?

Linux `ipchains` is a rewrite of the Linux IPv4 firewalling code (which was mainly stolen from BSD) and a rewrite of `ipfwadm`, which was a rewrite of BSD's `ipfw`, I believe. It is required to administer the IP packet filters in Linux kernel versions 2.1.102 and above.

Why?

The older Linux firewalling code doesn't deal with fragments; has 32-bit counters (on Intel at least); doesn't allow specification of protocols other than TCP, UDP or ICMP; can't make large changes atomically; can't specify inverse rules; has some quirks; and can be tough to manage (making it prone to user error).

How?

Currently the code is in the mainstream kernel from 2.1.102. For the 2.0 kernel series, you will need to download a kernel patch from the Web page. If your 2.0 kernel is more recent than the supplied patch, the older patch should be OK; this part of the 2.0 kernels is fairly stable (that is, the 2.0.34 kernel patch works just fine on the 2.0.35 kernel). Since the 2.0 patch is incompatible with the `ipportfw` and `ipautofw` patches, I don't recommend applying it unless you really need the functionality that `ipchains` offer.

Where?

At the Linux IP Firewall Chains Page (`http://www.adelaide.net.au/~rustcorp/linux/ipchains`)you can find a mailing list for bug reports, discussion, development, and usage. Join the mailing list by sending a message containing the word "subscribe to ipchains-request" at `wantree.com.au`. To send mail to the list use "ipchains"instead of "ipchains-request."

PACKET FILTERING BASICS

The following section describes the what, why, and how of packet filtering, kernels, and `ipchains`.

What?

All traffic through a network is sent in the form of packets. For example, downloading this package (say it's 50k long) might cause you to receive 36 or so packets of 1460 bytes each.

The start of each packet says where it's going, where it came from, the type of packet, and other administrative details. This start of the packet is called the *header*. The rest of the packet, containing the actual data being transmitted, is usually called the *body*.

Some protocols (like as TCP, which is used for Web traffic, mail, and remote logins) use the concept of a connection. This means that before any packets with actual data are sent, various setup packets (with special headers) are exchanged saying "I want to connect," "OK," and "Thanks." Then normal packets are exchanged.

A packet filter is a piece of software that looks at the header of packets as they pass through and decides the fate of the entire packet. It might decide to *deny* the packet (that is, discard the packet as if it had never received it), *accept* the packet (that is, let the packet go through), or *reject* the packet (like deny, it discards the packet, but it also tells the source of the packet that it has done so).

Under Linux, packet filtering is built into the kernel.There are a few tricky things we can do with packets, but the general principle of looking at the headers and deciding the fate of the packet is still there.

Why?

Control. Security. Watchfulness.

Control When you are using a Linux box to connect your internal network to another network (say, the Internet), you have an opportunity to allow certain types of traffic and disallow others. For example, the header of a packet contains the destination address of the packet, so you can prevent packets from going to a certain part of the outside network. For example, I use Netscape to access the Dilbert archives. There are advertisements from `doubleclick.net` on the page, and Netscape wastes my time by cheerfully downloading them. Telling the packet filter not to allow any packets to or from the addresses owned by `doubleclick.net` solves that problem (there are better ways of doing this though).

Security When your Linux box is the only thing between the chaos of the Internet and your nice, orderly network, it's nice to know you can restrict what comes tromping in your door. For example, you might allow anything to go out from your network, but you might be worried about the well-known "Ping of Death" coming in from malicious outsiders. As another example, you might not want outsiders telnetting to your Linux box, even though all your accounts have passwords; maybe you want (like most people) to be an observer on the Internet and not a server (willing or otherwise). To do this, simply don't let anyone connect in, by having the packet filter reject incoming packets used to set up connections.

Watchfulness Sometimes a badly configured machine on the local network will decide to spew packets to the outside world. It's nice to tell the packet filter to let you know if anything abnormal occurs; maybe you can do something about it or maybe you're just curious by nature.

How?

A Kernel with Packet Filtering

You need a kernel that has the new IP firewall chains in it. You can tell if the kernel you are running right now has this installed by looking for the file `/proc/net/ipfwchains`. If it exists, you're in.

If not, you need to make a kernel that has IP firewall chains. First, download the source to the kernel you want. If you have a kernel numbered 2.1.102 or higher, you won't need to patch it (it's in the mainstream kernel now). Otherwise, apply the patch from the Web page listed previously and set the configuration as detailed below. If you don't know how to do this, don't panic; read the Kernel-HOWTO.

The configuration options you will need to set for the 2.0-series kernel are:

```
CONFIG_EXPERIMENTAL=y
CONFIG_FIREWALL=y
CONFIG_IP_FIREWALL=y
CONFIG_IP_FIREWALL_CHAINS=y
```

For the 2.1 or 2.2 series kernels:

```
CONFIG_FIREWALL=y
CONFIG_IP_FIREWALL=y
```

The tool `ipchains` talks to the kernel and tells it what packets to filter. Unless you are a programmer, or overly curious, this is how you will control the packet filtering.

ipchains

This tool replaces `ipfwadm`, which was used for the old IP Firewall code. The package also contains a shell script called `ipfwadm-wrapper` that allows you to do packet filtering as it was done before. You should not use this script unless you want a quick way of upgrading a system that uses `ipfwadm` (it's slower, doesn't check arguments, and so on). In that case, you don't need this HOWTO much either. See the "Differences between `ipchains` and `ipfwadm`" sections later in this chapter for more details on `ipfwadm` issues.

I'm Confused! Routing, Masquerading, Portforwarding, ipautofw...

This HOWTO is about packet filtering. This means deciding whether a packet should be allowed to pass or not. However, Linux being the hacker's playground that it is, you probably want to do more than that.

One problem is that the same tool (`ipchains`) is used to control both masquerading and transparent proxying, although these are notionally separate from packet filtering. (The current Linux implementation blurs these together unnaturally, leaving the impression that they are closely related.)

Masquerading and proxying are covered by separate HOWTOs, and the auto forwarding and port forwarding features are controlled by separate tools, but since so many people keep asking me about it, I'll include a set of common scenarios and indicate when each one should be applied. The security merits of each setup will not be discussed here.

Rusty's Three-Line Guide to Masquerading

This assumes that your external interface is called ppp0. Use `ifconfig` to find out and adjust to taste.

```
# echo 1 > /proc/sys/net/ipv4/ip_forward
# ipchains -P forward -j DENY
# ipchains -A forward -i ppp0 -j MASQ
```

Gratuitous Promotion: WatchGuard Rules

You can buy off-the-shelf firewalls. An excellent one is WatchGuard's FireBox. It's excellent because I like it, it's secure, it's Linux-based, and because they are funding the maintenance of `ipchains` as well as the new firewalling code (aimed for 2.3). In short, WatchGuard is paying for me to eat while I work for you. So please consider their stuff. Watchguard's URL is: `http://www.watchguard.com`.

Common Firewall-like Setups

You run `littlecorp.com`. You have an internal network and a single dialup (PPP) connection to the Internet (`firewall.littlecorp.com`,which is 1.2.3.4). You run ethernet on your local network, and your personal machine is called "`myhost`".

Private Network: Traditional Proxies

In this scenario, packets from the private network never traverse the Internet, and vice versa. The IP addresses of the private network should be assigned from the RFC1597 Private Network Allocations (i.e., 10.*.*.*, 172.16.*.* or 192.168.*.*).

The only way things ever connect to the Internet is by connecting to the firewall, which is the only machine on both networks that connects onward. You run a program (on the firewall) called a proxy to do this (there are proxies for FTP, Web access, telnet, RealAudio, Usenet News and other services). See the Firewall HOWTO.

Any services you wish the Internet to access must be on the firewall. (But see the "Limited Internal Services" section later in this chapter).

Example: Allowing Web access from private network to the Internet.

- The private network is assigned 192.168.1.* addresses, with `myhost` being 192.168.1.100 and the firewall's ethernet interface being assigned 192.168.1.1.
- A Web proxy (for example, "squid") is installed and configured on the firewall, running on, say, port 8080.
- Netscape on the private network is configured to use the firewall port 8080 as a proxy.
- DNS does not need to be configured on the private network.
- DNS does need to be configured on the firewall.
- No default route (aka gateway) needs to be configured on the private network.

Netscape on `myhost` reads `http://slashdot.org`.

1. Netscape connects to the firewall port 8080, using port 1050 on `myhost`. It asks for the Web page of `http://slashdot.org`.
2. The proxy looks up the name `slashdot.org`, and gets 207.218.152.131. It then opens a connection to that IP address (using port 1025 on the firewall's external interface) and asks the Web server (port 80) for the Web page.
3. As it receives the Web page from its connection to the Web server, it copies the data to the connection from Netscape.
4. Netscape renders the page.

From `slashdot.org`'s point of view, the connection is made from 1.2.3.4 (firewall's PPP interface) port 1025 to 207.218.152.131 (`slashdot.org`) port 80. From `myhost`'s point of view, the connection is made from 192.168.1.100 (`myhost`) port 1050, to 192.168.1.1 (firewall's ethernet interface) port 8080.

Private Network: Transparent Proxies

In this scenario, packets from the private network never traverse the Internet, and vice versa. The IP addresses of the private network should be assigned from the RFC1597 Private Network Allocations (i.e., 10.*.*.*, 172.16.*.* or 192.168.*.*).

The only way things ever connect to the Internet is by connecting to the firewall, which is the only machine on both networks that connects onward. You run a program (on the firewall) called a transparent proxy to do this; the kernel sends outgoing packets to the transparent proxy instead of sending them onward (that is, it bastardizes routing).

Transparent proxying means that the clients don't need to know there is a proxy involved.

Any services you wish the Internet to access must be on the firewall. (But see the "Limited Internal Services" section later in this chapter).

Example: Allowing Web access from private network to the Internet.

1. The private network is assigned 192.168.1.* addresses, with `myhost` being 192.168.1.100 and the firewall's ethernet interface being assigned 192.168.1.1.
2. A transparent Web proxy (I believe there are patches for squid to allow it to operate in this manner, or try "`transproxy`") is installed and configured on the firewall, running on, say, port 8080.
3. The kernel is told to redirect connections to port 80 to the proxy, using `ipchains`.
4. Netscape on the private network is configured to connect directly.
5. DNS needs to be configured on the private network (that is, you need to run a DNS server as a proxy on the firewall).
6. The default route (aka gateway) needs to be configured on the private network to send packets to the firewall.

Netscape on `myhost` reads `http://slashdot.org`.

1. Netscape looks up the name `slashdot.org` and gets 207.218.152.131. It then opens a connection to that IP address, using local port 1050, and asks the Web server (port 80) for the Web page.

2. As the packets from `myhost` (port 1050) to `slashdot.org` (port 80) pass through the firewall, they are redirected to the waiting transparent proxy on port 8080. The transparent proxy opens a connection (using local port 1025) to 207.218.152.131 port 80 (which is where the original packets were going).

3. As the proxy receives the Web page from its connection to the Web server, it copies the data to the connection from Netscape.

4. Netscape renders the page.

From `slashdot.org`'s point of view, the connection is made from 1.2.3.4 (firewall's PPP interface) port 1025 to 207.218.152.131 (`slashdot.org`) port 80. From `myhost`'s point of view, the connection is made from 192.168.1.100 (`myhost`) port 1050, to 207.218.152.131 (`slashdot.org`) port 80, but it's actually talking to the transparent proxy.

Private Network: Masquerading

In this scenario, packets from the private network never traverse the Internet without special treatment, and vice versa. The IP addresses of the private network should be assigned from the RFC1597 Private Network Allocations (that is, 10.*.*.*, 172.16.*.* or 192.168.*.*).

Instead of using a proxy, we use a special kernel facility called "*masquerading*." Masquerading rewrites packets as they pass through the firewall, so that they always seem to come from the firewall itself. It then rewrites the responses so they look like they are going to the original recipient.

Masquerading has separate modules to handle "tricky" protocols, such as FTP, RealAudio, Quake, etc. For really hard-to-handle protocols, the auto forwarding facility can handle some of them by automatically setting up port forwarding for related sets of ports: look for `ipportfw` (2.0 kernels) or `ipmasqadm` (2.1 kernels).

Any services you wish the Internet to access must be on the firewall. (But see the "Limited Internal Services" section later in this chapter).

Example: Allowing Web access from private network to the Internet.

1. The private network is assigned 192.168.1.* addresses, with `myhost` being 192.168.1.100, and the firewall's ethernet interface being assigned 192.168.1.1.

2. The firewall is set up to masquerade any packets coming from the private network and going to port 80 on an Internet host.
3. Netscape is configured to connect directly.
4. DNS must be configured correctly on the private network.
5. The firewall should be the default route (aka gateway) for the private network.

Netscape on `myhost` reads `http://slashdot.org`.

1. Netscape looks up the name `slashdot.org`, and gets 207.218.152.131. It then opens a connection to that IP address, using local port 1050 and asks the Web server (port 80) for the Web page.
2. As the packets from `myhost` (port 1050) to `slashdot.org` (port 80) pass through the firewall, they are rewritten to come from the PPP interface of the firewall, port 65000. The firewall has a valid Internet address (1.2.3.4) so reply packets from `www.linuxhq.com` get routed back OK.
3. As packets from `slashdot.org` (port 80) to `firewall.littlecorp.com` (port 65000) come in, they are rewritten to go to `myhost`, port 1050. This is the real magic of masquerading: it remembers when it rewrites outgoing packets so it can write them back as replies come in.
4. Netscape renders the page.

From `slashdot.org`'s point of view, the connection is made from 1.2.3.4 (firewall's PPP interface) port 65000 to 207.218.152.131 (`slashdot.org`) port 80. From `myhost`'s point of view, the connection is made from 192.168.1.100 (`myhost`) port 1050, to 207.218.152.131 (`slashdot.org`) port 80.

Public Network

In this scenario, your personal network is a part of the Internet: Packets can flow without change across both networks. The IP addresses of the internal network must be assigned by applying for a block of IP addresses, so the rest of the network will know how to get packets to you. This implies a permanent connection.

In this role, packet filtering is used to restrict which packets can be forwarded between your network and the rest of the Internet, i.e., to restrict the rest of the Internet to only accessing your internal Web servers.

Example: Allowing Web access from private network to the Internet.

1. Your internal network is assigned according to the IP address block you have registered (say 1.2.3.*).
2. The firewall is set up to allow all traffic.
3. Netscape is configured to connect directly.
4. DNS must be configured correctly on your network.
5. The firewall should be the default route (aka gateway) for the private network.

Netscape on `myhost` reads `http://slashdot.org`.

1. Netscape looks up the name `slashdot.org`, and gets 207.218.152.131. It then opens a connection to that IP address, using local port 1050, and asks the Web server (port 80) for the Web page.
2. Packets pass through your firewall, just as they pass through several other routers between you and `slashdot.org`.
3. Netscape renders the page.

There is only one connection: from 1.2.3.100 (`myhost`) port 1050, to 207.218.152.131 (`slashdot.org`) port 80.

Limited Internal Services

There are a few tricks you can pull to allow the Internet to access your internal services, rather than running the services on the firewall. These will work with either a proxy- or masquerading-based approach for external connections.

The simplest approach is to run a *redirector*, which is a poor-man's proxy. This waits for a connection on a given port, opens a connection a fixed internal host and port, and then copies data between the two connections. An example of this is the `redir` program. From the Internet point of view, the connection is made to your firewall. From your internal server's point of view, the connection is made from the internal interface of the firewall to the server.

Another approach (which requires a 2.0 kernel patched for `ipportfw`, or a 2.1 or later kernel) is to use port forwarding in the kernel. This does the same job as `redir` in a different way: The kernel rewrites packets as they pass through, changing their destination address and ports to point them at an internal host and port. From the Internet's point of view, the connection is made to your firewall. From your internal server's point of view, a direct connection is made from the Internet host to the server.

IP Firewalling Chains

This section describes all you really need to know to build a packet filter that meets your needs.

How Packets Traverse the Filters

The kernel starts with three lists of rules; these lists are called firewall chains or just chains. The three chains are called `input`, `output`, and `forward`. When a packet comes in (say, through the Ethernet card) the kernel uses the input chain to decide its fate. If it survives that step, then the kernel decides where to send the packet next (this is called *routing*). If it is destined for another machine, it consults the `forward` chain. Finally, just before a packet is to go out, the kernel consults the `output` chain.

A chain is a checklist of rules. Each rule says 'if the packet header looks like this, then here's what to do with the packet'. If the rule doesn't match the packet, then the next rule in the chain is consulted. Finally, if there are no more rules to consult, then the kernel looks at the chain policy to decide what to do. In a security-conscious system, this policy usually tells the kernel to reject or deny the packet.

The following and Figure 14.1 show the complete path of a packet coming into a machine.

Here is a blow-by-blow description of each stage:

Checksum This is a test that the packet hasn't been corrupted in some way. If it has, it is denied.

Sanity There is actually one of these sanity checks before each firewall chain, but the `input` chain's is the most important. Some malformed packets might confuse the rule-checking code, and these are denied here (a message is printed to the syslog if this happens).

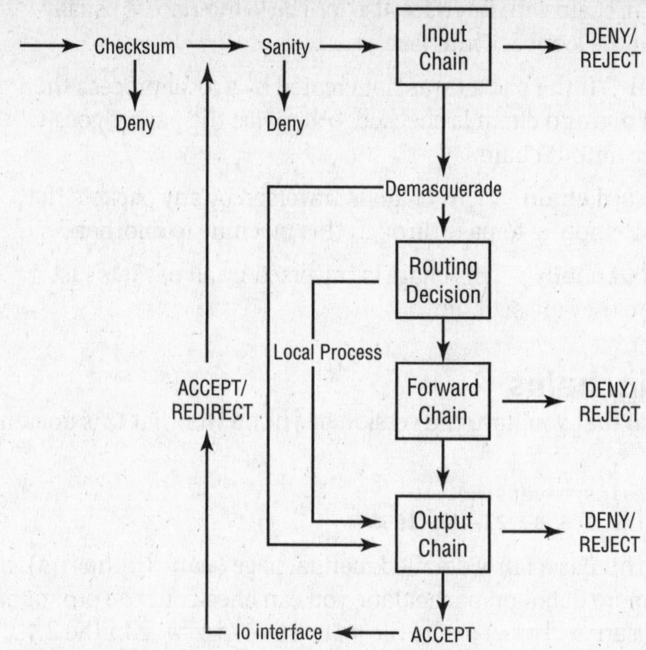

FIGURE 14.1: A packet coming into a machine

Input chain This is the first firewall chain against which the packet will be tested. If the verdict of the chain is not DENY or `REJECT`, the packet continues on.

De-masquerade If the packet is a reply to a previously masqueraded packet, it is de-masqueraded and skips straight to the `output` chain. If you don't use IP Masquerading, you can mentally erase this from the diagram.

Routing decision The destination field is examined by the routing code, to decide if this packet should go to a local process (see "local process" defined next) or be forwarded to a remote machine (see the "forward chain" definition).

Local process A process running on the machine can receive packets after the Routing Decision step and send packets. (These go through the Routing Decision step, then traverse the output chain).

Lo interface This interface is for packets from a local process that are destined for a local process. They will go through the `output` chain with interface set to lo, then return through the `input` chain with interface also lo. The lo interface is usually called the loopback interface.

Local If the packet was not created by a local process then the `forward` chain is checked, otherwise the packet goes to the output chain.

Forward chain This chain is traversed by any packets that are attempting to pass through this machine to another.

Output chain This chain is traversed by all packets just before they are sent out.

Using ipchains

First, check that you have the version of `ipchains` that this document refers to:

```
$ ipchains --version
ipchains 1.3.8, 27-Oct-1998
```

`ipchains` has a fairly detailed manual page (`man ipchains`), but if you need more detail on particulars, you can check out the programming interface (`man 4 ipfw`) or the file `net/ipv4/ipfw.c` in the 2.1.*x* kernel source, which is (obviously) authoritative.

There is also an excellent quick reference card by Scott Bronson in the source package, in both A4 and US Letter PostScript™.

There are several different things you can do with `ipchains`. First, there are operations to manage whole chains. You start with three built-in chains, `input`, `output`, and `forward`, which you can't delete. The command line options for whole-chain operations are

- Create a new chain (-N)
- Delete an empty chain (-X)
- Change the policy for a built-in chain. (-P)
- List the rules in a chain (-L)
- Flush the rules out of a chain (-F)
- Zero the packet and byte counters on all rules in a chain (-Z)

There are several ways to manipulate rules inside a chain:

- Append a new rule to a chain (-A)
- Insert a new rule at some position in a chain (-I)
- Replace a rule at some position in a chain (-R)

- Delete a rule at some position in a chain (-D)
- Delete the first rule that matches in a chain (-D)

There are a few operations for masquerading, which are in `ipchains` for want of a good place to put them:

- List the currently masqueraded connections (-M -L)
- Set masquerading timeout values (-M -S) (But read about a common masquerading timeout problem in the "Common Problems" section later in this chapter).

The final (and perhaps the most useful) function allows you to check what would happen to a given packet if it were to traverse a given chain.

Operations on a Single Rule

This is the bread and butter of `ipchains`—manipulating rules. Most commonly, you will probably use the append (-A) and delete (-D) commands. The others (-I for insert and -R for replace) are simple extensions of these concepts.

Each rule specifies a set of conditions the packet must meet and what to do if it meets them (a target). For example, you might want to deny all ICMP packets coming from the IP address 127.0.0.1. In this case our conditions are that the protocol must be ICMP and the source address must be 127.0.0.1. Our target is DENY.

127.0.0.1 is the loopback interface, which you will have even if you have no real network connection. You can use the ping program to generate such packets (it simply sends an ICMP type 8 [echo request], which all cooperative hosts should obligingly respond to with an ICMP type 0 [echo reply] packet). This makes it useful for testing.

```
# ping -c 1 127.0.0.1
PING 127.0.0.1 (127.0.0.1): 56 data bytes
64 bytes from 127.0.0.1: icmp_seq=0 ttl=64 time=0.2 ms

--- 127.0.0.1 ping statistics ---
1 packets transmitted, 1 packets received, 0% packet loss
round-trip min/avg/max = 0.2/0.2/0.2 ms
# ipchains -A input -s 127.0.0.1 -p icmp -j DENY
# ping -c 1 127.0.0.1
PING 127.0.0.1 (127.0.0.1): 56 data bytes

--- 127.0.0.1 ping statistics ---
1 packets transmitted, 0 packets received, 100% packet loss
#
```

You can see here that the first ping succeeds (the `-c 1` tells ping to only send a single packet).

Then we append (-A) to the `input` chain, a rule specifying that for packets from 127.0.0.1 (-s 127.0.0.1) with protocol ICMP (-p ICMP) we should jump to DENY (-j DENY).

Then we test our rule, using the second ping. There will be a pause before the program gives up waiting for a response that will never come.

We can delete the rule in one of two ways. First, since we know that it is the only rule in the `input` chain, we can use a numbered delete, such as:

```
# ipchains -D input 1
#
```

This will delete rule number 1 in the input chain.

The second way is to mirror the -A command, but replace the -A with -D. This is useful when you have a complex chain of rules and you don't want to have to count them to figure out that it's rule 37 that you want to get rid of. In this case, we would use:

```
# ipchains -D input -s 127.0.0.1 -p icmp -j DENY
#
```

The syntax of -D must have exactly the same options as the -A (or -I or -R) command. If there are multiple identical rules in the same chain, only the first one will be deleted.

Filtering Specifications

We have seen the use of -p to specify protocol and -s to specify source address, but there are other options we can use to specify packet characteristics. What follows is an exhaustive compendium.

Specifying Source and Destination IP Addresses Source (-s) and destination (-d) IP addresses can be specified in four ways. The most common way is to use the full name, such as `localhost` or `www.linuxhq.com`. The second way is to specify the IP address such as 127.0.0.1.

The third and fourth ways allow specification of a group of IP addresses, such as 199.95.207.0/24 or 199.95.207.0/255.255.255.0. These both specify any IP address from 192.95.207.0 to 192.95.207.255 inclusive; the digits after the "/" tell which parts of the IP address are significant. /32 or

/255.255.255.255 is the default (match all of the IP address). To specify any IP address at all, /0 can be used, like so:

```
# ipchains -A input -s 0/0 -j DENY
#
```

This is rarely used, as the effect above is the same as not specifying the -s option at all.

Specifying Inversion Many flags, including the -s and -d flags can have their arguments preceded by "!" (pronounced "not") to match addresses not equal to the ones given. For example. -s ! localhost matches any packet not coming from localhost.

Specifying Protocol The protocol can be specified with the -p flag. Protocol can be a number (if you know the numeric protocol values for IP) or a name for the special cases of TCP, UDP, or ICMP. Case doesn't matter, so tcp works as well as TCP.

The protocol name can be prefixed by a ! to invert it, as in -p ! TCP.

Specifying UDP and TCP Ports For the special case where a protocol of TCP or UDP is specified, there can be an extra argument indicating the TCP or UDP port or an (inclusive) range of ports (but see the "Handling Fragments" section later in this chapter). A range is represented using a ":" character, such as 6000:6010, which covers 11 port numbers from 6000 to 6010 inclusive. If the lower bound is omitted, it defaults to 0. If the upper bound is omitted, it defaults to 65535. To specify TCP connections coming from ports under 1024, the syntax would be -p TCP -s 0.0.0.0/0 :1023. Port numbers can be specified by name, e.g., www.

Note that the port specification can be preceded by a "!," which inverts it. So to specify every TCP packet BUT a www packet, you would specify -p TCP -d 0.0.0.0/0 ! www.

It is important to realize that the specification -p TCP -d ! 192.168.1.1 www is very different from -p TCP -d 192.168.1.1 ! www.

The first specifies any TCP packet to the www port on any machine but 192.168.1.1. The second specifies any TCP connection to any port on 192.168.1.1 but the www port.

Finally, this case means not the www port and not 192.168.1.1: -p TCP -d ! 192.168.1.1 ! www.

Specifying ICMP Type and Code ICMP also allows an optional argument, but since ICMP doesn't have ports, (ICMP has a *type* and a *code*) they have a different meaning.

You can specify them as ICMP names (use `ipchains -h icmp` to list the names) after the -s option or as a numeric ICMP type and code, where the type follows the -s option and the code follows the -d option.

The ICMP names are fairly long; you only need to use enough letters to make the name distinct from any other.

Here is a small table of some of the most common ICMP packets.

NUMBER	NAME	REQUIRED BY:
0	echo-reply	ping
3	destination-unreachable	any tcp/udp traffic
5	redirect	routing if not running routing daemon
8	echo-request	ping
11	time-exceeded	traceroute

Note that the ICMP names cannot be preceeded by ! at the moment.

WARNING

Do not block all ICMP type 3 messages! (See the "ICMP Packets" section later in this chapter).

Specifying an Interface The -i option specifies the name of an interface to match. An *interface* is the physical device the packet came in on or goes out on. You can use the `ifconfig` command to list the interfaces which are up (that is, working at the moment).

The interface for incoming packets (that is, packets traversing the input chain) is considered to be the interface they came in on. Logically, the interface for outgoing packets (packets traversing the `output` chain) is the interface they will go out on. The interface for packets traversing the `forward` chain is also the interface they will go out on (a fairly arbitrary decision it seems to me).

It is perfectly legal to specify an interface that currently does not exist; the rule will not match anything until the interface comes up. This is extremely useful for dial-up PPP links (usually interface ppp0) and the like.

As a special case, an interface name ending with a + will match all interfaces (whether they currently exist or not) that begin with that string. For example, to specify a rule which matches all PPP interfaces, the `-i ppp+` option would be used.

The interface name can be preceded by a ! to match a packet that does not match the specified interface(s).

Specifying TCP SYN Packets Only It is sometimes useful to allow TCP connections in one direction but not the other. For example, you might want to allow connections to an external WWW server, but not connections from that server.

The naive approach would be to block TCP packets coming from the server. Unfortunately, TCP connections require packets going in both directions to work at all.

The solution is to block only the packets used to request a connection. These packets are called SYN packets (OK, technically they're packets with the SYN flag set and the FIN and ACK flags cleared, but we call them SYN packets). By disallowing only these packets, we can stop attempted connections in their tracks.

The -y flag is used for this; it is only valid for rules which specify TCP as their protocol. For example, to specify TCP connection attempts from 192.168.1.1: -p TCP -s 192.168.1.1 -y

Once again, this flag can be inverted by preceding it with a !, which means every packet other than the connection initiation.

Handling Fragments Sometimes a packet is too large to fit down a wire all at once. When this happens, the packet is divided into fragments and sent as multiple packets. The other end reassembles the fragments to reconstruct the whole packet.

The problem with fragments is that some of the specifications listed above (in particular source port, destinations port, ICMP type, ICMP code, or TCP SYN flag) require the kernel to peek at the start of the packet, which is only contained in the first fragment.

If your machine is the only connection to an external network, then you can tell the Linux kernel to reassemble all fragments that pass through it by compiling the kernel with `IP: always defragment` set to Y. This sidesteps the issue neatly.

Otherwise, it is important to understand how fragments get treated by the filtering rules. Any filtering rule that asks for information we don't have will not match. This means that the first fragment is treated like any other packet. Second and further fragments won't be. Thus a rule `-p TCP -s 192.168.1.1` www (specifying a source port of www) will never match a fragment (other than the first fragment). Neither will the opposite rule `-p TCP -s 192.168.1.1 !` www.

However, you can specify a rule specifically for second and further fragments using the -f flag. Obviously, it is illegal to specify a TCP or UDP port, ICMP type, ICMP code, or TCP SYN flag in such a fragment rule.

It is also possible to specify that a rule does not apply to second and further fragments by preceding the -f with !.

Usually it is considered safe to let second and further fragments through, since filtering will effect the first fragment and thus prevent reassembly on the target host. However, bugs have been known to allow machines to crash simply by sending fragments. Your call.

Note for network-heads: Malformed packets (TCP, UDP, and ICMP packets too short for the firewalling code to read the ports or ICMP code and type) are treated as fragments as well. Only TCP fragments starting at position 8 are explicitly dropped by the firewall code (a message should appear in the syslog if this occurs).

As an example, the following rule will drop any fragments going to 192.168.1.1:

```
# ipchains -A output -f -D 192.168.1.1 -j DENY
#
```

Filtering Side Effects

OK, so now we know all the ways we can match a packet using a rule. If a packet matches a rule, the following things happen:

- The byte counter for that rule is increased by the size of the packet (header and all).
- The packet counter for that rule is incremented.
- If the rule requests it, the packet is logged.

- If the rule requests it, the packet's Type of Service field is changed.
- If the rule requests it, the packet is marked (not in 2.0 kernel series).
- The rule target is examined to decide what to do to the packet next.

I'll address these in order of importance.

Specifying a Target A *target* tells the kernel what to do with a packet that matches a rule. `ipchains` uses -j (think "jump-to") for the target specification.

The simplest case is when there is no target specified. This type of rule (often called an accounting rule) is useful for simply counting a certain type of packet. Whether this rule matches or not, the kernel simply examines the next rule in the chain. For example, to count the number of packets from 192.168.1.1, we could do this:

```
# ipchains -A input -s 192.168.1.1
#
```

(Using ipchains -L -v we can see the byte and packet counters associated with each rule).

There are six special targets. The first three, `ACCEPT`, `REJECT` and `DENY` are fairly simple. `ACCEPT` allows the packet through. `DENY` drops the packet as if it had never been received. `REJECT` drops the packet but (if it's not an ICMP packet) generates an ICMP reply to the source to tell it that the destination was unreachable.

The next one, `MASQ`, tells the kernel to masquerade the packet. For this to work, your kernel needs to be compiled with IP Masquerading enabled. For details on this, see the Masquerading-HOWTO in Chapter 12 and the "Differences between `ipchains` and `ipfwadm`" section later in this chapter. This target is only valid for packets traversing the forward chain.

The other major special target is `REDIRECT`, which tells the kernel to send a packet to a local port instead of wherever it was heading. This can only be specified for rules specifying TCP or UDP as their protocol. Optionally, a port (name or number) can be specified following -j REDIRECT, which will cause the packet to be redirected to that particular port, even if it was addressed to another port. This target is only valid for packets traversing the `input` chain.

The final special target is `RETURN`, which is identical to falling off the end of the chain immediately (see the "Setting Policy" section later in this chapter).

Any other target indicates a user-defined chain (as described in the "Operations on Masquerading" section later in this chapter). The packet will begin traversing the rules in that chain. If that chain doesn't decide the fate of the packet, then once traversal on that chain has finished traversal resumes on the next rule in the current chain.

Consider two (silly) chains in Figure 14.2: `input` (the built-in chain) and `Test` (a user-defined chain).

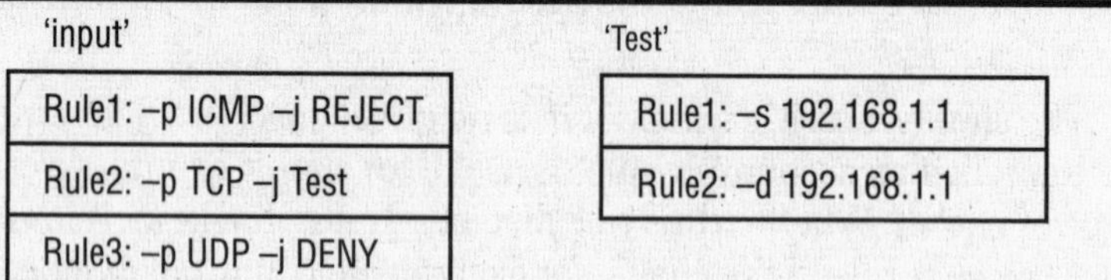

FIGURE 14.2: A built-in chain and a user-defined chain

Consider a TCP packet coming from 192.168.1.1, going to 1.2.3.4. It enters the `input` chain and gets tested against Rule1 - no match. Rule2 matches and its target is `Test`, so the next rule examined is the start of `Test`. Rule1 in `Test` matches but doesn't specify a target, so the next rule is examined, Rule2. This doesn't match, so we have reached the end of the chain. We return to the `input` chain, where we had just examined Rule2, so we now examine Rule3, which doesn't match either.

The packet path is shown in Figure 14.3.

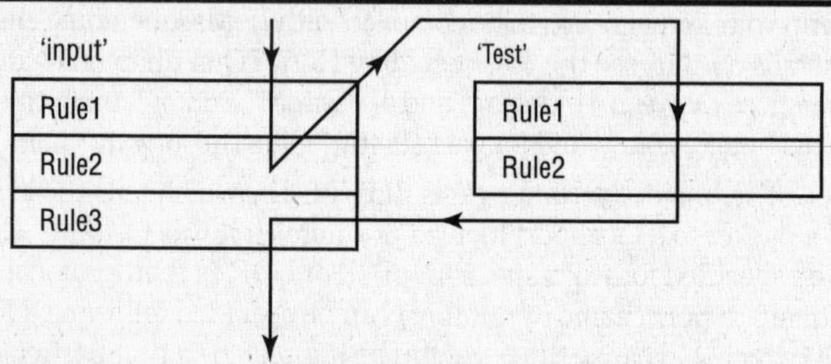

FIGURE 14.3: The packet path

See the "How to Organize Your Firewall Rules" section later in this chapter for ways to use user-defined chains effectively.

Logging Packets A side effect of matching a rule is that you can have the matching packet logged using the -l flag. You will usually not want this for routine packets, but it is a useful feature if you want to look for exceptional events.

The kernel logs this information and looks like:

```
Packet log: input DENY eth0 PROTO=17 192.168.2.1:53
192.168.1.1:1025 L=34 S=0x00 I=18 F=0x0000 T=254
```

This log message is designed to be terse and contain technical information useful only to networking gurus, but it can be useful to the rest of us. It breaks down like so:

input The chain that contained the rule that matched the packet, causing the log message.

DENY What the rule said to do to the packet. If this is "-" then the rule didn't effect the packet at all (an accounting rule).

eth0 The interface name. Because this was the input chain, it means that the packet came in eth0.

PROTO=17 The packet was protocol 17. A list of protocol numbers is given in `/etc/protocols`. The most common are 1 (ICMP), 6 (TCP), and 17 (UDP).

192.168.2.1 The packet's source IP address was 192.168.2.1.

:53 The source port was port 53. Looking in `/etc/services` shows that this is the domain port (that is, this is probably an DNS reply). For UDP and TCP, this number is the source port. For ICMP, it's the ICMP type. For others, it will be 65535.

192.168.1.1 The destination IP address.

:1025 The destination port was 1025. For UDP and TCP, this number is the destination port. For ICMP, it's the ICMP code. For others, it will be 65535.

L=34 The packet was a total of 34 bytes long.

S=0x00 The Type of Service field (divide by 4 to get the Type of Service as used by ipchains).

I=18 The IP ID.

F=0x0000 The 16-bit fragment offset plus flags. A value starting with 0x4 or 0x5 means that the Don't Fragment bit is set. 0x2 or 0x3 means the More Fragments bit is set; expect more fragments after this. The rest of the number is the offset of this fragment, divided by 8.

T=254 The Time to Live of the packet. One is subtracted from this value for every hop; it usually starts at 15 or 255.

On standard Linux systems, this kernel output is captured by `klogd` (the kernel logging daemon) which hands it to `syslogd` (the system logging daemon). The `/etc/syslog.conf` controls the behavior of `syslogd`, by specifying a destination for each facility (in our case, the facility is kernel) and level (for `ipchains`, the level used is info).

For example, my (Debian) `/etc/syslog.conf` contains two lines which match kern.info:

```
kern.*                    -/var/log/kern.log
*.=info;*.=notice;*.=warn;\
   auth,authpriv.none;\
   cron,daemon.none;\
   mail,news.none         -/var/log/messages
```

These mean that the messags are duplicated in `/var/log/kern.log` and `/var/log/messages`. For more details, see `man syslog.conf`.

Manipulating the Type of Service There are four seldom-used bits in the IP header, called the Type of Service (TOS) bits. They effect the way packets are treated; the four bits are Minimum Delay, Maximum Throughput, Maximum Reliability, and Minimum Cost. Only one of these bits is allowed to be set. Rob van Nieuwkerk, the author of the TOS-mangling code, puts it as follows:

> **Especially the "Minimum Delay" is important for me. I switch it on for "interactive" packets in my upstream (Linux) router. I'm behind a 33k6 modem link. Linux prioritizes packets in 3 queues. This way I get acceptable interactive performance while doing bulk downloads at the same time. (It could even be better if there wasn't such a big queue in the serial driver, but latency is kept down 1.5 seconds now.)**

NOTE

Obviously, you have no control over incoming packets; you can only control the priority of packets leaving your box. To negotiate priorities with the other end, a protocol like RSVP (which I know nothing about, so don't ask me) must be used.

The most common use is to set telnet and ftp control connections to Minimum Delay and FTP data to Maximum Throughput. This would be done as follows:

```
ipchains -A output -p tcp -d 0.0.0.0/0 telnet -t 0x01 0x10
ipchains -A output -p tcp -d 0.0.0.0/0 ftp -t 0x01 0x10
ipchains -A output -p tcp -s 0.0.0.0/0 ftp-data \ -t 0x01 0x08
```

The -t flag takes two extra parameters, both in hexadecimal. These allow complex twiddling of the TOS bits: The first mask is ANDed with the packet's current TOS, and then the second mask is XORed with it. If this is too confusing, just use the following table:

TOS Name	Value	Typical Uses
Minimum delay	0x01 0x10	ftp, telnet
Maximum throughput	0x01 0x08	ftp-data
Maximum reliability	0x01 0x04	Snmp
Minimum cost	0x01 0x02	nntp

Andi Kleen goes on to point out the following (mildly edited for posterity):

> **Maybe it would be useful to add a reference to the txqueuelen parameter of ifconfig to the discussion of TOS bits. The default device queue length is tuned for ethernet cards, on modems it is too long and makes the 3 band scheduler (which queues based on TOS) work suboptimally. It is a good idea to set it to a value between 4-10 on modem or single b channel ISDN links; on bundled devices an longer queue is needed. This is a 2.0 and 2.1 problem, but in 2.1 it is an ifconfig flag (with recent nettools), while in 2.0 it requires source patches in the device drivers to change.**

So, to see maximal benifits of TOS manipulation for modem PPP links, do `ifconfig $1 txqueuelen` in your `/etc/ppp/ip-up script`. The number to use depends on the modem speed and the amount of buffering in the modem; here's Andi to set me straight again:

> **The best value for a given configuration needs experiment. If the queues are too short on a router then packets will get dropped. Also, of course one gets benefits even without TOS rewriting, just that TOS rewriting helps to give the benefits to non-cooperating programs (but all standard Linux programs are cooperating).**

Marking a Packet This allows complex and powerful interactions with Alexey Kuznetsov's new Quality of Service implementation, as well as the mark-based forwarding in later 2.1 series kernels. More news as it comes to hand. This option is ignored altogether in the 2.0 kernel series.

Operations on an Entire Chain A very useful feature of `ipchains` is the ability to group related rules into chains. You can call the chains whatever you want, as long as the names don't clash with the built-in chains (`input`, `output`, and `forward`) or the targets (MASQ, REDIRECT, ACCEPT, DENY, REJECT, or RETURN). I suggest avoiding upper-case labels entirely, since I may use these for future extensions. The chain name can be up to 8 characters long.

Creating a New Chain Let's create a new chain. Because I am such an imaginative fellow, I'll call it `test`.

```
# ipchains -N test
#
```

It's that simple. Now you can put rules in it as detailed previously.

Deleting a Chain Deleting a chain is simple as well.

```
# ipchains -X test
#
```

Why -X? Well, all the good letters were taken.

There are a couple of restrictions to deleting chains: they must be empty (see "Flushing a Chain" next) and they must not be the target of any rule. You can't delete any of the three built-in chains.

Flushing a Chain There is a simple way of emptying all rules out of a chain, using the -F command.

```
# ipchains -F forward
#
```

If you don't specify a chain, then all chains will be flushed.

Listing a Chain You can list all the rules in a chain by using the -L command.

```
# ipchains -L input
Chain input (refcnt = 1): (policy ACCEPT)
target  prot  opt   source          destination  ports
ACCEPT  icmp  ----- anywhere        anywhere     any
# ipchains -L test
Chain test (refcnt = 0):
target  prot  opt   source          destination  ports
DENY    icmp  ----- localnet/24     anywhere     any
#
```

The `refcnt` listed for `test` is the number of rules that have `test` as their target. This must be zero (and the chain be empty) before this chain can be deleted.

If the chain name is omitted, all chains are listed, even empty ones.

There are three options that can accompany -L. The -n (numeric) option is very useful as it prevents `ipchains` from trying to lookup the IP addresses, which (if you are using DNS like most people) will cause large delays if your DNS is not set up properly or you have filtered out DNS requests. It also causes ports to be printed out as numbers rather than names.

The -v option shows you all the details of the rules, such as the packet and byte counters, the TOS masks, the interface, and the packet mark. Otherwise these values are omitted. For example:

```
# ipchains -v -L input
Chain input (refcnt = 1): (policy ACCEPT)
 pkts  bytes  target  prot  opt    tosa  tosx
   10    840  ACCEPT  icmp  -----  0xFF  0x00
 ifname  mark  source    destination  ports
 lo            anywhere  anywhere     any
```

Note that the packet and byte counters are printed out using the suffixes K, M, and G for 1000, 1,000,000, and 1,000,000,000 respectively. Using the -x (expand numbers) flag as well prints the full numbers, no matter how large they are.

Resetting (Zeroing) Counters It is useful to be able to reset the counters. This can be done with the -Z (zero counters) option. For example:

```
# ipchains -v -L input
Chain input (refcnt = 1): (policy ACCEPT)
 pkts bytes target     prot opt   tosa tosx
   10   840 ACCEPT     icmp ----- 0xFF 0x00
 ifname  mark  source    destination  ports
 lo            anywhere  anywhere     any
# ipchains -Z input
# ipchains -v -L input
Chain input (refcnt = 1): (policy ACCEPT)
 pkts bytes target     prot opt   tosa tosx
    0     0 ACCEPT     icmp ----- 0xFF 0x00
 ifname  mark  source    destination  ports
 lo            anywhere  anywhere     any
#
```

The problem with this approach is that sometimes you need to know the counter values immediately before they are reset. In the previous example, some packets could pass through between the -L and -Z commands. For this reason, you can use the -L and -Z together, to reset the counters while reading them. Unfortunately, if you do this you can't operate on a single chain; you have to list and zero all the chains at once.

```
# ipchains -L -v -Z
Chain input (policy ACCEPT):
 pkts bytes target     prot opt   tosa tosx
   10   840 ACCEPT     icmp ----- 0xFF 0x00
 ifname  mark  source    destination  ports
 lo            anywhere  anywhere     any

Chain forward (refcnt = 1): (policy ACCEPT)
Chain output (refcnt = 1): (policy ACCEPT)
Chain test (refcnt = 0):
    0     0 DENY       icmp ----- 0xFF 0x00   ppp0
    localnet/24                anywhere               any
# ipchains -L -v
Chain input (policy ACCEPT):
 pkts bytes target     prot opt   tosa tosx
   10   840 ACCEPT     icmp ----- 0xFF 0x00
 ifname  mark  source    destination  ports
 lo            anywhere  anywhere     any

Chain forward (refcnt = 1): (policy ACCEPT)
Chain output (refcnt = 1): (policy ACCEPT)
```

```
Chain test (refcnt = 0):
    0     0 DENY       icmp ----- 0xFF 0x00  ppp0
    localnet/24            anywhere              any
#
```

Setting Policy In the "Specifying a Target" section earlier in this chapter, we glossed over what happens when a packet hits the end of a built-in chain when we discussed how a packet walks through chains. In this case, the policy of the chain determines the fate of the packet. Only built-in chains (`input`, `output`, and `forward`) have policies, because if a packet falls off the end of a user-defined chain traversal resumes at the previous chain.

The policy can be any of the first four special targets: ACCEPT, DENY, REJECT, or MASQ. MASQ is only valid for the `forward` chain.

It is also important to note that a RETURN target in a rule in one of the built-in chains is useful to explicitly target the chain policy when a packet matches a rule.

Operations on Masquerading

There are several parameters you can tweak for IP Masquerading. They are bundled with `ipchains` because it's not worth writing a separate tool for them (although this will change).

The IP Masquerading command is -M; and it can be combined with -L to list currently masqueraded connections or with -S to set the masquerading parameters.

The -L command can be accompanied by -n (show numbers instead of hostnames and port names) or -v (show deltas in sequence numbers for masqueraded connection, just in case you care).

The -S command should be followed by three timeout values, each in seconds: for TCP sessions, for TCP sessions after a FIN packet, and for UDP packets. If you don't want to change any of these values, simply give a value of 0.

The default values are listed in `/usr/include/net/ipmasq.h`, currently 15 minutes, 2 minutes, and 5 minutes respectively.

The most common value to change is the first one, for FTP. (See the "FTP Nightmares" section later in this chapter.)

Note the problems with setting masquerading timeouts listed in the "Common Problems" section later in this chapter.

Checking a Packet

Sometimes you want to see what happens when a certain packet enters your machine. `ipchains` has the -C command to allow this, using the exact same routines that the kernel uses to diagnose real packets.

You specify which chain to test the packet on by following the -C argument with its name. Whereas the kernel always starts traversing on the `input`, `output`, or `forward` chains, you are allowed to begin traversing on any chain for testing purposes.

The details of the packet are specified using the same syntax used to specify firewall rules. In particular, a protocol (-p), source address (-s), destination address (-d), and interface (-i) are compulsory. If the protocol is TCP or UDP, then a single source and a single destination port must be specified and an ICMP type and code must be specified for the ICMP protocol (unless the -f flag is specified to indicate a fragment rule, in which case these options are illegal).

If the protocol is TCP (and the -f flag is not specified), the -y flag may be specified to indicate that the test packet should have the SYN bit set.

Here is an example of testing a TCP SYN packet from 192.168.1.1 port 60000 to 192.168.1.2 port www, coming in the eth0 interface, entering the `input` chain (this is a classic incoming WWW connection initiation):

```
# ipchains -C input -p tcp -y -i eth0 -s 192.168.1.1 60000 \
                                   -d 192.168.1.2 www
packet accepted
#
```

Multiple Rules at Once and Watching What Happens

Sometimes a single command line can result in multiple rules being effected. This is done in two ways. First, if you specify a hostname which resolves (using DNS) to multiple IP addresses, `ipchains` will act as if you had typed multiple commands with each combination of addresses.

So if the hostname `www.foo.com` resolves to three IP addresses and the hostname `www.bar.com` resolves to two IP addresses, then the command `ipchains -A input -j reject -s www.bar.com -d www.foo.com` would append six rules to the `input` chain.

The other way to have `ipchains` perform multiple actions is to use the bidirectional flag (-b). This flag makes `ipchains` behave as if you had typed the command twice; the second time with the -s and -d arguments reversed. So, to avoid forwarding either to or from 192.168.1.1, you could do the following:

```
# ipchains -b -A forward -j reject -s 192.168.1.1
#
```

Personally, I don't like the -b option much; if you want convenience, see the "Using `ipchains-save`" section later in this chapter.

The -b option can be used with the insert (-I), delete (-D, but not the variation which takes a rule number), append (-A), and check (-C) commands.

Another useful flag is -v (verbose), which prints out exactly what `ipchains` is doing with your commands. This is useful if you are dealing with commands that may effect multiple rules. For example, here we check the behavior of fragments between 192.168.1.1 and 192.168.1.2.

```
# ipchains -v -b -C input -p tcp -f \
                    -s 192.168.1.1 -d 192.168.1.2 -i lo
  tcp opt   ---f- tos 0xFF 0x00  via lo
    192.168.1.1  -> 192.168.1.2    * ->   *
packet accepted
  tcp opt   ---f- tos 0xFF 0x00  via lo
    192.168.1.2  -> 192.168.1.1    * ->   *
packet accepted
#
```

Useful Examples

I have a dial-up PPP connection (`-i ppp0`). I grab news (`-p TCP -s news.virtual.net.au nntp`) and mail (`-p TCP -s mail.virtual .net.au pop-3`) every time I dial up. I use Debian's FTP method to update my machine regularly (`-p TCP -y -s ftp.debian.org.au ftp-data`). I surf the Web through my ISP's proxy while this is going on (`-p TCP -d proxy.virtual.net.au 8080`) but hate the ads from `doubleclick.net` on the Dilbert archive (`-p TCP -y -d 199.95.207.0/24` & `-p TCP -y -d 199.95.208.0/24`).

I don't mind people trying to ftp to my machine while I'm online (`-p TCP -d $LOCALIP ftp`), but I don't want anyone outside pretending to have the IP address of my internal network (`-s 192.168.1.0/24`). This is commonly called IP spoofing, and there is a better way to protect yourself from it in the 2.1.*x* kernels and above (see the "How Do I Set Up IP Spoof Protection" section later in this chapter).

This setup is fairly simple, because there are currently no other boxes on my internal network.

I don't want any local process (i.e., Netscape, Lynx, etc.) to connect to `doubleclick.net`:

```
# ipchains -A output -d 199.95.207.0/24 -j REJECT
# ipchains -A output -d 199.95.208.0/24 -j REJECT
#
```

Now I want to set priorities on various outgoing packets (there isn't much point in doing it on incoming packets). Since I have a fair number of these rules, it makes sense to put them all in a single chain, called `ppp-out`.

```
# ipchains -N ppp-out
# ipchains -A output -i ppp0 -j ppp-out
#
```

Minimum delay for Web traffic & telnet.

```
# ipchains -A ppp-out -p TCP -d proxy.virtual.net.au 8080 \
                          -t 0x01 0x10
# ipchains -A ppp-out -p TCP -d 0.0.0.0 telnet -t 0x01 0x10
#
Low cosr for ftp data, nntp, pop-3:
# ipchains -A ppp-out -p TCP -d 0.0.0.0/0 ftp-data \
                          -t 0x01 0x02
# ipchains -A ppp-out -p TCP -d 0.0.0.0/0 nntp -t 0x01 0x02
# ipchains -A ppp-out -p TCP -d 0.0.0.0/0 pop-3 -t 0x01 0x02
#
```

There are a few restrictions on packets coming in the ppp0 interface. Let's create a chain called ppp-in:

```
# ipchains -N ppp-in
# ipchains -A input -i ppp0 -j ppp-in
#
```

Now, no packets coming in `ppp0` should be claiming a source address of 192.168.1.*, so we log and deny them:

```
# ipchains -A ppp-in -s 192.168.1.0/24 -l -j DENY
#
```

I allow UDP packets in for DNS (I run a caching nameserver that forwards all requests to 203.29.16.1, so I expect DNS replies from them only), incoming ftp, and return ftp-data only (which should only be going to a port above 1023 and not the X11 ports around 6000).

```
# ipchains -A ppp-in -p UDP -s 203.29.16.1 \
                   -d $LOCALIP dns -j ACCEPT
```

```
# ipchains -A ppp-in -p TCP -s 0.0.0.0/0 ftp-data \
                -d $LOCALIP 1024:5999 -j ACCEPT
# ipchains -A ppp-in -p TCP -s 0.0.0.0/0 ftp-data \
                 -d $LOCALIP 6010: -j ACCEPT
# ipchains -A ppp-in -p TCP -d $LOCALIP ftp -j ACCEPT
#
```

Finally, local-to-local packets are OK:

```
# ipchains -A input -i lo -j ACCEPT
#
```

Now, my default policy on the `input` chain is DENY, so everything else gets dropped:

```
# ipchains -P input DENY
#
```

NOTE

I wouldn't set up my chains in this order as packets might get through while I'm setting up. It's safer usually to set the policy to DENY first, then insert the rules. Of course, if your rules require DNS lookups to resolve hostnames, you could be in trouble.

Using ipchains-save

Setting up firewall chains just the way you want them and then trying to remember the commands you used so you can do them next time is a pain.

So, `ipchains-save` is a script which reads your current chains setup and saves it to a file. For the moment I'll keep you in suspense with regards to what `ipchains-restore` does.

`ipchains-save` can save a single chain or all chains (if no chain name is specified). The only option currently permitted is -v that prints the rules (to `stderr`) as they are saved. The policy of the chain is also saved for `input`, `output`, and `forward` chains.

```
$ ipchains-save > my_firewall
Saving 'input'.
Saving 'output'.
Saving 'forward'.
Saving 'ppp-in'.
Saving 'ppp-out'.
$
```

Using ipchains-restore

`ipchains-restore` restores chains as saved with `ipchains-save`. It can take two options: -v , which describes each rule as it is added, and -f, which forces flushing of user-defined chains if they exist, as described below.

If a user-defined chain is found in the `input`, `ipchains-restore` checks to see if that chain already exists. If it does, then you will be prompted as to whether the chains should be flushed (cleared of all rules) or whether restoring this chain should be skipped. If you specified -f on the command line, you will not be prompted; the chain will be flushed.

You must be root to run this script; it uses `ipchains` to attempt to restore the rules.

For example:

```
# ipchains-restore < my_firewall
Restoring 'input'.
Restoring 'output'.
Restoring 'forward'.
Restoring 'ppp-in'.
Chain 'ppp-in' already exists. Skip or flush? [S/f]? s
Skipping 'ppp-in'.
Restoring 'ppp-out'.
Chain 'ppp-out' already exists. Skip or flush? [S/f]? f
Flushing 'ppp-out'.
#
```

MISCELLANEOUS

This section contains all the information and FAQs that I couldn't fit inside the structure above.

How to Organize Your Firewall Rules

This process requires some thought. You can try to organize them to optimize speed (minimize the number of rule-checks for the most common packets) or to increase manageability.

If you have an intermittent link, say a PPP link, you might want to set the first rule in the `input` chain to be set to `-i ppp0 -j DENY` at boot time, then have something like this in your `ip-up` script:

```
# Re-create the 'ppp-in' chain.
ipchains-restore -f < ppp-in.firewall
```

```
# Replace DENY rule with jump to ppp-handling chain.
ipchains -R input 1 -i ppp0 -j ppp-in
```

Your ip-down script would look like:

```
ipchains -R input 1 -i ppp0 -j DENY
```

What Not to Filter Out

There are some things you should be aware of before you start filtering out everything you don't want.

ICMP Packets

ICMP packets are used (among other things) to indicate failure for other protocols (such as TCP and UDP); "Destination-unreachable" packets in particular. Blocking these packets means that you will never get "Host unreachable" or "No route to host" errors; any connections will just wait for a reply that never comes. This is irritating but rarely fatal.

A worse problem is the role of ICMP packets in MTU discovery. All good TCP implementations (Linux included) use MTU discovery to figure out what is the largest packet that can get to a destination without being fragmented. (Fragmentation slows performance, especially when occasional fragments are lost.) MTU discovery works by sending packets with the "Don't Fragment" bit set, and then sending smaller packets if it gets an ICMP packet indicating "Fragmentation needed but DF set" (fragmentation-needed). This is a type of "Destination-unreachable" packet, and if it is never received, the local host will not reduce MTU and performance will be abysmal or non-existent.

TCP Connections to DNS (Nameservers)

If you're trying to block outgoing TCP connections, remember that DNS doesn't always use UDP; if the reply from the server exceeds 512 bytes, the client uses a TCP connection (still going to port number 53) to get the data.

This can be a trap because DNS will mostly work if you disallow such TCP transfers; you may experience strange long delays and other occasional DNS problems if you do.

If your DNS queries are always directed at the same external source (either directly by using the nameserver line in `/etc/resolv.conf` or by using a caching nameserver in forward mode), then you need only allow TCP connections to port `domain` on that nameserver from the local `domain` port (if using a caching nameserver) or from a high port (1023) if using `/etc/resolv.conf`.

FTP Nightmares

The classic packet filtering problem is FTP. FTP has two modes; the traditional one is called active mode and the more recent one is called passive mode. Web browsers usually default to passive mode, but command-line FTP programs usually default to active mode.

In active mode, when the remote end wants to send a file (or even the results of an `ls` or `dir` command), it tries to open a TCP connection to the local machine. This means you can't filter out these TCP connections without breaking active FTP.

If you have the option of using passive mode, then fine; passive mode makes data connections from client to server, even for incoming data. Otherwise, it is recommended that you only allow TCP connections to ports above 1024 and not between 6000 and 6010 (6000 is used for X Windows).

Filtering Out the Ping of Death

Linux boxes are now immune to the famous Ping of Death, which involves sending an illegally-large ICMP packet that overflows buffers in the TCP stack on the receiver and causes havoc.

If you are protecting boxes that might be vulnerable, you could simply block ICMP fragments. Normal ICMP packets aren't large enough to require fragmentation, so you won't break anything except big pings. I have heard (unconfirmed) reports that some systems required only the last fragment of an oversize ICMP packet to corrupt them, so blocking only the first fragment is not recommended.

While the exploit programs I have seen all use ICMP, there is no reason that TCP or UDP fragments (or an unknown protocol) could not be used for this attack, so blocking ICMP fragments is only a temporary solution.

Filtering Out Teardrop and Bonk

Teardrop and Bonk are two attacks (mainly against Microsoft Windows NT machines) that rely on overlapping fragments. Having your Linux router do defragmentation or disallowing all fragments to your vulnerable machines are the other options.

Filtering Out Fragment Bombs

Some less reliable TCP stacks are said to have problems dealing with large numbers of fragments of packets when they don't receive all the fragments. Linux does not have this problem. You can filter out fragments (that might break legitimate uses) or compile your kernel with IP: always defragment set to Y (only if your Linux box is the only possible route for these packets).

Changing Firewall Rules

There are some timing issues involved in altering firewall rules. If you are not careful, you can let packets through while you are halfway through your changes. A simplistic approach is to do the following:

```
# ipchains -I input 1 -j DENY
# ipchains -I output 1 -j DENY
# ipchains -I forward 1 -j DENY
```

... make changes ...

```
# ipchains -D input 1
# ipchains -D output 1
# ipchains -D forward 1
#
```

This drops all packets for the duration of the changes.

If your changes are restricted to a single chain, you might want to create a new chain with the new rules and then replace (-R) the rule that pointed to the old chain with one that points to the new chain. Then you can delete the old chain. This replacement will occur atomically.

How Do I Set Up IP Spoof Protection?

IP spoofing is a technique where a host sends out packets that claim to be from another host. Since packet filtering makes decisions based on this source address, IP spoofing is used to fool packet filters. It is also used to hide the identity of attackers using SYN attacks, Teardrop, Ping of Death, and the like (don't worry if you don't know what they are).

The best way to protect from IP spoofing is called Source Address Verification; it is done by the routing code and not firewalling at all. Look for a file called `/proc/sys/net/ipv4/conf/all/rpfilter`. If this exists, then turning on Source Address Verification at every boot is the right solution for you. To do that, insert the following lines somewhere in your init scripts before any network interfaces are initialized (for example, Debian users would put them in /etc/init.d/netbase if they are not already there):

```
# This is the best method: turn on Source Address
# Verification and get spoof protection on all current
# and future interfaces.
if [ -e /proc/sys/net/ipv4/conf/all/rp_filter ]; then
 echo -n "Setting up IP spoofing protection..."
 for f in /proc/sys/net/ipv4/conf/*/rp_filter; do
   echo 1 > $f
 done
 echo "done."
else
 echo PROBLEMS SETTING UP SPOOFING PROTECTION. BE WORRIED.
 echo "CONTROL-D will exit this shell and continue startup."
 echo
 # Start a single user shell on the console
 /sbin/sulogin $CONSOLE
fi
```

If you cannot do this, you can manually insert rules to protect every interface. This requires knowledge of each interface. The 2.1 kernels automatically reject packets claiming to come from the 127.* addresses (reserved for the local loopback interface, lo).

For example, say we have three interfaces, eth0, eth1, and ppp0. We can use ifconfig to tell us the address and netmask of the interfaces. Say eth0 was attached to a network 192.168.1.0 with netmask 255.255.255.0, eth1 was attached to a network 10.0.0.0 with netmask 255.0.0.0, and ppp0 connected to the Internet (where any address except the reserved private IP addresses are allowed), we would insert the following rules:

```
# ipchains -A input -i eth0 -s ! 192.168.1.0/255.255.255.0 \
                           -j DENY
# ipchains -A input -i ! eth0 -s 192.168.1.0/255.255.255.0 \
                           -j DENY
# ipchains -A input -i eth1 -s ! 10.0.0.0/255.0.0.0 -j DENY
# ipchains -A input -i ! eth1 -s 10.0.0.0/255.0.0.0 -j DENY
#
```

This approach is not as good as the Source Address Verification approach, because if your network changes you have to change your firewalling rules to keep up.

If you are running a 2.0 series kernel, you might want to protect the loopback interface as well, using a rule like this:

```
# ipchains -A input -i ! lo -s 127.0.0.0/255.0.0.0 -j DENY
#
```

Advanced Projects

There is a userspace library I have written that is included with the source distribution called `libfw`. It uses the ability of IP Chains 1.3 and above to copy a packet to userspace (using the `IPFIREWALLNETLINK` config option).

Things such as stateful inspection (I prefer the term dynamic firewalling) can be implemented in userspace using this library. Other nifty ideas include controlling packets on a per user basis by doing a lookup in a userspace daemon. This should be pretty easy.

The mark capability of the firewalls is underutilized; it could easily be used to represent a priority for the Quality of Service code, which would make it simple to control packet priorities.

Future Enhancements

Firewalling and NAT are being redesigned for 2.3. Plans and discussions are available on the `netdev` archive. These enhancements should clear up many outstanding usability issues (really, firewalling and masquerading shouldn't be this hard) and allow growth for far more flexible firewalling.

Common Problems

ipchains -L freezes! You're probably blocking DNS lookups; it will eventually time out. Try using the -n (numeric) flag to `ipchains`, which suppresses the lookup of names.

Masquerading/forwarding doesn't work! Make sure that packet forwarding is enabled (in recent kernels it is disabled by default, meaning that packets never even try to traverse the forward chain). You can override this (as root) by typing

```
# echo 1 > /proc/sys/net/ipv4/ip_forward
#
```

If this works for you, you can put this somewhere in your bootup scripts so it is enabled every time; you'll want to set up your firewalling before this command runs, though, otherwise there's an opportunity for packets to slip through.

Wildcard interfaces don't work! There was a bug in versions 2.1.102 and 2.1.103 of the kernel (and some old patches I produced) which made ipchains commands that specified a wildcard interface (such as `-i ppp+`) fail.

This is fixed in recent kernels, and in the 2.0.34 patch on the Web site. You can also fix it by hand in the kernel source by changing line 63 or so in `include/linux/ipfw.h`:

```
#define IP_FW_F_MASK 0x002F /* All possible flag bits
                               mask  */
```

This should read 0x003F. Fix this and recompile the kernel.

TOS doesn't work! This was my mistake: setting the Type of Service field did not actually set the Type of Service in kernel versions 2.1.102 through 2.1.111. This problem was fixed in 2.1.112.

`ipautofw` and `ipportfw` don't work! For 2.0.*x*, this is true; I haven't time to create and maintain a jumbo patch for ipchains and ipautofw/ipportfw.

For 2.1.*x*, download Juan Ciarlante's `ipmasqadm` from `http://juanjox.linuxhq.com/` and use it exactly as you would have used `ipautofw` or `ipportfw`, except instead of `ipportfw` you type `ipmasqadm portfw`, and instead of `ipautofw` you type `ipmasqadm autofw`.

xosview is broken! Upgrade to version 1.6.0 or above, which doesn't require any firewall rules at all for 2.1.*x* kernels. This seems to have broken again in the 1.6.1 release; but it's not my fault!.

Segmentation fault with -j REDIRECT! This was a bug in `ipchains` version 1.3.3. Please upgrade.

I can't set masquerading timeouts! True (for 2.1.*x* kernels) up to 2.1.123. In 2.1.124, trying to set the masquerading time-outs causes a kernel lockup (change `return` to `ret =` on line 1328 of `net/ipv4/ipfw.c`). In 2.1.125, it works fine.

I want to firewall IPX! So do a number of others, it seems. My code only covers IP, unfortunately. On the good side, all the hooks are there to firewall IPX! You just need to write the code; I will happily help where possible.

Differences between IPCHAINS and IPFWADM

Some of these changes are a result of kernel changes and some a result of `ipchains` being different from `ipfwadm`.

- Many arguments have been remapped; capitals now indicates a command and lower-case now indicates an option.
- Arbitrary chains are supported, so even built-in chains have full names instead of flags (for example, input instead of -I).
- The -k option has vanished; use ! -y.
- The -b option actually inserts/appends/deletes two rules, rather than a single bidirectional rule.
- The -b option can be passed to -C to do two checks (one in each direction).
- The -x option to -l has been replaced by -v.
- Multiple source and destination ports are not supported anymore. Hopefully being able to negate the port range will somewhat make up for that.
- Interfaces can only be specified by name (not address). The old semantics got silently changed in the 2.1 kernel series anyway.
- Fragments are examined, not automatically allowed through.
- Explicit accounting chains have been done away with.
- Arbitrary protocols over IP can be tested for.
- The old behavior of SYN and ACK matching (which was previously ignored for non-TCP packets) has changed; the SYN option is not valid for non-TCP-specific rules.
- Counters are now 64-bit on 32-bit machines, not 32-bit.
- Inverse options are now supported.
- ICMP codes are now supported.
- Wildcard interfaces are now supported.

- TOS manipulations are now sanity-checked; the old kernel code would silently stop you from (illegally) manipulating the Must Be Zero TOS bit; ipchains now returns an error if you try, as well as for other illegal cases.

Quick-Reference Table

NOTE

Masquerading is specified by -j MASQ; it is completely different from -j ACCEPT and (unlike `ipfwadm`) is not treated as merely a side effect. Mainly, command arguments are UPPER CASE and option arguments are lower case.

IPFWADM	IPCHAINS	NOTES

`-A [both]`	`-N acct`
	`& -I 1 input -j acct`
	`& -I 1 output -j acct`
	`& acct`
		Create an acct chain and have output and input packets traverse it

`-A in`	`input`	A rule with no target
`-A out`	`output`	A rule with no target
`-F`	`forward`	Use this as `[chain]`
`-I`	`input`	Use this as `[chain]`
`-O`	`output`	Use this as `[chain]`
`-M -L`	`-M -L`	
`-M -S`	`-M -S`	
`-a policy`	`-A [chain] -j POLICY`	(but see `-r` and `-m`)
`-d policy`	`-D [chain] -j POLICY`	(but see `-r` and `-m`)
`-i policy`	`-I 1 [chain] -j POLICY`	(but see `-r` and `-m`)
`-l`	`-L`	
`-z`	`-Z`	
`-f`	`-F`	
`-p`	`-P`	

IPFWADM	IPCHAINS	NOTES
-c	-C	
-S	-s	Only takes on port or range, not multiples
-D	-d	Only takes on port or range, not multiples
-V	<none>	Use -I [name]
-W	-I	
-b	-b	Now actually makes 2 rules
-e	-v	
-k	! -y	Doesn't work unless -p tcp also specified
-m	-j MASQ	
-n	-n	
-o	-l	
-r [redirpt]	-j REDIRECT [redirpt]	
-t	-t	
-v	-v	
-x	-x	
-y	-y	Doesn't work unless -p also specified

Examples of Translated ipfwadm Commands

Old command: `ipfwadm -F -p deny`; New command: `ipchains -P forward DENY`

Old command: `ipfwadm -F -a m -S 192.168.0.0/24 -D 0.0.0.0/0`; New command: `ipchains -A forward -j MASQ -s 192.168.0.0/24 -d 0.0.0.0/0`

Old command: `ipfwadm -I -a accept -V 10.1.2.1 -S 10.0.0.0/8 -D 0.0.0.0/0`; New command: `ipchains -A input -j ACCEPT -i eth0 -s 10.0.0.0/8 -d 0.0.0.0/0`

NOTE

There is no equivalent for specifying interfaces by address; use the interface name. On this machine, 10.1.2.1 corresponds to eth0.

Using the ipfwadm-wrapper-script

The `ipfwadm-wrapper` shell script should be a plug-in replacement of `ipfwadm` for backward compatibility with `ipfwadm` 2.3a.

The only feature it can't really handle is the -V option. When this is used, a warning is given. If the -W option is also used, the -V option is ignored. Otherwise, the script tries to find the interface name associated with that address, using `ifconfig`. If that fails (such as for an interface that is down), then it will exit with an error message.

This warning can be suppressed by either changing the -V to a -W or directing the standard output of the script to `/dev/null`.

If you should find any mistakes in this script, or any changes between the real ipfwadm and this script, please report a bug to me: send an email to `ipchains@wantree.com.au` with "BUG-REPORT" in the subject. Please list your old version of `ipfwadm` (`ipfwadm -h`), your version of `ipchains` (`ipchains --version`), and the version of the `ipfwadm wrapper script` (`ipfwadm-wrapper --version`). Also send the output of `ipchains-save`. Thanks in advance.

Mix `ipchains` with this `ipfwadm-wrapper` script at your own peril.

Thanks

Many thanks have to go to Michael Neuling, who wrote the first releasable cut of the IP chains code while working for me. Public apologies for nixing his result-caching idea, which Alan Cox later proposed and I have finally begun implementing, having seen the error of my ways.

Thanks to Alan Cox for his 24-hour email tech support and encouragement.

Thanks to all the authors of the `ipfw` and `ipfwadm` code, especially Jos Vos. Standing on the shoulders of giants and all that... This applies to Linus Torvalds and all the kernel and userspace hackers as well.

Thanks to the diligent beta testers and bughunters, especially Jordan Mendelson, Shaw Carruthers, Kevin Moule, Dr. Liviu Daia, Helmut Adams, Franck Sicard, Kevin Littlejohn, Matt Kemner, John D. Hardin, Alexey Kuznetsov, Leos Bitto, Jim Kunzman, Gerard Gerritsen, Serge Sivkov, Andrew Burgess, Steve Schmidtke, Richard Offer, Bernhard Weisshuhn, and Pavel Krauz for beating sense into me on the TCP DNS stuff.

PART V
LINUX ON THE DESKTOP

Chapter 15

GNOME User's Guide

Introducing GNOME

GNOME is a user-friendly desktop environment that enables users to easily use and configure their computers. GNOME includes a panel (for starting applications and displaying status), a desktop (where data and applications can be placed), a set of standard desktop tools and applications, and a set of conventions that make it easy for applications to cooperate and be consistent with each other. Users of other operating systems or environments should feel right at home using the powerful graphics-driven environment GNOME provides.

GNOME is completely open source (free software), with freely available source code developed by hundreds of programmers around the world. If you would like to learn more about the GNOME project please visit the GNOME Web site at `http://www.gnome.org`.

GNOME has a number of advantages for users. GNOME makes it easy to use and configure applications without using text-only interfaces.

GNOME is highly configurable, enabling you to set your desktop the way you want it to look and feel. GNOME's Session Manager remembers previous settings, so once you've set things the way you like they'll stay that way. GNOME supports many human languages, and you can add more without changing the software. GNOME even supports several drag-and-drop protocols for maximum interoperability with applications that aren't GNOME compliant.

GNOME also has a number of advantages for developers which indirectly also help users. Developers don't need to purchase an expensive software license to make their commercial application GNOME compliant. In fact, GNOME is vendor neutral—no component of the interface is controlled solely by one company or restricted from modification and redistribution. GNOME applications can be developed in a variety of computer languages, so you're not stuck with a single language. GNOME uses the Common Object Request Broker Architecture (CORBA) to allow software components to interoperate seamlessly, regardless of the computer language in which they are implemented or even what machine they are running on. Finally, GNOME runs on a number of Unix-like operating systems, including Linux.

GNOME is an acronym for the GNU Network Object Model Environment, so GNOME is a part of the larger GNU project. The GNU Project started in 1984 to develop a completely free Unix-like operating system. If you'd like to learn more about the GNU project you can read about it at `http://www.gnu.org`.

About This Guide

This user's guide is designed to help you find your way around GNOME with ease. Both new and experienced computer users can benefit from this guide. If you're new to GNOME, or even computers, you'll gain an idea of how to use your desktop. If you're an advanced user, you can work with expert tips which will help you to become familiar with GNOME.

Although this was written originally in English, there are many translations of the guide available now or in the near future. If you would like to have this guide in another language you should check your operating system distribution or visit the GNOME Web site to find out more information on translation.

GNOME QUICK START

Figure 15.1 shows an example of GNOME running. GNOME is very configurable, so your screen may look quite different.

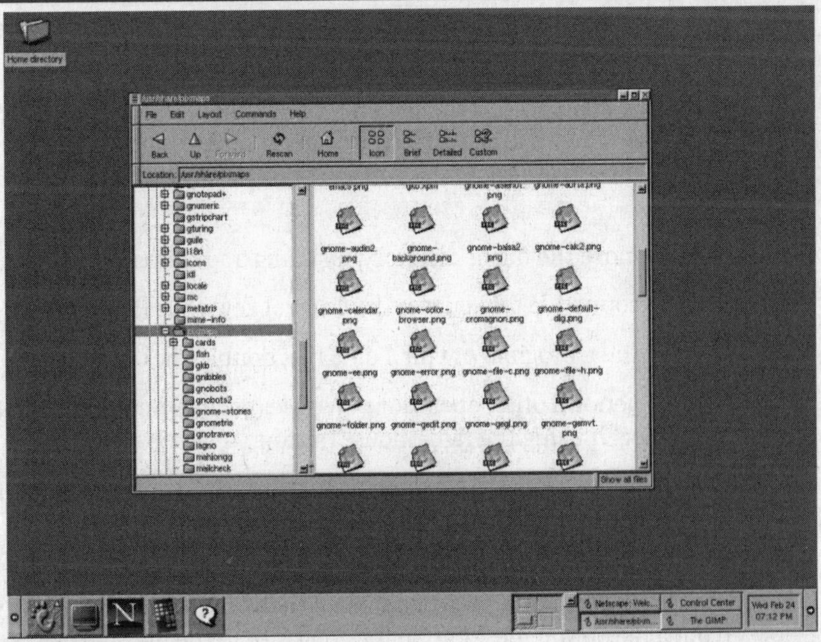

FIGURE 15.1: Sample GNOME display

The long bar at the bottom of Figure 15.1 is a GNOME Panel that contains a collection of useful panel applets and menus. Panel applets are tiny programs designed to be placed in a panel; for example, the clock applet on the far right shows the current time. The arrows on each side of the panel hide (and unhide) the panel.

The button in the panel containing a stylized foot is the Main Menu button. Just click the Main Menu button and you'll see a menu of preloaded applications and actions, including a logout command.

The rest of the screen space is called the *desktop*. Just place on your desktop the items you use most often and you can double-click an item (with the left mouse button) to use it. When you double-click the item, the following will happen:

- If the item is a program, that program will start.
- If the item is data, the appropriate program will start with that data loaded.
- If the item is a directory, the file manager application will start and show the contents of that directory. Your desktop will probably have a folder icon labelled "Home Directory." Double-clicking it will start a file manager at your home directory.

The file manager application lets you manipulate your files. The left side of its window shows directories, and the right side shows the selected directory's contents. You can manipulate your files in the following ways:

- To move the file or directory, just drag-and-drop it.
- To copy a file, hold down the Control key while dragging.
- To run a program or edit a data file, double-click it.
- To perform other operations on a file (such as rename or delete), select it using the right mouse button.
- To select more than one item at a time, click the items after the first one while holding down the Shift key.

You can easily move or copy files between directories by starting two file manager applications, each one showing a different directory. If you want to put a file on your desktop, simply drag it from the file manager onto the desktop. In fact, dragging and dropping items onto other items generally "does the right thing" in GNOME, making it easy to get work done.

GNOME is very configurable; for example, you can have multiple panels (horizontal and vertical), choose what goes in them, and have them hide automatically. There are many panel applets you can include in your panel. You can also change how the screen looks—later portions of this document tell you how.

GNOME follows several Unix conventions you should be aware of. The left mouse button is used to select and drag items. The right mouse button brings up a menu for the selected object (if a menu applies). Most Unix mice have three buttons, and the middle button is used to paste text (if in a text area) or to move things. If you only have two buttons, press the left and right buttons simultaneously to simulate the middle button. To copy text, use the left button to drag across the text you want to copy, move to the place you want the text to be, and press the middle button.

When an application window is displayed, there will be some buttons in its borders for controlling the window. These include buttons to minimize, maximize, and close the window. Their appearance can be configured and is controlled by a component called a *window manager*.

Two examples of border styles are the Clean style (Figure 15.2) and the ICE style (Figure 15.3):

- In the Clean border style, the underscore is used to minimize, the square is used to maximize (use the whole screen), and the X button is used to close the window.
- In the ICE style, the X button will close the window. Clicking the arrow with the left mouse button minimizes the window, while clicking with the right mouse button shows a menu of other options.

users-guide.sgml

FIGURE 15.2: Clean border style

users-guide.sgml

FIGURE 15.3: ICE border style

If you are using a default installation of GNOME, you may notice that minimizing a window actually causes that window to disappear from your desktop. To regain that window, you may use the GNOME Pager which is located on the panel. The Pager will show you which tasks are running and where they are on your desktops. You will find the application you minimized in the task list on the right side of the GNOME Pager (Figure 15.4). Press the button for that application and it will return to your desktop.

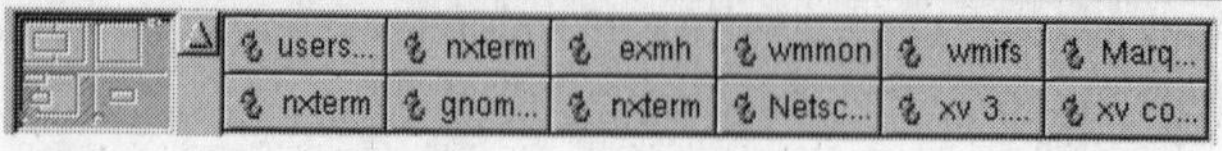

FIGURE 15.4: The GNOME Pager

The following sections go into more detail, describing each component of the system.

WINDOW MANAGERS AND GNOME

About Window Managers

The window manager is the piece of software that controls the windows in the X window environment. The placement, borders, and decorations of any window is managed by the window manager. This is very different from many other operating systems, and the way GNOME deals with window managers is different from other desktop environments.

As stated earlier in this guide, GNOME is not dependent on any one window manager. This means that major parts of your desktop environment will not change when you decide to switch window managers. GNOME works with the window manager to give you the easiest work environment you can have. GNOME does not worry about window placement but gets information from the window manager about their placement. The GNOME Pager will only work with a GNOME-compliant window manager as will drag-and-drop on the desktop.

At the time of this version of the GNOME User's Guide the Enlightenment Window Manager is the only window manager that is 100 percent compliant. There are many other window managers that are partially compliant or are being worked to meet compliance.

Some of the window managers that have partial to full compliance at the time of this version of the GNOME User's Guide are the following:

- Enlightenment (`http://www.enlightenment.org`)
- Icewm (`http://www.kiss.uni-lj.si/~k4fr0235/icewm/`)
- Window Maker (`http://www.windowmaker.org`)
- FVWM (`http://www.fvwm.org/`)

Changing Window Managers

At any time you may change the window manager you are using by utilizing the Window Manager Capplet in the GNOME Control Center. You may read more about this Capplet in the "Window Manager Capplet" section later in this chapter.

NOTE

Keep in mind that the window manager you choose to use may not be compliant with GNOME and you may not benefit from some of GNOME features if you use it.

Using the GNOME Panel

The Panel is the heart of the GNOME interface and acts as a repository for all of your system applications, applets, and the Main menu. The Panel is also designed to be highly configurable. The Panel gives you a place that always contains menus and applications as you want them to be.

The Basics

Using the GNOME Panel is very simple and will come easily to anyone who has used a graphical-based operating system. You can add new panels, add applications to the panel, and add various applets. All of these functions and more will be described in this section.

Using the Main Menu

To start using any preloaded application, press the Main Menu button (Figure 15.5). The Main menu has the picture of the stylized foot that, on first use, is on the bottom left of the screen. You should release the mouse button after pressing the Main Menu button so that you can take advantage of other features (such as right-clicks and drag-and-drop from the menu) in the Main menu.

FIGURE 15.5: The Main Menu button

The Main menu is the starting point for all of the applications on your system. Later in this manual you will learn how to customize the Main menu to suit your work environment, but for now you can use the menu that is established when you install GNOME. The Main menu works like any other menu you might have used in other graphical desktop environments. Simply press the Main Menu button and select from the menu that pops up.

Hiding the Panel

At any time you may hide the GNOME Panel by pressing the Hide button (see Figure 15.6).

FIGURE 15.6: The Hide button

This will hide the GNOME Panel in the direction of the arrow on the Hide button. There are Hide buttons on both sides of a Panel so you can hide it in either direction.

You may decide that you want the Panel to hide on its own when you are not using it. This can be a helpful function if you are unable to run your system in a high resolution. You can find out how to autohide the Panel in "Configuring the Panel" section later in this chapter.

Moving and Adding Panels

Any Panel you have on your desktop can be moved by using the middle mouse button (or by simultaneously pressing the left and right mouse buttons) to drag the panel to the desired edge of your screen. If you do not have a middle mouse button or did not configure your mouse to emulate a middle button, you may also move a Panel by changing its location in the Panel Configuration dialog box. You can read more in the "Configuring the Panel" section later in this chapter.

You may also add a new Panel to your desktop by selecting Add New Panel from the Main Menu ➢ Panel menu. You will be given a choice of Edge or Corner Panels. Both of these Panel types are described below:

Edge Panel An Edge Panel is exactly like the main Panel that starts up with GNOME. By selecting this type of panel, you can add a new Panel to another edge of your screen to give yourself more functionality.

Corner Panel The Corner Panel is a small Panel that will not stretch to the edge of the screen it is on. The Corner Panel will, however, stretch to the extent of icons and applets it contains.

NOTE

The Hide buttons work just a bit differently with Corner Panels. The hide button closest to the edge of your screen will hide the Panel as usual, but the other hide button will send the whole Panel to the opposite edge. When the latter move is made, it will not hide the Panel because it is changing the side of the screen it resides on. If you want to hide it, you will have to press the hide button once again.

At any time you can change the current panel to the opposite type by selecting either the Convert to Edge Panel or the Convert to Corner Panel options from the pop-up menu. The selection that is available depends on which type of panel you right-click. The selection displayed will be the opposite of the current panel.

Adding Applications and Applets to the Panel

Adding Application Launchers

If you would like to add an Application Launcher (an icon that starts a particular application) to the Panel, right-click the Panel and select Add New Launcher from the pop-up menu.

After selecting the Add New Launcher menu item, you will see a dialog box that will allow you to set the properties for the application launcher you wish to add (see Figure 15.7).

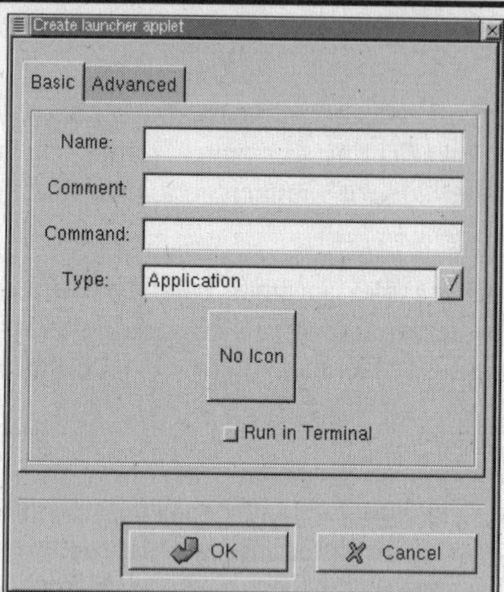

FIGURE 15.7: The Create Launcher dialog box

In the Create launcher applet dialog box, you may add a name for your launcher, include a comment, use the command line to launch the application, and define the application type. You may also press the Icon button and choose an icon to represent the application from the icon picker. If no icon is chosen a default icon will be used.

A quicker method of adding an application launcher to the Panel is to go into the Main menu and right-click an application menu item. You will be given another menu selection which contains Add This Launcher to Panel item. If you select this menu item, it will automatically add a launcher for that application to the Panel in which you invoked the Main menu. At this point, you may right-click the launcher and select the Properties menu item to change any options for that launcher.

Grouping Items with Drawers

If you would like to group a subset of applications together, you can use a Drawer (see Figure 15.8). A Drawer is simply a small menu-like button that sits on your panel, and it groups application launchers together in one place. Once you have placed a Drawer on the Panel you may click it to raise the menu of applications and click again to lower them.

FIGURE 15.8: A Drawer running on the Panel

There are a couple of ways to place a Drawer on your Panel. First, you can right-click the Panel and select Add Drawer from the pop-up menu. Second, if you want a whole subset of menus from the Main menu to become a drawer, you can right-click the title bar of that menu and select the Add This as Drawer to Panel from the pop-up menu.

You can add menus to your Panel in the same way you add Drawers. Menus are very similar to Drawers except that they do not use large icons to represent application launchers; instead, they use a style similar to the Main menu (i.e. small icons and the application name). You can add a menu by right-clicking the title bar of a menu and select the Add This as Menu to Panel from the pop-up menu. You may also add system directories as menus to the Panel by dragging a directory out of the GNOME File Manager and dropping it on the Panel.

Adding Applets

There are many applets which you can add to the Panel. Applets are small applications which can perform tasks within the Panel itself. The applets you can add are covered in more detail in the GNOME documentation. As an example of how to add an applet, you could add another clock applet to your Panel. To add the clock applet (see Figure 15.9) to your Panel:

1. Right-click the Panel.
2. From the pop-up menu, choose the Add New Applet menu item. This will bring up more levels of pop-up menus.
3. Choose the Utility ➤ Clock menu item. The Clock will be added to your Panel.

FIGURE 15.9: The clock applet

To remove the clock applet you added you can right-click the clock and select Remove from Panel from the pop-up menu.

Running Applications

There are many ways to launch applications within GNOME. Remember that one of GNOME's strong points is that it allows you to start and control applications using only an easy-to-use graphical interface. There are many ways to start the applications you wish to use.

As you saw in the previous section, you can use the Main menu to find applications which have been preloaded or that you provided using the Menu Editor. You can read more about the Menu Editor in the "Editing the Main Menu" section later in this chapter.

You can also add application launchers from the Panel (see "Adding Application Launchers" earlier in this chapter).

If you are using the GNOME File Manager you can double-click any executable file and it will run.

You can use the GNOME Run program to launch any application. To use it select the Run Program from the Main menu. This will launch a simple dialog which allows you to type in the command for launching the application. For example, if you wish to start the Emacs editor and it is not in a menu or on your Panel, you may start the GNOME Run Program and type **emacs** in the text box in the dialog box.

Logging Out of GNOME

GNOME has a couple of helpful methods for logging out. You may either use the Logout menu item or the Logout button.

The Logout menu item is the first menu item in the Main menu. Simply select Logout and you will be prompted on whether you would like to log out. Select Yes and your GNOME session will end.

You can add the Logout button to the Panel. This is just another method for logging out, it does not provide you any additional functionality than the Logout menu item other than a pretty button. To add the Logout button to the Panel, right-click the Panel and select Add Logout Button from the pop-up menu. Once the button is there, you may press it to log out.

NOTE

If you are running a window manager that is GNOME compliant, the logout feature will quit the window manager as well as GNOME. If you are not running such a window manager, you will have to end that window manager yourself.

The Logout dialog box (Figure 15.10) will display when you log out of GNOME. This dialog will ask you whether you really want to log out. It also provides you with different methods of quitting GNOME. You have three choices for quitting GNOME. You can Logout (which will simply take you to a terminal), Halt (which will shut down the whole system), or Reboot (which will reboot the whole system).

If you do not want to log out, press the No button, and you will be returned to your GNOME session.

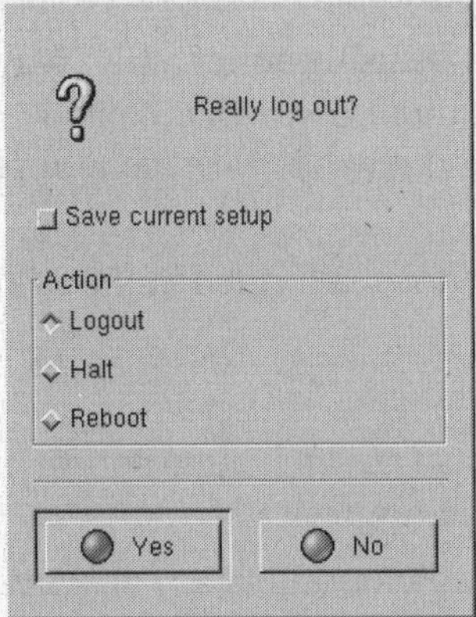

FIGURE 15.10: The Logout dialog box

Within the Logout dialog box there is one option you can choose before you leave GNOME.

If you would like to save your current setup, select the Save Current Setup check box. This will save which programs you have open and the configuration of your Panel.

The GNOME Desktop

The GNOME Desktop provides you with all the functionality of any traditional operating system desktop. You can drag files, programs, and directory folders to the desktop. You can also drag those items back into GNOME-compliant applications.

NOTE

The GNOME Desktop is actually provided by a backend process in the GNOME File Manager. If, for any reason, that backend process has stopped running, you may start the GNOME File Manager again and your desktop will be restored. If you do have to do this, you will not need to keep the GNOME File Manager window open to enable the desktop.

Using the Desktop

Using the desktop is as simple as routinely dragging items you wish to use to the desktop. The default desktop will include a folder of your home directory (/home/[*user name*]). By default, the GNOME File Manager window will also appear for you to access other areas of your system.

To utilize drag-and-drop, you need to be using either a GNOME-compliant application or a Motif application. GNOME is compliant with Motif drag-and-drop, so you will find it works with many applications you already have installed.

All items that are stored on your desktop are located in the following directory:

```
$/home/[user name]/.gnome-desktop/
```

This is helpful to remember when you want an item to appear on your desktop that you can not utilize drag-and-drop with.

Once you have started GNOME, you will notice that any drives you have connected to your system will be shown on your desktop with the appropriate icons. You may mount and access these drives utilizing these icons.

NOTE

You must have permission to mount the device shown on your desktop before you can utilize these icons. You must have the root password to accomplish this. If you do not have this password, you should consult your system administrator.

Gaining mount access can be done quite easily if you have *linuxconf* installed on your machine. Just select the drive you want to access in the Access Local Drive section. From the Options tab, select User Mountable. Your drive will now be mountable by users.

If you do not have *linuxconf,* you must edit your `/etc/fstab` to include user access. This is done by adding user access to the drive. For example, if your fstab file looks like

```
/dev/cdrom /mnt/cdrom iso9660 exec,dev,ro,noauto 0 0
```

add "user" to the fourth column, as follows:

```
/dev/cdrom /mnt/cdrom iso9660 user,exec,dev,ro,noauto 0 0
```

There could be some security risks involved with this, depending on your system and work environment. Please consult your system administrator before making any drive user mountable.

Once you have permission to mount a drive, you may right-click the drive icon on your desktop. This will bring up a small pop-up menu. Select Mount Device to mount it and Eject Device to eject it. Once it is mounted, you may either double-click it or choose Open from the pop-up menu to open a GNOME File Manager window so that you can view the contents of the device.

If you are missing any drives that you might have added to your machine, you may right-click an empty space on the desktop and select Rescan Mountable Devices from the pop-up menu.

Desktop Areas

Desktop areas allow you to keep a well-organized system when you have many tasks to perform at one time. Just like adding a new desk when you have too much stuff for one, desktop areas allow you to move to another area to launch more programs.

GNOME is aware of desktop areas even though they are controlled by another software program called the window manager. You can set the number of desktop areas within the configuration of the window manager you are using. If you are using the default window manager or your window manager has a graphical configuration tool, you may be able to launch it from the Window Manager Capplet. You may read more about this Capplet in the "Window Manager Capplet" section later in this chapter.

NOTE

Most window managers will give you the option of having multiple desktops, which are different from desktop areas. Desktop areas are virtual extensions of one desktop; whereas multiple desktops are actually separate desktops.

The default setup of GNOME is to use desktop areas with only one desktop. This is because in older applications, such as those which use Motif, users can experience problems with some drag-and-drop functionality across desktops.

Other Desktop Menus

You can choose from a few desktop menus in GNOME. These menus are accessed by right- clicking any clean space on the desktop. This will bring up the pop-up menu that contains the following items:

New ➢ Terminal This will launch a new GNOME Terminal window that will automatically navigate to the `~/.gnome-desktop` directory.

New ➢ Directory This allows you to create a new directory on your desktop. This can be a convenient tool to use if you wish to clean up your desktop by placing files in a new directory.

New ➢ Launcher This allows you to place a new application launcher on the desktop. When you select this menu item it will launch an Application Launcher dialog box that allows you to specify which application and its properties.

New ➢ [*application*] Some applications may put items for you in the New menu. For example, the Gnumeric spreadsheet will put a New Gnumeric Spreadsheet menu item in the New menu so you can start up a new spreadsheet easily.

Arrange Icons This will automatically arrange your desktop icons.

Create New Window This will launch a new GNOME File Manager window displaying your Home directory.

Rescan Mountable Devices This will rescan the mountable devices on your machine and display an icon for any new device it might find.

Rescan Desktop This will rescan the files in your `~/.gnome-desktop` directory.

The GNOME File Manager

GNOME includes a file manager that allows you to manipulate the files on your system in a comfortable, powerful, graphical environment. This file manager is known as GMC for GNU Midnight Commander. GMC is based on the Midnight Commander file manager which can be run in a terminal.

Midnight Commander has long been known for its power and ease of use. GMC has taken that power and ease of use from MC and added the GNOME graphical frontend.

As mentioned in the previous chapter, the GNOME File Manager (see Figure 15.11) provides the desktop functionality for GNOME. The GNOME File Manager also provides a place to manipulate files on your system by using the GNOME File Manager window.

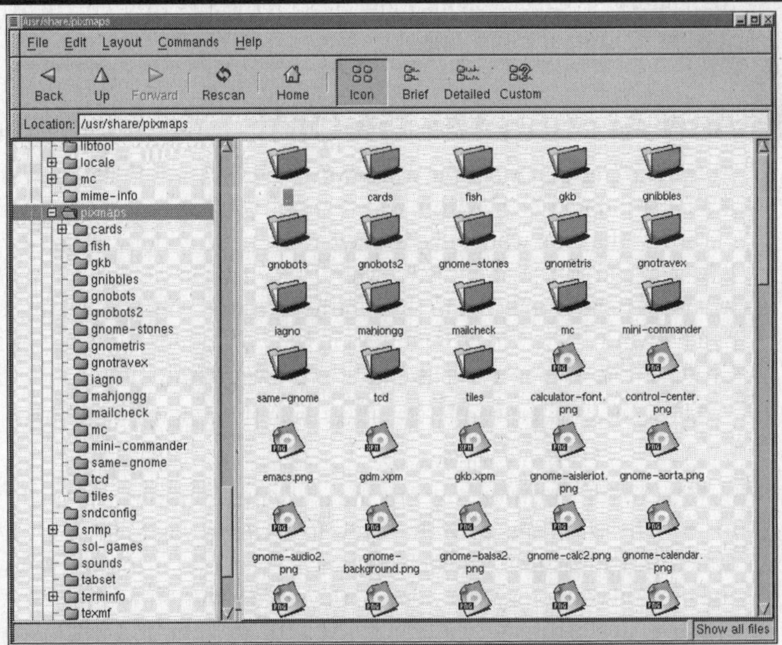

FIGURE 15.11: GNU Midnight Commander—the GNOME File Manager

There are two main windows within the GNOME File Manager. On the left is the tree view which represents all of the directories on your system by their hierarchical position. On the right is the directory window which will show you the contents of the directory that you have selected in the tree view.

To select a directory in the tree view, simply single-click the directory. This will change the main directory view, showing the files in the directory you have chosen. If there are directories contained within the directory, you may click the plus sign in the tree view to expand the directory. You may wish to take advantage of the Icon view and Detailed view in the main file view. The Icon view is the default view and will display large icons for each file. The Brief view shows the files and directories in a list but without any extra information shown.The Detailed view will display a list view of the files in the directory and information about the files. The Custom view is a list view which allows you to select the information you want to view about files.

In the Brief, Detailed, and Custom views, you can click one of the information titles on the top of the window and it will sort the files according to that information. For example, if you want to find the largest files in the directory, you can click the Size title and the files will be sorted by size from largest to smallest. One more click on the Size title will change the sorting from smallest to largest.

Moving Around the GNOME File Manager

Above the tree and main file windows in the GNOME File Manager there is a Location text box. Within this text box you can type the path location of the file that you would like to view in the main window. The GNOME File Manager is also equipped to view FTP sites. To view an FTP site, you will need to be connected to the Internet either through a dial-up account or a network. Type the FTP address in the Location text box and the GNOME File Manager will attempt to connect to the site.

Make sure you type in FTP addresses in the following manner:

```
ftp://[site address]
```

Next to the Location text box are navigation buttons you might wish to use. These buttons with the arrow icons allow you to move within the directories adjacent to the one you are in. The left button will take you to the previous directory you were in, the middle button will take you up one level in the directory hierarchy, and the right button will take you to the next directory if you have just moved backwards.

TIP

You can open a secondary window by using your middle mouse button on any directory. Press the middle mouse button (or both left and right mouse buttons if you have emulation) on a directory in the main window and a new window will open showing the contents of the directory you clicked.

Selecting Files

Selecting files is done with your mouse by clicking the file or files in the GNOME File Manager. The file that is selected will then highlight to show you that it has been selected.There are a couple of ways to select more than one file. One way is to use the "rubber band" select (see Figure 15.12) by clicking and dragging the mouse cursor around several files. This action will produce a small dotted line, the "rubber band," to show you the area in which files will be selected.

If you wish to be more selective about the files you are choosing or the files you need do not reside next to one another, you may use the Control key to keep the files you have selected while you are selecting more. This works by selecting a file, pressing and holding the Control key, and selecting another file. While the Control key is pressed, you will be able to add to the "list" of files that are selected. Once you have selected multiple files by either method, you may copy or move the files.

You may also select all files in a directory by selecting the Select All menu item from the Edit menu.You may also filter your selection by using the Select Files menu item in the Edit menu. Using Select Files will display a simple dialog box which will allow you to type in criteria for your selection. In this field, the symbol * is interpreted as a wildcard (e.g., it matches any string). For example, if you would like to select all files in the directory that start with the letter *D*, you can type **D*** (note that filenames in Unix are case-sensitive).

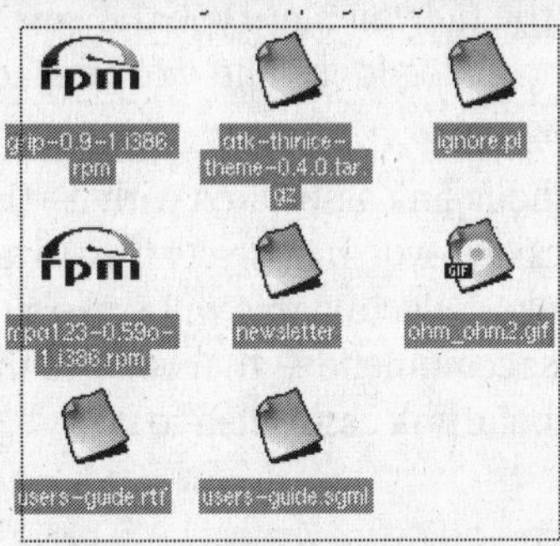

FIGURE 15.12: "Rubber Band Select"

Copying and Moving Files

The default action for drag-and-drop in the GNOME File Manager is to move files. But you can also use drag-and-drop to copy a file by pressing the Shift key while dragging the file(s). This will work the same for any files you drag to the desktop.You may also toggle a menu which lets you decide what action to perform with a drag by using the middle mouse button to drag a file or pressing the Alt Key while dragging a file. Once you release the drag you will get a pop-up menu which contains the options Copy, Move, Link, and Cancel Drag.

Another way to copy or move files is to take advantage of the right-click pop-up menu. Right-click the file you want to copy or move and select Move/Rename or Copy from the pop-up menu. This will bring up a dialog box (see Figure 15.13) in which to perform these tasks.

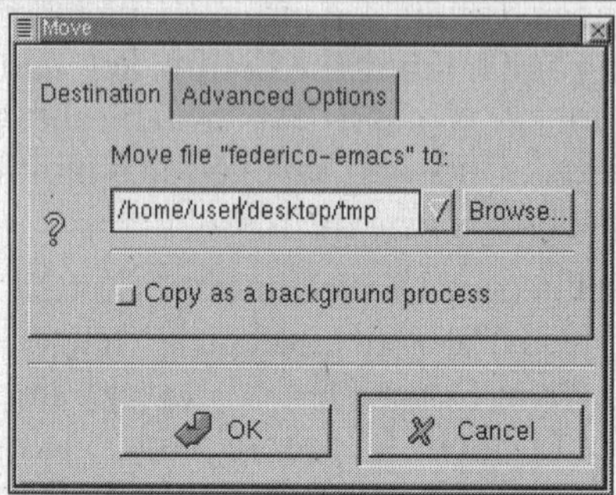

FIGURE 15.13: The Move dialog box

To use the move dialog you simply type in the path where you wish to move the file. If you want to rename the file you may type the new name of the file in the path string. The Copy dialog looks and works exactly the same way as the Move/Rename dialog box.

If the file you are moving has a symbolic link associated with it—that is, a virtual link to where the file actually resides—you may select the Advanced Options tab and select Preserve symlinks. Selecting this will make sure the link is preserved despite the move. It is recommended that you use this method of moving a file if it has a symbolic link associated to it.

Renaming Files

Renaming files in the GNOME File Manager window or on the desktop can be achieved in two ways. One method of renaming a file is to right-click the file and choose the Properties from the pop-up menu. In the File-name text box, you may type in the new name as you wish it to appear (see Figure 15.14).

A shortcut method to rename a file is to slowly double-click the file. Make sure this is slow so you do not launch the file but you simply highlight and then click again. At this point the name of the file will enter into the editing mode, your cursor will change to an editing line, and you can type in the new name.

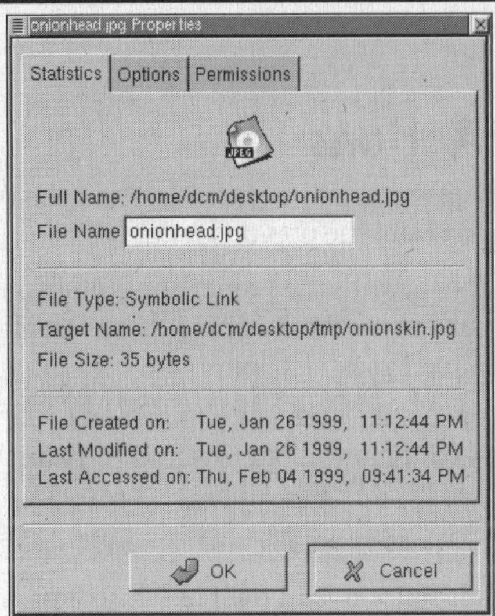

FIGURE 15.14: File properties

Launching Applications From the GNOME File Manager

The GNOME File Manager allows you to launch applications from the main window by simply double-clicking your mouse on a file that has an application associated with it. You can change the way file types are handled by reading the "GNOME Mime Types" section. If the file does not have an associated application, you can right-click the file and select Open with from the pop-up menu. This will bring up a dialog box that allows you to define the application that will launch the file. For example, if you want to edit file names `test.txt` with Emacs (a popular text editor), you can right-click `test.txt` and choose Open With. When you get the Open With dialog box (see Figure 15.15), simply type **emacs** in front of the `test.txt` file name. When you press OK, Emacs will open the file.

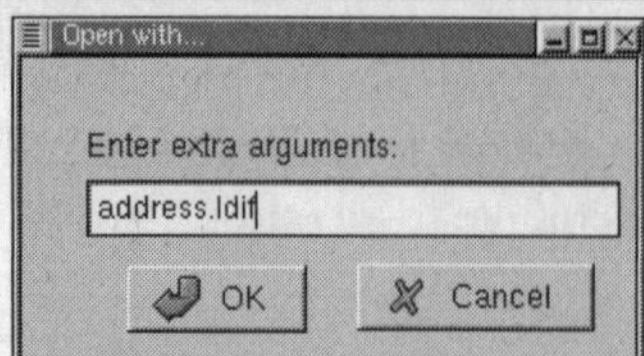

FIGURE 15.15: The Open With dialog box

File Properties and Actions

For any file in the main file display you may right-click it and choose a variety of properties and actions from the pop-up menu:

Open This will open the file with the proper application associated with it. You may read more about editing these associations in the "GNOME Mime Types" section.

Open With You may open a file with any application using this menu item. You may read more about this in the "Launching Applications from the GNOME File Manager" section.

View This will view the file with a basic text viewer.

Edit This will launch an editor to edit the file. The editor launched is determined by the application associated with that file type. You may read more about editing this association in the "GNOME Mime Types" section.

Copy This will copy the file to the clipboard so that it can be pasted elsewhere.

Delete This will delete the file.

Move This will bring up the Move dialog which will allow you to move the file. You can read more about this dialog and moving files in the "Copying and Moving Files" section.

Properties The Properties menu item will launch the Properties dialog box. The Properties dialog box allows you to edit and view the properties for the selected file.

The Properties dialog box (see Figure 15.16) consists of three tabs: Statistics, Options, and Permissions.

Statistics This tab will show you the file information including the name, type, size, and history. You may change the name of the file in the File Name text box.

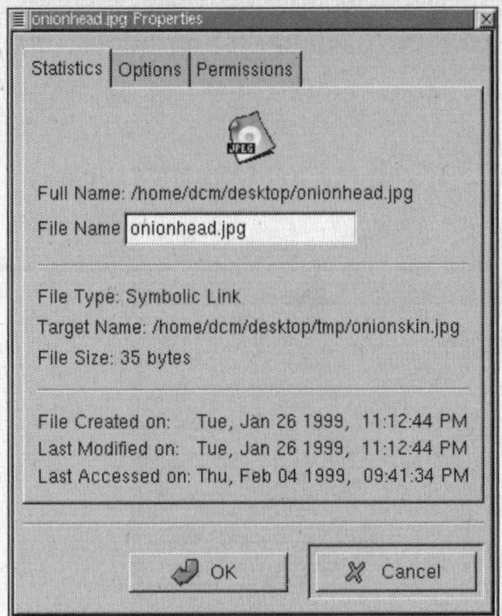

FIGURE 15.16: File properties

Options This tab will allow you to change the action options for the file. You can define how to open, view, and edit the file. If you need to open it in a terminal window, you may select the Needs Terminal to Run check box.

NOTE

If you bring up the Properties dialog box from an icon on the desktop, you will be able to change the icon for that file in the Options tab.

Permissions This tab allows you to change the permissions and ownership of a file if you have access to do so. You may select Read, Write, and Exec Permissions for the User, Group, and Others. You may also set the UID, GID and Sticky, as well as define who owns the file.

Changing Your Preferences in the File Manager

There are many settings you can configure for the GNOME File Manager. These settings may be accessed from the GMC Preferences dialog box. You can launch this dialog box by selecting Preferences from the Edit menu.

The GMC Preferences dialog is divided into five major sections: File Display, Confirmation, Custom View, Caching Optimizations, and VFS.

File Display

The File Display tab (Figure 15.17) allows you to change the way files are displayed in GMC.

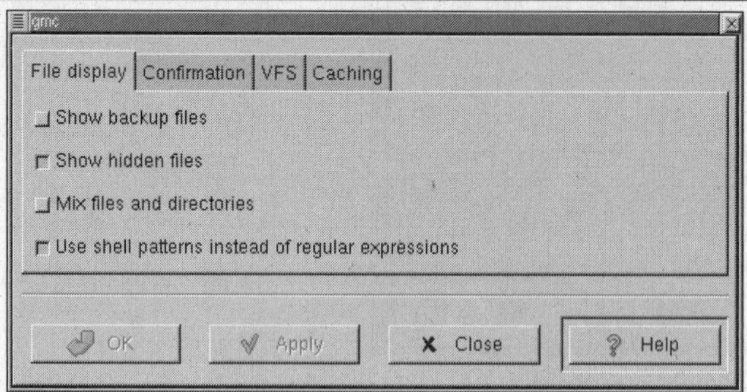

FIGURE 15.17: File Display preferences

Show Backup Files This will show any backup file that is on your system.

Show Hidden Files This will show all "dot files" or files that begin with a dot. This files typically include configuration files and directories.

Mix Files and Directories This option will display files and directories in the order you sort them instead of always having directories shown above files.

Use Shell Patterns Instead of Regular Expressions This option is for advanced users only. If you are unfamiliar with regular expressions, you should not use this option. If you are familiar with how to create regular expressions, you may select this option to use them in your sorts and filters.

Confirmation

This tab (see Figure 15.18) allows you to change which functions ask for your confirmation before continuing.

Confirm When Deleting File This will bring up a confirmation screen before deleting a file.

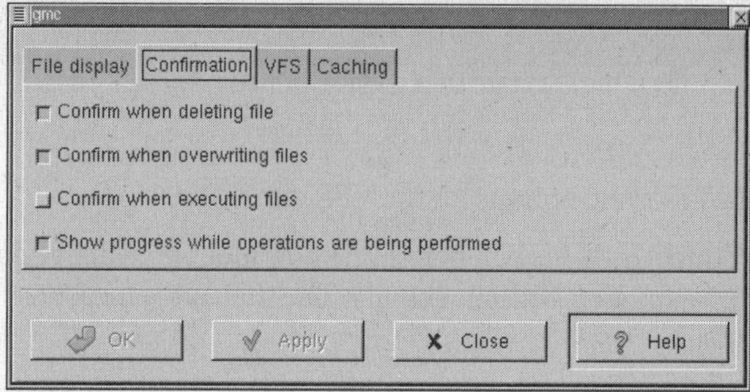

FIGURE 15.18: Confirmation preferences

Confirm When Overwriting Files This will bring up a confirmation screen before overwriting a file.

Confirm When Executing Files This will bring up a confirmation screen before executing a file.

Show Progress While Operations Are Being Performed This will bring up a progress bar while certain operations are being performed such as copying, moving, deleting, etc.

VFS

This tab (see Figure 15.19) allows you to configure the options for your Virtual File System.

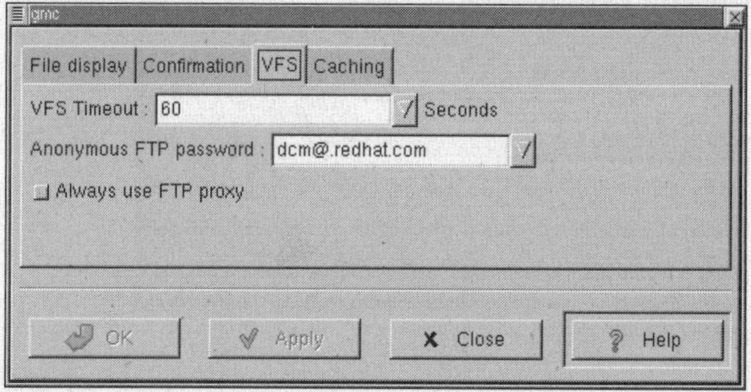

FIGURE 15.19: VFS Preferences

The Virtual File System allows you to manipulate files that are not located on your local file system. There are different versions of the VFS including ftpfs and tarfs. The ftpfs allows you to work on FTP sites while the tarfs gives you access inside `.tar` files.

NOTE

The `.tar` file is the standard Unix archive format

You have the following options on the VFS tab:

VFS Timeout This will determine how long you will be connected to any VFS without activity. The timeout is measured in seconds.

Anonymous FTP Password - This allows you to set a password for logging into anonymous FTP sites. Usually you will want to make this your e-mail address.

Always Use FTP Proxy - If you need to use a proxy to connect to FTP sites, you will want to enable this.

Caching

This tab allows you to configure items that will enhance the speed of GMC by using caching (see Figure 15.20).

Fast Directory Reload This option will store directory information in cache so that it can load faster.

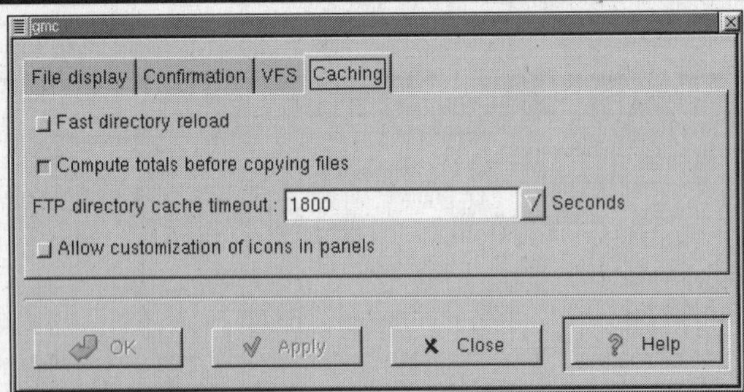

FIGURE 15.20: Caching preferences

NOTE

If you enable the Fast directory reload you may experience problems with not seeing new files that have been added to directories.

Compute Totals Before Copying Files This will make GMC determine the number of files you are copying before it performs the task so that it can give you information about the process as it's happening.

FTP Directory Cache Timeout - This option will keep recently visited FTP site information in cache for the amount of time you specify. The time is measured in seconds.

Allow Customization of Icons in Icon View - This will allow you to change the icons in the icon view by right-clicking them and selecting the Properties menu item. You can always change the icons of items that are on your desktop, but you can only change the icons in the Icon view with this option turned on.

NOTE

Turning on the Allow Customization of Icons in Icon View function may result in a slower system.

Custom View

The Custom View dialog box (see Figure 15.21) allows you to set the way you would like the Custom view to look in the GNOME File Manager.

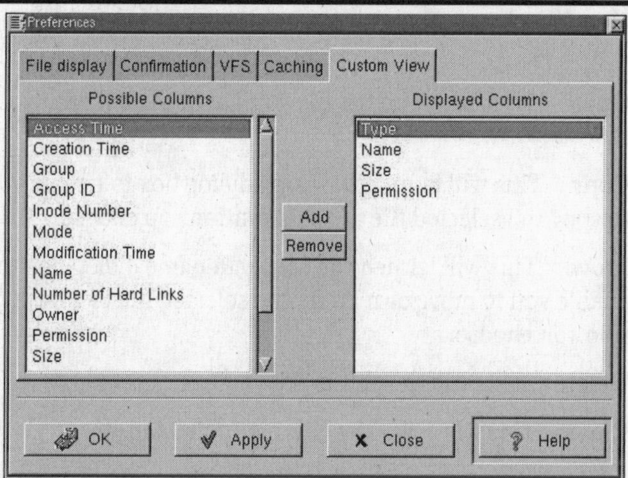

FIGURE 15.21: The Custom View dialog box

There are two main columns in the Custom View tab: Possible Columns and Displayed Columns.

Possible Columns list includes all of the information types that can be displayed. If you would like to include an information type, you may press the Add button and it will be added to the Displayed Columns list.

The Displayed Columns list shows you the current information types that will be included in your Custom View. If you wish to remove any, press the Remove button.

If you would like to re-arrange the items in the Displayed Columns list, drag them to the desired location with your mouse.

Menu Guide to the GNOME File Manager

This section describes each menu item in the GNOME File Manager.

TIP

All menus in the GNOME File Manager are enabled with the tear-away feature. If you would like any menu to "float" on the desktop in its own window, simply select the perforation line at the top of the menu.

File The File Menu contains items associated with files and higher level activity.

New Window This will open a new File Manager Window.

Open This will open the file you have selected with your mouse cursor.

Copy This will launch the Copy dialog box to enable you to copy the selected file to a destination you choose.

Move This will launch the Move/Rename dialog box to enable you to move or rename the selected file to a destination you choose.

Delete This will delete the file you have selected.

Close This will close the GNOME File Manager

Edit The Edit menu contains items that are associated with editing and selecting files.

Select All This will select all of the files in the directory you are currently working with in the GNOME File Manager.

Select Files This will launch a simple dialog box which will allow you to specify a file selection range. For example, if you wish to select all files beginning with the letter *D*, you can simple type **D*** and press OK.

Invert Selection This will invert the current selection. For example, if you have seven files selected in a directory with 10 files, selecting Invert Selection will select the three remaining files and unselect the seven files that were previously selected.

Rescan Directory This will rescan the current directory in case the files in the directory have changed.

Preferences This will launch the Preferences dialog box so that you can customize the GNOME File Manager.

Layout This menu contains items that are associated with the layout in GNOME File Manager.

Sort By This will launch a dialog box which will allow you to select how you wish the files to be sorted in the current directory. You may sort by one of the following: Name, File Type, Size, Time Last Accessed, Time Last Modified, or Time Last Changed.

Filter View This will bring up a simple dialog box which allows you to only view files with certain attributes. For example, if you wish to only view files in the directory that start with the letter *D*, you can type **D*** into the dialog box and press OK. If you wish to see all files again, you will need to launch the Filter View dialog box again and clear the dialog or type **a** *.

Icon View Selecting this will display the files in the main view as large icons.

Partial View Selecting this will display the files in the main view as a list with only file names.

Full View Selecting this will display the files in the main view as a list with all file information.

Custom View The Custom View's main item switches your view to the Custom View which is a list view displaying the information about the files that you specify. To customize the Custom View, you will need to use the Custom View Editor in the Preferences dialog box. You may read more about the Preferences dialog box in the "Changing Your Preferences in the File Manager" section.

Commands The Command menu contains items that are commands to run on files in the GNOME File Manager.

Find File Find File brings up a dialog box that allows you to search for particular files on your system.

Edit Mime Types This option will launch the GNOME Control Center Capplet that allows you to edit mime types for GNOME. Mime types determine, among other things, what application will handle particular file types. You can read more about mime types in the "GNOME Mime Types" section later in this chapter.

Run Command This menu item allows you to run a command from GMC.

Run Command in Panel This menu item lets you run preloaded commands or commands you specify within the directory that you are currently in. These commands include finding SUID or SGID programs as well as other commands.

Exit This will allow you to exit out of the GNOME File Manager.

NOTE

The Exit command will exit all GNOME File Manager processes that include the GNOME Desktop. If you exit, you will lose all functionality on your desktop. This option is not recommended.

A Drag-and-Drop Tour of GNOME

There are many tips and tricks to the desktop in GNOME. The drag-and-drop functionality extends to many areas of GNOME, making it easy to interconnect GNOME in many interesting ways. Following is a series of tips and tricks to using GNOME Drag-and-Drop. This is a good tour of GNOME and will show you how to utilize GNOME to its fullest extent.

Drag a Color onto the Panel Whenever you have a color selector displayed, you may drag a color from the selected color bar to the Panel and it will change the Panel to that color.

Drag a Pixmap to the Background Selector If you would like to change the background to an image, you can drag that image from your GNOME File Manager to the Monitor Image in the Background Capplet of the Control Center, and it will change to that image.

Drag to an Application Many GNOME-compliant applications will accept drag-and-drop. If you would like to open a file in Gnumeric, a GNOME-compliant spreadsheet application, drag the file from the GNOME File Manager onto Gnumeric, and it will open the file. The same is true for applications built using Motif. You may drag a saved URL onto Netscape 4.*x* and it will open the URL. This can be very useful if you are working within the GNOME File Manager and wish to quickly open a file.

Adding an Application Launcher to the Panel If you would like to add an application launcher to the Panel you may drag-and-drop any executable file from the GNOME File Manager or the desktop onto the Panel. This will display the Create Launcher Applet dialog box which will allow you to select a name and an icon for that launcher.

Dragging Files There are many ways to use drag-and-drop to help you manage your system. You can open two GNOME File Manager windows to two different directories, and then drag files between the two windows to copy, move, or link files. You can drag files from the File Manager to the desktop to make it more accessible. Use the middle mouse button or the right and left mouse buttons together to drag a directory folder to the desktop. Choose the link option from the pop-up menu to make a link to the desktop. This will give you a quick way to launch the File Manager to that directory.

Dragging Directories You can drag a directory out of the GNOME File Manger and place it on the Panel. This will create a new menu which allows you easy access to the files in that directory.

You may drag any submenu from the Main menu to the Panel and a new menu launcher is added to the Panel. This allows easier access to that subset of menus.

Configuring the Panel

The GNOME Panel is highly configurable and comes equipped with many graphical tools to help you do the configuration. In this section you will learn how to configure any GNOME Panel the way you would like it.

Global Panel Properties

To start configuring the GNOME panel, right-click the panel and select the Global Properties menu item. You may also press the Main menu button and select the Panel ➢ Global Properties menu item.

This will bring up the Global Panel Configuration dialog box (Figure 15.22). With this dialog box you can set the global properties for all panels you use now and any panels you add in the future.

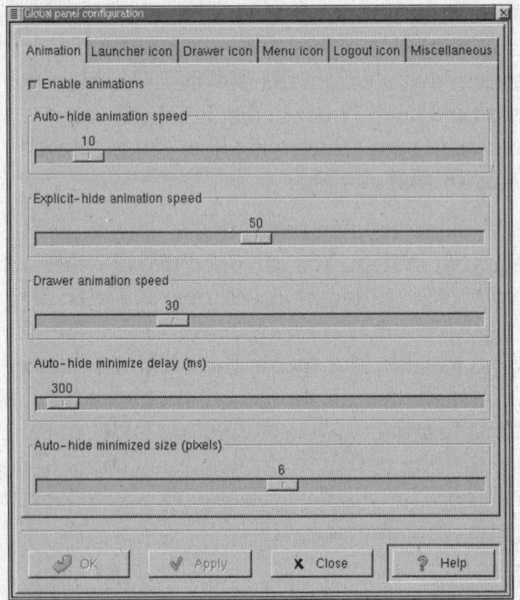

FIGURE 15.22: The Global Panel Configuration dialog box

The Global Panel Configuration dialog box contains six tabs that help you configure the global properties of the GNOME Panel: Animation, Launcher Icon, Drawer Icon, Menu Icon, Logout Icon, and Miscellaneous. Each of these tabs is explained below.

Animation Tab

Enable Animations This allows the animations configurable on this tab to be visible. The animations must be enabled to use the other features of this tab. The default position is on.

Auto-Hide Animation Speed If you have the panel hiding automatically, this will control how fast it occurs.

Explicit-Hide Animation Speed This controls the hide speed when you press the Panel's Hide Button.

Drawer Animation Speed If you use a Drawer panel, this will control how fast the Drawer menu will raise.

Auto-Hide Minimize Delay (ms) If you have the Panel set to minimize automatically, this will allow you to control how much time passes before it minimizes. The Panel will start the time count once the mouse is no longer over it. It will appear again when the mouse is passed to the area it occupies when up. This time is measured in milliseconds.

Auto-Hide Minimized Size (pixels) If you have the Panel hiding automatically, this determines the number of pixels that will show while the Panel is minimized.

Launcher Icon Tab

Tiles Enabled This check box will enable background tiles for all icons on the Panel.

Tile Filename (Up) This is the name and path of the image file you wish to use for the tile in the up position (inactive, not pressed). You may press the Browse button to search for the file. Tiles must be enabled to access this option.

Tile Filename (Down) This is the name and path of the image file you wish to use for the tile in the down position (active, pressed). You may press the Browse button to search for the file. Tiles must be enabled to access this option.

Border Width (Tile Only) This determines the width of the border around an icon. This is very useful if you have an icon that would normally cover up a tile. You can set the border to a smaller size and still be able to see your tile.

Depth (Displacement When Pressed) This determines the depth an icon will displace when pressed. Tiles must be enabled to access this option.

Drawer Icon Tab

Tiles Enabled This check box will enable background tiles for all drawers on the Panel.

Tile Filename (Up) This is the name and path of the image file you wish to use for the tile in the up position (inactive, not pressed). You may press the Browse button to search for the file. Drawer tiles must be enabled to access this option.

Tile Filename (Down) This is the name and path of the image file you wish to use for the tile in the down position (active, pressed). You may press the Browse button to search for the file. Drawer tiles must be enabled to access this option.

Border Width (Tile Only) This determines the width of the border around a tile. Drawer tiles must be enabled to access this option.

Depth (Displacement When Pressed) This determines the depth a tile will displace when pressed. Drawer tiles must be enabled to access this option.

Menu Icon Tab

Tiles Enabled This check box will enable background tiles for the Main Menu button on the Panel.

Tile Filename (Up) This is the name and path of the image file you wish to use for the tile in the up position (inactive, not pressed). You may press the Browse button to search for the file. Menu tiles must be enabled to access this option.

Tile Filename (Down) This is the name and path of the image file you wish to use for the tile in the down position (active, pressed). You may press the Browse button to search for the file. Menu tiles must be enabled to access this option.

Border Width (Tile Only) This determines the width of the border around a tile. Menu tiles must be enabled to access this option.

Depth (Displacement When Pressed) This determines the depth a tile will displace when pressed. Menu tiles must be enabled to access this option.

Logout Icon Tab

Tiles Enabled This checkbox will enable background tiles for all Logout buttons on the Panel.

Tile Filename (Up) This is the name and path of the image file you wish to use for the tile in the up position (inactive, not pressed). You may press the Browse button to search for the file. Logout button tiles must be enabled to access this option.

Tile Filename (Down) This is the name and path of the image file you wish to use for the tile in the down position (active, pressed). You may press the Browse button to search for the file. Logout button tiles must be enabled to access this option.

Border Width (Tile Only) This determines the width of the border around a tile. Logout button tiles must be enabled to access this option.

Depth (Displacement When Pressed) This determines the depth a tile will displace when pressed. Logout button tiles must be enabled to access this option.

Miscellaneous Tab

Tooltips Enabled This enables tooltips for items on the panel. Tooltips are pop-up help dialog boxes that appear when your cursor is over an element on the panel.

Show Small Icons This will enable small icons in the Main menu.

Show... Buttons This will enable three small dots to appear on Main menu items that launch dialog boxes.

Show Popup Menus Outside of Panels This allows pop-up menus to appear away from the Panel when it is on. When toggled off, the pop-ups will appear over the Panel. This can be useful on smaller screens or cluttered desktops.

Keep Menus in Memory This will keep your menus in memory so that they do not rescan for added items. This can increase the speed of GNOME but may also result in you missing new items in your menu that are GNOME-compliant.

Switched Movement This allows launcher buttons on the Panel to switch places with other icons when being moved.

Free Movement (Doesn't Disturb Other Applets) This feature locks the arrangement of your icons on the Panel. This is a good feature to use if you like the way your icons are arranged.

Prompt Before Logout This will bring up a Yes/No dialog box that asks you if you would really like to log out.

Raise Panels on Mouse-Over If you are using a window manager that is not GNOME-compliant, it will not understand its relationship with the Panel. This can cause your Panel to be covered by applications. If you enable this feature you can have the Panel automatically raise when your mouse is over it.

Keep Panel Below Windows If you are using a GNOME-compliant window manager, the window manager will understand its relationship with the Panel. If you choose this feature, the window manager and GNOME will allow applications to appear over the Panel. This can be useful on smaller screens.

Close Drawer If a Launcher Inside It Is Pressed By default, drawers will remain open when you select an item within one. This can be annoying as the drawer will remain open until you close it with a click. With this option selected, drawers will close automatically when you select any item within a drawer.

Applet Padding This changes the amount of space (padding) between icons and applets.

This Panel Properties

Each Panel's properties can be configured individually. To change the configuration of the active Panel, right-click the Panel and select This Panel Properties from the pop-up menu. You may also press the Main Menu button and select the Panel ➢ This Panel Properties. This will bring up the Panel Properties dialog box as shown in Figure 15.23. In this box you can change the properties for the active Panel.

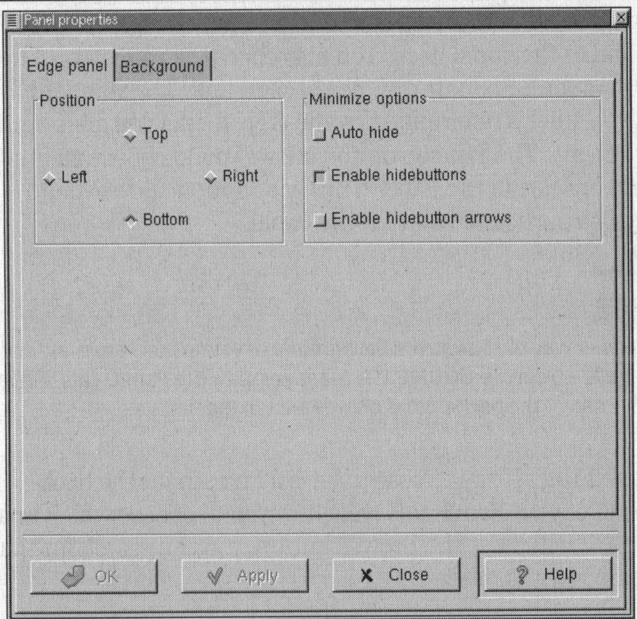

FIGURE 15.23: This Panel Properties dialog box

The Panel Properties dialog box contains two tabs to help you set the active Panel properties: Edge Panel and Background. An explanation for both of these tabs follows.

Edge Panel Tab

Position This changes the position of the Panel on the screen. You may select either Top, Right, Left, or Bottom. The Panel will change position once you have pressed the Apply button.

Minimize Options The options here will enable you to either explicitly hide the Panel yourself using the hide buttons or auto hide when the mouse is not over the Panel. If you choose Auto Hide, you might want to disable the hide buttons here as well. You may also disable the hide button arrows graphics on the Panel as well.

Background Tab

Background These options allow you to change the background of the Panel itself. You may choose, if you wish, to have the standard, Pixmap, or Color background. The standard look for the Panel is determined by the GTK theme you are running at the time. The Pixmap option allows you to choose an image to tile or scale to the Panel. The Color option allows you to specify a particular color for the Panel.

NOTE

An easier way to change the background of your panel is to drag-and-drop an image file from the GNOME File Manager onto the Panel. This will automatically change the background of the Panel to that image.

Image File If you choose to have a Pixmap for the background of your Panel, this will allow you to choose which image to use. If you press the Browse button, you can search for the file you want to use.

Scale Image to Fit Panel This allows a background image to scale to the size of the Panel. If not selected, images will tile to the panel.

Background Color If you choose to have your Panel one color, this button will launch a dialog box that allows you to specify which color to use.

EDITING THE MAIN MENU

The Main menu is a repository for your applications and can be found on the Panel. The Main menu is preloaded with GNOME, but it can be configured to fit your work habits. The Main menu is broken up into two main subdirectories: System menus and User menus. The Menu Editor is available for you to add new applications to the Main menu but you can not add applications to the System menus if you are not the system administrator (root). In this section you will learn how to configure the Main menu with applications you wish to use everyday.

Configuring the Main Menu

If you want to change properties of the Main menu or any other menu you have on your Panel, right-click the menu button and select Properties. This will launch the Menu Properties dialog box as shown in Figure 15.24.

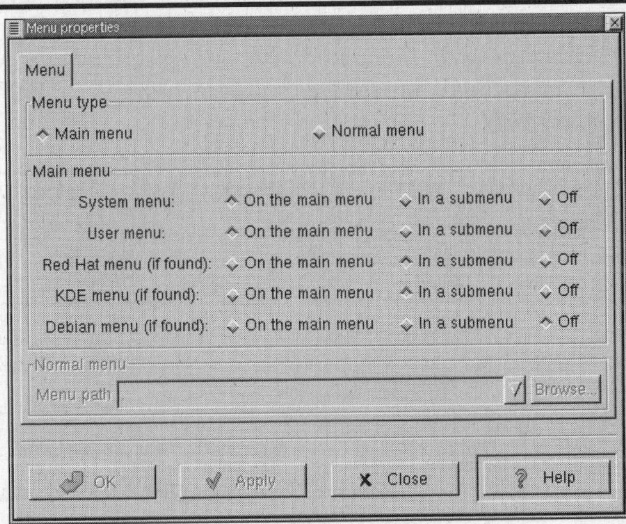

FIGURE 15.24: Menu Properties dialog box

The first selection item in the Menu properties dialog box is Menu Type. This will allow you to change the menu from a Main menu to a Normal Menu.

The other choices in the Menu Properties dialog box are submenu selections for Main menus. These selections allow you to choose what is in your Main menu in a submenu, or off:

System Menus These menu items are the default applications that come with GNOME.

User Menu This contains any menu item you added using the Menu Editor for your user account.

Another Level Menu If you are using the Red Hat Linux build, this is the default set of applications that ship with it.

KDE Menu If you are a user of the Kool Desktop Environment, you may choose to include the applications included in the KDE menus.

Debian Menu If you are using the Debian Linux build, this is the set of applications that ship with it by default.

Using the Menu Editor

The Menu Editor is a configuration tool for the Main menu. It is very useful in setting up your system to your requirements. The Menu Editor is started by clicking the Main Menu Launcher and selecting Settings ➢ Menu Editor from the Main menu. This will launch the Menu Editor as shown in Figure 15.25.

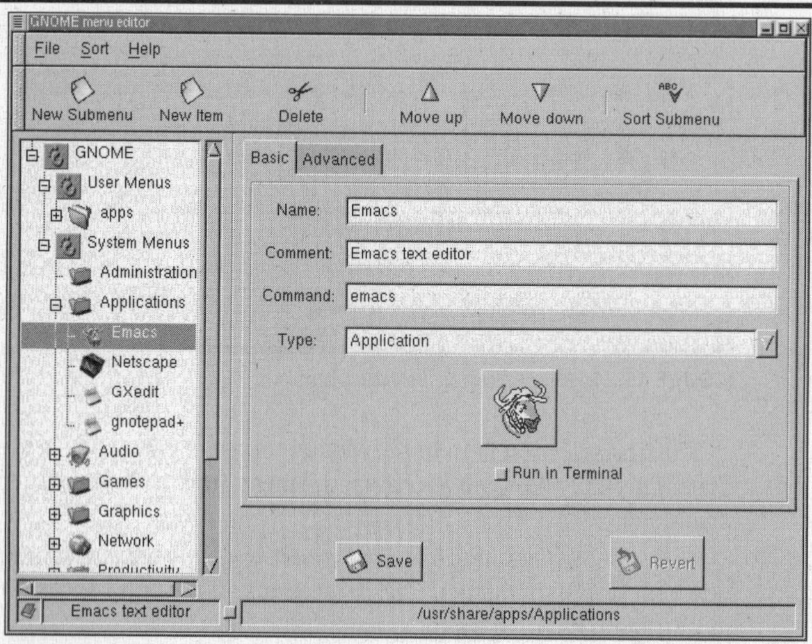

FIGURE 15.25: The Menu Editor

The Menu Editor is divided into two main panels. The left side contains the menu in its default state. The right side contains a tabbed dialog box that allows you to add new applications to the menu.

On the left side in the menu tree, notice that there are two main menu lists, one for User menus and one for System menus. The User menus are for the current user and the System menus are for all users on the system. The prepackaged applications are all located in the System menus.

Within the menu list on the left side you may open and close folders and see what is in your current menu by clicking the small plus signs beside the menus.

Adding a New Menu Item

If you want to add a new menu item, press the New Item button on the toolbar. A new menu item will be placed where the highlighted menu is. If you do not have a menu highlighted, it will be placed at the top of the menu tree. Select the new item and type in the information for the item in the dialog box on the right. Once the information is complete, press the Save button and the new menu item will be inserted where your cursor is on the menu tree on the right. You may then move the menu item by pressing the up or down buttons on the toolbar. You may also move the menu item by dragging it with your left mouse button.

NOTE

Keep in mind that you can not change the System menus unless you are logged in as root. If not, you can only add to and edit the User menus.

Drag-and-Drop in the Main Menu

The Menu Editor supports drag-and-drop functionality which will make your work easier. You may drag applications to the folders you wish them to reside in or re-arrange you folders completely.

If you would like to place a menu item onto the Panel, you can drag-and-drop the item from the menu to the Panel, and it will place a launcher there with all the appropriate properties set for you. If you prefer not to use drag-and-drop, you may also right-click the menu item and choose Add This Launcher to Panel from the pop-up menu.

The GNOME Control Center

The GNOME Control Center (see Figure 15.26) allows you to configure various parts of your system using a collection of tools called *capplets*.

These capplets may be associated with the core set of GNOME applications or other applications for which the developers have written capplets.

Your Control Center may contain more capplets than are documented here, depending on the applications installed on your system.

The Control Center is divided into two main sections: the menu of configurable capplets and the main work space.

Working with the Control Center simply requires you to select a capplet from the menu on the left and double-click it. Once this is done, the workspace will change, allowing you to configure the item.

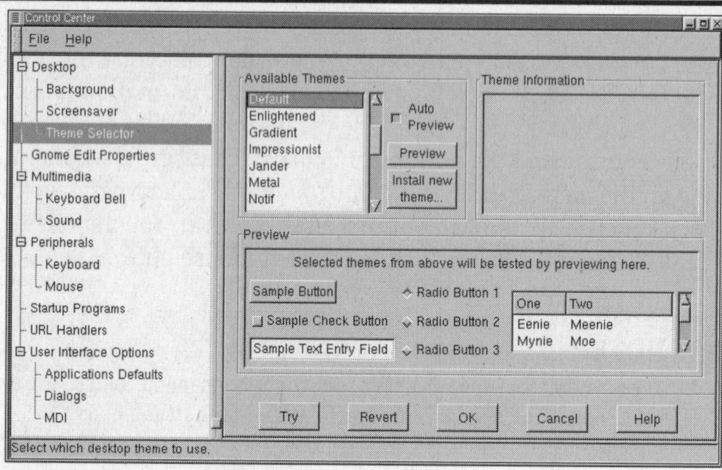

FIGURE 15.26: The GNOME Control Center

You may start the Control Center in one of two ways. To launch the Control Center without any particular active capplet, select the Control Center menu item from the System menu. If you know which capplet you would like to edit, start that capplet by selecting the correct menu item in the Control Center menu.

Desktop Capplets

The Background Properties Capplet

The properties for your background image can be set in the Background Properties capplet (see Figure 15.27) by either selecting a color or an image. If you select a color, you have the option of having solid or gradient colors. If you choose to have gradient colors, you may choose between a vertical or horizontal gradient and you may choose the second color for the gradient to end on.

If you decide to have an image as wallpaper, you may browse for the image you wish to use. Once you have found your image, you need to decide whether you would like to have the image tiled, centered, scaled keeping aspect, or simply scaled. Once you have changed your background properties, you may press the Try button at the bottom of the Control Center to make the change.

If you would like to set the background by any other means, disable this capplet by selecting Disable Background Selection.

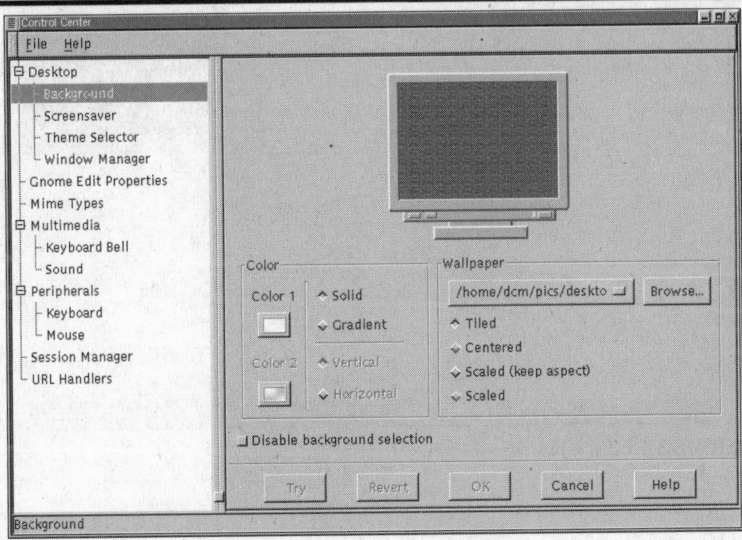

FIGURE 15.27: The Background Properties Capplet

The Screen Saver Capplet

In the Screen Saver capplet (see Figure 15.28), you can change your xscreensaver properties. This capplet contains a list of available screen savers you may choose and a demo screen. Below these two dialogs you will see a set of tools that allow you to change the settings for the global screen saver properties. If the screen saver you choose has particular settings, you can change those by pressing the Settings button that appears below the Screen Saver list.

In the Global Screen Saver Settings section of the capplet, you can change the time, password, and power management properties. You can decide how long you would like the screen saver to wait before starting by typing the number of minutes in the Start After text box. If you would like a password to return to your desktop, click the Require Password button. Your account login password is the password set for the screen saver.

You are also given the option of using power management—if your monitor is capable of it. You may set the time to wait before the monitor is shut off by typing the time in the Shutdown Monitor text box.

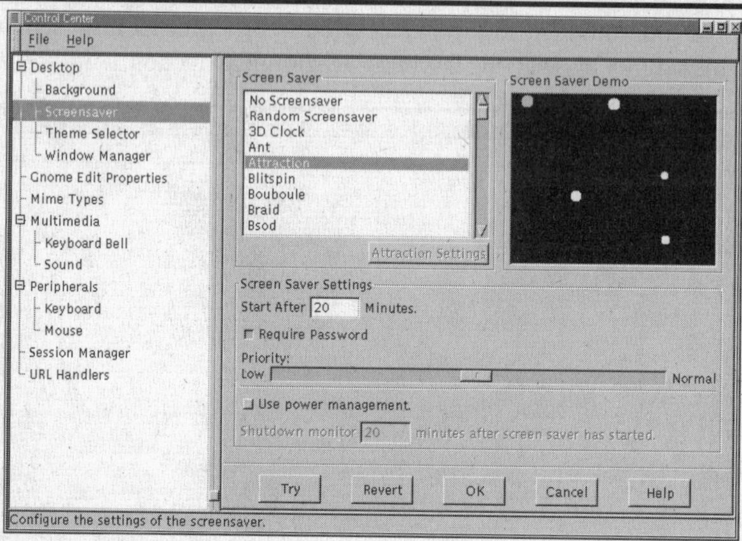

FIGURE 15.28: The Screen Saver Properties capplet

Theme Selector

The Appearances capplet contains the Theme Selector (see Figure 15.29) which allows you to select which GTK theme you would like to run. GTK themes are themes that allow the GTK widget set to change look and feel. The widget set is the set of tools that provide buttons, scrollbars, check boxes, etc. to applications. GNOME-compliant applications use the GTK tool set so most of your GNOME applications will change look and feel if you change the GTK theme.

To change your GTK theme, select a theme from the Available Themes list on the left side of the main workspace. If you have Auto Preview selected you will be able to see what the theme looks like in the preview window. If you like the theme, press the Try button on the bottom of the GNOME Control Center to install it.

There are a few GTK themes that come loaded with GNOME when you install it. If you would like more themes you can check resources on the Internet (such as `http://gtk.themes.org`). Once you have found and downloaded a theme you like, press the Install New Theme button. This will launch a file browser that allows you to find the theme you have just downloaded. The theme files should be in a **tar.gz** or **.tgz** format (otherwise known as a "tarball"). Once you have found the file, press the OK button and it will automatically install the theme for you. Now you can look in the Available Themes list for the theme you have installed.

Once the theme has been unpacked into the themes directory, it will be listed in the available themes window the next time you start the GNOME Control Center.

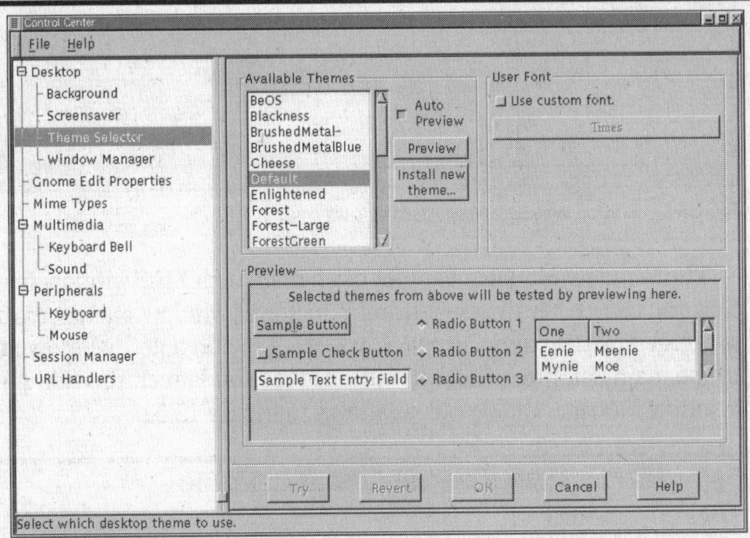

FIGURE 15.29: The Theme Selector capplet

If you would like to change the font used in the current theme, select the Use Custom Font checkbox and select the font from the Font button. This will bring up a Font Selection dialog box that allows you to specify the font, style, and size.

Window Manager Capplet

Because GNOME is not dependent on any one window manager, the Window Manager capplet allows you to select which window manager you wish to use. The Window Manager capplet (see Figure 15.30) does not determine which window managers you have available but allows you to define what and where they are.

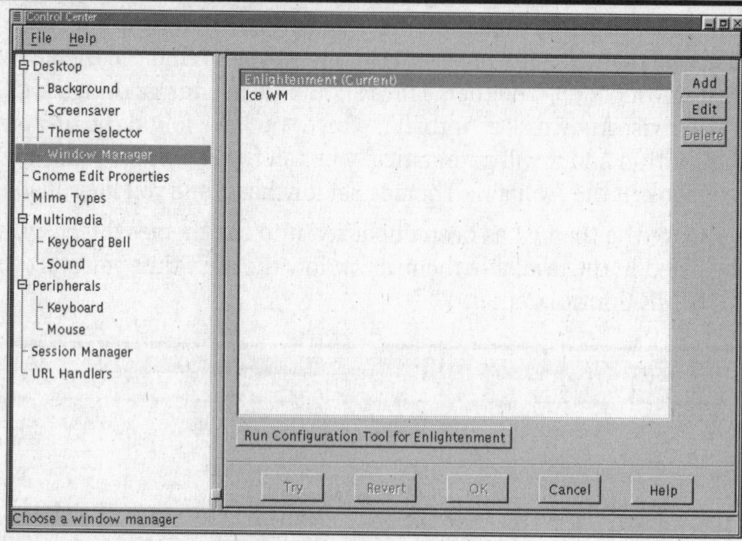

FIGURE 15.30: Window Manager capplet

The Window Manager capplet has a main list of the window managers that you can currently select from. Whichever window manager is active is notated by the word *Current*. If you wish to add a new window manager to the main list, press the Add button. This will launch the Add New Window Manager dialog box as shown in Figure 15.31.

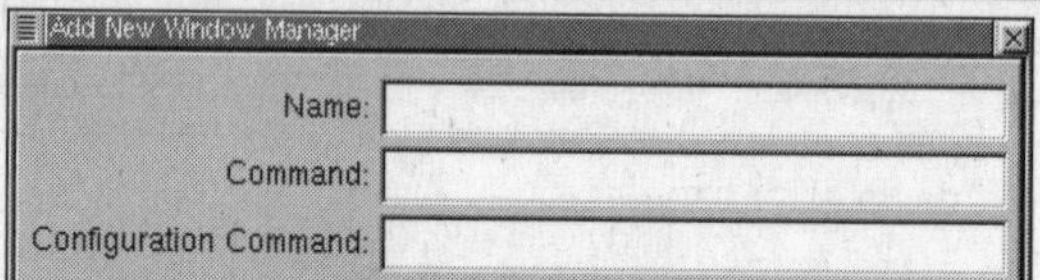

FIGURE 15.31: Add New Window Manager dialog box

In the Add New Window Manager dialog box, you may specify the name you wish to give the window manager, the command to launch that window manager, and the command to launch any configuration tool that might be available for that window manager. If you know that the window manager is fully GNOME-compliant and can be session managed, you may select the Window Manager Is Session Managed button. If you are unsure, you should check the documentation of your window manager. Press OK when you are done.

Once you have finished adding your new window manager, you will see it appear in the main list of window managers. If you need to change any of the properties you set in the Add New Window Manager dialog box, you may select the window manager from the main list and press the Edit button.

You may also delete any window manager in the main list by selecting it and pressing the Delete button.

If you are ready to switch the current window manager, select the manager you wish to run from the main list and press the Try button. If you would like to run the configuration tool before or after you switch, make sure the manager you want to configure is selected and press the Run Configuration Tool for [*window manager name*] button.

GNOME Edit Properties

The GNOME Edit Properties capplet (see Figure 15.32) allows you to select which editor will be your default editor while using GNOME. This will allow applications like the GNOME File Manager to launch the correct editor when you try to open files associated with editing. All popular available editors are included in the selection list. This capplet is very similar to the Mime Type capplet but is used in association with certain applications.

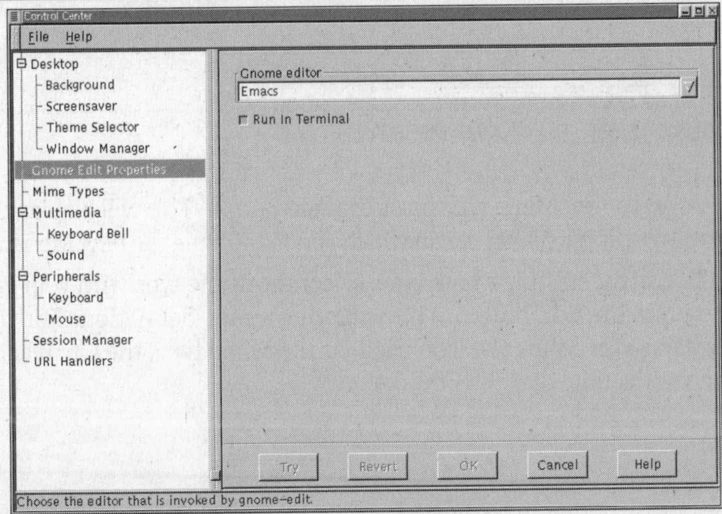

FIGURE 15.32: The GNOME Edit Properties

GNOME Mime Types

The GNOME Mime Types capplet (see Figure 15.33) allows you to determine how you wish to handle certain file types or Mime types. Mime stands for Multipurpose Internet Mail Extensions and was originally developed to allow e-mail to carry various forms of data. In GNOME you can define certain Mime types to be handled in any manner you wish. For example, if you use `.sgml` files frequently and you wish to always use Emacs to edit them you can configure the `.sgml` Mime type to always be handled by Emacs. This means that any program that wishes to launch the Mime type for you will bring up Emacs. This includes double-clicking the file type in the GNOME File Manager.

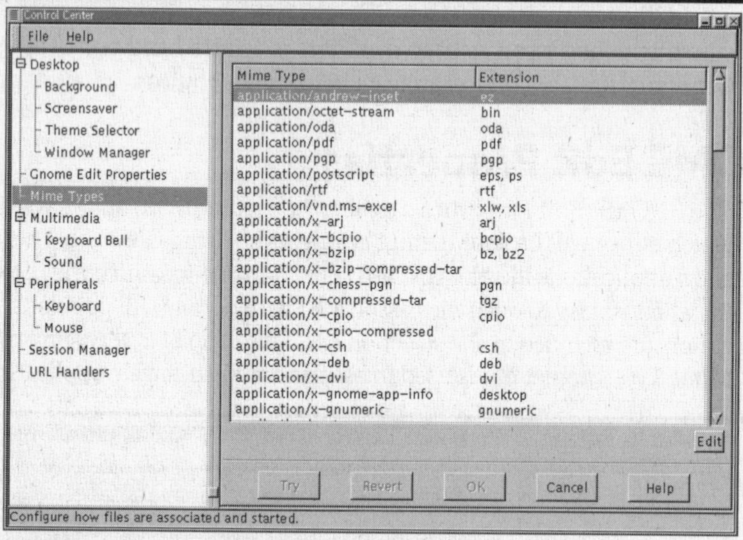

FIGURE 15.33: The GNOME Mime Types capplet

To add a new Mime type press the Add button. This will display the Add New Mime Type dialog box in which you may define the new Mime type.

To edit an existing Mime type, select the Mime type with your cursor and press the Edit button. This will bring up the Set Actions For...dialog box. You may define the icon used for the Mime type, the Open action, the View action, and the Edit action.

Multimedia Capplets

Keyboard Bell

The Keyboard Bell capplet (see Figure 15.34) allows you to change the bell sound that is produced by your CPU speaker when a keyboard error or message is sent.

Volume Changes the actual volume of the bell.

Pitch Slider Changes the pitch of the note that is played. By default it is set to 440Hz or the A above middle C.

Duration Changes the length of time the tone is played.

Test Allows you to hear the current settings of your keyboard bell.

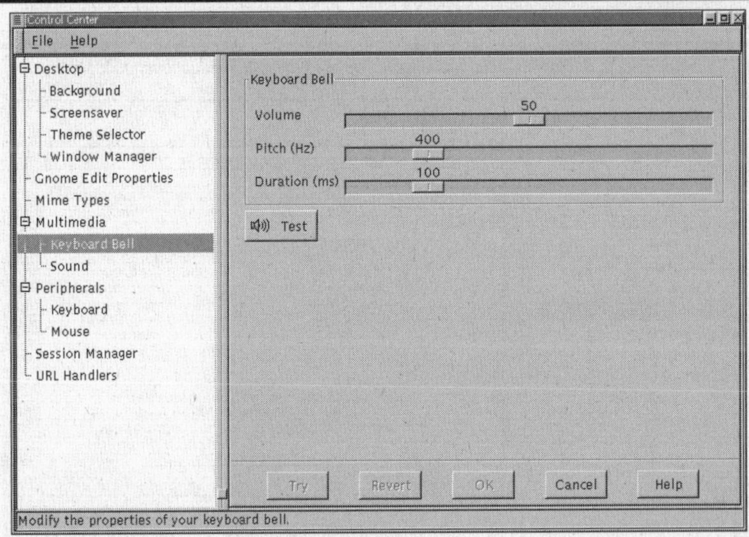

FIGURE 15.34: The Keyboard Bell capplet

The Sound Capplet

The Sound capplet (see Figure 15.35) allows you to set the system sounds for your GNOME session. There are two tabs to select in the sound capplet: General and Sound Events.

General At this point you have two options to choose from in the General tab: Enable Sound for GNOME and Enable Sound for Events. If you select Enable Sound for GNOME you will make sure that GNOME's sound engine (ESD) will be launched every session of GNOME you run. Enable Sound for Events will launch any sound files you have set in the Sound Events tab when those events occur. With these two items enabled you will utilize GNOME's session management which will remember your sound settings whenever you log in or out.

Sound Events This tab allows you to navigate through the sound events in GNOME and change their sounds.

To change a sound associated with a GNOME event, select the event in the hierarchical list on the left and press the Browse button to find a sound file on your system that you wish to associate with that event. Once you have found a sound file, press the Play button to test the sound and see if you like it enough to hear it every time the event occurs.

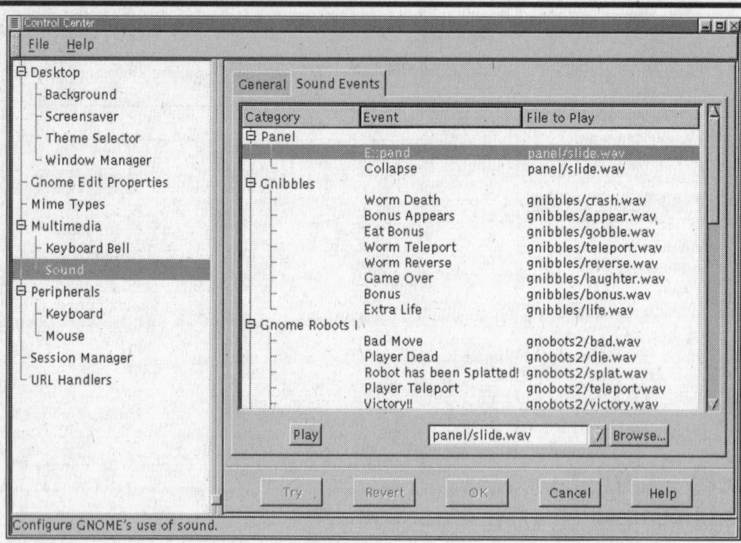

FIGURE 15.35: The Sound capplet

Peripherals

The capplets in this section of the Control Center will help you configure hardware input devices including keyboard and mouse properties.

The Keyboard Properties Capplet

There are currently two settings for the keyboard in the Keyboard Properties capplet (see Figure 15.36): Auto-repeat and Keyboard Click. You may change the properties of Auto-repeat and Keyboard Click. Auto-repeat enables you to hold a key down and have it repeat the character at the rate and delay you set in this capplet. Keyboard Click enables a small click sound to play at each key press.

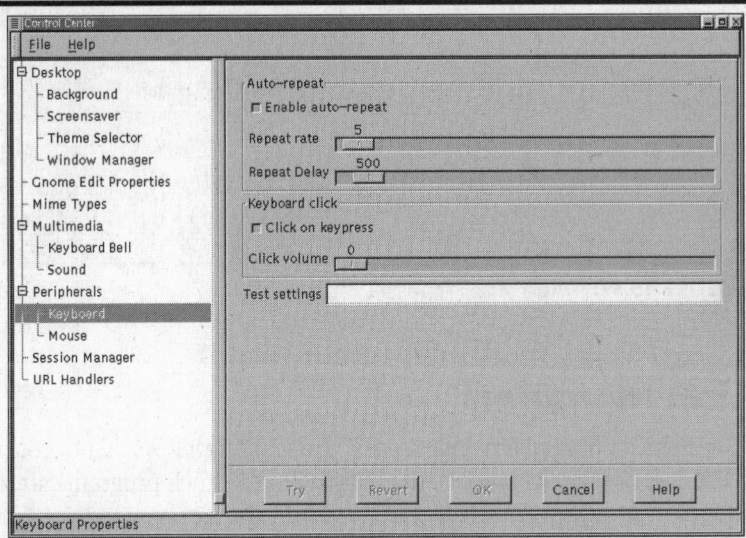

FIGURE 15.36: The Keyboard Properties capplet

The Mouse Properties Capplet

The Mouse Properties capplet (see Figure 15.37) allows you to change between left- and right-handed mouse buttons and define the Acceleration and Threshold properties.

The Acceleration setting allows you to change the speed the mouse moves across the screen in relation to the movement of the mouse on your mouse pad. The Threshold setting allows you to set the speed at which you have to move your mouse before it starts the acceleration speed you have defined in the Acceleration setting.

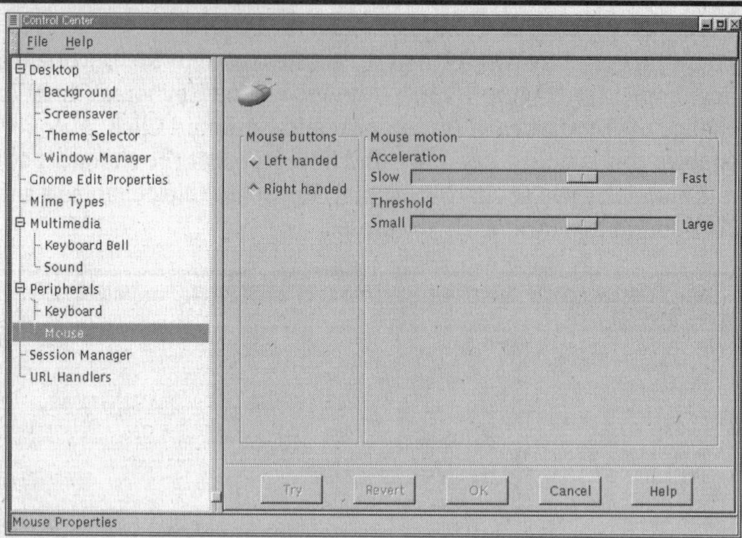

FIGURE 15.37: The Mouse Properties capplet

Session Manager

The Session Manager capplet (see Figure 15.38) allows you to control the GNOME Session Management. This includes which programs start up, how you save your GNOME configuration, and how you log out. You can find out more information about Session Management in "A Word about Session Management" section later in this chapter.

Prompt on Logout This first option allows you to disable the prompt when logging out.

Automatically Save Changes to Session This will make the Session Management always save changes made to your GNOME session when you log out.

Non–Session-Managed Startup Programs This allows you to start non–session-managed applications whenever you start a GNOME session.

NOTE

Programs that are not GNOME-compliant are not session-managed so you do not need to put GNOME applications in here; you can simply leave them running and save the current session when you log out.

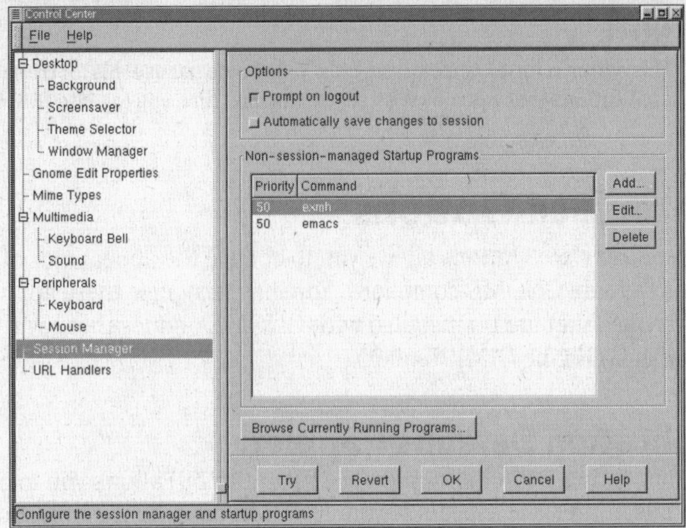

FIGURE 15.38: The Session Manager capplet

If you wish to add a new program to the Non–Session-Managed Startup Programs list, press the Add button. This will launch a simple dialog box that allows you to specify the command to launch the application and what priority it will receive.

The priority for most applications you wish to start is 50. If you have an application that needs to be started before other applications, such as a window manager, set the priority to a lower number.

NOTE

This option is for advanced users. Unless you are familiar with the Priority settings you should keep you applications running with a priority of 50.

Browse Currently Running Programs This allows you to see what applications are currently running. You may shut down those applications if you wish to and those applications will be removed from your GNOME session. The applications in this list are mostly higher-level applications and should not be shut down. However, if there are parts of GNOME that you do not wish to have, such as the Panel, this is where you would shut it down for now and your next GNOME session.

NOTE

This option is for advanced users only. You should not use this tool to shut down applications that you may wish to use the next time you log into GNOME.

User Interface Options

The User Interface Options allows you to change the appearance of applications that are GNOME-compliant. You may recognize these applications as ones that are preinstalled with GNOME or ones that say they are built with GTK (the GIMP Toolkit).

Application Defaults Capplet

The Application Defaults capplet (see Figure 15.39) allows you to change certain user interface aspects of your GNOME-compliant applications.

NOTE

Although this capplet gives you great control over the look and feel of your applications, you should consider these tools for advanced use only.

Can Detach and Move Toolbars By default toolbars in GNOME applications may be dragged from their usual location and placed anywhere within the application or desktop. If you do not wish to use this feature, you may turn it off.

Can Detach and Move Menubars By default, menubars in GNOME applications may be dragged from their usual location and placed anywhere within the application or desktop. If you do not wish to use this feature, you may turn it off.

Menubars Have Relieved Borders By default, menubars have relieved borders. If you do not like this look, you may turn this feature off.

Toolbars Have Relieved Borders By default, toolbars have relieved borders. If you do not like this look, you may turn this feature off.

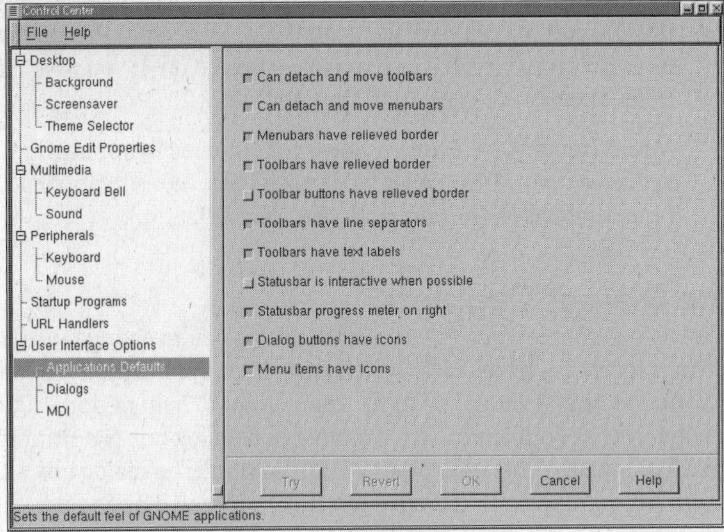

FIGURE 15.39: Applications Defaults capplet

Toolbar Buttons Have Relieved Borders By default toolbar buttons do not have relieved borders in their natural state. They do, however, change when the mouse is over them. If you wish them to be relieved at all times, you may turn on this feature.

Toolbars Have Line Separators By default, toolbar buttons have small line separators between them. If you so not wish to have the line separators, you may turn this feature off.

Toolbars Have Text Labels By default, toolbar buttons have images and text to identify them. If you are familiar with the buttons and do not need the text, you may turn on this feature.

Statusbar in Interactive When Possible Some applications can have the status bar at the bottom become separated into its own window. If you would like to have those applications separate the status bar into another window, you may turn on this option.

Statusbar Progress Meter on Right Some applications have progress meters in their statusbars. By default, these progress meters are on the right side of the statusbar. If you wish them to be on the left, you may turn off this feature.

Dialog Buttons Have Icons Some dialog buttons (for example the OK button) can have icons on them. By default, the applications that provide this have the icons turned on. If you wish not to see them, you may turn off this feature.

Menu Items Have Icons Some menu items in applications will have icons. If you wish not to see these icons in applications that use them, you may turn off this feature.

The Dialogs Capplet

The Dialogs capplet (see Figure 15.40) allows you to change the default settings for dialog boxes in GNOME-compliant applications. A dialog box is a window that is launched by an application to help perform a task needed by that application. An example of a dialog box is a Print dialog box that appears when you press a Print button. The dialog box allows you to set print options and start the print process. The Dialogs capplet will allow you to change the following options:

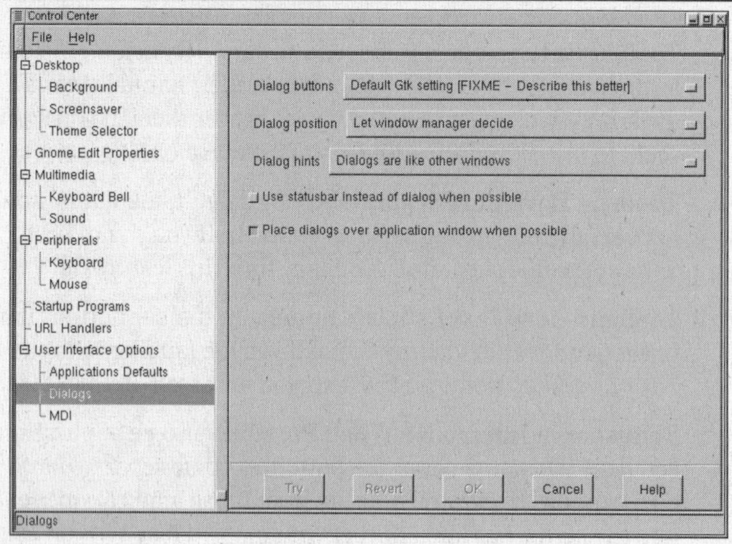

FIGURE 15.40: The Dialog capplet

Dialog Buttons Choose to use the default buttons, to spread the buttons out, to put buttons on the edges, to put the buttons on the left with left justify, and to put buttons on the right with right justify.

Default Position This will let you choose how the dialogs appear when launched. You can let the window manager decide for you (or how you have defined it in the window manager configuration), center the dialogs on the screen, or drop them where the mouse pointer is when they are launched.

Dialog Hints This will let you change the behavior of the Dialog Hints which are the tooltips that appear when you move your mouse button over a button or part of the dialog box. You may choose to have hints handled like other windows or let the window manager decide how to display them.

You may tell applications to use the status bar instead of a dialog box if the application will allow it. This will only work with dialog boxes that provide information, not ones that require some interaction on your part.

You may choose to place dialog boxes over the applications, when possible, which will help you keep your windows organized on your screen. If you are familiar with other operating systems, you may wish to keep this selected as this is how most operating systems handle dialog boxes.

NOTE

Although this capplet gives you great control over the look and feel of your applications, you should consider these tools for advanced use only.

MDI Capplet

The MDI capplet (see Figure 15.41) allows you to change the MDI mode for GNOME applications. MDI stands for Multiple Document Interface and refers to the how more than one document is displayed in GNOME applications.

NOTE

Although this capplet gives you great control over the look and feel of your applications you should consider these tools for advanced use only.

The default style in GNOME-compliant applications for MDI is usually tabs or "notebooks." If you do not like the tab look, you may change it here.

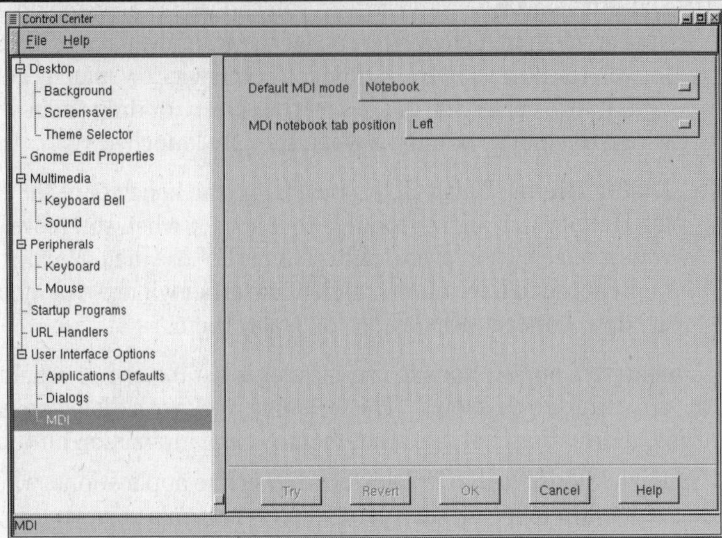

FIGURE 15.41: MDI capplet

In addition to Notebook, you will find, Top-level and Modal. Notebook is the default tab look, Top-level displays only the active document on the top view until it is closed, and Modal has only one top-level which can contain any of the documents at any one time; however only one can be displayed. If you have ever used Emacs, Modal is very similar to the way Emacs handles buffers.

If you choose to use the Notebook style you can then decide where you want the tabs to appear in your applications. You may have them at the top, left, right, or bottom of your application. Keep in mind that these choices will only work in applications that are GNOME-compliant.

A Word About Session Management

You might have seen a little bit about session management when you read about GNOME. Session management can be a very useful tool for you in your use of GNOME and GNOME applications.

The main idea of session management is that your work will be saved whenever you log out of GNOME. Your GNOME "session" is currently saved when you log out; however, you may not notice all that it can do.

Probably one of the most useful features of session management is the ability to start applications you had open when you logged out of GNOME. This is easily demonstrated as you exit GNOME and then enter again. You will see your applications re-appear in the same location on your desktop as they were when you logged out.

If there are certain applications you wish to start up whenever you log in, even if they were not open the last time your session was saved, you can add them to the Session Manager capplet that is disscussed in the previous "Session Manager" section of this chapter.

NOTE

If you have heard about application data being session managed, you have heard about the future of GNOME. For application data to be saved correctly, you must be using a fully compliant GNOME application. At the time of publication of this book, there were not any applications that offer full session management for your data. Until there are some and you are aware of its capabilities, you should not rely on session management to save your application data.

Resetting the GNOME Session

One advanced feature of the GNOME Session Manager is the ability to recover a "clean session" if anything goes wrong for you. To do this you must hold down the Control and Shift keys together when you log in to GNOME. This will bring up a dialog box that gives you two different options for restoring your GNOME Session (see Figure 15.42).

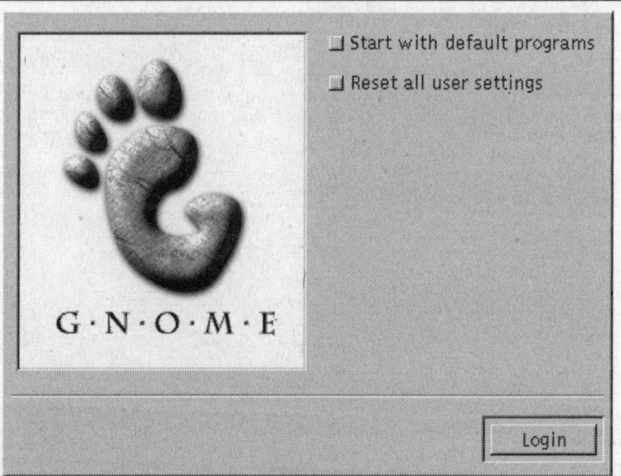

FIGURE 15.42: Login screen for Resetting GNOME Session

The first option is to Start With Default Programs. This option will remove all of the session configuration setting in respect to applications. This will only erase the GNOME session data for applications you had running when you logged out last; it will not change any information you may have set in the Session Manager capplet in the GNOME Control Center.

The second option is to Reset All User Settings. This will reset all GNOME application and core configuration data. This option will destroy any configurations you have made to the Panel, the GNOME File Manager, the Session Manager Capplet, and any GNOME application. This option will not remove files on your desktop.

NOTE

These options are for advanced users and should only be used in case there is a problem with your GNOME Session. You can lose data for many applications if you utilize the functionality provided by these options.

ipfwadm -O -a deny
masquera
V your.static
outgoing to
ipfwadm
such as ip masq
define the CONFIG
bin:/usr/sbin

Chapter 16

The K Desktop Environment

This chapter is a complete documentation of the K Desktop Environment from the user perspective. The K Desktop Environment is a collection of tools that will make your Unix life easier and more enjoyable.

This chapter is reprinted from the K Desktop Environment version 1.1 of 24 February 1999 by the KDE Team.

About This Preview

Although this information will need to be rewritten for the final version of KDE, I hope this preview version will be useful in answering some of the questions that a new KDE user may have.

Status of This Chapter

This chapter includes a complete introduction, a guide to KDE installation, a description of the user interface, three practical examples on how to use KDE for daily work, and a description of how to customize the KDE desktop. Also included is a table of shortcuts and some tips and tricks.

Introduction

640 kB ought to be enough for everybody.

—The CEO of a big software company, at the beginning of the 80s

Since the beginning of Unix development, there were stable kernels, and good, powerful software, but there has been one great problem: Only a few people could use Unix because it was written mainly for those students and professionals who had studied the system for a long time. For example, the standard method for reading USENET news was:

```
find /var/spool/news -name '[0-9]*' -exec cat {} \;|more
```

Today, however, this problem has been solved. There are many good frontends available, like tin and knews, which provide easy-to-use, intuitive graphical user interfaces (GUIs). Unfortunately, the GUIs lack a common "look-and-feel." Commercial libraries for programmers, like Motif, promised a solution to this, but these libraries remain far too expensive and far too slow.

The configuration of programs is also often difficult. Compiling is usually done with:

```
./configure && make && make install
```

Only a very few programs can be configured with menus or scripts. In most cases, you must edit text configuration files yourself. It often happens that a misplaced period ruins the whole file, forcing you to restart the configuration process. Whenever you need to change your settings or reconfigure a program, this problem comes up again.

All this contributes to the fact that Linux and other versions of Unix fail to reach a wider audience. At the same time, many people are not satisfied with their current operating system, mainly because of the lack of stability and performance found in those operating systems. Other people hate to buy a new computer each time a new version of the program they cannot live without comes out, because it needs more RAM and more disk space. Often the new version provides functions few people really need.

KDE is different. Although we're not trying to replace the standard Unix shell, we are working on a tool that will make using Unix easier. We also want to attract more users to the Unix environment. Simple things will be made easy and complex things will still be possible. Also, a single interface will be provided, instead of the dozens currently required.

What KDE Can Do for You

We designed KDE mainly for those new to Unix and others who wish to avoid the complicated process of learning new technologies and commands not found in their old operating systems. We also provide, however, something for experienced Unix users.

If you are new to Unix, do not even try to use anything else, because you are exactly the sort of person for whom we wrote this software. `:-)` For you, we provide:

- A good-looking, easy-to-use windowing environment
- A powerful, easy to use file manager
- A simple, centralized configuration
- An online help that will support you in every situation

If you already have experience in Unix, you will welcome the new features KDE has to offer:

- A good, handy, and fast window manager.
- A consistent interface for your applications. You will no longer need to guess if the right or the left mouse button does what you expect.
- A lean terminal emulator that does not fill up your memory when multiple windows are open simultaneously.
- A stylish desktop that makes your friends jealous.

Background of KDE

In October 1996, German LyX developer Matthias Ettrich initiated the development of KDE with a USENET posting. Soon after, a couple of interested developers began planning and programming parts of the new project. One year later, the window manager, file manager, the terminal emulator, the help system and the display configuration tool were released for ALPHA and BETA testing and proved to be relatively stable.

In July 1998, KDE 1.0 was released. It was a stable version for the next six months, while developers continued work on improving KDE without stability constraints. In January 1999, their improvements were consolidated and integrated to produce KDE 1.1, the new standard, stable version.

Developers and interested users communicate via several mailing lists as described in the "Contacting the Authors" section later in this chapter.

Legal Notices

KDE is free software under the GNU General Public License (see Appendix D), which is included with every KDE component. You can copy and distribute KDE and its components as you like, as long as you always include the complete source code.

How to Get New Components

The main site for KDE is `http://www.kde.org/`. Here, you can find all important information relating to KDE, including announcements, bugfixes, developer info, style guides, documentation, and much more. For software upgrades, please visit our ftp site, `ftp://ftp.kde.org/`, or use a mirror if one exists near you. (Mirrors are listed at `www.kde.org/`.)

The directory `unstable` always contains brand new software, but it often is untested and may not even compile. If you are looking for more reliable components, please take a look in the `stable` directory, where we put Beta and release versions.

If you are interested in developing KDE applications on your own, you should also visit Troll Tech's server (`http://www.troll.no/`), which features a great deal of information concerning the Qt library used by KDE. For development work, it is also advisable to join KDE mailing lists. (See the "Other Sources for Help" section at the end of this chapter.)

Contacting the Authors

Contact rwilliam@kde.org1 for questions about and critiques of this chapter. Because several people contributed material to this chapter, everyone is also listed in "The K Documentation Staff" section at the end of this chapter.

INSTALLATION

Core dumping fsck's tend to make me nervous.

—Linus Torvalds, after finding one of his file systems smashed by a new Beta kernel

Don't worry! Although the use of some Beta software can cause considerable grief, it is unlikely that the installation of KDE will smash your hard disk. In fact, this chapter is designed to guide you through the installation process so that you can take a look at your new desktop as quickly (and with as little grief) as possible. As with all new Window Manager installs, it is recommended that you back up all your X11-specific configuration files before you begin the install. If you do not know the exact location of them, try all the hidden (.*) files in your home directory and the directory /usr/X11/lib/X11/xdm.

WARNING

Because the software is in Beta stage at the moment, we strongly recommend that you back up ALL the critical data on your hard disk. We are NOT liable for any damage caused by the installation and usage of KDE!

Requirements

Before installing KDE, ascertain that your system fulfills the following requirements:

- A running POSIX compatible Unix system. Versions of Unix that are known to work with KDE include: Linux, FreeBSD, Solaris, HP-UX, and MkLinux. We are working to make KDE available for more platforms soon.
- Some free hard disk space on the partition where /opt/kde will be created. We recommend that you reserve about 50MB if your

system supports shared libraries, and considerably more if it does not. Due to the fact that this software is currently in Beta stage, the requirements may change from one week to another. I recommend that you reserve additional space for forthcoming KDE applications. If you need or want to build KDE from the source tree, please remember to reserve about 100MB in `/usr/src`.

- A running X11 system with or without xdm. If you have not installed the X Window System yet, first check your Unix installation media for an installable version. If you cannot find any version working, visit the XFree86 web site at `http://www.xfree86.org/` for more information on how to get and install the X Window System, or contact your Unix vendor support.
- The qt-libraries, version 1.42. You can get these at Troll Tech's FTP Server at `ftp://ftp.troll.no/pub/qt/` in both `rpm` and `tgz` format.

A warning before you start: Before upgrading from a previous version of KDE, we recommend that you do the following:

```
cd /opt/kde
tar cfvz ~/KDE-old-version-backup.tar.gz *
```

Linux: Installing RPMs for Red Hat, Caldera and SuSE

Using RPMs is the easiest method to get KDE up and running. Just visit your favorite KDE mirror and visit the directory `/pub/kde/stable/distribution/rpm`. There, you can see directories for different operating systems. Currently, the i386, alpha, and sparc architectures are supported. The RPM packages can also be found on the Red Hat contrib sites like `MetaLab.unc.edu` or `ftp.redhat.com`.

The basic system consists of the files `kde-(component).(architecture).rpm`. You need at least `kdesupport`, `kdelibs` and `kdebase`. After getting the base distribution, feel free to download any other RPMs that you think may come in handy.

Next, start installing with the base package. If you are installing KDE for the first time, use:

```
rpm -i kdesupport.arch.rpm
rpm -i kdelibs.arch.rpm
rpm -i kdebase.arch.rpm
```

NOTE

It is important that these components are installed in the order listed and that they are installed before any other KDE component.

If you are upgrading from a previous release, try:

```
rpm -Uvh kde-component.arch.rpm
```

Once again, the order given above should be preserved, and the given components should be installed before any other KDE components.

This will unpack the base distribution and install it in `/opt/kde`. If the installation of the base packages has been successful, you can install the remaining packages (use -Uvh instead of -i once again to update an existing version) the same way.

Linux: Installing on Top of a Debian/GNU Linux Distribution

An important note before you start: Due to various problems arising from the Linux filesystem standard, building .deb packages is very complex. Therefore, you will probably not find the most current version. If you want to see the newest in KDE development, we recommend you get the source distribution (see the following section on "Using TGZ to Install on Top of Other Systems" for details).

Retrieve the following files in order to get KDE installed on your Debian/GNU Linux system. You can find them in `/pub/kde/unstable/distribution/dpkg`.

- `libgif22.3-1i386.deb`
- `libkde00.10.01-1i386.deb`
- `kdeapps0.10.01-2i386.deb`

In addition, KDE requires components from the following packages: Make sure they are installed before beginning the KDE installation:

- `qt1.42`
- `libjpeg6`
- `libg++27`

NOTE

We highly recommend that you install the debian menu package before installing KDE (it makes kpanel much nicer).

To install kde use dselect or do it manually using the following:

```
dpkg -i libgif2_2.3-1_i386.deb
dpkg -i libkde0_0.10.01-1_i386.deb
dpkg -i kdeapps_0.10.01-2_i386.deb
```

If dpkg gives dependency errors, you'll have to find the packages, listed above, upon which KDE depends, install them, then rerun the dpkg commands.

Using TGZ to Install on Top of Other Systems

If your Linux distribution did not come with an RPM or DEB archive format, or you are not using Linux at all, you must compile KDE on your own. In the future, we are planning to provide a binary distribution which includes its own installation program.

In order to compile and install KDE properly, you need to have the following items installed on your hard disk:

- An ANSI-C compiler, e.g., the GNU C compiler
- An ANSI-C++ compiler, e.g., GNU C++
- The make utility
- Qt development version 1.41 or higher
- X11 development version (include files are often missing)

Once you have all of the needed helper applications, go to your favorite KDE mirror and retrieve the following files from the directory `/pub/kde/stable/`(newest version):

- `kdesupport-(version).tar.gz`
- `kdelibs-(version).tar.gz`
- `kdebase-(version).tar.gz`
- any other packages you wish to install (we advise you to get at least `kdeutils`)

In the above filenames, "(version)" stands for the current version number. Once you have downloaded all you need, extract these files to `/usr/src`. This process should yield the following directory structure:

- `/usr/src/kdesupport`
- `/usr/src/kdelibs`
- `/usr/src/kdebase`
- `/usr/src/...` (any other packages)

Make sure you have write permissions to `/opt/kde`. Next you must compile and install the packages using the following:

- `cd` into the directory of the package, you want to install (see above)
- `./configure` (with the options you want to apply)
- `make`
- `make install`

Apply the above steps to every package you want to install. (These instructions can be used for almost every source package available.)

Every configure script has several options available. Some are common between the packages, while others are specific to an individual package. The following is the result of `configure --help` in `kdebase`:

```
% configure --help
```

`--enable-debug`	creates debugging code [default=no]
`--disable-nls`	do not use Native Language Support
`--with-qt-dir`	where the root of qt is installed
`--with-qt-includes`	where the qt includes are
`--with-qt-libraries`	where the qt library is installed
`--with-extra-includes`	adds non standard include paths
`--with-extra-libs`	adds non standard library paths
`--disable-path-check`	don't try to find out where to install

`--with-install-root`	the root, where to install to [default=/]
`--disable-rpath`	do not use the rpath feature of ld
`--with-xdmdir`	if the xdm config dir can't be found automatically
`--without-pam`	disable Pluggable Authentication Modules
`--with-shadow`	if you want shadow password support
`--without-gl`	disable 3-D GL modes
`--without-xpm`	disable color pixmap XPM tests

Several options are not required and are only useful as workarounds for known problems (e.g., `--disable-path-check`). Since some are important options, for instance `--with-shadow`, you should always check the available options.

An important option is `--prefix`. This option specifies the path where configure should install (for `kdesupport` and `kdelibs`) or where to look for libraries (for the other packages). By default, configure will look in `/usr/local/kde`. If you want to install KDE into `/opt/kde`, you have to use `configure --prefix /opt/kde`.

If you have installed the Qt libraries in an uncommon place, for instance in `$HOME/src/qt`, you must use `configure --with-qt-dir=$HOME/src/qt`. By default configure looks in the most common places for QT before it gives up.

If you have problems that you are not able to solve, send a copy of the file `config.log` to the address in the README file in the offending package.

You must install KDE in the following order: `kdesupport`, `kdelibs`, then the application packages (for example `kdebase`). All of the application packages should only depend on `kdelibs`, so you can compile them at the same time (if you have a powerful machine).

If you want to take advantage of multiprocessor systems, try `make -j` <*Number of processors*> instead of `make`.

Platform-Specific Building Notes for Linux

For Linux, most of the utilities needed to build KDE can be found either at `ftp://MetaLab.unc.edu/pub/Linux/GCC` or `ftp://MetaLab.unc.edu/pub/GNU`. The Qt libraries can be found at `ftp://ftp.troll.no/pub/qt/linux`, available in source or RPM format for Linux. Both contain detailed instruction on how to install them. Include files for X11 programs should be available at `ftp://ftp.xfree86.org` in the "xdevel" section.

If you want to start your system in runlevel 3 using `kdm`, you need to replace the `xdm` call in `/etc/rc.d/xdm` with `/opt/kde/bin/kdm`. In any case, here is a version that should work:

```
#! /bin/sh
# Copyright (c) 1996 S.u.S.E. GmbH Fuerth, Germany.
# All rights reserved.
#
# Author: Florian La Roche <florian@suse.de>, 1996
#     Werner Fink <werner@suse.de>, 1996
#
# Modified on October, 13th by
#    Andreas Buschka <andi@bonn-online.com>, 1997
# for the KDE documentation project.
#
# /sbin/init.d/xdm
#

. /etc/rc.config

case "$1" in
  start)
    echo "Starting kdm."
    /opt/kde/bin/kdm
    ;;
  stop)
    echo -n "Shutting down kdm:"
    killproc -TERM /opt/kde/bin/kdm
    echo
    ;;
  *)
    echo "Usage: $0 {start|stop}"
    exit 1
esac

exit 0
```

You also need to change the default runlevel in `/etc/inittab` to 3 in order to start `kdm` when the system comes up.

NOTE

Do not forget to re-login in order to let the system read your new configuration settings!

Required Changes to Your Configuration Files

After you have placed the KDE binaries into their destination directory, there are a few adjustments you must make to your startup scripts.

The following procedure was tested on SuSE Linux 5.0 and should be compatible with the other popular versions of Unix as well.

NOTE

Always make backups of configuration files before changing them!

Add the following to the end of your `/etc/profile`:

```
export PATH=$PATH:/opt/kde/bin
export KDEDIR=/opt/kde
```

Next, edit the `.xinitrc` file in your home directory. Look for the line that calls your window manager and replace it with startkde.

Now that everything needed to run KDE has been installed, you can go on to Chapter 4 where you will start KDE for the first time. If something goes wrong, you may need to compile KDE on your own. Read the "Platform-Specific Building Notes for Linux" earlier in this chapter for more information.

We have made the installation as bulletproof as possible, so you should not encounter any serious problems unless your configuration is exotic. If you do experience difficulties, feel free to use the KDE mailing lists (see the "Other Sources for Help" section at the end of this book).

First Impressions

You see to sea to see that all you can see is sea.

—Unknown origin

First impressions are so important—this is not only true for Agatha Christie's famous thriller *The Mousetrap*—but also for KDE. As we mentioned before, KDE is supposed to be the most intuitive, easy-to-learn user interface available. In fact, we will have reached our goal when users no longer need this book in order to work with KDE, causing the authors to lose their (unpaid and voluntary) jobs as documentors.

Starting KDE

When you boot a Unix system, one of two things should happen. (If the system works correctly, that is; everything else is an undocumented third case.) Either you stay in text mode and get a login prompt or you are presented with a graphical login window. In the former case, you must log into your system and type:

```
startx
```

If the installation was successful, the KDE desktop should appear after a few seconds of initialization.

If a graphical login window is presented, then all that should be required is your login name and password. Assuming the KDE installation was successful, KDE should start without further intervention.

If you have not done so already, we recommend changing your X display manager from `xdm` to `kdm`, which includes the same functionality, but with the advanced features of the K Desktop Environment.

Desktop Components

After everything has come up, take some time to explore the new environment. If you have already worked with Windows 95 or OS/2 Warp 4, many things should look familiar to you. The three main parts of a KDE desktop are the desktop itself, the panel, and the task list.

Panel

When you start KDE for the first time, the panel is situated at the bottom of the screen. From here, you will start your programs and switch between the virtual screens.

K button Clicking this button removes the panel from the screen and replaces it with a mini panel. The K button stays on the screen so you can bring the main panel back. This feature only applies to the current desktop; the other desktops will keep the mini or main panel.

NOTE

When the panel is minimized, the application menu and the task list are available on top of the taskbar with the same functionality, but they use less space there.

Application starter The button next to the K button is one of the most important places on your KDE desktop. From here, you can start all of the KDE applications installed. Later, when you learn how to use programs (see the "Programs" section later in this chapter), you can also add other programs here as well. To start a program, just click the button. You will see a list of different categories, plus some special entries. Whenever you move your mouse over an entry that has an arrow to the right, a new menu will appear. When you find the program you want to start, just click it with the left mouse button.

Task list The button located to the right of the application menu (the one with the monitor on it) is a menu containing all the windows active on your desktops, sorted by desktop name. This feature makes it easy to quickly find a particular window and reduces overall desktop clutter when many windows are open.

Logout button Located to the right of the list of active windows, there are two more buttons. The top button, which looks like a big "X," is used when you want to quit the current KDE session. If any other applications are still open, three things may happen:

1. Applications that are written for KDE will prompt you to save your work. When you start KDE again, all the KDE windows will be opened again and you can start at the same point where you left your workstation the day before.
2. Applications which were not written explicitly for KDE, but comply with the X Window System standard, will also prompt you to save your work.
3. Applications which do not fully correspond to this standard (like Netscape Navigator 4.03) cannot ask you whether you want to save your work. KDE will warn you about these programs and provide you with the option to stop the logout process.

Remember, there are not many things to save when you are using a Web browser, but, for example, a CAD-program with a valuable drawing loaded should be quit using its own menus before logging out.

Lock screen button If you happen to live in a house with others who cannot stop spying on your work, this button could be handy. One click and it will lock your screen, preventing unwanted persons from reading your private mail or playing around with your work.

WARNING

The X Window System can still be terminated with Ctrl+Alt+Backspace, but this will destroy all your work on the KDE desktops. If you do not disable the use of Ctrl-Alt-Enter, Ctrl-Alt-Backspace, and the switching keys to your text consoles; this protection is not secure!

Desktop buttons When you start KDE for the first time, note the four buttons labeled, appropriately enough, "One," "Two," "Three," and "Four." These represent your four desktops. Just click one of them. Don't worry; though they have "disappeared"; any open windows are still active (just take a look at the task list!). Using multiple desktops is one of the most powerful features of KDE and the X Window System. Instead of placing one window over another, as you would when using Windows or OS/2, you can say, "Well, on the first desktop, I will write the KDE User Guide. On the second desktop I'll run the sgml2latex compiler and see my results while compiling my linux kernel on the third desktop, and on the fourth I'll read my e-mail."

Icon bar Some people are so lazy that they consider even the two or three motions through the applications menu to be too much (me included). For them, additional buttons can be placed next to the desktop buttons (for example, shortcuts to your home directory, to your trashcan, to the kvt terminal emulator and to the documents you use often). For information on how to add icons to the taskbar, read the "Shortcut Icons" section later in this chapter.

Time and date At the far right end of the KDE panel, you can always see the time and date.

The task list Move your mouse to the upper left corner of the screen. There, you will find a button for each open window. Just click on the button corresponding to the windows you want to open. This is an alternative to using the task list on the KDE panel.

Using Windows

When KDE comes up, the first opened window contains your home directory. We'll cover the contents of this window later. Right now, let's investigate the actual window widget.

Window menu On the top-left corner of each window, you can see a window manipulation icon. When you click it, a context menu containing commands to manipulate the window is presented. Maximize will expand the window to the largest size possible.

NOTE

KDE will take the size of your virtual desktop, which means that the window could be bigger than your screen.

Iconify will make the window invisible. Take a look at the Taskbar. You will notice that the window title is now shown in parentheses. To bring the window to the desktop again, click the window title. Move will let you move the window with your mouse. Click the left mouse button when you have the window where you want it to be. Resize enables you to make the window smaller or larger. Move your mouse around and click when you are satisfied with the new size. Sticky will stick the window to your desktop. Whenever you change the desktop, the "sticky" window will move with you. To stop this effect, select UnSticky.

NOTE

UnSticky is useful, for example, when you are debugging programs or network problems and you always want to see the tail -f window of the logfiles.

To desktop… enables you to send a window to another desktop. Choose the desktop where you want the window to be. The window will disappear at once. To see your window again, select its name in the taskbar or click the appropriate desktop button on the KDE panel. Close will close the window. Sometimes the application will allow you to save your work, but it some cases (e.g., old X11 applications) this does not work. It is best to close an application with its own commands, using this menu item only as a last resort.

Sticky button This button looks like a thumbtack. It performs the same operation as the sticky command in the Window menu but requires fewer steps to invoke.

Title bar The title bar containing the name of the window can be double-clicked in order to maximize it. Use the right mouse button: The Window menu will reappear, allowing you to (un)maximize, iconify, move, resize, (un)sticky the window, and move it to another desktop (this works faster than the method with the sticky button). When a program does not react anymore, you can close it (this will sometimes give you the opportunity to save your work).

Iconify, maximize, and close buttons To the right of the title bar, there are three buttons that can also be used to iconify, maximize, and close the window (this is faster than using the window manipulation menu). Iconified windows can be brought back with a click on the taskbar.

To move a window, place the cursor on the title bar and hold down the left mouse button. Without releasing the mouse button, move the window to the location of your choice, then release the mouse button. If you want to resize a window, move the mouse cursor to the window border you wish to change. Once you have reached the correct spot, the cursor will change from an arrow to a bracket and an arrow. Hold down the left mouse button and drag the side in question to the location you wish, then release the button. Note that you may drag sides or corners, which will adjust the size in two dimensions at once.

Using the menu bar of each KDE window is easy. Just click what you want to do, and it will be done. But the menu bar can do even more for you. Notice the sparkled stripe on the left of the menu and icon bars? Depress your right mouse button and a context menu will appear, allowing you to put the menu bar on the top or bottom of the window. You can even take the menu bar out of the window and have it "floating" around.

Below the menu bar, there is a set of tool symbols you can use to execute commands. Whenever you move over them, an active picture will be marked. You can also put the toolbar wherever you want: left, right, top, bottom, or floating.

Getting Help

Help is available basically everywhere. On the desktop, just use the right mouse button and choose Help On Desktop. On the KDE panel, open the application menu and choose Help. Every KDE program has a help menu. Every help is HTML-based, so using the help system is as easy as using your favorite Web browser!

Getting Started

Using only what you see, can you get from A to B?

–Help for one of the toughest riddles in The 7th Guest

Thus far, KDE may appear to be little more than another window manager with some handy desktop features. But hold onto your seat; in the next few sections, we'll introduce you to features that'll assure you will never again try to operate your system Unix without KDE!

Editing Files

Since you do not only have KDE applications installed on your system, you probably know the mess of editing ASCII-style configuration files. But there are a lot of other file types that need to be edited this way. For example, the raw SGML source for this guide was written ASCII style, as was the source code for the KDE programs themselves. We will now show you how you can use the KEdit facility in KDE to edit ASCII files of your own.

Opening a Window Containing Your Home Directory

Click the Application Starter and choose Home Directory. A window showing the contents of your home directory will pop up. To see a more detailed listing of files in your home directory, do the following:

- Select Show Dot Files from the View menu
- Select Show Tree from the View menu

On the left hand of the screen, a tree view of your file system structure should appear, including any "hidden files" (files or directories beginning with a period).

The File Manager Screen

We tried to make the File Manager as easy as possible to use, and if you know other window managers (including those built into other operating systems) with integrated file management, many of the following concepts should be familiar to you.

On the top, there is a File menu which contains functions to open and close file manager windows. You can also print the current contents.

NOTE

Want to visit the Internet? Just choose File > Open Location (or press Alt+L) and enter an URL. For example, if you want to visit the KDE homepage, enter `http://www.kde.org`. You can also quickly FTP files using this method. KDE is "Internet ready," which means that you can load and save files not only on your local hard disk but also on remote FTP and HTTP servers. While other operating systems and desktops make a distinction between local and remote file systems, KDE does not.

The Edit menu offers functions to select, copy, and move files. We will use them later. Already having used the View menu, you have probably seen that you can view the content in many different ways. Just play around a bit and see what happens.

You will undoubtedly find the bookmarks to be extremely useful. Now you can remember virtually any link, be it on the local machine or somewhere on the Internet.

The Tools menu helps you find the notorious files-that-I-put-somewhere-I-do-not-remember-anymore.

Navigating through Directories

We will now pick one of your configuration files and edit it. First, we must change the directory in the File Manager. Scroll down the tree view on the left side of the screen until you find the directory `/etc`. Double-click `etc`. You will see a list of files in the right window.

Editing a File

Scroll down until you find the file `motd` and click it with the right mouse button. In the Context Menu, select Open With. In the new window that pops up, enter:

```
kedit
```

and click OK or press Enter. Voila!

The Editor Screen

The more you work with KDE, the more you will notice that most screens and applications look and feel the same. The KEdit File menu is a great example of this. Almost every other KDE program has the same menu, allowing you to create new files, open existing files from your local file system or (coming soon) even the Web, save them (soon even on the Web, too!), and print or mail them to somebody else. The Edit menu can also be found in most KDE applications, allowing you to cut and paste information between programs. You can also search and replace text. Using the Options menu, you can customize the editor in many different ways. For example, you can increase the font size to suit your monitor resolution–and your eyes. Of course, as in any other KDE application, you'll find a Help Menu, offering you on-line help whenever you need it.

Using the Editor

Most `motd` files contain useless stuff like "Do not forget to back up your data" or "Do not annoy the system manager." Boring. Let's change the text so that users logging in get the really important information. You can navigate through the text using the arrow keys, and mark sections of text with Shift+Arrows or by using the mouse with the left button pressed. Use the Edit Menu to cut and paste text. Enter whatever you want, or use the following (great) example:

```
Welcome!

This machine now has KDE installed, providing you with a
great, easy-to-use interface and a consistent Look-and-Feel
for all your applications. For more information on how to get
KDE running on your account, please e-mail the administrator.
```

Saving Your Work

Now that you have changed the `motd` file, it is time to save the file, putting the changes into effect. To do this, you can use either the File

Menu, or you can use the Save icon on the toolbar. Finally, finish your work by closing the editor and file manager window. You can do this by clicking the "X" button on the top right of the window, by using the window menu of the title bar, or by choosing File ➢Quit. Simple and elegant, isn't it?

Moving Files with Drag-and-Drop

As you have seen in the previous section, working with files is as easy as 1-2-3. However, when you want to copy and move files, the whole copy-and-paste business can get annoying. Don't worry–a procedure called "drag-and-drop" allows you to copy and move files quickly and easily.

Opening Two File Manager Windows

Before you can start, you will need to open two file manager windows. The simplest way to open a new window is to press the white wheel button on the right of the icon bar. If you do not see the tree view in the new window, activate it (View ➢ Tree View).

Dragging a File from One Window to Another

In the first window, open the `/etc` folder and scroll until you see the `motd` file we modified in the previous section. In the second window, open your home directory. Click the `motd` file. Hold your left mouse button and drag your file into your home directory. Release the left mouse button (this is called *dropping* the file). You will be presented with three options: Copy, Move, and Link. Link will create a symbolic link to the file, while Copy and Move do exactly what they say. Select Copy. You should now have a copy of the `motd` file in your home directory.

Using Command Line and Terminals

So far, you have only worked with the tools and programs KDE provides. Undoubtedly, you will want to use other Unix programs as well. There are two ways of running them: The quick command line and the terminal.

Quick Command Line

Pressing Alt+F2 pops up a small window where you can enter a command to run. Please note that you will not see any text output generated from a program started in this manner! This method is only recommended for starting X Window System programs or for running tools where you do not need to see or type anything. For other programs, you will still need to use the terminal.

The Unix Terminal Emulator

From the application menu, choose Utilities ➢ Terminal. A terminal window will open. Here you can use regular Unix shell commands: `ls`, `cat`, `less`, and so forth. Using the options menu, you can customize the terminal emulator to suit your needs.

Finding Your Lost Files

Everyone has undoubtedly encountered the following problem: You start ftp, log into a great site like `ftp.kde.org` and start downloading files. It is late in the evening and you shut down your machine after completing the transfer. The next morning, you are at the keyboard again, and you start wondering into which directory you placed the recently transferred files. Using KDE's KFind utility makes finding those lost files a snap.

Starting KFind

Starting KFind is simple: Choose Find Files in the Application Starter. KFind uses an interface part you probably do not know yet: register tabs. When KFind starts, you see that Name Location is selected. When you click on Date Modified, the register content changes. Since you have never run a search before, most of the icons on the toolbar and most of the menu entries are disabled. We will change this now.

Finding a File by Knowing Parts of Its Name

As long as you know a bit of the file name, searching is easy. Select the Name Location tab, and enter the file name. Wildcards may be used as needed. As a test, type `*.tar.gz`. By default, the search begins in your home directory, but you can select any starting directory you wish by clicking the Look in or Browse.... To start searching, click the icon that looks like a magnifying glass over a sheet of paper on the left of the toolbar. After a moment, a list of files will appear in the search results window. If they do not appear, you started the search in the wrong directory, made a spelling mistake in the name field, or no files ending with a *`.tar.gz`* extension are located on your machine.

Finding a File by More Complex Criteria

There are many categories you can use to make your search more precise. The more you know about the file, the better are your chances of finding it.

Date modified Here, you can specify that you only want to see files that were last touched in a given period of time or since a specified number of months or days ago.

File type If you know that the file was of a special type (e.g., a `tar/gzip` archive or a `jpeg` picture), you can tell KFind to find only this type of file.

Text string You can specify text that the file must contain.

Size If you know the file size, you can limit your search in this regard as well.

Using Multiple Desktops

Using multiple desktops helps you organize your work. You can place your programs on different desktops, and name the desktops so you know what you do there. This increases and optimizes your workspace. It also helps you when you are surfing the net instead of doing your work and your boss comes in. But, of course, this is rare—at least in the office where I work .

You can switch between desktops by clicking the desktop buttons on the KDE panel. If you want to rename them, you can do so by double-clicking them.

You can use windows on multiple desktops. If you want to have a window present everywhere, just click the sticky button on the top-left of the window. To send a window to another desktop, click the title bar with the right mouse button, choose To Desktop, and select the desktop where you would like the window moved.

Quitting KDE

To quit working with KDE, you can use the Logout entry in the Application Starter menu or the corresponding button on the panel. You will be asked if you really want to quit KDE. Quitting will close all windows and return you to your console or display manager. For information on how programs can save your work during logout, please read about the Logout button in the "Panel" section earlier in this chapter.

All About Your Desktop

Grandma, what big eyes you have.

–Little Red Riding Hood

The better to see you with.

–The Wolf

The more you see, the more efficiently you can use your desktop. KDE gives you the opportunity to make the desktop look and work the you way prefer, enabling you to work faster and more productively. It even gives you the opportunity to be warned if a wolf is trying to eat you, or (if you happen to be a granny) alert you when Little Red Riding Hood is on her way to bring you the goodies. Now that's service.

The Autostart Folder

Before I discovered the Autostart folder, my daily startup routine with KDE consisted of starting KDE, starting KEdit, starting `kvt`, starting Netscape, and starting `kscd`. This took time I could have spent better. As of the first Beta release, native KDE programs left open at the end of a session will save their state and reappear when you login again, but there are some programs (like Netscape) that will not. You can use the Autostart folder for these programs.

To launch programs when KDE is started, do the following:

1. Open the Autostart folder found on the upper-left corner of your desktop.
2. Open a file manager window containing the program you want to add. If you do not know how to do this, see "The File Manager Screen" section earlier in this chapter.
3. Drag-and-drop the desired program from its source folder into the Autostart folder. When asked, choose Link to create a symbolic link instead of a full copy. This saves a great deal of disk space.
4. Repeat this step for every program you want started when KDE is launched. Of course, you may select applications not native to KDE, including Netscape, tin, pine and many others.
5. Restart KDE.

Your programs should now launch automatically when KDE is restarted. If you want to add something special (e.g., you want to see a certain Web site when your system goes up), read the "Using Templates" section later in this chapter. The procedures described there works for any folder, so you can also apply them to the Autostart folder.

Adding Programs and Shortcut Icons to Your Panel

The KDE panel is not limited to the setup you find right after installing KDE. The KDE panel is designed to be extended, and there are two ways of doing that: Adding new programs and adding shortcut icons.

Programs

To add your favorite programs to the KDE panel, you must use the KDE Menu Editor. To start it, use the Application Starter and choose Utilities ➢ Menu Editor. A window containing an empty button will appear. To change it, click it using the right mouse button and choose Change. Next, you should see another window with various options you can set. The Type dropdown menu contains some types of links you can create. Choose Application. Now choose the Name field and enter the description that will appear in the Application Starter. For example, you can type Netscape Communicator. Next, click the large and the small picture using the left mouse button and Select an Icon for the Application. In the Comment field you can optionally enter a remark about the application. Be sure to choose a helpful comment, because it will appear as tool-tip in the Application Starter. For Netscape, you might enter **WWW-Browser with Mail and News software.**

If not already selected, choose the Execute tab and enter the Execute field. Here, you must type the complete path to your application, for example `/usr/local/netscape/netscape`. Set the Working Directory to a value that makes sense, such as `/usr/local/netscape`. If your application runs in a terminal, you must select Run In Terminal and specify the Terminal Options. The terminal options are the command-line switches of `kvt`; you can see them by using

```
kvt --help
```

in a terminal window. After you have made all the adjustments needed, choose the Ok button and select File ➢ Save from the main menu. Next, restart your panel by choosing Panel ➢Restart from the Application Starter. You should now find a new entry Personal with the new menu entries.

Shortcut Icons

Although KDE is much more comfortable than the average Unix window manager, everyone wants a solution for a one-click way to start a program. Later, you will learn how to create links and files on your desktop, but this also has some disadvantages: sometimes all of your desktops are filled up with windows, and you cannot reach your icons without minimizing all of the windows that cover them. For commonly used programs, you can minimize this problem and speed access by creating shortcut icons on the KDE panel.

To create a shortcut on the KDE panel, do the following:

1. Click the Application Starter and choose Panel ➢ Add application.
2. You will see the top level of the Application Starter again. Go through the menus to find the program for which you want to create the shortcut, such as "Home Directory" or "`kvt`." Click the program you want.

A new icon will appear on the KDE panel. Click it, and the program will start . If you want to move the icon, click it using the right mouse button and choose Move. Move the icon to the position you want and press the left mouse button. If you wish to remove the icon, click it using the right mouse button and choose Remove.

Creating New Files on Your Desktop

Your desktop can be an efficient place to work. Every time you start KDE, you can see the complete files, folders, and URLs that you often use.

There are two ways to create and edit files on your desktop. In any application, you can say that you want to save your work in the desktop subfolder of your home directory. For example, my home directory is `/home/stupiddog`, so my desktop directory is `/home/stupiddog/Desktop`. Everything you save there will be put on your desktop.

If you want to move existing files to your desktop, the best way to achieve this is to use the K file manager (kfm). Open a file manager window and drag the files you need to your desktop. You can choose to copy them if you want to keep all your common stuff on the desktop now, or you can create symbolic links to the real files. Everything you change in the link files will be automatically updated in the originals. For more information on how to use drag-and-drop and the file manager, see the "Moving Files with Drag-and-Drop" section earlier in this chapter.

Placing Links on Your Desktop

Placing files on your desktop may shorten the paths you need to enter. However, sometimes it would be nice if you could start KEdit with a commonly edited file already opened in it. And how often do you find yourself frustrated after browsing through endless lists of bookmarks to find a site you visit often? Wouldn't it be nice if everything necessary to deliver you to that site was done automatically after clicking a single icon?

Using Templates

Templates provide a convenient mechanism for performing tasks such as those outlined above. Templates can also be used to associate particular file extensions with a specific application. When a file ending in a known extension is double-clicked, the application associated with that extension is automatically started. In short, Templates help you get the most out of KDE.

Example*:* You want to put an icon for visiting the KDE Web site on your desktop.

1. Open the Template folder on your desktop. Here, you can see all the templates you can use for creating new links and resources. Ftpurl is a template you can use for creating a link to an FTP site and even to a particular directory. For example, you could create a link straight to `ftp://ftp.kde.org/pub/kde/stable` to be informed when a new release is available. MimeType is a very powerful tool. Because of its complexity I have decided to explain it in the following "Using MIME Types" section. Program is a general template you can use to start a particular program with an argument. For example, you could use this to start `/usr/src/linux/make xconfig` to configure the kernel. URL is also something general: It is a link to a URL which does not start with `http://` or `ftp://`. Make sure that your link makes sense; kfm cannot handle Quake servers (yet). WWWUrl is the template we will be using now. It creates a link to a specific Web site.

WARNING

If you started KDE as the system administrator (root), make sure you do not change the templates unless you know exactly what you are doing! If you destroy a template, only a new installation of KDE can recreate it!

2. Drag the WWWUrl to your desktop. When asked, choose Copy to create your own copy of the template you can manipulate.

NOTE

If you do not know about how to use Drag-and-Drop, see the "Moving Files with Drag-and-Drop" section earlier in this chapter for more information.

3. Click the template copy using the right mouse button and choose Properties.
4. In the dialog box that appears, you will see three tabs: Program, Permission, and URL. Change the filename and permissions as needed, then click the URL tab.
5. In the URL field, you must enter the URL you want to be shown when you click the icon. For our example, type **`http://www.kde.org`**.
6. You can click the icon to change the icon for this new shortcut.
7. If you are satisfied, click OK to save your changes.

This will update the icon. When you click it, you will be transferred to the KDE homepage. I suggest that you play around with templates a bit. They are extremely powerful and can be customized for almost any need.

Using MIME Types

MIME Types are very powerful. Employing them, you can easily customize your system such that clicking a file of a specific type starts the application with which that file type has been associated. For example, all `.mod` files could be set to start `kmodplayer`, `.html` files could open a `kfm` window showing the file, and a core file can be viewed with the Hex Editor by simply clicking on the core file.

WARNING

Although MIME types are very powerful, they are not without dangers. Playing around with MIME types as the system administrator (root) can damage a KDE system so severely that it cannot be restarted!

In this example, you will create your personal MIME style, which is only relevant for you. It will only affect other users if you copy or move it to `/opt/share/mimelnk`.

To link a certain file type with a particular application:

1. Make sure that the application that you want to link to the file type has an entry in the KDE panel. If it is missing, see the "Programs" section earlier in this chapter for instructions on how to create an entry.
2. Choose Edit ➢ MIME types in the `kfm` file manager window.
3. Think about the type of file for which you want to create an entry. By default, there are five top level types: Application is for files that are usually created or edited with one specific application, for example, tar, gzip, and pdfs. Audio is for everything that generates any kind of tones: waves, midis, mods, etc. Image is for any graphics files like gif, jpeg or tiff. Text is for everything that is text, for example, plain text, html, C and Pascal source code, tex documents and tcl scripts. Finally, Video is for any type of video streaming like mpeg. Decide to which category your type belongs and change to the matching directory.
4. Open the Template folder, which is accessible as an icon on your desktop.
5. Drag-and-drop the Mimetype icon into the other window and copy it.
6. Right-click the copied icon and select Properties. Edit the properties of your type.
7. Click Binding. You will now see a mask that requires five entries.
8. The first field must be filled with the file suffix. For example, if you want to create a new type for SGML documents, you should type `*.sgml`; `*.SGML`; here. Any file ending with `.sgml` or `.SGML` will now be handled with the new type.
9. Enter a description for the type in the Comment field. For the SGML example, it could be "SGML document."

10. Enter the MIME type. It is built with the directory (`text/` for the SGML example) and a name you choose. For the SGML example, you would enter `text/sgml` as the Mime type. KDE will inform you if there already is a convention on which prefix to use for your type. The kfm Web browser will also depend on this setting when you download a document of this type from the Web!
11. Choose an application that is used to edit this file from the drop-down menu. For the SGML example, we simply use the Editor.
12. Click the icon to choose it. Every file matching the suffix you entered will appear with this icon when shown in the file manager window.
13. Click OK to save the new type.

Try your new association by opening a directory containing a file of the type you just selected. Click the file, and the program needed to edit it should start. If something goes wrong or your system cannot even start anymore, use a text console (or `kdm`'s emergency shell function) to delete the link. That should make everything fine.

Defining Your Own Templates

By default, KDE provides you with five default templates which can build new links on your desktop. However, sometimes you will want to create a new template. Doing this is simple:

1. Login with root privileges.
2. Create the file as usual.
3. Move or copy it into the Template folder.
4. Whenever you want to reuse your new template, copy it from the template folder onto your desktop or into a directory, rename it, and use it. Since the Template folder is only writable by you, nobody can accidentally destroy the template (that is, if he or she is not you. It might be a good idea to prevent even you from being able to write to this file, to avoid accidentally damaging it).

Using the Font Manager

The KDE font manager takes care that you only work with the fonts you really need. You can decide whether or not to use the set of fonts in your X11 font directory. You can start the font manager using the Application Starter. The font manager can be found in the System folder. When you start it, you will see the list of X11 fonts available in the left window and the fonts used by KDE in the right window. If you wish to add or remove the ability to use these fonts in KDE, click any of them and decide to add or to remove it.

The Font Test tab can be used to preview how a font will look. Choose the font family, subtype, size, and attributes and you will get a preview.

Understanding the Raw X11 Font List

There are many entries when you click the Tab raw X11 fonts. The KDE font manager already shows you the combinations which make sense, and lets you see which entries were useless to it. There is nothing you can do with this list except view it.

Using the Trashcan

Under normal circumstances, deleting a file under Unix is something that cannot be undone. However, with the KDE file manager, you can choose Move to Trashcan instead of Delete. This will move the file into the Trash Folder, which, by default, is accessible as an icon on your desktop. In the Trash Folder, you can always recover deleted files. Remember to empty the trashcan regularly by clicking it using the right mouse button, then choosing Empty Trashcan, otherwise you might run out of disk space because the files still need space. Note, however, that once you empty the Trash Folder, the files contained therein are lost forever.

Customizing KDE: The K Control Center

Actually, we are talking about peanuts.

—The president of a well-known German bank after the financial scandal surrounding Dr. Juergen Schneider

The K Control Center gives you full control over your desktop, giving it its individual touch by changing the setting of all those little peanuts. To start it, choose KDE Control Panel from the Application Starter. The K Control Center comes up and gives you some basic information about your system.

Desktop

When you start KDE for the first time, you can see a white background and buttons for your desktops. You might agree with me that this does not look very exciting, so we need something to change it. Click the Desktop in the selection list.

Background

Maybe the first feature that everyone wants to customize, the background tab gives you full control over the background you are working with. There are two types of backgrounds: colors (and color gradients) and "real" background images. You can change the settings for every desktop individually by choosing it with the left and right arrows.

Notice the color window first. You can see the currently selected color (some type of gray or white if you have not customized KDE yet) and the options Flat and Gradient. If you choose Flat, then your background will only consist of one single, unmodified color you can select. Try selecting Gradient. You will see another color selector and two more options appear. Click the color selector and pick a color of your choice. When you get back, you already have a preview of how the screen will look. If you choose Portrait, the color gradient will be vertically (from the top to the bottom of the screen), otherwise it will be painted horizontally (from the left to the right).

If you prefer to have a "real" background image instead of a color gradient, take a look at the right end of the window.

NOTE

Be sure to disable the color gradient, otherwise the background picture will not appear!

There is a drop-down control from where you can select a background picture. KDE provides you with three samples, but you can use the Browse... button to take any one you have available. Next, you should choose what to do with pictures that do not fit the screen exactly (this happens almost every time). If your picture is too small, Tiled is a good solution. Your picture will be copied as often as needed to fill the screen. This is the default. Centered will place your picture in the middle of the screen. The rest will be painted with the color you selected earlier (be sure to have its state set to Flat). The last option, Scaled, will stretch the picture until it matches the desktop in size.

Colors

If the backgrounds did not provide you with the level of individuality you need, these options surely will. Click the Color Schemes tab. Here, you can set the colors for all the screen elements individually. Click the Widget box on the left and select an element whose color you want to change. If you do not know what everything is, you can also click the sample. Next, click the Color Selector below the widget box and choose a color you like. Play around a little bit and see what you like best. If you do not get the results you want, you can also try one of the predefined schemes in the list box on the right. Once you get it the way you want it, be sure to save it using the Save button. You can also set the level of contrast for your color scheme; this is especially handy if you are working with a portable computer and light makes it difficult to decipher the display.

Screen Saver

Many older monitors have a very bad habit if you forget to turn them off when going out of your room; when they display a picture too long, they tend to like it so much that they want to display it as a shadow forever. Unfortunately, there is no way of stopping this unholy friendship between your monitor and the picture, but there are ways of preventing it: Screen Savers.

Click the Screen Savers register tab. Here you can set the screen saver delay. You can also password protect the screen saver so that it will be necessary to enter your password to continue. If you decide to set this, make sure to set the wait period not too short! It is annoying to type in the password every minute because the screen saver was activated while you were thinking about some project. The priority slider enables you to control how much CPU time the screen saver is allowed to take. If you compile big programs in the background or you are using your Unix box as a server, you better set this to Low.

Next, click around the screen saver list and pick a saver that you like. You can test it using the Test button, located to the right of the screen saver list. Many screen savers have additional options you can set by using the Setup button.

Style

You can change the general appearance of the KDE controls ("widgets") if you prefer a desktop that looks more like Windows 95. You can also set the default font. For example, if your display is small and the resolution high, you might find this handy.

Titlebar

After the installation, KDE applications always have the full KDE title bar, containing the window menu, sticky button, title bar itself, minimize, maximize and close buttons. If you do not want to have all of these buttons or want to change their positions, you can change the title bar settings in the register buttons. Choose whether you want to have a button or menu on the left or the right side. Off means that it will not be displayed at all.

WARNING

If you do not know alternative methods for the window actions (like the "Shortcut Table" later in this chapter), you can get into serious problems using your desktop. Beware!

The Appearance register contains two settings: At first, you can decide if the window title bar should be drawn using a color gradient or just (this is faster) with a plain color. If a window title is wider than the title bar, the text will be scrolled from left to right and backwards. With the Title Animation setting, you can decide how fast this happens.

Windows

The following will change the behavior of the windows themselves:

Window Movement You can tell KDE to move the windows with their entire content (this may be slow on your machine) or only to move the opaque, which is slightly faster.

Resize Animation This will animate the window while you resize it. Turn this off if KDE gets too slow.

Focus Policy It often can be helpful to switch to a window without having to press a button. If you want to be able to do this, choose Focus Follows Mouse and set the number of seconds to wait before raising the window under the mouse cursor.

Maximize Style For some reason, you may want your windows only to be maximized vertically. See the "Shortcuts" section later in this chapter for information on how to achieve the same with mouse and keyboard.

Sound System

Using the sound system panel, you can easily adjust settings to the sound output KDE and its applications produce.

Bell

KDE generates various warning signals, called beeps, when you make a mistake (e.g., copying a file into a folder you do not have access to). You can adjust the settings for these beeps here:

Volume Sets the volume of the beep. You can set it from 0 (no beep) to 100 (you should think carefully before making a mistake after setting this.)

Pitch Adjusts the frequency of the tone. Ranges go from 0 (no beep) up to 2000 (you should not set this unless you have no pets, like dogs or bats, around).

Duration Tells KDE how long the tone is played.

Input Devices

You can use several input devices with the X Window System (and thus with KDE). You can change their settings here:

Keyboard

Here, you can set whether a character is repeated when you keep pressing its key. If you have a bad keyboard and need the clicking after you hit a key, you can also turn on the key click volume.

Mouse

The Mouse is the most frequently used pointing device around, and for the majority of computer owners, the most intuitive method of navigating through KDE. (For some owners with bad mice, it is also a reason for visiting the doctor very often, see the "Moving Files with Drag-and-Drop" section earlier in this chapter for information.)

Acceleration Sets the speed of the mouse. The higher the setting, the faster your mouse will move around the screen.

Threshold Threshold is the distance the pointer must move (in a small amount of time) before accelerated movement occurs. 0 disables it.

Try to experiment with these settings; the right combination will allow you to point exactly on short distances and to move fast over long ones.

Panel Settings

You can also access the Panel Settings by selecting the Application Starter and choosing Panel ➢ Configure. A new window containing three register tabs will pop up.

Panel and Taskbar

On the first tab, you can tell KDE where you want the panel and the taskbar to be displayed. You can also use the drop-down field to set the size of the panel bar if your display is always too full.

Options

On this tab you can enable or diasable tool tips. If you enable tool tips you should set the duration between the time the mouse over a menu and when the tool tip for that menu pops up. Next you can set if you want the panel bar and/or the taskbar to auto hide when the mouse is not over them. The final option lets you set the clock to 24-hour or AM/PM format.

NOTE

The previous information relates to the KPanel Configuration window. The K Control Center part will be updated.

Desktops

As discussed earlier, desktops give you more space and help you organize your work. By clicking the Desktops register tab, you can customize them. Notice the two sliders at the bottom of the window. The Visible sliders let you set the number of desktops you can access, Width sets the size of their icons on the panel bar. Activate as many desktops as you need. You can now edit their names in the upper part of the windows.

System Information

There are no settings to be changed here. Instead, you will be given information about the available memory and information about your processor(s).

Network

KDE offers you complete network management via the KDE Control Centre (Kcc). Note that Kcc is still under development. This makes your life as a potential Unix system administrator very easy: From now on, setting up servers will be faster and easier. Because configuration is easier, there will be fewer mistakes and fewer security problems caused by them.

Samba Network Status

This point gives you information about the users that are connected to your Unix box via the SMB (Session Message Block) Protocol. SMB is the protocol used mainly by Windows 95 and Windows NT machines to share files and folders.

Tips and Tricks for Your Daily Work

Everyone can make an omelet with eggs. The trick is to make one with none.

—A fortune cookie

Nearly everyone can use KDE; this is why the developers made it. There are no cryptic switches with which to cope, and few configuration files you need edit in ASCII style. However, there are some ways you can do your work more elegantly, saving you time for the truly important things, like Tetris.

Shortcuts

Alt+Esc or **Control+Esc** Shows the KDE session manager, from which you can switch to a specific application or log out of KDE.

Alt+Tab or **Alt+Shift+Tab** Cycle through the windows

Ctrl+Tab or **Ctrl+Shift+Tab** Cycle through your desktops

Alt+F2 Command line

Alt+F3 Window Menu

Alt+F4 Close the current window

Ctrl+F1–8 Switch to a specific desktop

Ctrl+Alt+Esc Window destroyer (every window you click will be destroyed)

Ctrl+Alt+Backspace This exits KDE (without saving!); use this as a last resort

Ctrl+Alt+Numpad + Cycles to the next screen resolution

Ctrl+Alt+Numpad – Cycles to the previous screen resolution

Mouse Techniques

Click the border or the titlebar Left: Activates and raises the window, Middle: Activates and lowers the window, Right: Shows window menu if the window is active, activates it otherwise.

Double-click the window title Maximizes the window

Drag the titlebar Moves the window around

Drag corners or edges Resizes the window

Alt+Left button Moves the window around

Alt+Middle button Raises the window

Alt+Right button Resizes the window

Click the Icon on the top left Window Menu

Click the Sticky Button Toggles sticky

Click Maximize Left: Maximizes the window, Middle: Maximizes only vertically, Right: Maximizes horizontally

Click Close Closes the window, program asks you whether to save your work or not.

Activating the Screen Saver by Moving Your Mouse to a Corner

Besides the Lock Screen Button on the K Panel, there is another way you can invoke the K screen savers: Go into the screen saver settings (Application Starter ➢ System ➢ Screen Settings) and click one of the corners of the sample screen. Three options will be presented. Ignore will ignore any movement of the mouse into that corner. Save will invoke the screen saver after the mouse pointer resides in the corner for more than 5 seconds. Lock will do the same as Save, but it will ask for your login password.

FREQUENTLY ASKED QUESTIONS ABOUT KDE

What are you?

I'm your worst nightmare.

–*Batman* animated series

There are some questions that are always raised on the KDE mailing lists. To keep the traffic as low as possible (making the lists more readable), we have included them in this section. So please be kind and do not ask them in the mailing lists anymore–think of the quote above!

What Does "KDE" Stand For?

KDE stands for the K Desktop Environment, which itself is intended to be a collection of small tools, a window manager, a file manager, and tools that bring all this together. It is created to make your life with Unix easier.

I Cannot Compile Package XXX

Always be sure that you have the newest version of the KDE libraries installed. The software is in constant development, so the dependencies can change from one day to another. You may also find the "Using TGZ to Install on Top of Other Systems" section earlier in this chapter helpful. Another problem could be that you are using a program written for a very old version of KDE, which depends on outdated include files. Please check the file dates. They should be more recent than the dates of your current KDE version.

KDE Is Not Stable

KDE is being developed in two forks, one for bleeding edge development, the other for normal use (where stability is considered to be important). One can, in general, obtain KDE in many ways. Obtaining pre-compiled binaries in a package format (`rpm`,`deb`,`tgz`) labelled with a particular version (e.g., 1.1) is the best way to encourage stability on your KDE desktop.

The price of stability is that one must wait for each release to get new features. If you want the latest and greatest versions of software, you may have to go with source code, perhaps even to the point of CVS snapshots. These are daily snapshots of whatever the developers are working on, and some things are guaranteed to be broken.

WARNING

Do not rely on CVS snapshots to maintain operational desktops! You will get burned eventually!

Other Sources for Help

Take a look at the KDE Web-Site at `http://www.kde.org` for the most up-to-date information available about KDE on the Web. You may also want to subscribe to our mailing lists.

Send mail to the specified address with "subscribe your email address" in the subject line in order to get subscribed:

- KDE common mailing list: `kde-request@kde.org`
- KDE developers' mailing list: `kde-devel-request@kde.org`
- KDE look and feel discussions: `kde-look-request@kde.org`
- KDE announcements: `kde-announce-request@kde.org`
- KDE licensing questions: `kde-licensing-request@kde.org`
- KDE users' list: `kde-user-request@kde.org`
- KDE Documentors' list: `kde-doc-request@kde.org`

EPILOGUE

She had her moments, she had some style, the best show in town was the crowd, outside the Casa Rossada crying "Eva Peron;" but that's all gone now.

—The end of *Evita*

We hope that you found this documentation useful, informative, and perhaps even entertaining. If you would like to tell us your opinion or suggest improvements, see the "Contacting the Authors" section earlier in this chapter for further information. The following things are not necessary to understand the KDE Desktop Environment, but you still may want to read it.

The K Documentation Staff

Andreas Buschka The one responsible for the greatest part of this. Read about KDE in the German computer magazine *c't* and has been addicted to it ever since. Likes: Italian food, swimming, role playing games (GURPS, DSA), Sabrina Setlur's music and everything that has to do with romance. Hates: Mondays, seeing KDE not compiling, sunny weather, senseless lyrics, a famous software company from Redmond. E-mail: `andi@circe.tops.net`.

Robert D. Williams Created the first version and currently the coordinator. E-mail: `rwilliam@kde.org`

Poul Gerhard Contributed corrections and changes

John Waalkes Contributed corrections and changes

Vernon Wells Contributed corrections and changes

Kay Lutz Contributed corrections and changes

Stephan Kulow Our professional Installer. E-mail: `coolo@kde.org`

French Translation John B. Perr. E-mail: `jperro@mail.change-espace.fr`

German Translation Oliver Hensel. E-mail: `Oliver.Hensel@gmx.net`

Italian Translation Antonio Esposito. E-mail: `antonio.esposito@star1.change-espace.fr`

Polish Translation Piotr Roszatycki. E-mail: `dexter@fnet.com.pl`

Portuguese Translation Goncalo Valverde. E-mail: `grumbler@esoterica.pt`

Spanish Translation Gustavo Cavazos. E-mail: `gcavazos@yahoo.com`

Russian Translation Sergey Orlovsky. E-mail: `cyberian@cyberia.math.nsc.ru`

English Reviewer Peter Silva. E-mail: `Peter.Silva@kde.org`

We Still Need People!

KDE is a huge project, and every KDE supporter has already realized that. All of us are trying very hard to create a user interface that is easy to use and maybe also has the potential to make Unix ready for the desktop PC. You have the chance to participate in this project too, and we would be thankful if you did. Developers and interested users communicate via several mailing lists described in the "Other Sources for Help" section earlier in this chapter. If you would like to help, please do so! We are still looking for helpers in the following departments:

- Development (Libraries and Applications)
- Documentation
- Graphics
- Beta-Testing
- and everywhere else, too :-)

Legal Notices

This document may be freely published under the terms of the GNU General Public License (see Appendix D) and contains copyrighted material from Andreas Buschka, Gerhard Poul, and Robert David Williams. All trademarks and branded names mentioned are properties of their legal owners.

Sources of Information Used During the Creation of This Chapter

During the creation of this documentation, the authors used the following sources for information:

- The KDE Mailing lists
- Various README and HTML help files that came with the KDE components
- `ksgml2html` for creating the web version of this document

Greetings

Andreas Buschka

For keeping my working morale up: Robert David Williams

For musical support during the work: Madonna (and the *Evita* soundtrack), Enigma (and *MCMXC*, *The Cross Of Changes*, and *Le Roi Est Mort, Vive Le Roi!*), the Verve (and *Bittersweet Symphony*), and Sabrina Setlur (and *Die neue S-Klasse*)

No thanks to: A famous software company, located in Redmond, USA.

Severin: "Stop this boring stuff and get playing volleyball," L.

Stefan: "You do not seriously believe they will take this s...," L.

APPENDICES

Appendix A

Command Reference

This appendix contains reference documentation for some commonly used commands as well as for some other commands discussed in this book. This style of documentation is known as *man pages.* Each command on a Unix system comes with a man page. You can view man pages for a program with the command "man program."

There are many more commands than are documented in this chapter, and some commands on your system may be newer than the versions documented here, so you are encouraged to check the pages on your particular system for updates.

Man pages are organized into "sections." Here we include pages from the following sections:

1–User Commands

5–File Formats

8–Administrative Commands

The man page will search the sections for a page in a particular order, so if both foo(1) and foo(8) exist, you will probably be shown foo(1). Read the man page for man(1) for more information on this and on how to specify foo(8).

User Commands

AT(1)

NAME

at, batch, atq, atrm Queue, examine, or delete jobs for later execution.

SYNOPSIS

at [**-V**] [**-q** *queue*] [**-f** *file*] [**-mldbv**] **TIME at -c** *job* [*job...*]

atq [**-V**] [**-q** *queue*] [**-v**]

atrm [**-V**] *job* [*job...*]

batch [**-V**] [**-q** *queue*] [**-f** *file*] [**-mv**] [**TIME**]

DESCRIPTION

at and **batch** read commands from standard input or a specified file which are to be executed at a later time, using **/bin/sh**.

at Executes commands at a specified time.

atq Lists the user's pending jobs, unless the user is the superuser; in that case, everybody's jobs are listed.

atrm Deletes jobs.

batch Executes commands when system load levels permit; in other words, when the load average drops below 0.8, or the value specified in the invocation of **atrun**.

at allows fairly complex time specifications, extending the POSIX.2 standard. It accepts times of the form **HH:MM** to run a job at a specific time of day. (If that time is already past, the next day is assumed.) You may also specify **midnight, noon,** or **teatime** (4pm) and you can have a time-of-day suffixed with **AM** or **PM** for running in the morning or the evening. You can also say what day the job will be run, by giving a date in the form **month-name day** with an optional **year,** or giving a date of the form **MMDDYY** or **MM/DD/YY** or **DD.MM.YY.** The specification of a date *must* follow the specification of the time of day. You can also give times like **now +** ***count***

time-units, where the time-units can be **minutes, hours, days,** or **weeks** and you can tell **at** to run the job today by suffixing the time with **today** and to run the job tomorrow by suffixing the time with **tomorrow.**

For example, to run a job at 4pm three days from now, you would do **at 4pm + 3 days;** to run a job at 10am on July 31, you would do **at 10am Jul 31;** and to run a job at 1am tomorrow, you would do **at 1am tomorrow.**

The exact definition of the time specification can be found in `/usr/doc/at-3.1.7/timespec`.

For both **at** and **batch**, commands are read from standard input or the file specified with the **-f** option and executed. The working directory, the environment (except for the variables **TERM**, **DISPLAY** and _) and the umask are retained from the time of invocation. An **at** - or **batch** command invoked from a su(1) shell will retain the current userid. The user will be mailed standard error and standard output from his commands, if any. Mail will be sent using the command **/usr/sbin/sendmail**. If **at** is executed from a su(1) shell, the owner of the login shell will receive the mail.

The superuser may use these commands in any case; for other users, permission to use **at** is determined by the files `/etc/at.allow` and `/etc/at.deny`.

If the file `/etc/at.allow` exists, only usernames mentioned in it are allowed to use **at**.

If `/etc/at.allow` does not exist, `/etc/at.deny` is checked, every username not mentioned in it is then allowed to use **at**.

If neither exists, only the superuser is allowed to use **at**.

An empty `/etc/at.deny` means that every user is allowed to use these commands; this is the default configuration.

OPTIONS

-V Prints the version number to standard error.

-q *queue* Uses the specified queue. A queue designation consists of a single letter; valid queue designations range from a to z. and A to Z. The a queue is the default for **at** and the b queue for **batch**. Queues with higher letters run with increased niceness. The special queue "=" is reserved for jobs which are currently running.

If a job is submitted to a queue designated with an uppercase letter, it is treated as if it had been submitted to **batch** at that time. If **atq** is given a specific queue, it will only show jobs pending in that queue.

-m Sends mail to the user when the job has completed even if there was no output.

-f *file* Reads the job from file rather than standard input.

-l Is an alias for **atq**.

-d Is an alias for **atrm**.

-v For **atq**, shows completed but not yet deleted jobs in the queue; otherwise shows the time the job will be executed.

Times displayed will be in the format "1997-02-20 14:50" unless the environment variable *POSIXLY_CORRECT* is set; then, it will be "Thu Feb 20 14:50:00 1996".

-c cats the jobs listed on the command line to standart output.

FILES

```
/var/spool/at
/var/spool/at/spool
/proc/loadavg
/var/run/utmp
/etc/at.allow
/etc/at.deny
```

SEE ALSO

cron(1), nice(1), sh(1), umask(2), atd(8)

BUGS

The correct operation of **batch** for Linux depends on the presence of a `proc`- type directory mounted on */proc*.

If the file `/var/run/utmp` is not available or corrupted, or if the user is not logged on at the time **at** is invoked, the mail is sent to the userid found in the environment variable *LOGNAME*. If that is undefined or empty, the current userid is assumed.

at and **batch** as presently implemented are not suitable when users are competing for resources. If this is the case for your site, you might want to consider another batch system, such as **nqs**.

AUTHOR

at was mostly written by Thomas Koenig, `ig25@rz.uni-karlsruhe.de`.

CAL(1)

NAME

cal Displays a calendar.

SYNOPSIS

cal [-jy] [month [year]]

DESCRIPTION

Cal displays a simple calendar. If arguments are not specified, the current month is displayed. The options are as follows:

-j Display Julian dates (days one-based, numbered from January 1).

-y Display a calendar for the current year.

A single parameter specifies the year (1–9999) to be displayed; note the year must be fully specified: "cal 89" will *not* display a calendar for 1989. Two parameters denote the month (1–12) and year. If no parameters are specified, the current month's calendar is displayed.

A year starts on Jan 1.

The Gregorian Reformation is assumed to have occurred in 1752 on the 3rd of September. By this time, most countries had recognized the reformation (although a few did not recognize it until the early 1900s.) Ten days following that date were eliminated by the reformation, so the calendar for that month is a bit unusual.

HISTORY

A **cal** command appeared in Version 6 AT&T Unix.

CAT(1)

NAME

cat Concatenate files and print on the standard output.

SYNOPSIS

cat [-benstuvAET] [--number] [--number-nonblank] [--squeeze-blank] [--show-nonprinting] [--show-ends] [--show-tabs] [--show-all] [--help] [--version] [file...]

DESCRIPTION

This documentation is no longer being maintained and may be inaccurate or incomplete. The Texinfo documentation is now the authoritative source.

This manual page documents the GNU version of **cat**. **cat** writes the contents of each given file, the standard input if none are given or when a file named "-" is given, to the standard output.

OPTIONS

-b, --number-nonblank Number all nonblank output lines, starting with 1.

-e Equivalent to *-vE*.

-n, --number Number all output lines, starting with 1.

-s, --squeeze-blank Replace multiple adjacent blank lines with a single blank line.

-t Equivalent to *-vT*.

-u Ignored; for Unix compatibility.

-v, --show-nonprinting Display control characters except for LFD and TAB using '^' notation and precede characters that have the high bit set with *'M-'*.

-A, --show-all Equivalent to *-vET*.

-E, --show-ends Display a *'$'* after the end of each line.

-T, --show-tabs Display TAB characters as '^*I*'.

--help Print a usage message and exit with a status code indicating success.

--version Print version information on standard output then exit.

DATE(1)

NAME

cp Copy files.

SYNOPSIS

cp [*options*] source dest

cp [*options*] source... directory

Options:

[-abdfilprsuvxPR] [-S backup-suffix] [-V {numbered,existing, simple}] [--backup] [--no-dereference] [--force] [--interactive] [--one-file-system] [--preserve] [--recursive] [--update] [--verbose] [--suffix=backup-suffix] [--version-control={numbered, existing,simple}] [--archive] [--parents] [--link] [--symbolic-link] [--help] [--version]

DESCRIPTION

This documentation is no longer being maintained and may be inaccurate or incomplete. The Texinfo documentation is now the authoritative source.

This manual page documents the GNU version of cp. If the last argument names an existing directory, **cp** copies each other given file into a file with the same name in that directory. Otherwise, if only two files are given, it copies the first onto the second. It is an error if the last argument is not a directory and more than two files are given. By default, it does not copy directories.

OPTIONS

-a, --archive Preserve as much as possible of the structure and attributes of the original files in the copy. The same as -dpR.

-b, --backup Make backups of files that are about to be overwritten or removed.

-d, --no-dereference Copy symbolic links as symbolic links rather than copying the files that they point to, and preserve hard link relationships between source files in the copies.

-f, --force Remove existing destination files.

-i, --interactive Prompt whether to overwrite existing regular destination files.

-l, --link Make hard links instead of copies of non-directories.

-P, --parents Form the name of each destination file by appending to the target directory a slash and the specified name of the source file. The last argument given to cp must be the name of an existing directory. For example, the command cp --parents a/b/c existing_dir copies the file *a/b/c* to *existing_dir/a/b/c*, creating any missing intermediate directories.

-p, --preserve Preserve the original files' owner, group, permissions, and timestamps.

-r Copy directories recursively, copying all nondirectories as if they were regular files.

-s,--symbolic-link Make symbolic links instead of copies of non-directories. All source filenames must be absolute (starting with /) unless the destination files are in the current directory. This option produces an error message on systems that do not support symbolic links.

-u,--update Do not copy a nondirectory that has an existing destination with the same or newer modification time.

-v, --verbose Print the name of each file before copying it.

-x, --one-file-system Skip subdirectories that are on different filesystems from the one that the copy started on.

-R, --recursive Copy directories recursively.

--help Print a usage message on standard output and exit successfully.

--version Print version information on standard output then exit successfully.

-S, --suffix backup-suffix The suffix used for making simple backup files can be set with the *SIMPLE_BACKUP_SUFFIX* environment variable, which can be overridden by this option. If neither of those is given, the default is ~, as it is in Emacs.

-V, --version-control {numbered,existing,simple} The type of backups made can be set with the *VERSION_CONTROL* environment variable, which can be overridden by this option. If *VERSION_CONTROL* is not set and this option is not given, the default backup type is *existing*. The value of the *VERSION_CONTROL* environment variable and the argument to this option are like the GNU Emacs *version-control* variable; they also recognize synonyms that are more descriptive. The valid values are (unique abbreviations are accepted):

t or **numbered** Always make numbered backups.

nil or **existing** Make numbered backups of files that already have them, simple backups of the others.

never or **simple** Always make simple backups.

CRONTAB(1)

NAME

crontab Maintain crontab files for individual users (V3).

SYNOPSIS

crontab [*-u user*] file

crontab [*-u user*] { -l | -r | -e }

DESCRIPTION

Crontab is the program used to install, deinstall, or list the tables used to drive the cron(8) daemon in Vixie Cron. Each user can have their own crontab, and though these are files in /var, they are not intended to be edited directly.

If the `allow` file exists, then you must be listed therein in order to be allowed to use this command. If the `allow` file does not exist but the `deny` file does exist, then you must not be listed in the `deny` file in order to use this command. If neither of these files exists, then depending on site-dependent configuration parameters, only the superuser will be allowed to use this command, or all users will be able to use this command.

If the *-u* option is given, it specifies the name of the user whose crontab is to be tweaked. If this option is not given, crontab examines "your" crontab, i.e., the crontab of the person executing the command. Note that su(8) can confuse crontab and that if you are running inside of su(8) you should always use the *-u* option for safety's sake.

The first form of this command is used to install a new crontab from some named file or standard input if the pseudo-filename "-" is given.

The *-l* option causes the current crontab to be displayed on standard output.

The *-r* option causes the current crontab to be removed.

The *-e* option is used to edit the current crontab using the editor specified by the VISUAL or EDITOR environment variables. After you exit from the editor, the modified crontab will be installed automatically.

SEE ALSO

crontab(5), cron(8)

FILES

```
/etc/cron.allow
/etc/cron.deny
```

STANDARDS

The **crontab** command conforms to IEEE Std1003.2-1992 (POSIX). This new command syntax differs from previous versions of Vixie Cron, as well as from the classic SVR3 syntax.

DIAGNOSTICS

A fairly informative usage message appears if you run it with a bad command line.

AUTHOR

Paul Vixie <paul@vix.com>

DATE(1)

NAME

date Print or set the system date and time.

SYNOPSIS

date [-u] [-d datestr] [-s datestr] [--utc] [--universal] [--date=datestr] [--set=datestr] [--help] [--version] [+FORMAT] [MMDDhhmm[[CC]YY][.ss]]

DESCRIPTION

This documentation is no longer being maintained and may be inaccurate or incomplete. The Texinfo documentation is now the authoritative source.

This manual page documents the GNU version of date; **date** with no arguments prints the current time and date (in the format of the **%c** directive described below). If given an argument that starts with a **+**, it prints the current time and date in a format controlled by that argument, which has the same format as the format string passed to the **strftime** function. Except for directives that start with **%**, characters in that string are printed unchanged.

The directives are

%	A literal **%**
n	A newline
t	A horizontal tab

Time fields

%H	Hour (00..23)
%I	Hour (01..12)

Time fields

%k	Hour (0..23)
%l	Hour (1..12)
%M	Minute (00..59)
%p	Locale's AM or PM
%r	Time, 12-hour (hh:mm:ss [AP]M)
%s	Seconds since 1970-01-01 00:00:00 UTC (a nonstandard extension)
%S	Second (00..61)
%T	Time, 24-hour (hh:mm:ss)
%X	Locale's time representation (%H:%M:%S)
%Z	Time zone (e.g., EDT), or nothing if no time zone is determinable

Date fields

%a	Locale's abbreviated weekday name (Sun..Sat)
%A	Locale's full weekday name, variable length (Sunday..Saturday)
%b	Locale's abbreviated month name (Jan..Dec)
%B	Locale's full month name, variable length (January..December)
%c	Locale's date and time (Sat Nov 04 12:02:33 EST 1989)
%d	Day of month (01..31)
%D	Date (mm/dd/yy)
%h	Same as %b
%j	Day of year (001..366)
%m	Month (01..12)
%U	Week number of year with Sunday as first day of week (00..53)
%w	Day of week (0..6) with 0 corresponding to Sunday

%W	Week number of year with Monday as first day of week (00..53)
%x	Locale's date representation (mm/dd/yy)
%y	Last two digits of year (00..99)
%Y	Year (1970...)

By default, **date** pads numeric fields with zeroes. GNU **date** recognizes the following nonstandard numeric modifiers:

-	(hyphen) do not pad the field.
_	(underscore) pad the field with spaces.

If given an argument that does not start with **+**, **date** sets the system clock to the time and date specified by that argument. The argument must consist entirely of digits, which have the following meaning:

MM	Month
DD	Day within month
hh	Hour
mm	Minute
CC	First two digits of year (optional)
YY	Last two digits of year (optional)
ss	Second (optional)

Only the superuser can set the system clock.

OPTIONS

-d datestr, --date datestr Display the time and date specified in *datestr*, which can be in almost any common format. The display is in the default output format, or if an argument starting with + is given to date, in the format specified by that argument.

--help Print a usage message on standard output and exit successfully.

-s datestr, --set datestr Set the time and date to *datestr*, which can be in almost any common format. It can contain month names, timezones, *am* and *pm*, etc.

-u, --universal Print or set the time and date in Coordinated Universal Time (also known as Greenwich Mean Time) instead of in local (wall clock) time.

--version Print version information on standard output then exit successfully.

EXAMPLES

To print the date of the day before yesterday

date --date '2 days ago'

To print the date of the day three months and one day hence

date --date '3 months 1 day'

To print the day of year of Christmas in the current year

date --date '25 Dec' +%j

To print the current date in a format including the full month name and the day of the month

date '+%B %d'

But this may not be what you want because for the first nine days of the month, the **%d** expands to a zero-padded two-digit field, for example **date -d 1-may +%B %d** will print **May 01**.

To print the same date but without the leading zero for one-digit days of month, you can use the nonstandard **-** modifier to suppress the padding altogether.

date -d 1-may '+%B %-d'

DF(1)

NAME

df Summarize free disk space.

SYNOPSIS

df [-aikPv] [-t fstype] [-x fstype] [--all] [--inodes] [--type=fstype] [--exclude-type=fstype] [--kilobytes] [--portability] [--print-type] [--help] [--version] [filename...]

DESCRIPTION

This documentation is no longer being maintained and may be inaccurate or incomplete. The Texinfo documentation is now the authoritative source.

This manual page documents the GNU version of df. df displays the amount of disk space available on the filesystem containing each file name argument. If no file name is given, the space available on all currently mounted filesystems is shown. Disk space is shown in 1K blocks by default, unless the environment variable *POSIXLY_CORRECT* is set, in which case 512-byte blocks are used.

If an argument is the absolute file name of a disk device node containing a mounted filesystem, **df** shows the space available on that filesystem rather than on the filesystem containing the device node (which is always the root filesystem). This version of **df** cannot show the space available on unmounted filesystems, because on most kinds of systems doing so requires very nonportable intimate knowledge of filesystem structures.

OPTIONS

-a, --all Include in the listing filesystems that have 0 blocks, which are omitted by default. Such filesystems are typically special-purpose pseudo-filesystems, such as automounter entries. On some systems, filesystems of type "ignore"' or "auto" are also omitted by default and included in the listing by this option.

-i, --inodes List inode usage information instead of block usage. An inode (short for "index node") is a special kind of disk block that contains information about a file, such as its owner, permissions, timestamps, and location on the disk.

-k, --kilobytes Print sizes in 1K blocks instead of 512-byte blocks. This overrides the environment variable POSIXLY_CORRECT.

-P, --portability Use the POSIX output format. This is like the default format except that the information about each filesystem is always printed on exactly one line; a mount device is never put on a line by itself. This means that if the mount device name is more than 20 characters long (as for some network mounts), the columns are misaligned.

-T, --print-type Print a type string for each filesystem. Any such printed filesystem type name may be used as an argument to either of the *--type=* or *--exclude-type=* options.

-t, --type=fstype Limit the listing to filesystems of type *fstype*. Multiple filesystem types can be shown by giving multiple *-t* options. By default, all filesystem types are listed.

-x, --exclude-type=fstype Limit the listing to filesystems not of type *fstype*. Multiple filesystem types can be eliminated by giving multiple *-x* options. By default, all filesystem types are listed.

-v Ignored; for compatibility with System V versions of df.

--help Print usage message on standard output and exit successfully.

--version Print version information on standard output then exit successfully.

DU(1)

NAME

du Summarize disk usage.

SYNOPSIS

du [-abcklsxDLS] [--all] [--total] [--count-links] [--summarize] [--bytes] [--kilobytes] [--one-file-system] [--separate-dirs] [--dereference] [--dereference-args] [--help] [--version] [filename...]

DESCRIPTION

This documentation is no longer being maintained and may be inaccurate or incomplete. The Texinfo documentation is now the authoritative source.

This manual page documents the GNU version of du. du displays the amount of disk space used by each argument and for each subdirectory of directory arguments. The space is measured in 1K blocks by default, unless the environment variable *POSIXLY_CORRECT* is set, in which case 512-byte blocks are used.

OPTIONS

-a, --all Display counts for all files, not just directories.

-b, --bytes Print sizes in bytes.

-c, --total Write a grand total of all of the arguments after all arguments have been processed. This can be used to find out the disk usage of a directory, with some files excluded.

-k, --kilobytes Print sizes in kilobytes. This overrides the environment variable POSIXLY_CORRECT.

-l, --count-links Count the size of all files, even if they have appeared already in another hard link.

-s, --summarize Display only a total for each argument.

-x, --one-file-system Skip directories that are on different filesystems from the one that the argument being processed is on.

-D, --dereference-args Dereference symbolic links that are command line arguments. Does not affect other symbolic links. This is helpful for finding out the disk usage of directories like /usr/tmp where they are symbolic links.

-L, --dereference Dereference symbolic links (show the disk space used by the file or directory that the link points to instead of the space used by the link).

-S, --separate-dirs Count the size of each directory separately, not including the sizes of subdirectories.

--help Print a usage message on standard output and exit successfully.

--version Print version information on standard output then exit successfully.

BUGS

On BSD systems, **du** reports sizes that are half the correct values for files that are NFS-mounted from HP-UX systems. On HP-UX systems, it reports sizes that are twice the correct values for files that are NFS-mounted from BSD systems. This is due to a flaw in HP-UX; it also affects the HP-UX **du** program.

EJECT(1)

NAME

eject Eject removable media.

SYNOPSIS

eject -h

eject [-f][-u][-v]

eject [-f][-u][-v] <nickname>

eject [-f][-u][-v] <device-name>

eject -d

eject -n

eject -a on|1|off|0 [-v]

eject -c <slot> [-v]

DESCRIPTION

eject allows removable media (typically a CD-ROM, floppy disk, or Iomega Jaz or Zip disk) to be ejected under software control. The command can also control some multi-disc CD-ROM changers and the auto-eject feature supported by some devices.

If no device is specified, a default device is used. The environment variable CDROM can be used to set the default device, otherwise the compiled in default is used.

Other devices can be specified either using the full device name (e.g. /dev/cdrom) or a nickname.

COMMAND-LINE OPTIONS

-h This option causes eject to display a brief description of the command options.

-f Normally eject will not eject a device if it has determined that the device is being used for a mounted file system. This option overrides that behaviour, and attempts to force an eject even for a mounted device.

-u This option instructs eject to first try to unmount the device before ejecting it.

-v This makes eject run in verbose mode; more information is displayed about what the command is doing.

-d If invoked with this option, eject lists the default device.

-n If this option is used, eject will list the supported nicknames and corresponding devices.

-a on|1|off|0 This option controls the auto-eject mode, supported by some devices.

-c <slot> With this option a CD slot can be selected from an ATAPI/IDE CD-ROM changer. Linux 2.0 or higher is required to use this feature. The CD-ROM drive can not be in use (mounted data CD or playing a music CD) for a change request to work. Please also note that the first slot of the changer is referred to as 0, not 1.

BUGS/LIMITATIONS

eject only works with devices that support the CDROMEJECT or FDEJECT ioctl. It also works with the Jaz and Zip drive using normal SCSI commands. Most CD-ROM drives under Linux should work. The only ejectable floppy devices that it has been tested with are Sun workstation drives running Linux on the SPARC platform.

eject may not always be able to determine if the device is mounted (e.g. if it has several names). If the device name is a symbolic link, **eject** will follow the link and use the device that it points to. It will also properly check if any partitions of the device you are trying to eject are mounted (which could be the case on the Jaz, Zip, or even a CD-ROM, really).

If the auto-eject feature is enabled, then the drive will always be ejected after running this command, even if it is mounted and the *-f* option is used. Not all Linux kernel CD-ROM drivers support the auto-eject mode.

The nicknames are set when **eject** is compiled.

There is no way to find out the state of the auto-eject mode.

You probably shouldn't be able to eject a mounted disc, but most kernel drivers allow it.

The *-u* option will only succeed in unmounting if the user has privileges to run umount(8), or **eject** is installed setuid root, and it is not busy.

AUTHOR

eject was written by Jeff Tranter <`jeff_tranter@pobox.com`> and is released under the conditions of the GNU General Public License. See the file COPYING and notes in the source code for details.

For suggestions and patches, special thanks go out to: Ben Galliart <`bgallia@luc.edu`>,Dick Streefland, Donnie Barnes <`djb@redhat.com`>, Doug L. Hoffman <`hoffman@cs.unc.edu`>, Grant Guenther <`grant@torque.net`>, Mark Lord <`mlord@pobox.com`>, Markus Pilzecker <`markus.pilzecker@rhein-neckar.netsurf.de`>

SEE ALSO

mount(2), umount(2), mount(8), umount(8)
`/usr/src/linux/Documentation/cdrom/`

GREP(1)

NAME

grep, egrep, fgrep Print lines matching a pattern.

SYNOPSIS

grep [-AB] num] [-CEFGVbchiLlnqsvwxyUu] [-e pattern | -f file] [--extended-regexp] [--fixed-strings] [--basic-regexp] [--regexp=PATTERN] [--file=FILE] [--ignore-case] [--word-regexp] [--line-regexp] [--line-regexp] [--no-messages] [--revert-match] [--version] [--help] [--byte-offset] [--line-number] [--with-filename] [--no-filename] [--quiet] [--silent] [--files-without-match] [--fileswith-matcces] [--count] [--before-context=NUM] [--aftercontext=NUM] [--context] [--binary] [--unix-byte-offsets] *files...*

DESCRIPTION

grep searches the named input *files* (or standard input if no files are named, or the file name **-** is given) for lines containing a match to the given *pattern*. By default, **grep** prints the matching lines.

There are three major variants of grep, controlled by the following options:

-G, --basic-regexp Interpret *pattern* as a basic regular expression (see below). This is the default.

-E, --extended-regexp Interpret *pattern* as an extended regular expression (see below).

-F, --fixed-strings Interpret *pattern* as a list of fixed strings, separated by newlines, any of which is to be matched.

In addition, two variant programs **egrep** and **fgrep** are available. **egrep** is similar (but not identical) to **grep -E**, and is compatible with the historical Unix **egrep**. **Fgrep** is the same as **grep -F**.

All variants of grep understand the following options:

-num Matches will be printed with *num* lines of leading and trailing context. However, **grep** will never print any given line more than once.

-A num , --after-context=NUM Print *num* lines of trailing context after matching lines.

-B num , --before-context=NUM Print *num* lines of leading context before matching lines.

-C, --context Equivalent to **-2**.

-V, --version Print the version number of **grep** to standard error. This version number should be included in all bug reports (see below).

-b, --byte-offset Print the byte offset within the input file before each line of output.

-c, --count Suppress normal output; instead print a count of matching lines for each input file. With the *-v, --revert-match* option (see below), count non-matching lines.

-e *pattern,--regexp=PATTERN* Use *pattern* as the pattern; useful to protect patterns beginning with **-**.

-f *file,--file=FILE* Obtain the pattern from *file*.

-h, --no-filename Suppress the prefixing of filenames on output when multiple files are searched.

-i, --ignore-case Ignore case distinctions in both the *pattern* and the input files.

-L, --files-without-match Suppress normal output; instead print the name of each input file from which no output would normally have been printed. The scanning will stop on the first match.

-l, --files-with-matches Suppress normal output; instead print the name of each input file from which output would normally have been printed. The scanning will stop on the first match.

-n, --line-number Prefix each line of output with the line number within its input file.

-q, --quiet Quiet; suppress normal output. The scanning will stop on the first match.

-s, --silent Suppress error messages about nonexistent or unreadable files.

-v, --revert-match Invert the sense of matching, to select non-matching lines.

-w, --word-regexp Select only those lines containing matches that form whole words. The test is that the matching substring must either be at the beginning of the line, or preceded by a non-word constituent character. Similarly, it must be either at the end of the line or followed by a non-word constituent character. Word-constituent characters are letters, digits, and the underscore.

-x, --line-regexp Select only those matches that exactly match the whole line.

-y Obsolete synonym for **-i**.

-U, --binary Treat the file(s) as binary. By default, under MSDOS and MS-Windows, **grep** guesses the file type by looking at the contents of the first 32KB read from the file. If **grep** decides the file is a text file, it strips the CR characters from the original file contents (to make regular expressions with **^** and **$** work correctly). Specifying **-U** overrules this guesswork, causing all files to be read and passed to the matching mechanism verbatim; if the file is a text file with CR/LF pairs at the end of each line, this will cause some regular expressions to fail. This option is only supported on MS-DOS and MS-Windows.

-u, --unix-byte-offsets Report Unix-style byte offsets. This switch causes **grep** to report byte offsets as if the file were Unix-style text file, i.e. with CR characters stripped off. This will produce results identical to running **grep** on a Unix machine. This option has no effect unless **-b** option is also used; it is only supported on MS-DOS and MS-Windows.

REGULAR EXPRESSIONS

A regular expression is a pattern that describes a set of strings. Regular expressions are constructed analogously to arithmetic expressions, by using various operators to combine smaller expressions.

grep understands two different versions of regular expression syntax: "basic" and "extended."' In GNU **grep**, there is no difference in available functionality using either syntax. In other implementations, basic regular expressions are less powerful. The following description applies to extended regular expressions; differences for basic regular expressions are summarized afterwards.

The fundamental building blocks are the regular expressions that match a single character. Most characters, including all letters and digits, are regular expressions that match themselves. Any metacharacter with special meaning may be quoted by preceding it with a backslash.

A list of characters enclosed by **[** and **]** matches any single character in that list; if the first character of the list is the caret (^) then it matches any character *not* in the list. For example, the regular expression **[0123456789]** matches any single digit. A range of ASCII characters may be specified by giving the first and last characters, separated by a hyphen. Finally, certain named classes of characters are predefined. Their names are self explanatory, and they are: **[:alnum:]**, **[:alpha:]**, **[:cntrl:]**, **[:digit:]**, **[:graph:]**, **[:lower:]**, **[:print:]**, **[:punct:]**, **[:space:]**, **[:upper:]**, and **[:xdigit:]**. For example, **[[:alnum:]]** means **[0-9A-Za-z]**, except the latter form is dependent upon the ASCII character encoding, whereas the former is portable. (Note that the brackets in these class names are part of the symbolic names, and must be included in addition to the brackets delimiting the bracket list.) Most metacharacters lose their special meaning inside lists. To include a literal **]** place it first in the list. Similarly, to include a literal **^** place it anywhere but first. Finally, to include a literal **-** place it last.

The period (.) matches any single character. The symbol **\w** is a synonym for **[[:alnum:]]** and **\W** is a synonym for **[^[:alnum]]**.

The caret **^** and the dollar sign **$** are metacharacters that respectively match the empty string at the beginning and end of a line. The symbols **\<** and **\>** respectively match the empty string at the beginning and end of a word. The symbol **\b** matches the empty string at the edge of a word, and **\B** matches the empty string provided it's *not* at the edge of a word.

A regular expression matching a single character may be followed by one of several repetition operators:

?	The preceding item is optional and matched at most once.
*****	The preceding item will be matched zero or more times.
+	The preceding item will be matched one or more times.
{n}	The preceding item is matched exactly *n* times.
{n,}	The preceding item is matched *n* or more times.
{,m}	The preceding item is optional and is matched at most *m* times.
{n,m}	The preceding item is matched at least *n* times, but not more than *m* times.

Two regular expressions may be concatenated; the resulting regular expression matches any string formed by concatenating two substrings that respectively match the concatenated subexpressions.

Two regular expressions may be joined by the infix operator **|**; the resulting regular expression matches any string matching either subexpression.

Repetition takes precedence over concatenation, which in turn takes precedence over alternation. A whole subexpression may be enclosed in parentheses to override these precedence rules.

The backreference *n*, where *n* is a single digit, matches the substring previously matched by the *n*th parenthesized subexpression of the regular expression.

In basic regular expressions the metacharacters **?**, **+**, **{**, **|**, **(**, and **)** lose their special meaning; instead use the backslashed versions **\?**, **\+**, **\{**, **\|**, **\(**, and **\)**.

In **egrep** the metacharacter **{** loses its special meaning; instead use **\{**.

DIAGNOSTICS

Normally, exit status is 0 if matches were found, and 1 if no matches were found. (The **-v** option inverts the sense of the exit status.) Exit status is 2 if there were syntax errors in the pattern, inaccessible input files, or other system errors.

BUGS

E-mail bug reports to `bug-gnu-utils@prep.ai.mit.edu`. Be sure to include the word "grep" somewhere in the Subject: field.

Large repetition counts in the {*m,n*} construct may cause **grep** to use lots of memory. In addition, certain other obscure regular expressions require exponential time and space, and may cause **grep** to run out of memory.

Backreferences are very slow, and may require exponential time.

GZIP(1)

NAME

gzip, gunzip, zcat Compress or expand files.

SYNOPSIS

gzip [**-acdfhlLnNrtvV19**] **[-S suffix]** [*name* ...] **gunzip** [**-acfhlLnNrtvV**] **[-S suffix]** [*name* ...] **zcat** [**-fhLV**] [*name* ...]

DESCRIPTION

gzip reduces the size of the named files using Lempel-Ziv coding (LZ77). Whenever possible, each file is replaced by one with the extension .gz, while keeping the same ownership modes, access and modification times. (The default extension is -gz for VMS, **z** for MSDOS, OS/2 FAT, Windows NT FAT and Atari.) If no files are specified, or if a file name is **-**, the standard input is compressed to the standard output. gzip will only attempt to compress regular files. In particular, it will ignore symbolic links.

If the compressed file name is too long for its file system, gzip truncates it. gzip attempts to truncate only the parts of the file name longer than three characters. (A part is delimited by dots.) If the name consists of small parts only, the longest parts are truncated. For example, if file names are limited to 14 characters, gzip.msdos.exe is compressed to gzi.msd.exe.gz. Names are not truncated on systems which do not have a limit on file name length.

By default, gzip keeps the original file name and timestamp in the compressed file. These are used when decompressing the file with the *-N* option. This is useful when the compressed file name was truncated or when the time stamp was not preserved after a file transfer.

Compressed files can be restored to their original form using gzip -d or gunzip or zcat. If the original name saved in the compressed file is not suitable for its file system, a new name is constructed from the original one to make it legal.

gunzip takes a list of files on its command line and replaces each file whose name ends with .gz, -gz, .z, -z, _z or .Z and that begins with the correct magic number with an uncompressed file without the original extension. gunzip also recognizes the special extensions .tgz and .taz as shorthands for .tar.gz and .tar.Z respectively. When compressing, gzip uses the .tgz extension if necessary instead of truncating a file with a .tar extension.

gunzip can currently decompress files created by gzip, zip, compress, compress -H or pack. The detection of the input format is automatic. When using the first two formats, gunzip checks a 32-=bit CRC. For pack, gunzip checks the uncompressed length. The standard compress format was not designed to allow consistency checks. However gunzip is sometimes able to detect a bad .Z file. If you get an error when uncompressing a .Z file, do not assume that the .Z file is correct simply because the standard uncompress does not complain. This generally means that the standard uncompress does not check its input, and happily generates garbage output. The SCO compress -H format (lzh compression method) does not include a CRC but also allows some consistency checks.

Files created by zip can be uncompressed by gzip only if they have a single member compressed with the "deflation" method. This feature is only intended to help conversion of tar.zip files to the tar.gz format. To extract zip files with several members, use unzip instead of gunzip.

zcat is identical to gunzip -c. (On some systems, zcat may be installed as gzcat to preserve the original link to **compress**.*)* Zcat uncompresses either a list of files on the command line or its standard input and writes the uncompressed data on standard output. Zcat will uncompress files that have the correct magic number whether they have a .gz suffix or not.

gzip uses the Lempel-Ziv algorithm used in zip and PKZIP. The amount of compression obtained depends on the size of the input and the distribution of common substrings. Typically, text such as source code or English is reduced by 60–70%. Compression is generally much better than that achieved by LZW (as used in *compress*), Huffman coding (as used in *pack*), or adaptive Huffman coding (*compact*).

Compression is always performed, even if the compressed file is slightly larger than the original. The worst case expansion is a few bytes for the gzip file header, plus 5 bytes every 32K block, or an expansion ratio of 0.015% for large files. Note that the actual number of used disk blocks almost never increases. gzip preserves the mode, ownership and timestamps of files when compressing or decompressing.

OPTIONS

-a --ascii Ascii text mode: convert end-of-lines using local conventions. This option is supported only on some non-Unix systems. For MSDOS, CR LF is converted to LF when compressing, and LF is converted to CR LF when decompressing.

-c --stdout --to-stdout Write output on standard output; keep original files unchanged. If there are several input files, the output consists of a sequence of independently compressed members. To obtain better compression, concatenate all input files before compressing them.

-d --decompress --uncompress Decompress.

-f --force Force compression or decompression even if the file has multiple links or the corresponding file already exists, or if the compressed data is read from or written to a terminal. If the input data is not in a format recognized by *gzip,* and if the option --stdout is also given, copy the input data without change to the standard ouput: let *zcat* behave as *cat.* If -f is not given, and when not running in the background, *gzip* prompts to verify whether an existing file should be overwritten.

-h --help Display a help screen and quit.

-l --list For each compressed file, list the following fields:

compressed size: size of the compressed file
uncompressed size: size of the uncompressed file

ratio: compression ratio (0.0% if unknown)
uncompressed_name: name of the uncompressed file

The uncompressed size is given as -1 for files not in gzip format, such as compressed .Z files. To get the uncompressed size for such a file, you can use

```
zcat file.Z | wc -c
```

In combination with the --verbose option, the following fields are also displayed:

method: compression method

crc: the 32-bit CRC of the uncompressed data

date & time: time stamp for the uncompressed file

The compression methods currently supported are deflate, compress, lzh (SCO compress -H) and pack. The crc is given as ffffffff for a file not in gzip format.

With --name, the uncompressed name, date, and time are those stored within the compress file if present.

With --verbose, the size totals and compression ratio for all files is also displayed, unless some sizes are unknown. With --quiet, the title and totals lines are not displayed.

-L --license Display the *gzip* license and quit.

-n --no-name When compressing, do not save the original file name and time stamp by default. (The original name is always saved if the name had to be truncated.) When decompressing, do not restore the original file name if present (remove only the *gzip* suffix from the compressed file name) and do not restore the original time stamp if present (copy it from the compressed file). This option is the default when decompressing.

-N --name When compressing, always save the original file name and time stamp; this is the default. When decompressing, restore the original file name and time stamp if present. This option is useful on systems which have a limit on file name length or when the time stamp has been lost after a file transfer.

-q --quiet Suppress all warnings.

-r --recursive Travel the directory structure recursively. If any of the file names specified on the command line are directories, gzip will descend into the directory and compress all the files it finds there (or decompress them in the case of gunzip).

-S .suf --suffix .suf Use suffix .suf instead of .gz. Any suffix can be given, but suffixes other than .z and .gz should be avoided to avoid confusion when files are transferred to other systems. A null suffix forces gunzip to try decompression on all given files regardless of suffix, as in

gunzip -S "" * (*.* for MSDOS)

Previous versions of gzip used the .z suffix. This was changed to avoid a conflict with pack(1).

-t --test Check the compressed file integrity.

-v --verbose Display the name and percentage reduction for each file compressed or decompressed.

-V --version Display the version number and compilation options then quit.

-# --fast --best Regulate the speed of compression using the specified digit #, where -1 or --fast indicates the fastest compression method (less compression) and -9 or --best indicates the slowest compression method (best compression). The default compression level is -6 (that is, biased towards high compression at expense of speed).

ADVANCED USAGE

Multiple compressed files can be concatenated. In this case, gunzip will extract all members at once. For example:

```
gzip -c file1 > foo.gz
gzip -c file2 >> foo.gz
```

Then

```
gunzip -c foo
```

is equivalent to

```
cat file1 file2
```

In case of damage to one member of a .gz file, other members can still be recovered (if the damaged member is removed). However, you can get better compression by compressing all members at once:

```
cat file1 file2 | gzip > foo.gz
```

compresses better than

```
gzip -c file1 file2 > foo.gz
```

If you want to recompress concatenated files to get better compression, do

```
gzip -cd old.gz | gzip > new.gz
```

If a compressed file consists of several members, the uncompressed size and CRC reported by the --list option applies to the last member only. If you need the uncompressed size for all members, you can use

```
gzip -cd file.gz | wc -c
```

If you wish to create a single archive file with multiple members so that members can later be extracted independently, use an archiver such as tar or zip. GNU tar supports the -z option to invoke gzip transparently. gzip is designed as a complement to tar, not as a replacement.

ENVIRONMENT

The environment variable *GZIP* can hold a set of default options for gzip. These options are interpreted first and can be overwritten by explicit command line parameters. For example:

for sh: `GZIP="-8v -name"`; export GZIP

for csh: `setenv GZIP "-8v -name"`

for MSDOS: `set GZIP=-8v --name`

On Vax/VMS the name of the environment variable is GZIP_OZP, to avoid a conflict with the symbol set for invocation of the program.

SEE ALSO

znew(1), zcmp(1), zmore(1), zforce(1), gzexe(1), zip(1), unzip(1), compress(1), pack(1), compact(1)

DIAGNOSTICS

Exit status is normally 0; if an error occurs, exit status is 1. If a warning occurs, exit status is 2.

Usage: gzip [-cdfhlLnNrtvV19] [-S suffix] [file ...] Invalid options were specified on the command line.

***file*: not in gzip format** The file specified to gunzip has not been compressed.

***file:* Corrupt input. Use zcat to recover some data.** The compressed file has been damaged. The data up to the point of failure can be recovered using

zcat file > recover

***file*: compressed with *xx* bits, can only handle *yy* bits** *File* was compressed (using LZW) by a program that could deal with more bits than the decompress code on this machine. Recompress the file with gzip, which compresses better and uses less memory.

***file*: already has .gz suffix--no change** The file is assumed to be already compressed. Rename the file and try again.

***file* already exists; do you wish to overwrite (y or n)?** Respond "y" if you want the output file to be replaced; "n" if not.

gunzip: corrupt input A SIGSEGV violation was detected which usually means that the input file has been corrupted.

xx.x% Percentage of the input saved by compression. (Relevant only for **-v** and **-l**.)

--not a regular file or directory: ignored When the input file is not a regular file or directory (e.g., a symbolic link, socket, FIFO, device file), it is left unaltered.

--has *xx* other links: unchanged The input file has links; it is left unchanged. See ln(1) for more information. Use the **-f** flag to force compression of multiply-linked files.

CAVEATS

When writing compressed data to a tape, it is generally necessary to pad the output with zeroes up to a block boundary. When the data is read and the whole block is passed to gunzip for decompression, gunzip detects that there is extra trailing garbage after the compressed data and emits a warning by default. You have to use the --quiet option to suppress the warning. This option can be set in the *GZIP* environment variable as in

for sh: GZIP="-q" tar -xfz --block-compress /dev/rst0

for csh: (setenv GZIP -q; tar -xfz --block-compr /dev/rst0

In the above example, **gzip** is invoked implicitly by the -*z* option of GNU tar. Make sure that the same block size (-b option of tar) is used for reading and writing compressed data on tapes. (This example assumes you are using the GNU version of tar.)

BUGS

The --list option reports incorrect sizes if they exceed 2 gigabytes. The --list option reports sizes as -1 and crc as ffffffff if the compressed file is on a nonseekable media.

In some rare cases, the --best option gives worse compression than the default compression level (-6). On some highly redundant files, compress compresses better than gzip.

LN(1)

NAME

ln Make links between files.

SYNOPSIS

ln [options] source [dest]

ln [options] source... directory

OPTIONS

[-bdfinsvF] [-S backup-suffix] [-V {numbered,existing,simple}] [--version-control={numbered,existing,simple}] [--backup] [--directory] [--force] [--interactive] [--no-dereference] [--symbolic] [--verbose] [--suffix=backup-suffix] [--help] [--version]

DESCRIPTION

This documentation is no longer being maintained and may be inaccurate or incomplete. The Texinfo documentation is now the authoritative source. This manual page documents the GNU version of **ln**. If the last argument names an existing directory, **ln** links each other given file into a file with the same name in that directory. If only one file is given, it links that file into the current directory. Otherwise, if only two files are given, it links the first onto the second. It is an error if the last argument is not a directory and more than two files are given. It makes hard links by default. By default, it does not remove existing files.

OPTIONS

-b, --backup Make backups of files that are about to be removed.

-d, -F, --directory Allow the superuser to make hard links to directories.

-f, --force Remove existing destination files.

-i, --interactive Prompt whether to remove existing destination files.

-n, --no-dereference When the specified destination is a symbolic link to a directory, attempt to replace the symbolic link rather than dereferencing it to create a link in the directory to which it points. This option is most useful in conjunction with --force.

-s, --symbolic Make symbolic links instead of hard links. This option produces an error message on systems that do not support symbolic links.

-v, --verbose Print the name of each file before linking it.

--help Print a usage message on standard output and exit successfully.

--version Print version information on standard output then exit successfully.

-S, --suffix backup-suffix The suffix used for making simple backup files can be set with the *SIMPLE_BACKUP_SUFFIX* environment variable, which can be overridden by this option. If neither of those is given, the default is ~, as it is in Emacs.

-V, --version-control {numbered,existing,simple} The type of backups made can be set with the *VERSION_CONTROL* environment variable, which can be overridden by this option. If *VERSION_CONTROL* is not set and this option is not given, the default backup type is "existing". The value of the *VERSION_CONTROL* environment variable and the argument to this option are like the GNU Emacs *version-control* variable; they also recognize synonyms that are more descriptive. The valid values are (unique abbreviations are accepted)

t or **numbered** Always make numbered backups.

nil or **existing** Make numbered backups of files that already have them, simple backups of the others.

never or **simple** Always make simple backups.

LPQ(1)

NAME

lpq Spool queue examination program.

SYNOPSIS

lpq [**-l**] [**-Pprinter**] [job # ...] [user ...]

DESCRIPTION

lpq examines the spooling area used by lpd(8) for printing files on the line printer, and reports the status of the specified jobs or all jobs associated with a user. lpq invoked without any arguments reports on any jobs currently in the queue.

OPTIONS

-P Specify a particular printer, otherwise the default line printer is used (or the value of the PRINTER variable in the environment). All other arguments supplied are interpreted as user names or job numbers to filter out only those jobs of interest.

-l Information about each of the files comprising the job entry is printed. Normally, only as much information as will fit on one line is displayed.

For each job submitted (i.e. invocation of lpr(1)) lpq reports the user's name, current rank in the queue, the names of files comprising the job, the job identifier (a number which may be supplied to lprm(1) for removing a specific job), and the total size in bytes. Job ordering is dependent on the algorithm used to scan the spooling directory and is supposed to be FIFO (First in First Out). File names comprising a job may be unavailable (when lpr(1) is used as a sink in a pipeline) in which case the file is indicated as *(standard input)*.

If lpq warns that there is no daemon present (i.e. due to some malfunction), the lpc(8) command can be used to restart the printer daemon.

ENVIRONMENT

If the following environment variable exists, it is used by lpq:

PRINTER specifies an alternate default printer.

FILES

`/etc/printcap`	To determine printer characteristics.
`/var/spool/*`	The spooling directory, as determined from printcap.
`/var/spool/*/cf*`	Control files specifying jobs.
`/var/spool/*/lock`	The lock file to obtain the currently active job.
`/usr/share/misc/termcap`	For manipulating the screen for repeated display.

SEE ALSO

lpr(1), lprm(1), lpc(8), lpd(8)

HISTORY

lpq appeared in 3BSD.

BUGS

Due to the dynamic nature of the information in the spooling directory lpq may report unreliably. Output formatting is sensitive to the line length of the terminal; this can result in widely spaced columns.

DIAGNOSTICS

Unable to open various files. The lock file being malformed. Garbage files when there is no daemon active, but files in the spooling directory.

LPR(1)

NAME

lpr Off line print.

SYNOPSIS

lpr [**-Pprinter**] [**-#num**] [**-C** *class*] [**-J** *job*] [**-T** *title*] [**-U** *user*] [**-i** [*numcols*]] [**-1234** *font*] [**-wnum**] [**-cdfghlnmprstv**] [*name ...*]

DESCRIPTION

lpr uses a spooling daemon to print the named files when facilities become available. If no names appear, the standard input is assumed. The following single letter options are used to notify the line printer spooler that the files are not standard text files. The spooling daemon will use the appropriate filters to print the data accordingly.

-c The files are assumed to contain data produced by cifplot(1)

-d The files are assumed to contain data from *tex* (DVI format from Stanford).

-f Use a filter which interprets the first character of each line as a standard FORTRAN carriage control character.

-g The files are assumed to contain standard plot data as produced by the plot routines (see also plot for the filters used by the printer spooler).

-l Use a filter which allows control characters to be printed and suppresses page breaks.

-n The files are assumed to contain data from *ditroff* (device independent troff).

-p Use pr(1) to format the files (equivalent to print).

-t The files are assumed to contain data from troff(1) (cat phototypesetter commands).

-v The files are assumed to contain a raster image for devices like the Benson Varian.

These options apply to the handling of the print job:

-P Force output to a specific printer. Normally, the default printer is used (site dependent), or the value of the environment variable *PRINTER* is used.

-h Suppress the printing of the burst page.

-m Send mail upon completion.

-r Remove the file upon completion of spooling or upon completion of printing (with the -s option).

-s Use symbolic links. Usually files are copied to the spool directory. The *-s* option will use symlink(2) to link data files rather than trying to copy them, so large files can be printed. This means the files should not be modified or removed until they have been printed.

The remaining options apply to copies, the page display, and headers:

- #num The quantity num is the number of copies desired of each file named. For example,

```
lpr -#3 foo.c bar.c more.c
```

would result in 3 copies of the file foo.c, followed by 3 copies of the file bar.c, etc. On the other hand,

```
cat foo.c bar.c more.c | lpr -#3
```

will give three copies of the concatenation of the files. Often a site will disable this feature to encourage use of a photocopier instead.

-[1234]font Specifies a *font* to be mounted on font position *i*. The daemon will construct a .railmag file referencing the font pathname.

-C *class* Job classification to use on the burst page. For example,

```
lpr -C EECS foo.c
```

causes the system name (the name returned by hostname(1)) to be replaced on the burst page by EECS, and the file foo.c to be printed.

-J job Job name to print on the burst page. Normally, the first file's name is used.

-T *title* Title name for pr(1), instead of the file name.

-U *user* User name to print on the burst page, also for accounting purposes. This option is only honored if the real user-id is daemon (or that specified in the printcap file instead of daemon), and is intended for those instances where print filters wish to requeue jobs.

-i [numcols] The output is indented. If the next argument is numeric (*numcols*), it is used as the number of blanks to be printed before each line; otherwise, 8 characters are printed.

-w*num* Uses *num* as the page width for pr(1).

ENVIRONMENT

If the following environment variable exists, it is used by lpr:

PRINTER specifies an alternate default printer.

FILES

`/etc/passwd`	Personal identification.
`/etc/printcap`	Printer capabilities database.
`/usr/sbin/lpd*`	Line printer daemons.
`/var/spool/output/*`	Directories used for spooling.
`/var/spool/output/*/cf*`	Daemon control files.
`/var/spool/output/*/df*`	Data files specified in "cf" files.
`/var/spool/output/*/tf*`	Temporary copies of "cf" files.

SEE ALSO

lpq(1), lprm(1), pr(1), symlink(2), printcap(5), lpc(8), lpd(8)

HISTORY

The **lpr** command appeared in 3BSD.

DIAGNOSTICS

If you try to spool too large a file, it will be truncated. **lpr** will object to printing binary files. If a user other than root prints a file and spooling is disabled, **lpr** will print a message saying so and will not put jobs in the queue. If a connection to lpd(1) on the local machine cannot be made, **lpr** will say that the daemon cannot be started. Diagnostics may be printed in the daemon's log file regarding missing spool files by lpd(1).

BUGS

Fonts for troff(1) and tex reside on the host with the printer. It is currently not possible to use local font libraries.

LPRM(1)

NAME

lprm Remove jobs from the line printer spooling queue.

SYNOPSIS

lprm [**-Pprinter**] [**-**] [job # ...] [*user* ...]

DESCRIPTION

lprm will remove a job, or jobs, from a printer's spool queue. Since the spooling directory is protected from users, using **lprm** is normally the only method by which a user may remove a job. The owner of a job is determined by the user's login name and host name on the machine where the lpr(1) command was invoked.

OPTIONS AND ARGUMENTS

-Pprinter Specify the queue associated with a specific *printer* (otherwise the default printer is used).

- If a single - is given, lprm will remove all jobs which a user owns. If the superuser employs this flag, the spool queue will be emptied entirely.

User Causes **lprm** to attempt to remove any jobs queued belonging to that user (or users). This form of invoking **lprm** is useful only to the superuser.

job # A user may dequeue an individual job by specifying its job number. This number may be obtained from the lpq(1) program, e.g.:

```
% lpq -l
1st:ken [job #013ucbarpa]
(standard input) 100 bytes
% lprm 13
```

If neither arguments nor options are given, **lprm** will delete the currently active job if it is owned by the user who invoked **lprm**.

lprm announces the names of any files it removes and is silent if there are no jobs in the queue which match the request list.

lprm will kill off an active daemon, if necessary, before removing any spooling files. If a daemon is killed, a new one is automatically restarted upon completion of file removals.

ENVIRONMENT

If the following environment variable exists, it is utilized by **lprm**.

PRINTER If the environment variable *PRINTER* exists, and a printer has not been specified with the *P* option, the default printer is assumed from *PRINTER*.

FILES

`/etc/printcap`	Printer characteristics file.
`/var/spool/*`	Spooling directories.
`/var/spool/*/lock`	Lock file used to obtain the pid of the current daemon and the job number of the currently active job.

SEE ALSO

lpr(1), lpq(1), lpd(8)

DIAGNOSTICS

"Permission denied" if the user tries to remove files other than his own.

BUGS

Since there are race conditions possible in the update of the lock file, the currently active job may be incorrectly identified.

HISTORY

The **lprm** command appeared in 3.0BSD.

LS(1)

NAME

ls, dir, vdir List contents of directories.

SYNOPSIS

ls [-abcdfgiklmnpqrstuxABCFGLNQRSUX1] [-w cols] [-T cols]
[-I pattern] [--all] [--escape] [--directory] [--inode] [--kilobytes]
[--numeric-uid-gid] [--no-group] [--hidecontrol-chars]
[--reverse] [--size] [--width=cols] [--tabsize=cols] [--almost-all]
[--ignore-backups] [--classify] [--file-type] [--full-time]
[--ignore=pattern] [--dereference] [--literal] [--quote-name]
[--recursive] [--sort={none,time,size,extension}]
[--format={long,verbose,commas,across,vertical,single-column}]
[--time={atime,access,use,ctime,status}] [--help] [--version]
[--color[={yes,no,tty}]] [--colour[={yes,no,tty}]] [name...]

DESCRIPTION

This documentation is no longer being maintained and may be inaccurate or incomplete. The Texinfo documentation is now the authoritative source.

This manual page documents the GNU version of ls; dir and **vdir** are versions of **ls** with different default output formats. These programs list each given file or directory name. Directory contents are sorted alphabetically. For **ls**, files are by default listed in columns, sorted vertically, if the standard output is a terminal; otherwise they are listed one per line. For **dir**, files are by default listed in columns, sorted vertically. For **vdir**, files are by default listed in long format.

OPTIONS

-a, --all List all files in directories, including all files that start with '.'.

-b, --escape Quote nongraphic characters in file names using alphabetic and octal backslash sequences like those used in C.

-c, --time=ctime, --time=status Sort directory contents according to the files' status change time instead of the modification time. If the long listing format is being used, print the status change time instead of the modification time.

-d, --directory List directories like other files, rather than listing their contents.

-f Do not sort directory contents; list them in whatever order they are stored on the disk. The same as enabling *-a* and *-U* and disabling *-l, -s,* and *-t*.

--full-time List times in full, rather than using the standard abbreviation heuristics.

-g Ignored; for Unix compatibility.

-i, --inode Print the index number of each file to the left of the file name.

-k, --kilobytes If file sizes are being listed, print them in kilobytes. This overrides the environment variable *POSIXLY_CORRECT*.

-l, --format=long, --format=verbose In addition to the name of each file, print the file type, permissions, number of hard links, owner name, group name, size in bytes, and timestamp (the modification time unless other times are selected). For files with a time that is more than six months old or more than one hour into the future, the timestamp contains the year instead of the time of day.

-m, --format=commas List files horizontally, with as many as will fit on each line, separated by commas.

-n, --numeric-uid-gid List the numeric UID and GID instead of the names.

-p Append a character to each file name indicating the file type.

-q, --hide-control-chars Print question marks instead of nongraphic characters in file names.

-r, --reverse Sort directory contents in reverse order.

-s, --size Print the size of each file in 1K blocks to the left of the file name. If the environment variable *POSIXLY_CORRECT* is set, 512-byte blocks are used instead.

-t, --sort=time Sort directory contents by timestamp instead of alphabetically, with the newest files listed first.

-u, --time=atime, --time=access, --time=use Sort directory contents according to the files' last access time instead of the modification time. If the long listing format is being used, print the last access time instead of the modification time.

-x, --format=across, --format=horizontal List the files in columns, sorted horizontally.

-A, --almost-all List all files in directories, except for "." and "..".

-B, --ignore-backups Do not list files that end with ~, unless they are given on the command line.

-C, --format=vertical List files in columns, sorted vertically.

-F, --classify Append a character to each file name indicating the file type. For regular files that are executable, append a *. The file type indicators are / for directories, @ for symbolic links, | for FIFOs, = for sockets, and nothing for regular files.

-G, --no-group Inhibit display of group information in a long format directory listing.

-L, --dereference List the files linked to by symbolic links instead of listing the contents of the links.

-N, --literal Do not quote file names.

-Q, --quote-name Enclose file names in double quotes and quote nongraphic characters as in C.

-R, --recursive List the contents of all directories recursively.

-S, --sort=size Sort directory contents by file size instead of alphabetically, with the largest files listed first.

-U, --sort=none Do not sort directory contents; list them in whatever order they are stored on the disk. This option is not called *-f* because the Unix ls *-f* option also enables *-a* and disables *-l*, *-s*, and *-t*. It seems useless and ugly to group those unrelated things together in one option. Since this option doesn't do that, it has a different name.

-X, --sort=extension Sort directory contents alphabetically by file extension (characters after the last "."); files with no extension are sorted first.

-1, --format=single-column List one file per line.

-w, --width *cols* Assume the screen is *cols* columns wide. The default is taken from the terminal driver if possible; otherwise the environment variable COLUMNS is used if it is set; otherwise the default is 80.

-T, --tabsize *cols* Assume that each tabstop is *cols* columns wide. The default is 8.

-I, --ignore pattern Do not list files whose names match the shell pattern *pattern* unless they are given on the command line. As in the shell, an initial '.' in a filename does not match a wildcard at the start of *pattern.*

--color, --colour, --color=yes, --colour=yes Colorize the names of files depending on the type of file. See *DISPLAY COLORIZATION* below.

--color=tty, --colour=tty Same as *--color* but only if standard output is a terminal. This is very useful for shell scripts and command aliases, especially if your favorite pager does not support color control codes.

--color=no, --colour=no Disables colorization. This is the default. Provided to override a previous color option.

--help Print a usage message on standard output and exit successfully.

--version Print version information on standard output then exit successfully.

DISPLAY COLORIZATION

When using the --*color* option, this version of **ls** will colorize the file names printed according to the name and type of file. By default, this colorization is by type only, and the codes used are ISO 6429 (ANSI) compliant.

You can override the default colors by defining the environment variable *LS_COLORS* (or *LS_COLOURS*). The format of this variable is reminiscent of the termcap(5) file format; a colon-separated list of expressions of the form "*xx*=string", where *xx* is a two-character variable name. The variables with their associated defaults are:

no	0	Normal (non-filename) text
fi	0	Regular file
di	32	Directory
ln	36	Symbolic link
pi	31	Named pipe (FIFO)
so	33	Socket
bd	44;37	Block device
cd	44;37	Character device
ex	35	Executable file
mi	(none)	Missing file (defaults to fi)
or	(none)	Orphaned symbolic link (defaults to ln)
lc	\e[	Left code
rc	m	Right code
ec	(none)	End code (replaces lc+no+rc)

You only need to include the variables you want to change from the default.

File names can also be colorized based on filename extension. This is specified in the *LS_COLORS* variable using the syntax "*ext=string".

For example, using ISO 6429 codes, to color all C-language source files blue you would specify "*.c=34". This would color all files ending in .c in blue (34) color.

Control characters can be written either in C-style escaped notation, or in **stty**-like ^-notation. The C-style notation adds for Escape, - for a normal space characer, and for Delete. In addition, the escape character can be used to override the default interpretation of ^, : and =.

Each file will be written as <lc> <color code> <rc> <filename> <ec>. If the <ec> code is undefined, the sequence <lc> <no> <rc> will be used instead. This is generally more convenient to use, but less general. The left, right and end codes are provided so you don't have to type common parts over and over again and to support weird terminals; you will generally not need to change them at all unless your terminal does not use ISO 6429 color sequences but a different system.

If your terminal does use ISO 6429 color codes, you can compose the type codes (i.e. all except the **lc**, **rc**, and **ec** codes) from numerical commands separated by semicolons. The most common commands are:

0	To restore default color
1	For brighter colors
4	For underlined text
5	For flashing text
30	For black foreground
31	For red foreground
32	For green foreground
33	For yellow (or brown) foreground
34	For blue foreground
35	For purple foreground
36	For cyan foreground
37	For white (or gray) foreground
40	For black background
41	For red background
42	For green background

43 For yellow (or brown) background

44 For blue background

45 For purple background

46 For cyan background

47 For white (or gray) background

Not all commands will work on all systems or display devices.

A few terminal programs do not recognize the default end code properly. If all text gets colorized after you do a directory listing, try changing the **no** and **fi** codes from 0 to the numerical codes for your standard fore- and background colors.

BUGS

On BSD systems, the *-s* option reports sizes that are half the correct values for files that are NFS-mounted from HP-UX systems. On HP-UX systems, it reports sizes that are twice the correct values for files that are NFS-mounted from BSD systems. This is due to a flaw in HP-UX; it also affects the HP-UX **ls** program.

If there was a single standard for the English language it would not be necessary to support redundant spellings.

LSMOD(1)

NAME

lsmod List loaded modules.

SYNOPSIS

lsmod

DESCRIPTION

Lsmod shows information about all loaded modules.

The format is name, size, use count, list of referring modules. The information displayed is identical to that available from /proc/modules.

SEE ALSO

insmod(1), modprobe(1), depmod(1), rmmod(1), ksyms(1), modules(2)

HISTORY

Module support was first concieved by Anonymous.

Initial Linux version by Bas Laarhoven `<bas@vimec.nl>`.

Version 0.99.14 by Jon Tombs `<jon@gtex02.us.es>`.

Extended by Bjorn Ekwall `<bj0rn@blox.se>`.

Updated for 2.1.17 by Richard Henderson `<rth@tamu.edu>`.

MAKE(1L)

NAME

make GNU make utility to maintain groups of programs.

SYNOPSIS

make [**-f** makefile] [option] ... target ...

WARNING

This man page is an extract of the documentation of *GNU make.* It is updated only occasionally, because the GNU project does not use nroff. For complete, current documentation, refer to the Info file **make** or the DVI file **make.dvi**, which are made from the Texinfo source file **make.texinfo**.

DESCRIPTION

The purpose of the *make* utility is to determine automatically which pieces of a large program need to be recompiled, and issue the commands to recompile them. This manual describes the GNU implementation of *make*, which was written by Richard Stallman and Roland McGrath. Our examples show C programs, since they are most common, but you can use *make* with any programming language whose compiler can be run with a shell command. In fact, *make* is not limited to programs. You can use it to describe any task where some files must be updated automatically from others whenever the others change.

To prepare to use make, you must write a file called the *makefile* that describes the relationships among files in your program, and the states the commands for updating each file. In a program, typically the executable file is updated from object files, which are in turn made by compiling source files.

Once a suitable makefile exists, each time you change some source files, this simple shell command

make

suffices to perform all necessary recompilations. The *make* program uses the makefile database and the last-modification times of the files to decide which of the files need to be updated. For each of those files, it issues the commands recorded in the database.

make executes commands in the makefile to update one or more target *names*, where *name* is typically a program. If no **-f** option is present, *make* will look for the makefiles *GNUmakefile*, *makefile*, and *Makefile*, in that order.

Normally you should call your makefile either makefile or *Makefile*. (We recommend *Makefile* because it appears prominently near the beginning of a directory listing, right near other important files such as *README*.) The first name checked, *GNUmakefile*, is not recommended for most makefiles. You should use this name if you have a makefile that is specific to GNU *make*, and will not be understood by other versions of *make*. If *makefile* is -, the standard input is read.

make updates a target if it depends on prerequisite files that have been modified since the target was last modified, or if the target does not exist.

OPTIONS

-b -m These options are ignored for compatibility with other versions of *make*.

-C *dir* Change to directory *dir* before reading the makefiles or doing anything else. If multiple **-C** options are specified, each is interpreted relative to the previous one: **-C** / **-C** etc is equivalent to **-C** /etc. This is typically used with recursive invocations of *make*.

-d Print debugging information in addition to normal processing. The debugging information says which files are being considered for remaking, which file-times are being compared and with what results, which files actually need to be remade, which implicit rules are considered and which are applied--everything interesting about how *make* decides what to do.

-e Give variables taken from the environment precedence over variables from makefiles.

-f *file* Use *file* as a makefile.

-i Ignore all errors in commands executed to remake files.

-I *dir* Specifies a directory *dir* to search for included makefiles. If several **-I** options are used to specify several directories, the directories are searched in the order specified. Unlike the arguments to other flags of *make*, directories given with **-I** flags may come directly after the flag: -Idir is allowed, as well as **-I** *dir.* This syntax is allowed for compatibility with the C preprocessor's **-I** flag.

-j *jobs* Specifies the number of jobs (commands) to run simultaneously. If there is more than one -j option, the last one is effective. If the **-j** option is given without an argument, *make* will not limit the number of jobs that can run simultaneously.

-k Continue as much as possible after an error. While the target that failed, and those that depend on it, cannot be remade, the other dependencies of these targets can be processed all the same.

-l -l *load* Specifies that no new jobs (commands) should be started if there are others jobs running and the load average is at least *load* (a floating-point number). With no argument, removes a previous load limit.

-n Print the commands that would be executed, but do not execute them.

-o *file* Do not remake the file *file* even if it is older than its dependencies, and do not remake anything on account of changes in *file*. Essentially the file is treated as very old and its rules are ignored.

-p	Print the database (rules and variable values) that results from reading the makefiles; then execute as usual or as otherwise specified. This also prints the version information given by the **-v** switch (see below). To print the database without trying to remake any files, use **make -p -f**/*dev*/*null*.
-q	"Question mode". Do not run any commands, or print anything; just return an exit status that is zero if the specified targets are already up to date, nonzero otherwise.
-r	Eliminate use of the built-in implicit rules. Also clear out the default list of suffixes for suffix rules.
-s	Silent operation; do not print the commands as they are executed.
-S	Cancel the effect of the **-k** option. This is never necessary except in a recursive *make* where **-k** might be inherited from the top-level *make* via MAKEFLAGS or if you set **-k** in MAKEFLAGS in your environment.
-t	Touch files (mark them up to date without really changing them) instead of running their commands. This is used to pretend that the commands were done, in order to fool future invocations of *make*.
-v	Print the version of the *make* program plus a copyright, a list of authors and a notice that there is no warranty. After this information is printed, processing continues normally. To get this information without doing anything else, use **make -v -f**/*dev*/*null*.
-w	Print a message containing the working directory before and after other processing. This may be useful for tracking down errors from complicated nests of recursive *make* commands.
-W *file*	Pretend that the target *file* has just been modified. When used with the **-n** flag, this shows you what would happen if you were to modify that file. Without **-n**, it is almost the same as running a *touch* command on the given file before running *make*, except that the modification time is changed only in the imagination of *make*.

SEE ALSO

`/usr/local/doc/gnumake.dvi` *The GNU Make Manual*

BUGS

See the chapter "Problems and Bugs" in *The GNU Make Manual.*

AUTHOR

This manual page contributed by Dennis Morse of Stanford University. It has been reworked by Roland McGrath.

MAN

NAME

man Format and display the on-line manual pages manpath - determine user's search path for man pages.

SYNOPSIS

man [-acdfhkKtwW] [-m system] [-p string] [-C config_file] [-M path] [-P pager] [-S section_list] [section] name ...

DESCRIPTION

man formats and displays the on-line manual pages. This version knows about the *MANPATH* and *(MAN)PAGER* environment variables, so you can have your own set(s) of personal man pages and choose whatever program you like to display the formatted pages. If *section* is specified, **man** only looks in that section of the manual. You may also specify the order to search the sections for entries and which preprocessors to run on the source files via command line options or environment variables. If *name* contains a / then it is first tried as a filename, so that you can do **man ./foo.5** or even **man /cd/foo/bar.1.gz**.

OPTIONS

-C config_file Specify the man.config file to use; the default is /etc/man.config. See man.config(5).

-M path Specify the list of directories to search for man pages. If no such option is given, the environment variable *MANPATH* is used. If no such environment variable is found, the default list is found by consulting /etc/man.config. An empty substring of *MANPATH* denotes the default list.

-P pager Specify which pager to use. This option overrides the *MANPAGER* environment variable, which in turn overrides the *PAGER* variable. By default, man uses /usr/bin/less-is.

-S section_list List is a colon-separated list of manual sections to search. This option overrides the *MANSECT* environment variable.

-a By default, **man** will exit after displaying the first manual page it finds. Using this option forces **man** to display all the manual pages that match **name,** not just the first.

-c Reformat the source man page, even when an up-to-date cat page exists. This can be meaningful if the cat page was formatted for a screen with a different number of columns.

-d Don't actually display the man pages, but do print gobs of debugging information.

-D Both display and print debugging info.

-f Equivalent to whatis.

-h Print a one-line help message and exit.

-k Equivalent to **apropos**.

-K Search for the specified string in *all* man pages. Warning: this is probably very slow! It helps to specify a section. (Just to give a rough idea, on my machine this takes about a minute per 500 man pages.)

-m system Specify an alternate set of man pages to search based on the system name given.

-p string Specify the sequence of preprocessors to run before **nroff** or **troff**. Not all installations will have a full set of preprocessors. Some of the preprocessors and the letters used to designate them are: eqn (e), grap (g), pic (p), tbl (t), vgrind (v), refer (r). This option overrides the *MANROFFSEQ* environment variable.

-t Use /usr/bin/groff -Tps -mandoc to format the manual page, passing the output to stdout. The output from /usr/bin/groff -Tps -mandoc may need to be passed through some filter or another before being printed.

-w or --**path** Don't actually display the man pages, but do print the location(s) of the files that would be formatted or displayed. If no argument is given: display (on stdout) the list of directories that is searched by **man** for man pages. If **manpath** is a link to man, then "manpath" is equivalent to "man −path".

-W Like -w, but print file names one per line, without additional information. This is useful in shell commands like man -aW man | xargs ls -l

CAT PAGES

Man will try to save the formatted man pages, in order to save formatting time the next time these pages are needed. Traditionally, formatted versions of pages in DIR/manX are saved in DIR/catX, but other mappings from man dir to cat dir can be specified in /etc/man.config. No cat pages are saved when the required cat directory does not exist.

It is possible to make man suid to a user man. Then, if a cat directory has owner man and mode 0755 (only writable by man), and the cat files have owner man and mode 0644 or 0444 (only writable by man, or not writable at all), no ordinary user can change the cat pages or put other files in the cat directory. If **man** is not made suid, then a cat directory should have mode 0777 if all users should be able to leave cat pages there.

The option -c forces reformatting a page, even if a recent cat page exists.

ENVIRONMENT

MANPATH If **MANPATH** is set, its value is used as the path to search for manual pages.

MANROFFSEQ If **MANROFFSEQ** is set, its value is used to determine the set of preprocessors run before running **nroff** or **troff**. By default, pages are passed through the table preprocessor before **nroff**.

MANSECT If **MANSECT** is set, its value is used to determine which manual sections to search.

MANWIDTH If **MANWIDTH** is set, its value is used as the width man pages should be displayed. Otherwise the pages may be displayed over the whole width of your screen.

MANPAGER If **MANPAGER** is set, its value is used as the name of the program to use to display the man page. If not, then **PAGER** is used. If that has no value either, /usr/bin/less -is is used.

LANG If **LANG** is set, its value defines the name of the subdirectory where man first looks for man pages. Thus, the command **LANG=dk man 1 foo** will cause man to look for the foo man page in .../dk/man1/foo.1, and if it cannot find such a file, then in .../man1/foo.1, where ... is a directory on the search path.

NLSPATH, LC_MESSAGES, LANG The environment variables *NLSPATH* and *LC_MESSAGES* (or *LANG* when the latter does not exist) play a role in locating the message catalog. (But the English messages are compiled in, and for English no catalog is required.) Note that programs like col(1) called by man also use e.g. LC_CTYPE.

PATH **PATH** is used in the construction of the default search path for man pages.

SYSTEM **SYSTEM** is used to get the default alternate system name (for use with the *-m* option).

SEE ALSO

apropos(1), whatis(1), less(1), groff(1).

BUGS

The *-t* option only works if a troff-like program is installed.

If you see blinking 55 or <AD> instead of hyphens, put 'LESSCHARSET=latin1' in your environment.

MKDIR(1)

NAME

mkdir Make directories.

SYNOPSIS

mkdir [-p] [-m mode] [--parents] [--mode=mode] [--help] [--version] dir...

DESCRIPTION

This documentation is no longer being maintained and may be inaccurate or incomplete. The Texinfo documentation is now the authoritative source.

This manual page documents the GNU version of mkdir. **mkdir** creates a directory with each given name. By default, the mode of created directories is 0777 minus the bits set in the umask.

OPTIONS

-m, --mode mode Set the mode of created directories to *mode*, which is symbolic as in chmod and uses the default mode as the point of departure.

-p, --parents Ensure that each given directory exists. Create any missing parent directories for each argument. Parent directories default to the umask modified by *u+wx*. Do not consider an argument directory that already exists to be an error.

--help Print a usage message on standard output and exit successfully.

--version Print version information on standard output then exit successfully.

MORE(1)

NAME

more File perusal filter for crt viewing.

SYNOPSIS

more [**-dlfpcsu**] [**-num**] [+/ pattern] [+ linenum] [*file* ...]

DESCRIPTION

more is a filter for paging through text one screenful at a time. This version is especially primitive. Users should realize that less(1) provides more(1) emulation and extensive enhancements.

OPTIONS

Command line options are described below. Options are also taken from the environment variable ***MORE*** (make sure to precede them with a dash (-)) but command line options will override them.

-num This option specifies an integer which is the screen size (in lines).

-d **more** will prompt the user with the message "[Press space to continue, *q* to quit.]" and will display "[Press *h* for instructions.]" instead of ringing the bell when an illegal key is pressed.

-l **more** usually treats **^L** (form feed) as a special character, and will pause after any line that contains a form feed. The **-l** option will prevent this behavior.

-f Causes **more** to count logical, rather than screen lines (i.e., long lines are not folded).

-p Do not scroll. Instead, clear the whole screen and then display the text.

-c Do not scroll. Instead, paint each screen from the top, clearing the remainder of each line as it is displayed.

-s Squeeze multiple blank lines into one.

-u Suppress underlining.

+/ The **+/** option specifies a string that will be searched for before each file is displayed.

+num Start at line number **num**.

COMMANDS

Interactive commands for **more** are based on vi(1). Some commands may be preceded by a decimal number, called *k* in the descriptions below. In the following descriptions, ^X means Ctrl-X.

Command	Description
h or **?**	Help: display a summary of these commands. If you forget all the other commands, remember this one.
SPACE	Display next *k* lines of text. Defaults to current screen size.
z	Display next *k* lines of text. Defaults to current screen size. Argument becomes new default.
RETURN	Display next *k* lines of text. Defaults to 1. Argument becomes new default.
d or **^D**	Scroll *k* lines. Default is current scroll size, initially 11. Argument becomes new default.
q or **Q** or **INTERRUPT**	Exit.
s	Skip forward *k* lines of text. Defaults to 1.
F	Skip forward *k* screenfuls of text. Defaults to 1.
B or **^B**	Skip backwards *k* screenfuls of text. Defaults to 1.
'	Go to place where previous search started.
=	Display current line number.
/pattern	Search for *k*th occurrence of regular expression. Defaults to 1.
N	Search for *k*th occurrence of last r.e. Defaults to 1.
!<cmd> or **:!<cmd>**	Execute <cmd> in a subshell
V	Start up /usr/bin/vi at current line
^L	Redraw screen

:n	Go to *k*th next file. Defaults to 1.
:p	Go to *k*th previous file. Defaults to 1.
:f	Display current file name and line number
.	Repeat previous command

ENVIRONMENT

more utilizes the following environment variables, if they exist:

MORE This variable may be set with favored options to **more**.

SHELL Current shell in use (normally set by the shell at login time).

TERM Specifies terminal type, used by more to get the terminal characteristics necessary to manipulate the screen.

SEE ALSO

vi(1) less(1)

AUTHORS

Eric Shienbrood, UC Berkeley.

Modified by Geoff Peck, UCB to add underlining, single spacing.

Modified by John Foderaro, UCB to add -c and MORE environment variable.

HISTORY

The **more** command appeared in 3.0BSD. This man page documents **more** version 5.19 (Berkeley 6/29/88), which is currently in use in the Linux community. Documentation was produced using several other versions of the man page, and extensive inspection of the source code.

MTOOLS.1(3)

NAME

mtools Utilities to access DOS disks in Unix.

INTRODUCTION

Mtools is a public domain collection of tools to allow Unix systems to manipulate MS-DOS files: read, write, and move around files on an MS-DOS filesystem (typically a floppy disk). Where reasonable, each program attempts to emulate the MS-DOS equivalent command. However, unnecessary restrictions and oddities of DOS are not emulated. For instance, it is possible to move subdirectories from one subdirectory to another.

COMMON FEATURES OF ALL MTOOLS COMMANDS

OPTIONS AND FILENAMES MS-DOS filenames are composed of a drive letter followed by a colon, a subdirectory, and a filename. Only the filename part is mandatory, the drive letter and the subdirectory are optional. Filenames without a drive letter refer to Unix files. Subdirectory names can use either the / or ` separator. The use of the ` separator or wildcards requires the names to be enclosed in quotes to protect them from the shell. However, wildcards in Unix filenames should not be enclosed in quotes, because here we *want* the shell to expand them.

The regular expression "pattern matching" routines follow the Unix-style rules. For example, * matches all MS-DOS files in lieu of *.*. The archive, hidden, read-only and system attribute bits are ignored during pattern matching.

All options use the - (minus) as their first character, not / as you'd expect in MS-DOS.

Most mtools commands allow multiple filename parameters, which doesn't follow MS-DOS conventions, but which is more user-friendly.

Most mtools commands allow options that instruct them how to handle file name clashes. See section name clashes, for more details on these. All commands accept the -V flags which print the version, and most accept the -v flag, which switches on verbose mode. In verbose mode, these commands print out the name of the MS-DOS files upon which they act, unless stated otherwise. See section "Commands," for a description of the options which are specific to each command.

DRIVE LETTERS The meaning of the drive letters depends on the target architectures. However, on most target architectures, drive A is the first floppy drive, drive B is the second floppy drive (if available), drive J is a Jaz drive (if available), and drive Z is a Zip drive (if available). On those systems where the device name is derived from the SCSI id, the Jaz drive is assumed to be at SCSI target 4, and the Zip at SCSI target 5 (factory default settings). On Linux, both drives are assumed to be the second drive on the SCSI bus (/dev/sdb). The default settings can be changed using a configuration file (see section on Configuration).

CURRENT WORKING DIRECTORY The mcd command (mcd) is used to establish the device and the current working directory (relative to the MS-DOS filesystem), otherwise the default is assumed to be A:/. However, unlike MS-DOS, there is only one working directory for all drives, and not one per drive.

VFAT-STYLE LONG FILE NAMES This version of mtools supports VFAT style long filenames. If a Unix filename is too long to fit in a short DOS name, it is stored as a VFAT long name, and a companion short name is generated. This short name is what you see when you examine the disk with a pre-7 version of DOS. The following table shows some examples of short names:

Long name	MS-DOS name	Reason for the change
thisisatest	THISIS~1	Filename too long
alain.knaff	ALAIN~1.KNA	Extension too long
prn.txt	PRN~1.TXT	PRN is a device name
.abc	ABC~1	Null filename
hot+cold	HOT_CO~1	Illegal character

As you see, the following transformations happen to derive a short name:

- Illegal characters are replaced by underscores. The illegal characters are ;+=[]',*\<>/?:|.
- Extra dots, which cannot be interpreted as a main name/extension separator are removed
- A ~*n* number is generated,
- The name is shortened so as to fit in the 8+3 limitation

The initial Unix-style file name (whether long or short) is also called the *primary* name, and the derived short name is also called the *secondary* name.

Example:

```
mcopy /etc/motd a:ReallylongNAME
```

Mtools creates a VFAT entry for Reallylongname, and uses REALLYLO as a short name. Reallylongname is the primary name, and REALLYLO is the secondary name.

```
mcopy /etc/motd a:motd
```

Motd fits into the DOS filename limits. Mtools doesn't need to derive another name. Motd is the primary name, and there is no secondary name.

In a nutshell: The primary name is the long name, if one exists, or the short name if there is no long name.

Although VFAT is much more flexible than FAT, there are still names that are not acceptable, even in VFAT. There are still some illegal characters left (*\<>/?:|), and device names are still reserved.

Unix name	Long name	Reason for the change
prn	prn-1	PRN is a device name.
ab:c	ab_c-1	Illegal character.

As you see, the following transformations happen if a long name is illegal:

- Illegal characters are replaces by underscores.
- A *-n* number is generated.

NAME CLASHES When writing a file to disk, its long name (primary name) or short name may collide with an already existing file or directory. This may happen for all commands which create new directory entries, such as mcopy, mmd, mren, mmove, mwrite, and mread. When a name clash happens, mtools asks you what it should do. It offers several choices:

`overwrite` Overwrites the existing file. It is not possible to overwrite a directory with a file.

`rename` Renames the newly created file. Mtools prompts for the new filename

`autorename` Renames the newly created file. Mtools chooses a name by itself, without prompting.

`skip` Gives up on this file, and moves on to the next (if any).

To choose one of these actions, type its first letter at the prompt. If you use a lowercase letter, the action only applies for this file only, if you use an uppercase letter, the action applies to all files, and you won't be prompted again.

You may also choose actions (for all files) on the command line, when invoking mtools:

-o	Overwrites primary names by default.
-O	Overwrites secondary names by default.
-r	Renames primary name by default.
-R	Renames secondary name by default.
-a	Autorenames primary name by default.
-A	Autorenames secondary name by default.
-s	Skip primary name by default.
-S	Skip secondary name by default.
-m	Ask user what to do with primary name.
-M	Ask user what to do with secondary name.

By default, the user is prompted if the primary name clashes, and the secondary name is autorenamed.

If a name clash occurs in a Unix directory, mtools only asks whether to overwrite the file, or to skip it.

CASE SENSITIVITY OF THE VFAT FILESYSTEM The VFAT filesystem is able to remember the case of the filenames. However, filenames which differ only in case are not allowed to coexist in the same directory. For example if you store a file called LongFileName on a VFAT filesystem, mdir shows this file as LongFileName, and not as Longfilename. However, if you then try to add LongFilename to the same directory, it is refused, because case is ignored for clash checks.

The VFAT filesystem allows you to store the case of a filename in the attribute byte, if all letters of the filename are the same case, and if all letters of the extension are the same case too. Mtools uses this information when displaying the files, and also to generate the Unix filename when mcopying to a Unix directory. This may have unexpected results when applied to files written using an pre-7 version of DOS: Indeed, the old style filenames map to all uppercase. This is different from the behavior of the old version of mtools which used to generate lowercase Unix filenames.

HIGH CAPACITY FORMATS Mtools supports a number of formats which allow you to store more data on disk than usual. Due to different operating system abilities, these formats are not supported on all OSes. Mtools recognizes these formats transparently where supported.

In order to format these disks, you need to use an operating-system-specific tool. For Linux, suitable floppy tools can be found in the fdutils package at the following locations:

```
ftp://linux.wauug.org/pub/knaff/fdutils/.
ftp://tsx-11.mit.edu/pub/linux/sources/sbin/fdutils*
ftp://sunsite.unc.edu/pub/Linux/system/Misc/fdutils-*
```

See the manpages included in that package for further details: Use superformat to format all formats except XDF, and use xdfcopy to format XDF.

MORE SECTORS The oldest method of fitting more data on a disk is to use more sectors and more tracks. Although the standard format uses 80 tracks and 18 sectors (on a 3 1/2 inch high-density disk), it is possible to use up to 83 tracks (on most drives) and up to 21 sectors. This method allows to store up to 1743K on a 3 1/2 HD disk. However, 21 sector disks are twice as slow as the standard 18 sector disks because the sectors are packed so close together that we need to interleave them. This problem doesn't exist for 20 sector formats.

These formats are supported by numerous DOS shareware utilities such as fdformat and vgacopy. In his infinite hubris, Bill Gate$ believed that he invented this, and called it "DMF disks," or "Windows formatted disks." But in reality, it had already existed years before! Mtools supports these formats on Linux, on SunOs and on the Dell Unix PC.

BIGGER SECTORS By using bigger sectors it is possible to go beyond the capacity which can be obtained by the standard 512-byte sectors. This is because of the sector header. The sector header has the same size, regardless of how many data bytes are in the sector. Thus, we save some space by using *fewer*, but bigger sectors. For example, 1 sector of 4K only takes up header space once, whereas 8 sectors of 512 bytes have also 8 headers, for the same amount of useful data.

This method allows you to store up to 1992K on a 3 1/2 HD disk.

Mtools supports these formats only on Linux.

2m The 2m format was originally invented by Ciriaco Garcia de Celis. It also uses bigger sectors than usual in order to fit more data on the disk.

However, it uses the standard format (18 sectors of 512 bytes each) on the first cylinder, in order to make these disks easier to handle by DOS. Indeed this method allows a standard sized bootsector, which contains a description of how the rest of the disk should be read.

However, the drawback of this is that the first cylinder can hold less data than the others. Unfortunately, DOS can only handle disks where each track contains the same amount of data. Thus 2m hides the fact that the first track contains less data by using a *shadow FAT*. (DOS usually stores the FAT in two identical copies, for additional safety. XDF stores only one copy, and it tells DOS that it stores two. Thus the space that would be taken up by the second FAT copy is saved.) This also means that you should *never use a 2m disk to store anything else than a DOS fs*.

Mtools supports these formats only on Linux.

XDF XDF is a high capacity format used by OS/2. It can hold 1840K per disk. That's lower than the best 2m formats, but its main advantage is that it is fast: 600 milliseconds per track. That's faster than the 21 sector format, and almost as fast as the standard 18 sector format. In order to access these disks, make sure mtools has been compiled with XDF support, and set the *use_xdf* variable for the drive in the configuration file. See section "Compiling mtools and misc variables," for details on how to do this. Fast XDF access is only available for Linux kernels more recent than 1.1.34.

Mtools supports this format only on Linux.

WARNING

Caution / Attention distributors: If mtools is compiled on a Linux kernel more recent than 1.3.34, it won't run on an older kernel. However, if it has been compiled on an older kernel, it still runs on a newer kernel, except that XDF access is slower. It is recommended that distribution authors only include mtools binaries compiled on kernels older than 1.3.34 until 2 comes out. When 2 is out, mtools binaries compiled on newer kernels may (and should) be distributed. Mtools binaries compiled on kernels older than 1.3.34 won't run on any 2.1 kernel or later.

EXIT CODES All the Mtools commands return 0 on success, 1 on utter failure, or 2 on partial failure. All the Mtools commands perform a few sanity checks before going ahead, to make sure that the disk is indeed an MS-DOS disk (as opposed to, say, an ext2 or minix disk).

These checks may reject partially corrupted disks, which might otherwise still be readable. To avoid these checks, set the *MTOOLS_SKIP_CHECK* environmental variable or the corresponding configuration file variable (see section "Global Variables").

BUGS An unfortunate side effect of not guessing the proper device (when multiple disk capacities are supported) is an occasional error message from the device driver. These can be safely ignored.

The FAT checking code chokes on 1.72 MB disks mformatted with pre-2.0.7 mtools. Set the environmental variable *MTOOLS_FAT_COMPATIBILITY* (or the corresponding configuration file variable, *global variables*) to bypass the FAT checking.

HOW TO CONFIGURE MTOOLS FOR YOUR ENVIRONMENT

DESCRIPTION This sections explains the syntax of the configurations files for mtools. The configuration files are called `/usr/local/etc/mtools.conf` and `~/.mtoolsrc`. If the environmental variable *MTOOLSRC* is set, its contents are used as the filename for a third configuration file. These configuration files describe the following items:

- Global configuration flags and variables
- Per drive flags and variables
- Character translation tables

LOCATION OF THE CONFIGURATION FILES `/usr/local/etc/mtools.conf` is the system-wide configuration file, and `~/.mtoolsrc` is the user's private configuration file.

On some systems, the system-wide configuration file is called `/etc/defaults/mtools.conf` instead.

GENERAL CONFIGURATION FILE SYNTAX The configuration file is made up of sections. Each section starts with a keyword identifying the section followed by a colon. Then follow variable assignments and flags. Variable assignments take the following form: name=value

Flags are lone keywords without an equal sign and value following them. A section either ends at the end of the file or where the next section begins.

Lines starting with a hash (#) are comments. Newline characters are equivalent to whitespace (except where ending a comment). The configuration file is case insensitive, except for items enclosed in quotes (such as filenames).

DEFAULT VALUES For most platforms, mtools contains reasonable compiled-in defaults for physical floppy drives. Thus, you usually don't need to bother with the configuration file, if all you want to do with mtools is to access your floppy drives. On the other hand, the configuration file is needed if you also want to use mtools to access your hard disk partitions and dosemu image files.

GLOBAL VARIABLES Global variables may be set to 1 or to 0. The following global flags are recognized:

`MTOOLS_SKIP_CHECK` If this is set to 1, mtools skips most of its sanity checks. This is needed to read some Atari disks which have been made with the earlier ROMs, and which would not be recognized otherwise.

`MTOOLS_FAT_COMPATIBILITY` If this is set to 1, mtools skips the fat size checks. Some disks have a bigger FAT than they really need to. These are rejected if this option is not set.

`MTOOLS_LOWER_CASE` If this is set to 1, mtools displays all-uppercase short filenames as lowercase. This has been done to allow a behavior which is consistent with older versions of mtools which didn't know about the case bits.

`MTOOLS_NO_VFAT` If this is set to 1, mtools won't generate VFAT entries for filenames which are mixed-case, but otherwise legal DOS filenames. This is useful when working with DOS versions which can't grok VFAT longnames, such as Caldera's FreeDos.

Example: Inserting the following line into your configuration file instructs mtools to skip the sanity checks:

```
MTOOLS_SKIP_CHECK=1
```

Global variables may also be set via the environment:

```
export MTOOLS_SKIP_CHECK=1
```

PER DRIVE FLAGS AND VARIABLES

GENERAL INFORMATION Per drive flags and values may be described in a drive section. A drive section starts with drive "*driveletter*" :

Then follow variable-value pairs and flags.

This is a sample drive description:

```
drive a:file="/dev/fd0" use_xdf=1
```

DISK GEOMETRY CONFIGURATION Geometry information describes the physical characteristics about the disk. Its has three purposes:

formatting The geometry information is written into the boot sector of the newly made disk. However, you may also describe the geometry information on the command line. See section mformat for details.

filtering On some versions of Unix there are device nodes which only support one physical geometry. For instance, you might need a different node to access a disk as high density or as low density. The geometry is compared to the actual geometry stored on the boot sector to make sure that this device node is able to correctly read the disk. If the geometry doesn't match, this drive entry fails, and the next drive entry bearing the same drive letter is tried. See section "Multiple Descriptions" for more details on supplying several descriptions for one drive letter.

If no geometry information is supplied in the configuration file, all disks are accepted. On Linux (and on SPARC) there exist device nodes with configurable geometry ('`/dev/fd0`', '`/dev/fd1`', etc.), and thus filtering is not needed (and ignored) for disk drives. Mtools still does do filtering on plain files (disk images) in Linux: this is mainly intended for test purposes, as I don't have access to a Unix which would actually need filtering.

initial geometry The geometry information (if available) is also used to set the initial geometry on configurable device nodes. This initial geometry is used to read the boot sector, which contains the real geometry. If no geometry information is supplied in the configuration file, no initial configuration is done. On Linux, this is not really needed either, as the configurable devices are able to auto-detect the disk type accurately enough (for most common formats) to read the boot sector.

Wrong geometry information may lead to very bizarre errors. That's why I strongly recommend that you don't use geometry configuration unless you actually need it.

The following geometry related variables are available:

`cylinders` The number of cylinders. (`cylinders` is the preferred form, `tracks` is considered obsolete.)

`heads` The number of heads (sides).

`sectors` The number of sectors per track.

For example, the following drive section describes a 1.44M drive:

```
drive a:file="/dev/fd0H1440"
fat_bits=12
cylinders=80 heads=2 sectors=18
```

The following shorthand geometry descriptions are available:

`1.44m` High density 3 1/2 disk. Equivalent to: `fat_bits=12 cylinders=80 heads=2 sectors=18`

`1.2m` High density 5 1/4 disk. Equivalent to: `fat_bits=12 cylinders=80 heads=2 sectors=15`

`720k` Double density 3 1/2 disk. Equivalent to: `fat_bits=12 cylinders=80 heads=2 sectors=9`

`360k` Double density 5 1/4 disk. Equivalent to: `fat_bits=12 cylinders=40 heads=2 sectors=9`

The shorthand format descriptions may be amended. For example, `360k sectors=8` describes a 320k disk and is equivalent to: `fat_bits=12 cylinders=40 heads=2 sectors=8`

OPEN FLAGS Moreover, the following flags are available:

`sync` All i/o operations are done synchronously

`nodelay` The device or file is opened with the O_NDELAY flag. This is needed on some non-Linux architectures.

`exclusive` The device or file is opened with the O_EXCL flag. On Linux, this ensures exclusive access to the floppy drive. On most other architectures, and for plain files it has no effect at all.

GENERAL PURPOSE DRIVE VARIABLES The following general purpose drive variables are available:

`file` The name of the file or device holding the disk image. This is mandatory. The file name should be enclosed in quotes.

`use_xdf` If this is set to a nonzero value, mtools also tries to access this disk as an XDF disk. XDF is a high capacity format used by OS/2. This is off by default. See section "XDF" for more details.

`partition` Tells mtools to treat the drive as a partitioned device, and to use the given partition. Only primary partitions are accessible using this method, and they are numbered from 1 to 4. For logical partitions, use the more general `offset` variable. The `partition` variable is intended for removable media such as Syquests, ZIP drives, and magneto-optical disks. Although traditional DOS sees Syquests and magneto-optical disks as '`giant floppy disks`' which are unpartitioned, OS/2 and Windows NT treat them like hard disks, i.e. partioned devices. The `partition` flag is also useful DOSEMU hdimages. It is not recommended for hard disks for which direct access to partitions is available through mounting.

`scsi` When set to 1, this option tells mtools to use raw SCSI I/O instead of the standard read/write calls to access the device. Currently, this is supported on HP/UX, Solaris, and SunOs. This is needed because on some architectures, such as SunOs or Solaris, PC media can't be accessed using the `read` and `write` syscalls, because the OS expects them to contain a Sun specific "disk label".

As raw SCSI access always uses the whole device, you need to specify the "partition" flag in addition.

On some architectures, such as Solaris, mtools needs root privileges to be able to use the `scsi=1` option. Thus mtools should be installed set uid root on Solaris if you want to access Zip/Jaz drives. Mtools uses its root privileges to open the device, and to issue the actual SCSI I/O calls. Moreover, root privileges are only used for drives described in a system-wide configuration file such as '`/usr/local/etc/mtools.conf`', and not for those described in '`~/.mtoolsrc`' or '`$MTOOLSRC`'.

`privileged` When set to 1, this instructs mtools to use its set-uid and set-gid privileges for opening the given drive. This option is only valid for drives described in the system-wide configuration files (such as '`/usr/local/etc/mtools.conf`', not '`~/.mtoolsrc`' or '`$MTOOLSRC`'). Obviously, this option is also a no op if mtools is not installed setuid or setgid. This option is implied by 'scsi=1', but again only for drives defined in system-wide configuration files. Privileged may also be set explicitely to 0, in order to tell mtools not to use its privileges for a given drive even if `scsi=1` is set.

Mtools only needs to be installed setuid if you use the `privileged` or `scsi` drive variables. If you do not use these options, mtools works perfectly well even when not installed setuid root.

`nolock` Instructs mtools not to use locking on this drive. This is needed on systems with buggy locking semantics. However, enabling this makes operation less safe in cases where several users may access the same drive at the same time.

`offset` Describes where in the file the MS-DOS filesystem starts. This is useful for logical partitions in DOSEMU hdimages, and for ATARI ram disks. By default, this is zero, meaning that the filesystem starts right at the beginning of the device or file.

`fat_bits` The number of FAT bits. This may be 12 or 16. This is very rarely needed, as it can almost always be deduced from information in the boot sector. On the contrary, describing the number of fat bits may actually be harmful if you get it wrong. You should only use it if mtools gets the autodetected number of fat bits wrong, or if you want to mformat a disk with a weird number of fat bits.

`precmd` On some variants of Solaris, it is necessary to call 'volcheck -v' before opening a floppy device, in order for the system to notice that there is indeed a disk in the drive. `precmd="volcheck -v"` in the drive clause establishes the desired behavior.

Only the file variable is mandatory. The other parameters may be left out. In that case a default value or an autodetected value is used.

SUPPLYING MULTIPLE DESCRIPTIONS FOR A DRIVE It is possible to supply multiple descriptions for a drive. In that case, the descriptions are tried in order until one is found that fits. Descriptions may fail for several reasons:

- The geometry is not appropriate.
- There is no disk in the drive.
- There are other problems.

Multiple definitions are useful when using physical devices which are only able to support one single disk geometry. Example:

```
drive a: file="/dev/fd0H1440" 1.44m
drive a: file="/dev/fd0H720" 720k
```

This instructs mtools to use /dev/fd0H1440 for 1.44m (high density) disks and /dev/fd0H720 for 720k (double density) disks. On Linux, this feature is not really needed, as the /dev/fd0 device is able to handle any geometry.

You may also use multiple drive descriptions to access both of your physical drives through one drive letter:

```
drive z: file="/dev/fd0"
drive z: file="/dev/fd1"
```

With this description, `mdir z:` accesses your first physical drive if it contains a disk. If the first drive doesn't contain a disk, mtools checks the second drive.

When using multiple configuration files, drive descriptions in the files parsed last override descriptions for the same drive in earlier files. In order to avoid this, use the `drive+` or `+drive` keywords instead of `drive`. The first adds a description to the end of the list (i.e. it will be tried last), and the first adds it to the start of the list.

CHARACTER SET TRANSLATION TABLES

If you live in the USA, in Western Europe, or in Australia, you may skip this section.

WHY CHARACTER SET TRANSLATION TABLES ARE NEEDED

DOS uses a different character code mapping than Unix. Seven-bit characters still have the same meaning, only characters with the eight-bit set are affected. To make matters worse, there are several translation tables available depending on the country where you are. The appearance of the characters is defined using code pages. These code pages aren't the same for all countries. For instance, some code pages don't contain uppercase accented characters. On the other hand, some code pages contain characters which don't exist in Unix, such as certain line-drawing characters or accented consonants used by some Eastern European countries. This affects two things, relating to filenames:

upper case characters In short names, only uppercase characters are allowed. This also holds for accented characters. For instance, in a code page which doesn't contain accented uppercase characters, the accented lowercase characters get transformed into their unaccented counterparts.

long file names Micro$oft has finally come to their senses and uses a more standard mapping for the long file names. They use Unicode, which is basically a 32 bit version of ASCII. Its first 256 characters are identical to Unix ASCII. Thus, the code page also affects the correspondence between the codes used in long names and those used in short names

Mtools considers the filenames entered on the command line as having the Unix mapping, and translates the characters to get short names. By default, code page 850 is used with the Swiss uppercase/lowercase mapping. I chose this code page, because its set of existing characters most closely matches Unix's. Moreover, this code page covers most characters in use in the USA, Australia and Western Europe. However, it is still possible to chose a different mapping. There are two methods: the country variable and explicit tables.

CONFIGURATION USING COUNTRY

The `COUNTRY` variable is recommended for people who also have access to MS-DOS system files and documentation. If you don't have access to these, I'd suggest you'd rather use explicit tables instead.

SYNTAXCOUNTRY="country[,[codepage], country-file]"

This tells mtools to use a Unix-to-DOS translation table which matches *codepage* and an lowercase-to-uppercase table for *country* and to use the *country-file* file to get the lowercase-to-uppercase table. The country code is most often the telephone prefix of the country. Refer to the DOS help page on "country" for more details. The *codepage* and the *country-file* parameters are optional. Please don't type in the square brackets, they are only there to say which parameters are optional. The *country-file* file is supplied with MS-DOS, and is usually called `'COUNTRY.SYS'`, and stored in the 'C:{DOS' directory. In most cases you don't need it, as the most common translation tables are compiled into mtools. So, don't worry if you run a Unix only box which lacks this file.

If *codepage* is not given, a per country default code page is used. If the *country-file* parameter isn't given, compiled-in defaults are used for the lowercase-to-uppercase table. This is useful for versions of Unix other than Linux, which may have no 'COUNTRY.SYS' file available online.

The Unix-to-DOS tables are not contained in the 'COUNTRY.SYS' file, and thus mtools always uses compiled-in defaults for those. Thus, only a limited amount of code pages are supported. If your preferred code page is missing, or if you know the name of the Windows 95 file which contains this mapping, could you please drop me a line at `Alain.Knaff@poboxes.com`.

The COUNTRY variable can also be set using the environment.

CONFIGURATION USING EXPLICIT TRANSLATION TABLES

Translation tables may be described in line in the configuration file. Two tables are needed: first the DOS-to-Unix table, and then the Lowercase-to-Uppercase table. A DOS-to-Unix table starts with the `tounix` keyword, followed by a colon, and 128 hexadecimal numbers. A lower-to-upper table starts with the `fucase` keyword, followed by a colon, and 128 hexadecimal numbers.

The tables only show the translations for characters whose codes are greater than 128, because translation for lower codes is trivial.

EXAMPLE

tounix 0xc7 0xfc 0xe9 0xe2 0xe4 0xe0 0xe5 0xe7 0xea 0xeb 0xe8 0xef 0xee 0xec 0xc4 0xc5 0xc9 0xe6 0xc6 0xf4 0xf6 0xf2 0xfb 0xf9 0xff 0xd6 0xdc 0xf8 0xa3 0xd8 0xd7 0x5f 0xe1 0xed 0xf3 0xfa 0xf1 0xd1 0xaa 0xba 0xbf 0xae 0xac 0xbd 0xbc 0xa1 0xab 0xbb 0x5f 0x5f 0x5f 0x5f 0x5f 0xc1 0xc2 0xc0 0xa9 0x5f 0x5f 0x5f 0x5f 0xa2 0xa5 0xac 0x5f 0x5f 0x5f 0x5f 0x5f 0x5f 0xe3 0xc3 0x5f 0x5f 0x5f 0x5f 0x5f 0x5f 0x5f 0xa4 0xf0 0xd0 0xc9 0xcb 0xc8 0x69 0xcd 0xce 0xcf 0x5f 0x5f 0x5f 0x5f 0x7c 0x49 0x5f 0xd3 0xdf 0xd4 0xd2 0xf5 0xd5 0xb5 0xfe 0xde 0xda 0xd9 0xfd 0xdd 0xde 0xaf 0xb4 0xad 0xb1 0x5f 0xbe 0xb6 0xa7 0xf7 0xb8 0xb0 0xa8 0xb7 0xb9 0xb3 0xb2 0x5f 0x5f

fucase 0x80 0x9a 0x90 0xb6 0x8e 0xb7 0x8f 0x80 0xd2 0xd3 0xd4 0xd8 0xd7 0xde 0x8e 0x8f 0x90 0x92 0x92 0xe2 0x99 0xe3 0xea 0xeb 0x59 0x99 0x9a 0x9d 0x9c 0x9d 0x9e

0x9f 0xb5 0xd6 0xe0 0xe9 0xa5 0xa5 0xa6 0xa7 0xa8 0xa9
0xaa 0xab 0xac 0xad 0xae 0xaf 0xb0 0xb1 0xb2 0xb3 0xb4
0xb5 0xb6 0xb7 0xb8 0xb9 0xba 0xbb 0xbc 0xbd 0xbe 0xbf
0xc0 0xc1 0xc2 0xc3 0xc4 0xc5 0xc7 0xc7 0xc8 0xc9 0xca 0xcb
0xcc 0xcd 0xce 0xcf 0xd1 0xd1 0xd2 0xd3 0xd4 0x49 0xd6
0xd7 0xd8 0xd9 0xda 0xdb 0xdc 0xdd 0xde 0xdf 0xe0 0xe1
0xe2 0xe3 0xe5 0xe5 0xe6 0xe8 0xe8 0xe9 0xea 0xeb 0xed
0xed 0xee 0xef 0xf0 0xf1 0xf2 0xf3 0xf4 0xf5 0xf6 0xf7 0xf8
0xf9 0xfa 0xfb 0xfc 0xfd 0xfe 0xff

The first table maps DOS character codes to Unix character codes. For example, the DOS character number 129. This is a u with to dots on top of it. To translate it into Unix, we look at the character number 1 in the first table (1 = 129 - 128). This is 0xfc. (Beware, numbering starts at 0.) The second table maps lower case DOS characters to upper case DOS characters. The same lower case u with dots maps to character 0x9a, which is an uppercase U with dots in DOS.

UNICODE CHARACTERS GREATER THAN 256 If an existing MS-DOS name contains Unicode characters greater than 256, these are translated to underscores or to characters which are close in visual appearance. For example, accented consonants are translated into their unaccented counterparts. This translation is used for mdir and for the Unix filenames generated by mcopy. Linux does support Unicode too, but unfortunately too few applications support it yet to bother with it in mtools. Most importantly, xterm can't display Unicode yet. If there is sufficient demand, I might include support for Unicode in the Unix filenames as well.

WARNING

When deleting files with mtools, the underscore matches all characters which can't be represented in Unix. Be careful with mdel!

LOCATION OF CONFIGURATION FILES AND PARSING ORDER

The configuration files are parsed in the following order:

1. Compiled-in defaults
2. `'/usr/local/etc/mtools.conf'`
3. `'/etc/mtools'` for backwards compatibility only, and is only parsed if `'mtools.conf'` doesn't exist

4. '~/.mtoolsrc'
5. '$MTOOLSRC' (file pointed by the MTOOLSRC environmental variable)

Options described in the later files override those described in the earlier files. Drives defined in earlier files persist if they are not overridden in the later files. For instance, drives A and B may be defined in '/usr/local/etc/mtools.conf' and drives C and D may be defined in '~/.mtoolsrc'. However, if '~/.mtoolsrc' also defines drive A, this new description would override the description of drive A in '/usr/local/etc/mtools.conf' instead of adding to it. If you want to add a new description to a drive already described in an earlier file, you need to use either the +drive or drive+ keyword.

BACKWARDS COMPATIBILITY WITH OLD CONFIGURATION FILE SYNTAX The syntax described herein is new for version mtools-3.0. The old line-oriented syntax is still supported. Each line beginning with a single letter is considered to be a drive description using the old syntax. Old style and new style drive sections may be mixed within the same configuration file, in order to make upgrading easier. Support for the old syntax will be phased out eventually, and in order to discourage its use, I purposefully omit its description here.

COMMAND LIST

This section describes the available mtools commands, and the command line parameters that each of them accepts. Options that are common to all mtools commands are not described here, see 'arguments' for a description of those.

MATTRIB Mattrib is used to change MS-DOS file attribute flags. It has the following syntax:

```
mattrib [-a|+a] [-h|+h] [-r|+r] [-s|+s] msdosfile _
    [ msdosfiles ... ]
```

Mattrib adds attribute flags to an MS-DOS file (with the '+' operator) or removes attribute flags (with the '-' operator).

Mattrib supports the following attribute bits:

a   Archive bit. Used by some backup programs to indicate a new file.

r Read-only bit. Used to indicate a read-only file. Files with this bit set cannot be erased by DEL nor modified.

s System bit. Used by MS-DOS to indicate a operating system file.

h Hidden bit. Used to make files hidden from DIR.

MBADBLOCKS The mbadblocks command is used to scan an MS-DOS floppy and mark its unused bad blocks as bad. It uses the following syntax:

```
mbadblocks drive:
```

Mbadblocks scans an MS-DOS floppy for bad blocks. All unused bad blocks are marked as such in the FAT. This is intended to be used right after mformat. It is not intended to salvage bad disks.

BUGS

Mbadblocks should (but doesn't yet :-( ) also try to salvage bad blocks which are in use by reading them repeatedly, and then mark them bad.

MCD The mcd command is used to change the mtools working directory on the MS-DOS disk. It uses the following syntax:

mcd [*msdosdirectory*]

Without arguments, mcd reports the current device and working directory. Otherwise, mcd changes the current device and current working directory relative to an MS-DOS filesystem.

The environmental variable MCWD may be used to locate the file where the device and current working directory information is stored. The default is '$HOME/.mcwd'. Information in this file is ignored if the file is more than 6 hours old.

Mcd returns 0 on success or 1 on failure.

Unlike MS-DOS versions of CD, mcd can be used to change to another device. It may be wise to remove old '.mcwd' files at logout.

MCOPY The mcopy command is used to copy MS-DOS files to and from Unix. It uses the following syntax:

```
mcopy [-tnvmoOsSrRA] sourcefile targetfile
mcopy [-tnvmoOsSrRA] sourcefile [ sourcefiles... ] _
    targetdirectory
mcopy [-tnvm] MSDOSsourcefile
```

`Mcopy` copies the specified file to the named file, or copies multiple files to the named directory. The source and target can be either MS-DOS or Unix files.

The use of a drive letter designation on the MS-DOS files, 'a:' for example, determines the direction of the transfer. A missing drive designation implies a Unix file whose path starts in the current directory. If a source drive letter is specified with no attached file name (e.g. `mcopy a: .`), all files are copied from that drive.

If only a single, MS-DOS source parameter is provided (e.g. "mcopy a:foo.exe"), an implied destination of the current directory ('.') is assumed.

A filename of '-' means standard input or standard output, depending on its position on the command line.

`Mcopy` accepts the following command line options:

`Q` When mcopying multiple files, quits as soon as one copy fails (for example due to lacking storage space on the target disk).

`t` Text file transfer. `Mcopy` translates incoming carriage return/line feeds to line feeds.

`n` No confirmation when overwriting Unix files. `Mcopy` doesn't warn the user when overwriting an existing Unix file. In order to switch off confirmation for DOS files, use `-o`.

`m` Preserve the file modification time. If the target file already exists, and the `-n` option is not in effect, `mcopy` asks whether to overwrite the file or to rename the new file ('name clashes') for details.

BUGS

Unlike MS-DOS, the '+' operator (append) from MS-DOS is not supported. However, you may use mtype to produce the same effect:

```
mtype a:file1 a:file2 a:file3 >unixfile
mtype a:file1 a:file2 a:file3 | mcopy - a:msdosfile
```

MDEL The `mdel` command is used to delete an MS-DOS file. Its syntax is

`mdel` [`-v`] msdosfile [msdosfiles ...]

`Mdel` deletes files on an MS-DOS filesystem.

`Mdel` asks for verification prior to removing a read-only file.

MDELTREE The `mdeltree` command is used to delete an MS-DOS file. Its syntax is

`mdeltree` [-v] msdosdirectory [msdosdirectories...]

`Mdeltree` removes a directory and all the files and subdirectories it contains from an MS-DOS filesystem. An error occurs if the directory to be removed does not exist.

MDIR The `mdir` command is used to display an MS-DOS directory. Its syntax is

`mdir [-w]` *msdosdirectory*

`mdir [-f] [-w] [-a]` *msdosfile* [*msdosfiles...*]

`Mdir` displays the contents of an MS-DOS directory.

`Mdir` supports the following command line options:

- `w` Wide output. With this option, `mdir` prints the filenames across the page without displaying the file size or creation date.
- `a` Also list hidden files.
- `f` Fast. Do not try to find free space. On larger disks, finding out the amount of free space takes up some non trivial amount of time, as the whole FAT must be read in and scanned. The `-f` flag bypasses this step. This flag is not needed on FAT32 filesystems, which store the size explicitely.

An error occurs if a component of the path is not a directory.

MFORMAT The `mformat` command is used to add an MS-DOS filesystem to a low-level formatted diskette. Its syntax is

`mformat` [-t cylinders] [-h heads] [-s sectors] [-l vol*ume_label*] [-F] [-I *fsVersion*] [-S *sizecode*] [-2 *sectors_on_track_0*] [-M *software_sector_size*] [-a] [-X] [-C] [-H *hidden_sectors*] [-r *root_sectors*] *drive:*

`Mformat` adds a minimal MS-DOS filesystem (boot sector, FAT, and root directory) to a diskette that has already been formatted by a Unix low-level format.

The following options are supported: (The S, 2, 1 and M options may not exist if this copy of mtools has been compiled without the USE_2M option.)

`t` The number of cylinders.

`h` The number of heads (sides).

`s` The number of sectors per track. If the 2m option is given, number of 512-byte sector equivalents on generic tracks (i.e. not head 0 track 0). If the 2m option is not given, number of physical sectors per track (which may be bigger than 512 bytes).

`l` An optional volume label.

`S` The sizecode. The size of the sector is 2 ^ (sizecode + 7).

`2` 2m format. The parameter to this option describes the number of sectors on track 0, head 0. This option is recommended for sectors bigger than normal.

`1` Don't use a 2m format, even if the current geometry of the disk is a 2m geometry.

`M` Software sector size. This parameter describes the sector size in bytes used by the MS-DOS filesystem. By default it is the physical sector size.

`a` If this option is given, an Atari-style serial number is generated. Ataris store their serial number in the OEM label.

`X` Formats the disk as an XDF disk. See section "XDF" for more details. The disk has first to be lowlevel formatted using the xdfcopy utility included in the fdutils package.

`C` Creates the disk image file to install the MS-DOS filesystem on it. Obviously, this is useless on physical devices such as floppies and hard disk partitions.

`H` Number of hidden sectors. This parameter is useful for formatting hard disk partitions, which are not aligned on track boundaries (i.e. first head of first track doesn't belong to the partition, but contains a partition table). In that case the number of hidden sectors is in general the number of sectors per cylinder. This is untested.

`n` Serial number

F Format the partition as FAT32 (experimental).

I Sets the fsVersion id when formatting a FAT32 drive. In order to find this out, run minfo on an existing FAT32 drive, and mail me about it, so I can include the correct value in future versions of mtools.

c Sets the size of a cluster (in sectors). If this cluster size would generate a FAT that is too big for its number of bits, mtools automatically increases the cluster size, until the FAT is small enough.

r Sets the size of the root directory (in sectors). Only applicable to 12 and 16 bit FATs.

To format a diskette at a density other than the default, you must supply (at least) those command line parameters that are different from the default.

`Mformat` returns 0 on success or 1 on failure.

It doesn't record bad block information to the Fat, use mkmanifest for that.

MKMANIFEST The `mkmanifest` command is used to create a shell script (packing list) to restore Unix filenames. Its syntax is:

`mkmanifest` [*files*]

`Mkmanifest` creates a shell script that aids in the restoration of Unix filenames that got clobbered by the MS-DOS filename restrictions. MS-DOS filenames are restricted to 8 character names, 3 character extensions, upper case only, no device names, and no illegal characters.

The mkmanifest program is compatible with the methods used in `pcomm`, `arc`, and `mtools` to change perfectly good Unix filenames to fit the MS-DOS restrictions. This command is only useful if the target system which will read the diskette cannot handle vfat long names.

EXAMPLE

You want to copy the following Unix files to a MS-DOS diskette (using the `mcopy` command).

```
very_long_name
2.many.dots
illegal:
good.c
prn.dev
Capital
```

Mcopy converts the names to

```
very_lon
2xmany.dot
illegalx
good.c xprn.dev
capital
```

The command

```
mkmanifest very_long_name 2.many.dots illegal: _
    good.c prn.dev Capital >manifest
```

would produce the following:

```
mv very_lon very_long_name
mv 2xmany.dot 2.many.dots
mv illegalx illegal:
mv xprn.dev prn.dev
mv capital Capital
```

Notice that "good.c" did not require any conversion, so it did not appear in the output.

Suppose I've copied these files from the diskette to another Unix system, and I now want the files back to their original names. If the file "manifest" (the output captured above) was sent along with those files, it could be used to convert the filenames.

BUGS

The short names generated by `mkmanifest` follow the old convention (from mtools-2.0.7) and not the one from Windows 95 and mtools-3.0.

MINFO The `minfo` command prints the parameters of a Dos filesystem, such as number of sectors, heads and cylinders. It also prints an `mformat` command line which can be used to create a similar Dos filesystem on another media. However, this doesn't work with 2m or Xdf media, and with Dos 1.0 filesystems `minfo` *drive*.

Mlabel supports the following option:

v   Prints a hexdump of the bootsector, in addition to the other information

MLABEL The `mlabel` command adds a volume label to a disk. Its syntax is

`mlabel` [-vcs] *drive*:[*new_label*]

`Mlabel` displays the current volume label, if present. If *new_label* is not given, and if neither the `c` nor the `s` options are set, it prompts the user for a new volume label. To delete an existing volume label, press return at the prompt.

Reasonable care is taken to create a valid MS-DOS volume label. If an invalid label is specified, `mlabel` changes the label (and displays the new label if the verbose mode is set). `Mlabel` returns 0 on success or 1 on failure.

`Mlabel` supports the following options:

c	Clears an existing label, without prompting the user.
s	Shows the existing label, without prompting the user.

MMD The `mmd` command is used to make an MS-DOS subdirectory. Its syntax is

`mmd [-voOsSrRA]` *msdosdirectory* [*msdosdirectories...*]

`Mmd` makes a new directory on an MS-DOS filesystem. An error occurs if the directory already exists.

MMOUNT The `mmount` command is used to mount an MS-DOS disk. It is only available on Linux, as it is only useful if the OS kernel allows you to configure the disk geometry. Its syntax is

`mmount` *msdosdrive* [*mountargs*]

`Mmount` reads the boot sector of a MS-DOS disk, configures the drive geometry, and finally mounts it passing `mountargs` to `mount`. If no mount arguments are specified, the name of the device is used. If the disk is write protected, it is automatically mounted read-only.

MMOVE The `mmove` command is used to move or rename an existing MS-DOS file or subdirectory. Its syntax is

`mmove [-voOsSrRA]` *sourcefile targetfile* `mmove`
`[-voOsSrRA]` *sourcefile* [*sourcefiles...*] *targetdirectory*

`Mmove` moves or renames an existing MS-DOS file or subdirectory. Unlike the MS-DOS version of `MOVE`, `mmove` is able to move subdirectories.

MPARTITION The `mpartition` command is used to create MS-DOS filesystems as partitions. This is intended to be used on non-Linux systems, i.e. systems where fdisk and easy access to SCSI devices are not available. This command only works on drives whose partition variable is set. Its syntax is

`mpartition -p` drive `mpartition -r` *drive* `mpartition -I` *drive* `mpartition -a` *drive* `mpartition -d` *drive* `mpartition -c` [`-s` *sectors*] [`-h` *heads*] [`-t` *cylinders*] [`-v` [`-T` *type*] [`-b` *begin*] [`-l` length] [`-f`]

Mpartition supports the following operations:

`p` Prints a command line to recreate the partition for the drive. Nothing is printed if the partition for the drive is not defined, or an inconsistency has been detected. If verbose (-v) is also set, prints the current partition table.

`r` Removes the partition described by *drive*.

`I` Initializes the partition table, and removes all partitions.

`c` Creates the partition described by *drive*.

`a` "Activates" the partition, i.e. makes it bootable. Only one partition can be bootable at a time.

`d` "Deactivates" the partition, i.e. makes it unbootable.

If no operation is given, the current settings are printed.

For partition creations, the following options are available:

`s` *sectors* The number of sectors per track of the partition (which is also the number of sectors per track for the whole drive).

`h` *heads* The number of heads of the partition (which is also the number of heads for the whole drive). By default, the geometry information (number of sectors and heads) is figured out from neighboring partition table entries, or guessed from the size.

`t` *cylinders* The number of cylinders of the partition (not the number of cylinders of the whole drive).

`b` *begin* The starting offset of the partition, expressed in sectors. If begin is not given, mpartition lets the partition begin at the start of the disk (partition number 1), or immediately after the end of the previous partition.

`l` *length* The size (length) of the partition, expressed in sectors. If end is not given, mpartition figures out the size from the number of sectors, heads and cylinders. If these are not given either, it gives the partition the biggest possible size, considering disk size and start of the next partition.

The following option is available for all operations that modify the partition table:

`f` Usually, before writing back any changes to the partition, mpartition performs certain consistency checks, such as checking for overlaps and proper alignment of the partitions. If any of these checks fails, the partition table is not changed. The -f allows you to override these safeguards.

The following option is available for all operations:

`v` Together with `-p` prints the partition table as it is now (no change operation), or as it is after it is modified.

`vv` If the verbosity flag is given twice, mpartition will print out a hexdump of the partition table when reading it from and writing it to the device.

MRD The `mrd` command is used to remove an MS-DOS subdirectory. Its syntax is

`mrd [-v]` *msdosdirectory* [*msdosdirectories...*]

`Mrd` removes a directory from an MS-DOS filesystem. An error occurs if the directory does not exist or is not empty.

MREN The `mren` command is used to rename or move an existing MSDOS file or subdirectory. Its syntax is

`mren [-voOsSrRA]` *sourcefile targetfile*

`Mren` renames an existing file on a MS-DOS filesystem.

In verbose mode, `Mren` displays the new filename if the name supplied is invalid.

If the first syntax is used (only one sourcefile), and if the target name doesn't contain any slashes or colons, the file (or subdirectory) is renamed in the same directory, instead of being moved to the current mcd directory as would be the case with `mmove`. Unlike the MS-DOS version of `REN`, `mren` can be used to rename directories.

MTOOLSTEST The `mtoolstest` command is used to tests the mtools configuration files. To invoke it, just type `mtoolstest` without any arguments. `Mtoolstest` reads the mtools configuration files, and prints the cumulative configuration to `stdout`. The output can be used as a configuration file itself (although you might want to remove redundant clauses). You may use this program to convert old-style configuration files into new style configuration files.

MTYPE The `mtype` command is used to display contents of a MS-DOS file. Its syntax is

`mtype [-ts]` *msdosfile* [*msdosfiles...*]

`Mtype` displays the specified MS-DOS file on the screen.

In addition to the standard options, Mtype allows the following command line options:

t	Text file viewing. Mtype translates incoming carriage return/line feeds to line feeds.
s	Mtype strips the high bit from the data.

The `mcd` command may be used to establish the device and the current working directory (relative to MS-DOS), otherwise the default is A:/.

`Mtype` returns 0 on success, 1 on utter failure, or 2 on partial failure.

Unlike the MS-DOS version of TYPE, `mtype` allows multiple arguments.

MZIP The mzip command is used to issue ZIP disk specific commands on Solaris or HP-UX. Its syntax is

mzip [-epqrwx]

Mzip allows the following command line options:

`e`	Ejects the disk.
`f`	Force eject even if the disk is mounted.
`r`	Write protect the disk.
`w`	Remove write protection.
`p`	Password write protect.
`x`	Password protect.
`q`	Queries the status.

To remove the password, set it to one of the passwordless modes `-r` or `-w`:, mzip will then ask you for the password, and unlock the disk. If you have forgotten the password, you can get rid of it by low-level formatting the disk (using your SCSI adaptor's BIOS setup). The ZipTools disk included with the drive is also password protected. This password is automatically removed once the ZipTools have been installed.

XCOPY The `xcopy` script is used to recursively copy one directory to another. Its syntax is

`xcopy` *sourcedirectory targetdirectory*

If *targetdirectory* does not exist, it is created. If it does exist, the files of *sourcedirectory* are directly copied into it, and no subdirectory called *sourcedirectory* is created, unlike with `cp -rf`.

BUGS

This command is a big kludge. A proper implementation would take a rework of significant parts of mtools, but unfortunately I don't have the time for this right now. The main downside of this implementation is that it is inefficient on some architectures (several successive calls to mtools, which defeats mtools' caching).

ARCHITECTURE SPECIFIC COMPILATION FLAGS

To compile mtools, first invoke `./configure` before make. In addition to the standard autoconfigure flags, there are two architecture specific flags available.

```
./configure --enable-xdf
./configure --disable-xdf
```

Enables support for XDF disks. This is on by default. See section "XDF," for details.

```
./configure --enable-vold
./configure --disable-vold
```

Enables support for vold on Solaris. When used in conjunction with vold, mtools should use different device nodes as for direct access.

PORTING MTOOLS TO ARCHITECTURES WHICH ARE NOT SUPPORTED YET

This chapter is only interesting for those who want to port mtools to an architecture which is not yet supported. For most common systems, default drives are already defined. If you want to add default drives for a still unsupported system, run config.guess, to see which identification autoconf uses for that system. This identification is of the form cpu-vendor-os (for example, sparc-sunsunos). The cpu and the os parts are passed to the compiler as preprocessor flags.
The OS part is passed to the compiler in three forms.

1. The complete os name, with dots replaced by underscores. sco3.2v2 would yield sco3_2v2.
2. The base os name. Sco3.2v2 would yield Sco.
3. The base os name plus its major version. Sco3.2v2 would yield Sco3.

All three versions are passed, if they are different.

To define the devices, use the entries for the systems that are already present as templates. In general, they have the following form:

```
#if (defined (my_cpu) && defined(my_os))
#define predefined_devices
struct device devices[] = {
    { "/dev/first_drive", 'drive_letter', drive_description},
    { "/dev/last_drive", 'drive_letter', drive_description}
}
#define INIT_NOOP
#endif
```

"/dev/first_drive" is the name of the device or image file representing the drive. Drive_letter is a letter ranging from a to z giving access to the drive. Drive_description describes the type of the drive:

ED312	Extra density (2.88M) 3$^1/_2$"disk
HD312	High density 3$^1/_2$" disk
DD312	Double density 3$^1/_2$" disk
HD514	High density 5$^1/_4$" disk
DD514	Double density 5$^1/_4$" disk
Ddsmall	8 sector double density 5$^1/_4$" disk

SS514	Single sided double density $5^1/4''$ disk
Sssmall	Single sided 8 sector double density $5^1/4''$ disk
GENFD	Generic floppy drive (12 bit FAT)
GENHD	Generic hard disk (16 bit FAT)
GEN	Generic device (all parameters match)
ZIPJAZ(flags)	Generic ZIP drive using normal access. This uses partition 4. Flags are any special flags to be passed to open.
RZIPJAZ(flags)	Generic ZIP drive using raw SCSI access. This uses partition 4. Flags are any special flags to be passed to open.

Entries may be described in more detail:

fat_bits,open_flags,cylinders,heads,sectors,DEF_ARG

or, if you need to describe an offset (filesystem doesn't start at beginning of filesystem):

fat_bits, open_flags, cylinders, heads, sectors, offset, DEF_ARGO

`fat_bits` Is either 12, 16 or 0. 0 means that the device accepts both types of FAT.

`open_flags` May include flags such as O_NDELAY, or O_RDONLY, which might be necessary to open the device. 0 means no special flags are needed.

`cylinders,heads,sectors` Describe the geometry of the disk. If cylinders is 0, the heads and sectors parameters are ignored, and the drive accepts any geometry.

`offset` Is used if the DOS filesystem doesn't begin at the start of the device or image file. This is mostly useful for Atari Ram disks (which contain their device driver at the beginning of the file) or for DOS emulator images (which may represent a partitioned device).

Definition of defaults in the devices file should only be done if these same devices are found on a large number of hosts of this type. In that case, could you also let me know about your new definitions, so that I can include them into the next release. For a purely local file, I recommend that you use the `/usr/local/etc/mtools.conf` and `~/.mtoolsrc` configuration files.

However, the devices file also allows you to supply geometry setting routines. These are necessary if you want to access high capacity disks.

Two routines should be supplied:

1. Reading the current parameters:

   ```
   static inline int get_parameters(int fd, struct
   generic_floppy_struct *floppy)
   ```

   This probes the current configured geometry, and returns it in the structure generic_floppy_struct (which must also be declared).

   Fd is an open file descriptor for the device, and buf is an already filled in stat structure, which may be useful.

This routine should return 1 if the probing fails, and 0 otherwise.

2. Setting new parameters:

   ```
   static inline int set_parameters(int fd, struct
   generic_floppy_struct *floppy) struct stat *buf)
   ```

   This configures the geometry contained in floppy on the file descriptor fd. Buf is the result of a stat call (already filled in). This should return 1 if the new geometry cannot be configured, and 0 otherwise.

A certain number of preprocessor macros should also be supplied:

`TRACKS(floppy)` Refers to the track field in the floppy structure

`HEADS(floppy)` Refers to the heads field in the floppy structure

`SECTORS(floppy)` Refers to the sectors per track field in the floppy structure

`SECTORS_PER_DISK(floppy)` Refers to the sectors per disk field in the floppy structure (if applicable, otherwise leave undefined)

`BLOCK_MAJOR` Major number of the floppy device, when viewed as a block device

`CHAR_MAJOR` Major number of the floppy device, when viewed as a character device (a.k.a. "raw" device, used for fsck) (leave this undefined, if your OS doesn't have raw devices)

For the truly high-capacity formats (XDF, 2m, etc), there is no clean and documented interface yet.

SEE ALSO

mattrib mbadblocks mcd mcopy mdel mdeltree mdir `mformat` mkmanifest mlabel mmd mmount mmove mrd mread mren mtoolstest mtype mwrite

MV(1)

NAME

mv Rename files

SYNOPSIS

mv [options] source dest

mv [options] source... directory

OPTIONS

[-bfiuv] [-S backup-suffix] [-V {numbered,existing,simple}] [--backup] [--force] [--interactive] [--update] [--verbose] [--suffix=backup-suffix] [--version-control={numbered, existing,simple}] [--help] [--version]

DESCRIPTION

This documentation is no longer being maintained and may be inaccurate or incomplete. The Texinfo documentation is now the authoritative source.

This manual page documents the GNU version of mv. If the last argument names an existing directory, **mv** moves each other given file into a file with the same name in that directory. Otherwise, if only two files are given, it moves the first onto the second. It is an error if the last argument is not a directory and more than two files are given. It can move only regular files across filesystems.

If a destination file is unwritable, the standard input is a tty, and the *-f* or *--force* option is not given, **mv** prompts the user for whether to overwrite the file. If the response does not begin with 'y' or 'Y', the file is skipped.

OPTIONS

-b, --backup Make backups of files that are about to be removed.

-f, --force Remove existing destination files and never prompt the user.

-i, --interactive Prompt whether to overwrite each destination file that already exists. If the response does not begin with 'y' or 'Y', the file is skipped.

-u, --update Do not move a nondirectory that has an existing destination with the same or newer modification time.

-v, --verbose Print the name of each file before moving it.

--help Print a usage message on standard output and exit successfully.

--version Print version information on standard output then exit successfully.

-S, --suffix backup-suffix The suffix used for making simple backup files can be set with the **SIMPLE_BACKUP_SUFFIX** environment variable, which can be overridden by this option. If neither of those is given, the default is '~', as it is in Emacs.

-V, --version-control {numbered,existing,simple} The type of backups made can be set with the **VERSION_CONTROL** environment variable, which can be overridden by this option. If **VERSION_CONTROL** is not set and this option is not given, the default backup type is 'existing'. The value of the **VERSION_CONTROL** environment variable and the argument to this option are like the GNU Emacs 'version-control' variable; they also recognize synonyms that are more descriptive. The valid values are (unique abbreviations are accepted):

't' or 'numbered' Always make numbered backups.

'nil' or 'existing' Make numbered backups of files that already have them, simple backups of the others.

'never' or 'simple' Always make simple backups.

PASSWD(1)

NAME

passwd Update a user's authentication tokens(s).

SYNOPSIS

passwd **[-u] [username]**

DESCRIPTION

Passwd is used to update a user's authentication token(s).

Only the superuser may update another user's password by supplying a **username**. The option, **-u**, is used to indicate that the update should only be for expired authentication tokens (passwords); the user wishes to keep their nonexpired tokens as before.

Passwd is configured to work through the Linux-PAM API. Essentially, it initializes itself as a "passwd" service with *Linux-PAM* and utilizes configured *password* modules to authenticate and then update a user's password.

A simple entry in the *Linux-PAM* configuration file for this service would be

```
#
# passwd service entry that does strength checking of
# a proposed password before updating it.
#
passwd password requisite pam_cracklib.so retry=3
passwd password required pam_pwdb.so use_authtok #
```

Note, other module-types are not required for this application to function correctly.

EXIT CODE

On successful completion of its task, **passwd** will complete with exit code 0. An exit code of 1 indicates an error occurred. Textual errors are written to the standard error stream.

CONFORMING TO

Linux-PAM (Pluggable Authentication modules for Linux)

FILES

/etc/pam.conf The **Linux-PAM** configuration file

BUGS

None known.

SEE ALSO

pam(8), and pam_chauthok(2).

For more complete information on how to configure this application with **Linux-PAM**, see the **Linux-PAM System Administrators' Guide** at

`<http://parc.power.net/morgan/Linux-PAM/index.html>`

RM(1)

NAME

rm Remove files.

SYNOPSIS

rm [-dfirvR] [--directory] [--force] [--interactive] [--recursive] [--help] [--version] [--verbose] name...

DESCRIPTION

This documentation is no longer being maintained and may be inaccurate or incomplete. The Texinfo documentation is now the authoritative source.

This manual page documents the GNU version of **rm**. **rm** removes each specified file. By default, it does not remove directories.

If a file is unwritable, the standard input is a tty, and the *-f* or *--force* option is not given, **rm** prompts the user for whether to remove the file. If the response does not begin with 'y' or 'Y', the file is skipped.

GNU **rm**, like every program that uses the getopt function to parse its arguments, lets you use the -- option to indicate that all following arguments are non-options. To remove a file called '-f' in the current directory, you could type either

```
rm -- -f
```

or

```
rm ./-f
```

The Unix **rm** program's use of a single '-' for this purpose predates the development of the getopt standard syntax.

OPTIONS

-d, --directory Remove directories with 'unlink' instead of 'rmdir', and don't require a directory to be empty before trying to unlink it. Only works for the superuser. Because unlinking a directory causes any files in the deleted directory to become unreferenced, it is wise to **fsck** the filesystem after doing this.

-f, --force Ignore nonexistent files and never prompt the user.

-i, --interactive Prompt whether to remove each file. If the response does not begin with 'y' or 'Y', the file is skipped.

-r, -R, --recursive Remove the contents of directories recursively.

-v, --verbose Print the name of each file before removing it.

--help Print a usage message on standard output and exit successfully.

--version Print version information on standard output then exit successfully.

RMDIR(1)

NAME

rmdir Remove empty directories.

SYNOPSIS

rmdir [-p] [--parents] [--help] [--version] dir...

DESCRIPTION

This documentation is no longer being maintained and may be inaccurate or incomplete. The Texinfo documentation is now the authoritative source.

This manual page documents the GNU version of rmdir. **rmdir** removes each given empty directory. If any nonoption argument does not refer to an existing empty directory, it is an error.

OPTIONS

-p, --parents Remove any parent directories that are explicitly mentioned in an argument, if they become empty after the argument file is removed.

--help Print a usage message on standard output and exit successfully.

--version Print version information on standard output then exit successfully.

SSH(1)

NAME

ssh Secure shell client (remote login program)

SYNOPSIS

ssh [**-l** *login_name*] **hostname** [*command*]

ssh [**-a**] [**-c** idea|des|3des|arcfour|tss|none] [**-e** *escape_char*] [**-i** *identity_file*] [**-l** *login_name*] [**-n**] [**-o** *option*] [**-p** *port*] [**-q**] [**-t**] [**-v**] [**-x**] [**-C**] [**-L** *port:host:hostport*] [**-R** *port:host:hostport*] *hostname* [*command*]

DESCRIPTION

ssh (Secure Shell) is a program for logging into a remote machine and for executing commands in a remote machine. It is intended to replace rlogin and rsh, and provide secure encrypted communications between two untrusted hosts over an insecure network. X11 connections and arbitrary TCP/IP ports can also be forwarded over the secure channel.

Ssh connects and logs into the specified hostname. The user must prove his/her identity to the remote machine using one of several methods.

First, if the machine the user logs in from is listed in */etc/hosts.equiv* or */etc/shosts.equiv* on the remote machine, and the user names are the same on both sides, the user is immediately permitted to log in. Second, if *.rhosts* or *.shosts* exists in the user's home directory on the remote machine and contains a line containing the name of the client machine and the name of the user on that machine, the user is permitted to log in. This form of authentication alone is normally not allowed by the server because it is not secure.

The second (and primary) authentication method is the **rhosts** or **hosts.equiv** method combined with RSA-based host authentication. It means that if the login would be permitted by *.rhosts*, *.shosts*, */etc/hosts.equiv, or /etc/shosts.equiv*, and additionally it can verify the client's host key (see *$HOME/.ssh/known_hosts* and */etc/ssh_known_hosts* in the **FILES** section), only then is login permitted. This authentication method closes security holes due to IP spoofing, DNS spoofing and routing spoofing. [Note to the administrator: */etc/hosts.equiv*, *.rhosts*, and the rlogin/rsh protocol in general, are inherently insecure and should be disabled if security is desired.]

As a third authentication method, ssh supports RSA based authentication. The scheme is based on public-key cryptography: there are cryptosystems where encryption and decryption are done using separate keys, and it is not possible to derive the decryption key from the encryption key. RSA is one such system. The idea is that each user creates a public/private key pair for authentication purposes. The server knows the public key, and only the user knows the private key. The file *$HOME/.ssh/authorized_keys* lists the public keys that are permitted for logging in. When the user logs in, the **ssh** program tells the server which key pair it would like to use for authentication. The server checks if this key is permitted, and if so, sends the user (actually the **ssh** program running on behalf of the user) a challenge, a random number, encrypted by the user's public key. The challenge can only be decrypted using the proper private key. The user's client then decrypts the challenge using the private key, proving that he/she knows the private key but without disclosing it to the server.

Ssh implements the RSA authentication protocol automatically. The user creates his/her RSA key pair by running ssh-keygen(1). This stores the private key in *.ssh/identity* and the public key in *.ssh/identity.pub* in the user's home directory. The user should then copy the *identity.pub* to

.ssh/authorized_keys in his/her home directory on the remote machine. (The *authorized_keys* file corresponds to the conventional *.rhosts* file and has one key per line, though the lines can be very long.) After this, the user can log in without giving the password. RSA authentication is much more secure than rhosts authentication.

The most convenient way to use RSA authentication may be with an authentication agent. See ssh-agent(1) for more information.

If other authentication methods fail, **ssh** prompts the user for a password. The password is sent to the remote host for checking; however, since all communications are encrypted, the password cannot be seen by someone listening on the network.

When the user's identity has been accepted by the server, the server either executes the given command, or logs into the machine and gives the user a normal shell on the remote machine. All communication with the remote command or shell will be automatically encrypted.

If a pseudo-terminal has been allocated (normal login session), the user can disconnect with "~.", and suspend **ssh** with "~^Z". All forwarded connections can be listed with "~#", and if the session blocks waiting for forwarded X11 or TCP/IP connections to terminate, it can be backgrounded with "~&" (this should not be used while the user shell is active, as it can cause the shell to hang). All available escapes can be listed with "~?".

A single tilde character can be sent as "~~" (or by following the tilde by a character other than those described above). The escape character must always follow a new line to be interpreted as special. The escape character can be changed in configuration files or on the command line.

If no pseudo tty has been allocated, the session is transparent and can be used to reliably transfer binary data. On most systems, setting the escape character to "none" will also make the session transparent even if a tty is used.

The session terminates when the command or shell in on the remote machine exists and all X11 and TCP/IP connections have been closed. The exit status of the remote program is returned as the exit status of **ssh.**

If the user is using X11 (the DISPLAY environment variable is set), the connection to the X11 display is automatically forwarded to the remote side in such a way that any X11 programs started from the shell (or command) will go through the encrypted channel, and the connection to the real X server will be made from the local machine. The user should not manually set **DISPLAY**. Forwarding of X11 connections can be configured on the command line or in configuration files.

The DISPLAY value set by ssh will point to the server machine, but with a display number greater than zero. This is normal, and happens because **ssh** creates a "proxy" X server on the server machine for forwarding the connections over the encrypted channel.

Ssh will also automatically set up Xauthority data on the server machine. For this purpose, it will generate a random authorization cookie, store it in Xauthority on the server, and verify that any forwarded connections carry this cookie and replace it by the real cookie when the connection is opened. The real authentication cookie is never sent to the server machine (and no cookies are sent in the plain).

If the user is using an authentication agent, the connection to the agent is automatically forwarded to the remote side unless disabled on command line or in a configuration file.

Forwarding of arbitrary TCP/IP connections over the secure channel can be specified either on command line or in a configuration file. One possible application of TCP/IP forwarding is a secure connection to an electronic purse; another is going trough firewalls.

Ssh automatically maintains and checks a database containing RSA-based identifications for all hosts it has ever been used with. The database is stored in *.ssh/known_hosts* in the user's home directory. Additionally, the file */etc/ssh_known_hosts* is automatically checked for known hosts. Any new hosts are automatically added to the user's file. If a host's identification ever changes, **ssh** warns about this and disables password authentication to prevent a trojan horse from getting the user's password. Another purpose of this mechanism is to prevent man-in-the-middle attacks which could otherwise be used to circumvent the encryption. The **StrictHostKeyChecking** option (see below) can be used to prevent logins to machines whose host key is not known or has changed.

OPTIONS

-a Disables forwarding of the authentication agent connection. This may also be specified on a per-host basis in the configuration file.

-c *idea|des|3des|arcfour|tss|none* Selects the cipher to use for encrypting the session. **idea** is used by default. It is believed to be secure. **des** is the data encryption standard, but is breakable by governments, large corporations, and major criminal organizations. **3des** (triple-des) is encrypt-decrypt-encrypt triple with three different keys. It is presumably more secure than DES. It is used as default if both sites do not support IDEA. **arcfour** is an algorithm published in the Usenet News in 1995. This algorithm is believed to be equivalent with the RC4 cipher from RSA Data Security (RC4 is a trademark of RSA Data Security). This is the fastest algorithm currently supported. **TSS** is a fast home-grown algorithm based on MD5. **none** disables encryption entirely; it is only intended for debugging, and it renders the connection insecure.

-e *ch* | *^ch* | *none* Sets the escape character for sessions with a pty (default: ~). The escape character is only recognized at the beginning of a line. The escape character followed by a dot (.) closes the connection, followed by control-Z suspends the connection, and followed by itself sends the escape character once. Setting the character to 'none' disables any escapes and makes the session fully transparent.

-f Requests ssh to go to background after authentication is done and forwardings have been established. This is useful if ssh is going to ask for passwords or passphrases, but the user wants it in the background. This may also be useful in scripts. This implies **-n.** The recommended way to start X11 programs at a remote site is with something like "ssh -f host xterm".

-i *identity_file* Selects the file from which the identity (private key) for **RSA** authentication is read. Default is *.ssh/identity* in the user's home directory. Identity files may also be specified on a per-host basis in the configuration file. It is possible to have multiple -i options (and multiple identities specified in configuration files).

-l *login_name* Specifies the user to log in as on the remote machine. This may also be specified on a per-host basis in the configuration file.

-n Redirects stdin from /dev/null (actually, prevents reading from stdin). This must be used when **ssh** is run in the background. A common trick is to use this to run X11 programs in a remote machine. For example, "ssh -n shadows.cs.hut.fi emacs &" will start an emacs on shadows.cs.hut.fi, and the X11 connection will be automatically forwarded over an encrypted channel. The **ssh** program will be put in the background. (This does not work if **ssh** needs to ask for a password or passphrase; see also the -f option.)

-o *'option'* Can be used to give options in the format used in the config file. This is useful for specifying options for which there is no separate command-line flag. The option has the same format as a line in the configuration file.

-p *port* Port to connect to on the remote host. This can be specified on a per-host basis in the configuration file.

-q Quiet mode. Causes all warning and diagnostic messages to be suppressed. Only fatal errors are displayed.

-t Force pseudo-tty allocation. This can be used to execute arbitary screen-based programs on a remote machine, which can be very useful e.g. when implementing menu services.

-v Verbose mode. Causes **ssh** to print debugging messages about its progress. This is helpful in debugging connection, authentication, and configuration problems.

-x Disables X11 forwarding. This can also be specified on a per-host basis in a configuration file.

-C Requests compression of all data (including stdin, stdout, stderr, and data for forwarded X11 and TCP/IP connections). The compression algorithm is the same used by gzip, and the "level" can be controlled by the **CompressionLevel** option (see below). Compression is desirable on modem lines and other slow connections, but will only slow down things on fast networks. The default value can be set on a host-by-host basis in the configuration files; see the **Compress** option below.

-L *port:host:hostport* Specifies that the given port on the local (client) host is to be forwarded to the given host and port on the remote side. This works by allocating a socket to listen to **port** on the local side, and whenever a connection is made to this port, the connection is forwarded over the secure channel, and a connection is made to **host:hostport** from the remote machine. Port forwardings can also be specified in the configuration file. Only root can forward privileged ports.

-R *port:host:hostport* Specifies that the given port on the remote (server) host is to be forwarded to the given host and port on the local side. This works by allocating a socket to listen to **port** on the remote side, and whenever a connection is made to this port, the connection is forwarded over the secure channel, and a connection is made to **host:hostport** from the local machine. Port forwardings can also be specified in the configuration file. Privileged ports can be forwarded only when logging in as root on the remote machine.

CONFIGURATION FILES

Ssh obtains configuration data from the following sources (in this order): command line options, user's configuration file (*$HOME/.ssh/config*), and system-wide configuration file (*/etc/ssh_config*). For each parameter, the first obtained value will be used. The configuration files contain sections bracketed by "Host" specifications, and that section is only applied for hosts that match one of the patterns given in the specification. The matched host name is the one given on the command line. Since the first obtained value for each parameter is used, more host-specific declarations should be given near the beginning of the file, and general defaults at the end.

The configuration file has the following format:

- Empty lines and lines starting with '#' are comments.
- Otherwise a line is of the format "keyword arguments". The possible keywords and their meanings are as follows (note that the configuration files are case-sensitive):

  Host Restricts the following declarations (up to the next **Host** keyword) to be only for those hosts that match one of the patterns given after the keyword. '*' and '?' can be as wildcards in the patterns. A single '*' as a pattern can be used to provide global defaults for all hosts. The host is the *hostname* argument given on the command line (i.e., the name is not converted to a canonicalized host name before matching).

  BatchMode If set to "yes", passphrase/password querying will be disabled. This option is useful in scripts and other batch jobs where you have no user to supply the password. The argument must be "**yes**" or "**no**".

Cipher Specifies the cipher to use for encrypting the session. Currently, *idea, des, 3des, arcfour, tss,* and *none* are supported. The default is "idea" (or "3des" if "idea" is not supported by both hosts). Using "none" (no encryption) is intended only for debugging, and will render the connection insecure.

Compression Specifies whether to use compression. The argument must be "**yes**" or "**no**".

CompressionLevel Specifies the compression level to use if compression is enabled. The argument must be an integer from 1 (fast) to 9 (slow, best). The default level is 6, which is good for most applications. The meaning of the values is the same as in GNU GZIP.

ConnectionAttempts Specifies the number of tries (one per second) to make before falling back to rsh or exiting. The argument must be an integer. This may be useful in scripts if the connection sometimes fails.

EscapeChar Sets the escape character (default: ~). The escape character can also be set on the command line. The argument should be a single character, '^' followed by a letter, or "none" to disable the escape character entirely (making the connection transparent for binary data).

FallBackToRsh Specifies that if connecting via **ssh** fails due to a connection refused error (there is no **sshd** listening on the remote host), **rsh** should automatically be used instead (after a suitable warning about the session being unencrypted). The argument must be "**yes**" or "**no**".

ForwardAgent Specifies whether the connection to the authentication agent (if any) will be forwarded to the remote machine. The argument must be "yes" or "no".

ForwardX11 Specifies whether X11 connections will be automatically redirected over the secure channel and **DISPLAY** set. The argument must be "**yes**" or "**no**".

GlobalKnownHostsFile Specifies a file to use instead of */etc/ssh_known_hosts*.

HostNAME Specifies the real host name to log into. This can be used to specify nicnames or abbreviations for hosts. Default is the name given on the command line. Numeric IP addresses are also permitted (both on the command line and in **HostName** specifications).

IdentityFile Specifies the file from which the user's RSA authentication identity is read (default *.ssh/identity* in the user's home directory). Additionally, any identities represented by the authentication agent will be used for authentication. The file name may use the tilde syntax to refer to a user's home directory. It is possible to have multiple identity files specified in configuration files; all these identities will be tried in sequence.

KeepAlive Specifies whether the system should send keepalive messages to the other side. If they are sent, death of the connection or crash of one of the machines will be properly noticed. However, this means that connections will die if the route is down temporarily, and some people find it annoying.

The default is "yes" (to send keepalives), and the client will notice if the network goes down or the remote host dies. This is important in scripts, and many users want it too.

To disable keepalives, the value should be set to "no" in both the server and the client configuration files.

LocalForward Specifies that a TCP/IP port on the local machine be forwarded over the secure channel to given host:port from the remote machine. The first argument must be a port number, and the second must be host:port. Multiple forwardings may be specified, and additional forwardings can be given on the command line. Only the root can forward privileged ports.

PasswordAuthentication Specifies whether to use password authentication. The argument to this keyword must be "**yes**" or "**no**".

Port Specifies the port number to connect on the remote host. Default is 22.

ProxyCommand Specifies the command to use to connect to the server. The command string extends to the end of the line, and is executed with /bin/sh. In the command string, %h will be substituted by the host name to connect and %p by the port. The command can be basically anything, and should read from its stdin and write to its stdout. It should eventually connect an **sshd** server running on some machine, or execute "sshd -i" somewhere. Host key management will be done using the HostName of the host being connected (defaulting to the name typed by the user).Note that ssh can also be configured to support the SOCKS system using the --with-socks compile-time configuration option.

RemoteForward Specifies that a TCP/IP port on the remote machine be forwarded over the secure channel to given host:port from the local machine. The first argument must be a port number, and the second must be host:port. Multiple forwardings may be specified, and additional forwardings can be given on the command line. Only the root can forward privileged ports.

RhostsAuthentication Specifies whether to try rhosts-based authentication. Note that this declaration only affects the client side and has no effect whatsoever on security. Disabling rhosts authentication may reduce authentication time on slow connections when rhosts authentication is not used. Most servers do not permit RhostsAuthentication because it is not secure (see RhostsRSAAuthentication). The argument to this keyword must be "**yes**" or "**no**".

RhostsRSAAuthentication Specifies whether to try rhosts-based authentication with RSA host authentication. This is the primary authentication method for most sites. The argument must be "**yes**" or "**no**".

RSAAuthentication Specifies whether to try RSA authentication. The argument to this keyword must be "**yes**" or "**no**". RSA authentication will only be attempted if the identity file exists, or an authentication agent is running.

StrictHostKeyChecking If this flag is set to "yes", **ssh** will never automatically add host keys to the

$HOME/.ssh/known_hosts file, and refuses to connect hosts whose host key has changed. This provides maximum protection against trojan horse attacks. However, it can be somewhat annoying if you don't have good */etc/ssh_known_hosts* files installed and frequently connect new hosts. Basically this option forces the user to manually add any new hosts. Normally this option is disabled, and new hosts will automatically be added to the known host files. The host keys of known hosts will be verified automatically in either case. The argument must be "**yes**" or "**no**".

User Specifies the user to log in as. This can be useful if you have a different user name in different machines. This saves the trouble of having to remember to give the user name on the command line.

UserKnownHostsFile Specifies a file to use instead of *$HOME/.ssh/known_hosts.*

UseRsh Specifies that rlogin/rsh should be used for this host. It is possible that the host does not at all support the **ssh** protocol. This causes **ssh** to immediately exec **rsh.** All other options (except **HostName**) are ignored if this has been specified. The argument must be "**yes**" or "**no**".

ENVIRONMENT

ssh will normally set the following environment variables:

DISPLAY The DISPLAY variable indicates the location of the X11 server. It is automatically set by **ssh** to point to a value of the form "hostname:n" where hostname indicates the host where the shell runs, and n is an integer >= 1. Ssh uses this special value to forward X11 connections over the secure channel. The user should normally not set DISPLAY explicitly, as that will render the X11 connection insecure (and will require the user to manually copy any required authorization cookies).

HOME Set to the path of the user's home directory.

LOGNAME Synonym for USER; set for compatibility with systems that use this variable.

MAIL Set to point to the user's mailbox.

PATH Set to the default PATH, as specified when compiling **ssh** or, on some systems, */etc/environment* or */etc/default/login*.

SSH_AUTHENTICATION_FD This is set to an integer value if you are using the authentication agent and a connection to it has been forwarded. The value indicates a file descriptor number used for communicating with the agent. On some systems, **SSH_AUTHENTICATION_SOCKET** may be used instead to indicate the path of a unixdomain socket used to communicate with the agent. (This method is less secure, and is only used on systems that don't support the first method.)

SSH_CLIENT Identifies the client end of the connection. The variable contains three space-separated values: client ip-address, client port number, and server port number.

SSH_TTY This is set to the name of the tty (path to the device) associated with the current shell or command. If the current session has no tty, this variable is not set.

TZ The timezone variable is set to indicate the present timezone if it was set when the daemon was started (e.i., the daemon passes the value on to new connections).

USER Set to the name of the user logging in.

Additionally, **ssh** reads */etc/environment* and *$HOME/.ssh/environment*, and adds lines of the format *VARNAME=value* to the environment. Some systems may have still additional mechanisms for setting up the environment, such as */etc/default/login* on Solaris.

FILES

$HOME/.ssh/known_host Records host keys for all hosts the user has logged into (that are not in */etc/ssh_known_hosts*). See **sshd** manual page.

$HOME/.ssh/random_seed Used for seeding the random number generator. This file contains sensitive data and should be read/write for the user and not accessible for others. This file is created the first time the program is run and updated automatically. The user should never need to read or modify this file.

$HOME/.ssh/identity Contains the RSA authentication identity of the user. This file contains sensitive data and should be

readable by the user but not accessible by others. It is possible to specify a passphrase when generating the key; the passphrase will be used to encrypt the sensitive part of this file using **IDEA**.

$HOME/.ssh/identity.pub Contains the public key for authentication (public part of the identity file in human-readable form). The contents of this file should be added to *$HOME/.ssh/authorized_keys* on all machines where you wish to log in using RSA authentication. This file is not sensitive and can (but need not) be readable by anyone. This file is never used automatically and is not necessary; it is only provided for the convenience of the user.

$HOME/.ssh/config This is the per-user configuration file. The format of this file is described above. This file is used by the **ssh** client. This file does not usually contain any sensitive information, but the recommended permissions are read/write for the user, and not accessible by others.

$HOME/.ssh/authorized_keys Lists the RSA keys that can be used for logging in as this user. The format of this file is described in the **sshd** manual page. In the simplest form the format is the same as the .pub identity files (that is, each line contains the number of bits in modulus, public exponent, modulus, and comment fields, separated by spaces). This file is not highly sensitive, but the recommended permissions are read/write for the user, and not accessible by others.

/etc/ssh_known_hosts Systemwide list of known host keys. This file should be prepared by the system administrator to contain the public host keys of all machines in the organization. This file should be world-readable. This file contains public keys, one per line, in the following format (fields separated by spaces): system name, number of bits in modulus, public exponent, modulus, and optional comment field. When different names are used for the same machine, all such names should be listed, separated by commas. The format is described on the **sshd** manual page.

The canonical system name (as returned by name servers) is used by **sshd** to verify the client host when logging in; other names are needed because **ssh** does not convert the user-supplied name to a canonical name before checking the key because someone with access to the name servers would then be able to fool host authentication.

/etc/ssh_config Systemwide configuration file. This file provides defaults for those values that are not specified in the user's configuration file, and for those users who do not have a configuration file. This file must be world-readable.

$HOME/.rhosts This file is used in .rhosts authentication to list the host/user pairs that are permitted to log in. (Note that this file is also used by rlogin and rsh, which makes using this file insecure.) Each line of the file contains a host name (in the canonical form returned by name servers), and then a user name on that host, separated by a space. This file must be owned by the user, and must not have write permissions for anyone else. The recommended permission is read/write for the user, and not accessible by others.

Note that by default sshd will be installed so that it requires successful RSA host authentication before permitting .rhosts authentication. If your server machine does not have the client's host key in */etc/ssh_known_hosts*, you can store it in *$HOME/.ssh/known_hosts*. The easiest way to do this is to connect back to the client from the server machine using ssh; this will automatically add the host key in *$HOME/.ssh/known_hosts*.

$HOME/.shosts This file is used exactly the same way as .rhosts. The purpose for having this file is to be able to use rhosts authentication with **ssh** without permitting login with rlogin or rsh.

/etc/hosts.equiv This file is used during .rhosts authentication. It contains canonical hosts names, one per line (the full format is described on the **sshd** manual page). If the client host is found in this file, login is automatically permitted provided client and server user names are the same. Additionally, successful RSA host authentication is normally required. This file should only be writable by root.

/etc/shosts.equiv This file is processed exactly as */etc/hosts.equiv*. This file may be useful to permit logins using **ssh** but not using rsh/rlogin.

/etc/sshrc Commands in this file are executed by **ssh** when the user logs in just before the user's shell (or command) is started. See the **sshd** manual page for more information.

$HOME/.ssh/rc Commands in this file are executed by **ssh** when the user logs in just before the user's shell (or command) is started. See the **sshd** manual page for more information.

INSTALLATION

Ssh is normally installed as suid root. It needs root privileges only for rhosts authentication (rhosts authentication requires that the connection must come from a privileged port, and allocating such a port requires root privileges). It also needs to be able to read */etc/ssh_host_key* to perform **RSA** host authentication. It is possible to use **ssh** without root privileges, but rhosts authentication will then be disabled. **Ssh** drops any extra privileges immediately after the connection to the remote host has been made.

Considerable work has been put into making **ssh** secure. However, if you find a security problem, please report it immediately to `<ssh-bugs@cs.hut.fi>`.

AUTHOR

Tatu Ylonen `<ylo@cs.hut.fi>`

Information about new releases, mailing lists, and other related issues can be found from the ssh WWW home page at `http://www.cs.hut.fi/ssh`.

SEE ALSO

sshd(8), ssh-keygen(1), ssh-agent(1), ssh-add(1), scp(1), make-ssh-known-hosts(1), rlogin(1), rsh(1), telnet(1)

SU(1)

NAME

su Run a shell with substitute user and group Ids.

SYNOPSIS

su [-flmp] [-c command] [-s shell] [--login] [--fast] [--preserve-environment] [--command=command] [--shell=shell] [-] [--help] [--version] [user [arg...]]

DESCRIPTION

This documentation is no longer being maintained and may be inaccurate or incomplete. The Texinfo documentation is now the authoritative source.

This manual page documents the GNU version of su. su allows one user to temporarily become another user. It runs a shell with the real and effective user ID, group ID, and supplemental groups of USER. If no USER is given, the default is root, the superuser. The shell run is taken from USER's password entry, or /bin/sh if none is specified there. If USER has a password, **su** prompts for the password unless run by a user with real user ID 0 (the superuser).

By default, su does not change the current directory. It sets the environment variables 'HOME' and 'SHELL' from the password entry for USER, and if USER is not the superuser, sets 'USER' and 'LOGNAME' to USER. By default, the shell is not a login shell.

If one or more ARGs are given, they are passed as additional arguments to the shell.

su does not handle /bin/sh or other shells specially (setting argv[0] to "-su", passing -c only to certain shells, etc.).

On systems that have syslog, su can be compiled to report failed, and optionally successful, **su** attempts using syslog.

OPTIONS

-c COMMAND, --command=COMMAND Pass COMMAND, a single command line to run, to the shell with a *-c* option instead of starting an interactive shell.

-f, --fas Pass the *-f* option to the shell. This probably only makes sense with **csh** and **tcsh**, for which the *-f* option prevents reading the startup file (.cshrc). With Bourne-like shells, the *-f* option disables filename pattern expansion, which is not a generally desirable thing to do.

--help Print a usage message on standard output and exit successfully.

-, -l, --login Make the shell a login shell. This means the following: Unset all environment variables except 'TERM', 'HOME', and 'SHELL' (which are set as described above), and 'USER' and 'LOGNAME' (which are set, even for the superuser, as described above), and set 'PATH' to a compiled-in default value. Change to USER's home directory. Prepend "-" to the shell's name, to make it read its login startup file(s).

-m, -p, --preserve-environment Do not change the environment variables 'HOME', 'USER', 'LOGNAME', or 'SHELL'. Run the shell given in the environment variable 'SHELL' instead of USER's shell from /etc/passwd, unless the user running **su** is not the superuser and USER's shell is restricted. A restricted shell is one that is not listed in the file /etc/shells, or in a compiled-in list if that file does not exist. Parts of what this option does can be overridden by *--login* and *--shell.*

-s, --shell shell Run SHELL instead of USER's shell from /etc/passwd, unless the user running **su** is not the superuser and USER's shell is restricted.

--version Print version information on standard output then exit successfully.

TAR(1)

NAME

tar The GNU version of the tar archiving utility.

SYNOPSIS

tar [-] A --catenate --concatenate | c --create | d --diff --compare | r --append | t --list | u --update | x -extract --get [--atime-preserve] [-b, --block-size N] [-B, --read-full-blocks] [-C, --directory DIR] [--checkpoint] [-f, --file [HOSTNAME:]F] [--forcelocal] [-F, --info-script F --new-volume-script F] [-G, --incremental] [-g, --listed-incremental F] [-h, --dereference] [-i, --ignore-zeros] [--ignore-failedread] [-k, --keep-old-files] [-K, --starting-file F]

[-l, --one-file-system] [-L, --tape-length N]
[-m, --modification-time] [-M, --multi-volume]
[-N, --after-date DATE, --newer DATE]
[-o, --old-archive, --portability] [-O, --to-stdout]
[-p, --same-permissions, --preserve-permissions]
[-P, --absolute-paths] [--preserve] [-R, --record-number]
[--remove-files] [-s, --same-order, --preserve-order]
[--same-owner] [-S, --sparse] [-T, --files-from F] [--null]
[--totals] [-v, --verbose] [-V, --label NAME] [--version]
[-w, --interactive, --confirmation] [-W, --verify] [--exclude FILE]
[-X, --exclude-from FILE] [-Z, --compress, --uncompress]
[-z, --gzip, --ungzip] [--use-compress-program PROG]
[--blockcompress] [-[0-7][lmh]

filename1 [*filename2*, ... *filenameN*]

directory1 [directory2, ...directoryN]

DESCRIPTION

This manual page documents the GNU version of **tar** , an archiving program designed to store and extract files from an archive file known as a *tarfile.* A *tarfile* may be made on a tape drive, however, it is also common to write a *tarfile* to a normal file. The first argument to **tar** must be one of the options: **Acdrtux**, followed by any optional functions. The final arguments to **tar** are the names of the files or directories which should be archived. The use of a directory name always implies that the subdirectories below should be included in the archive.

FUNCTION LETTERS

One of the following options must be used:

-A, --catenate, --concatenate Append tar files to an archive.

-c, --create Create a new archive.

-d, --diff, --compare Find differences between archive and file system.

--delete Delete from the archive (not for use on mag tapes!).

-r, --append Append files to the end of an archive.

-t, --list List the contents of an archive.

-u, --update Only append files that are newer than copy in archive.

-x, --extract, --get Extract files from an archive.

OTHER OPTIONS

--atime-preserve Don't change access times on dumped FILES.

-b, --block-size N Block size of Nx512 bytes (default N=20).

-B, --read-full-blocks Reblock as we read (for reading 4.2BSD pipes).

-C, --directory DIR Change to directory DIR.

--checkpoint Print directory names while reading the archive.

-f, --file [HOSTNAME:]F Use archive file or device F (default /dev/rmt0).

--force-local Archive file is local even if it has a colon.

-F, --info-script F --new-volume-script F Run script at end of each tape (implies -M).

-G, --incremental Create/list/extract old GNU-format incremental backup.

-g, --listed-incremental F Create/list/extract new GNU-format incremental backup.

-h, --dereference Don't dump symlinks; dump the files they point to.

-i, --ignore-zeros Ignore blocks of zeros in archive (normally mean EOF).

--ignore-failed-read Don't exit with nonzero status on unreadable FILES.

-k, --keep-old-files Keep existing files; don't overwrite them from archive.

-K, --starting-file F Begin at file F in the archive.

-l, --one-file-system Stay in local file system when creating an archive.

-L, --tape-length N Change tapes after writing N*1024 bytes.

-m, --modification-time Don't extract file modified time.

-M, --multi-volume Create/list/extract multi-volume archive.

-N, --after-date DATE, --newer DATE Only store files newer than DATE.

-o, --old-archive, --portability Write a V7 format archive, rather than ANSI format.

-O, --to-stdout Extract files to standard output.

-p, --same-permissions, --preserve-permissions Extract all protection information.

-P, --absolute-paths Don't strip leading '/'s from file names.

--preserve Like -p –s.

-R, --record-number Show record number within archive with each message.

--remove-files Remove files after adding them to the archive.

-s, --same-order, --preserve-order List of names to extract is sorted to match archive.

--same-owner Create extracted files with the same ownership.

-S, --sparse Handle sparse files efficiently.

-T, --files-from F Get names to extract or create from file F.

--null -T reads null-terminated names, disable –C.

--totals Print total bytes written with –create.

-v, --verbose Verbosely list files processed.

-V, --label NAME Create archive with volume name NAME.

--version Print tar program version number.

-w, --interactive, --confirmation Ask for confirmation for every action.

-W, --verify Attempt to verify the archive after writing it.

--exclude FILE Exclude file FILE.

-X, --exclude-from FILE Exclude files listed in FILE.

-Z, --compress, --uncompress Filter the archive through compress.

-z, --gzip, --ungzip Filter the archive through gzip.

--use-compress-program PROG Filter the archive through PROG (which must accept -d).

--block-compress Block the output of compression program for tapes.

-[0-7][lmh] Specify drive and density.

UNZIP(1L)

NAME

unzip List, test, and extract compressed files in a ZIP archive.

SYNOPSIS

unzip [**-Z**] [**-cflptuvz**[**abjnoqsCLMVX$**]] *file*[*.zip*] [*file(s)* ...] [**-x** *xfile(s)* ...] [**-d** *exdir*]

DESCRIPTION

unzip will list, test, or extract files from a ZIP archive, commonly found on MS-DOS systems. The default behavior (with no options) is to extract into the current directory (and subdirectories below it) all files from the specified ZIP archive. A companion program, zip(1L), creates ZIP archives; both programs are compatible with archives created by PKWARE's *PKZIP* and *PKUNZIP* for MS-DOS, but in many cases the program options or default behaviors differ.

ARGUMENTS

file[*.zip*] Path of the ZIP archive(s). If the file specification is a wildcard, each matching file is processed in an order determined by the operating system (or filesystem). Only the filename can be a wildcard; the path itself cannot. Wildcard expressions are similar to Unix egrep(1) (regular) expressions and may contain:

*	matches a sequence of 0 or more characters
?	matches exactly 1 character
[...]	matches any single character found inside the brackets; ranges are specified by a beginning character, a hyphen, and an ending character. If an exclamation point or a caret ('!' or '^') follows the left bracket, then the range of characters within the brackets is complemented (that is, anything *except* the characters inside the brackets is considered a match).

(Be sure to quote any character that might otherwise be interpreted or modified by the operating system, particularly under Unix and VMS.) If no matches are found, the specification is assumed to be a literal filename; and if that also fails, the suffix .zip is appended. Note that self-extracting ZIP files are supported, as with any other ZIP archive; just specify the .exe suffix (if any) explicitly.

[*file(s)*] An optional list of archive members to be processed, separated by spaces. (VMS versions compiled with VMSCLI defined must delimit files with commas instead. See **-v** in **OPTIONS** below.) Regular expressions (wildcards) may be used to match multiple members; see above. Again, be sure to quote expressions that would otherwise be expanded or modified by the operating system.

[**-x** *xfile(s)*] An optional list of archive members to be excluded from processing. Since wildcard characters match directory separators ('/'), this option may be used to exclude any files that are in subdirectories. For example, "unzip foo *.[ch] -x */*" would extract all C source files in the main directory, but none in any subdirectories. Without the **-x** option, all C source files in all directories within the zipfile would be extracted.

[**-d** *exdir*] An optional directory to which to extract files. By default, all files and subdirectories are recreated in the current directory; the **-d** option allows extraction in an arbitrary directory (always assuming one has permission to write to the directory).

This option need not appear at the end of the command line; it is also accepted before the zipfile specification (with the normal options), immediately after the zipfile specification, or between the *file(s)* and the **-x** option. The option and directory may be concatenated without any white space between them, but note that this may cause normal shell behavior to be suppressed. In particular, "-d ~" (tilde) is expanded by Unix C shells into the name of the user's home directory, but "-d~" is treated as a literal subdirectory "~" of the current directory.

OPTIONS

Note that, in order to support obsolescent hardware, *unzip*'s usage screen is limited to 22 or 23 lines and should therefore be considered only a reminder of the basic *unzip* syntax rather than an exhaustive list of all possible flags. The exhaustive list follows:

-Z *zipinfo*(1L) mode. If the first option on the command line is **-Z**, the remaining options are taken to be zipinfo(1L) options. See the appropriate manual page for a description of these options.

-A [OS/2, Unix DLL] Print extended help for the DLL's programming interface (API).

-c Extract files to stdout/screen ("CRT"). This option is similar to the **-p** option except that the name of each file is printed as it is extracted, the **-a** option is allowed, and ASCII-EBCDIC conversion is automatically performed if appropriate. This option is not listed in the *unzip* usage screen.

-f Freshen existing files, i.e., extract only those files that already exist on disk and that are newer than the disk copies. By default *unzip* queries before overwriting, but the **-o** option may be used to suppress the queries. Note that under many operating systems, the TZ (timezone) environment variable must be set correctly in order for **-f** and **-u** to work properly (under Unix, the variable is usually set automatically). The reasons for this are somewhat subtle but have to do with the differences between DOS-format file times (always local time) and Unix-format times (always in GMT/UTC) and the necessity to compare the two. A typical TZ value is "PST8PDT" (US Pacific time with automatic adjustment for Daylight Savings Time or "summer time").

-l List archive files (short format). The names, uncompressed file sizes and modification dates and times of the specified files are printed, along with totals for all files specified. If UnZip was compiled with OS2_EAS defined, the **-l** option also lists columns for the sizes of stored OS/2 extended attributes (EAs) and OS/2 access control lists (ACLs). In addition, the zipfile comment and individual file comments (if any) are displayed. If a file was archived from a single-case file system (for example, the old MS-DOS FAT file system) and the **-L** option was given, the filename is converted to lowercase and is prefixed with a caret (^).

-p Extract files to pipe (stdout). Nothing but the file data is sent to stdout, and the files are always extracted in binary format, just as they are stored (no conversions).

-t Test archive files. This option extracts each specified file in memory and compares the CRC (cyclic redundancy check, an enhanced checksum) of the expanded file with the original file's stored CRC value.

-T [Unix only] Set the timestamp on the archive(s) to that of the newest file in each one. This corresponds to *zip*'s **-go** option except that it can be used on wildcard zipfiles (e.g., "`unzip -T .zip`") and is much faster.

-u Update existing files and create new ones if needed. This option performs the same function as the **-f** option, extracting (with query) files that are newer than those with the same name on disk, and in addition it extracts those files that do not already exist on disk. See **-f** above for information on setting the timezone properly.

-v Be verbose or print diagnostic version info. This option has evolved and now behaves as both an option and a modifier. As an option it has two purposes: when a zipfile is specified with no other options, **-v** lists archive files verbosely, adding to the basic **-l** info the compression method, compressed size, compression ratio and 32-bit CRC. When no zipfile is specified (that is, the complete command is simply "`unzip -v`"), a diagnostic screen is printed. In addition to the normal header with release date and version, *unzip* lists the home Info-ZIP ftp site and where to find a list of other ftp and non-ftp sites; the target operating system for which it was compiled, as well as (possibly) the hardware on which it was compiled, the compiler and version used, and the compilation date; any special compilation options that might affect the program's operation (see also **DECRYPTION** below); and any options stored in environment variables that might do the same (see **ENVIRONMENT OPTIONS** below). As a modifier it works in conjunction with other options (e.g., **-t**) to produce more verbose or debugging output; this is not yet fully implemented but will be in future releases.

-z Display only the archive comment.

MODIFIERS

-a Convert text files. Ordinarily all files are extracted exactly as they are stored (as "binary" files). The **-a** option causes files identified by *zip* as text files (those with the 't' label in *zipinfo* listings, rather than 'b') to be automatically extracted as such, converting line endings, end-of file characters and the character set itself as necessary. (For example, Unix files use line feeds (LFs) for end-of-line (EOL) and has no end-of-file (EOF) marker; Macintoshes use carriage returns (CRs) for EOLs; and most PC operating systems use CR+LF for EOLs and Control-Z for EOF. In addition, IBM mainframes and the Michigan Terminal System use EBCDIC rather than the more common ASCII character set, and NT supports Unicode.) Note that *zip*'s identification of text files is by no means perfect; some "text" files may actually be binary and vice versa. *unzip* therefore prints "`[text]`" or "`[binary]`" as a visual check for each file it extracts when using the **-a** option. The **-aa** option forces all files to be extracted as text, regardless of the supposed file type.

-b [non-VMS] Treat all files as binary (no text conversions). This is a shortcut for **---a**.

-b [VMS] Auto-convert binary files (see **-a** above) to fixed-length, 512-byte record format. Doubling the option (**-bb**) forces all files to be extracted in this format.

-B [Unix only, and only if compiled with UNIXBACKUP defined] Save a backup copy of each overwritten file with a tilde appended (e.g., the old copy of "`foo`" is renamed to "`foo~`"). This is similar to the default behavior of *emacs*(1) in many locations.

-C Match filenames case-insensitively. *unzip*'s philosophy is "you get what you ask for" (this is also responsible for the **-L**/**-U** change; see the relevant options below). Because some file systems are fully case-sensitive (notably those under the Unix operating system) and because both ZIP archives and *unzip* itself are portable across platforms, *unzip*'s default behavior is to match both wildcard and literal filenames case-sensitively. That is, specifying "`makefile`" on the command line will *only* match "makefile" in the archive, not "Makefile" or "MAKEFILE" (and similarly for wildcard specifications). Since this does not correspond to the behavior of many other operating/file systems (for example, OS/2 HPFS, which preserves mixed case but is not sensitive to it), the **-C** option may be used to force all filename matches to be case-insensitive. In the example above, all three files would then match "`makefile`" (or "`make*`", or similar). The **-C** option affects files in both the normal file list and the excluded-file list (xlist).

-j Junk paths. The archive's directory structure is not recreated; all files are deposited in the extraction directory (by default, the current one).

-L Convert to lowercase any filename originating on an uppercase-only operating system or filesystem. (This was *unzip*'s default behavior in releases prior to 5.11; the new default behavior is identical to the old behavior with the **-U** option, which is now obsolete and will be removed in a future release.) Depending on the archiver, files archived under single-case file systems (VMS, old MS-DOS FAT, etc.) may be stored as all-uppercase names; this can be ugly or inconvenient when extracting to a case-preserving file system such as OS/2 HPFS or a case-sensitive one such as under Unix. By default *unzip* lists and extracts such filenames exactly as they're stored (excepting truncation, conversion of unsupported characters, etc.); this option causes the names of all files from certain systems to be converted to lowercase.

-M Pipe all output through an internal pager similar to the Unix *more*(1) command. At the end of a screenful of output, *unzip* pauses with a "--More--" prompt; the next screenful may be viewed by pressing the Enter (Return) key or the space bar. *unzip* can be terminated by pressing the "q" key and, on some systems, the Enter/Return key. Unlike Unix *more*(1), there is no forward-searching or editing capability. Also, *unzip* doesn't notice if long lines wrap at the edge of the screen, effectively resulting in the printing of two or more lines and the likelihood that some text will scroll off the top of the screen before being viewed. On some systems the number of available lines on the screen is not detected, in which case *unzip* assumes the height is 24 lines.

-n Never overwrite existing files. If a file already exists, skip the extraction of that file without prompting. By default *unzip* queries before extracting any file that already exists; the user may choose to overwrite only the current file, overwrite all files, skip extraction of the current file, skip extraction of all existing files, or rename the current file.

-N [Amiga] Extract file comments as Amiga filenotes. File comments are created with the -c option of *zip*(1L), or with the -N option of the Amiga port of *zip*(1L), which stores filenotes as comments.

-o Overwrite existing files without prompting. This is a dangerous option, so use it with care. (It is often used with -f, however, and is the only way to overwrite directory EAs under OS/2.)

-P *password* Use *password* to decrypt encrypted zipfile entries (if any). **THIS IS INSECURE!** Many multi-user operating systems provide ways for any user to see the current command line of any other user; even on stand-alone systems there is always the threat of over-the-shoulder peeking. Storing the plaintext password as part of a command line in an automated script is even worse. Whenever possible, use the non-echoing, interactive prompt to enter passwords. (And where security is truly important, use strong encryption such as Pretty Good Privacy instead of the relatively weak encryption provided by standard zipfile utilities.)

-q Perform operations quietly (**-qq** = even quieter). Ordinarily *unzip* prints the names of the files it's extracting or testing, the extraction methods, any file or zipfile comments that may be stored in the archive, and possibly a summary when finished with each archive. The **-q**[**q**] options suppress the printing of some or all of these messages.

-s [OS/2, NT, MS-DOS] convert spaces in filenames to underscores. Since all PC operating systems allow spaces in filenames, *unzip* by default extracts filenames with spaces intact (e.g., "`EA DATA. SF`"). This can be awkward, however, since MS-DOS in particular does not gracefully support spaces in filenames. Conversion of spaces to underscores can eliminate the awkwardness in some cases.

-U (Obsolete; to be removed in a future release.) Leave filenames uppercase if created under MS-DOS, VMS, etc. See **-L** above.

-V Retain (VMS) file version numbers. VMS files can be stored with a version number, in the format `file .ext;`##. By default the "`;`##" version numbers are stripped, but this option allows them to be retained. (On file systems that limit filenames to particularly short lengths, the version numbers may be truncated or stripped regardless of this option.)

-X [VMS, Unix, OS/2, NT] Restore owner/protection info (UICs) under VMS, or user and group info (UID/GID) under Unix, or access control lists (ACLs) under certain network-enabled versions of OS/2 (Warp Server with IBM LAN Server/Requester 3.0 to 5.0; Warp Connect with IBM Peer 1.0), or security ACLs under

Windows NT. In most cases this will require special system privileges, and doubling the option (**-XX**) under NT instructs *unzip* to use privileges for extraction; but under Unix, for example, a user who belongs to several groups can restore files owned by any of those groups, as long as the user IDs match his or her own. Note that ordinary file attributes are always restored--this option applies only to optional, extra ownership info available on some operating systems. [NT's access control lists do not appear to be especially compatible with OS/2's, so no attempt is made at cross-platform portability of access privileges. It is not clear under what conditions this would ever be useful anyway.]

-$** [MS-DOS, OS/2, NT] Restore the volume label if the extraction medium is removable (e.g., a diskette). Doubling the option (**-$$) allows fixed media (hard disks) to be labelled as well. By default, volume labels are ignored.

ENVIRONMENT OPTIONS

unzip's default behavior may be modified via options placed in an environment variable. This can be done with any option, but it is probably most useful with the **-a**, **-L**, **-C**, **-q**, **-o**, or **-n** modifiers: make *unzip* auto-convert text files by default, make it convert filenames from uppercase systems to lowercase, make it match names case-insensitively, make it quieter, or make it always overwrite or never overwrite files as it extracts them. For example, to make *unzip* act as quietly as possible, only reporting errors, one would use one of the following commands:

`UNZIP=-qq; export UNZIP`	Unix Bourne shell
`setenv UNZIP -qq`	Unix C shell
`set UNZIP=-qq`	OS/2 or MS-DOS
`define UNZIP_OPTS "-qq"`	VMS (quotes for *lowercase*)

Environment options are, in effect, considered to be just like any other command-line options, except that they are effectively the first options on the command line. To override an environment option, one may use the "minus operator" to remove it. For instance, to override one of the quiet-flags in the example above, use the command

```
unzip --q[other options] zipfile
```

The first hyphen is the normal switch character, and the second is a minus sign, acting on the q option. Thus the effect here is to cancel one quantum of quietness. To cancel both quiet flags, two (or more) minuses may be used:

```
unzip -t--q zipfile
unzip ---qt zipfile
```

(The two are equivalent.) This may seem awkward or confusing, but it is reasonably intuitive: just ignore the first hyphen and go from there. It is also consistent with the behavior of Unix *nice*(1).

As suggested by the examples above, the default variable names are UNZIP_OPTS for VMS (where the symbol used to install *unzip* as a foreign command would otherwise be confused with the environment variable), and UNZIP for all other operating systems. For compatibility with *zip*(1L), UNZIPOPT is also accepted. (Don't ask.) If both UNZIP and UNZIPOPT are defined, however, UNZIP takes precedence. *unzip*'s diagnostic option (**-v** with no zipfile name) can be used to check the values of all four possible *unzip* and *zipinfo* environment variables.

The timezone variable (TZ) should be set according to the local timezone in order for the **-f** and **-u** to operate correctly. See the description of **-f** above for details. This variable may also be necessary in order for timestamps on extracted files to be set correctly. Under Windows 95/NT *unzip* should know the correct timezone even if TZ is unset, assuming the timezone is correctly set in the Control Panel.

DECRYPTION

Encrypted archives are fully supported by Info-ZIP software, but due to United States export restrictions, the encryption and decryption sources are not packaged with the regular *unzip* and *zip* distributions. Since the crypt sources were written by Europeans, however, they are freely available at sites throughout the world; see the file "Where" in any Info-ZIP source or binary distribution for locations both inside and outside the US.

Because of the separate distribution, not all compiled versions of *unzip* support decryption. To check a version for crypt support, either attempt to test or extract an encrypted archive, or else check *unzip*'s diagnostic screen (see the **-v** option above) for "`[decryption]`" as one of the special compilation options.

As noted above, the **-P** option may be used to supply a password on the command line, but at a cost in security. The preferred decryption method is simply to extract normally; if a zipfile member is encrypted, *unzip* will prompt for the password without echoing what is typed. *unzip* continues to use the same password as long as it appears to be valid, by testing a 12-byte header on each file. The correct password will always check out against the header, but there is a 1-in-256 chance that an incorrect password will as well. (This is a security feature of the PKWARE zipfile format; it helps prevent brute-force attacks that might otherwise gain a large speed advantage by testing only the header.) In the case that an incorrect password is given but it passes the header test anyway, either an incorrect CRC will be generated for the extracted data or else *unzip* will fail during the extraction because the "decrypted" bytes do not constitute a valid compressed data stream.

If the first password fails the header check on some file, *unzip* will prompt for another password, and so on until all files are extracted. If a password is not known, entering a null password (that is, just a carriage return or "Enter") is taken as a signal to skip all further prompting. Only unencrypted files in the archive(s) will thereafter be extracted. (In fact, that's not quite true; older versions of *zip*(1L) and *zipcloak*(1L) allowed null passwords, so *unzip* checks each encrypted file to see if the null password works. This may result in "false positives" and extraction errors, as noted above.)

Archives encrypted with 8-bit passwords (for example, passwords with accented European characters) may not be portable across systems and/or other archivers. This problem stems from the use of multiple encoding methods for such characters, including Latin-1 (ISO 8859-1) and OEM code page 850. DOS *PKZIP* 2.04g uses the OEM code page; Windows *PKZIP* 2.5 uses Latin-1 (and is therefore incompatible with DOS *PKZIP*); Info-ZIP uses the OEM code page on DOS, OS/2 and Win3.*x* ports but Latin-1 everywhere else; and Nico Mak's *WinZip* 6.*x* does not allow 8-bit passwords at all. *UnZip* 5.3 attempts to use the default character set first (e.g., Latin-1), followed by the alternate one (e.g., OEM code page) to test passwords. On EBCDIC systems, if both of these fail, EBCDIC encoding will be tested as a last resort. (Since there are no known archivers that encrypt using EBCDIC encoding, EBCDIC is not tested on non-EBCDIC systems.) ISO character encodings other than Latin-1 are not supported.

EXAMPLES

To use *unzip* to extract all members of the archive *letters.zip* into the current directory and subdirectories below it, creating any subdirectories as necessary:

```
unzip letters
```

To extract all members of letters.zip into the current directory only:

```
unzip -j letters
```

To test letters.zip, printing only a summary message indicating whether the archive is OK or not:

```
unzip -tq letters
```

To test all zipfiles in the current directory, printing only the summaries:

```
unzip -tq .zip
```

(The backslash before the asterisk is only required if the shell expands wildcards, as in Unix; double quotes could have been used instead, as in the source examples below.) To extract to standard output all members of *letters.zip* whose names end in *.tex*, auto-converting to the local end-of-line convention and piping the output into more(1):

```
unzip -ca letters .tex | more
```

To extract the binary file paper1.dvi to standard output and pipe it to a printing program:

```
unzip -p articles paper1.dvi | dvips
```

To extract all FORTRAN and C source files--*.f, *.c, *.h, and Makefile--into the /tmp directory:

```
unzip source.zip "*.[fch]" Makefile -d /tmp
```

(The double quotes are necessary only in Unix and only if globbing is turned on.) To extract all FORTRAN and C source files, regardless of case (e.g., both *.c and *.C, and any makefile, Makefile, MAKEFILE or similar):

```
unzip -C source.zip "*.[fch]" makefile -d /tmp
```

To extract any such files but convert any uppercase MS-DOS or VMS names to lowercase and convert the line-endings of all of the files to the local standard (without respect to any files that might be marked "binary"):

```
unzip -aaCL source.zip "*.[fch]" makefile -d /tmp
```

To extract only newer versions of the files already in the current directory, without querying (NOTE: be careful of unzipping in one timezone a zipfile created in another--ZIP archives other than those created by Zip 2.1

or later contain no timezone information, and a "newer" file from an eastern timezone may, in fact, be older):

```
unzip -fo sources
```

To extract newer versions of the files already in the current directory and to create any files not already there (same caveat as previous example):

```
unzip -uo sources
```

To display a diagnostic screen showing which unzip and *zipinfo* options are stored in environment variables, whether decryption support was compiled in, the compiler with which *unzip* was compiled, etc.:

```
unzip -v
```

In the last five examples, assume that UNZIP or UNZIP_OPTS is set to -q. To do a singly quiet listing:

```
unzip -l file.zip
```

To do a doubly quiet listing:

```
unzip -ql file.zip
```

(Note that the ".zip" is generally not necessary.) To do a standard listing:

```
unzip --ql file.zip
```

or

```
unzip -l-q file.zip
```

or

```
unzip -l--q file.zip
```

Extra minuses don't hurt.

TIPS

The current maintainer, being a lazy sort, finds it very useful to define a pair of aliases: `tt` for "`unzip -tq`" and ii for "`unzip -Z`" (or "`zipinfo`"). One may then simply type "`tt zipfile`" to test an archive, something that is worth making a habit of doing. With luck *unzip* will report "`No errors detected in compressed data of zipfile.zip`," after which one may breathe a sigh of relief.

The maintainer also finds it useful to set the UNZIP environment variable to "`-aL`" and is tempted to add "`-C`" as well. His ZIPINFO variable is set to "`-z`".

DIAGNOSTICS

The exit status (or error level) approximates the exit codes defined by PKWARE and takes on the following values, except under VMS:

0	Normal; no errors or warnings detected.
1	One or more warning errors were encountered, but processing completed successfully anyway. This includes zipfiles where one or more files was skipped due to unsupported compression method or encryption with an unknown password.
2	A generic error in the zipfile format was detected. Processing may have completed successfully anyway; some broken zipfiles created by other archivers have simple workarounds.
3	A severe error in the zipfile format was detected. Processing probably failed immediately.
4	*unzip* was unable to allocate memory for one or more buffers during program initialization.
5	*unzip* was unable to allocate memory or unable to obtain a tty to read the decryption password(s).
6	*unzip* was unable to allocate memory during decompression to disk.
7	*unzip* was unable to allocate memory during in-memory decompression.
8	[Currently not used]
9	The specified zipfiles were not found.
10	Invalid options were specified on the command line.
11	No matching files were found.
50	The disk is (or was) full during extraction.
51	The end of the ZIP archive was encountered prematurely.
80	The user aborted *unzip* prematurely with Control-C (or similar)
81	No files were found due to unsupported compression methods or unsupported decryption. (If even one additional file is successfully processed, however, the exit status is 1.)

82 No files were found due to bad decryption password(s). (This is also the exit status if no files were found due to a combination of unsupported compression and bad passwords. As in the previous case, however, a single successful file will result in an exit status of 1 instead.)

VMS interprets standard Unix (or PC) return values as other, scarier-looking things, so *unzip* instead maps them into VMS-style status codes. The current mapping is as follows: 1 (success) for normal exit, 0x7fff0001 for warning errors, and (0x7fff000?+ 16*normal_unzip_exit_status) for all other errors, where the '?' is 2 (error) for *unzip* values 2, 9-11 and 80-82, and 4 (fatal error) for the remaining ones (3-8, 50, 51). In addition, there is a compilation option to expand upon this behavior: defining RETURN_CODES results in a human-readable explanation of what the error status means.

BUGS

Multi-part archives are not yet supported, except in conjunction with *zip*. (All parts must be concatenated together in order, and then "zip -F" must be performed on the concatenated archive in order to "fix" it.) This will definitely be corrected in the next major release.

Archives read from standard input are not yet supported, except with *funzip* (and then only the first member of the archive can be extracted).

Archives encrypted with 8-bit passwords (e.g., passwords with accented European characters) may not be portable across systems and/or other archivers. See the discussion in **DECRYPTION** above.

unzip's -M ("more") option is overly simplistic in its handling of screen output; as noted above, it fails to detect the wrapping of long lines and may thereby cause lines at the top of the screen to be scrolled off before being read. *unzip* should detect and treat each occurrence of line-wrap as one additional line printed. This requires knowledge of the screen's width as well as its height. In addition, *unzip* should detect the true screen geometry on all systems.

Dates, times and permissions of stored directories are not restored except under Unix.

[MS-DOS] When extracting or testing files from an archive on a defective floppy diskette, if the "Fail" option is chosen from DOS's "Abort, Retry, Fail?" message, older versions of *unzip* may hang the system, requiring a reboot. This problem appears to be fixed, but Control-C (or Control-Break) can still be used to terminate *unzip*.

[DEC Ultrix] Under DEC Ultrix, unzip would sometimes fail on long zipfiles (bad CRC, not always reproducible). This was apparently due either to a hardware bug (cache memory) or an operating system bug (improper handling of page faults?). Since Ultrix has been abandoned in favor of Digital Unix (OSF/1), this may not be an issue anymore.

[Unix] Unix special files such as FIFO buffers (named pipes), block devices and character devices are not restored even if they are somehow represented in the zipfile, nor are hard-linked files relinked. Basically the only file types restored by *unzip* are regular files, directories and symbolic (soft) links.

[OS/2] Extended attributes for existing directories are only updated if the **-o** ("overwrite all") option is given. This is a limitation of the operating system; because directories only have a creation time associated with them, *unzip* has no way to determine whether the stored attributes are newer or older than those on disk. In practice this may mean a two-pass approach is required: first unpack the archive normally (with or without freshening/updating existing files), then overwrite just the directory entries (e.g., "unzip -o foo */").

[VMS] When extracting to another directory, only the *[.foo]* syntax is accepted for the **-d** option; the simple Unix *foo* syntax is silently ignored (as is the less common VMS *foo.dir* syntax).

[VMS] When the file being extracted already exists, *unzip*'s query only allows skipping, overwriting or renaming; there should additionally be a choice for creating a new version of the file. In fact, the "overwrite" choice does create a new version; the old version is not overwritten or deleted.

SEE ALSO

funzip(1L), *zip*(1L), *zipcloak*(1L), *zipgrep*(1L), *zipinfo*(1L), *zipnote*(1L), *zipsplit*(1L)

URL

The Info-ZIP home page is currently at `http://www.cdrom.com/pub/infozip/`.

AUTHORS

The primary Info-ZIP authors (current semi-active members of the Zip-Bugs workgroup) are: Greg "Cave Newt" Roelofs (UnZip); Onno van der Linden (Zip); Jean-loup Gailly (compression); Mark Adler (decompression, fUnZip); Christian Spieler (VMS, MS-DOS, Windows 95, NT, shared code, general Zip and UnZip integration and optimization); Mike White (Windows GUI, Windows DLLs); Kai Uwe Rommel (OS/2); Paul Kienitz (Amiga, Windows 95); Chris Herborth (BeOS, QNX, Atari); Jonathan Hudson (SMS/QDOS); Karl Davis and Sergio Monesi (Acorn RISC OS); Harald Denker (Atari, MVS); John Bush (Solaris, Amiga); Hunter Goatley (VMS); Steve Salisbury (Windows 95, NT); Steve Miller (Windows CE GUI), Johnny Lee (MS-DOS, Windows 95, NT); and Robert Heath (Windows GUI). The author of the original unzip code upon which Info-ZIP's was based is Samuel H. Smith; Carl Mascott did the first Unix port; and David P. Kirschbaum organized and led Info-ZIP in its early days with Keith Petersen hosting the original mailing list at WSMR-SimTel20. The full list of contributors to UnZip has grown quite large; please refer to the CONTRIBS file in the UnZip source distribution for a relatively complete version.

VERSIONS

v1.2	15 Mar 89	Samuel H. Smith
v2.0	9 Sep 89	Samuel H. Smith
v2.*x*	fall 1989	Many Usenet contributors
v3.0	1 May 90	Info-ZIP (DPK, consolidator)
v3.1	15 Aug 90	Info-ZIP (DPK, consolidator)
v4.0	1 Dec 90	Info-ZIP (GRR, maintainer)
v4.1	12 May 91	Info-ZIP
v4.2	20 Mar 92	Info-ZIP (Zip-Bugs subgroup, GRR)
v5.0	21 Aug 92	Info-ZIP (Zip-Bugs subgroup, GRR)
v5.01	15 Jan 93	Info-ZIP (Zip-Bugs subgroup, GRR)
v5.1	7 Feb 94	Info-ZIP (Zip-Bugs subgroup, GRR)
v5.11	2 Aug 94	Info-ZIP (Zip-Bugs subgroup, GRR)
v5.12	28 Aug 94	Info-ZIP (Zip-Bugs subgroup, GRR)
v5.2	30 Apr 96	Info-ZIP (Zip-Bugs subgroup, GRR)
v5.3	22 Apr 97	Info-ZIP (Zip-Bugs subgroup, GRR)
v5.31	31 May 97	Info-ZIP (Zip-Bugs subgroup, GRR)

FILE FORMATS

ALIASES(5)

NAME

`aliases` Aliases file for sendmail.

SYNOPSIS

`aliases`

DESCRIPTION

This file describes user ID aliases used by `/usr/sbin/sendmail`. The file resides in `/etc` and is formatted as a series of lines of the form

name: name_1, name2, name_3,...

The *name* is the name to alias, and the *name_n* are the aliases for that name. Lines beginning with white space are continuation lines. Lines beginning with '#' are comments.

Aliasing occurs only on local names. Loops can not occur, since no message will be sent to any person more than once.

After aliasing has been done, local and valid recipients who have a "`.forward`" file in their home directory have messages forwarded to the list of users defined in that file.

This is only the raw data file; the actual aliasing information is placed into a binary format in the file `/etc/aliases.db` using the program `newaliases(1)`. A `newaliases` command should be executed each time the aliases file is changed for the change to take effect.

SEE ALSO

`newaliases(1), dbopen(3), dbm(3), sendmail(8)`

SENDMAIL Installation and Operation Guide.

SENDMAIL An Internetwork Mail Router.

BUGS

If you have compiled `sendmail` with DBM support instead of NEWDB, you may have encountered problems in dbm(3) restricting a single alias to about 1000 bytes of information. You can get longer aliases by "chaining"; that is, make the last name in the alias be a dummy name which is a continuation alias.

HISTORY

The **`aliases`** file format appeared in 4.0BSD.

CRONTAB(5)

NAME

crontab Tables for driving cron.

DESCRIPTION

A *crontab* file contains instructions to the cron(8) daemon of the general form: "run this command at this time on this date". Each user has their own crontab, and commands in any given crontab will be executed as the user who owns the crontab. Uucp and News will usually have their own crontabs, eliminating the need for explicitly running su(1) as part of a cron command.

Blank lines and leading spaces and tabs are ignored. Lines whose first non-space character is a pound-sign (#) are comments, and are ignored. Note that comments are not allowed on the same line as cron commands, since they will be taken to be part of the command. Similarly, comments are not allowed on the same line as environment variable settings.

An active line in a crontab will be either an environment setting or a cron command. An environment setting is of the form,

name = value

where the spaces around the equal-sign (=) are optional, and any subsequent non-leading spaces in *value* will be part of the value assigned to *name*. The *value* string may be placed in quotes (single or double, but matching) to preserve leading or trailing blanks.

Several environment variables are set up automatically by the *cron*(8) daemon. SHELL is set to /bin/sh, and LOGNAME and HOME are set from the /etc/passwd line of the crontab's owner. HOME and SHELL may be overridden by settings in the crontab; LOGNAME may not.

(Another note: the LOGNAME variable is sometimes called USER on BSD systems... on these systems, USER will be set also.)

In addition to LOGNAME, HOME, and SHELL, *cron*(8) will look at MAILTO if it has any reason to send mail as a result of running commands in "this" crontab. If MAILTO is defined (and non-empty), mail is sent to the user so named. If MAILTO is defined but empty (MAILTO=""), no mail will be sent. Otherwise mail is sent to the owner of the crontab. This option is useful if you decide on /bin/mail instead of /usr/lib/sendmail as your mailer when you install cron -- /bin/mail doesn't do aliasing, and UUCP usually doesn't read its mail.

The format of a cron command is very much the V7 standard, with a number of upward-compatible extensions. Each line has five time and date fields, followed by a user name if this is the system crontab file, followed by a command. Commands are executed by *cron*(8) when the minute, hour, and month of year fields match the current time, *and* when at least one of the two day fields (day of month, or day of week) match the current time (see "Note" below). *cron*(8) examines cron entries once every minute. The time and date fields are

Field	Allowed Values
minute	0-59
hour	0-23
day of month	0-31
month	0-12 (or names, see below)
day of week	0-7 (0 or 7 is Sun, or use names)

A field may be an asterisk (*), which always stands for "first-last."

Ranges of numbers are allowed. Ranges are two numbers separated with a hyphen. The specified range is inclusive. For example, 8-11 for an "hours" entry specifies execution at hours 8, 9, 10 and 11.

Lists are allowed. A list is a set of numbers (or ranges) separated by commas. Examples: "1,2,5,9" and "0-4,8-12."

Step values can be used in conjunction with ranges. Following a range with "/<number>" specifies skips of the number's value through the range. For example, "0-23/2" can be used in the hours field to specify command execution every other hour. (The alternative in the V7 standard is "0,2,4,6,8,10,12,14,16,18,20,22".) Steps are also permitted after an asterisk, so if you want to say "every two hours", just use "*/2".

Names can also be used for the "month" and "day of week" fields. Use the first three letters of the particular day or month (case doesn't matter). Ranges or lists of names are not allowed.

The "sixth" field (the rest of the line) specifies the command to be run. The entire command portion of the line, up to a new line or % character, will be executed by /bin/sh or by the shell specified in the SHELL variable of the cronfile. Percent-signs (%) in the command, unless escaped with backslash , will be changed into newline characters, and all data after the first % will be sent to the command as standard input.

NOTE

The day of a command's execution can be specified by two fields -- day of month, and day of week. If both fields are restricted (ie, aren't *), the command will be run when *either* field matches the current time. For example, "30 4 1,15 * 5" would cause a command to be run at 4:30 am on the 1st and 15th of each month, plus every Friday.

EXAMPLE CRON FILE

```
# use /bin/sh to run commands,no matter what /etc/passwd says
SHELL=/bin/sh
# mail any output to `paul', no matter whose crontab this is
MAILTO=paul
#
# run five minutes after midnight, every day
5 0 * * *      $HOME/bin/daily.job >> $HOME/tmp/out 2>&1
# run at 2:15pm on the 1st of month -- output mailed to paul
15 14 1 * *   $HOME/bin/monthly
# run at 10 pm on weekdays, annoy Joe
0 22 * * 1-5  mail -s "It's 10pm" joe%Where are your kids?%
23 0-23/2 * * * echo "run 23 mins after midn, 2, 4..., daily"
5 4 * * sun     echo "run at 5 after 4 every sunday"
```

SEE ALSO

cron(8), crontab(1)

EXTENSIONS

When specifying day of week, both day 0 and day 7 will be considered Sunday. BSD and ATT seem to disagree about this.

Lists and ranges are allowed to co-exist in the same field. "1-3,7-9" would be rejected by ATT or BSD cron -they want to see "1-3" or "7,8,9" ONLY.

Ranges can include "steps", so "1-9/2" is the same as "1,3,5,7,9".

Names of months or days of the week can be specified by name.

Environment variables can be set in the crontab. In BSD or ATT, the environment handed to child processes is basically the one from /etc/rc.

Command output is mailed to the crontab owner (BSD can't do this), can be mailed to a person other than the crontab owner (SysV can't do this), or the feature can be turned off and no mail will be sent at all (SysV can't do this either).

AUTHOR

Paul Vixie <paul@vix.com>

HOST.ACCESS(5)

NAME

hosts_access Format of host access control files.

DESCRIPTION

This manual page describes a simple access control language that is based on client (host name/address, user name), and server (process name, host name/address) patterns. Examples are given at the end. The impatient reader is encouraged to skip to the EXAMPLES section for a quick introduction.

An extended version of the access control language is described in the *hosts_options*(5) document. The extensions are turned on at program build time by building with -DPROCESS_OPTIONS.

In the following text, *daemon* is the the process name of a network daemon process, and *client* is the name and/or address of a host requesting service. Network daemon process names are specified in the inetd configuration file.

ACCESS CONTROL FILES

The access control software consults two files. The search stops at the first match:

- Access will be granted when a (daemon,client) pair matches an entry in the */etc/hosts.allow* file.
- Otherwise, access will be denied when a (daemon,client) pair matches an entry in the */etc/hosts.deny* file.
- Otherwise, access will be granted.

A non-existing access control file is treated as if it were an empty file. Thus, access control can be turned off by providing no access control files.

ACCESS CONTROL RULES

Each access control file consists of zero or more lines of text. These lines are processed in order of appearance. The search terminates when a match is found.

- A newline character is ignored when it is preceded by a backslash character. This permits you to break up long lines so that they are easier to edit.
- Blank lines or lines that begin with a '#' character are ignored. This permits you to insert comments and whitespace so that the tables are easier to read.
- All other lines should satisfy the following format, things between [] being optional:

  daemon_list : client_list [: shell_command]

daemon_list is a list of one or more daemon process names (argv[0] values) or wildcards (see below).

client_list is a list of one or more host names, host addresses, patterns or wildcards (see below) that will be matched against the client host name or address.

The more complex forms `daemon@host` and `user@host` are explained in the sections on server endpoint patterns and on client username lookups, respectively.

List elements should be separated by blanks and/or commas.

With the exception of NIS (YP) netgroup lookups, all access control checks are case-insensitive.

PATTERNS

The access control language implements the following patterns:

- A string that begins with a '.' character. A host name is matched if the last components of its name match the specified pattern. For example, the pattern '.tue.nl' matches the host name 'wzv.win.tue.nl'.
- A string that ends with a '.' character. A host address is matched if its first numeric fields match the given string. For example, the pattern '131.155.' matches the address of (almost) every host on the Eindhoven University network (131.155.x.x).
- A string that begins with an @ character is treated as an NIS (formerly YP) netgroup name. A host name is matched if it is a host member of the specified netgroup. Netgroup matches are not supported for daemon process names or for client user names.
- An expression of the form 'n.n.n.n/m.m.m.m' is interpreted as a 'net/mask' pair. A host address is matched if 'net' is equal to the bitwise AND of the address and the 'mask'. For example, the net/mask pattern '131.155.72.0/255.255.254.0' matches every address in the range '131.155.72.0' through '131.155.73.255'.

WILDCARDS

The access control language supports explicit wildcards:

ALL The universal wildcard, always matches.

LOCAL Matches any host whose name does not contain a dot character.

UNKNOWN Matches any user whose name is unknown, and matches any host whose name *or* address are unknown. This pattern should be used with care: host names may be unavailable due to temporary name server problems. A network address will be unavailable when the software cannot figure out what type of network it is talking to.

KNOWN Matches any user whose name is known, and matches any host whose name *and* address are known. This pattern should be used with care: host names may be unavailable due to temporary name server problems. A network address will be unavailable when the software cannot figure out what type of network it is talking to.

PARANOID Matches any host whose name does not match its address. When tcpd is built with -DPARANOID (default mode), it drops requests from such clients even before looking at the access control tables. Build without -DPARANOID when you want more control over such requests.

OPERATORS

EXCEPT Intended use is of the form: 'list_1 EXCEPT list_2'; this construct matches anything that matches *list_1* unless it matches *list_2*. The EXCEPT operator can be used in daemon_lists and in client_lists. The EXCEPT operator can be nested: if the control language would permit the use of parentheses, 'a EXCEPT b EXCEPT c' would parse as '(a EXCEPT (b EXCEPT c))'.

SHELL COMMANDS

If the first-matched access control rule contains a shell command, that command is subjected to %<letter> substitutions (see next section). The result is executed by a */bin/sh* child process with standard input, output and error connected to */dev/null*. Specify an '&' at the end of the command if you do not want to wait until it has completed.

Shell commands should not rely on the PATH setting of the inetd. Instead, they should use absolute path names, or they should begin with an explicit PATH=whatever statement.

The hosts_options(5) document describes an alternative language that uses the shell command field in a different and incompatible way.

% EXPANSIONS

The following expansions are available within shell commands:

%a (%A) The client (server) host address.

%c Client information: `user@host`, `user@address`, a host name, or just an address, depending on how much information is available.

%d The daemon process name (argv[0] value).

%h (%H) The client (server) host name or address, if the host name is unavailable.

%n (%N) The client (server) host name (or "unknown" or "paranoid").

%p The daemon process id.

%s Server information: `daemon@host`, `daemon@address`, or just a daemon name, depending on how much information is available.

%u The client user name (or "unknown").

%% Expands to a single '%' character.

Characters in % expansions that may confuse the shell are replaced by underscores.

SERVER ENDPOINT PATTERNS

In order to distinguish clients by the network address that they connect to, use patterns of the form:

```
process_name@host_pattern : client_list ...
```

Patterns like these can be used when the machine has different Internet addresses with different Internet hostnames. Service providers can use this facility to offer FTP, GOPHER or WWW archives with Internet names that may even belong to different organizations. See also the 'twist' option in the hosts_options(5) document. Some systems (Solaris, FreeBSD) can have more than one Internet address on one physical interface; with other systems you may have to resort to SLIP or PPP pseudo interfaces that live in a dedicated network address space.

The host_pattern obeys the same syntax rules as host names and addresses in client_list context. Usually, server endpoint information is available only with connection-oriented services.

CLIENT USERNAME LOOKUP

When the client host supports the RFC 931 protocol or one of its descendants (TAP, IDENT, RFC 1413) the wrapper programs can retrieve additional information about the owner of a connection. Client username information, when available, is logged together with the client host name, and can be used to match patterns like

```
daemon_list : ... user_pattern@host_pattern ...
```

The daemon wrappers can be configured at compile time to perform rule-driven username lookups (default) or to always interrogate the client host. In the case of rule-driven username lookups, the above rule would cause username lookup only when both the *daemon_list* and the *host_pattern* match.

A user pattern has the same syntax as a daemon process pattern, so the same wildcards apply (netgroup membership is not supported). One should not get carried away with username lookups, though.

- The client username information cannot be trusted when it is needed most, i.e. when the client system has been compromised. In general, ALL and (UN)KNOWN are the only user name patterns that make sense.
- Username lookups are possible only with TCP-based services, and only when the client host runs a suitable daemon; in all other cases the result is "unknown".
- A well-known Unix kernel bug may cause loss of service when username lookups are blocked by a firewall. The wrapper README document describes a procedure to find out if your kernel has this bug.
- Username lookups may cause noticeable delays for non-Unix users. The default timeout for username lookups is 10 seconds: too short to cope with slow networks, but long enough to irritate PC users.

Selective username lookups can alleviate the last problem. For example, a rule like

```
daemon_list : @pcnetgroup ALL@ALL
```

would match members of the pc netgroup without doing username lookups, but would perform username lookups with all other systems.

DETECTING ADDRESS SPOOFING ATTACKS

A flaw in the sequence number generator of many TCP/IP implementations allows intruders to easily impersonate trusted hosts and to break in via, for example, the remote shell service. The IDENT (RFC931 etc.) service can be used to detect such and other host address spoofing attacks.

Before accepting a client request, the wrappers can use the IDENT service to find out that the client did not send the request at all. When the client host provides IDENT service, a negative IDENT lookup result (the client matches 'UNKNOWN@host') is strong evidence of a host spoofing attack.

A positive IDENT lookup result (the client matches 'KNOWN@host') is less trustworthy. It is possible for an intruder to spoof both the client connection and the IDENT lookup, although doing so is much harder than spoofing just a client connection. It may also be that the client's IDENT server is lying.

NOTE

IDENT lookups don't work with UDP services.

EXAMPLES

The language is flexible enough that different types of access control policy can be expressed with a minimum of fuss. Although the language uses two access control tables, the most common policies can be implemented with one of the tables being trivial or even empty.

When reading the examples below it is important to realize that the allow table is scanned before the deny table, that the search terminates when a match is found, and that access is granted when no match is found at all.

The examples use host and domain names. They can be improved by including address and/or network/netmask information, to reduce the impact of temporary name server lookup failures.

MOSTLY CLOSED

In this case, access is denied by default. Only explicitly authorized hosts are permitted access.

The default policy (no access) is implemented with a trivial deny file:

```
/etc/hosts.deny:
    ALL: ALL
```

This denies all service to all hosts, unless they are permitted access by entries in the allow file.

The explicitly authorized hosts are listed in the allow file. For example:

```
/etc/hosts.allow:
      ALL: LOCAL @some_netgroup
      ALL: .foobar.edu EXCEPT terminalserver.foobar.edu
```

The first rule permits access from hosts in the local domain (no '.' in the host name) and from members of the *some_netgroup* netgroup. The second rule permits access from all hosts in the *foobar.edu* domain (notice the leading dot), with the exception of *terminalserver.foobar.edu*.

MOSTLY OPEN

Here, access is granted by default; only explicitly specified hosts are refused service.

The default policy (access granted) makes the allow file redundant so that it can be omitted. The explicitly nonauthorized hosts are listed in the deny file. For example:

```
/etc/hosts.deny:
      ALL: some.host.name, .some.domain
      ALL EXCEPT in.fingerd: other.host.name, .other.domain
```

The first rule denies some hosts and domains all services; the second rule still permits finger requests from other hosts and domains.

BOOBY TRAPS

The next example permits tftp requests from hosts in the local domain (notice the leading dot). Requests from any other hosts are denied. Instead of the requested file, a finger probe is sent to the offending host. The result is mailed to the superuser.

```
/etc/hosts.allow:
      in.tftpd: LOCAL, .my.domain
/etc/hosts.deny:
      in.tftpd: ALL: (/some/where/safe_finger -l @%h |
      /usr/ucb/mail -s %d-%h root) &
```

The safe_finger command comes with the tcpd wrapper and should be installed in a suitable place. It limits possible damage from data sent by the remote finger server. It gives better protection than the standard finger command.

The expansion of the %h (client host) and %d (service name) sequences is described in the section on shell commands.

WARNING

Do not booby-trap your finger daemon unless you are prepared for infinite finger loops.

On network firewall systems this trick can be carried even further. The typical network firewall only provides a limited set of services to the outer world. All other services can be "bugged" just like the above tftp example. The result is an excellent early-warning system.

DIAGNOSTICS

An error is reported when a syntax error is found in a host access control rule; when the length of an access control rule exceeds the capacity of an internal buffer; when an access control rule is not terminated by a newline character; when the result of %<letter> expansion would overflow an internal buffer; when a system call fails that shouldn't. All problems are reported via the syslog daemon.

FILES

`/etc/hosts.allow` (daemon,client) pairs that are granted access

`/etc/hosts.deny` (daemon,client) pairs that are denied access

SEE ALSO

tcpd(8) tcp/ip daemon wrapper program

tcpdchk(8), tcpdmatch(8), test programs

BUGS

If a name server lookup times out, the host name will not be available to the access control software, even though the host is registered.

Domain name server lookups are case-insensitive; NIS (formerly YP) netgroup lookups are case-sensitive.

AUTHOR

Wietse Venema <wietse@wzv.win.tue.nl>

Department of Mathematics and Computing Science

Eindhoven University of Technology

Den Dolech 2, P.O. Box 513

5600 MB Eindhoven, The Netherlands

PASSWD(5)

NAME

passwd Password file.

DESCRIPTION

passwd is an ASCII file which contains a list of the system's users and the passwords they must use for access. The password file should have general read permission (many utilities, like *ls*(1) use it to map user IDs to user names), but write access only for the superuser.

In the good old days there was no great problem with this general read permission. Everybody could read the encrypted passwords, but the hardware was too slow to crack a well-chosen password, and moreover, the basic assumption used to be that of a friendly user-community. These days many people run some version of the shadow password suite, where */etc/passwd* has *'s instead of passwords, and the encrypted passwords are in */etc/shadow* which is readable by root only.

When you create a new login, leave the password field empty and use passwd(1) to fill it. A star (*) in the password field means that this user can not login via login(1).

There is one entry per line, and each line has the format

```
login_name:passwd:UID:GID:user_name:directory:shell
```

The field descriptions are

login_name	the name of the user on the system
password	the encrypted optional user password
UID	the numerical user ID
GID	the numerical group ID for this user

user_name	the (optional) comment field (often a full user name.
Directory	the user's $HOME directory
shell	the program to run at login (if empty, use */bin/sh*)

NOTE

If your root file system is on */dev/ram*, you must save a changed password file to your root file system floppy before you shut down the system and check the access rights. If you want to create user groups, their GIDs must be equal and there must be an entry in */etc/group*, or no group will exist.

FILES

/etc/passwd

SEE ALSO

passwd(1), **login**(1), **group**(5), **shadow**(5)

PRINTCAP(5)

NAME

printcap Printer capability database.

SYNOPSIS

printcap

DESCRIPTION

The **printcap** function is a simplified version of the termcap(5) database used to describe line printers. The spooling system accesses the **printcap** file every time it is used, allowing dynamic addition and deletion of printers. Each entry in the database is used to describe one printer. This database may not be substituted for, as is possible for `termcap`, because it may allow accounting to be bypassed.

The default printer is normally *lp*, though the environment variable PRINTER may be used to override this. Each spooling utility supports an option, **-P** *printer*, to allow explicit naming of a destination printer.

Refer to the *4.3 BSD Line Printer Spooler Manual* for a complete discussion on how setup the database for a given printer.

CAPABILITIES

Refer to `termcap`(5) for a description of the file layout.

Name	Type	Default	Description
af	str	`NULL`	name of accounting file
br	num	none	if lp is a tty, set the baud rate (`ioctl`(2) call)
cf	str	`NULL`	cifplot data filter
df	str	`NULL`	tex data filter (DVI format)
fc	num	0	if lp is a tty, clear flag bits (`sgtty.h`)
ff	str	`` `\f ``	string to send for a form feed
fo	bool	false	print a form feed when device is opened
fs	num	0	like `fc' but set bits
gf	str	`NULL`	graph data filter (`plot`(3) format)
hl	bool	false	print the burst header page last
ic	bool	false	driver supports (non standard) ioctl to indent printout
if	str	`NULL`	name of text filter which does accounting
lf	str	`/dev/console`	error logging file name
lo	str	`lock`	name of lock file
lp	str	`/dev/lp`	device name to open for output
mx	num	1000	maximum file size (in `BUFSIZ` blocks), zero = unlimited
nd	str	`NULL`	next directory for list of queues (unimplemented)
nf	str	`NULL`	ditroff data filter (device independent troff)

Name	Type	Default	Description
of	str	NULL	name of output filtering program
pc	num	200	price per foot or page in hundredths of cents
pl	num	66	page length (in lines)
pw	num	132	page width (in characters)
px	num	0	page width in pixels (horizontal)
py	num	0	page length in pixels (vertical)
rf	str	NULL	filter for printing FORTRAN style text files
rg	str	NULL	restricted group. Only members of group allowed access
rm	str	NULL	machine name for remote printer
rp	str	"lp"	remote printer name argument
rs	bool	false	restrict remote users to those with local accounts
rw	bool	false	open the printer device for reading and writing
sb	bool	false	short banner (one line only)
sc	bool	false	suppress multiple copies
sd	str	`/var/spool/lpd`	spool directory
sf	bool	false	suppress form feeds
sh	bool	false	suppress printing of burst page header
st	str	*status*	status file name
tf	str	NULL	troff data filter (cat phototypesetter)
tr	str	NULL	trailer string to print when queue empties
vf	str	NULL	raster image filter

If the local line printer driver supports indentation, the daemon must understand how to invoke it.

FILTERS

The lpd(8) daemon creates a pipeline of *filters* to process files for various printer types. The filters selected depend on the flags passed to lpr(1). The pipeline set up is

p	pr	if regular text + pr(1)
none	if	regular text
c	cf	cifplot
d	df	DVI (tex)
g	gf	plot(3)
n	nf	ditroff
f	rf	Fortran
t	tf	troff
v	vf	raster image

The **if** filter is invoked with arguments:

`if [-c]` **-w***width* **-l***length* **-i***indent* **-n** *login* **-h** *host acct-file*

The **-c** flag is passed only if the **-l** flag (pass control characters literally) is specified to lpr. The *width* and *length* function specify the page width and length (from **pw** and **pl** respectively) in characters. The **-n** and **-h** parameters specify the login name and host name of the owner of the job respectively. The *Acct-file* function is passed from the **af printcap** entry.

If no **if** is specified, **of** is used instead, with the distinction that of is opened only once, while **if** is opened for every individual job. Thus, **if** is better suited to performing accounting. The **of** is only given the *width* and *length* flags.

All other filters are called as

filter -x*width* -y*length* **-n** *login* **-h** *host acct-file*

where *width* and *length* are represented in pixels, specified by the **px** and **py** entries respectively.

All filters take *stdin* as the file, *stdout* as the printer, may log either to *stderr* or using syslog(3), and must not ignore SIGINT.

LOGGING

Error messages generated by the line printer programs themselves (that is, the `lp*` programs) are logged by `syslog(3)` using the LPR facility. Messages printed on *stderr* of one of the filters are sent to the corresponding **`lf`** file. The filters may, of course, use `syslog` themselves.

Error messages sent to the console have a carriage return and a line feed appended to them, rather than just a line feed.

SEE ALSO

`termcap(5)`, `lpc(8)`, `lpd(8)`, `pac(8)`, `lpr(1)`, `lpq(1)`, `lprm(1)`

4.3 BSD Line Printer Spooler Manual.

HISTORY

The **`printcap`** file format appeared in 4.2BSD.

ADMINISTRATIVE COMMANDS

DUMP(8)

NAME

dump Filesystem backup.

SYNOPSIS

dump [**0123456789BbhfusTdWn** [*argument* ...]] *filesystem*

dump [**0123456789BbhfusTdWn** [*argument* ...]] *directory*

DESCRIPTION

Dump examines files on a filesystem and determines which files need to be backed up. These files are copied to the given disk, tape or other storage medium for safe keeping (see the **`f`** option below for doing remote backups). A dump that is larger than the output medium is broken into multiple volumes. On most media the size is determined by writing until an end-of-media indication is returned. On media that cannot reliably return an end-of-media indication (such as some cartridge tape drives) each volume is of a fixed size; the actual size is determined by the tape size and density and/or block count options below. By default, the same output file name is used for each volume after prompting the operator to change media.

The following options are supported by **dump**:

0-9 Dump levels. A level 0, full backup, guarantees the entire file system is copied (but see also the **h** option below). A level number above 0, incremental backup, tells dump to copy all files new or modified since the last dump of lower level. The default level is 9.

B *records* The number of dump records per volume (this is interpreted as the size in kilobytes). This option overrides the calculation of tape size based on length and density.

b *blocksize* The number of kilobytes per dump record.

h *level* Honor the user "nodump" flag only for dumps at or above the given *level*. The default honor level is 1, so that incremental backups omit such files but full backups retain them.

f *file* Write the backup to `file`; `file` may be a special device file like `/dev/rmt12` (a tape drive), `/dev/rsd1c` (a disk drive), an ordinary file, or '-' (the standard output). Multiple file names may be given as a single argument separated by commas. Each file will be used for one dump volume in the order listed; if the dump requires more volumes than the number of names given, the last file name will used for all remaining volumes after prompting for media changes. If the name of the file is of the form "`host:file`," or "`user@host:file`," **dump** writes to the named file on the remote host using `rmt`(8).

d *density* Set tape density to `density`. The default is 1600BPI.

n Whenever **dump** requires operator attention, notify all operators in the group "operator" by means similar to a wall(1).

s *feet* Attempt to calculate the amount of tape needed at a particular density. If this amount is exceeded, **dump** prompts for a new tape. It is recommended to be a bit conservative on this option. The default tape length is 2300 feet.

u Update the file `/etc/dumpdates` after a successful dump. The format of `/etc/dumpdates` is readable by people, consisting of one free format record per line: filesystem name, increment level and `ctime(3)` format dump date. There may be only one entry per filesystem at each level. The file `/etc/dumpdates` may be edited to change any of the fields, if necessary.

T *date* Use the specified date as the starting time for the dump instead of the time determined from looking in `/etc/dumpdates`. The format of date is the same as that of `ctime(3)`. This option is useful for automated dump scripts that wish to dump over a specific period of time. The **T** option is mutually exclusive from the **u** option.

W **dump** tells the operator what file systems need to be dumped. This information is gleaned from the files `/etc/dumpdates` and `/etc/fstab`. The **W** option causes **dump** to print out, for each file system in `/etc/dumpdates` the most recent dump date and level, and highlights those file systems that should be dumped. If the **W** option is set, all other options are ignored, and **dump** exits immediately.

w Is like W, but prints only those filesystems which need to be dumped.

dump requires operator intervention on these conditions: end of tape, end of dump, tape write error, tape open error or disk read error (if there are more than a threshold of 32). In addition to alerting all operators implied by the **n** key, **dump** interacts with the operator on *dump's* control terminal at times when **dump** can no longer proceed, or if something is grossly wrong. All questions **dump** poses *must* be answered by typing "yes" or "no," appropriately.

Since making a dump involves a lot of time and effort for full dumps, **dump** checkpoints itself at the start of each tape volume. If writing that volume fails for some reason, **dump** will, with operator permission, restart itself from the checkpoint after the old tape has been rewound and removed, and a new tape has been mounted.

dump tells the operator what is going on at periodic intervals, including usually low estimates of the number of blocks to write, the number of tapes it will take, the time to completion, and the time to the tape change. The output is verbose, so that others know that the terminal controlling **dump** is busy, and will be for some time.

In the event of a catastrophic disk event, the time required to restore all the necessary backup tapes or files to disk can be kept to a minimum by staggering the incremental dumps. An efficient method of staggering incremental dumps to minimize the number of tapes follows:

> Always start with a level 0 backup, for example:
>
> `/sbin/dump 0uf /dev/nrstl /usr/src`

This should be done at set intervals, say once a month or once every two months, and on a set of fresh tapes that is saved forever.

> After a level 0, dumps of active file systems are taken on a daily basis, using a modified Tower of Hanoi algorithm, with this sequence of dump levels:
>
> `3 2 5 4 7 6 9 8 9 9...`

For the daily dumps, it should be possible to use a fixed number of tapes for each day, used on a weekly basis. Each week, a level 1 dump is taken, and the daily Hanoi sequence repeats beginning with 3. For weekly dumps, another fixed set of tapes per dumped file system is used, also on a cyclical basis.

After several months or so, the daily and weekly tapes should get rotated out of the dump cycle and fresh tapes brought in.

FILES

`/dev/rmt8`	Default tape unit to dump to
`/etc/dumpdates`	Dump date records
`/etc/fstab`	Dump table: file systems and frequency
`/etc/group`	Find group *operator*

SEE ALSO

`restore`(8), `rmt`(8), `dump`(5), `fstab`(5)

DIAGNOSTICS

Many, and verbose.

dump exits with zero status on success. Startup errors are indicated with an exit code of 1; abnormal termination is indicated with an exit code of 3.

BUGS

Fewer than 32 read errors on the filesystem are ignored. Each reel requires a new process, so parent processes for reels already written just hang around until the entire tape is written.

dump with the **W** or **w** options does not report filesystems that have never been recorded in `/etc/dumpdates`, even if listed in `/etc/fstab`.

It would be nice if **dump** knew about the dump sequence, kept track of the tapes scribbled on, told the operator which tape to mount when, and provided more assistance for the operator running restore.

The Linux port of **dump** is not able yet to produce correct multi-volume backups.

HISTORY

A **dump** command appeared in Version 6 AT&T Unix.

ICONFIG(8)

NAME

ifconfig Configure a network interface.

SYNOPSIS

ifconfig [interface]

ifconfig interface [aftype] options | address...

DESCRIPTION

ifconfig is used to set up (and maintain thereafter) the kernel-resident network interfaces. It is used at boot time to configure most of them to a running state. After that, it is usually only needed when debugging or when system tuning is needed.

If no arguments are given, ifconfig just displays the status of the currently defined interfaces. If the single **interface** argument is given, it displays the status of the given interface only. Otherwise, it assumes that things have to be set up.

ADDRESS FAMILIES

If the first argument after the interface name is recognized as the name of a supported address family, that address family is used for decoding and displaying all protocol addresses. Currently supported address families include **inet** (TCP/IP, default) **ax25** (AMPR Packet Radio), **ddp** (Appletalk Phase 2), **ipx** (Novell IPX) and **netrom** (AMPR Packet radio).

OPTIONS

interface The name of the NET interface. This usually is a name like **eth0** , **sl3** or something like that: a device driver name followed by a unit number.

up This flag causes the interface to be activated. It is implicitly specified if the interface is given a new address (see below).

down This flag causes the driver for this interface to be shut down, and is useful when things start going wrong.

[-]arp Enable or disable the use of the ARP protocol on this interface. If the minus **(-)** sign is present, the flag is turned OFF.

[-]trailers Enable or disable the use of trailers on Ethernet frames. This is not used in the current implementation of NET.

[-]allmulti Enable or disable the **promiscuous** mode of the interface. This means that all incoming frames get sent to the network layer of the system kernel, allowing for networking monitoring.

metric N This parameter sets the interface metric. It is not used at present, but we will implement it for the future.

mtu N This parameter sets the Maximum Transfer Unit (MTU) of an interface. For Ethernet, this is a number in the range of 1000-2000 (default is 1500). For SLIP, use something between 200 and 4096. Note, that the current implementation does not handle IP fragmentation yet, so you'd better make the MTU large enough!

dstaddr addr Set the "other end"'s IP address in case of a Point-To-Point link, like PPP. This keyword is made obsolete by the new **pointopoint** keyword.

netmask addr Set the IP network mask for this interface. This value defaults to the usual class A, B or C network mask (as deducted from the interface IP address), but it can be set to any value for the use of subnetting.

irq addr Set the interrupt line used by this device. Many devices don't support dynamic IRQ setting.

[-]broadcast [addr] If the address argument is also given, set the protocol broadcast address for this interface. Otherwise, it only sets the **IFF_BROADCAST** flag of the interface. If the keyword was preceded by a minus **(-)** sign, then the flag is cleared instead.

[-]pointopoint [addr] This keyword enables the **point-to-point** mode of an interface, meaning that it is a direct link between two machines with nobody else listening on it (or, at least we hope that this is the case, grin :-)). If the address argument is also given, set the protocol address of the other side of the link, just like the obsolete **dstaddr** keyword does. Otherwise, it only sets the **IFF_POINTOPOINT** flag of the interface. If the keyword is preceded by a minus **(-)** sign, then the flag is cleared instead.

hw Set the hardware address of this interface, if the device driver supports this operation. The keyword must be followed by the name of the hardware class and the printable ASCII equivalent of the hardware address. Hardware classes currently supported include **ether** (Ethernet), **ax25** (AMPR AX.25), **ARCnet** and **netrom** (AMPR NET/ROM).

multicast Set the multicast flag on the interface. This should not normally be needed as the drivers set the flag correctly themselves.

address The host name or IP address (a host name will be resolved into an IP address) of that interface. This parameter is required, although the syntax doesn't currently require it.

FILES

```
/proc/net/socket
/proc/net/dev
/etc/init.d/network
```

BUGS

While AppleTalk DDP and IPX addresses will be displayed they cannot be altered by this command.

AUTHORS

Fred N. van Kempen `<waltje@uwalt.nl.mugnet.org>`, Alan Cox `<Alan.Cox@linux.org>`

IPFWADM(8)

NAME

ipfwadm IP firewall and accounting administration.

SYNOPSIS

ipfwadm -A command parameters [options]

ipfwadm -I command parameters [options]

ipfwadm -O command parameters [options]

ipfwadm -F command parameters [options]

ipfwadm -M [-l | -s] [options]

DESCRIPTION

Ipfwadm is used to set up, maintain, and inspect the IP firewall and accounting rules in the Linux kernel. These rules can be divided into 4 different categories: accounting of IP packets, the IP input firewall, the IP output firewall, and the IP forwarding firewall. For each of these categories, a separate list of rules is maintained. See *ipfw*(4) for more details.

OPTIONS

The options that are recognized by **ipfwadm** can be divided into several different groups.

CATEGORIES The following flags are used to select the category of rules to which the given command applies:

-A [*direction*] IP accounting rules. Optionally, a *direction* can be specified (*in*, *out*, or *both*), indicating whether only incoming or outgoing packets should be counted. The default direction is *both*.

-I IP input firewall rules.

-O IP output firewall rules.

-F IP forwarding firewall rules.

-M IP masquerading administration. This category can only be used in combination with the **-l** (list) or **-s** (set timeout values) command.

Exactly one of these options has to be specified.

COMMANDS The next options specify the specific action to perform. Only one of them can be specified on the command line, unless something else is listed in the description.

-a [*policy*] Append one or more rules to the end of the selected list. For the accounting chain, no policy should be specified. For firewall chains, it is required to specify one of the following policies: *accept*, *deny*, or *reject*. When the source and/or destination names resolve to more than one address, a rule will be added for each possible address combination.

-i [*policy*] Insert one or more rules at the beginning of the selected list. See the description of the **-a** command for more details.

-d [*policy*] Delete one or more entries from the selected list of rules. The semantics are equal to those of the append/insert commands. The specified parameters should exactly match the parameters given with an append or insert command, otherwise no match will be found and the rule will not be removed from the list. Only the first matching rule in the list will be deleted.

-l List all the rules in the selected list. This command may be combined with the **-z** (reset counters to zero) command. In that case, the packet and byte counters will be reset immediately after listing their current values. Unless the **-x** option is present, packet and byte counters (if listed) will be shown as *number*K or *number*M, where 1K means 1000 and 1M means 1000K (rounded to the nearest integer value). See also the **-e** and **-x** flags for more capabilities.

-z Reset the packet and byte counters of all the rules in selected list. This command may be combined with the **-l** (list) command.

-f Flush the selected list of rules.

-p *policy* Change the default policy for the selected type of firewall. The given policy has to be one of accept, deny, or reject. The default policy is used when no matching rule is found. This operation is only valid for IP firewalls, that is, in combination with the **-I**, **-O**, or **-F** flag.

-s *tcp tcpfin udp* Change the timeout values used for masquerading. This command always takes 3 parameters, representing the timeout values (in seconds) for TCP sessions, TCP sessions after receiving a FIN packet, and UDP packets, respectively. A timeout value 0 means that the current timeout value of the corresponding entry is preserved. This operation is only allowed in combination with the **-M** flag.

-c Check whether this IP packet would be accepted, denied, or rejected by the selected type of firewall. This operation is only valid for IP firewalls, that is, in combination with the **-I**, **-O**, or **-F** flag.

-h Help. Give a (currently very brief) description of the command syntax.

PARAMETERS The following parameters can be used in combination with the append, insert, delete, or check commands:

-P *protocol* The protocol of the rule or of the packet to check. The specified protocol can be one of `tcp`, `udp`, `icmp`, or all. Protocol all will match with all protocols and is taken as default when this option is omitted. All may not be used in in combination with the check command.

-S *address*[/*mask*] [*port* ...] Source specification (optional). *Address* can be either a hostname, a network name, or a plain

IP address. The *mask* can be either a network mask or a plain number, specifying the number of 1's at the left side of the network mask. Thus, a mask of *24* is equivalent with *255.255.255.0*.

The source may include one or more port specifications or ICMP types. Each of them can either be a service name, a port number, or a (numeric) ICMP type. In the rest of this paragraph, a *port* means either a port specification or an ICMP type. One of these specifications may be a range of ports, in the format *port:port*. Furthermore, the total number of ports specified with the source and destination addresses should not be greater than **IP_FW_MAX_PORTS** (currently 10). Here a port range counts as 2 ports.

Packets not being the first fragment of a TCP, UDP, or ICMP packet are always accepted by the firewall. For accounting purposes, these second and further fragments are treated specially, to be able to count them in some way. The port number 0xFFFF (65535) is used for a match with the second and further fragments of TCP or UDP packets. These packets will be treated for accounting purposes as if both their port numbers are 0xFFFF. The number 0xFF (255) is used for a match with the second and further fragments of ICMP packets. These packets will be treated for acounting purposes as if their ICMP types are 0xFF. Note that the specified command and protocol may imply restrictions on the ports to be specified. Ports may only be specified in combination with the *tcp*, *udp*, or *icmp* protocol.

When this option is omitted, the default address/mask *0.0.0.0/0* (matching with any address) is used as source address. This option is required in combination with the check command, in which case also exactly one port has to be specified.

-D *address*[*/mask*] [*port* ...] Destination specification (optional). See the desciption of the **-S** (source) flag for a detailed description of the syntax, default values, and other requirements. Note that ICMP types are not allowed in combination with the **-D** flag: ICMP types can only be specified after the the **-S** flag.

-V *address* Optional address of an interface via which a packet is received, or via which a packet is going to be sent. Address can be either a hostname or a plain IP address. When a hostname is specified, it should resolve to exactly one IP address. When this option is omitted, the address 0.0.0.0 is assumed, which has a special meaning and will match with any interface address. For the check command, this option is mandatory.

-W *name* Optional name of an interface via which a packet is received, or via which a packet is going to be sent. When this option is omitted, the empty string is assumed, which has a special meaning and will match with any interface name. For the check command, this option is mandatory.

OTHER OPTIONS The following additional options can be specified:

-b Bidirectional mode. The rule will match with IP packets in both directions. This option is only valid in combination with the append, insert, or delete commands.

-e Extended output. This option makes the list command also show the interface address and the rule options (if any). For firewall lists, also the packet and byte counters (the default is to only show these counters for the accounting rules) and the TOS masks will be listed. When used in combination with **-M**, information related to delta sequence numbers will also be listed. This option is only valid in combination with the list command.

-k Only match TCP packets with the ACK bit set (this option will be ignored for packets of other protocols). This option is only valid in combination with the append, insert, or delete command.

-m Masquerade packets accepted for forwarding. When this option is set, packets accepted by this rule will be masqueraded as if they originated from the local host. Furthermore, reverse packets will be recognized as such and they will be demasqueraded automatically, bypassing the forwarding firewall. This option is only valid in forwarding firewall rules with policy *accept* (or when specifying *accept* as default policy) and can only be used when the kernel is compiled with **CONFIG_IP_MASQUERADE** defined.

-n Numeric output. IP addresses and port numbers will be printed in numeric format. By default, the program will try to display them as host names, network names, or services (whenever applicable).

-o Turn on kernel logging of matching packets. When this option is set for a rule, the Linux kernel will print some information of all matching packets (like most IP header fields) via *printk*(). This option will only be effective when the Linux kernel is compiled with **CONFIG_IP_FIREWALL_VERBOSE** defined. This option is only valid in combination with the append, insert or delete command.

-r [*port*] Redirect packets to a local socket. When this option is set, packets accepted by this rule will be redirected to a local socket, even if they were sent to a remote host. If the specified redirection port is 0, which is the default value, the destination port of a packet will be used as the redirection port. This option is only valid in input firewall rules with policy *accept* and can only be used when the Linux kernel is compiled with **CONFIG_IP_TRANSPARENT_PROXY** defined.

-t *andmask xormask* Masks used for modifying the TOS field in the IP header. When a packet is accepted (with or without masquerading) by a firewall rule, its TOS field is first bitwise and'ed with first mask and the result of this will be bitwise xor'ed with the second mask. The masks should be specified as hexadecimal 8-bit values. This option is only valid in combination with the append, insert or delete command and will have no effect when used in combination with accounting rules or firewall rules for rejecting or denying a packet.

-v Verbose output. Print detailed information of the rule or packet to be added, deleted, or checked. This option will only have effect with the append, insert, delete, or check command.

-x Expand numbers. Display the exact value of the packet and byte counters, instead of only the rounded number in K's (multiples of 1000) or M's (multiples of 1000K). This option will only have effect when the counters are listed anyway (see also the **-e** option).

-y Only match TCP packets with the SYN bit set and the ACK bit cleared (this option will be ignored for packets of other protocols). This option is only valid in combination with the append, insert, or delete command.

FILES

```
/proc/net/ip_acct
/proc/net/ip_input
/proc/net/ip_output
/proc/net/ip_forward
/proc/net/ip_masquerade
```

SEE ALSO

ipfw(4)

AUTHOR

Jos Vos `<jos@xos.nl>`

X/OS Experts in Open Systems BV, Amsterdam, The Netherlands

LPD(8)

NAME

lpd Line printer spooler daemon.

SYNOPSIS

lpd [-l] [*port#*]

DESCRIPTION

lpd is the line printer daemon (spool area handler) and is normally invoked at boot time from the `rc`(8) file. It makes a single pass through the `printcap`(5) file to find out about the existing printers and prints any files left after a crash. It then uses the system calls `listen`(2) and `accept`(2) to receive requests to print files in the queue, transfer files to the spooling area, display the queue, or remove jobs from the queue. In each case, it forks a child to handle the request so the parent can continue to listen for more requests.

OPTIONS

`-l` The `-l` flag causes **lpd** to log valid requests received from the network. This can be useful for debugging purposes.

port# The Internet port number used to rendezvous with other processes is normally obtained with `getservbyname(3)` but can be changed with the *port#* argument.

Access control is provided by two means. First, all requests must come from one of the machines listed in the file `/etc/hosts.equiv` or `/etc/hosts.lpd`. Second, if the `rs` capability is specified in the `printcap` entry for the printer being accessed, *lpr* requests will only be honored for those users with accounts on the machine with the printer.

The file *minfree* in each spool directory contains the number of disk blocks to leave free so that the line printer queue won't completely fill the disk. The *minfree* file can be edited with your favorite text editor.

The daemon begins processing files after it has successfully set the lock for exclusive access (descibed a bit later), and scans the spool directory for files beginning with *cf*. Lines in each *cf* file specify files to be printed or non-printing actions to be performed. Each such line begins with a key character to specify what to do with the remainder of the line.

J Job Name. String to be used for the job name on the burst page.

C Classification. String to be used for the classification line on the burst page.

L Literal. The line contains identification info from the password file and causes the banner page to be printed.

T Title. String to be used as the title for `pr(1)`.

H Host Name. Name of the machine where `lpr` was invoked.

P Person. Login name of the person who invoked `lpr`. This is used to verify ownership by `lprm`.

M Send mail to the specified user when the current print job completes.

f Formatted File. Name of a file to print which is already formatted.

l Like "f" but passes control characters and does not make page breaks.

p Name of a file to print using `pr(1)` as a filter.

t Troff File. The file contains `troff(1)` output (cat phototypesetter commands).

n	Ditroff File. The file contains device independent troff output.
r	DVI File. The file contains Tex l output DVI format from Stanford.
g	Graph File. The file contains data produced by `plot(3)`.
c	Cifplot File. The file contains data produced by *cifplot*.
v	The file contains a raster image.
r	The file contains text data with FORTRAN carriage control characters.
1	Troff Font R. Name of the font file to use instead of the default.
2	Troff Font I. Name of the font file to use instead of the default.
3	Troff Font B. Name of the font file to use instead of the default.
4	Troff Font S. Name of the font file to use instead of the default.
W	Width. Changes the page width (in characters) used by `pr(1)` and the text filters.
I	Indent. The number of characters to indent the output by (in ascii).
U	Unlink. Name of file to remove upon completion of printing.
N	File name. The name of the file which is being printed, or a blank for the standard input (when `lpr` is invoked in a pipeline).

If a file can not be opened, a message will be logged via `syslog(3)` using the *LOG_LPR* facility. **Lpd** will try up to 20 times to reopen a file it expects to be there, after which it will skip the file to be printed.

Lpd uses `flock(2)` to provide exclusive access to the lock file and to prevent multiple deamons from becoming active simultaneously. If the daemon should be killed or die unexpectedly, the lock file need not be removed. The lock file is kept in a readable ASCII form and contains two lines. The first is the process id of the daemon and the second is the control file name of the current job being printed. The second line is updated to reflect the current status of **lpd** for the programs lpq(1) and lprm(1).

FILES

/etc/printcap	printer description file
/var/spool/*	spool directories
/var/spool/*/minfree	minimum free space to leave
/dev/lp*	line printer devices
/dev/printer	socket for local requests
/etc/hosts.equiv	lists machine names allowed printer access
/etc/hosts.lpd	lists machine names allowed printer access, but not under same administrative control.

SEE ALSO

lpc(8), pac(1), lpr(1), lpq(1), lprm(1), syslog(3), printcap(5)

4.2 BSD Line Printer Spooler Manual.

HISTORY

An **lpd** daemon appeared in Version 6 AT&T UNIX.

MKE2FS(8)

NAME

mke2fs Create a Linux second extended file system.

SYNOPSIS

mke2fs [**-c** | **-l** *filename*] [**-b** *block-size*] [**-f** *fragment-size*]
[**-i** *bytes-per-inode*] [**-m** *reserved-blockspercentage*]
[**-o** *creator-os*] [**-q**] [**-r fs-revisionlevel**] [**-R raid_options**]
[**-s sparse-super-flag**] [**-v**] [**-F**] [**-L** *volume-label*]
[**-M** *last-mounted-directory*] [**-S**] *device* [*blocks-count*]

DESCRIPTION

mke2fs is used to create a Linux second extended file system on a device (usually a disk partition).

device is the special file corresponding to the device (e.g /dev/hdXX).

blocks-count is the number of blocks on the device. If omitted, **mke2fs** automagically figures the file system size.

OPTIONS

-b block-size Specify the size of blocks in bytes.

-c Check the device for bad blocks before creating the file system, using a fast read-only test.

-f fragment-size Specify the size of fragments in bytes.

-i bytes-per-inode Specify the bytes/inode ratio. **mke2fs** creates an inode for every bytes-per-inode bytes of space on the disk. This value defaults to 4096 bytes. bytes-per-inode must be at least 1024.

-l filename Read the bad blocks list from filename

-m reserved-blocks-percentage Specify the percentage of reserved blocks for the superuser. This value defaults to 5%.

-o Manually override the default value of the "creator os" field of the filesystem. Normally the creator field is set by default to the native OS of the mke2fs executable.

-q Quiet execution. Useful if mke2fs is run in a script.

-s sparse-super-flag If sparse-super-flag is 1, then turn on the sparse superblock flag. If 0, then turn off the sparse superblock flag. (Currently, the sparse superblock flag defaults to off.) **Warning:** The Linux 2 kernel does not properly support this feature. Neither do all Linux 2.1 kernels; please don't use this unless you know what you're doing!

-v Verbose execution.

-F Force mke2fs to run, even if the specified device is not a block special device.

-L Set the volume label for the filesystem.

-M Set the last mounted directory for the filesystem. This might be useful for the sake of utilities that key off of the last mounted directory to determine where the filesytem should be mounted.

-r revision Set the filesystem revision for the new filesystem. Note that 1.2 kernels only support revision 0 filesystems.

-R raid_options Set RAID-related options for the filesystem. RAID options are comma separated, and may take an argument using the equals ('=') sign. Currently the only supported argument is stride which takes as its argument the number of blocks in a RAID stripe.

-S Write superblock and group descriptors only. This is useful if all of the superblock and backup superblocks are corrupted, and a last-ditch recovery method is desired. It causes **mke2fs** to reinitialize the superblock and group descriptors, while not touching the inode table and the block and inode bitmaps. The **e2fsck** program should be run immediately after this option is used, and there is no guarantee that any data will be salvageable.

BUGS

mke2fs accepts the -f option but currently ignores it because the second extended file system does not support fragments yet.

There may be some other ones. Please, report them to the author.

AVAILABILITY

mke2fs is available for anonymous ftp from ftp.ibp.fr and tsx-11.mit.edu in `/pub/linux/packages/ext2fs`.

SEE ALSO

dumpe2fs(8), **e2fsck**(8), **tune2fs**(8)

AUTHOR

This version of **mke2fs** has been written by Theodore Ts'o <tytso@mit.edu>.

MKSWAP(8)

NAME

mkswap Set up a Linux swap area.

SYNOPSIS

mkswap [-c] *device* [size-in-blocks]

DESCRIPTION

mkswap sets up a Linux swap area on a device or in a file.

The *device* is usually of the following form:

/dev/hda[1-8]

/dev/hdb[1-8]

/dev/sda[1-8]

/dev/sdb[1-8]

The *size-in-blocks* parameter is the desired size of the file system, in blocks. This information is determined automatically by **mkswap** if it is omitted. Block counts are rounded down so that the total size is an integer multiple of the machine's page size. Only block counts in the range MINCOUNT..MAXCOUNT are allowed. If the block count exceeds the MAXCOUNT, it is truncated to that value and a warning message is issued.

The MINCOUNT and MAXCOUNT values for a swap area are

MINCOUNT = 10 * PAGE_SIZE / 1024

MAXCOUNT = (PAGE_SIZE - 10) * 8 * PAGE_SIZE / 1024

For example, on a machine with 4kB pages (e.g., x86), we get:

MINCOUNT = 10 * 4096 / 1024 = 40

MAXCOUNT = (4096 - 10) * 8 * 4096 / 1024 = 130752

As each block is 1kB large, the swap area in this example could have a size that is anywhere in the range from 40kB up to 127.6875MB.

If you don't know the page size that your machine uses, you may be able to look it up with "cat /proc/cpuinfo."

The reason for the limit on MAXCOUNT is that a single page is used to hold the swap bitmap at the start of the swap area, where each bit represents a single page. The reason for the -10, is that the signature is "SWAP-SPACE"--10 characters.

To setup a swap file, it is necessary to create that file before running **mkswap.** A sequence of commands similar to the following is reasonable for this purpose:

```
# dd if=/dev/zero of=swapfile bs=1024 count=8192

# mkswap swapfile 8192

# sync

# swapon swapfile
```

Note that a swap file must not contain any holes (so, using **cp**(1) to create the file is not acceptable).

OPTIONS

-c Check the device for bad blocks before creating the file system. If any are found, the count is printed. This option is meant to be used for swap partitions **only**, and should **not** be used for regular files! To make sure that regular files do not contain bad blocks, the partition that contains the regular file should have been created with **mkfs -c**.

SEE ALSO

fsck(8), **mkfs**(8), **fdisk**(8)

AUTHOR

Linus Torvalds <torvalds@cs.helsinki.fi>

MOUNT(8)

NAME

mount Mounts a file system.

SYNOPSIS

mount [-hV]

mount -a [-fFnrvw] [**-t** vfstype]

mount [-fnrvw] [**-o** *options* **[,...]**] *device* | *dir*

mount [-fnrvw] [**-t** *vfstype]* [**-o** *options] device dir*

DESCRIPTION

All files accessible in a Unix system are arranged in one big tree, the file hierarchy, rooted at /. These files can be spread out over several devices. The **mount** command serves to attach the file system found on some device to the big file tree. Conversely, the **umount(8)** command will detach it again.

The standard form of the **mount** command, is

mount -t *type device dir*

This tells the kernel to attach the file system found on *device* (which is of type *type*) at the directory *dir*. The previous contents (if any) and owner and mode of *dir* become invisible, and as long as this file system remains mounted, the pathname *dir* refers to the root of the file system on *device*.

Three forms of invocation do not actually mount anything:

mount -h prints a help message

mount -V prints a version string; and just

mount [-t *type]* lists all mounted file systems (of type *type*). See below.

The proc file system is not associated with a special device, and when mounting it, an arbitrary keyword, such as *proc* can be used instead of a device specification. (The customary choice *none* is less fortunate: the error message 'none busy' from **umount** can be confusing.)

Most devices are indicated by a file name (of a block special device), like */dev/sda1*, but there are other possibilities. For example, in the case of an NFS mount, *device* may look like *knuth.cwi.nl:/dir*.

The file */etc/fstab* (see **fstab**(5)), may contain lines describing what devices are usually mounted where, using which options. This file is used in three ways:

(i) The command

mount -a [**-t** *type*]

(usually given in a bootscript) causes all filesystems mentioned in *fstab* (of the proper type) to be mounted as indicated, except for those whose line contains the **noauto** keyword. Adding the **-F** option will make mount fork, so that the filesystems are mounted simultaneously.

(ii) When mounting a filesystem mentioned in fstab, it suffices to give only the device, or only the mount point.

(iii) Normally, only the superuser can mount file systems. However, when *fstab* contains the **user** option on a line, then anybody can mount the corresponding system.

Thus, given a line

/dev/cdrom /cd iso9660 ro,user,noauto,unhide

any user can mount the iso9660 file system found on his CDROM using the command

mount /dev/cdrom

or

mount /cd

For more details, see fstab(5).

The programs **mount** and **umount** maintain a list of currently mounted file systems in the file */etc/mtab*. If no arguments are given to **mount**, this list is printed. When the *proc* filesystem is mounted (say at */proc*), the files */etc/mtab* and */proc/mounts* have very similar contents. The former has somewhat more information, such as the mount options used, but is not necessarily up-to-date (cf. the **-n** option below). It is possible to replace */etc/mtab* by a symbolic link to */proc/mounts*, but some information is lost that way, and in particular working with the loop device will be less convenient.

OPTIONS

The full set of options used by an invocation of **mount** is determined by first extracting the options for the file system from the *fstab* table, then applying any options specified by the **-o** argument, and finally applying a **-r** or **-w** option, when present.

Options available for the mount command:

-V Output version.

-h Print a help message.

-v Verbose mode.

-a Mount all filesystems (of the given types) mentioned in *fstab*.

-F (Used in conjunction with **-a**.) Fork off a new incarnation of mount for each device. This will do the mounts on different devices in parallel. This has the advantage that it is faster; also NFS timeouts go in parallel. A disadvantage is that the mounts are done in undefined order. Thus, you cannot use this option if you want to mount both */usr* and */usr/spool*.

-f Causes everything to be done except for the actual system call; if it's not obvious, this "fakes" mounting the file system. This option is useful in conjunction with the **-v** flag to determine what the **mount** command is trying to do. It can also be used to add entries for devices that were mounted earlier with the -n option.

-n Mount without writing in */etc/mtab*. This is necessary for example when */etc* is on a read-only file system.

-r Mount the file system read-only. A synonym is **-o ro**.

-w Mount the file system read/write. This is the default. A synonym is **-o rw**.

-t *vfstype* The argument following the **-t** is used to indicate the file system type. The file system types which are currently supported are listed in *linux/fs/filesystems.c*: *minix*, *ext*, *ext2*, *xiafs*, *hpfs*, *msdos*, *umsdos*, *vfat*, *proc*, *nfs*, *iso9660*, *smbfs*, *ncpfs*, *affs*, *ufs*, *romfs*, *sysv*, *xenix*, *coherent*. Note that the last three are equivalent and that *xenix* and *coherent* will be removed at some point in the future--use *sysv* instead. Since kernel version 2.1.21 the types *ext* and *xiafs* do not exist anymore.

The type *iso9660* is the default. If no **-t** option is given, or if the **auto** type is specified, the superblock is probed for the filesystem type (*minix*, *ext*, *ext2*, *xiafs*, *iso9660*, *romfs* are supported). If this probe fails and */proc/filesystems* exists, then all of the filesystems listed there will be tried, except for those that are labeled "nodev" (e.g., *proc* and *nfs*).

Note that the auto type may be useful for usermounted floppies.

WARNING

The probing uses a heuristic (the presence of appropriate 'magic'), and could recognize the wrong filesystem type.

More than one type may be specified in a comma separated list. The list of file system types can be prefixed with **no** to specify the file system types on which no action should be taken. (This can be meaningful with the **-a** option.)

For example, the command

```
mount -a -t nomsdos,ext
```

mounts all file systems except those of type *msdos* and *ext*.

-o Options are specified with a -o flag followed by a comma separated string of options. Some of these options are only useful when they appear in the */etc/fstab* file. The following options apply to any file system that is being mounted:

async All I/O to the file system should be done asynchronously.

atime Update inode access time for each access. This is the default.

auto Can be mounted with the -a option.

defaults Use default options: **rw**, **suid**, **dev**, **exec**, **auto**, **nouser**, and **async.**

dev Interpret character or block special devices on the file system.

exec Permit execution of binaries.

noatime Do not update inode access times on this file system (e.g, for faster access on the news spool to speed up news servers).

noauto Can only be mounted explicitly (i.e., the **-a** option will not cause the file system to be mounted).

nodev Do not interpret character or block special devices on the file system.

noexec Do not allow execution of any binaries on the mounted file system. This option might be useful for a server that has file systems containing binaries for architectures other than its own.

nosuid Do not allow set-user-identifier or setgroup-identifier bits to take effect.

nouser Forbid an ordinary (i.e., non-root) user to mount the file system. This is the default.

remount Attempt to remount an already-mounted file system. This is commonly used to change the mount flags for a file system, especially to make a read-only file system writeable.

ro Mount the file system read-only.

rw Mount the file system read-write.

suid Allow set-user-identifier or set-group-identifier bits to take effect.

sync All I/O to the file system should be done synchronously.

user Allow an ordinary user to mount the file system. This option implies the options **noexec**, **nosuid**, and **nodev** (unless overridden by subsequent options, as in the option line **user,exec,dev,suid**).

FILESYSTEM SPECIFIC MOUNT OPTIONS

The following options apply only to certain file systems. We sort them by file system. They all follow the **-o** flag.

MOUNT OPTIONS FOR AFFS

uid=*value* and **gid=***value* Set the owner and group of the root of the file system (default: **uid**=**gid**=0, but with option uid or gid without specified value, the uid and gid of the current process are taken).

setuid=*value* and **setgid=***value* Set the owner and group of all files.

mode=*value* Set the mode of all files to *value* & 0777 disregarding the original permissions. Add search permission to directories that have read permission. The value is given in octal.

protect Do not allow any changes to the protection bits on the file system.

usemp Set uid and gid of the root of the file system to the uid and gid of the mount point upon the first sync or umount, and then clear this option. Strange...

verbose Print an informational message for each successful mount.

prefix=*string* Prefix used before volume name, when following a link.

volume=*string* Prefix (of length at most 30) used before '/' when following a symbolic link.

reserved=*value* (Default: 2.) Number of unused blocks at the start of the device.

root=*value* Give explicitly the location of the root block.

bs=*value* Give blocksize. Allowed values are 512, 1024, 2048, 4096.

grpquota / noquota / quota / usrquota These options are accepted but ignored.

MOUNT OPTIONS FOR COHERENT

None.

MOUNT OPTIONS FOR EXT

None. Note that the 'ext' file system is obsolete. Don't use it. Since Linux version 2.1.21 extfs is no longer part of the kernel source.

MOUNT OPTIONS FOR EXT2

The 'ext2' file system is the standard Linux file system. Due to a kernel bug, it may be mounted with random mount options (fixed in Linux 2.0.4).

bsddf / minixdf Set the behaviour for the *statfs* system call. The **minixdf** behaviour is to return in the *f_blocks* field the total number of blocks of the file system, while the **bsddf** behaviour (which is the default) is to subtract the overhead blocks used by the ext2 file system and not available for file storage. Thus

```
% mount /k -o minixdf; df /k; umount /k
```

Filesystem 1024-blocks Used Available Capacity Mounted on

```
/dev/sda6    2630655 86954 2412169    3% /k
% mount /k -o bsddf; df /k; umount /k
```

Filesystem 1024-blocks Used Available Capacity Mounted on

```
/dev/sda6    2543714    13 2412169    0% /k
```

NOTE

This example shows that one can add command line options to the options given in ***/etc/fstab*****.**

check / check=normal / check=strict Set checking level. When at least one of these options is set (and **check=normal** is set by default) the inodes and blocks bitmaps are checked upon mount (which can take half a minute or so on a big disk). With strict checking, block deallocation checks that the block to free is in the data zone.

check=none / nocheck No checking is done.

debug Print debugging info upon each (re)mount.

errors=continue / errors=remount-ro / errors=panic Define the behaviour when an error is encountered. (Either ignore errors and just mark the file system erroneous and continue, or remount the file system read-only, or panic and halt the system.) The default is set in the filesystem superblock, and can be changed using **tune2fs**(8).

grpid or **bsdgroups / nogrpid** or **sysvgroups** These options define what group id a newly created file gets. When **grpid** is set, it takes the group id of the directory in which it is created; otherwise (the default) it takes the fsgid of the current process, unless the directory has the setgid bit set, in which case it takes the gid from the parent directory, and also gets the setgid bit set if it is a directory itself.

resgid=*n* and **resuid**=*n* The ext2 file system reserves a certain percentage of the available space (by default 5%, see **mke2fs**(8) and **tune2fs**(8)). These options determine who can use the reserved blocks. (Roughly: whoever has the specified uid, or belongs to the specified group.)

sb=*n* Instead of block 1, use block n as superblock. This could be useful when the filesystem has been damaged. Usually, copies of the superblock are found every 8192 blocks: in block 1, 8193, 16385, ... (Thus, one gets hundreds or even thousands of copies of the superblock on a big filesystem. I do not know of options to mke2fs that would cause fewer copies to be written.)

grpquota / noquota / quota / usrquota These options are accepted but ignored.

MOUNT OPTIONS FOR FAT

NOTE

***Fat* is not a separate filesystem, but a common part of the *msdos*, *umsdos* and *vfat* filesystems.)**

blocksize=512 / blocksize=1024 Set blocksize (default 512).

uid=*value* and **gid=***value* Set the owner and group of all files. (Default: the uid and gid of the current process.)

umask=*value* Set the umask (the bitmask of the permissions that are **not** present). The default is the umask of the current process. The value is given in octal.

check=*value* Three different levels of pickyness can be chosen:

r[elaxed] Upper- and lowercase are accepted and equivalent, long name parts are truncated (e.g. *verylongname.foobar* becomes *verylong.foo*), leading and embedded spaces are accepted in each name part (name and extension).

n[ormal] Like "relaxed," but many special characters (*, ?, <, spaces, etc.) are rejected. This is the default.

s[trict] Like "normal," but names may not contain long parts and special characters that are sometimes used on Linux, but are not accepted by MS-DOS are rejected. (+, =, spaces, etc.)

conv=b[inary] / conv=t[ext] / conv=a[uto] The *fat* file system can perform CRLF<-->NL (MS-DOS text format to UNIX text format) conversion in the kernel. The following conversion modes are available:

binary no translation is performed. This is the default.

text CRLF<-->NL translation is performed on all files.

auto CRLF<-->NL translation is performed on all files that don't have a "well-known binary" extension. The list of known extensions can be found at the beginning of *fs/fat/misc.c* (as of 2.0, the list is: exe, com, bin, app, sys, drv, ovl, ovr, obj, lib, dll, pif, arc, zip, lha, lzh, zoo, tar, z, arj, tz, taz, tzp, tpz, gz, tgz, deb, gif, bmp, tif, gl, jpg, pcx, tfm, vf, gf, pk, pxl, dvi).

Programs that do computed lseeks won't like in-kernel text conversion. Several people have had their data ruined by this translation. Beware!

For file systems mounted in binary mode, a conversion tool (fromdos/todos) is available.

debug Turn on the debug flag. A version string and a list of file system parameters will be printed (these data are also printed if the parameters appear to be inconsistent).

fat=12 / fat=16 Specify either a 12 bit fat or a 16 bit fat. This overrides the automatic FAT type detection routine. Use with caution!

quiet Turn on the quiet flag. Attempts to chown or chmod files do not return errors, although they fail. Use with caution!

sys_immutable, showexec, dots, nodots, dotsOK=[yes|no] Various misguided attempts to force Unix or DOS conventions onto a FAT file system.

MOUNT OPTIONS FOR HPFS

uid=*value* and **gid=***value* Set the owner and group of all files. (Default: the uid and gid of the current process.)

umask=*value* Set the umask (the bitmask of the permissions that are not present). The default is the umask of the current process. The value is given in octal.

case=lower / case=asis Convert all files names to lowercase, or leave them. (Default: case=lower.)

conv=binary / conv=text / conv=auto For **conv=text**, delete some random CRs (in particular, all followed by NL) when reading a file. For **conv=auto**, choose more or less at randomly between **conv=binary** and **conv=text**. For **conv=binary**, just read what is in the file. This is the default.

nocheck Do not abort mounting when certain consistency checks fail.

MOUNT OPTIONS FOR ISO9660

Normal *iso9660* filenames appear in a 8.3 format (i.e., DOS-like restrictions on filename length), and in addition all characters are in uppercase. Also there is no field for file ownership, protection, number of links, provision for block/character devices, etc.

Rock Ridge is an extension to iso9660 that provides all of these Unix-like features. Basically there are extensions to each directory record that supply all of the additional information, and when Rock Ridge is in use, the filesystem is indistinguishable from a normal Unix file system (except that it is read-only, of course).

norock Disable the use of RockRidge extensions, even if available. Cf. **map**.

check=r[elaxed] / check=s[trict] With **check=relaxed**, a filename is first converted to lowercase before doing the lookup. This is probably only meaningful together with **norock** and **map=normal**. (Default: **check=strict**.)

uid=*value* and **gid=***value* Give all files in the file system the indicated user or group id, possibly overriding the information found in the Rock Ridge extensions. (Default: **uid=0,gid=0**.)

map=n[ormal] / map=o[ff] For non-Rock Ridge volumes, normal name translation maps upper- to lowercase ASCII, drops a trailing ';1', and converts ';' to '.'. With **map=off** no name translation is done. See **norock**. (Default: **map=normal**.)

mode=*value* For non-Rock Ridge volumes, give all files the indicated mode. (Default: read permission for everybody.) Since Linux 2.1.37 one no longer needs to specify the mode in decimal. (Octal is indicated by a leading 0.)

unhide Also show hidden and associated files.

block=[512|1024|2048] Set the block size to the indicated value. (Default: **block=1024**.)

conv=a[uto] / conv=b[inary] / conv=m[text] / conv=t[ext] (Default: **conv=binary**.) Since Linux 1.3.54 this option has no effect. (And non-binary settings used to be very dangerous, often leading to silent data corruption.)

cruft If the high byte of the file length contains other garbage, set this mount option to ignore the high order bits of the file length. This implies that a file cannot be larger than 16MB. The **cruft** option is set automatically if the entire CDROM has a weird size (negative, or more than 800MB). It is also set when volume sequence numbers other than 0 or 1 are seen.

MOUNT OPTIONS FOR MINUX

None.

MOUNT OPTIONS FOR MS-DOS

See mount options for FAT. If the *msdos* file system detects an inconsistency, it reports an error and sets the file system read-only. The file system can be made writeable again by remounting it.

MOUNT OPTIONS FOR NCP

Just like *nfs*, the *ncp* implementation expects a binary argument (a *struct ncp_mount_data*) to the mount system call. This argument is constructed by ncpmount(8) and the current version of **mount** (2.6h) does not know anything about ncp.

MOUNT OPTIONS FOR NFS

Instead of a textual option string, parsed by the kernel, the *nfs* filesystem expects a binary argument of type *struct nfs_mount_data*. The program **mount** itself parses the following options of the form 'tag=value', and puts them in the structure mentioned: **rsize=n, wsize=n, timeo=n, retrans=n, acregmin=n, acregmax=n, acdirmin=n, acdirmax=n, actimeo=n, retry=n, port=n, mountport=n, mounthost=name, mountprog=n, mountvers=n, nfsprog=n, nfsvers=n, namlen=n.** The option **addr=n** is accepted but ignored. Also the following Boolean options, possibly preceded by **no** are recognized: **bg**, **fg**, **soft**, **hard**, **intr**, **posix**, **cto**, **ac**, **tcp**, **udp**, **lock**. For details, see **nfs**(5).

Especially useful options include

rsize=8192,wsize=8192 This will make your nfs connection much faster than with the default buffer size of 1024.

hard The program accessing a file on a NFS mounted file system will hang when the server crashes. The process cannot be interrupted or killed unless you also specify **intr**. When the NFS server is back online the program will continue undisturbed from where it was. This is probably what you want.

soft This option allows the kernel to time out if the nfs server is not responding for some time. The time can be specified with **timeo=time**. This option might be useful if your nfs server sometimes doesn't respond or will be rebooted while some process tries to get a file from the server. Usually it just causes lots of trouble.

nolock Do not use locking. Do not start lockd.

MOUNT OPTIONS FOR PROC

uid=*value* and **gid=***value* These options are recognized, but have no effect as far as I can see.

MOUNT OPTIONS FOR ROMFS

None.

MOUNT OPTIONS FOR SMBFS

Just like *nfs*, the *smb* implementation expects a binary argument (a *struct smb_mount_data*) to the mount system call. This argument is constructed by **smbmount**(8) and the current version of **mount** (2.6c) does not know anything about smb.

MOUNT OPTIONS FOR SYSV

None.

MOUNT OPTIONS FOR UFS

None.

MOUNT OPTIONS FOR UMSDOS

See mount options for ms-dos. The **dotsOK** option is explicitly killed by *umsdos*.

MOUNT OPTIONS FOR VFAT

First of all, the mount options for *fat* are recognized. The **dotsOK** option is explicitly killed by *vfat*. Furthermore, there are

uni_xlate Translate unhandled Unicode characters to special escaped sequences. This lets you backup and restore filenames that are created with any Unicode characters. Without this option, a '?' is used when no translation is possible. The escape character is ':' because it is otherwise illegal on the vfat filesystem. The escape sequence that gets used, where u is the unicode character, is: ':', (u & 0x3f), ((u>>6) & 0x3f), (u>>12).

posix Allow two files with names that only differ in case.

nonumtail First try to make a short name without sequence number, before trying *name~num.ext*.

MOUNT OPTIONS FOR XENIX

None.

MOUNT OPTIONS FOR XIAFS

None. Although nothing is wrong with xiafs, it is not used much, and is not maintained. Probably one shouldn't use it. Since Linux version 2.1.21 xiafs is no longer part of the kernel source.

THE LOOP DEVICE

One further possible type is a mount via the loop device. For example, the command

mount /tmp/fdimage /mnt -t msdos -o loop=/dev/loop3,blocksize=1024

will set up the loop device /dev/loop3 to correspond to the file */tmp/fdimage*, and then mount this device on */mnt*. This type of mount knows about three options, namely **loop**, **offset** and **encryption**, that are really options to **losetup(8)**. If no explicit loop device is mentioned (but just an option '**-o loop**' is given), then **mount** will try to find some unused loop device and use that.

FILES

`/etc/fstab` file system table

`/etc/mtab` table of mounted file systems

`/etc/mtab~` lock file

`/etc/mtab.tmp` temporary file

SEE ALSO

mount(2), **umount**(2), **fstab**(5), **umount**(8), **swapon**(8), **nfs**(5), **mountd**(8), **nfsd**(8), **mke2fs**(8), **tune2fs**(8), **losetup**(8)

BUGS

It is possible for a corrupted file system to cause a crash.

Some Linux file systems don't support **-o sync** (the ext2fs *does* support synchronous updates [a la BSD] when mounted with the **sync** option).

The **-o remount** may not be able to change mount parameters (all *ext2fs*-specific parameters, except **sb**, are changeable with a remount, for example, but you can't change **gid** or **umask** for the *fatfs*).

HISTORY

A **mount** command appeared in Version 6 AT&T Unix.

NETSTAT(8)

NAME

netstat Display network connections, routing tables, interface statistics and masquerade connections.

SYNOPSIS

netstat [-venaoc] [--tcp|-t] [--udp|-u] [--raw|-w] [--unix|-u] [--inet|--ip] [--ax25] [--ipx] [--netrom]

netstat [-veenc] [--inet] [--ipx] [--netrom] [--ddp] [--ax25] {--route|-r}

netstat [-veenac] {--interfaces|-i} [*iface*]

netstat [-enc] {--masquerade|-M}

netstat {--statistics|-s}

netstat {-V|--version} {-h|--help}

DESCRIPTION

netstat displays information of the Linux networking subsystem.

(no option) You can view the status of network connections by listing the open sockets. This is the default operation: If you don't specify any address families, then the active sockets of all configured address families will be printed. With **-e** you get some additional information (userid). With the **-v** switch you can make **netstat** complain about known address families which are not supported by the kernel. The **-o** option displays some additional information on networking timers. **-a** print all sockets, including the listening server sockets. The address family **inet** will display raw, udp and tcp sockets.

-r, --route With the **-r, --route** option, you get the kernel routing tables in the same format as **route -e** use. **netstat -er** will use the output format of **route**. Please see **route**(8) for details.

-i, --interface iface If you use the **-i, --interfaces** option, a table of all (or the specified *iface*) networking interfaces will be printed. The output uses the **ifconfig -e** format, and is described in **ifconfig**(8). **netstat -ei** will print a table or a single interface entry just like **ifconfig** does. With the **-a** switch, you can include interfaces which are not configured (i.e. don't have the **U=UP** flag set).

-M, --masquerade A list of all masqueraded sessions can be viewed, too. With the **-e** switch you can include some more information about sequence numbering and deltas, caused by data rewrites on FTP sessions (PORT command). Masquerade support is used to hide hosts with unofficial network addresses from the outside world, as described in ipfw(4),ipfwadm(8) and, ipfw(8).

-s, --statistics Displays statistics about the networking subsystem of the Linux Kernel which are read from */proc/net/snmp*.

OPTIONS

-v, --verbose Tells the user what is going on by being verbose. Especially print some useful informations about unconfigured address families.

-n, --numeric Shows numerical addresses instead of trying to determine symbolic host, port or user names.

-A, --af family Use a different method to set the address families. *family* is a comma (',') seperated list of address family keywords like **inet**, **unix**, **ipx**, **ax25**, **netrom** and **ddp**. This has the same effect as using the long options **--inet**, **--unix**, **--ipx**, **--ax25**, **--netrom** and **--ddp**.

-c, --continous This will cause **netstat** to print the selected table every second continously on the screen until you interrupt it.

OUTPUT

ACTIVE INTERNET CONNECTIONS (TCP, UDP, RAW)

Proto The protocol (tcp, udp, raw) used by the socket.

Recv-Q The count of bytes not copied by the user program connected to this socket.

Send-Q The count of bytes not acknoledged by the remote host.

Local Address The local address (local hostname) and port number of the socket. Unless the -n switch is given, the socket address is resolved to its canonical hostname, and the port number is translated into the corresponding service name.

Foreign Address The remote address (remote hostname) and port number of the socket. As with the local address:port, the -n switch turns off hostname and service name resolution.

State The state of the socket. Since there are no states in RAW and usually no states used in UDP, this row may be left blank. Normally this can be one of several values:

ESTABLISHED The socket has an established connection.

SYN_SENT The socket is actively attempting to establish a connection.

SYN_RECV The connection is being initialized.

FIN_WAIT1 The socket is closed, and the connection is shutting down.

FIN_WAIT2 Connection is closed, and the socket is waiting for a shutdown from the remote end.

TIME_WAIT The socket is waiting after close for remote shutdown retransmission.

CLOSED The socket is not being used.

CLOSE_WAIT The remote end has shut down, waiting for the socket to close.

LAST_ACK The remote end shut down, and the socket is closed. Waiting for acknowledgement.

LISTEN The socket is listening for incoming connections. Those sockets are only displayed if the **-a,--listening** switch is set.

CLOSING Both sockets are shut down but we still don't have all our data sent.

UNKNOWN The state of the socket is unknown.

User The name or the UID of the owner of the socket.

Timer (This needs to be written.)

ACTIVE UNIX DOMAIN SOCKETS

Proto The protocol (usually unix) used by the socket.

RefCnt The reference count (i.e. attached processes via this socket).

Flags The flags displayed are SO_ACCEPTON (displayed as **ACC**), SO_WAITDATA (**W**) or SO_NOSPACE (**N**). SO_ACCECPTON is used on unconnected sockets if their corresponding processes are waiting for a connect request. The other flags are not of normal interest.

Type There are several types of socket access:

SOCK_DGRAM The socket is used in Datagram (connectionless) mode.

SOCK_STREAM This is a stream (connection) socket.

SOCK_RAW The socket is used as a raw socket.

SOCK_RDM This one serves reliably-delivered messages.

SOCK_SEQPACKET This is a sequential packet socket.

SOCK_PACKET RAW interface access socket.

UNKNOWN Who ever knows, what the future will bring us--just fill in here :-)

State This field will contain one of the following Keywords:

FREE The socket is not allocated

LISTENING The socket is listening for a connection request. Those sockets are only displayed if the -a,--listening switch is set.

CONNECTING The socket is about to establish a connection.

CONNECTED The socket is connected.

DISCONNECTING The socket is disconnecting.

(empty) The socket is not connected to another one.

UNKNOWN This state should never happen.

Path This displays the path name at which the corresponding processes attached to the socket.

Active IPX sockets (This needs to be done by somebody who knows it.)

Active NET/ROM sockets (This needs to be done by somebody who knows it.)

Active AX.25 sockets (This needs to be done by somebody who knows it.)

FILES

/etc/services The services translation file.

/proc/net/dev Devices information.

/proc/net/snmp Networking statistics.

/proc/net/raw RAW socket information.

/proc/net/tcp TCP socket information.

/proc/net/udp UDP socket information.

/proc/net/unix Unix domain socket information.

/proc/net/ipx IPX socket information.

/proc/net/ax25 AX25 socket information.

/proc/net/appeltalk DDP (appletalk) socket information.

/proc/net/nr NET/ROM socket information.

/proc/net/route Kernel IP routing information.

/proc/net/ax25_route Kernel AX25 routing information.

/proc/net/ipx_route Kernel IPX routing information.

/proc/net/nr_nodes Kernel NET/ROM nodelist.

/proc/net/nr_neigh Kernel NET/ROM neighbors.

/proc/net/ip_masquerade Kernel masqueraded connections.

SEE ALSO

route(8), **ifconfig**(8), **ipfw**(4), **ipfw**(8), **ipfwadm**(8)

BUGS

Occasionally strange information may appear if a socket changes as it is viewed. This is unlikely to occur. The **netstat -i** options is described as it should work after some code cleanup of the BETA release of the nettools package.

AUTHORS

The netstat user interface was written by Fred Baumgarten `<dc6iq@insu1.etec.uni-karlsruhe.de>`, the man page basically by Matt Welsh `<mdw@tc.cornell.edu>`. It was updated by Alan Cox `<Alan.Cox@linux.org>` but could do with a bit more work.

The man page and the command included in the net-tools package is totally rewritten from Bernd Eckenfels <ecki@linux.de>.

PING(8)

NAME

ping Send ICMP ECHO_REQUEST packets to network hosts.

SYNOPSIS

ping [**-dfnqrvR**] [-c *count*] [**-i** *wait*]
[**-l** *preload*] [**-p** *pattern*] [**-s** *packetsize*]

DESCRIPTION

Ping uses the ICMP protocol's mandatory ECHO_REQUEST datagram to elicit an ICMP ECHO_RESPONSE from a host or gateway. ECHO_REQUEST datagrams ("pings") have an IP and ICMP header, followed by a "struct timeval" and then an arbitrary number of "pad" bytes used to fill out the packet.

OPTIONS

-c *count* Stop after sending (and receiving) count ECHO_RESPONSE packets.

-d Set the SO_DEBUG option on the socket being used.

-f Flood ping. Outputs packets as fast as they come back or one hundred times per second, whichever is more. For every ECHO_REQUEST sent a period "." is printed, while for ever ECHO_REPLY received a backspace is printed. This provides a rapid display of how many packets are being dropped. Only the superuser may use this option. *This can be very hard on a network and should be used with caution.*

-i *wait* Wait *wait* seconds *between sending each packet*. The default is to wait for one second between each packet. This option is incompatible with the **-f** option.

`-l` *`preload`*	If *`preload`* is specified, **`ping`** sends that many packets as fast as possible before falling into its normal mode of behavior. Only the superuser may use this option.
`-n`	Numeric output only. No attempt will be made to lookup symbolic names for host addresses.
`-p` *`pattern`*	You may specify up to 16 "pad" bytes to fill out the packet you send. This is useful for diagnosing data-dependent problems in a network. For example, "`-p ff`" will cause the sent packet to be filled with all ones.
`-q`	Quiet output. Nothing is displayed except the summary lines at startup time and when finished.
`-R`	Record route. Includes the RECORD_ ROUTE option in the ECHO_REQUEST packet and displays the route buffer on returned packets. Note that the IP header is only large enough for nine such routes. Many hosts ignore or discard this option.
`-r`	Bypass the normal routing tables and send directly to a host on an attached network. If the host is not on a directly-attached network, an error is returned. This option can be used to ping a local host through an interface that has no route through it (e.g., after the interface was dropped by `routed`(8)).
`-s` *`packetsize`*	Specifies the number of data bytes to be sent. The default is 56, which translates into 64 ICMP data bytes when combined with the 8 bytes of ICMP header data.
`-v`	Verbose output. ICMP packets other than ECHO_RESPONSE that are received are listed.

When using **ping** for fault isolation, it should first be run on the local host, to verify that the local network interface is up and running. Then, hosts and gateways further and further away should be "pinged." Round-trip times and packet loss statistics are computed. If duplicate packets are received, they are not included in the packet loss calculation, although the round trip time of these packets is used in calculating the minimum/average/maximum round-trip time numbers. When the specified number of packets have been sent (and received) or if the program is terminated with a `SIGINT`, a brief summary is displayed.

If **ping** does not receive any reply packets at all it will exit with code 1. On error it exits with code 2. Otherwise it exits with code 0. This makes it possible to use the exit code to see if a host is alive or not.

This program is intended for use in network testing, measurement and management. Because of the load it can impose on the network, it is unwise to use **ping** during normal operations or from automated scripts.

ICMP PACKET DETAILS

An IP header without options is 20 bytes. An ICMP ECHO_REQUEST packet contains an additional 8 bytes worth of ICMP header followed by an arbitrary amount of data. When a *packetsize* is given, this indicates the size of this extra piece of data (the default is 56). Thus the amount of data received inside of an IP packet of type ICMP ECHO_REPLY will always be 8 bytes more than the requested data space (the ICMP header).

If the data space is at least eight bytes large, **ping** uses the first eight bytes of this space to include a timestamp which it uses in the computation of round trip times. If less than eight bytes of pad are specified, no round trip times are given.

DUPLICATE AND DAMAGED PACKETS

ping will report duplicate and damaged packets. Duplicate packets should never occur, and seem to be caused by inappropriate link-level retransmissions. Duplicates may occur in many situations and are rarely (if ever) a good sign, although the presence of low levels of duplicates may not always be cause for alarm.

Damaged packets are obviously serious cause for alarm and often indicate broken hardware somewhere in the **ping** packet's path (in the network or in the hosts).

TRYING DIFFERENT DATA PATTERNS

The (inter)network layer should never treat packets differently depending on the data contained in the data portion. Unfortunately, data-dependent problems have been known to sneak into networks and remain undetected for long periods of time. In many cases the particular pattern that will have problems is something that doesn't have sufficient "transitions," such as all ones or all zeros, or a pattern right at the edge, such as almost all zeros. It isn't necessarily enough to specify a data pattern of all zeros (for example) on the command line because the pattern that is of interest is at the data link level, and the relationship between what you type and what the controllers transmit can be complicated.

This means that if you have a data-dependent problem you will probably have to do a lot of testing to find it. If you are lucky, you may manage to find a file that either can't be sent across your network or that takes much longer to transfer than other similar length files. You can then examine this file for repeated patterns that you can test using the `-p` option of `ping`.

TTL DETAILS

The TTL value of an IP packet represents the maximum number of IP routers that the packet can go through before being thrown away. In current practice you can expect each router in the Internet to decrement the TTL field by exactly one.

The TCP/IP specification states that the TTL field for TCP packets should be set to 60, but many systems use smaller values (4.3 BSD uses 30, 4.2 used 15).

The maximum possible value of this field is 255, and most Unix systems set the TTL field of ICMP ECHO_REQUEST packets to 255. This is why you will find you can "ping" some hosts, but not reach them with `telnet`(1) or `ftp`(1).

In normal operation **ping** prints the TTL value from the packet it receives. When a remote system receives a ping packet, it can do one of three things with the TTL field in its response:

- Not change it; this is what Berkeley Unix systems did before the 4.3BSD-Tahoe release. In this case the TTL value in the received packet will be 255 minus the number of routers in the round-trip path.

- Set it to 255; this is what current Berkeley Unix systems do. In this case the TTL value in the received packet will be 255 minus the number of routers in the path `from` the remote system *to* the pinging host.
- Set it to some other value. Some machines use the same value for ICMP packets that they use for TCP packets, for example either 30 or 60. Others may use completely wild values.

BUGS

Many Hosts and Gateways ignore the RECORD_ROUTE option.

The maximum IP header length is too small for options like RECORD_ROUTE to be completely useful. There's not much that can be done about this, however.

Flood pinging is not recommended in general, and flood pinging the broadcast address should only be done under very controlled conditions.

SEE ALSO

netstat(1), **ifconfig**(8), **routed**(8)

HISTORY

The **ping** command appeared in 4.3BSD.

PPPD(8)

NAME

pppd Point to Point Protocol daemon.

SYNOPSIS

pppd [tty_name] [speed] [options]

DESCRIPTION

The Point-to-Point Protocol (PPP) provides a method for transmitting datagrams over serial point-to-point links. PPP is composed of three parts: a method for encapsulating datagrams over serial links, an extensible Link

Control Protocol (LCP), and a family of Network Control Protocols (NCP) for establishing and configuring different network-layer protocols.

The encapsulation scheme is provided by driver code in the kernel. **pppd** provides the basic LCP, authentication support, and an NCP for establishing and configuring the Internet Protocol (IP) (called the IP Control Protocol, IPCP).

FREQUENTLY USED OPTIONS

<tty_name> Communicates over the named device. The string "/dev/" is prepended if necessary. If no device name is given, or if the name of the terminal connected to the standard input is given, pppd will use that terminal, and will not fork to put itself in the background. This option is privileged if the noauth option is used.

<speed> Sets the baud rate to <speed> (a decimal number). On systems such as 4.4BSD and NetBSD, any speed can be specified. Other systems (e.g. SunOS) allow only a limited set of speeds.

active-filter *filter-expression* Specifies a packet filter to be applied to data packets to determine which packets are to be regarded as link activity, and therefore reset the idle timer, or cause the link to be brought up in demand-dialling mode. This option is useful in conjunction with the **idle** option if there are packets being sent or received regularly over the link (for example, routing information packets) which would otherwise prevent the link from ever appearing to be idle. The *filter-expression* syntax is as described for tcpdump(1), except that qualifiers which are inappropriate for a PPP link, such as **ether** and **arp**, are not permitted. Generally the filter expression should be enclosed in single quotes to prevent whitespace in the expression from being interpreted by the shell. This option is currently only available under NetBSD, and then only if both the kernel and pppd were compiled with PPP_FILTER defined.

asyncmap *<map>* Sets the async character map to *<map>*. This map describes which control characters cannot be successfully received over the serial line. Pppd will ask the peer to send these characters as a 2-byte escape sequence. The argument is a 32 bit hex number with each bit representing a character to escape. Bit 0 (00000001) represents the character 0x00; bit 31

(80000000) represents the character 0x1f or ^_. If multiple asyncmap options are given, the values are ORed together. If no asyncmap option is given, no async character map will be negotiated for the receive direction; the peer should then escape all control characters. To escape transmitted characters, use the escape option.

auth Requires the peer to authenticate itself before allowing network packets to be sent or received.

call *name* Reads options from the file /etc/ppp/peers/*name*. This file may contain privileged options, such as *noauth*, even if pppd is not being run by root. The *name* string may not begin with / or include .. as a pathname component. The format of the options file is described below.

connect *script* Uses the executable or shell command specified by script to set up the serial line. This script would typically use the chat(8) program to dial the modem and start the remote ppp session. This option is privileged if the *noauth* option is used.

crtscts Uses hardware flow control (i.e. RTS/CTS) to control the flow of data on the serial port. If neither the *crtscts* nor the *nocrtscts* option is given, the hardware flow control setting for the serial port is left unchanged.

defaultroute Adds a default route to the system routing tables, using the peer as the gateway, when IPCP negotiation is successfully completed. This entry is removed when the PPP connection is broken. This option is privileged if the *nodefaultroute* option has been specified.

disconnect *script* Runs the executable or shell command specified by *script* after pppd has terminated the link. This script could, for example, issue commands to the modem to cause it to hang up if hardware modem control signals were not available. The disconnect script is not run if the modem has already hung up. This option is privileged if the *noauth* option is used.

escape *xx,yy,...* Specifies that certain characters should be escaped on transmission (regardless of whether the peer requests them to be escaped with its async control character map). The characters to be escaped are specified as a list of hex numbers separated by commas. Note that almost any character can be specified for the *escape* option, unlike the *asyncmap* option which only allows control characters to be specified. The characters which may not be escaped are those with hex values 0x20 - 0x3f or 0x5e.

file *name* Reads options from file *name* (the format is described below). The file must be readable by the user who has invoked pppd.

lock Specifies that pppd should create a UUCP-style lock file for the serial device to ensure exclusive access to the device.

mru *n* Sets the MRU [Maximum Receive Unit] value to *n*. Pppd will ask the peer to send packets of no more than *n* bytes. The minimum MRU value is 128. The default MRU value is 1500. A value of 296 is recommended for slow links (40 bytes for TCP/IP header + 256 bytes of data).

mtu *n* Sets the MTU [Maximum Transmit Unit] value to *n*. Unless the peer requests a smaller value via MRU negotiation, pppd will request that the kernel networking code send data packets of no more than *n* bytes through the PPP network interface.

passive Enables the "passive" option in the LCP. With this option, pppd will attempt to initiate a connection; if no reply is received from the peer, pppd will then just wait passively for a valid LCP packet from the peer, instead of exiting, as it would without this option.

OPTIONS

<local_IP_address>:<remote_IP_address> Set the local and/or remote interface IP addresses. Either one may be omitted. The IP addresses can be specified with a host name or in decimal dot notation (e.g. 150.234.56.78). The default local address is the (first) IP address of the system (unless the *noipdefault* option is given). The remote address will be obtained from the peer if not specified in any option. Thus, in simple cases, this option is not required. If a local and/or remote IP address is specified with this option, pppd will not accept a different value from the peer in the IPCP negotiation, unless the *ipcp-accept-local* and/or *ipcp-accept-remote* options are given, respectively.

bsdcomp *nr,nt* Requests that the peer compress packets that it sends, using the BSD-Compress scheme, with a maximum code size of *nr* bits, and agree to compress packets sent to the peer with a maximum code size of *nt* bits. If *nt* is not specified, it defaults to the value given for *nr*. Values in the range 9 to 15 may be used for *nr* and *nt*; larger values give better compression but consume more kernel memory for compression dictionaries. Alternatively, a value of 0 for *nr* or *nt* disables compression in the corresponding direction. Use *nobsdcomp* or *bsdcomp 0* to disable BSD-Compress compression entirely.

chap-interval *n* If this option is given, pppd will rechallenge the peer every n seconds.

chap-max-challenge *n* Sets the maximum number of CHAP challenge transmissions to n (default 10).

chap-restart *n* Sets the CHAP restart interval (retransmission timeout for challenges) to n seconds (default 3).

debug Enables connection debugging facilities. If this option is given, pppd will log the contents of all control packets sent or received in a readable form. The packets are logged through syslog with facility *daemon* and level *debug*. This information can be directed to a file by setting up /etc/syslog.conf appropriately (see syslog.conf(5)).

default-asyncmap Disables asyncmap negotiation, forcing all control characters to be escaped for both the transmit and the receive direction.

default-mru Disables MRU [Maximum Receive Unit] negotiation. With this option, pppd will use the default MRU value of 1500 bytes for both the transmit and receive direction.

deflate *nr,nt* Requests that the peer compress packets that it sends, using the Deflate scheme, with a maximum window size of 2***nr* bytes, and agrees to compress packets sent to the peer with a maximum window size of 2***nt* bytes. If *nt* is not specified, it defaults to the value given for *nr*. Values in the range 8 to 15 may be used for *nr* and *nt*; larger values give better compression but consume more kernel memory for compression dictionaries. Alternatively, a value of 0 for *nr* or *nt* disables compression in the corresponding direction. Use *nodeflate* or *deflate 0* to disable Deflate compression entirely.

NOTE

pppd requests Deflate compression in preference to BSD-Compress if the peer can do either.

demand Initiates the link only on demand, i.e. when data traffic is present. With this option, the remote IP address must be specified by the user on the command line or in an options file. Pppd will initially configure the interface and enable it for IP traffic without connecting to the peer. When traffic is available, pppd will connect to the peer and perform negotiation, authentication, etc. When this is completed, pppd will commence passing data packets (i.e., IP packets) across the link.

NOTE

The *demand* option implies the persist option. If this behaviour is not desired, use the nopersist option after the *demand* option. The *idle* and *holdoff* options are also useful in conjuction with the demand option.

domain *d* Appends the domain name *d* to the local host name for authentication purposes. For example, if gethostname() returns the name porsche, but the fully qualified domain name is porsche.Quotron.COM, you could specify *domain Quotron.COM*. Pppd would then use the name *porsche.Quotron.COM* for looking up secrets in the secrets file, and as the default name to send to the peer when authenticating itself to the peer. This option is privileged.

holdoff *n* Specifies how many seconds to wait before re-initiating the link after it terminates. This option only has any effect if the *persist* or *demand* option is used. The holdoff period is not applied if the link was terminated because it was idle.

idle *n* Specifies that pppd should disconnect if the link is idle for *n* seconds. The link is idle when no data packets (i.e. IP packets) are being sent or received.

NOTE

It is not advisable to use this option with the *persist* option without the *demand* option. If the active-filter option is given, data packets which are rejected by the specified activity filter also count as the link being idle.

ipcp-accept-local With this option, pppd will accept the peer's idea of our local IP address, even if the local IP address was specified in an option.

ipcp-accept-remote With this option, pppd will accept the peer's idea of its (remote) IP address, even if the remote IP address was specified in an option.

ipcp-max-configure *n* Sets the maximum number of IPCP configure-request transmissions to *n* (default 10).

ipcp-max-failure *n* Sets the maximum number of IPCP configure-NAKs returned before starting to send configure-Rejects instead to *n* (default 10).

ipcp-max-terminate *n* Sets the maximum number of IPCP terminate-request transmissions to *n* (default 3).

ipcp-restart *n* Sets the IPCP restart interval (retransmission timeout) to *n* seconds (default 3).

ipparam *string* Provides an extra parameter to the ip-up and ipdown scripts. If this option is given, the *string* supplied is given as the 6th parameter to those scripts.

ipx Enables the IPXCP and IPX protocols. This option is presently only supported under Linux, and only if your kernel has been configured to include IPX support.

ipx-network *n* Sets the IPX network number in the IPXCP configure request frame to *n*, a hexadecimal number (without a leading 0x). There is no valid default. If this option is not specified, the network number is obtained from the peer. If the peer does not have the network number, the IPX protocol will not be started.

ipx-node *n:m* Sets the IPX node numbers. The two node numbers are separated from each other with a colon character. The first number *n* is the local node number. The second number *m* is the peer's node number. Each node number is a hexadecimal number, at most 10 digits long. The node numbers on the ipx-network must be unique. There is no valid default. If this option is not specified then the node numbers are obtained from the peer.

ipx-router-name <*string*> Sets the name of the router. This is a string and is sent to the peer as information data.

ipx-routing *n* Sets the routing protocol to be received by this option. More than one instance of *ipx-routing* may be specified. The *'none'* option (0) may be specified as the only instance of ipx-routing. The values may be *0* for *NONE*, *2* for *RIP/SAP*, and *4* for *NLSP*.

ipxcp-accept-local Accepts the peer's NAK for the node number specified in the ipx-node option. If a node number was specified, and nonzero, the default is to insist that the value be used. If you include this option then you will permit the peer to override the entry of the node number.

ipxcp-accept-network Accepts the peer's NAK for the network number specified in the ipx-network option. If a network number was specified, and nonzero, the default is to insist that the value be used. If you include this option then you will permit the peer to override the entry of the node number.

ipxcp-accept-remote Uses the peer's network number specified in the configure request frame. If a node number was specified for the peer and this option was not specified, the peer will be forced to use the value which you have specified.

ipxcp-max-configure *n* Sets the maximum number of IPXCP configure request frames which the system will send to *n*. The default is 10.

ipxcp-max-failure *n* Sets the maximum number of IPXCP NAK frames which the local system will send before it rejects the options. The default value is 3.

ipxcp-max-terminate *n* Sets the maximum nuber of IPXCP terminate request frames before the local system considers that the peer is not listening to them. The default value is 3.

kdebug *n* Enables debugging code in the kernel-level PPP driver. The argument *n* is a number which is the sum of the following values: 1 to enable general debug messages, 2 to request that the contents of received packets be printed, and 4 to request that the contents of transmitted packets be printed. On most systems, messages printed by the kernel are logged by syslog(1) to a file as directed in the /etc/syslog.conf configuration file.

lcp-echo-failure *n* If this option is given, pppd will presume the peer to be dead if *n* LCP echo-requests are sent without receiving a valid LCP echo-reply. If this happens, pppd will terminate the connection. Use of this option requires a nonzero value for the *lcp-echointerval* parameter. This option can be used to enable pppd to terminate after the physical connection has been broken (e.g., the modem has hung up) in situations where no hardware modem control lines are available.

lcp-echo-interval *n* If this option is given, pppd will send an LCP echo-request frame to the peer every *n* seconds. Normally the peer should respond to the echo-request by sending an echo-reply. This option can be used with the *lcp-echo-failure* option to detect that the peer is no longer connected.

lcp-max-configure *n* Sets the maximum number of LCP configure-request transmissions to *n* (default 10).

lcp-max-failure *n* Sets the maximum number of LCP configure-NAKs returned before starting to send configure-Rejects instead to *n* (default 10).

lcp-max-terminate *n* Sets the maximum number of LCP terminate-request transmissions to *n* (default 3).

lcp-restart *n* Sets the LCP restart interval (retransmission timeout) to *n* seconds (default 3).

local Don't use the modem control lines. With this option, pppd will ignore the state of the CD (Carrier Detect) signal from the modem and will not change the state of the DTR (Data Terminal Ready) signal.

login Uses the system password database for authenticating the peer using PAP, and record the user in the system wtmp file. Note that the peer must have an entry in the /etc/ppp/pap-secrets file as well as the system password database to be allowed access.

maxconnect *n* Terminates the connection when it has been available for network traffic for *n* seconds (i.e. *n* seconds after the first network control protocol comes up).

modem Uses the modem control lines. This option is the default. With this option, pppd will wait for the CD (Carrier Detect) signal from the modem to be asserted when opening the serial device (unless a connect script is specified), and it will drop the DTR (Data Terminal Ready) signal briefly when the connection is terminated and before executing the connect script. On Ultrix, this option implies hardware flow control, as for the *crtscts* option.

ms-dns <*addr*> If pppd is acting as a server for Microsoft Windows clients, this option allows pppd to supply one or two DNS (Domain Name Server) addresses to the clients. The first instance of this option specifies the primary DNS address; the second instance (if given) specifies the secondary DNS address. (This option was present in some older versions of pppd under the name **dns-addr**.)

ms-wins <*addr*> If pppd is acting as a server for Microsoft Windows or "Samba" clients, this option allows pppd to supply one or two WINS (Windows Internet Name Services) server addresses to the clients. The first instance of this option specifies the primary WINS address; the second instance (if given) specifies the secondary WINS address.

name *name* Sets the name of the local system for authentication purposes to *name*. This is a privileged option. With this option, pppd will use lines in the secrets files which have *name* as the second field when looking for a secret to use in authenticating the peer. In addition, unless overridden with the *user* option, *name* will be used as the name to send to the peer when authenticating the local system to the peer. (Note that pppd does not append the domain name to *name*.)

netmask *n* Sets the interface netmask to *n*, a 32 bit netmask in "decimal dot" notation (e.g. 255.255.255.0). If this option is given, the value specified is ORed with the default netmask. The default netmask is chosen based on the negotiated remote IP address; it is the appropriate network mask for the class of the remote IP address, ORed with the netmasks for any non point-to-point network interfaces in the system which are on the same network.

noaccomp Disables Address/Control compression in both directions (send and receive).

noauth Does not require the peer to authenticate itself. This option is privileged if the *auth* option is specified in /etc/ppp/options.

nobsdcomp Disables BSD-Compress compression; **pppd** will not request or agree to compress packets using the BSDCompress scheme.

noccp Disables CCP (Compression Control Protocol) negotiation. This option should only be required if the peer is buggy and gets confused by requests from pppd for CCP negotiation.

nocrtscts Disables hardware flow control (i.e. RTS/CTS) on the serial port. If neither the *crtscts* nor the *nocrtscts* option is given, the hardware flow control setting for the serial port is left unchanged.

nodefaultroute Disables the *defaultroute* option. The system administrator who wishes to prevent users from creating default routes with pppd can do so by placing this option in the /etc/ppp/options file.

nodeflate Disables Deflate compression; pppd will not request or agree to compress packets using the Deflate scheme.

nodetach Don't detach from the controlling terminal. Without this option, if a serial device other than the terminal on the standard input is specified, pppd will fork to become a background process.

noip Disables IPCP negotiation and IP communication. This option should only be required if the peer is buggy and gets confused by requests from pppd for IPCP negotiation.

noipdefault Disables the default behaviour when no local IP address is specified, which is to determine (if possible) the local IP address from the hostname. With this option, the peer will have to supply the local IP address during IPCP negotiation (unless it specified explicitly on the command line or in an options file).

noipx Disables the IPXCP and IPX protocols. This option should only be required if the peer is buggy and gets confused by requests from pppd for IPXCP negotiation.

nomagic Disables magic number negotiation. With this option, pppd cannot detect a looped-back line. This option should only be needed if the peer is buggy.

nopcomp Disables protocol field compression negotiation in both the receive and the transmit direction.

nopersist Exits once a connection has been made and terminated. This is the default unless the *persist* or *demand* option has been specified.

nopredictor1 Does not accept or agree to Predictor-1 compression.

noproxyarp Disables the *proxyarp* option. The system administrator who wishes to prevent users from creating proxy ARP entries with pppd can do so by placing this option in the /etc/ppp/options file.

novj Disables Van Jacobson style TCP/IP header compression in both the transmit and the receive direction.

novjccomp Disables the connection-ID compression option in Van Jacobson style TCP/IP header compression. With this option, pppd will not omit the connection-ID byte from Van Jacobson compressed TCP/IP headers, nor ask the peer to do so.

papcrypt Indicates that all secrets in the /etc/ppp/pap-secrets file which are used for checking the identity of the peer are encrypted, and thus pppd should not accept a password which, before encryption, is identical to the secret from the /etc/ppp/papsecrets file.

pap-max-authreq *n* Sets the maximum number of PAP authenticate-request transmissions to *n* (default 10).

pap-restart *n* Sets the PAP restart interval (retransmission timeout) to *n* seconds (default 3).

pap-timeout *n* Sets the maximum time that pppd will wait for the peer to authenticate itself with PAP to *n* seconds (0 means no limit).

pass-filter *filter-expression* Specifies a packet filter to apply to data packets being sent or received to determine which packets should be allowed to pass. Packets which are rejected by the filter are silently discarded. This option can be used to prevent specific network daemons (such as routed) using up link bandwidth, or to provide a basic firewall capability. The *filter-expression* syntax is as described for tcpdump(1), except that qualifiers which are inappropriate for a PPP link, such as **ether** and **arp**, are not permitted. Generally the filter expression should be enclosed in single-quotes to prevent whitespace in the expression from being interpreted by the shell. Note that it is possible to apply different constraints to incoming and outgoing packets using the **inbound** and **outbound** qualifiers. This option is currently only available under NetBSD, and then only if both the kernel and pppd were compiled with PPP_FILTER defined.

persist Does not exit after a connection is terminated; instead try to reopen the connection.

predictor1 Requests that the peer compress frames that it sends using Predictor-1 compression, and agree to compress transmitted frames with Predictor-1 if requested. This option has no effect unless the kernel driver supports Predictor-1 compression.

proxyarp Adds an entry to this system's ARP [Address Resolution Protocol] table with the IP address of the peer and the Ethernet address of this system. This will have the effect of making the peer appear to other systems to be on the local ethernet.

remotename *name* Sets the assumed name of the remote system for authentication purposes to *name*.

refuse-chap With this option, pppd will not agree to authenticate itself to the peer using CHAP.

refuse-pap With this option, pppd will not agree to authenticate itself to the peer using PAP.

require-chap Requires the peer to authenticate itself using CHAP [Challenge Handshake Authentication Protocol] authentication.

require-pap Requires the peer to authenticate itself using PAP [Password Authentication Protocol] authentication.

silent With this option, pppd will not transmit LCP packets to initiate a connection until a valid LCP packet is received from the peer (as for the 'passive' option with ancient versions of pppd).

usehostname Enforces the use of the hostname (with domain name appended, if given) as the name of the local system for authentication purposes (overrides the *name* option).

user *name* Sets the name used for authenticating the local system to the peer to *name*.

vj-max-slots *n* Sets the number of connection slots to be used by the Van Jacobson TCP/IP header compression and decompression code to *n*, which must be between 2 and 16 (inclusive).

welcome *script* Runs the executable or shell command specified by *script* before initiating PPP negotiation, after the connect script (if any) has completed. This option is privileged if the *noauth* option is used.

xonxoff Uses software flow control (i.e. XON/XOFF) to control the flow of data on the serial port.

OPTIONS FILES

Options can be taken from files as well as the command line. Pppd reads options from the files /etc/ppp/options, ~/.ppprc and /etc/ppp/options.*ttyname* (in that order) before processing the options on the command line. (In fact, the command-line options are scanned to find the terminal name before the options.*ttyname* file is read.) In forming the name of the options.*ttyname* file, the initial /dev/ is removed from the terminal name, and any remaining / characters are replaced with dots.

An options file is parsed into a series of words, delimited by whitespace. Whitespace can be included in a word by enclosing the word in quotes ("). A backslash quotes the following character. A hash (#) starts a comment, which continues until the end of the line. There is no restriction on using the *file* or *call* options within an options file.

SECURITY

pppd provides system administrators with sufficient access control that PPP access to a server machine can be provided to legitimate users without fear of compromising the security of the server or the network it's on. In part this is provided by the /etc/ppp/options file, where the administrator can place options to restrict the ways in which pppd can be used, and in part by the PAP and CHAP secrets files, where the administrator can restrict the set of IP addresses which individual users may use.

The normal way that pppd should be set up is to have the *auth* option in the /etc/ppp/options file. (This may become the default in later releases.)

If users wish to use pppd to dial out to a peer which will refuse to authenticate itself (such as an Internet service provider), the system administrator should create an options file under /etc/ppp/peers containing the *noauth* option, the name of the serial port to use, and the *connect* option (if required), plus any other appropriate options. In this way, pppd can be set up to allow nonprivileged users to make unauthenticated connections only to trusted peers.

As indicated above, some security-sensitive options are privileged, which means that they may not be used by an ordinary non-privileged user running a setuid-root pppd, either on the command line, in the user's ~/.ppprc file, or in an options file read using the *file* option. Privileged options may be used in /etc/ppp/options file or in an options file read using the *call* option. If pppd is being run by the root user, privileged options can be used without restriction.

AUTHENTICATION

Authentication is the process whereby one peer convinces the other of its identity. This involves the first peer sending its name to the other, together with some kind of secret information which could only come from the genuine authorized user of that name. In such an exchange, we will call the first peer the "client" and the other the "server." The client has a name by which it identifies itself to the server, and the server also has a name by which it identifies itself to the client. Generally the genuine client shares some secret (or password) with the server, and authenticates itself by proving that it knows that secret. Very often, the names used for authentication correspond to the Internet hostnames of the peers, but this is not essential.

At present, pppd supports two authentication protocols: the Password Authentication Protocol (PAP) and the Challenge Handshake Authentication Protocol (CHAP). PAP involves the client sending its name and a cleartext password to the server to authenticate itself. In contrast, the server initiates the CHAP authentication exchange by sending a challenge to the client (the challenge packet includes the server's name). The client must respond with a response which includes its name plus a hash value derived from the shared secret and the challenge, in order to prove that it knows the secret.

The PPP protocol, being symmetrical, allows both peers to require the other to authenticate itself. In that case, two separate and independent authentication exchanges will occur. The two exchanges could use different authentication protocols, and in principle, different names could be used in the two exchanges.

The default behaviour of pppd is to agree to authenticate if requested, and to not require authentication from the peer. However, pppd will not agree to authenticate itself with a particular protocol if it has no secrets which could be used to do so.

Pppd stores secrets for use in authentication in secrets files (/etc/ppp/pap-secrets for PAP, /etc/ppp/chap-secrets for CHAP). Both secrets files have the same format. The secrets files can contain secrets for pppd to use in authenticating itself to other systems, as well as secrets for pppd to use when authenticating other systems to itself.

Each line in a secrets file contains one secret. A given secret is specific to a particular combination of client and server - it can only be used by that client to authenticate itself to that server. Thus each line in a secrets file has at least 3 fields: the name of the client, the name of the server, and the secret. These fields may be followed by a list of the IP addresses that the specified client may use when connecting to the specified server.

A secrets file is parsed into words as for a options file, so the client name, server name and secrets fields must each be one word, with any embedded spaces or other special characters quoted or escaped. Any following words on the same line are taken to be a list of acceptable IP addresses for that client. If there are only 3 words on the line, or if the first word is "-", then all IP addresses are disallowed. To allow any address, use "*". A word starting with "!" indicates that the specified address is *not* acceptable. An address may be followed by "/" and a number *n*, to indicate a whole subnet, i.e. all addresses which have the same value in the most significant *n* bits. Note that case is significant in the client and server names and in the secret.

If the secret starts with an '@', what follows is assumed to be the name of a file from which to read the secret. A "*" as the client or server name matches any name. When selecting a secret, pppd takes the best match, i.e. the match with the fewest wildcards.

Thus a secrets file contains both secrets for use in authenticating other hosts, plus secrets which we use for authenticating ourselves to others. When pppd is authenticating the peer (checking the peer's identity), it chooses a secret with the peer's name in the first field and the name of the local system in the second field. The name of the local system defaults to the hostname, with the domain name appended if the *domain* option is used. This default can be overridden with the *name* option, except when the *usehostname* option is used.

When pppd is choosing a secret to use in authenticating itself to the peer, it first determines what name it is going to use to identify itself to the peer. This name can be specified by the user with the *user* option. If this option is not used, the name defaults to the name of the local system, determined as described in the previous paragraph. Then pppd looks for a secret with this name in the first field and the peer's name in the second field. Pppd will know the name of the peer if CHAP authentication is being used, because the peer will have sent it in the challenge packet. However, if PAP is being used, pppd will have to determine the peer's name from the options specified by the user. The user can specify the peer's name directly with the *remotename* option. Otherwise, if the remote IP address was specified by a name (rather than in numeric form), that name will be used as the peer's name. Failing that, pppd will use the null string as the peer's name.

When authenticating the peer with PAP, the supplied password is first compared with the secret from the secrets file. If the password doesn't match the secret, the password is encrypted using crypt() and checked against the secret again. Thus secrets for authenticating the peer can be stored in encrypted form if desired. If the *papcrypt* option is given, the first (unencrypted) comparison is omitted, for better security.

Furthermore, if the login option was specified, the username and password are also checked against the system password database. Thus, the system administrator can set up the pap-secrets file to allow PPP access only to certain users, and to restrict the set of IP addresses that each user can use. Typically, when using the *login* option, the secret in /etc/ppp/pap-secrets would be "", which will match any password supplied by the peer. This avoids the need to have the same secret in two places.

Authentication must be satisfactorily completed before IPCP (or any other Network Control Protocol) can be started. If the peer is required to authenticate itself, and fails to do so, pppd will terminate the link (by closing LCP). If IPCP negotiates an unacceptable IP address for the remote host, IPCP will be closed. IP packets can only be sent or received when IPCP is open.

In some cases it is desirable to allow some hosts which can't authenticate themselves to connect and use one of a restricted set of IP addresses, even when the local host generally requires authentication. If the peer refuses to authenticate itself when requested, pppd takes that as equivalent to authenticating with PAP using the empty string for the username and password. Thus, by adding a line to the pap-secrets file which specifies the empty string for the client and password, it is possible to allow restricted access to hosts which refuse to authenticate themselves.

ROUTING

When IPCP negotiation is completed successfully, pppd will inform the kernel of the local and remote IP addresses for the ppp interface. This is sufficient to create a host route to the remote end of the link, which will enable the peers to exchange IP packets. Communication with other machines generally requires further modification to routing tables and/or ARP (Address Resolution Protocol) tables. In most cases the *defaultroute* and/or *proxyarp* options are sufficient for this, but in some cases further intervention is required. The /etc/ppp/ip-up script can be used for this.

Sometimes it is desirable to add a default route through the remote host, as in the case of a machine whose only connection to the Internet is through the ppp interface. The *defaultroute* option causes pppd to create such a default route when IPCP comes up, and delete it when the link is terminated.

In some cases it is desirable to use proxy ARP, for example on a server machine connected to a LAN, in order to allow other hosts to communicate with the remote host. The *proxyarp* option causes pppd to look for a network interface on the same subnet as the remote host (an interface supporting broadcast and ARP, which is up and not a point-to-point or loopback interface). If found, pppd creates a permanent, published ARP entry with the IP address of the remote host and the hardware address of the network interface found.

When the *demand* option is used, the interface IP addresses have already been set at the point when IPCP comes up. If pppd has not been able to negotiate the same addresses that it used to configure the interface (for example when the peer is an ISP that uses dynamic IP address assignment), pppd has to change the interface IP addresses to the negotiated addresses. This may disrupt existing connections, and the use of demand dialling with peers that do dynamic IP address assignment is not recommended.

EXAMPLES

The following examples assume that the /etc/ppp/options file contains the *auth* option (as in the default /etc/ppp/options file in the ppp distribution).

Probably the most common use of pppd is to dial out to an ISP. This can be done with a command such as

```
pppd call isp
```

where the /etc/ppp/peers/isp file is set up by the system administrator to contain something like this

```
ttyS0 19200 crtscts
connect '/usr/sbin/chat -v -f /etc/ppp/chat-isp'
noauth
```

In this example, we are using chat to dial the ISP's modem and go through any logon sequence required. The /etc/ppp/chat-isp file contains the script used by chat; it could, for example, contain something like this

```
ABORT "NO CARRIER"
ABORT "NO DIALTONE"
ABORT "ERROR"
ABORT "NO ANSWER"
ABORT "BUSY"
ABORT "Username/Password Incorrect"
"" "at"
OK "at&d0&c1"
OK "atdt2468135"
"name:" "^Umyuserid"
"word:" ""
"ispts" "^Uppp"
"~-^Uppp-~"
```

See the chat(8) man page for details of chat scripts.

Pppd can also be used to provide a dial-in ppp service for users. If the users already have login accounts, the simplest way to set up the ppp service is to let the users log in to their accounts and run pppd (installed setuidroot) with a command such as

```
pppd proxyarp
```

To allow a user to use the PPP facilities, you need to allocate an IP address for that user's machine and create an entry in /etc/ppp/pap-secrets or /etc/ppp/chap-secrets (depending on which authentication method the PPP implementation on the user's machine supports), so that the user's machine can authenticate itself. For example, if Joe has a machine called "joespc" which is to be allowed to dial in to the machine called "server" and use the IP address joespc.my.net, you would add an entry like this to /etc/ppp/pap secrets or /etc/ppp/chap-secrets:

```
joespc   server   "joe's secret" joespc.my.net
```

Alternatively, you can create a username called (for example) "ppp," whose login shell is pppd and whose home directory is /etc/ppp. Options to be used when pppd is run this way can be put in /etc/ppp/.ppprc.

If your serial connection is any more complicated than a piece of wire, you may need to arrange for some control characters to be escaped. In particular, it is often useful to escape XON (^Q) and XOFF (^S), using *asyncmap a0000*. If the path includes a telnet, you probably should escape ^] as well (*asyncmap 200a0000*). If the path includes an rlogin, you will need to use the *escape ff* option on the end which is running the rlogin client, since many rlogin implementations are not transparent; they will remove the sequence [0xff, 0xff, 0x73, 0x73, followed by any 8 bytes] from the stream.

DIAGNOSTICS

Messages are sent to the syslog daemon using facility LOG_DAEMON. (This can be overriden by recompiling pppd with the macro LOG_PPP defined as the desired facility.) In order to see the error and debug messages, you will need to edit your /etc/syslog.conf file to direct the messages to the desired output device or file.

The debug option causes the contents of all control packets sent or received to be logged, that is, all LCP, PAP, CHAP or IPCP packets. This can be useful if the PPP negotiation does not succeed or if authentication fails. If debugging is enabled at compile time, the *debug* option also causes other debugging messages to be logged.

Debugging can also be enabled or disabled by sending a SIGUSR1 signal to the pppd process. This signal acts as a toggle.

FILES

/var/run/ppp*n*.pid (BSD or Linux), **/etc/ppp/pppn.pid** (others) Process-ID for pppd process on ppp interface unit *n*.

/etc/ppp/auth-up A program or script which is executed after the remote system successfully authenticates itself. It is executed with the parameters

```
interface-name peer-name user-name tty-device speed
```

and with its standard input, output and error redirected to /dev/null. This program or script is executed with the real and effective user-IDs set to root, and with an empty environment. (Note that this script is not executed if the peer doesn't authenticate itself, for example when the *noauth* option is used.)

/etc/ppp/auth-down A program or script which is executed when the link goes down, if /etc/ppp/auth-up was previously executed. It is executed in the same manner with the same parameters as /etc/ppp/auth-up.

/etc/ppp/ip-up A program or script which is executed when the link is available for sending and receiving IP packets (that is, IPCP has come up). It is executed with the parameters `interface-name tty-device speed local-IP-address remote-IP-address ipparam` and with its standard input, output and error streams redirected to /dev/null. This program or script is executed with the real and effective user-IDs set to root. This is so that it can be used to manipulate routes, run privileged daemons (e.g. *sendmail*), etc. Be careful that the contents of the /etc/ppp/ip-up and /etc/ppp/ip-down scripts do not compromise your system's security. This program or script is executed with an empty environment, so you must either specify a PATH or use full pathnames.

/etc/ppp/ip-down A program or script which is executed when the link is no longer available for sending and receiving IP packets. This script can be used for undoing the effects of the /etc/ppp/ip-up script. It is invoked in the same manner and with the same parameters as the ip-up script, and the same security considerations apply.

/etc/ppp/ipx-up A program or script which is executed when the link is available for sending and receiving IPX packets (that is, IPXCP has come up). It is executed with the parameters

```
interface-name tty-device speed network-number local-
IPX-node-address remote-IPX-node-address local-IPX-
routing-protocol remote-IPX-routing-protocol local-IPX-
router-name remote-IPX-router-name ipparam pppd-pid
```

and with its standard input, output and error streams redirected to /dev/null.

The local-IPX-routing-protocol and remote-IPX-routing-protocol field may be one of the following:

NONE	to indicate that there is no routing protocol
RIP	to indicate that RIP/SAP should be used
NLSP	to indicate that Novell NLSP should be used
RIP NLSP	to indicate that both RIP/SAP and NLSP should be used

This program or script is executed with the real and effective user-IDs set to root, and with an empty environment. This is so that it can be used to manipulate routes, run privileged daemons (e.g. *ripd*), etc. Be careful that the contents of the /etc/ppp/ipx-up and /etc/ppp/ipx-down scripts do not compromise your system's security.

/etc/ppp/ipx-down A program or script which is executed when the link is no longer available for sending and receiving IPX packets. This script can be used for undoing the effects of the /etc/ppp/ipx-up script. It is invoked in the same manner and with the same parameters as the ipx-up script, and the same security considerations apply.

/etc/ppp/pap-secrets Usernames, passwords and IP addresses for PAP authentication. This file should be owned by root and not be readable or writable by any other user. pppd will log a warning if this is not the case.

/etc/ppp/chap-secrets Names, secrets and IP addresses for CHAP authentication. As for /etc/ppp/pap-secrets, this file should be owned by root and not be readable or writable by any other user. Pppd will log a warning if this is not the case.

/etc/ppp/options System default options for pppd, read before user default options or command-line options.

~/.ppprc User default options, read before /etc/ppp/options.*ttyname*.

/etc/ppp/options.ttyNAME System default options for the serial port being used, read after ~/.ppprc. In forming the *ttyname* part of this filename, an initial /dev/ is stripped from the port name (if present), and any slashes in the remaining part are converted to dots.

/etc/ppp/peers A directory containing options files which may contain privileged options, even if pppd was invoked by a user other than root. The system administrator can create options files in this directory to permit non-privileged users to dial out without requiring the peer to authenticate, but only to certain trusted peers.

SEE ALSO

RFC1144 Jacobson, V. Compressing TCP/IP headers for lowspeed serial links. February 1990.

RFC1321 Rivest, R. The MD5 Message-Digest Algorithm. April 1992.

RFC1332 McGregor, G. PPP Internet Protocol Control Protocol (IPCP). May 1992.

RFC1334 Lloyd, B.; Simpson, W.A. *PPP authentication protocols.* October 1992.

RFC1661 Simpson, W.A. The Point-to-Point Protocol (PPP). July 1994.

RFC1662 Simpson, W.A. *PPP in HDLC-like Framing.* July 1994.

NOTES

The following signals have the specified effect when sent to pppd.

SIGINT, SIGTERM These signals cause pppd to terminate the link (by closing LCP), restore the serial device settings, and exit.

SIGHUP This signal causes pppd to terminate the link, restore the serial device settings, and close the serial device. If the *persist* or *demand* option has been specified, pppd will try to reopen the serial device and start another connection (after the holdoff period). Otherwise pppd will exit. If this signal is received during the holdoff period, it causes pppd to end the holdoff period immediately.

SIGUSR1 This signal toggles the state of the *debug* option.

SIGUSR2 This signal causes pppd to renegotiate compression. This can be useful to re-enable compression after it has been disabled as a result of a fatal decompression error. (Fatal decompression errors generally indicate a bug in one or other implementation.)

AUTHORS

Paul Mackerras <Paul.Mackerras@cs.anu.edu.au>, based on earlier work by Drew Perkins, Brad Clements, Karl Fox, Greg Christy, and Brad Parker.

RESTORE(8)

NAME

restore Restore files or file systems from backups made with dump.

SYNOPSIS

restore *key [name ...]*

DESCRIPTION

The **restore** command performs the inverse function of dump(8). A full backup of a file system may be restored and subsequent incremental backups layered on top of it. Single files and directory subtrees may be restored from full or partial backups. **Restore** works across a network; to do this see the **-f** flag described below. The actions of **restore** are controlled by the given **key**, which is a string of characters containing at most one function letter and possibly one or more function modifiers. Other arguments to the command are file or directory names specifying the files that are to be restored. Unless the **h** key is specified (see below), the appearance of a directory name refers to the files and (recursively) subdirectories of that directory.

The function portion of the key is specified by one of the following letters:

r Restore (rebuild a file system). The target file system should be made pristine with `newfs`(8), mounted and the user `cd`'d into the pristine file system before starting the restoration of the initial level 0 backup. If the level 0 restores successfully, the **r** key may be used to restore any necessary incremental backups on top of the level 0. The **r** key precludes an interactive file extraction and can be detrimental to one's health if not used carefully (not to mention the disk). An example:

```
newfs /dev/rrp0g eagle
mount /dev/rp0g /mnt
cd /mnt
restore rf /dev/rst8
```

NOTE

restore leaves a file restoresymtable in the root directory to pass information between incremental restore passes. This file should be removed when the last incremental has been restored.

Restore, in conjunction with newfs(8) and dump(8), may be used to modify file system parameters such as size or block size.

C **Restore** reads the backup and compares its contents with files present on the disk. It first changes its working directory to the root of the filesystem that was dumped and compares the tape with the files in its new current directory. This is useful to check that the backup is correct.

R **Restore** requests a particular tape of a multi volume set on which to restart a full restore (see the **r** key above). This is useful if the restore has been interrupted.

x The named files are read from the given media. If a named file matches a directory whose contents are on the backup and the **h** key is not specified, the directory is recursively extracted. The owner, modification time, and mode are restored (if possible). If no file argument is given, then the root directory is extracted, which results in the entire content of the backup being extracted, unless the **h** key has been specified.

t The names of the specified files are listed if they occur on the backup. If no file argument is given, then the root directory is listed, which results in the entire content of the backup being listed, unless the **h** key has been specified. Note that the **t** key replaces the function of the old dumpdir(8) program.

i This mode allows interactive restoration of files from a dump. After reading in the directory information from the dump, **restore** provides a shell-like interface that allows the user to move around the directory tree selecting files to be extracted. The available commands are given below; for those commands that require an argument, the default is the current directory.

add [*arg*] The current directory or specified argument is added to the list of files to be extracted. If a directory is specified, then it and all its descendents are added to the extraction list (unless the **h** key is specified on the command line). Files that are on the extraction list are prepended with a "*" when they are listed by **ls**.

cd *arg* Change the current working directory to the specified argument.

delete [*arg*] The current directory or specified argument is deleted from the list of files to be extracted. If a directory is specified, then it and all its descendents are deleted from the extraction list (unless the **h** key is specified on the command line). The most expedient way to extract most of the files from a directory is to add the directory to the extraction list and then delete those files that are not needed.

extract All the files that are on the extraction list are extracted from the dump. **Restore** will ask which volume the user wishes to mount. The fastest way to extract a few files is to start with the last volume, and work towards the first volume.

help List a summary of the available commands.

ls [*arg*] List the current or specified directory. Entries that are directories are appended with a "/". Entries that have been marked for extraction are prepended with a "*". If the verbose key is set the inode number of each entry is also listed.

pwd Print the full pathname of the current working directory.

quit Restore immediately exits, even if the extraction list is not empty.

`setmodes` All the directories that have been added to the extraction list have their owner, modes, and times set; nothing is extracted from the dump. This is useful for cleaning up after a restore has been prematurely aborted.

`verbose` The sense of the v key is toggled. When set, the verbose key causes the ls command to list the inode numbers of all entries. It also causes **`restore`** to print out information about each file as it is extracted.

The following characters may be used in addition to the letter that selects the function desired.

`b` The next argument to **`restore`** is used as the block size of the media (in kilobytes). If the **`-b`** option is not specified, **`restore`** tries to determine the media block size dynamically.

`D` The next argument to **`restore`** is used as the filesystem name used by the **`-C`** option in its comparison.

`f` The next argument to **`restore`** is used as the name of the archive instead of `/dev/rmt?`. If the name of the file is of the form "host:file," **`restore`** reads from the named file on the remote host using `rmt(8)`. If the name of the file is '-', **`restore`** reads from standard input. Thus, `dump(8)` and **`restore`** can be used in a pipeline to dump and restore a file system with the command

```
dump 0f - /usr | (cd /mnt; restore xf -)
```

`h` **`Restore`** extracts the actual directory, rather than the files that it references. This prevents hierarchical restoration of complete subtrees from the dump.

`m` **`Restore`** will extract by inode numbers rather than by file name. This is useful if only a few files are being extracted, and one wants to avoid regenerating the complete pathname to the file.

`N` **`Restore`** will not extract files. It will only print the file names.

`s` The next argument to **`restore`** is a number which selects the file on a multi-file dump tape. File numbering starts at 1.

T The next argument to **restore** is a directory to use for the storage of temporary files. The default value is /tmp. This option is most useful when restoring files after having booted from a floppy. There might be little or no space on the floppy filesystem, but another source of space might exist.

v Normally **restore** does its work silently. The **v** (verbose) key causes it to type the name of each file it treats preceded by its file type.

y **Restore** will not ask whether it should abort the restore if it gets an error. It will always try to skip over the bad block(s) and continue as best it can.

DIAGNOSTICS

Complaints about bad key characters.

Complaints if it gets a read error. If **y** has been specified, or the user responds 'y', **restore** will attempt to continue the restore.

If a backup was made using more than one tape volume, restore will notify the user when it is time to mount the next volume. If the **x** or **i** key has been specified, **restore** will also ask which volume the user wishes to mount. The fastest way to extract a few files is to start with the last volume, and work towards the first volume.

There are numerous consistency checks that can be listed by **restore**. Most checks are self-explanatory or can "never happen." Common errors are given below.

Converting to New File System Format

A dump tape created from the old file system has been loaded. It is automatically converted to the new file system format.

<filename>: Not Found on Tape

The specified file name was listed in the tape directory, but was not found on the tape. This is caused by tape read errors while looking for the file, and from using a dump tape created on an active file system.

Expected Next File <inumber>, Got <inumber>

A file that was not listed in the directory showed up. This can occur when using a dump created on an active file system.

Incremental Dump Too Low

When doing incremental restore, a dump that was written before the previous incremental dump, or that has too low an incremental level has been loaded.

Incremental Dump Too High

When doing incremental restore, a dump that does not begin its coverage where the previous incremental dump left off, or that has too high an incremental level has been loaded.

Tape Read Error While Restoring <filename>, Tape Read Error While Skipping Over Inode <inumber>, Tape Read Error While Trying To Resynchronize

A tape (or other media) read error has occurred. If a file name is specified, then its contents are probably partially wrong. If an inode is being skipped or the tape is trying to resynchronize, then no extracted files have been corrupted, though files may not be found on the tape.

Resync Restore, Skipped <num> Blocks

After a dump read error, **restore** may have to resynchronize itself. This message lists the number of blocks that were skipped over.

FILES

`/dev/rmt?`	the default tape drive
`/tmp/rstdir*`	file containing directories on the tape.
`/tmp/rstmode*`	owner, mode, and timestamps for directories.
`./restoresymtable`	information passed between incremental restores.

SEE ALSO

dump(8), newfs(8), mount(8), mkfs(8), rmt(8)

BUGS

`Restore` can get confused when doing incremental restores from dump that were made on active file systems.

A level zero dump must be done after a full restore. Because restore runs in user code, it has no control over inode allocation; thus a full dump must be done to get a new set of directories reflecting the new inode numbering, even though the contents of the files is unchanged.

The Linux port of **`restore`** is not able yet to restore multi-volume backups.

HISTORY

The **`restore`** command appeared in 4.2BSD.

ROUTE(8)

NAME

route Show / manipulate the IP routing table.

SYNOPSIS

route [-vnee]

route [-v] add [-net|-host] Target [**netmask** Nm] [**gw** Gw] [**metric** N] [**mss** M] [**window** W] [**irtt** I] [**reject**] [**mod**] [**dyn**] [**reinstate**] [[**dev**] If]

route [-v] **del** [**-net**|**-host**] Target [**gw** Gw] [**netmask** Nm] [**metric** N] [[**dev**] If]

route [-V] [--version] [-h] [--help]

DESCRIPTION

route manipulates the kernel's IP routing table. Its primary use is to set up static routes to specific hosts or networks via an interface after it has been configured with the **ifconfig**(8) program.

OPTIONS

-v	Is a flag for verbose (not used).
-n	Shows numerical addresses instead of trying to determine symbolic host names. This is useful if you are trying to determine why the route to your nameserver has vanished.
-e	Use **netstat**(8)-format for displaying the routing table. **-ee** will generate a very long line with all parametres from the routing table.
-net	The **Target** is the address of a network (found in */etc/networks* by the **getnetbyname**(2) library function).
-host	Is the address of a host (found with **gethostbyname**(2) library function).
(none)	Displays the kernel routing table. The layout can be changed with **-e** and **-ee**
del	Deletes a route.
add	Adds a route.
Target	The destination network or host. You can provide IP addresses in dotted decimal or host/network names.
netmask Nm	Modifier specifies the netmask of the route to be added. This only makes sense for a network route, and when the address Target actually makes sense with the specified netmask. If no netmask is given, **route** guesses it instead, so for most normal setups you won't need to specify a netmask.
gw Gw	Any IP packets for the target network/host will be routed through the specified gateway.

NOTE

The specified gateway must be reachable first. This usually means that you have to set up a static route to the gateway beforehand. If you specifiy the address of one of your local interfaces, it will be used to decide about the interface to which the packets should be routed to. This is a BSDism compatibility hack.

metric M	Modifier sets the metric field in the roting table, used from daemons for dynamic routing.
mss M	Modifier specifies the TCP Maximum Segment Size in Bytes (MSS) for TCP Connections over this route. This is normally used only for fine optimisation of routing setups. The default is 536.
window W	Modifier specifies the TCP window size for TCP Connections over this route. This is typically only used on AX.25 networks and with drivers unable to handle back-to-back frames.
irtt I	Modifier specifies the initial round trip time (irtt) for TCP Connections over this route. This is typically only used on AX.25 networks. The number is given in milliseconds (1-12000). If ommited the RFC 1122 default of 300ms is used.
reject	Modifier installs a blocking route, which will force a route lookup to fail. This is, for example, used to mask out networks before using the default route. This is NOT for firewalling.
mod, dyn, reinstate	Modifier installs a dynamic or modified route. Both flags are generally only set by a routing daemon. This is only for diagnostic purposes.
dev If	Modifier forces the route to be associated with the specified device, as the kernel will otherwise try to determine the device

on its own (by checking already existing routes and device specifications, and where the route is added to). In most normal networks you won't need this.

If **dev If** is the last option on the command line, the word **dev** may be omitted, as it's the default. Otherwise the order of the route modifiers (metric - netmask - gw - dev) doesn't matter.

EXAMPLES

route add -net 127.0.0.0 Adds the normal loopback entry, using netmask 255.0.0.0 (Class A net, determined from the destination address) and associated with the "lo" device (assuming this device was previously set up correctly with **ifconfig**(8)).

route add -net 192.56.76.0 netmask 255.255.255.0 dev eth0 Adds a route to the network 192.56.76.x via "eth0." The Class C netmask modifier is not really necessary here because 192.* is a Class C IP address. The word "dev" can be omitted here.

route add default gw mango-gw Adds a default route (which will be used if no other route matches). All packets using this route will be gatewayed through "mango-gw." The device which will actually be used for that route depends on how we can reach "mango-gw" - the static route to "mango-gw" will have to be set up before.

route add ipx4 sl0 Adds the route to the "ipx4" host via the SLIP interface (assuming that "ipx4" is the SLIP host).

route add -net 192.57.66.0 netmask 255.255.255.0 gw ipx4 This command adds the net "192.57.66.x" to be gatewayed through the former route to the SLIP interface.

route add -net 224.0.0.0 netmask 240.0.0.0 dev eth0 This is an obscure one documented so people know how to do it. This sets all of the class D (multicast) IP routes to go via "eth0." This is the correct normal configuration line with a multicasting kernel.

route add 10.0.0.0 netmask 255.0.0.0 reject This installs a rejecting route for the private network "10.x.x.x."

OUTPUT

The output of the kernel routing table is organized in the following columns:

Destination The destination network or destination host.

Gateway The Gateway host or '*' if none set.

Genmask The netmask for the destination net '255.255.255 .255' for a host destination and '0.0.0.0' for the **default** route.

Flags Possible flags are

U (route is **Up**)

H (target is a **host**)

G (use **gateway**)

R (**reinstate** route for dynamic routing)

D (**dynamically** installed by daemon or redirect)

M (**modified** from routing daemon or rederict)

! (**reject** route)

Metric The 'distance' to the target (usually counted in hops). It is not used by recent kernels, only routing daemons may use it.

Ref Number of references to this route. Not used in the Linux kernel, always 0.

Use Count of lookups for the route. With recent kernels these numbers are very low, since the sockets have its own cache and don't need to lookup routes.

Iface Interface to which the IP Packages will be send.

MSS Default maximum segement size for TCP Connections over this route.

Window Default windowsize for TCP Connections over this route.

irtt Initial RTT (Round Trip Time). The kernels use this to guess about the best TCP protocol parameters without waiting on (possible slow) answers.

FILES

`/proc/net/route`
`/etc/networks`
`/etc/hosts`
`/etc/init.d/network`

SEE ALSO

ifconfig(8), *netstat*(8), *arp*(8)

HISTORY

route for Linux was originally written by Fred N. van Kempen, `<waltje@uwalt.nl.mugnet.org>` and then modified by Johannes Stille and Linus Torvalds for pl15. Alan Cox added the mss and window options for Linux 1.1.22. irtt support and merged with netstat from Bernd Eckenfels.

BUGS

none :)

RPM(8)

NAME

rpm Red Hat Package Manager.

SYNOPSIS

rpm [options]

DESCRIPTION

rpm is a powerful *package manager*, which can be used to build, install, query, verify, update, and uninstall individual software packages. A *package* consists of an archive of files, and package information, including name, version, and description.

There are ten basic modes of operation, and each takes a different set of options. They are *Install*, *Query*, *Verify*, *Signature check*, *Uninstall*,

Build, *Rebuild Database*, *fix permissions*, *set owners and groups*, and *Show RC*.

Install mode **rpm -i [install-options] <package_file>+**

Query mode **rpm -q [query-options]**

Verify mode **rpm -V|-y|--verify [verify-options]**

Signature Check mode **rpm --checksig <package_file>+**

Uninstall mode **rpm -e <package_name>+**

Build mode **rpm -[b|t]O [build-options] <package_spec>+**

Rebuild database **rpm --rebuilddb**

Fix permissions **rpm --setperms [query-package-specifiers]**

Set owners and groups **rpm --setugids [query-package-specifiers]**

Show RC **rpm --showrc**

GENERAL OPTIONS

These options can be used in all the different modes:

-vv Print lots of ugly debugging information.

--keep-temps Do not remove temporary files (/tmp/rpm-*). Primarily only useful for debugging rpm.

--quiet Print as little as possible - normally only error messages will be displayed.

--help Print a longer usage message then normal.

--version Print a single line containing the version number of rpm being used.

--rcfile <file> Use <file> instead of /etc/rpmrc and $HOME/.rpmrc.

--root *<dir>* Use the system rooted at *<dir>* for all operations. Note that this means the database will be read or modified under *<dir>* and any *pre* or *post* scripts are run after a chroot() to *<dir>*.

--dbpath <path> Use RPM database in <path>.

--ftpproxy <host> Use <host> as an FTP proxy. See **FTP OPTIONS.**

--ftpport <port> Use <port> as the FTP port. See **FTP OPTIONS.**

INSTALL AND UPGRADE OPTIONS

The general form of an rpm install command is

rpm -i [install-options] <package_file>+

This installs a new package. The general form of an rpm upgrade command is

rpm -U [install-options] <package_file>+

This upgrades or installs the package currently installed to the version in the new RPM. This is the same as install, except all other version of the package are removed from the system.

The <package_file> may be specified as an ftp style URL, in which case the package will be downloaded before being installed. See **FTP OPTIONS** for information on RPM's built in ftp support.

--force Same as using both **--replacepkgs**, **--replacefiles**, and **--oldpackage**.

-h, --hash Print 50 hash marks as the package archive is unpacked. Use with **-v** for a nice display.

--oldpackage Allow an upgrade to replace a newer package with an older one.

--percent Print percentages as files are unpacked from the package archive. This is intended to make RPM easy to run from other tools.

--replacefiles Install the packages even if they replace files from other, already installed, packages.

--replacepkgs Install the packages even if some of them are already installed on this system.

--allfiles Installs or upgrades all the missingok files in the package, regardless if they exist.

--nodeps Don't do a dependency check before installing to upgrading a package.

--noscripts Don't execute the preinstall or postinstall scripts.

--notriggers Don't execute scripts which are triggered by the installation of this package.

--excludedocs Don't install any files which are marked as documentation (which includes man pages and texinfo documents).

--includedocs Install documentation files. This is only needed if *excludedocs: 1* is specified in an rpmrc file.

--test Do not install the package, simply check for and report potential conflicts.

--prefix <path> This sets the installation prefix to <path> for relocatable packages.

--ignorearch This allows installation or upgrading even if the architectures of the binary RPM and host don't match.

--ignoreos This allows installation or upgrading even if the operating systems of the binary RPM and host don't match.

QUERY OPTIONS

The general form of an rpm query command is

rpm -q [query-options]

You may specify the format that package information should be printed in. To do this, you use the **--queryformat** option, followed by the format string.

Query formats are modifed versions of the standard **printf**(3) formatting. The format is made up of static strings (which may include standard C character escapes for newlines, tabs, and other special characters) and **printf**(3) type formatters. As rpm already knows the type to print, the type specifier must be omitted however, and replaced by the name of the header tag to be printed, enclosed by **{}** characters. The **RPMTAG_** portion of the tag name may be omitted.

Alternate output formats may be requested by following the tag with **:typetag**. Currently, the following types are supported: **octal**, **date**, **shescape**, **perms**, **fflags**, and **depflags**.

For example, to print only the names of the packages queried, you could use **%{NAME}** as the format string. To print the package's name and distribution information in two columns, you could use **%-30{NAME}%{DISTRIBUTION}**.

rpm will print a list of all of the tags it knows about when it is invoked with the **--querytags** argument.

There are two subsets of options for querying: package selection, and information selection.

Package selection options:

<package_name> Query installed package named *<package_name>*.

-a Query all installed packages

--whatrequires *<capability>* Query all packages that require *<capability>* for proper functioning.

--whatprovides *<virtual>* Query all packages that provide the *<virtual>* capability.

-f <file> Query package owning *<file>*.

--requiredby *<package>* Query all of the packages which contain trigger scripts that are triggered by *<package>*.

-p <package_file> Query an (uninstalled) package *<package_file>*. The <package_file> may be specified as an ftp style URL, in which case the package header will be downloaded and queried. See **FTP OPTIONS** for information on RPM's built in ftp support.

Information selection options:

-i Display package information, including name, version, and description. This uses the **--queryformat** if one was specified.

-R List packages this one depends on (same as **--requires**).

--provides List capabilities this package provides.

--changelog Display change information for the package.

-l List files in package.

-s Display the *states* of files in the package (implies **-l**). The state of each file is either *normal*, *not installed*, or *replaced*.

-d List only documentation files (implies **-l**).

-c List only configuration files (implies **-l**).

--scripts List the package specific shell scripts that are used as part of the installation and uninstallation processes, if there are any.

--triggers Display the trigger scripts, if any, which are contained in the package.

--dump Dump file information as follows: path size mtime md5sum mode owner group isconfig isdoc rdev symlink. This must be used with at least one of **-l**, **-c**, **-d**.

VERIFY OPTIONS

The general form of an rpm verify command is

rpm -V|-y|--verify [verify-options]

Verifying a package compares information about the installed files in the package with information about the files taken from the original package and stored in the rpm database. Among other things, verifying compares the size, MD5 sum, permissions, type, owner and group of each file. Any discrepencies are displayed. The package specification options are the same as for package querying.

Files that were not installed from the package, for example documentation files excluded on installation using the "**--excludedocs**" option, will be silently ignored.

The format of the output is a string of 8 characters, a possible "**c**" denoting a configuration file, and then the file name. Each of the 8 characters denotes the result of a comparison of one attribute of the file to the value of that attribute recorded in the RPM database. A single "**.**" (period) means the test passed. The following characters denote failure of certain tests:

5	MD5 sum
S	File size
L	Symlink
T	Mtime
D	Device
U	User
G	Group
M	Mode (includes permissions and file type)

SIGNATURE CHECKING

The general form of an rpm signature check command is

rpm --checksig <package_file>+

This checks the PGP signature built into a package to ensure the integrity and the origin of the package. PGP configuration information is read from /etc/rpmrc. See the section on PGP SIGNATURES for details.

UNINSTALL OPTIONS

The general form of an rpm uninstall command is

rpm -e <package_name>+

--allmatches Remove all versions of the package which match <*package_name*>. Normally an error is issued if <*package_name*> matches multiple packages.

--noscripts Don't execute the preuninstall or postuninstall scripts.

--notriggers Don't execute scripts which are triggered by the removal of this package.

--nodeps Don't check dependencies before uninstalling the packages.

--test Don't really uninstall anything, just go through the motions. **-vv** option.

--nodeps Don't check for broken dependencies before removing the package.

BUILD OPTIONS

The general form of an rpm build command is

rpm -[b|t]O [build-options] <package_spec>+

The argument used is -b if a spec file is being used to build the package and **-t** if **RPM** should look inside of a gzipped (or compressed) tar file for the spec file to use. After the first argument, the next argument (*O*) specifies the stages of building and packaging to be done and is one of

-bp Executes the "%prep" stage from the spec file. Normally this involves unpacking the sources and applying any patches.

-bl Do a "list check." The "%files" section from the spec file is macro expanded, and checks are made to insure the files exist.

-bc Do the "%build" stage from the spec file (after doing the prep stage). This generally involves the equivalent of a "make."

-bi Do the "%install" stage from the spec file (after doing the prep and build stages). This generally involves the equivalent of a "make install."

-bb Build a binary package (after doing the prep, build, and install stages).

-ba Build binary and source packages (after doing the prep, build, and install stages).

The following options may also be used:

--short-circuit Skip straight to specified stage (ie, skip all stages leading up to the specified stage). Only valid with **-bc** and **-bi**.

--timecheck Set the "timecheck" age (0 to disable). This value can also be set in rpmrc with "timecheck:." The timecheck value expresses, in seconds, the maximum age of a file being packaged. Warnings will be printed for all files beyond the timecheck age.

--clean Remove the build tree after the packages are made.

--rmsource Remove the sources and spec file after the build (may also be used standalone, eg. "**rpm --rmsource foo.spec**").

--test Do not execute any build stages. Useful for testing out spec files.

--sign Embed a PGP signature in the package. This signature can be used to verify the integrity and the origin of the package. See the section on PGP SIGNATURES for /etc/rpmrc details.

REBUILD AND RECOMPILE OPTIONS

There are two other ways to invoke rpm:

rpm --recompile <source_package_file>+

rpm --rebuild <source_package_file>+

When invoked this way, rpm installs the named source package, and does a prep, compile and install. In addition, **--rebuild** builds a new binary package. When the build has completed, the build directory is removed (as in **--clean**) and the the sources and spec file for the package are removed.

SIGNING AN EXISTING RPM

rpm --resign <binary_package_file>+

This option generates and inserts new signatures for the listed packages. Any existing signatures are removed.

PGP SIGNATURES

In order to use the signature feature RPM must be able to run PGP (it must be installed and in your path), and it must be able to find a public key ring with RPM public keys in it. By default, RPM uses the PGP defaults to find the keyrings (honoring PGPPATH). If your key rings are not located where PGP expects them to be, you must set the following in your /etc/rpmrc:

pgp_path Replacement path for /usr/lib/rpm. Must contain your key rings.

If you want to be able to sign packages you create yourself, you also need to create your own public and secret key pair (see the PGP manual). In addition to the above /etc/rpmrc entries, you should add the following:

signature The signature type. Right now only pgp is supported.

pgp_name The name of the "user" whose key you wish to use to sign your packages.

When building packages you then add --sign to the command line. You will be prompted for your pass phrase, and your package will be built and signed.

REBUILD DATABASE OPTIONS

The general form of an rpm rebuild database command is

rpm --rebuilddb

The only options this mode supports are **--dbpath** and **--root**.

SHOWRC

Running

rpm --showrc

shows the values RPM will use for all of the options that may be set in *rpmrc* files.

FTP OPTIONS

RPM includes a simple FTP client to simplify installing and querying packages which are available over the Internet. Package files for install, upgrade, and query operations may be specified as an ftp style URL:

ftp://<user>:<password>@hostname/path/to/package.rpm

If the `@password` portion is omitted, the password will be prompted for (once per user/hostname pair). If both the user and password are omitted, anonymous ftp is used. In all cases passive (PASV) ftp transfers are used.

RPM allows the following options to be used with ftp URLs:

--ftpproxy <hostname> The host <hostname> will be used as a proxy server for all transfers, which allows users to ftp through firewall machines which use proxy systems. This option may also be specified in an *rpmrc* file.

--ftpport <port> Specifies the TCP port number to use for the ftp connection instead of the default port. This option may also be specified in an *rpmrc* file.

FILES

```
/etc/rpmrc
~/.rpmrc
/var/lib/rpm/packages
/var/lib/rpm/pathidx
/var/lib/rpm/nameidx
/tmp/rpm*
```

SEE ALSO

glint(8), *rpm2cpio*(8), `http://www.redhat.com/rpm`

AUTHORS

Marc Ewing <marc@redhat.com>

Erik Troan <ewt@redhat.com>

SHUTDOWN(8)

NAME

shutdown Bring the system down.

SYNOPSIS

/sbin/shutdown [**-t** *sec*] [**-rkhncf**] *time* [*warning-message*]

DESCRIPTION

Shutdown brings the system down in a secure way. All logged in users are notified that the system is going down, and *login(1)* is blocked. It is possible to shut the system down immideately, or after a delay. All processes are first notified that the system is going down by the signal SIGTERM. This gives programs like *vi(1)* the time to save the file being edited, mail and news processing programs a chance to exit cleanly, etc. **Shutdown** does it's job by signalling the **init** process, asking it to change the *runlevel*. *Runlevel 0* is used to halt the system, *runlevel 6* is used to reboot the system and *runlevel 1* is used to put the system into a state where administrative tasks can be performed; this is the default if neither the *-h* or *-r* flag is given to **shutdown**. To see which actions are taken on halt or reboot see the appropriate entries of these *runlevels* in the file */etc/inittab*.

OPTIONS

-t *sec* — Tell init to wait *sec* seconds between sending processes the warning and the kill signal, before changing to another *runlevel*.

-k — Don't really shutdown; only send the warning messages to everybody.

-r — Reboot after shutdown.

-h	Halt after shutdown.
-n	[DEPRECIATED] Don't call init to do the shutdown but do it ourself. The use of this option is discouraged, and its results are not always what you'd expect.
-f	Do a 'fast' reboot.
-c	Cancel an already running shutdown. With this option it is, of course, not possible to give the **time** argument, but you can enter a explanatory message on the command line that will be sent to all users.
time	When to shutdown.
warning-message	Message to send to all users.

The time argument can have different formats. First, it can be an absolute time in the format *hh:mm*, in which *hh* is the hour (1 or 2 digits) and *mm* is the minute of the hour (in two digits). Second, it can be in the format **+m**, in which *m* is the number of minutes to wait. The word **now** is an alias for **+0**.

The -f flag means 'reboot fast'. This only creates an advisory file **/fastboot** which can be tested by the system when it comes up again. The boot rc file can test if this file is present, and decide not to run *fsck(1)* since the system has been shut down in the proper way. After that, the boot process should remove **/fastboot**.

The **-n** flag causes shutdown not to call init, but to kill all running processes itself. After all processes are killed, **shutdown** will try to run the script */etc/rc.d/rc.halt fast* (or rc.reboot). It also tests for the presence of the equivalent files *rc.0* and *rc.6*. If this script returns or can't be executed (because it's not present for example) **shutdown** will turn off *quota* and *accounting*, turn off *swapping* and *unmount* all filesystems.

ACCESS CONTROL

Shutdown can be called from **init**(8) when the magic keys **CTRL-ALT-DEL** are pressed, by creating an appropriate entry in */etc/inittab*. This means that everyone who has physical access to the console keyboard can shut the system down. To prevent this, **shutdown** can check to see if an authorized user is logged in on one of the virtual consoles. If **shutdown** is called from **init**, it checks to see if the file */etc/shutdown.allow* is present. It then compares the login names in that file with the list of people that are logged in on a virtual console (from */var/run/utmp*). Only if one of those authorized users **or root** is logged in, it will proceed. Otherwise it will write the message

shutdown: no authorized users logged in

to the (physical) system console. The format of /etc/shut*down.allow* is one user name per line. Empty lines and comment lines (prefixed by a **#**) are allowed. Currently there is a limit of 32 users in this file.

FILES

```
/fastboot
/etc/inittab
/etc/rc.d/rc.halt
/etc/rc.d/rc.reboot
/etc/shutdown.allow
```

BUGS

Not really a bug, but most users forget to give the *time* argument and are then puzzled by the error message **shutdown** produces. The *time* argument is mandatory; in 90 percent of all cases this argument will be the word **now**.

AUTHOR

Miquel van Smoorenburg `<miquels@cistron.nl>`

SEE ALSO

fsck(8), init(1), halt(8), reboot(8)

USERADD(8)

NAME

useradd Create a new user or update default new user information.

SYNOPSIS

useradd [**-A** {*method*|**DEFAULT**},...] [**-c** *comment*] [**-d** *home_dir*]

[**-e** *expire_date*] [**-f** *inactive_time*] [**-g** *initial_group*]

[**-G** *group*[,...]] [**-m** [**-k** *skeleton_dir*] | *-M*] [**-s** *shell*]

[**-u** *uid* [**-o**]] [**-n**] [**-r**] *login*

useradd **-D** [**-g** default_group] [**-b** default_home] [**-f** *default_inactive*] [**-e** *default_expiration*] [**-s** *default_shell*]

DESCRIPTION

CREATING NEW USERS

When invoked without the -D option, the useradd command creates a new user account using the values specified on the command line and the default values from the system. The new user account will be entered into the system files as needed, the home directory will be created, and initial files copied, depending on the command line options. The version provided with Red Hat Linux will create a group for each user added to the system, unless -n option is given. The options which apply to the useradd command are

-A {method|**DEFAULT**},... The value of the user's authentication method. The authentication method is the name of a program which is responsible for validating the user's identity. The string **DEFAULT** may be used to change the user's authentication method to the standard system password method. This is a comma-separated list of program names. It may include **DEFAULT** exactly once.

-d *home_dir* The new user will be created using *home_dir* as the value for the user's login directory. The default is to append the *login* name to *default_home* and use that as the login directory name.

-e *expire_date* The date on which the user account will be disabled. The date is specified in the format *MM/DD/YY*.

-f *inactive_days* The number of days after a password expires until the account is permanently disabled. A value of 0 disables the account as soon as the password has expired, and a value of -1 disables the feature. The default value is -1.

-g *initial_group* The group name or number of the user's initial login group. The group name must exist. A group number must refer to an already existing group. The default group number is 1.

-G *group,[...]* A list of supplementary groups which the user is also a member of. Each group is separated from the next by a comma, with no intervening whitespace. The groups are subject to the same restrictions as the group given with the **-g** option. The default is for the user to belong only to the initial group.

-m The user's home directory will be created if it does not exist. The files contained in *skeleton_dir* will be copied to the home directory if the **-k** option is used, otherwise the files contained in */etc/skel* will be used instead. Any directories contained in *skeleton_dir* or */etc/skel* will be created in the user's home directory as well. The **-k** option is only valid in conjunction with the **-m** option. The default is to not create the directory and to not copy any files.

-M The user home directory will not be created, even if the system wide settings from */etc/login.defs* is to create home dirs.

-n A group having the same name as the user being added to the system will be created by default. This option will turn off this Red Hat Linux-specific behavior.

-r This flag is used to create a system account. That is, an user with an UID lower than value of UID_MIN defined in */etc/login.defs*. Note that **useradd** will not create a home directory for such an user, regardless of the default setting in */etc/login.defs*. You have to specify **-m** option if you want a home directory for a system account to be created. This is an option added by Red Hat.

-s *shell* The name of the user's login shell. The default is to leave this field blank, which causes the system to select the default login shell.

-u *uid* The numerical value of the user's ID. This value must be unique, unless the *-o* option is used. The value must be non-negative. The default is to use the smallest ID value greater than 99 and greater than every other user. Values between 0 and 99 are typically reserved for system accounts.

CHANGING THE DEFAULT VALUES

When invoked with the **-D** option, **useradd** will either display the current default values, or update the default values from the command line. The valid options are

-b *default_home* The initial path prefix for a new user's home directory. The user's name will be affixed to the end of *default_home* to create the new directory name if the **-d** *option is not used when creating a new account.*

-e *default_expire* The number of days after a password is changed before it must be changed again.

-f *default_inactive* The number of days after a password has expired before the account will be disabled.

-g *default_group* The group name or ID for a new user's initial group. The named group must exist, and a numerical group ID must have an existing entry.

-s *default_shell* The name of the new user's login shell. The named program will be used for all future new user accounts.

If no options are specified, **useradd** displays the current default values.

NOTES

The system administrator is responsible for placing the default user files in the */etc/skel* directory. This version of useradd was modified by Red Hat to suit Red Hat user/group convention.

CAVEATS

You may not add a user to an NIS group. This must be performed on the NIS server.

FILES

/etc/passwd User account information.

/etc/shadow Secure user account information **/etc/group** - group information.

/etc/default/useradd Default information **/etc/login.defs** - system-wide settings.

/etc/skel Directory containing default files.

SEE ALSO

chfn(1), **chsh**(1), **groupadd**(8), **groupdel**(8), **groupmod**(8), **passwd**(1), **userdel**(8), **usermod**(8)

AUTHOR

Julianne Frances Haugh <`jfh@tab.com`>

USERDEL(8)

NAME

userdel Delete a user account and related files.

SYNOPSIS

userdel [**-r**] *login*

DESCRIPTION

The **userdel** command modifies the system account files, deleting all entries that refer to *login*. The named user must exist.

-r Files in the user's home directory will be removed along with the home directory itself. Files located in other file system will have to be searched for and deleted manually.

FILES

`/etc/passwd` User account information.

`/etc/shadow-` Secure user account information.

`/etc/group-` Group information.

CAVEATS

userdel will not allow you to remove an account if the user is currently logged in. You must kill any running processes which belong to an account that you are deleting. You may not remove any NIS attributes on an NIS client. This must be performed on the NIS server.

SEE ALSO

chfn(1), **chsh**(1), **groupadd**(8), **groupdel**(8), **groupmod**(8), **passwd**(1), **useradd**(8), **usermod**(8)

AUTHOR

Julianne Frances Haugh <`jfh@tab.com`>

USERMOD(8)

NAME

usermod Modify a user account.

SYNOPSIS

usermod[**-A** {*method*|**DEFAULT**},...] [**-c** *comment*] [**-d** *home_dir* [**-m**]]

[**-e** *expire_date*] [**-f** *inactive_time*] [**-g** *initial_group*]

[**-G** *group*[,...]] [**-l** *login_name*] [**-s** *shell*] [**-u** *uid* [**-o**]] *login*

DESCRIPTION

The **usermod** command modifies the system account files to reflect the changes that are specified on the command line. The options which apply to the **usermod** command are

-A *method*|**DEFAULT** The new value of the user's authentication method. The authentication method is the name of a program which is responsible for validating the user's identity. The string **DEFAULT** may be used to change the user's authentication method to the standard system password method.

-c *comment* The new value of the user's password file comment field. It is normally modified using the chfn(1) utility.

-d *home_dir* The user's new login directory. If the **-m** option is given the contents of the current home directory will be moved to the new home directory, which is created if it does not already exist.

-e *expire_date* The date on which the user account will be disabled. The date is specified in the format *MM/DD/YY*.

-f *inactive_days* The number of days after a password expires until the account is permanently disabled. A value of 0 disables the account as soon as the password has expired, and a value of -1 disables the feature. The default value is -1.

-g *initial_group* The group name or number of the user's new initial login group. The group name must exist. A group number must refer to an already existing group. The default group number is 1.

-G *group,[...]* A list of supplementary groups which the user is also a member of. Each group is separated from the next by a comma, with no intervening whitespace. The groups are subject to the same restrictions as the group given with the **-g** option. If the user is currently a member of a group which is not listed, the user will be removed from the group

-l *login_name* The name of the user will be changed from *login* to *login_name*. Nothing else is changed. In particular, the user's home directory name should probably be changed to reflect the new login name.

-s *shell* The name of the user's new login shell. Setting this field to blank causes the system to select the default login shell.

-u *uid* The numerical value of the user's ID. This value must be unique, unless the *-o* option is used. The value must be non-negative. Values between 0 and 99 are typically reserved for system accounts. Any files which the user owns and which are located in the directory tree rooted at the user's home directory will have the file user ID changed automatically. Files outside of the user's home directory must be altered manually.

CAVEATS

usermod will not allow you to change the name of a user who is logged in. You must make certain that the named user is not executing any processes when this command is being executed if the user's numerical user ID is being changed. You must change the owner of any crontab files manually. You must change the owner of any at jobs manually. You must make any changes involving NIS on the NIS server.

FILES

`/etc/passwd` User account information.

`/etc/shadow` Secure user account information.

`/etc/group` Group information.

SEE ALSO

chfn(1), **chsh**(1), **groupadd**(8), **groupdel**(8), **groupmod**(8), **passwd**(1), **useradd**(8), **userdel**(8)

AUTHOR

Julianne Frances Haugh `<jfh@tab.com>`

Appendix B

Linux Reading List

This appendix is reprinted from the Linux Reading List HOWTO, version 1.4 of 22 November 1998, by Eric S. Raymond.

This document lists the books I think are most valuable to a person trying to learn Unix (especially Linux) top to bottom.

INTRODUCTION

This document lists what I consider to be the essential book-length references for learning Unix (especially Linux) and how to program under it.

New Versions of This Document

New versions of the Linux Reading List HOWTO will be periodically posted to `comp.os.linux.answers`. They will also be uploaded to various Linux Web and FTP sites, including the LDP home page.

You can also view the latest version of this on the World Wide Web at `http://MetaLab.unc.edu/LDP/HOWTO/Reading-List-HOWTO.html`.

Feedback and Corrections

If you have questions or comments about this document, or just want to suggest a book that you think should be on it, please feel free to e-mail Eric S. Raymond at `esr@thyrsus.com`. I welcome any suggestions or criticisms.

Related Resources

For online HOWTOs, magazines, and other non-book material, see the Linux Documentation Project home page (`http://MetaLab.unc.edu/LDP/HOWTO`).

Some years ago I wrote a less Linux-focused Unix bibliography that may still be of some interest and retains a certain amusement value. You can find the Loginataka at `http://www.tuxedo.org/~esr/faqs/loginataka.html`.

There's a collection of Web links to Linux book reviews called Opening Doors, Breaking Windows (`http://members.bellatlantic.net/~ptgeiger/guidehome.htm`).

Conventions Used in This Document

Comments not in quotation marks below are either mine, or I have seen no reason to change them from those of Jim Haynes (the previous maintainer of this document). Comments sent in by others are in quotation marks and have the name of the commentator before them (JH is Jim Haynes).

"See" URLs following publishing information point directly to the publisher's Web catalog and typically take you to a page containing a cover shot, blurbs, and ordering information. Books that don't have these lack them because the publisher is using frames and the catalog pages can't be bookmarked.

Topic listings go roughly from the outside in (culture to user-land programming to kernel programming to hardware). Within sections, I have tried to list the most useful books first. It's just an embarrassing coincidence that this lists one of my books first, honest! (Suggestions for a better organization are cheerfully accepted.)

Books on Culture, History, and Pragmatics

The New Hacker's Dictionary (Third Edition) Raymond, Eric S. MIT Press, 1996. ISBN 0-262-68092-0. 547 pages. See `http://www-mitpress.mit.edu/book-home.tcl?isbn=0262680920`.

Um, er. A guide to Internet culture. Lots of people like it. An HTML version is available at the Jargon File Resource Page (`http://www.tuxedo.org`).

A Quarter Century of Unix Salus, Peter H. Addison-Wesley, 1994. ISBN 0-201-54777-5. 256 pages. See `http://www.awl.com/cp/authors/salus/unix/unix.html`.

Linux is part of the Unix tradition. This book is an oral history of Unix—how it originated, how it evolved, how it spread—by the people who were there.

The Mythical Man Month (Anniversary Edition) Brooks, Frederick P. Addison-Wesley, 1995. ISBN 0-201-83595-9. See `http://heg-school.awl.com/cseng/authors/brooks/mmm-ae/mmm-ae.html`.

The one book on software engineering that everyone should read.

Alan Cox: "This I'd recommend not for its technical value but for its application of common sense and reality to computing projects." JH: "Ah, yes. What if Linus had been given 200 programmers and had been told to produce Linux in 3 months!"

Bell System Technical Journal 57 No. 6 (July-August 1978):416 pages.

Many early papers on Unix, including Ritchie Thompson, "The UNIX Time Sharing System"; Thompson, "UNIX Implementation"; Ritchie, "A Retrospective"; and Bourne, "The UNIX Shell".

Books on General Unix/Linux

This section is concerned with installing and maintaining Linux systems.

Linux Installation and Administration

Linux Installation and Getting Started Welsh, Matt. LDP, 1997. Available on the LDP home page or directly at `http://MetaLab.unc.edu/LDP/gs`.

How to bring up Linux. Explains a lot of Linux basics. Covers basic system administration.

Linux System Administrator's Guide Wirzenius, Lars. LDP, 1997. Available on the LDP home page or directly at `http://MetaLab.unc.edu/LDP/sag`.

An excellent first book on how to maintain and administer a Linux system.

Essential System Administration (Second Edition) Frisch, Aeleen. O'Reilly, 1995. ISBN 0-937175-80-3. 788 pages. $32.95. See `http://www.ora.com/catalog/esa2/noframes.html`.

More in-depth coverage of normal system-administration tasks. Not Linux-specific but contains Linux material.

Using Unix Linux

Linux in a Nutshell Hekman, Jessica P., et al. O'Reilly, 1997. ISBN 1-56592-167-4. 438 pages. $9.95. See `http://www.ora.com/catalog/linuxnut/noframes.html`.

According to O'Reilly, "The Desktop Reference for Linux." For Linux users this makes obsolete *Unix In a Nutshell*, which was SVr4/Solaris-oriented.

Running Linux (Second Edition) Welsh, Matt, and Lar Kaufman. O'Reilly, 1996. ISBN 1-56592-151-8. 650 pages. $24.95. See `http://www.ora.com/catalog/runux2/noframes.html`.

Everything you need in order to understand, install, and use the Linux operating system. Excellent beginner's book.

Hands-on-Linux Sobell, Mark G. Addison-Wesley, 1998. ISBN 0-201-32569-1. 1,015 pages.

Just what the title says—practical tutorials on basic Unix, shells, editors, mail programs, networking, Web tools, and utilities. Covers some system administration fundamentals. (This appears to be a repackaging of 1997's *A Practical Guide to Linux* from the same auther, with Caldera OpenLinux Lite included.)

System Security

Practical Unix Security Garfinkel, Simpson, and Gene Spafford. O'Reilly, 1991. ISBN 0-56592-148-8. See `http://www.ora.com/catalog/puis/noframes.html`.

Ronald P. Miller: "Some overlap with Essential System Admin., but all in all a solid book on security, especially for those aspiring to allow multiple-user, dial-up/net access to their Linux boxes."

Firewalls & Internet Security Cheswick, William R., and Steven M. Bellovin. Addison-Wesley, 1994. ISBN 0-201-63357-4. 320 pages. See `http://cseng.awl.com/bookdetail.qry?ISBN=0-201-63357-4=0`.

Books on Shell, Script, and Web Programming

Programming Perl (Second Edition) Wall, Larry, Tom Christiansen, and Randal Schwartz. O'Reilly, 1997. ISBN 0-56592-149-6.

644 pages. See `http://www.ora.com/catalog/pperl2/noframes.html`.

Shell (as a programming language for more than trivial scripting) is dead. Perl rules in its place. This is the second edition of the definitive Perl book—vastly better organized than the first, and it covers Perl 5.

Programming Python Lutz, Mark. O'Reilly, 1997. ISBN 0-56592-197-6. 880 pages. See `http://www.ora.com/catalog/python/noframes.html`.

The next step beyond Perl. Python is beautifully designed, has better integration with C, and scales up better to large projects.

HTML: The Definitive Guide (2nd Edition) Musciano, Chuck, and Bill Kennedy. O'Reilly, 1997. ISBN 0-56592-235-2. 552 pages. See `http://www.ora.com/catalog/html2/noframes.html`.

The best HTML tutorial/reference I have ever seen, and the only HTML book you need unless you want to do CGI.

The Unix Programming Environment Kernighan, Brian, and Rob Pike. Prentice-Hall, 1984. ISBN 0-13-937681-X.

A true classic—possibly the best single book exposition of the Unix philosophy.

Books on Text Formatting: TeX and LaTeX

The LaTeX Companion Goossens, Michael, Frank Mittlebach, and Alexander Samarin. Addison-Wesley, 1994. ISBN 0-201-54199-8. 530 pages. See `http://www.awl.com/cp/tlc.html`.

`If you are one of those users who would like to know how LaTeX can be extended to create the nicest documents possible without becoming a (La)TeX guru, then this book is for you'—from the Preface. Bruce Thompson adds, "A very nice book providing a lot of information about the new extensions to LaTeX, provides a large number of examples showing precisely how your document's layout can be manipulated."

LaTeX: A Document Preparation System (Second Edition)
Lamport, Leslie. Addison-Wesley, 1994. ISBN 0-201-52983-1. 256 pages. See `http://heg-school.awl.com/cseng/authors/lamport/latex/latex.html`.

Bruce Thompson: "The ultimate reference on LaTeX 2.09 by its author. A new edition covering LaTeX2e (the version included in the current TeX/LaTeX distribution) is in preparation. LaTeX 2.09 is fully supported by LaTeX2e. A must for anyone wanting to use LaTeX. Provides a gentle introduction to document preparation and the various tools that LaTeX provides for producing professional quality documents. Lots of examples."

The TeXbook, Volume A of Computers and Typesetting
Knuth, Donald A. Addison-Wesley, 1986. ISBN 0-201-13448. 496 pages. See `http://www.awl.com/cp/TeXbook.html`.

Bruce Thompson: "The definitive user's guide and complete reference manual for TeX. Probably not needed for casual LaTeX use, but a fascinating book nonetheless." I'll affirm that by adding that this book is not for the faint of heart.

The METAFONT Book, Volume C of Computers and Typesetting Knuth, Donald A. Addison-Wesley, 1986. 0-201-13444-6. 384 pages. See `http://www.awl.com/cp/METAFONTbook.html`.

Bruce Thompson: "The definitive user's guide and reference manual for METAFONT, the companion program to TeX for designing fonts. An excellent work if you're planning to design your own fonts for use in TeX and LaTeX. METAFONT is included with the normal TeX/LaTeX distribution." This book is *definitely* not for the faint of heart.

Books on C and C++ Programming

The C Programming Language (Second Edition)
Kernighan, Brian W., and Dennis M. Ritchie. Prentice-Hall, 1988. ISBN 0-13-110362-8. 272 pages.

The improved second edition, covering ANSI C, of the original classic C book coauthored by C's designer, "K R". Still the best!

Who's Afraid of C++? Heller, Steve. Academic Press, 1996. ISBN 0-12-339097. 508 pages.

The best introductory book on C++ I have seen.

C System Call Interface

POSIX Programmer's Guide: Writing Portable Unix Programs Lewine, Donald. O'Reilly, 1992. ISBN 0-937175-73-0. 607 pages. See `http://www.ora.com/catalog/posix/noframes.html`.

An excellent programmer's reference on the POSIX.1 standard. I like this one better than JH's choice.

The Posix.1 Standard: A Programmer's Guide Zlotnick, Fred. Benjamin/Cummings, 1991. ISBN 0-8053-9605-5. 379 pages. $35.95.

JH: "When I complained about the lack of Section 2 man pages in Linux, somebody told me just to get a POSIX book, because that's what Linux does. I like this book because I'm not a professional programmer and the author gives copious explanations and examples."

Books on Networking

Unix Network Programming Stevens, W. Richard. Prentice Hall, 1990. ISBN 0-13-949876-1. 772 pages. $54.

Everything you might want to know about the subject and some things you probably didn't want to know (really, XNS!?). Generally regarded as definitive on the basics, though it's pre-Web.

Linux Network Administrator's Guide Kirch, Olaf. O'Reilly, 1995. ISBN 1-56592-087-2. 335 pages. See `http://www.ora.com/catalog/linag/noframes.html`.

A practical guide to Linux's TCP/IP and related services. Accessible on the Web at the Linux Documentation Project (`http://MetaLab.unc.edu/LDP`) page or directly at `http://MetaLab.unc.edu/LDP/LDP/nag/nag.html`.

TCP/IP Network Adminstration Hunt, Craig. O'Reilly, 1992. ISBN 0-937175-82-X. 472 pages. See `http://www.ora.com/catalog/tcp2/noframes.html`.

Less Linux-specific than the Kirch book. Features deeper coverage of the TCP/IP core, including routing and BGP.

DNS and BIND (Second Edition) Albitz, Paul, and Cricket Liu. O'Reilly, 1996. ISBN 1-56592-236-0. 438 pages. $32.95. See `http://www.ora.com/catalog/dns2/noframes.html`.

In-depth coverage of DNS; useful for people running complicated multiple-subnet installations. Covers BIND library programming.

Sendmail (Second Edition) Costales, Bryan, and Eric Allman. O'Reilly, 1997. ISBN 1-56592-222-0. 1,050 pages. $32.95. See `http://www.ora.com/catalog/sendmail2/noframes.html`.

An exhaustive (and exhausting) guide to Linux and Unix's default mail-transfer agent.

Books on Unix Kernel Implementation

Here you'll find books on Linux and its ancestors and relatives.

Ancestors of Linux

The Design of the Unix Operating System Bach, Maurice J. Prentice-Hall. ISBN 0-13-201799-7. 470 pages. $60.

The book that got Linus started.

Operating Systems, Design and Implementation Tanenbaum, Andrew S. Prentice-Hall, 1987.

Alan Cox (one of the core kernel people) likes this book. Tanenbaum designed Minix, which is the system Linus bootstrapped Linux up from.

Linux

Linux Kernel Hackers' Guide Johnson, Michael K.

Accessible on the Web at the Linux Documentation Project page (`http://MetaLab.unc.edu/LDP`) or directly at `http://www.redhat.com:8080/HyperNews/get/khg.html`.

Linux Kernel Internals (Second Edition) Beck, Michael, Harold Bohme, Dziadzka Mirko, Ulrich Kunitz, Robert Magnus, Dick Verworner. Addison-Wesley, 1998. ISBN:0-201-33143-8. 480 pages. See `http://heg-school.awl.com/cseng/authors/beck.m/linux/linux.html`.

A guide to Linux kernel programming; covers 2.0.

Relatives of Linux

The Design and Implementation of the 4.4BSD Unix Operating System McKusick, Marshall Kirk, Keith Bostic, Michael J. Karels, and John S. Quarterman. Addison-Wesley, 1996. ISBN 0-201-54979-4. 608 pages. See `http://heg-school.awl.com/cseng/authors/mckusick/4.4bsd/4.4bsd.html`.

The successor to a classic book on the implementation of the 4.3BSD kernel, which influenced Linux's design (especially near sockets and networking). This book covers the 4.4BSD base of BSD/OS, FreeBSD, and NetBSD.

Porting Unix to the 386 Jolitz, William F., and Lynne G. Jolitz. Dr. Dobb's Journal (January 1991–July 1992).

Books on Intel Processor Architecture and Programming

80386 Programmer's Reference Manual Intel, 1986. ISBN 1-55512-022-9.

Part I: Applications Programming, data types, memory model, instruction set. Part II: Systems Programming, architecture, memory management, protection, multitasking, I/O, exceptions and interrupts, initialization, coprocessing and multiprocessing. Part III: Compatibility (with earlier x86 machines). Part IV: Instruction Set.

80386 System Software Writer's Guide Intel, 1987. ISBN 1-55512-023-7.

This explains the 386 features for operating system writers. It includes a chapter on Unix implementation. A lot of the 80386 architecture seems to have been designed with Multics in mind; the features are not used by DOS or by Unix.

Programming the 80386 Crawford, John H., Patrick P. Gelsinger. Sybex. ISBN 0-89588-381-3. 774 pages. $26.95.

This is the book the Jolitzes used when they ported BSD to the 386 architecture.

Pentium Processor User's Manual: Volume 3, Architecture and Programming Manual Intel, 1993. ISBN 1-55512-195-0.

Pretty much the Pentium version of the 80386 Programmer's manual listed above.

Books on PC-Class Hardware

WARNING

These books are four or five years old and possibly out of date. I don't really grok hardware...

80386 Hardware Reference Manual Intel, 1986. ISBN 1-55512-024-5.

Pin connections, timing, waveforms, block diagrams, voltages, all that kind of stuff.

The Indispensable PC Hardware Book Messmer, Hans-Peter. Addison-Wesley, 1993. ISBN 0-201-62424-9. 1,000 pages.

JH: "Covers the more recent stuff like EIDE and PCI."

Administrivia

This section contains the terms of use for this appendix, along with its history.

Terms of Use

This document is copyright ©1997 by Eric S. Raymond. You may use, disseminate, and reproduce it freely, provided you

- Do not omit or alter this copyright notice.
- Do not omit or alter the version number and date.
- Do not omit or alter the document's pointer to the current WWW version.
- Clearly mark any condensed or altered versions as such.

These restrictions are intended to protect potential readers from stale or mangled versions. If you think you have a good case for an exception, ask me.

History

This was originally a mini-HOWTO maintained by Jim Haynes. I have changed the emphasis somewhat, trying to make it more a standalone document and less reliant on the various Usenet bibliographic postings. The unattributed mini-reviews are mine rather than his.

Appendix C

The Linux HOWTO Index

"The Linux HOWTO Index" is reprinted from the Linux HOWTO Index, version 2.10.98 of 28 March 1999, by Tim Bynum <linux-howto@metalab.unc.edu>.

This document contains an index to the Linux HOWTOs and mini-HOWTOs, as well as other information about the HOWTO project.

What Are Linux HOWTOs?

Linux HOWTOs are documents which describe in detail a certain aspect of configuring or using Linux. For example, there is the Installation HOWTO, which gives instructions on installing Linux, and the Mail HOWTO, which describes how to set up and configure mail under Linux. Other examples include the NET-3 HOWTO and the Printing HOWTO.

HOWTOs are comprehensive docs—much like an FAQ but generally not in question-and-answer format. However, many HOWTOs contain an FAQ section at the end.

There are several HOWTO formats available: plain text, PostScript, DVI, and HTML.

In addition to the HOWTOs, there are a multitude of mini-HOWTOs on short, specific subjects. They are only available in plain text and HTML format.

Where Can I Get Linux HOWTOs?

HOWTOs can be retrieved via anonymous FTP from the following sites:

- `ftp://metalab.unc.edu/pub/Linux/docs/HOWTO`
- `ftp://tsx-11.mit.edu/pub/linux/docs/HOWTO`

There are also many mirror sites (see `ftp://metalab.unc.edu/pub/Linux/MIRRORS.html`).

You can also browse HOWTOs in HTML format (see `http://metalab.unc.edu/LDP/HOWTO/`). Many mirror sites mirror the HTML files (see `http://metalab.unc.edu/LDP/hmirrors.html`).

`metalab.unc.edu` is heavily used, so please use a mirror site if possible.

HOWTOs are also posted towards the beginning of the month to the Usenet newsgroup `comp.os.linux.answers`. There is a tool called NewstoHOWTO that will assemble the postings (see `ftp://metalab unc.edu/pub/Linux/system/news/misc/`).

HOWTO Translations

HOWTO translations are available on `metalab.unc.edu` and mirrors around the world. So far there are the following translations:

- Chinese (zh)
- Croatian (hr)
- French (fr)
- German (de)
- Hellenic (el)
- Indonesian (id)
- Italian (it)
- Japanese (ja)
- Korean (ko)
- Polish (pl)
- Slovenian (sl)
- Spanish (es)
- Swedish (sv)
- Turkish (tr)

If you know of any other translation projects, please let me know and I will add them to this list. If you are interested in getting your translations archived on `metalab.unc.edu`, please read the directory structure specification at `http://metalab.unc.edu/pub/Linux/docs/HOWTO/translations/Directory-Structure` and get in touch with me.

HOWTO INDEX

The following Linux HOWTOs are currently available:

- 3Dfx HOWTO, by Bernd Kreimeier <`bk@gamers.org`>. How to use 3Dfx graphics accelerator chip support. Updated 6 February 1998.

- AX25 HOWTO, by Terry Dawson <terry@perf.no.itg.telecom.com.au>. How to configure AX25 networking for Linux. Updated 17 October 1997.
- Access HOWTO, by Michael De La Rue <access-howto@ed.ac.uk>. How to use adaptive technology with Linux. Updated 28 March 1997.
- Alpha HOWTO, by David Mosberger <davidm@azstarnet.com>. Overview of Alpha systems and processors. Updated 6 June 1997.
- Assembly HOWTO, by François-René Rideau <rideau@ens.fr>. Information on programming in x86 assembly. Updated 16 November 1997.
- Bash Prompt HOWTO, by Giles Orr <giles@interlog.com>. Creating and controlling terminal and xterm prompts. Updated 7 January 1999.
- Benchmarking HOWTO, by André D. Balsa <andrewbalsa@usa.net>. How to do basic benchmarking. Updated 15 August 1997.
- Beowulf HOWTO, by Jacek Radajewski <jacek@usq.edu.au> & Douglas Eadline <deadline@plogic.com>. Introduces the Beowulf Supercomputer architecture and provides background information on parallel programming. Updated 22 November 1998.
- BootPrompt HOWTO, by Paul Gortmaker <gpg109@rsphy1.anu.edu.au>. List of boot time arguments and overview of booting software. Updated 1 February 1998.
- Bootdisk HOWTO, by Tom Fawcett <fawcett@croftj.net>. How to create a boot/root maintenance disk for Linux. Updated 1 February 1998.
- Busmouse HOWTO, by Chris Bagwell <cbagwell@sprynet.com>. Information on bus mouse compatibility with Linux. Updated 15 June 1998.
- CD Writing HOWTO, by Winfried Trümper <winni@xpilot.org>. How to write CDs. Updated 16 December 1997.

- CDROM HOWTO, by Jeff Tranter <jefftranter@pobox.com>. Information on CD-ROM drive compatibility for Linux. Updated 23 January 1998.
- Chinese HOWTO, by Chih-Wei Huang <cwhuang@phys.ntu.edu.tw>. How to configure Linux for use with the Chinese character set. Updated 2 June 1998.
- Commercial HOWTO, by Martin Michlmayr <tbm@cyrius.com>. Listing of commercial software products for Linux. Updated 21 September 1998.
- Config HOWTO, by Guido Gonzato <guido@ibogfs.cineca.it>. How to fine-tune and customize your Linux system. Updated 19 January 1999.
- Consultants HOWTO, by Martin Michlmayr <tbm@cyrius.com>. Listing of Linux consultants. Updated 8 November 1998.
- Cyrillic HOWTO, by Alexander L. Belikoff <abel@bfr.co.il>. How to configure Linux for use with the Cyrillic character set. Updated 23 January 1998.
- DNS HOWTO, by Nicolai Langfeldt <janl@math.uio.no>. How to set up DNS. Updated 12 November 1998.
- DOS/Win to Linux HOWTO, by Guido Gonzato <guido@ibogfs.cineca.it>. How to move from DOS/Windows to Linux. Updated 15 April 1998.
- DOSEMU HOWTO, by Uwe Bonnes <bon@elektron.ikp.physik.th-darmstadt.de>. HOWTO about the Linux MS-DOS Emulator, DOSEMU. Updated 15 March 1997 for dosemu-0.64.4 (in progress).
- Danish HOWTO, by Niels Kristian Bech Jensen <nkbj@image.dk>. How to configure Linux for use with the Danish character set. Updated 1 December 1998.
- Distribution HOWTO, by Eric S. Raymond <esr@snark.thyrsus.com>. A list of Linux distributions. Updated 10 September 1998.

- ELF HOWTO, by Daniel Barlow <daniel.barlow@linux.org>. How to install and migrate to the ELF binary file format. Updated 14 July 1996.
- Emacspeak HOWTO, by Jim Van Zandt <jrv@vanzandt.mv.com>. How to use 'emacspeak' with Linux. Updated 21 Dececember 1997.
- Esperanto HOWTO, by Wolfram Diestel <diestel@rzaix340.rz.uni-leipzig.de>. How to use Esperanto in general and ISO-8859-3 in particular with Linux. Updated June 1998.
- Ethernet HOWTO, by Paul Gortmaker <gpg109@rsphy1.anu.edu.au>. Information on Ethernet hardware compatibility for Linux. Updated 6 July 1998.
- Finnish HOWTO, by Pekka Taipale <pjt@iki.fi>. How to configure Linux for use with the Finnish character set. Updated 14 February 1996.
- Firewall HOWTO, by Mark Grennan <markg@netplus.net>. How to set up a firewall using Linux. Updated 8 November 1996.
- French HOWTO by Guylhem Aznar <guylhem@danmark.linux.eu.org>. How to configure Linux for use with the French character set.
- Ftape HOWTO, by Kevin Johnson <kjj@pobox.com>. Information on ftape drive compatibility with Linux. Updated August 1998.
- GCC HOWTO, by Daniel Barlow <daniel.barlow@linux.org>. How to set up the GNU C compiler and development libraries. Updated 28 February 1996.
- German HOWTO, by Winfried Trümper <winni@xpilot.org>. Information on using Linux with German-specific features. Updated 19 March 1997.
- Glibc2 HOWTO, by Eric Green <ejg3@cornell.edu>. How to install and migrate to the glibc2 library. Updated 8 February 1998.

- HAM HOWTO, by Terry Dawson <terry@perf.no.itg.telecom.com.au>. How to configure amateur radio software for Linux. Updated 1 April 1997.
- HOWTO Index, by Tim Bynum <linux-howto@metalab.unc.edu>. Index of HOWTO documents about Linux. Updated 28 March 1999.
- Hardware Compatibility HOWTO, by Patrick Reijnen <antispam.patrickr@antispam.bart.nl>. A list of hardware known to work with Linux. Updated 30 July 1998.
- Hebrew HOWTO, by Yair G. Rajwan <yair@hobbes.jct.ac.il>. How to configure Linux for use with the Hebrew character set. Updated 12 September 1995.
- INFO-SHEET, by Michael K. Johnson <johnsonm@redhat.com>. Generic introduction to the Linux operating system. Updated 1 September 1998.
- IPCHAINS HOWTO, by Paul Russell <Paul.Russell@rustcorp.com.au>. Install and configure the enhanced IP firewalling chains software. Updated 27 October 1998.
- IPX HOWTO, by Terry Dawson <terry@perf.no.itg.telecom.com.au>. How to install and configure IPX networking. Updated 6 May 1998.
- IR HOWTO, by Werner Heuser <r2d2c3po@zedat.fu-berlin.de>. An introduction to the software provided by the Linux/IR project. Updated 9 February 1999.
- ISP Hookup HOWTO, by Egil Kvaleberg <egil@kvaleberg.no>. Basic introduction to hooking up to an ISP. Updated 5 March 1998.
- Installation HOWTO, by Eric S. Raymond <esr@snark.thyrsus.com>. How to obtain and install Linux. Updated 20 November 1998.
- Intranet Server HOWTO, by Pramod Karnad <karnad@indiamail.com>. How to set up a Linux intranet server. Updated 7 August 1997.

- Italian HOWTO, by Marco "Gaio" Gaiarin <gaio@dei.unipd.it>. How to configure Linux for use with the Italian character set. Updated 3 November 1998.
- Java-CGI HOWTO, by David H. Silber <dhs@orbits.com>. How to set up Java-capable CGI bin. Updated 1 December 1998.
- Kernel HOWTO, by Brian Ward <ward@blah.math.tu-graz.ac.at>. Upgrading and compiling the Linux kernel. Updated 26 May 1997.
- Keyboard and Console HOWTO, by Andries Brouwer <aeb@cwi.nl>. Information about the Linux keyboard, console and non-ASCII characters. Updated 25 February 1998.
- KickStart HOWTO, by Martin Hamilton <martinh@gnu.org>. Briefly describes how to use the RedHat Linux KickStart system to rapidly install large numbers of identical Linux boxes. Updated 11 January 1999.
- LinuxDoc+Emacs+Ispell HOWTO, by Philippe Martin <feloy@wanadoo.fr>. Assist writers and translators of Linux HOWTOs or any other paper for the Linux Documentation Project. Updated 27 February 1998.
- META-FAQ, by Michael K. Johnson <johnsonm@redhat.com>. A listing of Linux sources of information. Updated 25 October 1997.
- MGR HOWTO, by Vincent Broman <broman@nosc.mil>. Information on the MGR graphics interface for Linux. Updated 30 May 1996.
- MILO HOWTO, by David A. Rusling <david.rusling@reo.mts.dec.com>. How to use the Alpha Linux Miniloader (MILO). Updated 6 December 1996.
- Mail HOWTO, by Guylhem Aznar <guylhem@danmark.linux.eu.org>. Information on electronic mail servers and clients. Updated 4 January 1999.
- Modem HOWTO, by David S. Lawyer <bf347@lafn.org>. Help with selecting, connecting, configuring, troubleshooting, and understanding modems for a PC. Updated January 1999.

- Multi-Disk HOWTO, by Stein Gjoen <sgjoen@nyx.net>. How to set up multiple hard disk drives. Updated 3 February 1998.
- Multicast HOWTO, by Juan-Mariano de Goyeneche <jmseyas@dit.upm.es>. This HOWTO tries to cover most aspects related to multicast over TCP/IP networks. Updated 20 March 1998.
- NET-3 HOWTO, by Terry Dawson <terry@perf.no.itg.telecom.com.au>. How to configure TCP/IP networking under Linux. Updated August 1998.
- NFS HOWTO, by Nicolai Langfeldt <janl@math.uio.no>. How to set up NFS clients and servers. Updated 3 November 1997.
- NIS HOWTO, by Thorsten Kukuk <kukuk@vt.uni-paderborn.de>. Information on using NIS/YP on Linux systems. Updated 12 June 1998.
- Networking Overview HOWTO, by Daniel López Ridrego <ridruejo@esi.us.es>. The purpose of this document is to give an overview of the networking capabilities of the Linux Operating System, providing pointers for further information and implementation details. Updated 10 July 1998.
- Optical Disk HOWTO, by Skip Rye <SkipRye@faneuil.com>. How to use optical disk drives with Linux. Updated 11 December 1998.
- Oracle HOWTO, by Paul Haigh <paul@nailed.demon.co.uk>. How to set up Oracle as a database server. Updated 4 August 1998.
- PCI HOWTO, by Michael Will <Michael.Will@student.uni-tuebingen.de>. Information on PCI-architecture compatibility with Linux. Updated 30 March 1997.
- PCMCIA HOWTO, by Dave Hinds <dhinds@allegro.stanford.edu>. How to install and use PCMCIA Card Services. Updated 08 February 1999.
- PPP HOWTO, by Robert Hart <hartr@interweft.com.au>. Information on using PPP networking with Linux. Updated 31 March 1997.

- PalmOS HOWTO, by David H. Silber <pilot@orbits.com>. How to use your Palm OS device with a Linux system. Updated 20 September 1998.
- Parallel Processing HOWTO, by Hank Dietz <pplinux@ecn.purdue.edu>. Discussion of parallel processing approaches for Linux. Updated 5 January 1998.
- Plug and Play HOWTO, by David Lawyer <bf347@lafn.org>. How to get your Linux system to support Plug-and-Play. Updated November 1998.
- Polish HOWTO, by Sergiusz Pawlowicz <ser@arch.pwr.wroc.pl>. Information on using Linux with Polish-specific features. Updated 1 June 1998.
- Portuguese-HOWTO, by Carlos Augusto Moreira dos Santos <casantos@cpmet.ufpel.tche.br>. Este documento pretende ser um guia de referência de configuraçao do Linux e seus programas.... Updated 1 January 1999.
- PostgreSQL HOWTO, by Al Dev (Alavoor Vasudevan) <aldev@hotmail.com>. How to set up PostgreSQL as a database server. Updated 8 January 1999.
- Printing HOWTO, by Grant Taylor <gtaylor+pht@picante.com>. HOWTO on printing software for Linux. Updated 2 February 1999.
- Printing Usage HOWTO, by Mark Komarinski <markk@auratek.com>. How to use the printing system for a variety of file types and options. Updated 6 February 1998.
- Quake HOWTO, by Bob Zimbinski <bobz@mr.net> and Thomas Mike Hallock <mikeh@medina.net>. This document explains how to install, run, and troubleshoot Quake, QuakeWorld, and Quake II on an Intel Linux system. Updated 30 August 1998.
- RPM HOWTO, by Donnie Barnes <djb@redhat.com>. How to use the Red Hat Package Manager (.rpm). Updated 8 April 1997.
- Reading List HOWTO, by Eric S. Raymond <esr@snark.thyrsus.com>. Interesting books pertaining to Linux subjects. Updated 22 November 1998.

- Root RAID HOWTO, by Michael A. Robinton <michael@bzs.org>. How to create a root-mounted RAID filesystem. Updated 25 March 1998.
- SCSI Programming HOWTO, by Heiko Eissfeldt <heiko@colossus.escape.de>. Information on programming the generic Linux SCSI interface. Updated 7 May 1996.
- SMB HOWTO, by David Wood <dwood@plugged.net.au>. How to use the Session Message Block (SMB) protocol with Linux. Updated 10 August 1996.
- SRM HOWTO, by David Mosberger <davidm@azstarnet.com>. How to boot Linux/Alpha using the SRM firmware. Updated 17 August 1996.
- Security HOWTO, by Kevin Fenzi <kevin@scrye.com>. General overview of security issues. Updated 1 May 1998.
- Serial HOWTO, by David Lawyer <bf347@lafn.org>. How to use serial devices (modems, terminals) with Linux. Updated July 1998.
- Serial Programming HOWTO, by Peter H. Baumann <Peter.Baumann@dlr.de>. How to use serial ports in programs. Updated 22 January 1998.
- Shadow Password HOWTO, by Michael H. Jackson <mhjack@tscnet.com>. How to obtain, install, and configure shadow passwords. Updated 3 April 1996.
- Slovenian HOWTO, by Primoz Peterlin <primoz.peterlin@biofiz.mf.uni-lj.si>. Information on using Linux with Slovenian-specific features. Updated 30 October 1996.
- Software Release Practice HOWTO, by Eric S. Raymond <esr@snark.thyrsus.com>. Describes good release practices for Linux open-source projects. Updated 21 November 1998.
- Sound HOWTO, by Jeff Tranter <jefftranter@pobox.com>. Sound hardware and software for the Linux operating system. Updated 23 January 1998.
- Sound Playing HOWTO, by Yoo C. Chung <wacko@laplace.snu.ac.kr>. How to play various sound formats under Linux. Updated 11 August 1998.

- Spanish HOWTO, by Gonzalo Garcia Agullo <Gonzalo.Garcia-Agullo@jrc.es>. Information on using Linux with Spanish-specific features. Updated 20 August 1996.
- teTeX HOWTO, by Robert Kiesling <kiesling@terracom.net>. How to install the teTeX package (TeX and LaTeX) under Linux. Updated 9 November 1998.
- Text-Terminal HOWTO, by David S. Lawyer <bf347@lafn.org>. This document explains what text terminals are, how they work, and how to install and configure them. Updated January 1999.
- Thai HOWTO, by Poonlap Veeratanabutr <poon-v@fedu.uec.ac.jp>. How to configure Linux for use with the Thai character set. Updated 4 August 1998.
- Tips HOWTO, by Paul Anderson <paul@geeky1.ebtech.net>. HOWTO on miscellaneous tips and tricks for Linux. Updated June 1998.
- UMSDOS HOWTO, by Jacques Gelinas <jacques@solucorp.qc.ca>. How to install and use the UMSDOS filesystem. Updated 13 November 1995.
- UPS HOWTO, by Harvey J. Stein <abel@netvision.net.il>. Information on using a UPS power supply with Linux. Updated 18 November 1997.
- UUCP HOWTO, by Guylhem Aznar <guylhem@danmark.linux.eu.org>. Information on UUCP software for Linux. Updated 6 February 1998.
- Unix and Internet Fundamentals HOWTO, by Eric S. Raymond <esr@snark.thyrsus.com>. Describes the working basics of PC-class computers, Unix-like operating systems, and the Internet in non-technical language. Updated 3 December 1998.
- User Group HOWTO, by Kendall Grant Clark <kclark@ntlug.org>. Tips on founding, maintaining, and growing a Linux User Group. Updated 24 April 1998.
- VAR HOWTO, by Martin Michlmayr <tbm@cyrius.com>. Listing of Linux value added resellers. Updated 25 October 1998.

- VME HOWTO, by John Huggins and Michael Wyrick <vmelinux@va.net>. How to run Linux on your VMEbus Pentium and other PCI local bus-based VMEbus processor designs. Updated 30 July 1998.
- VMS to Linux HOWTO, by Guido Gonzato <guido@ibogfs.cineca.it>. How to move from VMS to Linux. Updated 20 April 1998.
- Virtual Services HOWTO, by Brian Ackerman <brian@nycrc.net>. How to set up virtual hosting services. Updated 15 August 1998.
- WWW HOWTO, by Wayne Leister <n3mtr@qis.net>. How to set up WWW clients and servers. Updated 19 November 1997.
- WWW mSQL HOWTO, by Oliver Corff <corff@zedat.fu-berlin.de>. How to set up a Web server database with mSQL. Updated 17 September 1997.
- XFree86 HOWTO, by Eric S. Raymond <esr@snark.thyrsus.com>. How to obtain, install, and configure XFree86 3.2 (X11R6). Updated 2 January 1999.
- XFree86 Video Timings HOWTO, by Eric S. Raymond <esr@snark.thyrsus.com>. How to compose a mode line for XFree86. Updated 18 January 1999.
- X Window User HOWTO, by Ray Brigleb <ray@croftj.net>. Information on configuring the X Window environment for the Linux user. Updated 22 January 1999.

Mini-HOWTOs

The following mini-HOWTOs are available:

- 3 Button Mouse mini-HOWTO, by Geoff Short <geoff@kipper.york.ac.uk>. How to configure your mouse to use 3 buttons. Updated 31 May 1998.
- ADSM Backup mini-HOWTO by Thomas Koenig <Thomas.Koenig@ciw.uni-karlsruhe.de>. How to install and use the ADSM backup program. Updated 15 January 1997.

- Asymmetric Digital Subscriber Loop (ADSL) mini-HOWTO, by David Fannin <dfannin@dnai.com>. Addresses the ordering, installation, and configuration. Updated 7 June 1998.
- AI-Alife mini-HOWTO by John A. Eikenberry <jae@ai.uga.edu>. Information about AI software for Linux. Updated 13 January 1998.
- Advocacy mini-HOWTO by Paul L. Rogers <Paul.L.Rogers@li.org>. Suggestions on how to advocate the use of Linux. Updated 7 May 1998.
- Alsa Sound mini-HOWTO, by Valentijn Sessink. Describes the installation of the Alsa sound drivers for Linux. Updated 8 February 1999.
- Apache SSL PHP/FI frontpage mini-HOWTO, by Marcus Faure <marcus@faure.de>. Build a multipurpose Web server. Updated July 1998.
- Automount mini-HOWTO, by Don <don@sabotage.org>. This file describes the autofs automounter, how to configure it, and points out some problems to avoid. Updated 7 September 1998.
- Backup with MSDOS mini-HOWTO, by Christopher Neufeld <neufeld@physics.utoronto.ca>. How to back up Linux machines with MS-DOS. Updated 5 August 1997.
- Battery Powered mini-HOWTO, by Hanno Mueller <hanno@lava.de>. How to reduce a Linux system's power consumption. Updated 21 December 1997.
- Boca mini-HOWTO, by David H Dennis <david@freelink.net>. How to install a Boca 16-port serial card (Boca 2016). Updated 1 August 1997.
- BogoMips mini-HOWTO, by Wim C.A. van Dorst <baron@clifton.hobby.nl>. Information about BogoMips. Updated 8 February 1999.
- Bridge mini-HOWTO, by Chris Cole <cole@lynkmedia.com> How to set up an Ethernet bridge. Updated 7 September 1998.

- Bridge+Firewall mini-HOWTO, by Peter Breuer <ptb@it.uc3m.es>. How to set up an Ethernet bridge and firewall. Updated 19 December 1997.
- Bzip2 mini-HOWTO, by David Fetter <dfetter@best.com>. How to use the new bzip2 compression program. Updated 29 June 1998.
- Cable Modem mini-HOWTO, by Vladimir Vuksan <vuksan@veus.hr>. How to use a cable modem with a cable ISP. Updated 11 February 1999.
- Cipe+Masquerading mini-HOWTO, by Anthony Ciaravalo <acj@home.com>. How to set up a Virtual Private Network between your LAN and other LAN's using cipe through Linux-masquerading firewall machines. Updated 28 October 1998.
- Clock mini-HOWTO, by Ron Bean <rbean@execpc.com>. How to set and keep your clock on time. Updated December 1996.
- Coffee mini-HOWTO, by Georgatos Photis <gef@ceid.upatras.gr>. Thoughts about making coffee with Linux (humorous). Updated 15 January 1998.
- Colour ls mini-HOWTO, by Thorbjoern Ravn Andersen <ravn@dit.ou.dk>. How to set up the colours with 'ls'. Updated 7 August 1997.
- Cyrus IMAP mini-HOWTO, by Kevin Mitchell <kevin@iserv.net>. How to install the Cyrus IMAP server. Updated 21 January 1998.
- DHCP mini-HOWTO, by Vladimir Vuksan <vuksan@veus.hr>. How to set up a DHCP server and client. Updated 11 February 1999.
- DPT Hardware RAID mini-HOWTO, by Ram Samudrala <me@ram.org>. How to configure hardware RAID. Updated 15 December 1997.
- Diald mini-HOWTO, by Harish Pillay <h.pillay@ieee.org>. How to use 'diald' to dial an ISP. Updated 3 June 1996.

- Diskless mini-HOWTO, by Robert Nemkin <buci@math.klte.hu>. How to set up a diskless Linux box. Updated 12 September 1996.
- Ext2fs Undeletion mini-HOWTO, by Aaron Crane <aaronc@pobox.com>. How to retrieve deleted files from an ext2 filesystem. Updated 4 August 1997.
- Fax Server mini-HOWTO, by Erez Strauss <erez@newplaces.com>. How to set up a fax server. Updated 8 November 1997.
- Firewall Piercing mini-HOWTO, by François-René Rideau <rideau@ens.fr>. Using PPP over telnet transparently through an Internet firewall. Updated 27 November 1998.
- GIS-GRASS mini-HOWTO, by David A. Hastings <dah@ngdc.noaa.gov>. How to install Geographic Information System (GIS) software. Updated 13 November 1997.
- GTEK BBS-550 mini-HOWTO, by Wajihuddin Ahmed <wahmed@sdnpk.undp.org>. How to set up the GTEK BBS-550 multiport board with Linux. Updated 20 August 1997.
- Hard Disk Upgrade mini-HOWTO, by Yves Bellefeuille <yan@ottawa.com>. How to copy a Linux system from one hard disk to another. Updated 31 January 1998.
- IO Port Programming mini-HOWTO, by Riku Saikkonen <Riku.Saikkonen@hut.fi>. How to use I/O ports in C programs. Updated 28 December 1997.
- IP Alias mini-HOWTO, by Harish Pillay <h.pillay@ieee.org>. How to use IP aliasing. Updated 13 January 1997.
- IP Masquerade mini-HOWTO, by Ambrose Au <ambrose@writeme.com>. How to use IP masquerading. Updated 7 February 1999.
- IP Subnetworking mini-HOWTO, by Robert Hart <hartr@interweft.com.au>. Why and how to subnetwork an IP network. Updated 31 March 1997.
- ISP Connectivity mini-HOWTO, by Michael Strates <mstrates@croftj.net>. How to get mail and news over a dial-up connection. Updated 6 November 1997.

- Install From ZIP mini-HOWTO, by Kevin Snively <k.snively@seaslug.org>. How to install Linux from a parallel port ZIP drive. Updated 29 April 1998.
- Kerneld mini-HOWTO, by Henrik Storner <storner@osiris.ping.dk>. How to use 'kerneld' (dynamic module loading). Updated 19 July 1997.
- LBX mini-HOWTO, by Paul D. Smith <psmith@baynetworks.com>. How to use Low-Bandwidth X (LBX). Updated 11 December 1997.
- LILO mini-HOWTO, by Alessandro Rubini <rubini@linux.it>. Examples of typical LILO installations. Updated 16 August 1998.
- Large Disk mini-HOWTO, by Andries Brouwer <aeb@cwi.nl>. How to use disks with 1024 cylinders. Updated 22 January 1999.
- Leased Line mini-HOWTO, by Rob van der Putten <rob@sput.webster.nl>. How to set up leased line modems. Updated July 1998.
- Linux+DOS+Win95+OS2 mini-HOWTO, by Mike Harlan <r3mdh@raex.com>. How to use Linux and DOS and OS/2 and Win95 together. Updated 11 November 1997.
- Linux+FreeBSD mini-HOWTO, by Niels Kristian Bech Jensen <nkbj@image.dk>. How to use Linux and FreeBSD together. Updated 15 January 1999.
- Linux+NT-Loader mini-HOWTO, by Bernd Reichert <reichert@dial.eunet.ch>. How to use Linux and the Windows NT boot loader together. Updated 2 September 1997.
- Linux+Win95 mini-HOWTO, by Jonathan Katz <jkatz@in.net>. How to use Linux and Windows 95 together. Updated 26 October 1996.
- Loadlin+Win95 mini-HOWTO, by Chris Fischer <protek@brigadoon.com>. How to use Linux and Windows 95 together, using loadlin. Updated 13 March 1999.

- Mac Terminal mini-HOWTO, by Robert Kiesling <kiesling@terracom.net>. How to use an Apple Macintosh as a serial terminal. Updated 9 November 1997.
- Mail Queue mini-HOWTO, by Leif Erlingsson <leif@lege.com>. How to queue remote mail and deliver local mail. Updated 3 September 1997.
- Mail2News mini-HOWTO, by Robert Hart <iweft@ipax.com.au>. How to set up a mail to news gateway. Updated 4 November 1996.
- Man Page mini-HOWTO, by Jens Schweikhardt <schweikh@noc.dfn.de>. How to write man pages. Updated July 1998.
- Modules mini-HOWTO, by Riley H. Williams <rhw@bigfoot.com>. How to set up and configure kernel modules. Updated 14 November 1997.
- Multiboot using LILO mini-HOWTO, by Renzo Zanelli <rzanelli@southeast.net>. How to multiboot between Windows 95, Windows NT, and Linux. Updated 26 March 1998.
- NCD X Terminal mini-HOWTO, by Ian Hodge <ihodge@nortel.ca>. Describes how to connect an NCD X terminal to a Unix host. Updated 3 April 1998.
- NFS-Root mini-HOWTO, by Andreas Kostyrka <andreas@ag.or.at>. How to set up diskless Linux machines. Updated 8 August 1997.
- NFS-Root-Client mini-HOWTO, by Ofer Maor <ofer@hadar.co.il>. How to set up diskless Linux machines using NFS. Updated 2 February 1999.
- Netrom-Node mini-HOWTO, by Karl Larsen <k5di@yahoo.com>. How to set up the ax25-utilities package for Amateur Radio such as making Netrom Nodes. Updated 19 October 1998.
- Netscape+Proxy mini-HOWTO, by Sarma Seetamraju <sarma@usa.net>. How to set up a proxy server for Netscape. Updated 15 August 1997.
- Netstation mini-HOWTO, by Kris Buytaert <Kris.Buytaert@advalvas.be>. How to hook up a IBM Netstation to your local network using a Linux box as server. Updated 22 February 1998.

- News Leafsite mini-HOWTO, by Florian Kuehnert <sutok@gmx.de>. How to set up a leaf news site. Updated 4 January 1998.
- Offline Mailing mini-HOWTO, by Gunther Voet <freaker@tuc.ml.org>. How to set up e-mail addresses without a dedicated Internet connection. Updated 4 June 1998.
- PLIP mini-HOWTO, by Andrea Controzzi <controzz@cli.di.unipi.it>. How to set up PLIP (Parallel Line Interface Protocol). Updated 12 March 1998.
- Partition mini-HOWTO, by Kristian Koehntopp <kris@koehntopp.de>. How to choose disk partitions. Updated 3 November 1997.
- Partition Rescue mini-HOWTO, by Rolf Klausen <rolfk@romsdal.vgs.no>. How to rescue deleted Linux partitions. Updated 22 October 1997.
- Path mini-HOWTO, by Esa Turtiainen <etu@dna.fi>. How to use the PATH environment variable. Updated 15 November 1997.
- Pre-installation Checklist mini-HOWTO, by S. Parthasarathy <algolog@hd1.vsnl.net.in>. Pre-installation checklist and questionnaire. Updated 29 August 1998.
- Process Accounting mini-HOWTO, by Albert M.C. Tam <bertie@scn.org>. How to set up process accounting. Updated 8 August 1997.
- Proxy ARP Subnet mini-HOWTO, by Bob Edwards <bob@faceng.anu.edu.au>. How to use proxy ARP with subnetting. Updated August 1997.
- Public Web Browser mini-HOWTO, by Donald B. Marti Jr. <dmarti@best.com>. How to set up a guest account to use a Web browser. Updated 5 January 1998.
- Qmail+MH mini-HOWTO, by Christopher Richardson <rdn@tara.n.eunet.de>. How to install qmail and MH. Updated 5 March 1998.
- Quota mini-HOWTO, by Albert M.C. Tam <bertie@scn.org>. How to set up disk quotas. Updated 8 August 1997.

- RCS mini-HOWTO, by Robert Kiesling <kiesling@terra-com.net>. How to use RCS (Revision Control System). Updated 14 August 1997.
- RPM+Slackware mini-HOWTO, by Dave Whitinger <dave@whitinger.net>. How to install the Red Hat Package Manager (RPM) under Slackware. Updated 13 April 1998.
- Red Hat CD mini-HOWTO, by Morten Kjeldgaard <mok@imsb.au.dk> and Peter von der Ahé <pahe+rhcd@daimi.au.dk>. How to make your own CDs from the Red Hat Linux distribution equivalent to the ones commercially available from Red Hat. Updated 9 September 1998.
- Remote Boot mini-HOWTO, by Marc Vuilleumier Stckelberg <Marc.VuilleumierStuckelberg@cui.unige.ch>. How to set up a server-based boot selector. Updated February 1999.
- Remote X Apps mini-HOWTO, by Vincent Zweije <zweije@xs4all.nl>. How to run remote X applications. Updated 14 July 1998.
- SLIP-PPP Emulator mini-HOWTO, by Irish <irish@eskimo.com>. How to use SLIP-PPP emulators with Linux. Updated 7 August 1997.
- Sendmail Address Rewrite mini-HOWTO, by Thomas Roessler <roessler@guug.de>. Set up sendmail's configuration file for the home user's dial-up access. Updated 6 May 1998.
- Sendmail+UUCP mini-HOWTO, by Jamal Hadi Salim <jamal@glcom.com>. How to use sendmail and UUCP together. Updated August 1998.
- Secure POP via SSH mini-HOWTO, by Manish Singh <yosh@gimp.org>. How to set up secure POP connections using SSH. Updated 30 September 1998.
- Small Memory mini-HOWTO, by Todd Burgess <tburgess@uoguelph.ca>. How to run Linux on a system with a small amount of memory. Update 29 October 1997.
- Software Building mini-HOWTO, by Mendel Leo Cooper <thegrendel@theriver.com>. How to build software packages. Updated 6 July 1998.

- Software RAID mini-HOWTO, by Linas Vepstas <linas@fc.net>. How to configure software RAID. Updated 21 November 1998.
- Soundblaster AWE mini-HOWTO, by Marcus Brinkmann <Marcus.Brinkmann@ruhr-uni-bochum.de>. How to install the Soundblaster AWE 32/64. Updated 11 January 1998.
- StarOffice mini-HOWTO, by Matthew Borowski <mkb@poboxes.com>. Information on installing the StarOffice suite. Updated 2 June 1998.
- Term Firewall mini-HOWTO, by Barak Pearlmutter <bap@cs.unm.edu>. How to use 'term' over a firewall. Updated 15 July 1997.
- TkRat mini-HOWTO, by Dave Whitinger <dave@whitinger.net>. How to install and use the TkRat mail program. Updated 2 February 1998.
- Token Ring mini-HOWTO, by Mike Eckhoff <mike.e@emissary.aus-etc.com>. How to use Token Ring cards. Updated 7 January 1998.
- Ultra-DMA mini-HOWTO, by Brion Vibber <brion@pobox.com>. How to use Ultra-DMA drives and controllers. Updated 6 July 1998.
- Update mini-HOWTO, by Stein Gjoen <sgjoen@nyx.net>. How to stay updated about Linux development. Updated 3 February 1998.
- Upgrade mini-HOWTO, by Greg Louis <glouis@dynamicro.on.ca>. How to upgrade your Linux distribution. Updated 6 June 1996.
- VAIO mini-HOWTO, by Hideki Saito <hideki@chatlink.com>. This document explains installation of Linux on Sony VAIO computers. Updated 16 September 1998.
- Vesafb mini-HOWTO, by Alex Buell <alex.buell@tahallah.demon.co.uk>. How to use the vesafb device. Updated 2 August 1998.
- VPN mini-HOWTO, by Árpád Magosányi <mag@bunuel.tii.matav.hu>. How to set up a VPN (Virtual Private Network). Updated 7 August 1997.

- Visual Bell mini-HOWTO, by Alessandro Rubini <rubini @linux.it>. How to disable audible bells and enable visual bells. Updated 11 November 1997.
- Windows Modem Sharing mini-HOWTO, by Friedemann Baitinger <baiti@toplink.net>. How to set up Windows to use a shared modem on a Linux machine. Updated 2 November 1997.
- WordPerfect mini-HOWTO, by Wade Hampton <whampton @staffnet.com>. How to set up WordPerfect for Linux. Updated 13 August 1997.
- X Big Cursor mini-HOWTO, by Joerg Schneider <schneid @ira.uka.de>. How to use enlarged cursors with XWindows. Updated 11 August 1997.
- XFree86-XInside mini-HOWTO, by Marco Melgazzi <marco @techie.com>. How to convert XFree86 to XInside modelines. Updated September 1997.
- xterm Title mini-HOWTO, by Ric Lister <ric@giccs .georgetown.edu>. How to put strings into the titlebar of an xterm. Updated 7 January 1998.
- ZIP Install mini-HOWTO, by John Wiggins <jwiggins @comp.uark.edu>. How to install Linux onto a ZIP drive. Updated 10 January 1999.
- ZIP Drive mini-HOWTO, by Kyle Dansie <dansie@ibm.net>. Provides a quick reference guide on setting up and using the Iomega ZIP drive with Linux. Updated 10 January 1999.

Special HOWTOs

The High Availability HOWTO, by Harald Milz <hm@seneca.muc.de>, is available at http://metalab.unc.edu/pub/Linux/ALPHA/linux-ha/High-Availability-HOWTO.html. It is not included with the HOWTO collection because it relies on figures and cannot be distributed in all supported formats.

The Graphics mini-HOWTO, by Michael J. Hammel <mjhammel @graphics-muse.org>, is available at http://www.graphics-muse.org/linux/lgh.html. It is not included with the HOWTO collection because it needs to use a lot of images, which don't translate to other output formats.

Unmaintained HOWTOs and mini-HOWTOs

There are a number of unmaintained documents at `ftp://metalab.unc.edu/pub/Linux/docs/HOWTO/unmaintained`. These are kept around since old documentation is sometimes better than none. However, you should *be aware that you are reading old documentation.*

WRITING AND SUBMITTING A HOWTO

If you are interested in writing a HOWTO or mini-HOWTO, please get in touch with me *first* at `linux-howto@metalab.unc.edu`.

Here are a few guidelines that you should follow when writing a HOWTO or mini-HOWTO:

- Try to use meaningful structure and organization and write clearly. Remember that many of the people reading HOWTOs do not speak English as their first language.
- If you are writing a HOWTO, you *must* use the SGML-Tools package, available from `http://www.sgmltools.org/`, to format the HOWTO. This package allows us to produce LaTeX (for DVI and PostScript), plain text, and HTML from a single source document and was designed specifically for the HOWTOs. This also gives all of the HOWTOs a uniform look. It is very important that you format and review the output of the formatting in PostScript, plain text, and HTML.
- If you are writing a mini-HOWTO, you can either use SGML (as described above) or HTML. If you use SGML for your mini-HOWTO, it will be pubished along with the HOWTOs in LDP books.
- Make sure that all of the information is correct. I can't stress this enough. When in doubt, speculate, but make it clear that you're only guessing.
- Make sure that you are covering the most recent version of the available software. Also, be sure to include full instructions on where software can be downloaded from (FTP site name, full pathname) and the current version number and release date of the software.

- Include an FAQ section at the end, if appropriate. Many HOWTO documents need an "FAQ" or "Common Problems" section to cover information which can't be covered in the regular text.
- Use other HOWTOs or mini-HOWTOs as a model! The SGML source to the HOWTOs is available on Linux FTP sites. In addition, have a look at the LDP Style Guide for some guidelines.
- Make sure that your name, e-mail address, date, and a version number is near the beginning of the document. You could also include WWW addresses and a snail mail address if you want. The standard header is:

  Title

  Author's name and e-mail address

  Version number and date

  For example,

  The Linux HOWTO Index

  by Tim Bynum

  v2.10.29, 31 July 1997
- Lastly, be prepared to receive questions and comments about your writing. Several hundreds access the HOWTO collection every day from around the world!

After you have written the HOWTO, mail it to me. If you used SGML-Tools, simply mail me the SGML source; I take care of formatting the documents. I'll also take care of archiving the HOWTOs on `metalab.unc.edu` and posting them to the various newsgroups.

It is *important* that you go through me when submitting a HOWTO, as I maintain the archives and need to keep track of what HOWTOs are being written and who is doing what.

Then, all you have to do is send me periodic updates whenever appropriate.

Copyright

If you have questions, please contact Tim Bynum, the Linux HOWTO coordinator, at `linux-howto@metalab.unc.edu` via e-mail.

Appendix D

GNU General Public License

Version 2, June 1991

PREAMBLE

The licenses for most software are designed to take away your freedom to share and change it. By contrast, the GNU General Public License is intended to guarantee your freedom to share and change free software—to make sure the software is free for all its users. This General Public License applies to most of the Free Software Foundation's software and to any other program whose authors commit to using it. (Some other Free Software Foundation software is covered by the GNU Library General Public License instead.) You can apply it to your programs, too.

When we speak of free software, we are referring to freedom, not price. Our General Public Licenses are designed to make sure that you have the freedom to distribute copies of free software (and charge for this service if you wish), that you receive source code or can get it if you want it, that you can change the software or use pieces of it in new free programs; and that you know you can do these things.

To protect your rights, we need to make restrictions that forbid anyone to deny you these rights or to ask you to surrender the rights. These restrictions translate to certain responsibilities for you if you distribute copies of the software, or if you modify it.

For example, if you distribute copies of such a program, whether gratis or for a fee, you must give the recipients all the rights that you have. You must make sure that they, too, receive or can get the source code. And you must show them these terms so they know their rights.

We protect your rights with two steps: (1) copyright the software, and (2) offer you this license which gives you legal permission to copy, distribute and/or modify the software.

Also, for each author's protection and ours, we want to make certain that everyone understands that there is no warranty for this free software. If the software is modified by someone else and passed on, we want its recipients to know that what they have is not the original, so that any problems introduced by others will not reflect on the original authors' reputations.

Finally, any free program is threatened constantly by software patents. We wish to avoid the danger that re-distributors of a free program will individually obtain patent licenses, in effect making the program proprietary. To prevent this, we have made it clear that any patent must be licensed for everyone's free use or not licensed at all.

The precise terms and conditions for copying, distribution and modification follow.

Terms and Conditions for Copying, Distribution and Modification

1. This License applies to any program or other work which contains a notice placed by the copyright holder saying it may be distributed under the terms of this General Public License. The *Program*, below, refers to any such program or work, and a "work based on the Program" means either the Program or any derivative work under copyright law: that is to say, a work containing the Program or a portion of it, either verbatim or with modifications and/or translated into another language. (Hereinafter, translation is included without limitation in the term *modification.*) Each licensee is addressed as "you".

Activities other than copying, distribution and modification are not covered by this License; they are outside its scope. The act of running the Program is not restricted, and the output from the Program is covered only if its contents constitute a work based on the Program (independent of having been made by running the Program). Whether that is true depends on what the Program does.

2. You may copy and distribute verbatim copies of the Program's source code as you receive it, in any medium, provided that you conspicuously and appropriately publish on each copy an appropriate copyright notice and disclaimer of warranty; keep intact all the notices that refer to this License and to the absence of any warranty; and give any other recipients of the Program a copy of this License along with the Program.

You may charge a fee for the physical act of transferring a copy, and you may at your option offer warranty protection in exchange for a fee.

3. You may modify your copy or copies of the Program or any portion of it, thus forming a work based on the Program, and copy and distribute such modifications or work under the

terms of Section 1 above, provided that you also meet all of these conditions:

a. You must cause the modified files to carry prominent notices stating that you changed the files and the date of any change.

b. You must cause any work that you distribute or publish, that in whole or in part contains or is derived from the Program or any part thereof, to be licensed as a whole at no charge to all third parties under the terms of this License.

c. If the modified program normally reads commands interactively when run, you must cause it, when started running for such interactive use in the most ordinary way, to print or display an announcement including an appropriate copyright notice and a notice that there is no warranty (or else, saying that you provide a warranty) and that users may redistribute the program under these conditions, and telling the user how to view a copy of this License. (Exception: if the Program itself is interactive but does not normally print such an announcement, your work based on the Program is not required to print an announcement.)

These requirements apply to the modified work as a whole. If identifiable sections of that work are not derived from the Program, and can be reasonably considered independent and separate works in themselves, then this License, and its terms, do not apply to those sections when you distribute them as separate works. But when you distribute the same sections as part of a whole which is a work based on the Program, the distribution of the whole must be on the terms of this License, whose permissions for other licensees extend to the entire whole, and thus to each and every part regardless of who wrote it.

Thus, it is not the intent of this section to claim rights or contest your rights to work written entirely by you; rather, the intent is to exercise the right to control the distribution of derivative or collective works based on the Program.

In addition, mere aggregation of another work not based on the Program with the Program (or with a work based on the Program) on a volume of a storage or distribution medium does not bring the other work under the scope of this License.

4. You may copy and distribute the Program (or a work based on it, under Section 2) in object code or executable form under the terms of Sections 1 and 2 above provided that you also do one of the following:

   a. Accompany it with the complete corresponding machine-readable source code, which must be distributed under the terms of Sections 1 and 2 above on a medium customarily used for software interchange; or,

   b. Accompany it with a written offer, valid for at least three years, to give any third party, for a charge no more than your cost of physically performing source distribution, a complete machine-readable copy of the corresponding source code, to be distributed under the terms of Sections 1 and 2 above on a medium customarily used for software interchange; or,

   c. Accompany it with the information you received as to the offer to distribute corresponding source code. (This alternative is allowed only for noncommercial distribution and only if you received the program in object code or executable form with such an offer, in accord with Subsection b above.)

The source code for a work means the preferred form of the work for making modifications to it. For an executable work, complete source code means all the source code for all modules it contains, plus any associated interface definition files, plus the scripts used to control compilation and installation of the executable. However, as a special exception, the source code distributed need not include anything that is normally distributed (in either source or binary form) with the major components (compiler, kernel, and so on) of the operating system on which the executable runs, unless that component itself accompanies the executable.

If distribution of executable or object code is made by offering access to copy from a designated place, then offering equivalent access to copy the source code from the same place counts as distribution of the source code, even though third parties are not compelled to copy the source along with the object code.

5. You may not copy, modify, sub-license, or distribute the Program except as expressly provided under this License. Any attempt otherwise to copy, modify, sub-license or distribute the Program is void, and will automatically terminate your rights under this License. However, parties who have received copies, or rights, from you under this License will not have their licenses terminated so long as such parties remain in full compliance.

6. You are not required to accept this License, since you have not signed it. However, nothing else grants you permission to modify or distribute the Program or its derivative works. These actions are prohibited by law if you do not accept this License. Therefore, by modifying or distributing the Program (or any work based on the Program), you indicate your acceptance of this License to do so, and all its terms and conditions for copying, distributing or modifying the Program or works based on it.

7. Each time you redistribute the Program (or any work based on the Program), the recipient automatically receives a license from the original licensor to copy, distribute or modify the Program subject to these terms and conditions. You may not impose any further restrictions on the recipients' exercise of the rights granted herein. You are not responsible for enforcing compliance by third parties to this License.

8. If, as a consequence of a court judgment or allegation of patent infringement or for any other reason (not limited to patent issues), conditions are imposed on you (whether by court order, agreement or otherwise) that contradict the conditions of this License, they do not excuse you from the conditions of this License. If you cannot distribute so as to satisfy simultaneously your obligations under this License and any other pertinent obligations, then as a consequence you may not distribute the Program at all. For example, if a patent license would not permit royalty-free redistribution of the Program by all those who receive copies directly or indirectly through you, then the only way you could satisfy both it and this License would be to refrain entirely from distribution of the Program.

If any portion of this section is held invalid or unenforceable under any particular circumstance, the balance of the section is intended to apply and the section as a whole is intended to apply in other circumstances.

It is not the purpose of this section to induce you to infringe any patents or other property right claims or to contest validity of any such claims; this section has the sole purpose of protecting the integrity of the free software distribution system, which is implemented by public license practices. Many people have made generous contributions to the wide range of software distributed through that system in reliance on consistent application of that system; it is up to the author/donor to decide if he or she is willing to distribute software through any other system and a licensee cannot impose that choice.

This section is intended to make thoroughly clear what is believed to be a consequence of the rest of this License.

9. If the distribution and/or use of the Program is restricted in certain countries either by patents or by copyrighted interfaces, the original copyright holder who places the Program under this License may add an explicit geographical distribution limitation excluding those countries, so that distribution is permitted only in or among countries not thus excluded. In such case, this License incorporates the limitation as if written in the body of this License.

10. The Free Software Foundation may publish revised and/or new versions of the General Public License from time to time. Such new versions will be similar in spirit to the present version, but may differ in detail to address new problems or concerns.

Each version is given a distinguishing version number. If the Program specifies a version number of this License which applies to it and "any later version", you have the option of following the terms and conditions either of that version or of any later version published by the Free Software Foundation. If the Program does not specify a version number of this License, you may choose any version ever published by the Free Software Foundation.

11. If you wish to incorporate parts of the Program into other free programs whose distribution conditions are different, write to the author to ask for permission. For software which is copyrighted by the Free Software Foundation, write to the

Free Software Foundation; we sometimes make exceptions for this. Our decision will be guided by the two goals of preserving the free status of all derivatives of our free software and of promoting the sharing and reuse of software generally.

No Warranty

12. BECAUSE THE PROGRAM IS LICENSED FREE OF CHARGE, THERE IS NO WARRANTY FOR THE PROGRAM, TO THE EXTENT PERMITTED BY APPLICABLE LAW. EXCEPT WHEN OTHERWISE STATED IN WRITING THE COPYRIGHT HOLDERS AND/OR OTHER PARTIES PROVIDE THE PROGRAM "AS IS" WITHOUT WARRANTY OF ANY KIND, EITHER EXPRESSED OR IMPLIED, INCLUDING, BUT NOT LIMITED TO, THE IMPLIED WARRANTIES OF MERCHANTABILITY AND FITNESS FOR A PARTICULAR PURPOSE. THE ENTIRE RISK AS TO THE QUALITY AND PERFORMANCE OF THE PROGRAM IS WITH YOU. SHOULD THE PROGRAM PROVE DEFECTIVE, YOU ASSUME THE COST OF ALL NECESSARY SERVICING, REPAIR OR CORRECTION.

13. IN NO EVENT UNLESS REQUIRED BY APPLICABLE LAW OR AGREED TO IN WRITING WILL ANY COPYRIGHT HOLDER, OR ANY OTHER PARTY WHO MAY MODIFY AND/OR REDISTRIBUTE THE PROGRAM AS PERMITTED ABOVE, BE LIABLE TO YOU FOR DAMAGES, INCLUDING ANY GENERAL, SPECIAL, INCIDENTAL OR CONSEQUENTIAL DAMAGES ARISING OUT OF THE USE OR INABILITY TO USE THE PROGRAM (INCLUDING BUT NOT LIMITED TO LOSS OF DATA OR DATA BEING RENDERED INACCURATE OR LOSSES SUSTAINED BY YOU OR THIRD PARTIES OR A FAILURE OF THE PROGRAM TO OPERATE WITH ANY OTHER PROGRAMS), EVEN IF SUCH HOLDER OR OTHER PARTY HAS BEEN ADVISED OF THE POSSIBILITY OF SUCH DAMAGES.

End of Terms and Conditions

INDEX

Note to the Reader: Throughout this index **boldfaced** page numbers indicate primary discussions of a topic. *Italicized* page numbers indicate illustrations.

SYMBOLS AND NUMBERS

A

D

E

F

G

H

I

J

K

L

M

N

O

P

Q

R

S

T

U

Z

Summary of Common Linux Commands (*continued*)

COMMAND	ACTION
`nice`	Run a command at (usually) lower priority
`nohup`	Run a command after logout (inhibit hangups)
`nslookup`	Display IP information about a domain
`od`	Display file in octal
`psswd`	Create or change login password
`paste`	Merge lines of files
`pr`	Format and print file
`ps`	Report status of active processes
`pstat`	Report system status
`pwd`	Display current working directory
`recode`	Translate files to different formats
`rlogin`	Login to remote Unix systems insecurely
`rm`	Remove (erase) files or directories
`rmdir`	Remove (erase) empty directories
`sed`	The stream editor
`set`	Assign value to variable
`setenv`	Assign value to environmental variable (C Shell)
`sh`	Invoke Bourne shell
`shutdown`	Gracefully shut down system (`root`)
`sleep`	Suspend execution for given period
`slogin`	Login to remote Unix systems securely
`sort`	Sort and merge files
`spell`	Find spelling errors
`split`	Split a file into smaller files
`stty`	Set options for a terminal
`su`	Make a user a superuser (or a different user) without logging out first
`sum`	Compute checksums and number of blocks for files
`tail`	Display last few lines of a file
`tar`	Copy (archive) and restore files to diskette or tape
`tee`	Create a tee in a pipe
`telnet`	Access remote systems

CONTINUED →